WORKERS OF ALL COUNTRIES, UNITE!

LENIN

COLLECTED WORKS

1

В Ульянов (Ленин)

THE RUSSIAN EDITION WAS PRINTED
IN ACCORDANCE WITH A DECISION
OF THE NINTH CONGRESS OF THE R.C.P. (B.)
AND THE SECOND CONGRESS OF SOVIETS
OF THE U.S.S.R.

ИНСТИТУТ МАРКСИЗМА — ЛЕНИНИЗМА при ЦК КПСС

В. И. ЛЕНИН

СОЧИНЕНИЯ

Издание четвертое

ГОСУДАРСТВЕННОЕ ИЗДАТЕЛЬСТВО
ПОЛИТИЧЕСКОЙ ЛИТЕРАТУРЫ
МОСКВА

V. I. LENIN

COLLECTED WORKS

VOLUME
1
1893 - 1894

PROGRESS PUBLISHERS
MOSCOW 1972

PUBLISHER'S NOTE

This English edition of V. I. Lenin's *Collected Works* is a translation of the fourth, enlarged Russian edition prepared by the Institute of Marxism-Leninism, Central Committee of the C.P.S.U.

Corrections have been made to some of the texts and notes in accordance with the fifth Russian edition, and some further editorial comments have been added.

First printing 1960
Second printing 1963
Third printing 1972

CONTENTS

Preface to Volume One 9

1893

NEW ECONOMIC DEVELOPMENTS IN PEASANT LIFE (On V. Y. Postnikov's *Peasant Farming in South Russia*) 11

I 13
II 17
III 32
IV 43
V 69

ON THE SO-CALLED MARKET QUESTION 75

I 79
II 79
III 84
IV 89
V 93
VI 99
VII 107
VIII 122

1894

WHAT THE "FRIENDS OF THE PEOPLE" ARE AND HOW THEY FIGHT THE SOCIAL-DEMOCRATS. (A Reply to Articles in *Russkoye Bogatstvo* Opposing the Marxists) 129

Part I 131
Publisher's Note 201
Note to the Present Edition 202
Part III 203
Appendix I 301
Appendix II 308
Appendix III 326

THE ECONOMIC CONTENT OF NARODISM AND THE CRITICISM OF IT IN MR. STRUVE'S BOOK. (THE REFLECTION OF MARXISM IN BOURGEOIS LITERATURE.) P. Struve. *Critical Remarks on the Subject of Russia's Economic Development*. St. Petersburg, 1894 333

Chapter I A Line-by-Line Commentary on a Narodnik Profession de foi 340

Chapter II A Criticism of Narodnik Sociology 395
Chapter III The Presentation of Economic Problems by the Narodniks and by Mr. Struve 424
Chapter IV How Mr. Struve Explains Some Features of Russia's Post-Reform Economy 451
I 453
II 480
III 486
IV 489
V 493
VI 500

Notes 509

The Life and Work of V. I. Lenin. Outstanding Dates 537

ILLUSTRATIONS

V. I. Lenin, 1918 2-3

V. I. Lenin, 1890-1891 10-11

First manuscript page of Lenin's *New Economic Developments in Peasant Life*, 1893 12-13

First manuscript page of Lenin's *On the So-Called Market Question*, 1893 77

Last manuscript page of Lenin's *On the So-Called Market Question*, 1893 127

Cover of Part III, hectographed edition, of Lenin's *What the "Friends of the People" Are and How They Fight the Social-Democrats*, 1894 204-205

Last page of Part III, hectographed edition, of Lenin's *What the "Friends of the People" Are and How They Fight the Social-Democrats*, 1894 300-301

Title page of the miscellany containing Lenin's *The Economic Content of Narodism and the Criticism of It in Mr. Struve's Book*, 1895 335

PREFACE TO VOLUME ONE

The first volume contains four works (*New Economic Developments in Peasant Life*, *On the So-Called Market Question*, *What the "Friends of the People" Are and How They Fight the Social-Democrats*, *The Economic Content of Narodism and the Criticism of It in Mr. Struve's Book*) written by V. I. Lenin in 1893-1894, at the outset of his revolutionary activity, during the first years of the struggle to establish a workers' revolutionary party in Russia.

In these works, which are directed against the Narodniks and "legal Marxists," Lenin gives a Marxist analysis of Russia's social and economic system at the close of the nineteenth century, and formulates a number of programme principles and tasks for the revolutionary struggle of the Russian proletariat.

The paper, *On the So-Called Market Question*, is included in the fourth edition of V. I. Lenin's *Collected Works*; it did not appear in earlier editions. Lenin wrote the paper in the autumn of 1893. The manuscript was believed to be lost beyond recall and was discovered only in 1937, when it was published for the first time.

Lenin's work *What the "Friends of the People" Are* is published in the present edition according to a new copy of the hectographed edition of 1894 which came into the possession of the Institute of Marxism-Leninism only in 1936, and was not taken account of in previous editions of the *Works* of V. I. Lenin. The copy mentioned contains numerous editorial corrections apparently introduced by Lenin when preparing to have the book published abroad. All these corrections have been introduced into the present edition. This edition, therefore, contains the exact text of *What the "Friends of the People" Are and How They Fight the Social-Democrats*.

V. I. LENIN
1890-1891

NEW ECONOMIC DEVELOPMENTS IN PEASANT LIFE

(ON V. Y. POSTNIKOV'S *Peasant Farming in South Russia*)[1]

Written in the spring of 1893
First published in 1923

Published according to the manuscript

Новыя хозяйственныя движенія въ крестьянской жизни.

По поводу книги В. Е. Постникова — „Южно-русское крестьянское хозяйство".

I

Вышедшая въ прошломъ году книга В. Е. Постникова „Южнорусское крестьянское хозяйство" (Москва, 1891 г. Стр. XXXII + 391) представляетъ изъ себя чрезвычайно подробное и обстоятельное описаніе крестьянскаго хозяйства въ губерніяхъ Таврической, Херсонской и Екатеринославской, преимущественно же въ материковыхъ (сѣверныхъ) уѣздахъ Таврической губерніи. Описаніе это основано, во 1°, — и главнымъ образомъ — на земско-статистическихъ изслѣдованіяхъ трехъ указанныхъ губерній; во 2°, на личныхъ наблюденіяхъ автора, произведенныхъ имъ отчасти по долгу службы[1], от-

[1] Авторъ служилъ чиновникомъ по устройству казенныхъ земель въ Таврической губерніи.

First manuscript page of Lenin's *New Economic Developments in Peasant Life*, 1893

Reduced

I

V. Y. Postnikov's *Peasant Farming in South Russia* (Moscow, 1891, pp. XXXII+391), which appeared two years ago, is an extremely detailed and thorough description of peasant farming in the Taurida, Kherson and Yekaterinoslav gubernias,* but chiefly in the mainland (northern) uyezds of Taurida Gubernia. This description is based firstly—and primarily—on the Zemstvo[2] statistical investigations of the three gubernias mentioned; and, secondly, on the author's personal observations made partly in his official capacity,** and partly for the special purpose of studying peasant farming in 1887-1890.

An attempt to combine into one whole the Zemstvo statistical investigations for an entire region and to set forth the results in systematic form is in itself of tremendous interest, since the Zemstvo statistics provide a mass of detailed material on the economic conditions of the peasantry, but they do so in a form that renders these investigations practically useless to the public: the Zemstvo statistical abstracts comprise whole volumes of tables (a sep-

---

* *Administrative divisions*: the biggest territorial division in tsarist Russia was the *gubernia* (literally—governor's province); each gubernia had its capital city which was the seat of the governor. The gubernia was divided in *uyezds* (counties), each with its administrative centre and these, in turn, were divided into *volosts* (rural districts) containing a number of villages.—*Ed. Eng. ed.*

** The author was an official in the Government Land Department of Taurida Gubernia.

arate volume is usually devoted to each uyezd), the mere summarising of which under sufficiently definite and comprehensive headings is a labour in itself. The need to summarise and analyse Zemstvo statistical data has long been felt. It is for this purpose that the publication of the *Results of Zemstvo Statistical Investigations* was recently undertaken. The plan of this publication is as follows: a particular question related to peasant farming is taken, and a special investigation is carried out, bringing together all the data on this question contained in the Zemstvo statistics; data are brought together relating to the black-earth South of Russia and to the non-black-earth North, to the exclusively agricultural gubernias and to the gubernias where there are handicraft industries. The two published volumes of *Results* have been compiled according to this plan; the first is devoted to the "peasant community" (V. V.), the second to "peasant rentings of non-allotment land" (N. Karyshev).[3] It is quite reasonable to doubt the correctness of this method of summarising: firstly, data relating to different economic regions with different economic conditions have to be placed under one heading (the separate characterisation of each region involves tremendous difficulties due to the incompleteness of the Zemstvo investigations and the omission of many uyezds. These difficulties were already evident in the second volume of *Results*; Karyshev's attempt to assign the data contained in the Zemstvo statistics to definite regions was unsuccessful); secondly, it is quite impossible to give a separate description of one aspect of peasant farming without touching on others; the particular question has to be artificially abstracted, and the completeness of the picture is lost. Peasant rentings of non-allotment land are divorced from the renting of allotment land, from general data on the economic classification of the peasants and the size of the crop area; they are regarded only as part of peasant farming, whereas actually they are often a special method of private-landowner farming. That is why a summary of Zemstvo statistical data for a given region where the economic conditions are uniform would, I think, be preferable.

While expressing, in passing, my views on a more correct way of summarising Zemstvo statistical investigations, views to which I am led by comparing the *Results* with Postnikov's book, I must, however, make the reservation that Postnikov did not, in fact, aim at *summarising* materials: he pushes the figures into the background and concentrates his attention on a full and clear description.

In his description, the author pays almost equal attention to questions of an economic, administrative-legal character (forms of land tenure) and of a technical character (boundaries, farming system, harvests), but with the intention of keeping questions of the first kind in the foreground.

"I must confess," says Mr. Postnikov in the Preface, "that I devote less attention to the technique of peasant farming than I might have done; but I take this course because, in my view, conditions of an economic character play a much more important part in peasant farming than technique. In our press ... the economic aspect is usually ignored.... Very little attention is paid to investigating fundamental economic problems, such as the agrarian and boundary problems are for our peasant farming. It is to the elucidation of these problems, and of the agrarian problem in particular, that this book is chiefly devoted" (Preface, p. IX).

Fully sharing the author's views on the relative importance of economic and technical questions, I intend to devote my article only to that part of Mr. Postnikov's work in which peasant farming is subjected to political-economic investigation.*

In his preface the author defines the main points of the investigation as follows:

"The considerable employment of machines that has recently become evident in peasant farming and the marked increase in the size of farms belonging to the well-to-

* It seems to me that such an exposition is worth while, inasmuch as Mr. Postnikov's book, one of the most outstanding in our economic literature of recent years, has passed almost unnoticed. This may partly be explained by the fact that although the author recognises the great importance of economic problems, he treats them too fragmentarily and encumbers his exposition with details relating to other problems.

do section of the peasantry, constitute a new phase in our agrarian life, the development of which will undoubtedly receive a new stimulus from the severe economic conditions of the present year. The productivity of peasant labour and the working capacity of the family rise considerably with the increase in the size of the farm and the employment of machines, a point hitherto overlooked in defining the area that a peasant family can cultivate....

"The employment of machines in peasant farming causes substantial changes in peasant life: by reducing the demand for labour in agriculture and rendering the existing agricultural over-population still more acute for the peasants, it helps to increase the number of families which, having become superfluous in the villages, are forced to seek outside employment and virtually become landless. At the same time, the introduction of large machines in peasant farming raises the peasant's living standard, even under the prevailing methods and extensive character of agriculture, to a level hitherto undreamt-of. Therein lies the guarantee of the strength of the new economic developments in peasant life. To draw attention to and elucidate these developments among the peasantry of South Russia is the immediate purpose of this book" (Preface, p. X).

Before proceeding to outline what, in the opinion of our author, these new economic developments are, I must make two reservations.

Firstly, it has been said above that Postnikov provides data for Kherson, Yekaterinoslav and Taurida gubernias; data in sufficient detail are given only for the latter gubernia, however, and then not for the whole of it; the author gives no data for the Crimea, where the economic conditions are somewhat different, and confines himself exclusively to the three northern, mainland uyezds of Taurida Gubernia—Berdyansk, Melitopol and Dnieper uyezds. I shall confine myself to the data for these three uyezds.

Secondly, in addition to Russians, Taurida Gubernia is inhabited by Germans and Bulgarians, whose numbers, however, are small compared with the Russian population: in Dnieper Uyezd, there are 113 households of German colonists out of 19,586 households in the uyezd, i.e., only 0.6%; in Melitopol Uyezd, there are 2,159

(1,874+285) German and Bulgarian households out of 34,978, i.e., 6.1%. Lastly, in Berdyansk Uyezd, 7,224 households out of 28,794, i.e., 25%. Taken together, in all the three uyezds, the colonists account for 9,496 households out of 83,358, i.e., about one-ninth. Consequently, the number of colonists is, on the whole, very small, and in the Dnieper Uyezd is quite insignificant. The author describes the colonists' farming in detail, always separating it from that of the Russians. All these descriptions I omit, confining myself exclusively to the farming of the Russian peasants. True, the figures given combine the Russians and the Germans, but, owing to the small number of the latter, their addition cannot change the general picture, so that it is quite permissible, on the basis of these data, to describe Russian peasant farming. The Russian population of Taurida Gubernia, who have settled in this region during the past 30 years, differ from the peasantry of the other Russian gubernias only by their greater affluence. Community land tenure in these areas is, in the words of our author, "typical and stable."* In a word, if the colonists are omitted, peasant farming in Taurida Gubernia does not differ fundamentally from the general type of Russian peasant farming.

II

"At the present time," says Postnikov, "a South-Russian village of any size (and the same can probably be said of most localities in Russia) presents such a variegated picture as regards the economic status of the various groups of its inhabitants, that it is very difficult to speak of the living standard of separate villages as single units, or to depict this standard in average figures. Such average figures indicate certain general conditions that determine the economic life of the peasantry, but they do not give any idea of the great diversity of economic phenomena that actually exists" (p. 106).

A little further on, Postnikov expresses himself still more definitely:

* Individual land tenure prevails in only 5 villages.

"The diversity in economic level," he says, "makes it extremely difficult to settle the question of the general prosperity of the population. People who make a cursory tour through the large villages of Taurida Gubernia usually draw the conclusion that the local peasants are very prosperous. But can a village be called prosperous when half its peasants are rich, while the other half live in permanent poverty? And by what criteria is the relatively greater or lesser prosperity of a particular village to be determined? Obviously, average figures characterising the condition of the population of a whole village or district are here insufficient to draw conclusions as to the prosperity of the peasants. This latter may be judged only from the sum-total of many facts, *by dividing the population into groups*" (p. 154).

One might think that there is nothing new in this statement of the differentiation of the peasantry; it is referred to in practically every work dealing with peasant farming in general. But the point is that, as a rule, when mention is made of the fact, no significance is attached to it, it being regarded as unimportant or even incidental. It is deemed possible to speak of a type of peasant farming, the type being defined by average figures; discussion takes place about the significance of various practical measures in relation to the peasantry as a whole. In Postnikov's book we see a protest against such views. He points (and does so repeatedly) to the "tremendous diversity in the economic status of the various households within the village community" (p. 323), and takes up arms against "the tendency to regard the peasant *mir** as something integral and homogeneous, such as our urban intelligentsia still imagine it to be" (p. 351). "The Zemstvo statistical investigations of the past decade," he says, "have shown that our village community is by no means the homogeneous unit our publicists of the seventies thought it was, and that in the past few decades there has taken place within it a differentiation of the population into groups with quite different levels of economic prosperity" (p. 323).

---

* *Mir*—a peasant community. See Note 4 at the end of the book. —*Ed. Eng. ed.*

Postnikov supports his opinion with a mass of data dispersed throughout the book, and we must proceed to gather all these data systematically in order to test the truth of this opinion and to decide who is right—whether it is the "urban intelligentsia," who regard the peasantry as something homogeneous, or Postnikov, who asserts that there is tremendous heterogeneity—and then how profound is this heterogeneity, does it prevent a general description of peasant farming being given from the political-economic standpoint, on the basis of only average data, and can it alter the action and influence of practical measures in relation to the various categories of the peasantry?

Before citing figures that supply the material to settle these questions, it should be noted that Postnikov took all data of this kind from the Zemstvo statistical abstracts for Taurida Gubernia. Originally, the Zemstvo census statistics were confined to data covering whole village communities, no data being collected on individual peasant households. Soon, however, differences were noted in the property status of these households, and house-to-house censuses were undertaken; this was the first step towards a more thoroughgoing study of the economic status of the peasants. The next step was the introduction of combined tables: prompted by the conviction that the property differences among the peasants within the village community[4] are more profound than the differences between the various juridical categories of peasants, the statisticians began to classify all the indices of peasant economic status according to definite property differences; for example, they grouped the peasants according to the number of dessiatines* under crops, the number of draught animals, the amount of allotment arable per household, and so on.

The Taurida Zemstvo statistics classify the peasants according to the number of dessiatines under crops. Postnikov is of the opinion that this classification "is a happy one" (p. XII), as "under the farming conditions in the Taurida uyezds, the amount of land under crops is the most important criterion of the peasant's living standard" (p. XII). "In the South-Russian steppe territory," says Postnikov, "the

* A dessiatine=2.7 acres.—*Ed. Eng. ed.*

development among the peasants of various kinds of non-agricultural industries is as yet relatively insignificant, and the main occupation of the vast majority of the rural population today is agriculture based on the cultivation of grain." "The Zemstvo statistics show that in the northern uyezds of Taurida Gubernia, 7.6% of the native rural population engage exclusively in industries, while 16.3%, in addition to farming their own land, have some subsidiary occupation" (p. 108). As a matter of fact, classification according to area under crops is far more correct even for other parts of Russia than any other basis of classification adopted by the Zemstvo statisticians, as, for example, number of dessiatines of allotment land or allotment arable per household. For, on the one hand, the amount of allotment land is no direct indication of the household's prosperity, inasmuch as the size of the allotment is determined by the number of registered[5] or of actual males in the family, and is only indirectly dependent on the peasant's prosperity, and because, lastly, the peasant possibly does not use his allotment land and leases it to others, and when he has no implements he cannot use it. On the other hand, if the principal pursuit of the population is agriculture, the determination of the cultivated area is necessary in order to keep account of production, to determine the amount of grain consumed by the peasant, purchased by him, or placed on the market, for unless these points are ascertained, a highly important aspect of peasant economy will remain unexplained, the character of his farming, its significance relative to other earnings, etc., will not be made clear. Lastly, it is precisely the cultivated area that must be made the basis of classification, so that we can compare the economy of the household with the so-called norms of peasant land tenure and farming, with the food norm (Nahrungsfläche) and the labour norm (Arbeitsfläche).* In a word, clas-

* *Food norm* and *labour norm*—as can be seen from the text Lenin uses these expressions as translations of the German political-economic terms "Nahrungsfläche" and "Arbeitsfläche," the former being the amount of land required to feed one person (or any other unit, such as the family) and the latter the amount that can be cultivated by one person (or family).—*Ed. Eng. ed.*

sification according to area under crops not only seems to be a happy one; it is the best and is absolutely essential.

As to area under crops the Taurida statisticians divide the peasants into six groups: 1) those cultivating no land; 2) those cultivating up to 5 dessiatines; 3) from 5 to 10 dessiatines; 4) from 10 to 25 dessiatines; 5) from 25 to 50 dessiatines and 6) over 50 dessiatines per household. For the three uyezds the proportionate relation of these groups according to the number of households is as follows:

Percentages of households	Uyezds			Average area (dess.) under crops per household in all three uyezds
	Berdyansk %	Melitopol %	Dnieper %	
Cultivating no land	6	7.5	9	—
" up to 5 dess.	12	11.5	11	3.5
" 5 to 10 "	22	21	20	8
" 10 to 25 "	38	39	41.8	16.4
" 25 to 50 "	19	16.6	15.1	34.5
" over 50 "	3	4.4	3.1	75

The general proportions (these percentages are given for the whole population, including Germans) undergo little change if we omit the Germans. Thus, the author reckons that of the households in the Taurida uyezds 40% cultivate small areas (up to 10 dessiatines), 40% medium (from 10 to 25 dessiatines) and 20% large areas. If the Germans are excluded, the latter figure is reduced to one-sixth (16.7%, i.e., in all 3.3% less) and correspondingly increases the number of households with a small cultivated area.

To determine the degree to which these groups differ, let us begin with land tenure and land usage.

Postnikov gives the following table (the combined totals of the three categories of land mentioned in it were not calculated by him [p. 145]):

Peasant groups	AVERAGE ARABLE PER HOUSEHOLD (dessiatines)											
	Berdyansk Uyezd				Melitopol Uyezd				Dnieper Uyezd			
	Allotment	Purchased	Rented	Total	Allotment	Purchased	Rented	Total	Allotment	Purchased	Rented	Total
Cultivating no land	6.8	3.1	0.09	10	8.7	0.7	—	9.4	6.4	0.9	0.1	7.4
" up to 5 dess.	6.9	0.7	0.4	8.0	7.1	0.2	0.4	7.7	5.5	0.04	0.6	6.1
" 5 to 10 "	9	—	1.1	10.1	9	0.2	1.4	10.6	8.7	0.05	1.6	10.3
" 10 to 25 "	14.1	0.6	4	18.7	12.8	0.3	4.5	17.6	12.5	0.6	5.8	18.9
" 25 to 50 "	27.6	2.1	9.8	39.5	23.5	1.5	13.4	38.4	16.6	2.3	17.4	36.3
" over 50 "	36.7	31.3	48.4	116.4	36.2	21.3	42.5	100	17.4	30	44	91.4
Per uyezd	14.8	1.6	5	21.4	14.1	1.4	6.7	22.2	11.2	1.7	7.0	19.9

"These figures show," says Postnikov, "that the more affluent group of peasants in the Taurida uyezds not only have large allotments, which may be due to the large size of their families, but are at the same time the largest purchasers and the largest renters of land" (p. 146).

It seems to me that in this connection we need only say that the increase in the amount of allotted land, as we proceed from the bottom group to the top, cannot be explained *entirely* by the larger size of families. Postnikov gives the following table showing the family composition by groups for the three uyezds.

	Average per family					
	Berdyansk Uyezd		Melitopol Uyezd		Dnieper Uyezd	
	Persons, both sexes	Working members	Persons, both sexes	Working members	Persons, both sexes	Working members
Cultivating no land	4.5	0.9	4.1	0.9	4.6	1
" up to 5 dess.	4.9	1.1	4.6	1	4.9	1.1
" 5 to 10 "	5.6	1.2	5.3	1.2	5.4	1.2
" 10 to 25 "	7.1	1.6	6.8	1.5	6.3	1.4
" 25 to 50 "	8.2	1.8	8.6	1.9	8.2	1.9
" over 50 "	10.6	2.3	10.8	2.3	10.1	2.3
Per uyezd	6.6	1.5	6.5	1.5	6.2	1.4

The table shows that the amount of allotment land per household increases from the bottom group to the top much more rapidly than the number of persons of both sexes and the number of working members. Let us illustrate this by taking 100 as the figure for the bottom group in Dnieper Uyezd:

	Allotment land	Working members	Persons of both sexes
Cultivating no land	100	100	100
" up to 5 dess.	86	110	106
" 5 to 10 "	136	120	117
" 10 to 25 "	195	140	137
" 25 to 50 "	259	190	178
" over 50 "	272	230	219

It is clear that what determines the size of the allotment, apart from the composition of the family, is the prosperity of the household.

Examining the data for the amount of purchased land in the various groups, we see that the purchasers of land are almost exclusively the top groups, with over 25 dessiatines under crops, and chiefly the very big cultivators, those with 75 dessiatines under crops per household. Hence, the data for purchased land fully corroborate Postnikov's opinion regarding the differences between the peasant groups. The type of information as that given by the author on p. 147, for example, where he says that "the peasants of the Taurida uyezds purchased 96,146 dessiatines of land," does not in any way describe the real situation; almost all this land is in the hands of an insignificant minority, those already best provided with allotment land, the "affluent" peasants, as Postnikov calls them; and they constitute no more than one-fifth of the population.

The same must be said of rented land. The above table gives the total figure for rented land, allotment and non-allotment. It appears that the area of rented land grows quite regularly the greater the prosperity of the peasants, and that, consequently, the better supplied the peasant is with land, the more he rents, thus depriving the poorer groups of the land they need.

It should be noted that this phenomenon is common to the whole of Russia. Prof. Karyshev, summarising the facts of peasant non-allotment rentings throughout Russia, wherever Zemstvo statistical investigations are available, formulates the general law that the amount of rented land depends directly on the renter's degree of affluence.*

Postnikov, incidentally, cites even more detailed figures about the distribution of rented land (non-allotment and allotment together), which I give here:

	Berdyansk Uyezd			*Melitopol Uyezd*			*Dnieper Uyezd*		
	Arable			Arable			Arable		
	% of renting households	per renting household (dess.)	Price per dess. (rubles)	% of renting households	per renting household (dess.)	Price per dess. (rubles)	% of renting households	per renting household (dess.)	Price per dess. (rubles)
Cultivating up to 5 dess.	18.7	2.1	11	14.4	3	5.50	25	2.4	15.25
" 5 to 10 "	33.6	3.2	9.20	34.8	4.1	5.52	42	3.9	12
" 10 to 25 "	57	7	7.65	59.3	7.5	5.74	69	8.5	4.75
" 25 to 50 "	60.6	16.1	6.80	80.5	16.9	6.30	88	20	3:75
" over 50 "	78.5	62	4.20	88.8	47.6	3.93	91	48.6	3.55
Per uyezd	44.8	11.1	5.80	50	12.4	4.86	56.2	12.4	4.23

* *Results of the Economic Investigation of Russia According to Zemstvo Statistical Data*; Vol. II, N. Karyshev, *Peasant Rentings of Non-Allotment Land*, Dorpat, 1892. Pp. 122, 133 et al.

We see that here, too, average figures do not in any way describe the real situation. When we say, for example, that in Dnieper Uyezd 56% of the peasants rent land, we give a very incomplete picture of this renting, for the percentage of renters in the groups who (as will be shown later) have insufficient land of their own is much lower—only 25% in the first group, whereas the top group, those who have sufficient land of their own, almost all resort to renting (91%). The difference in the number of rented dessiatines per renting household is even more considerable: the top category rents 30, 15 and 24 times more than the bottom one. Obviously, this alters the very character of the renting, for in the top category it is already a commercial undertaking, whereas in the bottom one it may be an operation necessitated by dire need. This latter assumption is corroborated by data on rentals: they show that the bottom groups pay a higher rent for the land, sometimes four times as much as the top category (in Dnieper Uyezd). It should be recalled in this connection that the increase in rent as the amount of rented land grows smaller is not peculiar to South Russia; Karyshev's work shows the general applicability of this law.

"Land in the Taurida uyezds," says Postnikov with regard to these data, "is rented chiefly by the well-to-do peasants, who have enough allotment land and land of their own; this should be said in particular of the renting of non-allotment land, i.e., of privately-owned and government land, situated at greater distances from the villages. Actually this is quite natural: to be able to rent distant land the peasant must have sufficient draught animals, whereas the less prosperous peasants in these areas have not enough even to cultivate their allotment land" (p. 148).

It should not be thought that this distribution of rented land is due to its being rented by individuals. There is no difference at all where the land is rented by the community, and for the simple reason that the land is distributed on the same principle, that is, "according to where the money lies."

"According to the registers of the Administration of State Property," says Postnikov, "in 1890, out of 133,852 dessiatines of government land leased on contract in the

Peasant groups	Berdyansk Uyezd			Melitopol Uyezd			Dnieper Uyezd			All three uyezds			
	Number of renting households	Dessiatines rented	Per renting h'hold (dess.)	Number of renting households	Dessiatines rented	Per renting h'hold (dess.)	Number of renting households	Dessiatines rented	Per renting h'hold (dess.)	Number of renting households	Dessiatines rented	%	Per renting household (dess.)
Cultivating up to 5 dess.	39	66	1.7	24	383	16	20	62	3.1	83	511	1	6.1
" 5 to 10 "	227	400	1.8	159	776	4.8	58	251	4.3	444	1,427	3	3.2
" 10 to 25 "	687	2,642	3.8	707	4,569	6.4	338	1,500	4.4	1,732	8,711	20	5.0
" 25 to 50 "	387	3,755	9.7	672	8,564	12.7	186	1,056	5.7	1,245	13,375	30	10.7
" over 50 "	113	3,194	28.3	440	15,365	34.9	79	1,724	21.8	632	20,283	46	32.1
Totals	1,453	10,057	7	2,002	29,657	14.8	681	4,593	6.7	4,136	44,307	100	10.7

three uyezds, 84,756 dessiatines of good land, or about 63% of the total area, were used by peasant communities. But the land rented by the peasant communities was used by a comparatively small number of householders, mostly well-to-do at that. The Zemstvo house-to-house census makes this fact quite clear" (p. 150).*

"Thus," concludes Postnikov, "in Dnieper Uyezd more than half of all the rented arable, in Berdyansk Uyezd over two-thirds, and in Melitopol Uyezd, where mostly government land is rented, even more than four-fifths of the rented land was in the hands of the group of well-to-do peasants. On the other hand, the group of poor peasants (cultivating up to 10 dessiatines of arable), held in all the uyezds a total of 1,938 dessiatines, or about 4% of the rented land" (p. 150). The author then cites many examples of the uneven distribution of community-rented land, but there is no need to quote them here.

As to Postnikov's conclusion about the amount of rented land being dependent upon the degree of prosperity of the renter, it is highly interesting to note the opposite view of the Zemstvo statisticians.

Postnikov placed an article, "On Zemstvo Statistical Work in Taurida, Kherson and Yekaterinoslav Gubernias" (pp. XI-XXXII), at the beginning of his book. Here, among other things, he examines the *Taurida Gubernia Handbook*, published by the Taurida Zemstvo in 1889, in which the entire investigation was briefly summarised. Analysing the section of the book which deals with renting, Postnikov says:

"In our land-abundant southern and eastern gubernias, the Zemstvo statistics have revealed that a fairly substantial proportion of well-to-do peasants, in addition to having considerable allotments of their own, rent fairly large amounts of land on the side. Farming is here conducted not only to satisfy the requirements of the family itself, but also to obtain some surplus, an income with which to improve buildings, acquire machines and buy additional land. This

---

* The last section of this table (the totals for the three uyezds) is not given by Postnikov. In a note to the table he says that "under the terms of lease the peasants may plough up only one-third of the rented land."

is quite a natural desire, and there is nothing reprehensible about it, for in itself it contains no elements of kulakism." [There are no elements of kulakism here, it is true; but there undoubtedly are elements of exploitation: by renting land far in excess of their requirements, the prosperous peasants deprive the poor of land needed for their subsistence; by enlarging their farms they need extra hands and resort to hiring labour.] "But some of the Zemstvo statisticians, evidently regarding such manifestations in peasant life as something illegitimate, try to belittle their importance and to prove that it is chiefly the need for food that drives the peasant to rent land, and that even if the well-to-do peasants do rent a great deal of land, these renters constitute a percentage that decreases steadily as the size of the allotment increases" (p. XVII)—to prove this point, Mr. Werner, the compiler of the *Handbook*, grouped together, according to the size of their allotments, the peasant families of the *entire* Taurida Gubernia who had 1 or 2 working members and 2 or 3 draught animals. It turned out that "as the size of the allotment increases, there is a regular decrease in the percentage of renting households and a less regular decrease in the amount of land rented per household" (p. XVIII). Postnikov quite rightly says that this method is not conclusive at all, since a *section* of the peasants (only those possessing 2 or 3 draught animals) has been selected arbitrarily, it being precisely the well-to-do peasants who have been omitted, and that, moreover, to lump together the mainland uyezds of Taurida Gubernia and the Crimea is impermissible, since the conditions of renting in the two areas are not identical: in the Crimea, one half to three-fourths of the population are landless (so-called dessiatiners),[6] whereas in the northern uyezds only 3 or 4% are landless. In the Crimea, it is almost always easy to find land for hire; in the northern uyezds it is sometimes impossible. It is interesting to note that the Zemstvo statisticians of other gubernias have been observed to make similar attempts (of course, equally unsuccessful) to tone down such "illegitimate" manifestations in peasant life as renting land to provide an income. (See Karyshev, op. cit.)

If, accordingly, the distribution of peasant non-allotment renting reveals the existence among the various peasant farms of differences that are not only quantitative (he rents much, he rents little), but also qualitative (he rents through need of food; he rents for commercial purposes), still more has this to be said of the renting of *allotment* land.

"The total allotment arable rented by peasants from other peasants," says Postnikov, "as registered in the three Taurida uyezds by the 1884-1886 house-to-house census of the peasantry, amounted to 256,716 dessiatines, which here constitutes one-fourth of the total peasant allotment arable; and this does not include land let by peasants to all sorts of people who live in the countryside, or to clerks, teachers, priests and other persons who do not belong to the peasantry and are not covered by the house-to-house census. Practically all this land is rented by peasants who belong to the well-to-do groups, as the following figures show. The amount of allotment arable rented by peasants from their neighbours, as recorded by the census, was as follows:

Cultivating up to 10 dess. per household	16,594 dess., i.e.,	6%
Cultivating 10 to 25 dess. per household	89,526 " "	35%
Cultivating more than 25 dess. per household	150,596 " "	59%
Total	256,716 dess.	100%

"The major part, however, of this leased land, like most of the lessors themselves, belongs to the group of peasants who cultivate no land, do no farming of any sort, or to those who cultivate but little land. Thus, a considerable number of the peasants of the Taurida uyezds (approximately one-third of the total population) do not exploit their whole allotment—some for lack of desire, but mostly for lack of the necessary animals and implements with which to engage in farming—but lease it to others and thereby increase the land in use by the other, better-off section of the peasants. The majority of the lessors undoubtedly belong to the category of impoverished, declining householders" (pp. 136-37).

Corroboration of this is furnished by the following table "for two uyezds of Taurida Gubernia (the Zemstvo statistics provide no information for Melitopol Uyezd), which shows the proportion of householders who lease their allotments to others, and the percentage of allotment arable leased by them" (p. 135):

	Berdyansk Uyezd		Dnieper Uyezd	
	% of h'holders leasing their allotment land	% of leased allotment land	% of h'holders leasing their allotment land	% of leased allotment land
Cultivating no land	73	97	80	97.1
" up to 5 dess.	65	54	30	38.4
" 5 to 10 "	46	23.6	23	17.2
" 10 to 25 "	21.5	8.3	16	8.1
" 25 to 50 "	9	2.7	7	2.9
" over 50 "	12.7	6.3	7	13.8
For uyezd . .	32.7	11.2	25.7	14.9

Let us now pass from peasant land tenure and land usage to the distribution of farm stock and implements. Postnikov gives the following data—for all three uyezds together—on the number of draught animals possessed by the groups:

	Total		Average per household			
	Horses	Oxen	Draught animals	Other animals*	In all*	% of h'holds possessing no dr. animals
Cultivating no land	—	—	0.3	0.8	1.1	80.5
" up to 5 dess.	6,467	3,082	1.0	1.4	2.4	48.3
" 5 to 10 "	25,152	8,924	1.9	2.3	4.2	12.5
" 10 to 25 "	80,517	24,943	3.2	4.1	7.3	1.4
" 25 to 50 "	62,823	19,030	5.8	8.1	13.9	0.1
" over 50 "	21,003	11,648	10.5	19.5	30	0.03
Total . . .	195,962	67,627	3.1	4.5	7.6	—

* In terms of cattle.

These figures, by themselves, do not characterise the categories—that will be done below, when we describe the technique of agriculture and classify the peasants according to economic category. Here we shall only mention that the difference between peasant groups with regard to the number of draught animals they own is so profound that we see far more animals in the top groups than can possibly be required for the needs of the family, while the bottom groups have so few (especially draught animals) that independent farming becomes impossible.

Similar in every respect are data on the distribution of farm implements. "The house-to-house census, that registered the peasant-owned iron ploughs and drill ploughs, gives the following figures for the entire population of the uyezds" (p. 214):

	Percentage of households		
	with no ploughing implements	with only a drill plough	with an iron plough, etc.
Berdyansk Uyezd	33	10	57
Melitopol "	37.8	28.2	34
Dnieper "	39.3	7	53.7

This table shows how very large a group of peasants is unable to carry on *independent* farming. The situation among the top groups can be seen from the following data on the number of implements per household in the various groups, classified according to area under crops:

	Implements per household					
	Berdyansk Uyezd		Melitopol Uyezd		Dnieper Uyezd	
	Carting (waggons, etc.)	Ploughing (iron ploughs and drill ploughs)	Carting	Ploughing	Carting	Ploughing
Cultivating 5 to 10 dess.	0.8	0.5	0.8	0.4	0.8	0.5
" 10 to 25 "	1.2	1.3	1.2	1	1	1
" 25 to 50 "	2.1	2	2	1.6	1.7	1.5
" over 50 "	3.4	3.3	3.2	2.8	2.7	2.4

As regards the number of implements, the top group has 4 to 6 times more than the bottom one (the group with less than 5 dessiatines under crops is entirely disregarded by the author); as regards the number of working members in the families,* however, it has $\frac{23}{12}$ times, i.e., less than twice, as many as the same group. This alone shows that the top group has to resort to the hire of labour, while in the bottom group half the households are without farm implements (N.B.—this "bottom" group is the third from below) and, consequently, are unable to carry on independent farming.

Naturally, the above-mentioned differences in the amount of land and implements held are the cause of differences in the amount of land under crops. The area under crops per household in the six groups has been given above. The total area cultivated by the peasants of Taurida Gubernia is distributed by groups as follows:

	Dessiatines under crops	%	
Cultivating up to 5 dess.	34,070	2.4	12% of crop area held by 40% of population
" 5 to 10 "	140,426	9.7	
" 10 to 25 "	540,093	37.6	38% of crop area held by 40% of population
" 25 to 50 "	494,095	34.3	50% of crop area held by 20% of population
" over 50 "	230,583	16	
Total	1,439,267	100%	

These figures speak for themselves. It should only be added that for a family to live by farming alone, Postnikov estimates (p. 272), a crop area of 16 to 18 dessiatines per household is required.

III

In the previous chapter, data showing the property status of the different groups of peasants and the size of their farms were summarised. We must now sum up data indicating the character of the farming of the various groups of peasants and their methods and systems of farming.

* See above, the table showing the family composition of the various groups.

Let us first dwell on Postnikov's proposition that "the productivity of peasant labour and the working capacity of the family rise considerably with the increase in the size of the farm and the employment of machines" (p. X). The author demonstrates this proposition by calculating the number of workers and draught animals per *given* area under crops in the different economic groups. In so doing, however, it is impossible to use the data of family composition, as "the bottom economic groups release part of their working members for outside employment as farm labourers, while the top groups take labourers into employment" (p. 114). The Taurida Zemstvo statistics do not give the number of labourers hired or released for hire, and Postnikov estimates it approximately by taking the Zemstvo statistical data for the number of households which hired people and by calculating how many working people were needed for the given cultivated area. Postnikov admits that he can lay no claim to perfect accuracy for these estimates, but he believes that it is only in the two top groups that his calculations may considerably change the family composition, as the number of hired labourers in the other groups is small. By comparing the data on family composition given above with the following table the reader can test the correctness of this view:

In the three uyezds of Taurida Gubernia

	Working persons			Average per household	
	Hired	Released for hire	Difference	Number in family (with hired labourers)	Working persons*
Cultivating no land	239	1,077	— 838	4.3	0.9
" up to 5 dess.	247	1,484	—1,237	4.8	1.0
" 5 to 10 "	465	4,292	—3,827	5.2	1.0
" 10 to 25 "	2,846	3,389	— 543	6.8	1.6
" 25 to 50 "	6,041	—	+6,041	8.9	2.4
" over 50 "	8,241	—	+8,241	13.3	5
Total	18,079	10,242	+7,837	—	—

* *Working persons*—this somewhat un-English term is used for "working members, men and women of a peasant family or household" as opposed to hired labourers. *Ed. Eng. ed.*

Comparing the last column with the data of family composition, we see that Postnikov has somewhat understated the number of workers in the bottom and overstated it in the top groups. As his purpose was to prove that the number of workers per given area under crops decreases as the size of the farm increases, his approximate estimates succeeded in minimising rather than exaggerating this decrease.

Having made this preliminary calculation, Postnikov gives the following table showing the relation between the crop area and the number of working persons, draught animals, and then population generally for different groups of peasants (p. 117):

	Area under crops per pair of draught animals	*Per 100 dess. of crop area* Households	Persons (with hired labourers)	Workers (with hired labourers)	Number of draught animals
Cultivating up to 5 dess.	7.1 dess.	28.7	136	28.5	28.2
" 5 to 10 "	8.2 "	12.9	67	12.6	25
" 10 to 25 "	10.2 "	6.1	41.2	9.3	20
" 25 to 50 "	12.5 "	2.9	25.5	7	16.6
" over 50 "	14.5 "	1.3	18	6.8	14
Average	10.9 dess.	5.4	36.6	9	18.3

"Thus, with the increase in the size of the farm and in the area cultivated by the peasant, the expenditure on the maintenance of labour-power, human and animal, that prime item of expenditure in agriculture, progressively decreases, and among the groups that cultivate large areas, drops to nearly one-half per dessiatine under crops of what it is among the groups with small cultivated areas" (p. 117).

The proposition that the maintenance of working persons and draught animals is the predominant item of expenditure in agriculture is confirmed by the author later when he cites the detailed budget of a Mennonite[7] farm: of the total expenditure, 24.3% is general expenditure on the farm; 23.6% is expenditure on draught animals and 52.1% on working persons (p. 284).

Postnikov attributes great importance to his conclusion that the productivity of labour increases with the increase in the size of the farm (as is shown from the above quotation, taken from his preface); and, indeed, one cannot but admit its importance—firstly, for a study of the economic life of our peasantry and the character of the farming of the various groups; and, secondly, in connection with the general question of the relation between small-scale and large-scale farming. This latter question has been greatly confused by many writers, the chief cause of the confusion being that comparison was made between dissimilar farms, existing in different social conditions and differing in the type of farming; for example, farms whose income was derived from the output of agricultural produce were compared with farms whose income was derived from exploiting other households' need of land (e. g., peasant and landlord farms in the period immediately following the Reform of 1861).[8] Postnikov is entirely free of this error and does not forget the first rule of all comparisons, namely, that the things compared must be of a similar order.

The author gives a more detailed proof of his proposition in respect of the Taurida uyezds, and cites data, firstly, for each uyezd separately and, secondly, for the Russian population separately, or, rather, for its most numerous group, the former state peasants (pp. 273-74).

	Dessiatines under crops per pair of draught animals					
	For the uyezds in general			In the group of former state peasants		
	Berdyansk	Melitopol	Dnieper	Berdyansk	Melitopol	Dnieper
Cultivating up to 5 dess.	8.9	8.7	4.3	—	—	—
" 5 to 10 "	8.9	8.7	6.8	8.9	9.1	6.8
" 10 to 25 "	10.2	10.6	9.7	10.3	10.9	9.6
" 25 to 50 "	11.6	12.4	12.3	12.3	12.8	11.9
" over 50 "	13.5	13.8	15.7	13.7	14.3	15
Average	10.7	11.3	10.1	—	—	—

The conclusion reached is the same, that "on the small-scale farm the relative number of draught animals per given crop area is one and a half times or double the number on the 'full' peasant farm. The same law is revealed by the house-to-house census in the case of all the other, smaller, groups—former landlords' peasants, tenant farmers, etc.—and in all localities, even in the smallest, confined to one volost or even one village" (p. 274).

The relation between size of crop area and farm expenditure is also found to be unfavourable for the small farms in respect of another type of expenditure—the maintenance of implements and productive animals.

We have already seen how rapidly both these items increase per farm as we proceed from the bottom group to the top one. If we calculate the quantity of implements per given crop area, we find that it *decreases* from the bottom to the top group (p. 318):

	Per 100 dessiatines of crop area		
	Productive animals	Iron ploughs and drill ploughs	Waggons
Cultivating up to 5 dess.	42 head	4.7	10
" 5 to 10 "	28.8 "	5.9	9
" 10 to 25 "	24.9 "	6.5	7
" 25 to 50 "	23.7 "	4.8	5.7
" over 50 "	25.8 "	3.8	4.3
For the three uyezds	25.5 head	5.4	6.5

"This table shows that as the crop area per household increases, the biggest implements (for cultivation and cartage) progressively decrease in number per given crop area, and, consequently, on the farms of the top groups the cost of maintaining cultivation and cartage implements should be relatively less per dessiatine. The group with up to 10 dessiatines per household under crops constitutes an exception: there are comparatively fewer farm implements than in the next group, with its 16 dessiatines per household under crops, but that is only because many of the peasants do not work with their own implements, but with hired ones, which does not, however, in any way reduce the expenditure on implements" (p. 318).

"Zemstvo statistics," says Postnikov, "prove incontrovertibly that the larger the size of a peasant farm, the smaller the number of implements, workers and draught animals employed on a given cultivated area" (p. 162).

"In previous chapters," says Postnikov further on, "it has been shown that in the Taurida uyezds this phenomenon occurs in all the groups of peasants and in all localities. It can be seen in peasant farming, as the Zemstvo statistics show, in other gubernias as well, where agriculture is also the main branch of peasant economy. This phenomenon, therefore, is widespread and assumes the form of a law, economically of great importance, for it robs small crop farming, to a considerable degree, of all economic sense" (p. 313).

This last remark of Postnikov's is somewhat premature: to prove the inevitability of small farms being ousted by large ones, it is not enough to demonstrate the greater advantage of the latter (the lower price of the product); the predominance of money (more precisely, commodity) economy over natural economy must also be established; under natural economy, when the product is consumed by the producer himself and is not sent to the market, the cheap product does not encounter the more costly product on the market, and is therefore unable to oust it. But of that more anon.

To prove that the above-established law is applicable to all Russia, Postnikov takes those uyezds for which the Zemstvo statistics contain a detailed economic classification of the population, and calculates the cultivated area per pair of draught animals and per working person in the various groups. The conclusion is the same: "where the peasant farm is a small one the cultivated area has to bear a cost of maintaining labour-power one and a half times to twice as large as when the farm is of a more adequate size" (p. 316). This is true for both Perm (p. 314) and Voronezh gubernias, for both Saratov and Chernigov gubernias (p. 315), so that Postnikov has undoubtedly proved this law to be applicable to all Russia.

Let us now pass to the question of the "incomes and expenditures" (Chapter IX) of the different groups of peasant farms and of their relation to the market.

"The territory of every farm that is an independent unit," says Postnikov, "consists of the following four parts: one part produces food for the sustenance of the working family and of the labourers who live on the farm; this, in the narrow sense, is the *food* area of the farm. Another part provides fodder for the cattle working on the farm, and may be called the *fodder* area. A third part consists of the farmyard, roads, ponds, etc., and of that part of the crop area that produces seed; it may be called the *farm-service* area, as it serves the needs of the whole farm without distinction. Lastly, the fourth part produces grain and plants destined, either raw or processed, for sale on the market; this is the *market* or *commercial* area of the farm. The division of the territory into these four parts is determined in each separate farm, not by the crops grown, but by the immediate purpose of their cultivation.

"The cash income of the farm is determined by the commercial part of its territory, and the larger the latter and the greater the relative value of the produce obtained from it, the greater the demand made by the farmers on the market and the larger the amount of labour the country can maintain outside of agriculture within the vicinity of its market; the greater, too, is the state (fiscal) and cultural importance of agriculture to the country, and the greater, too, are the net income of the cultivator himself and the resources at his disposal for farm expenses and for improvements" (p. 257).

This argument of Postnikov's would be perfectly true, if one, fairly substantial, correction were made: the author speaks of the importance of the farm's commercial area to the country in general, whereas this can obviously be said only of a country where money economy predominates, where the greater part of the produce assumes the form of *commodities*. To forget this condition, to consider it self-evident, and to omit a precise investigation of how far it is applicable to the given country, would be to fall into the error of vulgar political economy.

To single out the market area from the farm as a whole is very important. For the home *market* it is by no means the producer's income in general (by which the level of his prosperity is determined) that is significant, but exclusively his income *in cash*. The producer's possession of monetary resources is not determined by his degree of prosperity: the peasant who obtains from his plot of land sufficient produce to satisfy his own requirements fully, but who engages in natural economy, is well-off, but he possesses no monetary resources; on the other hand, the half-ruined peasant who obtains from his plot of land only a small part of the grain he needs and who secures the rest (although in a lesser amount and of poorer quality) by casual earnings, is not well-off, but possesses monetary resources. It is clear from this that no discussion on the importance to the market of peasant farms and the incomes they yield can be of any value if not based on a calculation of the cash part of the income.

In order to determine the size of these four parts of the crop area on the farms of the different groups of peasants, Postnikov first estimates the annual consumption of grain, taking the round figure of two chetverts* of grain per head (p. 259), which means two-thirds of a dessiatine per head out of the crop area. He then estimates the fodder area at one and a half dessiatines per horse, and the seed area at 6% of the total under crops, and arrives at the following results** (p. 319):

	100 dess. under crops consist of				*Cash income*	
	Farm-service	Food	Fodder	Commercial	Per dess. under crops	Per household
	areas				(rubles)	
Cultivating up to 5 dess.	6	90.7	42.3	—39	—	—
" 5 to 10 "	6	44.7	37.5	+11.8	3.77	30
" 10 to 25 "	6	27.5	30	36.5	11.68	191
" 25 to 50 "	6	17	25	52	16.64	574
" over 50 "	6	12	21	61	19.52	1,500

"The difference indicated in the cash income of the various groups," says Postnikov, "is sufficient to illustrate the importance of the size of the farms; but, actually, this difference between the incomes of the various groups from cropping should be even greater, for it must be assumed that the top groups obtain larger harvests per dessiatine and secure better prices for the grain they sell.

* A chetvert equals about six bushels.—*Ed. Eng. ed.*

** To determine the cash income Postnikov proceeded as follows: he assumed that the entire commercial area is sown to the dearest kind of grain—wheat—and, knowing the average crop and prevailing prices, he calculated the value of the produce obtainable from this area.

"In this record of income obtained, we have included the cultivated, and not the total area of the farm, for we have no precise data on the way in which the peasant farms of the Taurida uyezds make use of other farmland for various kinds of livestock; but inasmuch as the cash income of the South-Russian peasant, whose sole pursuit is cropping, is almost entirely determined by the crop area, the above figures fairly accurately depict the difference in the cash income from farming between the various groups of peasants. These figures show how markedly this income changes with the size of the area under crops. A family with 75 dessiatines under crops obtains a cash income of as much as 1,500 rubles a year; a family with 34 $\frac{1}{2}$ dessiatines under crops obtains 574 rubles a year, whereas one with 16 $\frac{1}{3}$ dessiatines under crops obtains only 191 rubles. A family which cultivates 8 dessiatines obtains only 30 rubles, a sum insufficient to cover the cash expenditure of the farm without outside earnings. Of course, the figures quoted do not show the net income of the farms; to obtain this we have to deduct the expenditure of the household on taxes, implements, buildings, the purchase of clothing, footwear, etc. But such expenditure does not increase proportionately as the size of the farm increases. Expenditure on maintaining the family increases in proportion to its size, and the latter, as the table shows, increases far more slowly than the crop area of the various groups. As to total farm expenditure (payment of land tax and rental, repair of buildings and implements), they, at any rate, do not increase more than proportionately to the size of farms, whereas the gross cash income from the farm, as the previous table shows, increases in more than direct proportion to the size of the crop area. What is more, all these expenses are very small compared with the main item of farm expenditure, the maintenance of labour-power. We are thus able to formulate the rule that, in peasant economy, the net proceeds per dessiatine from cropping grow progressively smaller as the size of the farm decreases" (p. 320).

We thus see from Postnikov's figures that peasant farming in the different groups varies substantially with respect to the market: the top groups (with more than 25 dessiatines under crops per household) conduct what is already commercial farming; they grow grain for the income it provides. In the bottom groups, on the contrary, cropping does not cover the family's essential needs (this applies to those who cultivate up to 10 dessiatines per household); if we make an exact calculation of all farm expenditure we shall most certainly find that in these groups the farm is run at a loss.

It is also very interesting to make use of data cited by Postnikov to settle the problem of the relationship between the splitting of the peasantry into different groups and the extent of the market demand. We know that the extent of this demand depends on the size of the commercial area and that the latter becomes greater as the size of the farm increases; but parallel to this increase in the size of the farm in the top groups there is a decrease in its size in the bottom groups. As to the number of farms, the bottom groups contain twice as many as the top: the former constitute 40% in the Taurida uyezds, the latter only 20%. Do we not get the result, in general, that the above-mentioned economic split decreases the extent of the market demand? Properly speaking, we are entitled to answer this question in the negative on purely a priori grounds: the fact is that in the bottom groups, the farm is so small that the family's needs cannot be fully covered by agriculture; to avoid dying of starvation, the members of these bottom groups have to take their labour-power to the market, where its sale provides them with monetary resources and thus counterbalances (to some degree) the lesser demand due to the smaller size of the farms. But Postnikov's data enable us to give a more precise answer to the problem raised.

Let us take some crop area, say, 1,600 dessiatines, and let us imagine it divided in two ways: firstly, among an economically homogeneous peasantry, and, secondly, among peasants split up into different groups such as we find in the Taurida uyezds today. In the first case, assuming that an average peasant farm has 16 dessiatines under crops (as is actually the case in the Taurida uyezds), we get 100 farms that fully cover their needs by agriculture. The demand made on the market will equal $191 \times 100 = 19{,}100$ rubles. Second case: the 1,600 dessiatines under crops are divided among the 100 households differently, exactly as the crop area is actually divided among the peasants of the Taurida uyezds: 8 households have no crop area at all; 12 cultivate 4 dessiatines each; 20—8 dessiatines each; 40—16 dessiatines each; 17—34 dessiatines each, and 3—75 dessiatines (a total of 1,583 dessiatines, i.e., even a little less than 1,600 dessiatines). With such a distribution, a very considerable section of the peasants (40%) will not be in a position to derive a sufficient return from their land to cover all their needs. The extent of the monetary demand made on the market, counting only the farms with over 5 dessiatines under crops per household, will be as follows: (20×30)+(40×191)+(17×574)+(3×1,500)= 21,350 rubles. We thus find that, despite the omission of 20 households [undoubtedly these also have a cash income, but it is not obtained from the sale of their produce], and despite the reduction of the crop area to 1,535 dessiatines, the total monetary demand on the market is higher.[9]

It has already been said that the peasants of the bottom economic groups are forced to sell their labour-power; the members of the top groups, on the contrary, have to buy it, for the workers in their own families are inadequate for the cultivation of their large crop areas. We must now dwell in greater detail on this important fact. Postnikov apparently does not class it under the "new economic developments in peasant life" (at least, he does not mention it in his preface, where he sums up the results of his work), but it is deserving of far more attention than the introduction of machines or the extension of cropping by the well-to-do peasants.

"The more affluent peasantry in the Taurida uyezds," the author says, "generally employ hired labourers to a considerable extent and farm an area that far exceeds the working capacity of the families themselves. Thus, in the three uyezds the percentage of families in all categories of peasants employing hired labourers is as follows:

Cultivating no land	3.8%
" up to 5 dess.	2.5
" 5 to 10 "	2.6
" 10 to 25 "	8.7
" 25 to 50 "	34.7
" over 50 "	64.1
Average	12.9%

"These figures show that it is mostly the well-to-do farmers with the larger cultivated areas that employ hired labourers" (p. 144).

Comparing the data already given on family composition by groups without hired labourers (for the three uyezds separately) and with hired labourers (for the three uyezds together), we find that by hiring labourers, farmers who sow from 25 to 50 dessiatines per household increase the number of hands on their farms by about one-third (from 1.8 or 1.9 working persons per family to 2.4), while farmers with over 50 dessiatines under crops per household almost double the number of their workers (from 2.3 to 5); even more than double according to the estimate of the author, who considers that they have to hire 8,241 workers (p. 115), while they have only 7,129 of their own. That the bottom groups have to release workers on the side in very large numbers is clear from the very fact that cropping cannot provide them with the amount of produce which they need for their own subsistence. Unfortunately, we have no precise data as to the number of persons released for outside work. An indirect indication of this number may be found in the number of householders who lease their allotments; above we have cited Postnikov's statement to the effect that about one-third of the inhabitants of the Taurida uyezds do not exploit their allotment land to the full.

IV

It can be seen from the data given above that Postnikov has fully proved his point on the "tremendous diversity" in the economic status of the various households. This diversity applies not only to the property status of the peasants and the size of the areas they cultivate, but even to the character of the farming in the different groups. That is still not all. It turns out that the terms "diversity" and "differentiation" are inadequate for a full description of the phenomenon. When one peasant owns one draught animal and another 10, we call that differentiation; but when one rents scores of dessiatines of land above the allotment that satisfies his needs, with the sole object of deriving profit from its exploitation, thus depriving another peasant of the opportunity of renting land which he requires in order to feed his family, we obviously are faced with something much bigger; we have to call that sort of thing "strife" p. 323), a "struggle of economic interests" (p. XXXII). Although he employs these terms, Postnikov does not fully appreciate their importance; nor does he see that the terms themselves are inadequate. To rent allotment land from the impoverished section of the population, and to hire as a labourer the peasant who has ceased to run his own farm is something more than mere strife—it is downright exploitation.

Recognising the profound economic strife among the peasantry of today, we can no longer restrict ourselves to just dividing the peasants into several strata according to the property they possess. Such a division would suffice if the diversity mentioned above amounted to mere quantitative differences. But that is not so. If, in the case of one section of the peasants, the aim of agriculture is commercial profit and the result is a large cash income, whereas in the case of another, agriculture cannot cover even the family's essential needs; if the top peasant groups base their improved farming on the ruin of the bottom groups; if the prosperous peasantry employ hired labour on a considerable scale, while the poor are compelled to resort to the sale of their labour-power—these are undoubtedly qualitative differences, and our task must now be to classify the peasantry according to differences in the character of the farming itself (meaning by character of farming peculiarities not of a technical but of an economic order).

Postnikov has devoted too little attention to these latter differences. Therefore, while he recognises the need for a "more general division of the population into groups" (p. 110) and attempts to make such a division, this attempt, as we shall soon see, cannot be considered quite successful.

"To achieve a more general division of the population into economic groups," says Postnikov, "we shall adopt a different criterion which, although not of uniform economic significance in all localities, is more in conformity with the division into groups made by the peasants themselves and that has also been noted in all uyezds by the Zemstvo statisticians. This division is made according to the degree of the farmers' independence in the conduct of their farms, depending on the number of draught animals owned" (p. 110).

"At the present time the peasants of the South-Russian region may be divided, according to the degree of their economic independence and at the same time their methods of farming, into the three following main groups:

"1) Peasant households owning a full team of animals, i.e., with enough animals to work a plough or some other ploughing implement and who can cultivate their land with their own animals without having to hire or to yoke[10] with other peasants. When the implement used is a plough or a drill plough the peasant has two, three or more pairs of draught animals and, correspondingly, three or at least two adult workers and a part-time worker in the household.

"2) Peasants with insufficient animals, or yokers, i.e., peasants who yoke with one another for field work because their own animals do not suffice for independent harnessing. Such peasants have one or one and a half, in some cases even two pairs of draught animals and, correspondingly, one or two adult workers. Where the soil is heavy and a plough (or a drill plough) needs three pairs of draught animals the peasants invariably yoke with each other, even if they have two pairs of draught animals of their own.

"3) 'Footers,' or householders who have no animals whatever or have one (more often than not a horse, as oxen are generally kept in pairs and harnessed only in pairs). They work by hiring animals from others, or let their land for a part of the harvest and have no cultivated land of their own.

"This classification of the peasants according to an economic criterion fundamental to peasant life, such as in the present instance the number of draught animals and the manner of harnessing them, is usually made by the peasants themselves. But there are considerable variations of it, both within the bounds of each separate group enumerated above, and in the division of the groups themselves" (p. 121).

These groups constitute the following percentages of the total number of households (p. 125):

	I	II	III	
	Working with own animals	Working on yoking basis	Working with hired animals	With no land under crops
Berdyansk Uyezd	37	44.6	11.7	6.7
Melitopol "	32.7	46.8	13	7.5
Dnieper "	43	34.8	13.2	9

Side by side with this table, the author gives a classification of households according to the number of draught animals they own, in order to show how the animals are distributed in the uyezds described:

	Percentage of total number of households			
	Draught animals (per household)			
	4 or more	2 or 3	one	none
Berdyansk Uyezd	36.2	41.6	7.2	15
Melitopol "	34.4	44.7	5.3	15.6
Dnieper "	44.3	36.6	5.1	14

Consequently, in the Taurida uyezds, a full team consists of no less than four draught animals.

This classification, as made by Postnikov, cannot be considered altogether happy, first of all because marked differences are to be observed within each of the three groups: "In the group of householders owning a team of draught animals," the author says, "there is considerable diversity evident in South Russia: side by side with the large numbers of animals of the well-to-do peasants there are the small teams of the poorer peasants. The former, in their turn, may be subdivided into those with full working teams (6 to 8 or more animals) and those with less than a full team (4 to 6 animals).... The category of 'footer' householders also presents considerable variety in degree of affluence" (p. 124).

Another inconvenience in the division adopted by Postnikov is, as we have already indicated, that the Zemstvo statistics do not classify the population according to the number of draught animals owned, but according to cultivated area. In order, therefore, to be able to express accurately the property status of the various groups, this classification according to cultivated area has to be used.

On this basis Postnikov also divides the population into three groups: householders who are small cultivators—with up to 10 dessiatines under crops, or none at all; middle cultivators—with 10 to 25 dessiatines; and large cultivators—with over 25 dessiatines per household under crops. The author calls the first group "poor," the second middle, and the third well-to-do.

In respect of the size of these groups, Postnikov says: "In general, among the Taurida peasants (excluding the colonists), the large cultivators constitute about one-sixth of the total number of households; those with medium-sized crop areas about 40%, while the households with small crop areas and those with none at all constitute a little over 40%. Taking the population of the Taurida uyezds as a whole (including the colonists), the large cultivators constitute one-fifth, or about 20%, the middle 40%, and the small cultivators and those with no tillage about 40%" (p. 112).

Hence, the composition of the groups is altered very slightly by the inclusion of the German colonists, so that no error will arise from using the general data for a whole uyezd.

We now have to describe as accurately as possible the economic status of each of these groups separately, and to try to ascertain the extent and causes of the economic strife among the peasantry.

Postnikov did not set himself this task; that is why the data he quotes are markedly very scattered and his general observations on the groups are not definite enough.

Let us begin with the bottom group, the poor peasants, to which two-fifths of the population of the Taurida uyezds belong.

The number of draught animals (the chief instrument of production in agriculture) owned by this group is the best indication of how poor they really are. In the three uyezds of Taurida Gubernia, out of a total of 263,589 draught animals, the bottom group possess (p. 117) 43,625, or 17% in all, which is $2\frac{1}{3}$ times less than the average. The data on the percentage of households possessing no draught animals were given above (80%, 48% and 12% for the three subdivisions of the bottom group). On the basis of these data, Postnikov arrived at the conclusion that "the percentage of householders who possess no animals of their own is considerable only in the groups with no land under crops or with crop areas of up to 10 dessiatines per household" (p. 135). The crop area of this group corresponds to the number of animals: on their own land they cultivate 146,114 dessiatines out of the total of 962,933 dessiatines (in the three uyezds), that is, 15%. The addition of rented land raises the sown area to 174,496 dessiatines; but since the sown area of the other groups also increases and does so to a larger extent than in the bottom group, the result is that the area cultivated by the bottom group constitutes only 12% of the total; in other words, there is only one-eighth of the cultivated area to more than three-eighths of the population. If we remember that it is the medium-sized area cultivated by the Taurida peasant which the author regards as normal (i.e., covering all the family's needs) we can easily see how this group, with a sown area $3\frac{1}{3}$ times less than the average, is deprived of its just share.

It is quite natural that, under these circumstances, the farming of this group is in a very bad way. We have already seen that 33% to 39% of the population in the Taurida uyezds—consequently, the overwhelming majority of the bottom group—have no ploughing implements whatever. Lack of implements compels the peasants to give up the land, to lease their allotments: Postnikov estimates that such lessors (whose farms are undoubtedly already utterly ruined) comprise about one-third of the population, that is, again a considerable majority of the poor group. Let us note in passing that this practice of "selling" allotments (to borrow the customary expression of the peasants) has been reflected in Zemstvo statistics everywhere, and on a very large scale. The periodicals which have drawn attention to this fact have already managed to invent a remedy for it—the inalienability of allotments. Postnikov quite rightly questions the effectiveness of such measures, which reveal in their authors a purely bureaucratic faith in the power of the decrees of the authorities. "There can be no doubt," he says, "that merely to prohibit the leasing of land will not eliminate it when it is so deeply rooted in the present economic structure of peasant life. A peasant who has no implements and means with which to run his own farm is virtually unable to make use of his allotment and has to lease it to other peasants who are in a position to farm it. The direct prohibition of the leasing of land will force the peasant to do it surreptitiously, without control, and most likely on terms that are worse for the lessor than at present, since he is forced to lease his land. Furthermore, allotments will increasingly be leased through the village courts[11] in payment of taxation arrears, and such leasing is the least advantageous for the poor peasant" (p. 140).

Absolute economic decline is to be observed in the case of all the members of the poor group.

"At bottom," says Postnikov, "there is no great difference in economic status between the householders who sow nothing and those who sow little, cultivating their land with hired animals. The former lease the whole of their land to their fellow villagers, the latter only part; but both groups *either serve as labourers* for their fellow villagers, *or* engage in *outside employments, mostly agricultural*, while continuing to live at home. Hence, *both these categories of peasants—those who sow nothing and those who sow little—may be examined together*; both belong to the class of peasants who are losing their farms, who in most cases are ruined or on the verge of ruin, and are without the livestock and implements with which to work their farms" (p. 135).

"While the non-farming, non-cultivating households are in most cases those that are already ruined," says Postnikov a little later on, "those that cultivate little, that lease their land, are candidates for membership of that category. Every severe harvest failure, or chance calamity such as fire, loss of horses, etc., drives some of the householders out of this group into the category of non-farming peasants and farm labourers. A householder who, from one cause or another, loses his draught animals, takes the first step along the road to ruin. Cultivating the land with hired animals is too casual and unsystematic, and usually leads to a reduction of cropping. Such a muzhik is refused credit by the village loan-and-savings societies and by his fellow villagers" [a footnote says: "In the Taurida uyezds there are very many loan-and-savings societies in the big villages, operating with funds borrowed from the State Bank; but it is only the rich and well-to-do householders who obtain loans from them"]; "when he does get a loan, it is usually on worse terms than those obtained by the 'thriving' peasants. 'How can you lend him anything if he has nothing to pay with?' the peasants say. Once he gets involved in debt, the first stroke of ill luck robs him of his land too, especially if he is also in arrears with his taxes" (p. 139).

The extent of the decline of farming among the peasants of the poor group can best be seen from the fact that the author does not even attempt to answer the question of exactly how they run their farms. In the case of farms that cultivate less than 10 dessiatines per household, he says, "the conditions of farming are too fortuitous for it to be described by any definite system" (p. 278).

The characteristics of peasant farming in the bottom group that have been cited are, despite their considerable number, still quite inadequate; they are exclusively negative in character, although there surely must be positive characteristics. All we have heard so far is that the peasants of this group cannot be regarded as independent agriculturists, because their farms are in absolute decline, their cultivated area is far too inadequate and because, lastly, their farms are run haphazardly. "Only the prosperous and well-to-do farmers, who are not in need of seed," remark the statisticians in describing Bakhmut Uyezd, "can observe any sort of system in sowing crops; but the poor peasants sow whatever happens to be on hand, anywhere and anyhow" (p. 278). Nevertheless, the existence of all this mass of the peasantry embraced by the bottom group (in the three Taurida uyezds, over 30,000 households and over 200,000 persons of both sexes) cannot be accidental. If they do not live on the produce of their own farms, how do they live? Chiefly by the sale of their labour-power. We have seen above that Postnikov says of this group of peasants that they live by farm-labouring and other outside earnings. In view of the almost total absence of handicraft industries in the South, such earnings are mostly agricultural which means, in fact, that the peasants are *hiring themselves* for farm work. To prove in greater detail that the chief feature of the economy of the bottom group of peasants is the sale of their labour-power, let us proceed to examine this group according to the categories into which they are divided in the Zemstvo statistics. As to the non-farming householders, nothing need be said of them: they are farm labourers pure and simple. In the second category we have cultivators with crop areas of up to 5 dessiatines per household (the average is 3.5 dessiatines). The division of the cultivated area, given above, into farm-service, fodder, food and commercial, shows us that an area of this size is altogether inadequate. "The first group, with a cultivated area up to 5 dessiatines per household," says Postnikov, "have no market, or commercial, area at all; they can only exist with the help of outside earnings, obtained by working as farm labourers, or by other means" (p. 319). There remains the last category—the farmers with 5 to 10 dessiatines of cultivated land per household. The question is: what, among the peasants of this group, is the relation of independent farming to the so-called "earnings"? For a precise answer to this question, we should have several *typical* peasant budgets relating to the farmers of *this group*. Postnikov fully admits the need for and importance of budget data, but points out that the "collection of such data is extremely difficult, and in many cases simply beyond the power of the statisticians" (p. 107). We find it very difficult to agree to this view: Moscow statisticians have collected several extremely interesting and detailed budgets (see *Statistical Returns for Moscow Gubernia.* Section on Economic Statistics, Vols. VI and VII); in several uyezds of Voronezh Gubernia, as the author himself indicates, budget data have even been collected on a house-to-house basis.

It is a great pity that the budget material Postnikov himself gives is very inadequate: he cites the budgets of seven German colonists and of only one Russian peasant; moreover, all are those of big cultivators (the minimum—in the case of the Russian—is $39\frac{1}{2}$ dessiatines sown), that is, all belong to a group of whose economy one may obtain a clear enough idea from the facts contained in the Zemstvo statistics. Expressing his regret that he was "unable during his tour to gather a larger number of peasant budgets," Postnikov says that "to give an exact appreciation of these budgets is, in general, no easy matter. The Tauridians are quite frank in giving economic information, but often enough they themselves do not know the exact figures of their income and expenditure. The peasants recall with greater accuracy the general amount of their expenditure, or the biggest items of income and expenditure, but small amounts almost invariably escape their memory" (p. 288). It would, however, be better to collect a few budgets, even without minor details, than, as the author has done, to collect "about 90 descriptions and an evaluation" of the economic situation, which is elucidated with sufficient clarity in the Zemstvo house-to-house censuses.

In the absence of budgets, only two kinds of data are at our disposal for determining the character of the economy of the group under review: firstly, Postnikov's estimates of the cultivated area per household necessary to feed an average family; and, secondly, data on the division of the cultivated area into four parts, and on the average cash expenditure (per family per year) of the local peasants.

On the basis of detailed estimates of the cultivated area required for a family's food, for seed and for fodder, Postnikov arrives at the following final conclusion:

"A peasant family of average size and well-being, living exclusively by farming and balancing its income and expenditure without deficit, needs, given average harvests, 4 dessiatines to feed $6\frac{1}{2}$ members of the family, $4\frac{1}{2}$ dessiatines to feed 3 draught horses, $1\frac{1}{2}$ dessiatines for seed supply, and 6 to 8 dessiatines for the production of grain for sale, or in all, 16 to 18 dessiatines under crops. ...The average Tauridian has about 18 dessiatines under crops per household, but 40% of the population of the three Taurida uyezds have less than 10 dessiatines per household; and if they are nevertheless able to engage in farming, it is only because part of their income is derived from outside employments and by leasing part of their land. The economic position of this section of the population is abnormal and insecure, because in the majority of cases they are unable to accumulate the reserve to tide them over a difficult period" (p. 272).

As the average cultivated area per household in the group under review is 8 dessiatines, i.e., less than half the area required (17 dessiatines), we are entitled to conclude that the peasants of this group derive the greater part of their income from "employments," i.e., from the sale of their labour.

Here is another calculation: according to Postnikov's data, quoted above, on the division of the cultivated area, out of 8 dessiatines under crops, 0.48 dessiatines will go for seed; 3 dessiatines for fodder (in this group there are 2, not 3, draught animals per household); and 3.576 dessiatines for the food of the family (its size is also below the average—about $5\frac{1}{2}$ persons, not $6\frac{1}{2}$); so that less than one dessiatine (0.944) remains for the commercial area, the income from which the author estimates at 30 rubles. But the amount of a Tauridian's essential cash expenditure is much greater. It is much easier to collect information on the amount of cash expenditure than on budgets, says the author, because the peasants themselves often make calculations of this sort. These calculations show that:

"In the case of a family of average size, i.e., consisting of the working husband, the wife and 4 young children or adolescents, if they farm their own land (roughly about 20 dessiatines) and do not resort to renting, the essential cash expenditure, as estimated by the Tauridians, amounts to between 200 and 250 rubles per annum. A cash expenditure of 150 to 180 rubles is considered to be the minimum that a small family must make, even if they stint themselves in everything. An annual income of less than this amount is considered quite inadequate, for in these parts a working man and his wife can, by farm-labouring, earn 120 rubles a year, with board and lodging, without incurring the expense of maintaining livestock, implements and so forth, and, in addition, can get 'extras' from land leased to fellow villagers" (p. 289). As the group under examination is below the average, we take the minimum, not the average, cash expenditure, and the lowest figure of this minimum at that—150 rubles—which has to be derived from "employments." According to this calculation, a peasant of the group under examination derives from his own farming a total of 117.5

rubles (30+87.5*), and from the sale of his labour-power 120 rubles. Consequently, we again find that by independent farming the peasants of this group can only cover *less than half* of their minimum expenditure.**

Thus an examination of the character of the economy in all the subdivisions of the bottom group leads us to the unquestionable conclusion that although the majority of the peasants do cultivate small plots, the sale of their labour-power is their principal source of livelihood. All the peasants of this group are hired labourers rather than independent farmers.

Postnikov did not raise this question of the character of the economy of the bottom group of peasants, and did not elucidate the relation of outside employments to the peasant's own farming—and that is a big defect in his work. As a result, he does not adequately explain the, at first glance, strange fact that although the peasants of the bottom group have too little land of their own, they abandon it, lease it; as a result the important fact, that the means of production (i. e., land and implements) possessed by the bottom group of peasants are quantitatively far below the average, is not linked up with the general character of their

* A food area of $3\frac{1}{2}$ dessiatines will yield 25 rubles in produce per dessiatine (25 × 3.5 = 87.5)—Postnikov's calculation, p. 272.

** The calculations made by Mr. Yuzhakov in *Russkaya Mysl*,[12] No. 9, 1885 ("Quotas for People's Landownership") fully corroborate this conclusion. He considers that the food norm, i.e., the lowest norm, in Taurida Gubernia, is an allotment of 9 dessiatines under crops per household. But Mr. Yuzhakov sees the allotment as covering *only* the *cereal* foods and taxation, and assumes that the other expenditures will be covered by outside earnings. The budgets given in the Zemstvo statistics show that the latter expenditures constitute over half the total. For example, in Voronezh Gubernia the average expenditure of a peasant family is 495.39 rubles, reckoning expenditure both in cash and kind. Of this sum, 109.10 rubles go for the maintenance of livestock [N. V. Yuzhakov sees the maintenance of livestock as coming from hay-fields and other grounds, and not from arable land], 135.80 rubles for vegetable food and taxes, and 250.49 rubles for other expenditure—clothing, implements, rent, various household requirements, etc. [24 budgets in *Statistical Returns for Ostrogozhsk Uyezd*]. In Moscow Gubernia, the average annual expenditure per family is 348.83 rubles, of which 156.03 go for cereal foods and taxes, and 192.80 for other expenditure. [Average of 8 budgets collected by Moscow statisticians—loc. cit.]

farming. Since the average quantity of means of production, as we have seen, is only just enough to satisfy the essential needs of the family, it necessarily and inevitably follows from this fact—the fact of the poor peasants being deprived of their fair share—that they must seek means of production belonging to others to which to apply their labour, i.e., they must sell themselves.

Let us now pass to the second group—the *middle* one, also embracing 40% of the population. Under this category come farmers with a cultivated area of from 10 to 25 dessiatines per household. The term "middle" is fully applicable to the members of this group, with the reservation, however, that their means of production are somewhat (slightly) below the average: the cultivated area per household is 16.4 dessiatines, as against the average of 17 dessiatines for all peasants; livestock—7.3 head per household, as against an average of 7.6 (draught animals—3.2, as against an average of 3.1); total tillage per household—17 to 18 dessiatines (allotment, purchased, and rented), as against an average of 20 to 21 dessiatines for the uyezds. A comparison of the number of dessiatines under crops per household with the norm given by Postnikov, shows that the farming of their own land by this group yields them only just enough for their subsistence.

All these facts, it would seem, should lead us to think that the farming of this group of peasants is the most stable: the peasant covers all his expenses by it; he works not for profit but only to satisfy primary needs. As a matter of fact, however, we see the very opposite: the farming of this group of peasants is distinguished by its very considerable instability.

Firstly, an average cultivated area of 16 dessiatines is shown to be adequate. Consequently, peasants with 10 to 16 dessiatines under crops do not cover all their expenses by farming and are also obliged to resort to outside employments. From Postnikov's approximate estimates quoted above, we see that this group hires 2,846 workers, whereas it releases 3,389, or 543 more. Hence, about half the farms in the group are not fully provided for.

Further, in this group the number of draught animals per household is 3.2, whereas, as we have seen, the number needed for a team is four. Consequently, a large number of the households in this group have insufficient animals of their own with which to cultivate their land, and have to resort to yoking. The yokers in this group likewise constitute no less than one-half of the total: we may draw this conclusion from the fact that the proportion of households owning working teams is about 40%, of which 20% go to the prosperous upper group, the remaining 20% belonging to the middle group, so that no less than half of the middle group do not own a working team. Postnikov does not give the exact number of yokers in this group. Turning to the Zemstvo statistical abstracts we find the following data (for two uyezds):*

	Total in group cultivating 10 to 25 dess.		Distribution of the number of dessiatines cultivated							
			With own animals		By yoking		With hired animals		By other means	
	Households	Dess.	Households	Dess.	Households	Dess.	Households	Dess.	Households	Dess.
Melitopol Uyezd	13,789	226,389.21	4,218	79,726.55	9,201	141,483.26	321	4,405.8	49	773.3
Dnieper Uyezd	8,234	137,343.75	4,029	71,125.2	3,835	61,159.05	320	4,352.5	50	707.25

Thus, in the middle group of the two uyezds, a minority of the households cultivate their land with their own animals: in Melitopol Uyezd less than one-third of the households; in Dnieper Uyezd less than one-half. Hence, the number of yokers estimated above for all the three uyezds (one-half) is, if anything, too low and certainly not exaggerated. Of course, the peasant's inability to farm with animals of his own is in itself sufficiently indicative of the instability of his farm; but, as an illustration, let us quote

* *Statistical Returns for Melitopol Uyezd* (Appendix to *Returns for Taurida Gubernia*, Vol. I), Simferopol, 1885, p. B 195. *Statistical Returns for Dnieper Uyezd* (*Returns for Taurida Gubernia*, Vol. II), Simferopol, 1886, p. B 123.

the description of the yoking system given by Postnikov, who, unfortunately, pays too little attention to this phenomenon, interesting as it is economically and from the standpoint of life and customs.

"Among the peasants who work on a yoking basis," says Postnikov, "the standard working area is lower [than among the peasants who work with their own animals] by virtue of the law of mechanics which says that three horses harnessed together do not pull three times as much as one horse. Those who arrange to yoke may live at different ends of the village (they are usually relatives); furthermore, the number of plots belonging to the two householders (sometimes three householders yoke) is twice that of one. All this increases the time spent on travelling from one section to another." [A footnote says: "When the land is divided, each household receives for its members an unbroken patch in a particular field; hence small families receive smaller patches. The conditions of yoking in Taurida Gubernia vary considerably. If one of the yokers has a drill plough, he gets an extra dessiatine ploughed—e.g., one gets 10 dessiatines, the other 11—or the one who has no drill plough of his own has to bear all the expenses of repairing it while in use. Similarly, when the number of yoked animals is unequal, one gets an extra day's ploughing done, etc. In the village of Kamenka, the owner of a drill plough receives from three to six rubles in cash for the spring. Ouarrels among the yokers are generally very frequent."] "Some time is also spent in coming to terms, and it may happen that the yokers fall out before the work is finished. The yokers sometimes do not have enough horses for harrowing, in which case the drill plough horses are unharnessed: some go off for water, while the others harrow. In the village of Yuzkui, I was told that yokers often plough no more than one dessiatine a day, which is half the normal rate" (p. 233).

There is a shortage of implements in addition to the shortage of animals. From the table given above, showing the number of implements per household in the various groups, we see that in the middle group, in all the uyezds, there is not less than one ploughing implement per household. Actually, however, the distribution of implements even within the group is by no means uniform. Unfortunately, Postnikov does not give any data on this subject, and we have to turn to the Zemstvo statistical abstracts. In Dnieper Uyezd, 1,808 households out of 8,227 have no ploughing implements at all; in Melitopol Uyezd 2,954 out of 13,789; in the former uyezd the ill-provided households constitute 21.9% of the total; in the latter 21.4%. There can be no doubt that the householders who have no ploughing implements approximate the bottom group in economic status, while those who have more than one such implement per household approximate the top group. The number of householders who have no ploughs is even higher: 32.5% in Dnieper Uyezd and 65.5% in Melitopol. Lastly, the peasants of this group own an insignificant number of reaping machines (they are of very great importance in South-Russian peasant farming because of the shortage of workers for hand reaping and the long-tract system,[13] which drags out grain removal for months): in Dnieper Uyezd the whole group owns 20 mowing and reaping machines (one per 400 households); in Melitopol Uyezd, $178\frac{1}{2}$ (one per 700 households).

The general system of peasant farming in this group is described by Postnikov as follows:

"Householders having less than four draught animals invariably yoke together for the cultivation of their fields and for sowing. The householders of this category have either two working members or only one. The lower relative working capacity of such farmers is due to the smaller size of the farms, the yoking system, and the shortage of implements. The yokers mostly plough with small, three-share drill ploughs, which work more slowly. If such peasants harvest their grain with machines hired from neighbours, they get them only after the latter have cut their own crops. Harvesting by hand takes longer, in some cases necessitates the hiring of day labourers, and is more expensive. For single-handed peasants any urgent household matter, or the performance of public duties, interrupts the work. If the single-handed peasant goes to work in a distant field, where the peasants usually spend the whole week until the ploughing and sowing are completed, he has to return to the village more often to see how the family at home is faring" (p. 278). Such single-handed peasants (one working member in the family) constitute the majority in the group under examination, as will be seen from the following table given by Postnikov and showing the number of working members in the families in the different crop-sowing groups in all the three uyezds of Taurida Gubernia (p. 143):

	Per 100 households			
	With no male workers	With 1 worker	With 2 workers	With 3 or more workers
Cultivating no land	19	67	11	3
" up to 5 dess.	9	77.6	11.7	1.7
" 5 to 10 "	4.2	74.8	17.7	3.3
" 10 to 25 "	1.7	59	29	10.3
" 25 to 50 "	1.2	40	35.7	23.1
" over 50 "	0.9	25	34.3	39.8
Average	4.3	60.6	24.6	10.5

It will be seen from this table that three-fifths of the families in the middle group have one working member each or none at all.*

To illustrate the relation of the middle to the top group, and the stability of its farms in general, let us quote data from *Statistical Returns for Dnieper Uyezd* showing how all the land at the peasants' disposal, and the cultivated area** in particular, is distributed among the groups We get the following table:***

* In support of his point about the considerable advantages in farming enjoyed by the large-family householders (i.e., those with many working members) over the single-handed householders, Postnikov cites Trirogov's well-known book *The Village Community and the Peasant Tax*.

** The data relate to the entire Dnieper Uyezd, including villages not counted in the volosts. The figures in the "Total land in use" column I have calculated myself, by adding together the amounts of allotment, rented and purchased land and subtracting the amount leased. Dnieper Uyezd has been chosen because it is inhabited almost exclusively by Russians.

*** See table on p. 60.—*Ed.*

Peasant Groups	Percentage of total households	Allotment land		Purchased land		Rented land		Leased land	Total land in use by group		Sown area	
		Dessiatines	%	Dessiatines	%	Dessiatines	%		Dessiatines	%	Dessiatines	%
Poor	39.9	56,444.95	25.5	2,003.25	6	7,838.75	6	21,551.25	44,735.7	12.4	38,439.25	11
Middle	41.7	102,793.7	46.5	5,376	16	48,397.75	35	8,311	148,256.45	41.2	137,343.75	43
Prosperous	18.4	61.844.25	28	26,530.75	78	81,645.95	59	3,039.25	166,981.7	46.4	150,614.45	46
Total	100	221,082.9	100	33,910	100	137,882.45	100	32,901.5	359,973.85	100	326,397.45	100

This table shows that the middle group held more allotment arable than the others: 46.5% of the total. The peasants were forced by the inadequacy of their allotments to resort to renting, as a result of which the area cultivated by them increased all in all by more than 50%. The amount of land in the hands of the middle group also increased *absolutely*, but decreased *relatively*—to 41.2% of the total area and 43% of the cultivated area; first place was occupied by the top group. Hence, not only the bottom group, but the middle one, too, feels the direct pressure of the top group, which deprives them of the land.

All that has been said entitles us to describe the economic status of the middle group as follows. It comprises peasants who live exclusively on the returns from the land they cultivate themselves; the area of the latter is almost equal to the average area cultivated by the local peasantry (or somewhat less) and barely covers the family's essential needs. But the insufficiency of animals and implements, and their uneven distribution, render the farming of this group of peasants unstable, precarious, especially in view of the menacing tendency of the top group to squeeze out the bottom and middle groups.

Let us now turn to this top group, which comprises the affluent peasantry. In the Taurida uyezds it embraces one-fifth of the population, with a cultivated area of over 25 dessiatines per household. Sufficient facts have already been cited to show the extent to which this group is really richer than the others in draught animals, implements, and allotment and other land. To show how much better off the peasants of this group are than the middle peasants, we shall cite only the following data of crop areas: in Dnieper Uyezd, the well-to-do group have 41.3 dessiatines under crops per household, whereas the average for the uyezd is 17.8 dessiatines, or less than half as much. Generally speaking, this aspect of the matter—the greater prosperity of the big cultivators—has been sufficiently brought out by Postnikov, but he pays practically no attention to another and far more important question: what part is played by this group's farming in the total agricultural production of the region, and what price is paid by the other groups for the thriving condition of the top group.

The fact of the matter is that this group is numerically very small—in the most prosperous region of the South, Taurida Gubernia, it constitutes only 20% of the population. It might therefore be thought that its relative importance to the locality's general economy is not great.* Actually, however, we find the contrary to be true: this well-to-do minority plays a predominant part in the total output of agricultural produce. In the three Taurida uyezds, out of a total of 1,439,267 dessiatines under crops 724,678 dessiatines, or more than half, are in the hands of the well-to-do peasants. These figures, of course, are a far from accurate expression of the predominance of the top group, inasmuch as the well-to-do peasants' harvests are much larger than those of the poor and the middle peasants, who, as shown in Postnikov's description quoted above, do not run their farms on proper lines.

Thus, the principal grain producers are the top group of peasants, and hence (a fact of the utmost importance, and one particularly often ignored) all the various descriptions of agriculture and talk about agricultural improvements and so on, relate primarily and mostly (sometimes even exclusively) to the prosperous minority. Let us take, for example, the data relating to the distribution of improved implements.

Postnikov speaks of the Taurida peasant's implements as follows:

"With few exceptions, the implements of the peasant are the same as those of the German colonist, but less varied, sometimes of poorer quality, and therefore cheaper. An exception is the south-western, less densely populated part of Dnieper Uyezd, where the primitive Little-Russian implements, the heavy wooden plough and wooden iron-tipped drill plough, are still in vogue. In the rest of the Taurida uyezds, the ploughs used by the peasants are everywhere of an improved type, made of iron. Side by side with the iron plough the drill plough is everywhere of primary importance in the cultivation of the soil and in many cases

* This mistake, for example, is made by Mr. Slonimsky, who in an article on Postnikov's book says: "The well-to-do group of peasants is lost in the mass of the poor, and in some areas would seem to be altogether non-existent." (*Vestnik Yevropy*,[14] 1893, No. 3, p. 307.)

is the only ploughing implement used by the peasants. But most frequently the drill plough is used side by side with the iron plough.... The harrows everywhere are of wood, with iron teeth, and are of two types: two-horse harrows, with a 10-foot stretch, and one-horse harrows, with a stretch of about 7 feet.... The drill plough is an implement with 3, 4 or 5 shares.... Very often a small seed-drill is attached to the front of the drill plough and is operated by its wheel. It plants the seed while the drill plough fills in the drills. Of the other implements used by the peasants in cultivating the soil we meet, although not often, with the wooden roller, used to roll the soil after sowing. Reaping-machines have spread among the peasants particularly in the last 10 years. In the more prosperous villages, the peasants relate, almost half the households possess them.... Mowing-machines are far more rarely met with among the peasants than reapers.... Horse rakes and threshers are equally rare. The use of winnowing-machines is universal.... For carting purposes, the German farm waggon and *mazhara** are used exclusively; they are now built in many of the Russian villages.... Stone toothed rollers of various sizes are universally used for threshing" (pp. 213-15).

To learn how these implements are distributed, we have to turn to the Zemstvo statistical abstracts, although their data are not complete either: the Taurida statisticians registered only ploughs and drill ploughs, reapers and mowers, and vehicles (waggons and mazharas). If we combine the data for Melitopol and Dnieper uyezds we shall find that of the total number (46,522) of ploughs and cultivators the top group owns 19,987, or 42.9%; waggons, 23,747 out of 59,478, or 39.9%; and, finally, reapers and mowers, 2,841 out of 3,061, or 92.8%.

Data have already been cited to show that labour productivity in the top groups of the peasantry is considerably higher than in the bottom and middle groups. Let us now see what peculiarities of technique determine this specific feature of the economy of the big cultivators.

"The amount of land held and used by the peasants," says Postnikov, "largely determines the system and character of farming. Unfortunately, the dependence of one on the

* *Mazhara*—a long heavy farm cart with a light framework of poles for its sides.—*Ed. Eng. ed.*

other has so far been little studied by our investigators of peasant farming, who not infrequently conceive it to be of the same type among all sections of the rural population. Leaving aside the system of farming, I shall endeavour briefly to summarise the peculiarities in the farming technique of different peasant groups insofar as I have been able to ascertain them during my visits to the Taurida uyezds.

"Householders who work with their own animals and do not resort to yoking, own four, five, six or more draught animals.* Their economic status, however, varies considerably. A four-share drill plough requires a team of four animals, a five-share implement a team of five animals. Ploughing is followed by harrowing, and if the farmer has no extra horse, he cannot harrow immediately behind the plough, but only when the ploughing is finished, that is, the seed is covered when the soil is already slightly dry, a circumstance that does not favour germination. If the ploughing is done at a distance from the village, necessitating the carting of water and fodder, the absence of an extra horse also interrupts the work. In all such cases, the lack of a full complement of working animals leads to loss of time and delays the sowing. Given a larger number of draught animals and a multi-share drill plough, the peasants are able to plant their fields more quickly, to make the most of favourable weather, and to cover the seed with moister soil. Thus it is the "full" farmer, the one with six, or, better still, seven draught animals, that has the advantage in the technique of spring sowing. With seven horses, a five-share drill plough and two harrows can function simultaneously. Such a farmer, the peasants say, 'carries on without a stop.'

"Even more important is the difference in the status of the farmers in the period immediately following the reaping, when in a good harvest year the utmost exertion of labour-power is demanded on the farm. A farmer with six draught animals can thresh the grain as it is carted and does not need to stack it, thus, of course, saving time and manpower" (p. 277).

To complete the description of the big cultivator's economy, it should be mentioned that farming in the case of this group of cultivators is a "commercial" enterprise, as

* The peasants of the prosperous group own 6 to 10 draught animals per household (see above).

Postnikov puts it. The data given above showing the size of the commercial area fully bear out the author's description, inasmuch as the greater part of the cultivated area yields produce for the market—52% of the total area on farms with from 25 to 50 dessiatines under crops, and 61% on farms with over 50 dessiatines under crops. Further evidence of this is the amount of the cash income: even the minimum in the case of the well-to-do group—574 rubles per household—is more than double the essential cash expenditure (200 to 250 rubles), thus forming a surplus which is accumulated and serves for the farm's expansion and improvement. "In the case of the more affluent peasants, those with over 50 dessiatines under crops per household," even "one branch of animal husbandry—the breeding of coarse-fleece sheep—assumes a market character," as Postnikov informs us (p. 188).

Let us now pass to another question, one that is also inadequately treated (in fact, left practically untouched) by Postnikov: how does the economic success of the minority of the peasants affect the majority? Undoubtedly, the effect is completely negative: the data cited above (especially those relating to the renting of land) are sufficient proof of this, so that we may here confine ourselves merely to summing up. In all three uyezds of Taurida Gubernia, the peasants rent a total of 476,334 dessiatines of land (non-allotment and allotment), of which 298,727 dessiatines, or more than three-fifths (63%), are taken by the prosperous group. Only 6% falls to the share of the poor group, and 31% to that of the middle group. If we bear in mind that it is the two bottom groups that are most—if not exclusively—in need of rented land (the data given above regarding the distribution of land among the peasant groups in Dnieper Uyezd show that in the case of the top group the allotment arable alone is almost sufficient for a sown area of "normal" size), it will be obvious how severely they must suffer from lack of land due to the commercial expansion of the tillage of prosperous peasants.*

* "The German colonist presses hard upon the local peasant ... in depriving him of adjacent land, which he could otherwise rent or purchase," says Postnikov (p. 292) Obviously, in this respect the Russian well-to-do peasant stands closer to the German colonist than to his poor compatriot.

The distribution of the renting of allotment land, data for which have been given above, leads to exactly the same conclusions. To show the importance of the renting of allotment land to the different groups of peasants, let us quote the description of this type of renting given in Chapter IV of Postnikov's work.

"Allotment land," he says, "is now an object of extensive speculation among the South-Russian peasants. Land is used as security for loans on promissory notes, these latter circulating very widely here among the Taurida peasants, the proceeds from the land going to the money-lender until the debt is cleared. The land is leased or 'sold' for one or two years, and longer periods—8, 9 or 11 years. Such allotment leases are officially registered in the volost or village administration offices. On Sundays and holidays, I have seen large animated crowds in big villages standing in front of the village administration offices. In answer to my inquiry as to why the people were assembled, I was told that refreshments were being consumed and allotments 'sold,' the 'sales' being registered in the books of the village authorities.... The 'sale' of allotments is practised both in villages where the land is divided according to the number of registered persons in each family and no fundamental redistribution of the land takes place, and in villages where the land is divided according to the number of actual members in each family and is subject to periodical redistribution; only, in the latter case, the transactions are usually for shorter periods, until the next redistribution date, which in these parts has recently in most cases been determined in advance by the community's decision on land redistribution. Nowadays, these allotment-land transactions in the South-Russian villages are bound up with the most vital interests of the local prosperous peasants, who are so numerous here, especially in the Taurida uyezds. They are, incidentally, one of the principal conditions for the extensive cultivation of land practised by prosperous Taurida peasants, and of considerable economic advantage to them. That is why the prosperous peasants are so sensitive nowadays to every change in their manner of life which might deprive them of this renting of land that is mostly cheap and is, moreover, situated near by" (p. 140). He then goes on to tell of how the Melitopol Uyezd Board of Peasants' Affairs[15] demanded that each separate case of allotment leasing should be sanctioned by the village assembly, how the peasants were inconvenienced by this order and how "its only effect so far has been the disappearance of the land transaction records from the village courts, although they are probably still being kept unofficially" (p. 140).

Despite the large amount of land they rent, the prosperous peasants are also practically the only purchasers of land: in Dnieper Uyezd they own 78% of all the purchased land, and in Melitopol Uyezd 42,737 dessiatines out of a total of 48,099 dessiatines, or 88%.

Lastly, it is exclusively this category of peasants to whom credits are available. To supplement the author's remarks already cited on the village loan-and-savings societies in the South, we shall quote the following description of them.

"The village loan-and-savings societies now to be found here and there in our country—they are very numerous in the Taurida villages, for example—chiefly assist prosperous peasants, and, it is to be presumed, quite substantially. I have on several occasions heard peasants in the Taurida villages where these societies function saying: 'Thank God, we've got rid of the Jews!' But it is the prosperous peasants who say this. The economically weak peasants cannot find guarantors and do not get loans" (p. 368). There is nothing surprising in this monopoly of credit: the credit transaction is nothing more than deferred-payment purchase. Quite naturally, payment can only be made by those who have the means, and among the South-Russian peasants it is only the well-to-do minority that have them.

To complete the description of the economy of this group, which surpasses all the other groups taken together in the fruits of its productive activity, we have only to recall that it resorts "to a considerable extent" to hired labour, of which members of the lower group are perforce the suppliers. It should be remarked in this regard that it is a matter of immense difficulty to calculate exactly the hired labour employed in agriculture, a difficulty which, it seems, has not yet been overcome by our Zemstvo statistics. As agriculture does not require a constant and steady supply of labour all year round, but only an extra supply for a definite season, the registration of regular hired labourers alone will by no means indicate the degree of exploitation of hired labour, while the calculation of the number of seasonal (often casual) labourers is extremely difficult. In making a rough estimate of the number of hired labourers in each group, Postnikov sets the labour norm in the prosperous group at 15 dessiatines under crops per working member.* From Chapter VII of his book, where the author examines in detail the actual size of the area cultivated, we learn that this norm is achieved only when the crop is machine harvested. Yet the number of harvesting-machines is not very large even in the prosperous group—in Dnieper Uyezd, for example, it is about one per 10 households—so that even if we bear in mind the author's statement that when they have completed their own harvesting, the owners of the machines hire them out, we shall nevertheless find that the majority of the peasants have to go without machines, and, consequently, have to hire day labourers. The employment of hired labour in the top group must therefore be on a larger scale than the author estimates, so that the big money income obtained by the peasants of this group largely (if not entirely) represents income from *capital*, in the specific meaning of that term given to it by scientific political economy.

Summing up what has been said about the third group, we arrive at the following description of it: the prosperous peasants, who possess considerably more than the average quantity of means of production, and whose labour, as a consequence, is more productive, are the principal growers of agricultural produce in the district, and predominate over the remaining groups; this group's farming is commercial in character, and is very largely based on the exploitation of hired labour.

The brief survey we have made of the political-economic differences in the economy of the three groups of the population of this area has been based on a systematisation of

* For 1.8 to 2.3 working members it is 27 to 34.5 dessiatines; but, as we know, the peasants of the prosperous group sow 34.5 to 75 dessiatines. Hence, the general characteristic of this group is that the size of the farm far exceeds the family labour norm.

the material contained in Postnikov's book on South-Russian peasant farming. This survey, it seems to me, proves that a study of peasant farming (from the political-economic standpoint) is quite impossible unless the peasants are divided into groups. Postnikov, as has already been indicated, recognises this, and even flings the reproach at the Zemstvo statisticians that they do not do this, that the summaries they make, despite the abundance of figures given, are "unclear," and that "they do not see the wood for the trees" (p. XII). Postnikov is hardly entitled to cast this reproach at the Zemstvo statisticians, for he himself has not made a systematic division of the peasants into "clear" groups, but the correctness of his demand is beyond question. Once it is admitted that there are not only quantitative, but also qualitative* differences between the various farms, it becomes absolutely essential to divide the peasants into groups differing, not in "affluence," but in the social and economic character of their farming. One is justified in hoping that it will not be long before this is done by the Zemstvo statisticians.

V

Not confining himself to recording the economic strife among the peasantry, Postnikov points to the intensification of this process:

"Diversity in the prosperity of the peasant groups is to be found everywhere in this country," he says, "and has existed from time immemorial. But in the last few decades this differentiation among the peasant population is becoming very marked, and is apparently steadily progressing" (p. 130). The difficult economic conditions of the year 1891[16] should, in the opinion of the author, give new impetus to this process.

---

* Character of farming: self-consumer or commercial; character of exploitation of labour: sale of labour-power as the chief source of livelihood, or purchase of labour-power as the necessary consequence of the expansion of the cultivated area beyond the family's working capacity.

The question arises: what are the causes of this phenomenon which is exerting such an immense influence on the entire peasant population?

"Taurida Gubernia," says Postnikov, "is one of the most land-abundant in European Russia, and the one where the peasants' allotments are largest; communal landownership is universal there, and the land is distributed more or less evenly per head; agriculture is practically the sole pursuit of the rural population, yet the house-to-house census shows that 15% of the population have no draught animals at all, and that about one-third of the population have not enough implements to cultivate their allotments" (p. 106). "On what," asks the author, "does this wide diversity of the groups depend, and, in particular, what, in a purely agricultural economy, determines the high proportion of householders with no tillage or draught animals that we now find in the region described?" (P. 130.)

Setting out in search of the causes of this phenomenon, Postnikov goes completely astray (fortunately, not for long) and starts to talk about "indolence," "drunkenness," and even about fires and horse-stealing. Nevertheless, he arrives at the conclusion that it is not in these causes that "the most essential aspect of the matter is to be found." Nor is anything explained by talking about bereavement in families, i.e., absence of adult working members: in the Taurida uyezds, of the total number of non-farming households, i.e., that have no land under crops, bereaved families constitute only 18%.

"The chief reasons why households are non-farming," the author concludes, "must be sought in other factors of the peasants' economic life" (p. 134). Specifically, Postnikov is of the opinion that "of the enumerated causes contributing to the decline of farming among certain peasants, the one which may be considered the most fundamental, and which, unfortunately, our Zemstvo statisticians have done little to elucidate as yet, is the *fragmentation of the allotments* and the restricted amount of land in use by the peasant, the diminution in the average size of the peasant farm" (p. 141). "The root cause of Russia's economic poverty," the author says, "is the small size of the peasant's land and of his farm, which prevents him from making full use of the labour-power of his family" (p. 341).

To explain this proposition, which Postnikov expresses very inaccurately, for he himself has established that the average size of peasant farm (17 to 18 dessiatines under crops) is sufficient to maintain a family in comfort, and that a general, wholesale description of the entire peasantry in terms of the size of the farm is impossible—it should be recalled that he has already established the general law that the productivity of peasant labour grows with the increase in the size of the farm. Full utilisation of the family's labour-power (and draught animals) is achieved, according to his estimates, only in the top groups—in the Taurida uyezds, for example, only among the prosperous peasants; the vast majority of the population "pick at the land unproductively" (p. 340), uselessly wasting a vast amount of effort.

Despite the fact that the author has fully demonstrated the dependence of labour productivity on the size of the farm and the extremely low productivity in the bottom peasant groups, this law (Postnikov calls it agricultural over-population in Russia, agricultural over-saturation with labour) should not be regarded as the cause of the break-up of the peasantry—the question, after all, is why the peasantry have broken up into such different groups, whereas agricultural over-population already presupposes the existence of such a break-up; the author arrived at the very concept of over-population by comparing small and large farms and their profitability. Hence, the question—"on what does the wide diversity of the groups depend?"—cannot be answered by talking about agricultural over-population. This, apparently, Postnikov himself realised, but he did not set himself the definite aim of investigating the causes of the phenomenon, so that his observations suffer from a certain scrappiness: side by side with incomplete and inaccurate points, we find true ideas. For example, he says:

"It cannot be expected that the fierce struggle now going on in rural life over landownership will help in the future to further the principles of communality and harmony among the population. And this struggle is not a transitory one, the result of chance causes.... In our view it is not a struggle between communal traditions and the individualism that is developing in rural life, but a pure struggle of economic interests, which is bound to end fatally for one section of the population in view of the existing land poverty" (p. XXXII).

"It is quite an obvious truth," says Postnikov elsewhere, "that with this land poverty and the small size of the farms, and the absence of sufficient industries, there can be no prosperity among the peasantry, and all that is economically weak is bound, one way or another, sooner or later, to be ousted from peasant farming" (p. 368).

These remarks contain a much truer answer to the question, and one, moreover, that fully conforms to the above-established differentiation of the population. The answer is that the appearance of a mass of non-farming households and the increase in their numbers, are determined by the struggle of economic interests among the peasantry. On what basis is this struggle being waged, and by what means? As to the means, they are not only, and not even so much, the grabbing of land (as might be concluded from Postnikov's remarks just quoted), as the lower production costs following on the increase in the size of the farms—of which enough has already been said. As for the basis on which this struggle arises, Postnikov points to it quite clearly in the following remark:

"There is a definite minimum of farm-service area below which a peasant farm must not drop, because it would then become unprofitable, or even impossible to run. A definite food area is required for the maintenance of family and livestock (?); a farm which has no outside earnings, or where they are small, must possess a certain market area, the produce of which may be sold to provide the peasant family with money for the payment of taxes, for the acquisition of clothing and footwear, for necessary expenditure on farm implements, buildings, etc. If the size of a peasant farm falls below this minimum, farming becomes impossible. In such cases, the peasant will find it more profitable to give up farming and become a labourer, whose expenditure is more limited and whose needs can be more fully satisfied even with a smaller gross income" (p. 141).

If, on the one hand, a peasant finds it profitable to expand his sown area far beyond his own grain requirements, it is because he can sell his produce. If, on the other hand, a peasant finds it profitable to give up farming and become a labourer, it is because the satisfaction of the greater part of his needs entails cash expenditure, that is, sale;* and as, in selling his farm produce, he encounters a rival on the market with whom he cannot compete, the only thing left for him is to sell his labour-power. In a word, the soil in which the above-described phenomena grow is production for sale. The fundamental cause of the struggle of economic interests arising among the peasantry is the existence of a system under which the market is the regulator of social production.

Having concluded his description of the "new economic developments in peasant life" and his attempt to explain them, Postnikov goes on to outline practical measures to solve the "agrarian problem." We shall not follow the author into this field, firstly, because it does not enter the plan of the present article, and, secondly, because this part of Postnikov's work is the weakest of all. This will be quite obvious if we recall that most of the contradictions and incomplete statements in the work were to be met with precisely when the author tried to explain economic processes; and unless these are fully and accurately explained, there can be no question of indicating any practical measures.

* Cf. the data given above regarding the food and the commercial areas under crops (the income from only these areas goes to cover the needs of the farmer, and not of the farm, that is, represents income in the real sense, and not production costs), and also the data regarding the average cash expenditure of the Taurida peasant in connection with the quantity of grain used for food (two chetverts per person of either sex).

ON THE SO-CALLED MARKET QUESTION [17]

Written in the autumn of 1893

First published in 1937 in
No. 21 of the journal *Bolshevik*

Published according
to the manuscript

По поводу такъ-называемаго вопроса о рынкахъ.

I.

Можетъ-ли у насъ въ Россіи развиваться и впол-
нѣ развиться капитализмъ, когда масса народа
бѣдна и бѣднѣетъ все больше? Вѣдь для развитія
капитализма необходимъ широкій внутренній рынокъ, а разореніе крестьянства подрываетъ этотъ
рынокъ, грозитъ совершенно закрыть его и сдѣлать
невозможной организацію капиталистическихъ
порядковъ. Говорятъ, правда, что превращая нату-
ральное хозяйство нашихъ непосредственныхъ про-
изводителей въ товарное, капитализмъ тѣмъ самымъ
создаетъ себѣ рынокъ, но мыслимо-ли допустить,
чтобы на счетъ жалкихъ остатковъ натуральнаго хозяйства у полу-нищихъ крестьянъ могло раз-

First manuscript page of Lenin's *On the So-Called Market Question*, 1893 (*Reduced*)

I

Can capitalism develop in Russia and reach full development when the masses of the people are poor and are becoming still poorer? The development of capitalism certainly needs an extensive home market; but the ruin of the peasantry undermines this market, threatens to close it altogether and make the organisation of the capitalist order impossible. True, it is said that, by transforming the natural economy of our direct producers into a commodity economy, capitalism is creating a market for itself; but is it conceivable that the miserable remnants of the natural economy of indigent peasants can form the basis for the development in our country of the mighty capitalist production that we see in the West? Is it not evident that the one fact of the masses being impoverished already makes our capitalism something impotent and without foundation, incapable of embracing the entire production of the country and of becoming the *basis* of our social economy?

Such are the questions that are constantly being advanced in our literature in opposition to the Russian Marxists; the absence of a market is one of the principal arguments invoked against the possibility of applying the theory of Marx to Russia. To refute this argument is the aim, incidentally, of the paper *The Market Question*, which we are about to discuss.

II

The main premise of the author of the paper is the assumption of the "general and exclusive domination of capitalist production." Proceeding from that premise he expounds the contents of Chapter XXI of Volume II of *Capital* (Part III—"The Reproduction and Circulation of the Aggregate Social Capital").

Here Marx sets out to investigate how social production replaces the part of the product which serves to satisfy the personal needs of the workers and the capitalists, and that which goes to form the elements of productive capital. Hence, in Volume I, the investigation of the production and reproduction of an *individual* capital could be limited to an analysis of the component parts of capital and the product according to their value—[as is shown in Volume I of *Capital* the value of the product consists of *c* (constant capital) + *v* (variable capital) + *s* (surplus-value)]—but here the product must be divided into its material components, because that part of the product which consists of the elements of capital cannot be used for personal consumption, and vice versa. In view of that, Marx divides aggregate social production—and consequently, the aggregate social product—into two departments: I) the production of means of production, i.e., the elements of productive capital—commodities which can serve only for productive consumption, and II) the production of means of consumption, i.e., commodities that serve for the personal consumption of the working class and the capitalist class.

The investigation is based on the following scheme [Arabic numerals indicate units of value—millions of rubles, for example; Roman numerals indicate the above-mentioned departments of social production. The rate of surplus-value is taken at 100 per cent]:

$$\begin{array}{l} \text{I } 4{,}000\,c + 1{,}000\,v + 1{,}000\,s = 6{,}000 \\ \text{II } 2{,}000\,c + 500\,v + 500\,s = 3{,}000 \end{array} \left\{ \begin{array}{l} \text{Capital} = 7{,}500 \\ \text{Product} = 9{,}000 \end{array} \right\}$$

Let us begin by supposing that we are dealing with simple reproduction, i.e., let us assume that production does not expand, but remains permanently on its former scale; this means that the capitalists consume the whole surplus-value unproductively, that they expend it for their personal needs and not for accumulation. Under those circumstances it is obvious, firstly, that II 500 v and II 500 s must be consumed by the capitalists and the workers in the same department II, since that product exists in the form of means of consumption intended for the satisfaction of personal needs. Further, I 4,000 c in its natural form must be consumed by the capitalists in the same department I, because the condition that the scale of production remains unchanged demands the retention of the same capital for the next year's production of means of production; consequently, the replacement of this part of capital also presents no difficulty; the corresponding part of the product existing in the natural form of coal, iron, machines, etc., will be exchanged among the capitalists engaged in producing means of production and will serve them, as before, as constant capital. Thus, there remains I (v+s) and II c. I 1,000 v+I 1,000 s are products existing in the form of means of production, and II 2,000 c—in the form of means of consumption. The workers and capitalists in department I (under simple reproduction, i.e., consumption of the entire surplus-value) must consume means of consumption to the value of 2,000 [1,000 (v)+1,000 (s)]. To be able to continue production on the previous scale, the capitalists in department II must acquire means of production to the extent of 2,000 in order to replace their constant capital (2,000 II c). It is evident from this that I v+I s must be exchanged for II c, because, if they are not, production on the previous scale will be impossible. The condition for simple reproduction is that the sum of the variable capital and surplus-value in department I must be equal to the constant capital in department II: I (v + s) =II c. In other words, that law may be formulated as follows: the sum of *all the new* values produced in the course of a year (in both departments) must be equal to the gross value of the product existing in the form of means of consumption: I (v + s) + II (v + s) = II (c + v + s).

Actually, of course, there can be no simple reproduction, both because the production of the whole of society cannot remain on the previous scale every year, and because accumulation is a law of the capitalist system. Let us, therefore, examine how social production on an expanding scale, or accumulation, takes place. Where there is accumulation, only part of the surplus-value is consumed by the capitalists for their personal needs, the other part being consumed productively, i.e., converted into the elements of productive capital for the expansion of production. Therefore, where there is accumulation, I (v + s) and II c cannot be equal: I (v + s) must be greater than II c in order that part of the surplus-value in department I (Is) may be used for the expansion of production, and not exchanged for means of consumption. Thus we get

A. *Scheme of Simple Reproduction*:

I 4,000 c+1,000 v+1,000 s=6,000
II 2,000 c+ 500 v+ 500 s=3,000
I (v+s)=II c.

B. *Initial Scheme of Accumulation*:

I 4,000 c+1,000 v+1,000 s=6,000
II 1,500 c+ 750 v+ 750 s=3,000
I (v+s)>II c.

Let us now see how social production must proceed if there is accumulation.

First year.

I 4,000 c+1,000 v+1,000 s=6,000 { Capital =7,250 }
II 1,500 c+ 750 v+ 750 s=3,000 { Product =9,000 }

I (1,000 v+500 s) are exchanged for II 1,500 c (as in simple reproduction).

I 500 s are accumulated, i.e., go to expand production, are converted into *capital*. If we take the previous division into constant and variable capital we get

I 500 s=400 c+100 v.

The additional constant capital (400 c) is contained in the product I (its natural form is means of production); but the additional variable capital (100 v) must be obtained from the capitalists of department II, who, consequently, also have to accumulate: they exchange part of their surplus-value (II 100 s) for means of production (I 100 v) and convert these means of production into additional constant capital. Consequently, their constant capital grows from 1,500 c to 1,600 c; to process it additional labour-power is needed—*50 v*, which is also taken out of the surplus-value of the capitalists of department II.

By adding the additional capital from department I and department II to the original capital we get the following distribution of the product:

I 4,400 c+1,100 v+(500 s)=6,000
II 1,600 c+ 800 v+(600 s)=3,000

The surplus-value in parentheses represents the capitalists' consumption fund, i.e., the part of surplus-value that does not go for accumulation, but for the personal needs of the capitalists.

If production proceeds on the previous scale, at the end of the year we shall get:

I 4,400 c+1,100 v+1,100 s=6,600
II 1,600 c+ 800 v+ 800 s=3,200
{Capital=7,900; Product=9,800}

I (1,100 v+550 s) are exchanged for II 1,650 c; the additional 50 c are taken from 800 II s [and the increase of *c* by 50 causes an increase of *v* by 25].

Further, 550 I s are accumulated as before:

550 I s=440 c + 110 v
↙
165 II s=110 c + 55 v.

If to the original capital we now add the additional [to I 4,400 c—440 c; to I 1,100 v — 110 v; to II 1,600 c — 50 c and 110 c; and to II 800 v—25 v — and 55 v], we shall get:

I 4,840 c+1,210 v+(550 s)=6,600
II 1,760 c+ 880 v+(560 s)=3,200

With the further progress of production we get

I 4,840 c+1,210 v+1,210 s=7,260
II 1,760 c+ 880 v+ 880 s=3,520
{Capital= 8,690; Product=10,780}

and so forth.

Such, in essence, are the results of Marx's investigations in the reproduction of the aggregate social capital. These investigations (the reservation must be made) are given here in a most concise form; very much that Marx analyses in detail has been omitted—for example, circulation of money, replacement of fixed capital which is gradually worn out, and so forth—because all this has no direct bearing on the question under review.

III

What conclusions does the author of the paper draw from these investigations made by Marx? Unfortunately, he does not formulate his conclusions very precisely and definitely, so that we have to make our own judgement of them from certain remarks which do not fully harmonise with each other. Thus, for example, we read:

"We have seen here," says the author, "how accumulation takes place in department I, the production of means of production as means of production: ...this accumulation takes place independently both of the progress of the production of articles of consumption and of the personal consumption itself, no matter whose it is" (page $^{15}/_{8}$).

Of course, it is wrong to speak of accumulation being "independent" of the production of articles of consumption, if only because the expansion of production calls for new variable capital and, consequently, articles of consumption; evidently, by using that term the author merely wanted to stress the specific feature of the scheme, namely, that the reproduction of I c—constant capital in department I—takes place without exchanges with department II, i.e., every year a certain quantity of, say, coal is produced in society for the purpose of producing coal. It goes without saying that this production (of coal for the purpose of producing coal) links up, by a series of subsequent exchanges, with the production of articles of consumption—otherwise, neither the coal-owners nor their workers could exist.

Elsewhere, the author expresses himself much more feebly: "The *principal* movement of capitalist accumulation," he says, "takes place, and has taken place (except in very early periods) independently of any direct producers, independently of the personal consumption of any stratum of the population" (p. 8). Here, reference is made only to the predominance of the production of means of production over the production of articles of consumption in the course of the historical development of capitalism. This reference is repeated in another passage: "On the one hand, the typical feature of capitalist society is accumulation for accumulation, productive but not personal consumption; on the other hand, *typical* of it is precisely the production of means of production as means of production" (p. $^{21}/_{2}$). If by these references the author wanted to say that capitalist society is distinguished from the other economic organisations which preceded it precisely by the development of machines and the articles necessary for them (coal, iron, and so forth), then he is quite right. In technical level capitalist society is higher than all others, and technical progress is expressed precisely in the fact that the work of machines pushes human labour more and more into the background.

Instead of engaging in criticism of the author's insufficiently clear statements it will, therefore, be better to turn straight to Marx and see whether it is possible to draw from his theory the conclusion that department I "predominates" over department II, and in what sense this predominance is to be understood.

From Marx's scheme quoted above the conclusion cannot be drawn that department I predominates over department II: both develop on parallel lines. But that scheme does not take technical progress into consideration. As Marx proved in Volume I of *Capital*, technical progress is expressed by the gradual decrease of the ratio of variable capital to constant capital $\left(\frac{v}{c}\right)$, whereas in the scheme it is taken as unchanged.

It goes without saying that if this change is made in the scheme there will be a relatively more rapid increase in means of production than in articles of consumption. Nevertheless, it seems to me that it will be worth while making that calculation, firstly, for the sake of clarity, and secondly, to avoid possible wrong conclusions from that premise.

[In the following scheme the rate of accumulation is taken as constant: half of the surplus-value is accumulated and half is consumed personally.]

[The reader may skip the following scheme and pass straight to the conclusions on the next page. The letter *a* stands for additional capital used for the expansion of production, i.e., the accumulated part of surplus-value.]

1st year)
I 4,000 c + 1,000 v + 1,000 s = 6,000... v: (c + v) = 20.0%
II 1,500 c + 750 v + 750 s = 3,000... " " " 33.3%
I (1,000 v + 500 s) = II 1,500 c
a. I 500 s = 450 c + 50 v... " " " $\frac{1}{10}$
a. II 60 s = 50 c + 10 v... " " " $\frac{1}{6}$
I 4,450 c + 1,050 v + (500 s) = 6,000
II 1,550 c + 760 v + (690 s) = 3,000

2nd year)
I 4,450 c + 1,050 v + 1,050 s = 6,550 " " " 19.2%
II 1,550 c + 760 v + 760 s = 3,070 " " " 32.9%
I (1,050 v + 525 s) = II 1,575 c
II (1,550 c + 25 s)
a. II 28 s = 25 c + 3 v... " " " ab. $\frac{1}{9}$
a. I 525 s = 500 c + 25 v... " " " ab. $\frac{1}{21}$
a. II 28 s = 25 c + 3 v... " " " ab. $\frac{1}{9}$
I 4,950 c + 1,075 v + (525 s) = 6,550
II 1,602 c + 766 v + (702 s) = 3,070

3rd year)
I 4,950 c + 1,075 v + 1,075 s = 7,100... " " " 17.8%
II 1,602 c + 766 v + 766 s = 3,134... " " " 32.3%
I (1,075 v + 537 $\frac{1}{2}$ s) = II 1,612 $\frac{1}{2}$ c
II (1,602 c + 10 $\frac{1}{2}$ s)
a. II 11 $\frac{1}{2}$ s = 10 $\frac{1}{2}$ c + 1 v ... " " " ab. $\frac{1}{12}$
a. I 537 $\frac{1}{2}$ s = 517 $\frac{1}{2}$ c + 20 v ... " " " ab. $\frac{1}{26}$
a. II 22 s = 20 c + 2 v ... " " " $\frac{1}{11}$

$$\text{I } 5{,}467\tfrac{1}{2}\text{c} + 1{,}095\text{ v} + (537\tfrac{1}{2}\text{ s}) = 7{,}100$$
$$\text{II } 1{,}634\tfrac{1}{2}\text{c} + 769\text{ v} + (730\tfrac{1}{2}\text{ s}) = 3{,}134$$

4th year)
$$\text{I } 5{,}467\tfrac{1}{2}\text{c} + 1{,}095\text{ v} + 1{,}095\text{ s} = 7{,}657\tfrac{1}{2} \ldots \text{v:(c+v)} = 16.7\%$$
$$\text{II } 1{,}634\tfrac{1}{2}\text{c} + 769\text{ v} + 769\text{ s} = 3{,}172\tfrac{1}{2} \ldots \quad 32.0\%$$

and so forth.[18]

Let us now compare the conclusions drawn from this scheme concerning the growth of the various parts of the social product:[19]

	Means of production as means of		Means of production as means of		Means of consumption		Aggregate social product	
	Production	%	Consumption	%		%		%
1st year	4,000	100	2,000	100	3,000	100	9,000	100
2nd year	4,450	111.25	2,100	105	3,070	102	9,620	107
3rd year	4,950	123.75	2,150	107.5	3,134	104	10,234	114
4th year	5,467½	136.7	2,190	109.5	3,172	106	10,828½	120

We thus see that growth in the production of means of production as means of production is the most rapid, then comes the production of means of production as means of consumption, and the slowest rate of growth is in the production of means of consumption. That conclusion could have been arrived at, without Marx's investigation in Volume II of *Capital*, on the basis of the law that constant capital tends to grow faster than variable: the proposition that means of production grow faster is merely a paraphrase of this law as applied to social production as a whole.

But perhaps we should take another step forward? Since we have accepted that the ratio v to $c+v$ diminishes constantly, why not let v decrease to zero, the same number of workers being sufficient for a larger quantity of means of production? In that case, the accumulated part of surplus-value will be added straight to constant capital in department I, and social production will grow exclusively on account of means of production as means of production, complete stagnation reigning in department* II.**

That would, of course, be a misuse of the schemes, for such a conclusion is based on improbable assumptions and is therefore wrong. Is it conceivable that technical progress, which reduces the proportion of *v* to *c*, will find expression only in department I and leave department II in a state of complete stagnation? Is it in conformity with the laws governing capitalist society, laws which *demand* of every capitalist that he enlarge his enterprise on pain of ruin, that no accumulation at all should take place in department II?

Thus, the only correct conclusion that can be drawn from Marx's investigation, outlined above, is that *in capitalist society, the production of means of production increases faster than the production of means of consumption.* As has been stated already, this conclusion follows directly from the generally known proposition that capitalist production attains an immeasurably higher technical level than production in previous times.*** On this point specifically Marx expresses himself quite definitely only in one

---

* I do not mean to say that such a thing is absolutely impossible as an individual case. Here, however, we are not discussing special cases, but the general law of development of capitalist society.

** I shall explain the point by the following scheme:

I 4,000 c + 1,000 v + 1,000 s = 6,000
II 1,500 c + 750 v + 750 s = 3,000
I (1,000 v + 500 s) = II 1,500 c
I 500 s are accumulated, added to I 4,000 c:

I 4,500 c + 1,000 v + (500 s) = 6,000
II 1,500 c + 750 v + 750 s = 3,000
I 4,500 c + 1,000 v + 1,000 s = 6,500
II 1,500 c + 750 v + 750 s = 3,000
I (1,000 v + 500 s) = II 1,500 c
I 500 s are accumulated as before, and so forth.

*** That is why the conclusion drawn can be formulated somewhat differently: in capitalist society, production (and, consequently, "the market") can grow either on account of the growth of articles of consumption, or, and mainly, of technical progress, i.e., the ousting of hand by machine labour, for the change in the proportion of *v* to *c* expresses precisely the diminution of the role of hand labour.

passage, and that passage fully confirms the correctness of the formula given:

"What distinguishes capitalist society in this case from the savage is not, as Senior thinks, the privilege and peculiarity of the savage to expend his labour at times in a way that does not procure him any products resolvable (exchangeable) into revenue, i.e., into articles of consumption. No, the distinction consists in the following:

"α) Capitalist society employs more [Nota bene] of its available annual labour in the production of means of production (ergo, of constant capital), which are not resolvable into revenue in the form of wages or surplus-value, but can function only as capital." (*Das Kapital*, Bd. II, Seite 436.)[20]

IV

The question now is, what relation has the theory that has been expounded to "the notorious market question"? The theory is based on the assumption of the "general and exclusive domination of the capitalist mode of production," whereas the "question" is one of whether the full development of capitalism is "possible" in Russia? True, the theory introduces a correction into the ordinary conception of the development of capitalism, but, evidently, the explanation of how capitalism develops *in general* does not in the least help to clear up the question of the "possibility" (and necessity) of the development of capitalism in Russia.

The author of the paper, however, does not confine himself to expounding Marx's theory of the process of aggregate social production organised on capitalist lines. He points to the necessity of distinguishing "two *essentially different* features in the accumulation of capital: 1) the development of capitalist production in breadth, when it takes hold of already existing fields of labour, ousting natural economy and expanding at the latter's expense; and 2) the development of capitalist production in depth, if one may so express it, when it expands independently of natural economy, i.e., under the general and exclusive domination of the capitalist mode of production." Without, for the time being, stopping to criticise this division, let us proceed directly to find out what the author means by the development of capitalism in breadth: the explanation of that process, which consists in the replacement of natural economy by capitalist economy, should show us how Russian capitalism will "take hold of the whole country."

The author illustrates the development of capitalism in breadth by the following diagram:*

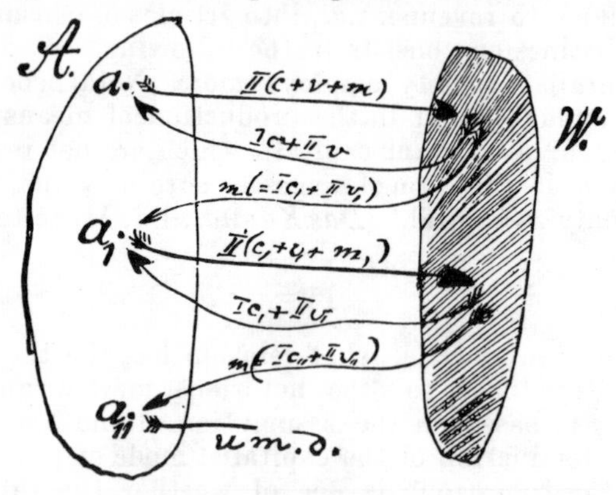

A—capitalists; *W*—direct producers
a, a_1, a_{11} — capitalist enterprises.
The arrows show the movement of the commodities exchanged.
c, v, m—component parts of the value of commodities.
I, II—commodities in their natural form: I—means of production; II—means of consumption.

"The essential difference between the spheres *A* and *W*," says the author, "is that in *A* the producers are capitalists who consume their surplus-value productively, whereas in *W* they are direct producers, who consume their surplus-value (here I mean the value of the product over and above the value of the means of production and necessary means of subsistence) unproductively.

"If we follow the arrows in the diagram we shall easily see how capitalist production in *A* develops at the expense of consumption in *W*, gradually absorbing it." The product of the capitalist enterprise *a* goes "to the direct producers" in

* m stands for "Mehrwert," i.e., surplus-value (s); "*u m. д.*" means "and so on."—*Ed. Eng. ed.*

the form of articles of consumption; in exchange for it the "direct producers" return the constant capital (c) in the form of means of production and the variable capital (v) in the form of means of consumption, and the surplus-value (s) in the form of the elements of additional productive capital: c_1+v_1. That capital serves as the basis of the new capitalist enterprise a_1, which in exactly the same way sends its product in the form of articles of consumption to the "direct producers," and so on. "From the above diagram of the development of capitalism in breadth it follows that the whole of production is most closely dependent upon consumption in 'foreign' markets, upon consumption by the masses (and from the general point of view it makes absolutely no difference where those masses are—alongside the capitalists, or somewhere across the ocean). Obviously, the expansion of production in *A*, i.e., the development of capitalism in this direction, will come to a stop as soon as all the direct producers in *W* turn into commodity producers, for, as we saw above, every new enterprise (or expansion of an old one) is calculated to supply a new circle of consumers in *W*." In conclusion the author says: "The current conception of capitalist accumulation, i.e., of capitalist reproduction on an expanded scale, is limited solely to this view of things, and has no suspicion of the development of capitalist production in depth, independently of any countries with direct producers, i.e., independently of so-called foreign markets."

The only thing we can agree with in this entire exposition is that this conception of the development of capitalism in breadth, and the diagram which illustrates it, is in complete accordance with the current, Narodnik views on the subject.

It would, indeed, be difficult to depict the utter absurdity and vapidity of current views more saliently and strikingly than is done in the diagram given.

"The current conception" always regarded capitalism in our country as something isolated from the "people's system," standing apart from it, exactly as it is depicted in the diagram from which it is quite impossible to see what connection there is between the two "spheres," the capitalist sphere and the people's sphere. Why do commodities sent from *A* find a market in *W*? What causes the transformation of natural economy in *W* into commodity economy? The current view has never answered these questions because it regards exchange as something accidental and not as a certain *system of economy.*

Further, the current view has never *explained* whence and how capitalism arose in our country any more than it is explained by the diagram: the matter is presented as though the capitalists have come from somewhere outside and not from among these very "direct producers." Where the capitalists get the "free workers" who are needed for enterprises a, a_1, etc., remains a mystery. Everybody knows that in reality those workers are obtained precisely from the "direct producers," but the diagram does not show at all that when commodity production embraced "sphere" *W*, it created there a body of free workers.

In short, the diagram—exactly like the current view—explains absolutely nothing about the phenomena of the capitalist system in our country and is therefore worthless. The object for which it was drawn—to explain how capitalism develops at the expense of natural economy, and embraces the whole country—is not achieved at all, because, as the author himself sees—"if we adhere consistently to the view under examination, then we must conclude that it is not possible for the development of the capitalist mode of production to become universal."

After this, one can only express surprise at the fact that the author himself adheres, if only in part, to that view when he says that "capitalism did indeed (?), in its infancy, develop in this very easy (sic!?) way (very easy because here existing branches of labour are involved) and is partly developing in the same direction even now (??), since there are still remnants of natural economy in the world, and since the population is growing."

Actually, this is not a "very easy" way of developing capitalism, but simply a "very easy" way of understanding the process; so "very easy" that it would be more correct to call it a total lack of understanding. The Russian Narodniks of all shades make shift to this very day with these "very easy" tricks: they never dream of *explaining* how capitalism arose in our country, and how it functions, but confine themselves to comparing the "sore spot" in our system, capitalism, with the "healthy spot," the direct producers, the "people"; the former is put on the left, the latter on the right, and all this profound thinking is rounded off with sentimental phrases about what is "harmful" and what is "useful" for "human society."

V

To correct the diagram given above we must begin by ascertaining the content of the concepts dealt with. By commodity production is meant an organisation of social economy in which goods are produced by separate, isolated producers, each specialising in the making of some one product, so that to satisfy the needs of society it is necessary to buy and sell products (which, therefore, become commodities) in the market. By capitalism is meant that stage of the development of commodity production at which not only the products of human labour, but human labour-power itself becomes a commodity. Thus, in the historical development of capitalism two features are important: 1) the transformation of the natural economy of the direct producers into commodity economy, and 2) the transformation of commodity economy into capitalist economy. The first transformation is due to the appearance of the social division of labour—the specialisation of isolated [N. B.: this is an essential condition of commodity economy], separate producers in only one branch of industry. The second transformation is due to the fact that separate producers, each producing commodities on his own for the market, enter into competition with one another: each strives to sell at the highest price and to buy at the lowest, a necessary result of which is that the strong become stronger and the weak go under, a minority are enriched and the masses are ruined. This leads to the conversion of independent producers into wage-workers and of numerous small enterprises into a few big ones. The diagram should, therefore, be drawn up to show both these features of the development of capitalism and the changes which this development brings about in the dimensions of the market, i.e., in the quantity of products that are turned into commodities.

The following table* has been drawn up on these lines: all extraneous circumstances have been abstracted, i.e., taken as constants (for example, size of population, productivity of labour, and much else) in order to analyse the influence on the market of *only those* features of the development of capitalism that are mentioned above.

Let us now examine this table showing the consecutive changes in the system of economy of a community consisting of 6 producers. It shows 6 periods expressing stages in the transformation of natural into capitalist economy.

1st period. We have 6 producers, each of whom expends his labour in all 3 branches of industry (in *a*, in *b* and in *c*). The product obtained (9 from each producer: a+b+c=9) is spent by each producer on himself in his own household. Hence, we have natural economy in its pure form; no products whatever appear in the market.

2nd period. Producer I changes the productivity of his labour: he leaves industry *b* and spends the time formerly spent in that industry in industry *c*. As a result of this specialisation by one producer, the others cut down production *c*, because producer I has produced more than he consumes himself, and increase production *b* in order to turn out a product for producer I. The division of labour which comes into being inevitably leads to commodity production: producer I sells 1 *c* and buys 1 *b*; the other producers sell 1 *b* (each of the 5 sells $\frac{1}{5}$ b) and buy 1 *c* (each buying $\frac{1}{5}$ c); a quantity of products appears in the market to the value of *6*. The dimensions of the market correspond exactly to the degree of specialisation of social labour: specialisation has taken place in the production of one *c* (1 c=3) and of one *b* (1 b=3), i.e., a ninth part of total social production [18 c (=a=b)], and a ninth part of the total social product has appeared in the market.

3rd period. Division of labour proceeds further, embracing branches of industry *b* and *c* to the full: three producers engage exclusively in industry *b* and three exclusively in industry *c*. Each sells 1 c (or 1 b), i.e., 3 units of value, and also buys 3—1 *b* (or 1 c). This increased division of labour leads to an expansion of the market, in which 18 units of

* See table on pp. 96-97.—*Ed.*

value now appear. Again, the dimensions of the market correspond exactly to the degree of specialisation (=division) of social labour: specialisation has taken place in the production of 3 *b* and 3 *c*, i.e., one-third of social production, and one-third of the social product appears in the market.

The 4th period already represents capitalist production: the process of the transformation of commodity into capitalist production did not go into the table and, therefore, must be described separately.

In the preceding period each producer was already a commodity producer (in the spheres of industry *b* and *c*, the only ones we are discussing): each producer separately, on his own, independently of the others, produced for the market, whose dimensions were, of course, not known to any one of them. This relation between isolated producers working for a common market is called competition. It goes without saying that an equilibrium between production and consumption (supply and demand) is, under these circumstances, achieved only by a series of fluctuations. The more skilful, enterprising and strong producer will become still stronger as a result of these fluctuations, and the weak and unskilful one will be crushed by them. The enrichment of a few individuals and the impoverishment of the masses—such are the inevitable consequences of the law of competition. The matter ends by the ruined producers losing economic independence and engaging themselves as wage-workers in the enlarged establishment of their fortunate rival. That is the situation depicted in the table. Branches of industry *b* and *c*, which were formerly divided among all 6 producers, are now concentrated in the hands of 2 producers (I and IV). The rest of the producers are their wage-workers, who no longer receive the whole product of their labour, but the product with the surplus-value deducted, the latter being appropriated by the employer [let me remind you that, by assumption, surplus-value equals one-third of the product, so that the producer of 2 *b* (=6) will receive from the employer two-thirds—i.e., 4]. As a result, we get an increase in division of labour—and a growth of the market, where 22 units now appear, notwithstanding the fact that the "masses" are "impoverished": the producers who have become (partly)

EXPLANATION OF THE TABLE

I—II...—VI are producers.

a, b, c are branches of industry (for example, agriculture, manufacturing and extractive industries).

a=*b*=*c*=3. The magnitude of value of the products *a*=*b*=*c* equals *3* (three units of value) of which *1* is surplus-value.*

The "market" column shows the magnitude of value of the *products* sold (and bought); the figures in parentheses show the magnitude of value of the labour-power (=l. p.) sold (and bought).

The arrows proceeding from one producer to another show that the first is a wage-worker for the second.

Simple reproduction is assumed: the capitalists consume the entire surplus-value unproductively.

	Producers	Production: Branch of industry a	b	c	Total	Natural consumption
1.	I	a	b	c	9	9
	II	a	b	c	9	9
	III	a	b	c	9	9
	IV	a	b	c	9	9
	V	a	b	c	9	9
	VI	a	b	c	9	9
	Total	6a	6b	6c	54	54
3.	I	a	—	2c	9	6
	II	a	2b	—	9	6
	III	a	—	2c	9	6
	IV	a	2b	—	9	6
	V	a	—	2c	9	6
	VI	a	2b	—	9	6
	Total	6a	6b	6c	54	36
5.	I	2a	—	6c ↑↑	24	11
	II	$\frac{1}{2}$a →	—	—	$1\frac{1}{2}$	$1\frac{1}{2}$
	III	$\frac{1}{2}$a →	—	—	$1\frac{1}{2}$	$1\frac{1}{2}$
	IV	2a	6b ↑↑	—	24	11
	V	$\frac{1}{2}$a →	—	—	$1\frac{1}{2}$	$1\frac{1}{2}$
	VI	$\frac{1}{2}$a →	—	—	$1\frac{1}{2}$	$1\frac{1}{2}$
	Total	6a	6b	6c	54	28

* The part of value which replaces constant capital is taken as unchanging, and is therefore ignored.

Market		Producers	Production				Natural consumption	Market		
			Branch of industry							
Sells	Buys		a	b	c	Total		Sells	Buys	
—	—	I	a	—	2c	9	6	3	3	2.
—	—	II	a	$\frac{6}{5}$b	$\frac{4}{5}$c	9	$8\frac{2}{5}$	$\frac{3}{5}$	$\frac{3}{5}$	
—	—	III	a	$\frac{6}{5}$b	$\frac{4}{5}$c	9	$8\frac{2}{5}$	$\frac{3}{5}$	$\frac{3}{5}$	
—	—	IV	a	$\frac{6}{5}$b	$\frac{4}{5}$c	9	$8\frac{2}{5}$	$\frac{3}{5}$	$\frac{3}{5}$	
—	—	V	a	$\frac{6}{5}$b	$\frac{4}{5}$c	9	$8\frac{2}{5}$	$\frac{3}{5}$	$\frac{3}{5}$	
—	—	VI	a	$\frac{6}{5}$b	$\frac{4}{5}$c	9	$8\frac{2}{5}$	$\frac{3}{5}$	$\frac{3}{5}$	
—	—	*Total*	6a	6b	6c	54	48	6	6	
3	3	I	a		6c	21	10	11	3 (+8 l.p.)	4.
3	3	II	a	—	—	3	3	(4 l.p.)	4	
3	3	III	a	—	—	3	3	(4 l.p.)	4	
3	3	IV	a	6b	—	21	10	11	3 (+8 l.p.)	
3	3	V	a	—	—	3	3	(4 l.p.)	4	
3	3	VI	a	—	—	3	3	(4 l.p.)	4	
18	18	*Total*	6a	6b	6c	54	32	22 (+16 l.p.)	22 (+16 l.p.)	
1	3 (+10 l.p.)	I	6a	—	—	18	6	12	6 (+6 l.p.)	6.
(5 l.p.)	5	II		—	—	—	—	(6 l.p.)	6	
(5 l.p.)	5	III	—	6b	—	18	6	12	6 (+6 l.p.)	
13	3 (+10 l.p.)	V	—		—	—	—	(6 l.p.)	6	
(5 l.p.)	5	V	—	—	6c	18	6	12	6 (+6 l.p.)	
(5 l.p.)	5	VI	—		—	—	—	(6 l.p.)	6	
26 (+20 l.p.)	26 (+20 l.p.)	*Total*	6a	6b	6c	54	18	36 (+18 l.p.)	36 (+18 l.p.)	

wage-workers no longer receive the whole product of 9, but only of 7—they receive 3 from their independent activity (agricultural—industry *a*) and 4 from wage-labour (from the production of 2 *b* or 2 *c*). These producers, now more wage-workers than independent masters, have lost the opportunity of bringing any product of their labour to the market because ruin has deprived them of the means of production necessary for the making of products. They have had to resort to "outside employments," i.e., to take their labour-power to the market and with the money obtained from the sale of this new commodity to buy the product they need.

The table shows that producers II and III, V and VI each sells labour-power to the extent of 4 units of value and buys articles of consumption to the same amount. As regards the capitalist producers, I and IV, each of them produces products to the extent of 21; of this, he himself consumes 10 [3 (=a)+3 (=c or b)+4 (surplus-value from 2 *c* or 2 *b*)] and sells 11; but he buys commodities to the extent of 3 (*c* or *b*)+8 (labour-power).

In this case, it must be observed, we do not get complete correspondence between the degree of specialisation of social labour (the production of 5 *b* and 5 *c*, i.e., to the sum of 30, was specialised) and the dimensions of the market (22), but this error in the table is due to our having taken simple reproduction,* i.e., with no accumulation; that is why the surplus-value taken from the workers (four units by each capitalist) is all consumed *in kind*. Since absence of accumulation is impossible in capitalist society, the appropriate correction will be made later.

5th period. The differentiation of the commodity producers has spread to the agricultural industry (*a*): the wage-workers could not continue their farming, for they worked mainly in the industrial establishments of others, and were ruined: they retained only miserable remnants of their farming, about a half (which, we assumed, was just enough to cover the needs of their families)—exactly as the present cultivated land of the vast mass of our peasant "agriculturists" are merely miserable bits of independent farming. The concentration of industry *a* in an insignificant

* This also applies to the 5th and 6th periods.

number of big establishments has begun in an exactly similar way. Since the grain grown by the wage-workers is now not enough to cover their needs, wages, which were kept low by their independent farming, increase and provide the workers with the money to buy grain (although in a smaller quantity than they consumed when they were their own masters): now the worker produces $1\frac{1}{2}(=\frac{1}{2}$ a) and buys 1, getting in all $2\frac{1}{2}$ instead of the former 3 (=a). The capitalist masters, having added expanded farming to their industrial establishments now each produce 2 *a* (=6), of which 2 goes to the workers in the form of wages and 1 ($\frac{1}{3}$ a)—surplus-value—to themselves. The development of capitalism depicted in this table is accompanied by the "impoverishment" of the "people" (the workers now consume only $6\frac{1}{2}$ each instead of 7, as in the 4th period), and by the growth of the market, in which 26 now appear. The "decline of farming," in the case of the majority of the producers, did not cause a shrinkage, but an expansion of the market for farm produce.

6th period. The specialisation of occupations, i.e., the division of social labour, is completed. All branches of industry have separated, and have become the speciality of separate producers. The wage-workers have completely lost their independent farms and subsist entirely on wage-labour. We get the same result: the development of capitalism [independent farming on one's own account has been fully eliminated], "impoverishment of the masses" [although the workers' wages have risen, their consumption has diminished from $6\frac{1}{2}$ to 6: they each produce *9* (3a, 3b, 3c) and give their masters one-third as surplus-value], and a further growth of the market, in which there now appears two-thirds of the social product (36).

VI

Let us now draw the conclusions which follow from the above table.

The first conclusion is that the concept "market" is quite inseparable from the concept of the social division of labour—that "general basis of all commodity [and consequently, let us add, of capitalist] production" as Marx calls it. The "market" arises where, and to the extent that, social division of labour and commodity production appear. The dimensions of the market are inseparably connected with the degree of specialisation of social labour.

"...It [a commodity] cannot acquire the properties of a socially recognised universal equivalent, except by being converted into money. That money, however, is in someone else's pocket. In order to entice the money out of that pocket, our friend's commodity must, above all things, be a use-value to the owner of the money. For this, it is necessary that the labour expended upon it be of a kind that is socially useful, of a kind that constitutes *a branch of the social division of labour.* But division of labour is a system of production which has grown up spontaneously and continues to grow behind the backs of the producers. The commodity to be exchanged may possibly be the product of some new kind of labour that pretends to satisfy newly arisen requirements, or even to give rise itself to new requirements. *A particular operation, though yesterday, perhaps, forming one out of the many operations conducted by one producer in creating a given commodity, may today separate itself from this connection, may establish itself as an independent branch of labour and send its incomplete product to market as an independent commodity*" (*Das Kapital*, Bd. I, S. 85.[21] My italics).

Thus, the limits of the development of the market, in capitalist society, are set by the limits of the specialisation of social labour. But this specialisation, by its very nature is as infinite as technical developments. To increase the productivity of human labour in, for instance, the making of some part of a whole product, the production of that part must be specialised, must become a special one concerned with mass production and, therefore, permitting (and engendering) the employment of machines, etc. That is on the one hand. On the other hand, technical progress in capitalist society consists in the socialisation of labour, and this socialisation necessarily calls for specialisation in the various functions of the production process, for their transformation from scattered, isolated functions repeated separately in every establishment engaged in this production, into socialised functions concentrated in one, new establishment, and calculated to satisfy the requirements of the whole of society. I shall quote an example:

"Recently, in the United States, the woodworking factories are becoming more and more specialised, 'new factories are springing up exclusively for the making of, for instance, axe handles, broom handles, or extensible tables.... Machine building is making constant progress, new machines are being continuously invented to simplify and cheapen some side of production.... Every branch of furniture making, for instance, has become a trade requiring special machines and special workers.... In carriage building, wheel rims are made in special factories (Missouri, Arkansas, Tennessee), wheel spokes are made in Indiana and Ohio, and hubs again are made in special factories in Kentucky and Illinois. All these separate parts are bought by factories which specialise in the making of whole wheels. Thus, quite a dozen factories take part in the building of some cheap kind of vehicle'" (Mr. Tverskoi, "Ten Years in America," *Vestnik Yevropy*, 1893, 1. I quote from Nik. —on,[22] p. 91, footnote 1).

This shows how wrong is the assertion that the growth of the market in capitalist society caused by the specialisation of social labour must cease as soon as all natural producers become commodity producers. Russian carriage building has long become commodity production, but wheel rims, say, are still made in every carriage builder's (or wheelwright's) shop; the technical level is low, production is split up among a mass of producers. Technical progress must entail the specialisation of different parts of production, their socialisation, and, consequently, the expansion of the market.

Here the following reservation must be made. All that has been said by no means implies the rejection of the proposition that a capitalist nation cannot exist without foreign markets. Under capitalist production, an equilibrium between production and consumption is achieved only by a series of fluctuations; the larger the scale of production, and the wider the circle of consumers it is calculated to serve, the more violent are the fluctuations. It can be understood, therefore, that when bourgeois production has reached a high degree of development it can no longer keep within the limits of the national state: competition compels the capitalists to keep on expanding production and to seek foreign markets for the mass sale of their products. Obviously, the fact that a capitalist nation must have foreign markets just as little violates the law that the market is a simple expression of the social division of labour under commodity economy and, consequently, that it can grow as infinitely as the division of labour, as crises violate the law of value. Lamentations about markets appeared in Russian literature only when certain branches of our capitalist production (for example, the cotton industry) had reached full development, embraced nearly the entire home market and become concentrated in a few huge enterprises. The best proof that the material basis of the idle talk and "questions" of markets is precisely the interests of our large-scale capitalist industry, is the fact that nobody in our literature has yet prophesied the ruin of our handicraft industry because of the disappearance of "markets," although the handicraft industry produces values totalling over a thousand million rubles and supplies the very same impoverished "people." The wailing about the ruin of our industry due to the shortage of markets is nothing more than a thinly disguised manoeuvre of our capitalists, who in this way exert pressure on policy, identify (in humble avowal of their own "impotence") the interests of their pockets with the interests of the "country" and are capable of making the government pursue a policy of colonial conquest, and even of involving it in war for the sake of protecting such "state" interests. The bottomless pit of Narodnik utopianism and Narodnik simplicity is needed for the acceptance of this wailing about markets—these crocodile tears of a quite firmly established and already conceited bourgeoisie—as proof of the "impotence" of Russian capitalism!

The second conclusion is that "the impoverishment of the masses of the people" (that indispensable point in all the Narodnik arguments about the market) not only does not hinder the development of capitalism, but, on the contrary, is the expression of that development, is a condition of capitalism and strengthens it. Capitalism needs the "free labourer," and impoverishment consists in the petty producers being converted into wage-workers. The impoverishment of the masses is accompanied by the enrichment of a few exploiters, the ruin and decline of small establishments is accompanied by the strengthening and development of bigger ones; both processes facilitate the growth of the market: the "impoverished" peasant who formerly lived by his own farming now lives by "earnings," i.e., by the sale of his labour-power; he now has to purchase essential articles of consumption (although in a smaller quantity and of inferior quality). On the other hand, the means of production from which this peasant is freed are concentrated in the hands of a minority, are converted into *capital*, and the product now appears on the market. This is the only explanation of the fact that the mass expropriation of our peasantry in the post-Reform epoch has been accompanied by an increase and not a decrease in the gross productivity of the country* and by the growth of the home market: it is a known fact that there has been an enormous increase in the output of the big factories and works and

* This may be a debatable point only in relation to the agricultural industry. "Grain production is in a state of absolute stagnation," says Mr. N. —on, for example. He bases his conclusion on the data for only eight years (1871-1878). Let us examine the data for a longer period; an eight-year period is, of course, too short. Let us compare the statistics for the 1860's [*Military Statistical Abstract*, 1871], the 1870's [N. —on's data] and the 1880's [*Returns for Russia*, 1890]. The data cover 50 gubernias of European Russia and all crops, including potatoes.

Annual average for	Sown		Harvested		Yield (times)	Population (thousands)	
	Thousands of chetverts (minus seed)						
1864-1866 (3)	71,696	100	151,840	100	3.12	61,421 (1867)	100
1871-1878 (8)	71,378	99.5	195,024	128.4	3.73	76,594 (1876)	124.7
1883-1887 (5)	80,293	111.9	254,914	167.8	4.17	85,395 (1886)	139.0

that there has been a considerable extension of the handicraft industries—both work mainly for the home market—and there has been a similar increase in the amount of grain circulating in the home markets (the development of the grain trade within the country).

The third conclusion—about the significance of the production of means of production—calls for a correction to the table. As has already been stated, that table does not at all claim to depict the whole process of development of capitalism, but only to show how the replacement of natural by commodity economy and of the latter by capitalist economy affects the market. That is why accumulation was disregarded in the table. Actually, however, capitalist society cannot exist without accumulating, for competition compels every capitalist on pain of ruin to expand production. Such expansion of production is depicted in the table: producer I, for example, in the interval between the 3rd and 4th periods, expanded his output of *c* threefold: from 2 *c* to 6 *c*; formerly he worked alone in his workshop—now he has two wage-workers. Obviously, that expansion of production could not have taken place without accumulation: he had to build a special workshop for several persons, to acquire implements of production on a larger scale, and to purchase larger quantities of raw materials and much else. The same applies to producer IV, who expanded the production of *b*. This expansion of individual establishments, the concentration of production, must of necessity have entailed (or increased, it makes no difference) the production of means of production for the capitalists: machines, iron, coal, etc. The concentration of production increased the productivity of labour, replaced hand by machine labour and discarded a certain number of workers. On the other hand, there was a development in the production of these machines and other means of production, converted by the capitalist into constant capital which now begins to grow more rapidly than variable capital. If, for example, we compare the 4th period with the 6th, we shall find that the production of means of production has increased 50 per cent (because in the former case there are two capitalist enterprises requiring an increase of constant capital, and in the latter, three): by comparing this increase with the growth in the production of articles of consumption we arrive at the more rapid growth of the production of means of production mentioned above.

The whole meaning and significance of this law of the more rapid growth of means of production lies in the one fact that the replacement of hand by machine labour—in general the technical progress that accompanies machine industry—calls for the intense development of the production of coal and iron, those real "means of production as means of production." It is clearly evident from the following statement that the author failed to understand the meaning of this law, and allowed the schemes depicting the process to screen its real nature from him: "Viewed from the side this production of means of production as means of production seems absolutely absurd, but the accumulation of money for money's sake by Plyushkin[23] was also (?!!) an absolutely absurd process. Both know not what they do." That is precisely what the Narodniks try their utmost to prove—the absurdity of Russian capitalism, which, they aver, is ruining the people, but is not providing a higher organisation of production. Of course, that is a fairy-tale. There is nothing "absurd" in replacing hand by machine labour: on the contrary, the progressive work of human technique consists precisely in this. The higher the level of technical development the more is human hand labour ousted, being replaced by machines of increasing complexity: an ever larger place is taken in the country's total production by machines and the articles needed for their manufacture.*

These three conclusions must be supplemented by two further remarks.

---

* Naturally, therefore, it is wrong to divide the development of capitalism into development in breadth and in depth: the entire development proceeds on account of division of labour; there is no "essential" difference between the two features. Actually, however, the difference between them boils down to different stages of technical progress. In the lower stages of the development of capitalist technique—simple co-operation and manufacture—the production of means of production as means of production does not yet exist: it emerges and attains enormous development only at the higher stage—large-scale machine industry.

Firstly, what has been said does not negate the "contradiction in the capitalist mode of production" which Marx spoke of in the following words: "The labourers as buyers of commodities are important for the market. But as sellers of their own commodity—labour-power—capitalist society tends to keep them down to the minimum price" (*Das Kapital*, Bd. II, S. 303, No. 32).[24] It has been shown above that in capitalist society that part of social production which produces articles of consumption must also grow. The development of the production of means of production merely sets the above-mentioned contradiction aside, but does not abolish it. It can only be eliminated with the elimination of the capitalist mode of production itself. It goes without saying, however, that it is utterly absurd to regard that contradiction as an obstacle to the full development of capitalism in Russia (as the Narodniks are fond of doing); incidentally, that is sufficiently explained by the table.

Secondly, when discussing the relation between the growth of capitalism and of the "market," we must not lose sight of the indubitable fact that the development of capitalism inevitably entails a rising level of requirements for the entire population, including the industrial proletariat. This rise is created in general by the increasing frequency of exchange of products, which results in more frequent contacts between the inhabitants of town and country, of different geographical localities, and so forth. It is also brought about by the crowding together, the concentration of the industrial proletariat, which enhances their class-consciousness and sense of human dignity and enables them to wage a successful struggle against the predatory tendencies of the capitalist system. This law of increasing requirements has manifested itself with full force in the history of Europe—compare, for example, the French proletariat of the end of the eighteenth and of the end of the nineteenth centuries, or the British worker of the 1840's* and of today.

---

* Cf. Frederick Engels, *The Condition of the Working-Class in England in 1844*. That was a state of most horrible and sordid poverty (in the literal sense of the word) and of utter loss of the sense of human dignity.

This same law operates in Russia, too: the rapid development of commodity economy and capitalism in the post-Reform epoch has caused a rise in the level of requirements of the "peasantry," too: the peasants have begun to live a "cleaner" life (as regards clothing, housing, and so forth). That this undoubtedly progressive phenomenon must be placed to the credit of Russian capitalism and of nothing else is proved if only by the generally known fact (noted by all the investigators of our village handicrafts and of peasant economy in general) that the peasants of the industrial localities live a far "cleaner" life than the peasants engaged exclusively in agriculture and hardly touched by capitalism. Of course, that phenomenon is manifested primarily and most readily in the adoption of the purely outward, ostentatious aspect of "civilisation," but only arrant reactionaries like Mr. V. V. are capable of bewailing it and seeing nothing in it but "decline."

VII

To understand what, in fact, the "market question" consists of, it is best to compare the Narodnik and Marxist conceptions of the process illustrated by the *diagram* (showing exchange between the capitalists of sphere *A* and the direct producers of sphere *W*) and by the *table* (showing the conversion of the natural economy of 6 producers into capitalist economy).

If we take the diagram we get no explanation at all. Why does capitalism develop? Where does it come from? It is represented as a sort of "accident"; its emergence is attributed either to "*we* took the wrong road"... or to "implantation" by the authorities. Why do "the masses become impoverished"? This again is not answered by the diagram, and in place of an answer the Narodniks dispose of the matter with sentimental phrases about a "time-hallowed system," deviation from the true path, and similar nonsense which the celebrated "subjective method in sociology" is so good at inventing.

The inability to explain capitalism, and preference for utopias instead of a study and elucidation of reality, lead to a denial of the significance and strength of capitalism. It is like a hopeless invalid who has no source from which to draw strength for development. And we shall introduce into the condition of that invalid an insignificant, almost impalpable improvement if we say that he can develop by producing "means of production as means of production."* That requires the technical development of capitalism, and "we see" that precisely this development is lacking. For that capitalism must embrace the whole country, but we see that "it is not possible for the development of capitalism to become universal."

If, however, we take the table, neither the development of capitalism nor the impoverishment of the people will appear to be accidental. They are necessary concomitants of the growth of commodity production based on the division of social labour. The question of the market is entirely eliminated, because the market is nothing other than the expression of that division of labour and commodity production. The development of capitalism is now seen not only as a possibility [something the author of the paper could at best** have proved], but also as a necessity, because once social economy is based on the division of labour and the commodity form of the product, technical progress must inevitably lead to the strengthening and deepening of capitalism.

The question now arises: why should we accept the second view? By what criterion is it correct?

By the facts of contemporary Russian economic reality.

The pivot of the table is the transition from commodity to capitalist economy, the differentiation of the commodity producers into capitalists and proletarians. And if we turn to the phenomena of the contemporary social economy of Russia we shall see that the foremost of them is precisely the *differentiation* of our small producers. If we take the peasant agriculturists, we shall find that, on

* That is, the replacement of small industrial units by big ones, the ousting of hand by machine labour.

** That is, if he correctly appraised and properly understood the significance of the production of means of production.

the one hand, masses of peasants are giving up the land, losing economic independence, turning into proletarians, and, on the other hand, peasants are continually enlarging their crop areas and adopting improved farming methods. On the one hand, peasants are losing farm property (livestock and implements) and, on the other hand, peasants are acquiring improved implements, are beginning to procure machines, and so forth. [*Cf.* V. V., *Progressive Trends in Peasant Farming.*] On the one hand, peasants are giving up the land, selling or leasing their allotments, and, on the other hand, peasants are renting allotments and are greedily buying privately-owned land. All these are commonly known facts,* established long, long ago, the only *explanation* of which lies in the laws of commodity economy, which splits our "community" peasants, too, into a bourgeoisie and a proletariat. If we take the village handicraftsmen we shall find that in the post-Reform epoch not only have new industries emerged and the old ones developed more rapidly [the result of the differentiation of the agricultural peasantry just mentioned, the result of the progressing social division of labour**], but, in addition, the mass of handicraftsmen have been growing poorer and poorer, sinking into dire poverty and losing economic independence, while an insignificant minority have been growing rich at the expense of that mass, accumulating vast amounts of capital, and turning into buyers-up, monopolising the market, and in the overwhelming majority of our handicraft industries, have, in the end, organised a completely capitalist *domestic system of large-scale production.*

The existence of these two polarising trends among our petty producers clearly shows that capitalism and mass impoverishment, far from precluding, actually condition each other, and irrefutably proves that capitalism is already the main background of the economic life of Russia.

* The peasants themselves very aptly call this process "*depeasantising.*" (See *Agricultural Survey of Nizhni-Novgorod Gubernia for 1892*, Nizhni-Novgorod, 1893, Vol. III, pp. 186-87.)

** One of Mr. Nikolai —on's biggest theoretical mistakes is that he ignores this phenomenon.

That is why it will be no paradox to say that the fact of the break-up of the peasantry provides the answer to the "question of markets."

One cannot help noting, also, that the very (current) presentation of the notorious "market question" harbours a number of absurdities. The usual formula (see § 1) is based on the most incredible assumptions—that the economic system of society can be built or destroyed at the will of some group of persons—"intellectuals" or the "government" (otherwise the question could not be raised—"can" capitalism develop?, "must" Russia pass through capitalism?, "should" the village community be preserved? and so forth)—that capitalism precludes the impoverishment of the people, that the market is something separate from and independent of capitalism, some special condition for its development. Unless these absurdities are corrected, the question cannot be answered.

Indeed, let us imagine that in answer to the question: "Can capitalism develop in Russia, when the masses of the people are poor and are becoming still poorer?" somebody would say the following: "Yes, it can, because capitalism will develop not on account of articles of consumption, but on account of means of production." Obviously, such an answer is based on the absolutely correct idea that the total productivity of a capitalist nation increases chiefly on account of means of production (i.e., more on account of means of production than of articles of consumption); but it is still more obvious that such an answer cannot advance the solution of the question one iota, just as you cannot draw a correct conclusion from a syllogism with a correct minor premise but an absurd major premise. Such an answer (I repeat) already presupposes that capitalism is developing, is embracing the whole country, passing to a higher technical stage (large-scale machine industry), whereas the question itself is based on the denial of the possibility of capitalism developing and of small-scale production being replaced by large-scale production.

The "market question" must be removed from the sphere of fruitless speculation about "possibility" and "necessity" to the solid ground of reality, that of studying and *ex-*

plaining what shape the Russian economic order is taking, and why it is taking that shape and no other.

I shall confine myself to quoting some examples from the material in my possession in order to show concretely on what data this proposition is based.

To illustrate the differentiation of the small producers and the fact that not only a process of impoverishment, but also of the creation of large-scale (relatively) bourgeois economy is taking place among them, I shall quote data for three purely agricultural uyezds in different gubernias of European Russia: Dnieper Uyezd in Taurida Gubernia, Novouzensk Uyezd in Samara Gubernia, and Kamyshin Uyezd in Saratov Gubernia. The data are taken from Zemstvo statistical abstracts. To forestall possible statements that the uyezds chosen are not typical (in our outlying regions, which hardly experienced serfdom and largely became populated only under post-Reform, "free" conditions, differentiation has, indeed, made more rapid strides than at the centre) let me say the following:

1) Of the three mainland uyezds of Taurida Gubernia I have chosen Dnieper Uyezd because it is wholly Russian [0.6% are colonist farms] and is inhabited by community peasants.

2) For Novouzensk Uyezd the data concern only the Russian (community) population [see *Statistical Returns for Novouzensk Uyezd*, pp. 432-39. Column *a*], and do not include the so-called farmstead peasants, i.e., those community peasants who have left the community and have settled separately on purchased or rented land. The addition of these direct representatives of capitalist farming* would show an even greater differentiation.

3) For Kamyshin Uyezd the data concern only the Great-Russian (community) population.

The classification in the abstracts is—for Dnieper Uyezd—according to dessiatines of crop area per household; for the others—according to number of draught animals.

---

* Indeed, 2,294 farmstead peasants have 123,252 dessiatines under crops (i.e., an average of 53 dessiatines per farmer). They employ 2,662 male labourers (and 234 women). They have over 40,000 horses and oxen. Very many improved implements: see p. 453 of *Statistical Returns for Novouzensk Uyezd*.

Groups of peasants according to economic strength	Dnieper Uyezd					Novouzensk	
	Number of households	%	Crop area (dess.)	%	Crop area per household (dess.)	Number of households	%
Poor group	7,880	40	38,439	11	4.8 } 10.9	10,504	37
Middle group	8,234	42	137,344	43	16.6 }	10,757	38
Prosperous group	3,643	18	150,614	46	41.3	7,014	25
Totals	19,757	100	326,397	100	17.8	28,275	100

The *poor* group includes households—in Dnieper Uyezd—cultivating no land, or with crop areas of up to 10 dessiatines per household; in Novouzensk and Kamyshin uyezds—households having no draught animals or one. The *middle* group includes households in Dnieper Uyezd having from 10 to 25 dessiatines of crop area; in Novouzensk Uyezd—households having from 2 to 4 draught animals; in Kamyshin Uyezd—households having from 2 to 3 draught animals. The *prosperous* group includes households having over 25 dessiatines (Dnieper Uyezd), or having more than 4 draught animals (Novouzensk Uyezd) and more than 3 (Kamyshin Uyezd).

From these data it is quite evident that the process going on among our agricultural and community peasants is not one of impoverishment and ruin in general, but a process of splitting into a bourgeoisie and a proletariat. A vast mass of peasants (the poor group)—about a half on the average—are losing economic independence. They

Uyezd			Kamyshin Uyezd				
Crop area (dess.)	%	Crop area per household (dess.)	Number of households	%	Crop area (dess.)	%	Crop area per household (dess.)
36,007	8	3.4 } 7.75	9,313	54	29,194	20	3.1 } 5.7
128,986	29	12	4,980	29	52,735	35	10.6
284,069	63	40.5	2,881	17	67,844	45	23.5
449,062	100	15.9	17,174	100	149,703	100	8.7

now have only an insignificant part of the total farming of the local peasants—some 13% (on the average) of the crop area; the area under crops is 3-4 dessiatines per household. To show what such a crop area means, let me say that in Taurida Gubernia, for a peasant household to subsist exclusively by independent farming, without resorting to so-called "outside employments," it must have 17-18 dessiatines* under crops. Obviously, the members of the bottom group already subsist far less by their farming than by outside employments, i.e., the sale of their labour-power. And if we turn to more detailed data characterising the conditions of the peasants in this group we shall see that precisely this group provides the largest contingent of those who give up their farming, lease their allotments, have

* In Samara and Saratov gubernias the amount will be about a third lower, as the local population is less prosperous.

no working implements and seek employment elsewhere. The peasants in this group represent our rural proletariat.

But, on the other hand, from among these very same community peasants quite another group, of an entirely opposite character, is emerging. The peasants in the top group have crop areas 7 to 10 times larger than those of the peasants in the bottom group. If we compare these crop areas (23-40 dessiatines per household) with the "normal" number of dessiatines under crops that a family needs in order to live comfortably by its farming alone, we shall find that they are double or treble that amount. Obviously, these peasants already engage in agriculture to obtain an income, to trade in grain. They accumulate considerable savings and use them to improve their farms and farming methods; for example, they buy agricultural machines and improved implements. In Novouzensk Uyezd as a whole, for instance, 14% of the householders have improved agricultural implements; of the peasants in the top group 42% of the householders have improved implements (so that the peasants in the top group account for 75% of the total number of households in the uyezd possessing improved agricultural implements), and concentrate in their hands 82% of the total improved implements owned by the "peasantry."* The peasants in the top group can no longer manage their crop sowing with their own labour force and therefore resort to the hiring of workers: for example, in Novouzensk Uyezd 35% of the householders in the top group employ regular wage-workers (not counting those hired, for instance, for the harvesting, etc.); it is the same in Dnieper Uyezd. In short, the peasants in the top group undoubtedly constitute a bourgeoisie. Their strength now is not based on plundering other producers (as is the strength of the usurers and "kulaks"), but on the independent organisation** of production: in the hands of this group, which constitutes only one-fifth of the peasantry, is concentrated more than one-half of the total crop area [I take the general average area for all three

* Altogether, the peasants in the uyezd have 5,724 improved implements.

** Which, of course, is also based on plunder, only not the plunder of independent producers, but of workers.

uyezds]. If we bear in mind that the productivity of labour (i.e., the harvests) of these peasants is immeasurably higher than that of the ground-scratching proletarians in the bottom group, we cannot but draw the conclusion that the chief motive force in grain production is the rural bourgeoisie.

What influence was this splitting of the peasantry into a bourgeoisie and a proletariat [the Narodniks see nothing in this process but the "impoverishment of the masses"] bound to have on the size of the "market," i.e., on the proportion of grain that is converted into a *commodity*? Obviously, that proportion was bound to grow considerably, because the mass of grain possessed by the peasants in the top group far exceeded their own needs and went to the market; on the other hand, the members of the bottom group had to buy extra grain with money earned by outside work.

To quote exact data on this point we must now turn not to Zemstvo statistical abstracts, but to V. Y. Postnikov's book: *Peasant Farming in South Russia*. Using Zemstvo statistical data, Postnikov describes peasant farming in three mainland uyezds of Taurida Gubernia (Berdyansk, Melitopol and Dnieper) and analyses that farming according to different groups of peasants [divided into 6 categories according to crop area: 1) cultivating no land; 2) cultivating up to 5 dessiatines; 3) from 5 to 10 dessiatines; 4) 10 to 25 dessiatines; 5) 25 to 50 dessiatines; 6) over 50 dessiatines]. Investigating the relation of the different groups to the market, the author divides the crop area of each farm into the following 4 parts: 1) the *farm-service area*—as Postnikov calls the part of the crop area which provides the seed necessary for sowing; 2) the *food area*—provides grain for the sustenance of the family and labourers; 3) the *fodder area*—provides fodder for the draught animals, and lastly, 4) the *commercial* or *market* area provides the product which is converted into a commodity and disposed of on the market. It goes without saying that only the last area provides income in *cash*, whereas the others yield it in kind, i.e., provide a product that is consumed on the farm.

Calculating the size of each of these plots in the different crop-area groups of the peasantry, Postnikov presents the following table:

	Out of 100 dess. under crops				Cash income		In the 3 uyezds of Taurida Gubernia		
	Farm-service area	Food area	Fodder area	Commercial area	Per dess. under crops (rubles)	Per household (rubles)	Total under crops (dessiatines)	Of which, commercial areas (dessiatines)	Average under crops in each group
Cultivating up to 5 dess.	6	90.7	42.3	—39	—	—	34,070	—	3.5 dess.
" 5 to 10 "	6	44.7	37.5	+11.8	3.77	30	140,426	16,851	8
" 10 to 25 "	6	27.5	30	36.5	11.68	191	540,093	194,433	16.4
" 25 to 50 "	6	17.0	25	52	16.64	574	494,095	256,929	34.5
" over 50 "	6	12.0	21	61	19.52	1,500	230,583	140,656	75
Totals	6			42			1,439,267	608,869	17-18 dess.

Note to table:

1) Postnikov does not give the penultimate column; I compiled it myself.

2) Postnikov calculates the cash income on the assumption that the entire commercial area is planted to wheat, and taking the average yield and the average price of grain.

We see from these data that the bigger the farm, the more it assumes a commodity character and the larger is the proportion of grain grown for sale [12-36-52-61% according to group]. The principal grain growers, the peasants in the two top groups (they have more than half the total area under crops), sell more than half of their total agricultural product [52% and 61%].

If the peasantry were not split up into a bourgeoisie and a proletariat, if, in other words, the area under crops were divided among all the "peasants" "equally," *all* of them would then belong to the middle group (those cultivating 10 to 25 dessiatines), and only 36% of the total grain, i.e., the product of 518,136 dessiatines of crop area (36% of 1,439,267 =518,136), would appear on the market. But now, as can be seen from the table, 42% of the total grain, the product of 608,869 dessiatines, goes to the market. Thus, the "impoverishment of the masses," the complete decline of the farms of 40% of the peasants (the poor group, i.e., those cultivating up to 10 dessiatines), the formation of a rural proletariat have led to the produce of *90,000** dessiatines of land under crops being thrown on to the market.

I do not at all want to say that the growth of the "market" as a consequence of the differentiation of the peasantry was limited only to this. Far from it. We have seen, for example, that the peasants acquire improved implements, i.e., turn their savings to the "production of means of production." We have seen that, in addition to grain, another commodity, human labour-power, has come on to the market. I do not refer to all this only because I have quoted this example for a narrow and specific purpose: to show that here in Russia the impoverishment of the masses is actually leading to the strengthening of commodity and capitalist economy. I deliberately chose a product like grain, which everywhere and always is the last and the slowest to be drawn into commodity circulation. And that is why I took an exclusively agricultural locality.

I shall now take another example, relating to a purely industrial area—Moscow Gubernia. Peasant farming is described by the Zemstvo statisticians in volumes VI and VII of *Statistical Returns for Moscow Gubernia*, which contain a number of excellent essays on the handicraft industries. I shall confine myself to quoting one passage from the essay on "The Lace Industry"** which explains how and why the post-Reform epoch saw a particularly rapid development of peasant handicrafts.

The lace industry arose in the twenties of the present century in two neighbouring villages of Voronovo Volost, Podolsk Uyezd. "In the 1840's it began to spread slowly to other nearby villages, although it did not yet cover a big area. But beginning with the sixties and especially during

---

* 90,733 dessiatines = 6.3% of the total crop area.

** *Statistical Returns for Moscow Gubernia*. Section of Economic Statistics. Vol. VI, Issue II, Handicraft Industries of Moscow Gubernia, Issue II, Moscow, 1880.

the last three or four years, it has spread rapidly to the surrounding countryside."

Of the 32 villages in which this industry is practised at the present time it began:

in	2	villages in	1820
"	4	" "	1840
"	5	" "	the 1860's
"	7	" "	1870-1875
"	14	" "	1876-1879

"If we investigate the causes of this phenomenon," says the author of the essay, "i.e., the extremely rapid spread of the industry precisely in the last few years, we shall find that, on the one hand, during that period the peasants' living conditions greatly deteriorated and, on the other hand, that the requirements of the population—that part of it which is in more favourable circumstances—considerably increased."

In confirmation of this the author borrows from the Moscow Zemstvo statistics the following data, which I give in the form of a table.*

"These figures," continues the author, "are eloquent proof that the *total* number of horses, cows and small livestock in that volost increased, but this increased prosperity fell to the lot of certain individuals, namely, the category of householders owning 2-3 and more horses....

"...Consequently, we see that, side by side with an increase in the number of peasants who have neither cows nor horses, there is an increase in the number of those who stop cultivating their land: they have no animals, and, therefore, not enough manure; the land becomes exhausted, it is not worth tilling; to get food for themselves and their families, to avert starvation, it is not enough for the males alone to engage in some industry—they did that previously, when they were free from farm work—now, other members of the family must also seek outside employment....

"...The figures we gave in the tables showed us something else; in those villages there was also an *increase* in the number

* I have omitted data on the distribution of cows (the conclusion is the same) and added the percentages. [See table on p. 119.—*Ed. Eng. ed.*]

VORONOVO VOLOST, PODOLSK UYEZD:

In Voronovo Volost	Number of householders	Number of		Per 100 persons of both sexes			Number of householders owning					Number of horses owned by householders having				Number of allotment-holding householders			
																	Cultivating allotment		
		Horses	Cows	Horses	Cows	Small livestock	No horses	1 horse	2 horses	3 horses	More than 3 horses	1 horse	2 horses	3 horses	More than 3 horses	Total	them-selves	with hired labour	Not cultivating land
In 1869 there were	1,233	1,473	1,472	22	22	30	276	567	298	70	22	567	596	210	100	1,067	900	92	75
							22%	46%	24%	6%	2%	39%	40%	14%	7%		84%	9%	7%
In 1877 there were	1,244	1,607	1,726	25	27	38	319	465	313	95	52	465	626	285	231	1,166	965	5	196
							26%	37%	25%	8%	4%	29%	39%	18%	14%		82.5%	0.5%	17%

of people having 2-3 horses, or cows. Consequently, the prosperity of those peasants increased, and yet, at the same time, we said that 'all the women and children in such and such a village engage in industry.' How is this to be explained?... To explain this phenomenon we must see what sort of life is lived in those villages, and become more closely acquainted with their domestic conditions, and then, perhaps, ascertain what accounts for this strong urge to produce goods for the market.

"We shall not, of course, stop here to investigate in detail under what fortunate circumstances there gradually emerge from the peasant population stronger individuals, stronger families, what conditions give rise to their prosperity and what social conditions enable that prosperity, once it has appeared, to grow rapidly and cause it to grow to such an extent as to considerably distinguish one section of the village inhabitants from the other. To follow this process it is sufficient to point to one of the most ordinary occurrences in a peasant village. In a village, a certain peasant is reputed among his fellow villagers to be a healthy, strong, sober working man. He has a large family, mostly sons, also distinguished for their physical strength and good traits. They all live together; there is no dividing up. They get an allotment for 4-5 persons. It does not, of course, require the labour of all the members of the family to cultivate it. And so, two or three of the sons regularly engage in some outside or local industry, and only during the haymaking season do they drop their industry for a short time and help the family with the field work. The individual members of the family do not keep their earnings, but pool them. Given other favourable circumstances, the combined income considerably exceeds the expenditure necessary to satisfy the family's requirements. Money is saved and, as a consequence, the family is able to engage in industry under better conditions: it can buy raw materials for cash at first hand, it can sell the goods produced when they fetch a good price, and can dispense with the services of all kinds of 'hirers-out of labour,' men and women dealers, and so forth.

"It becomes possible to hire a worker or two, or give out work to be done at home by poor peasants who have lost the possibility of doing any job quite independently. Due to these and similar circumstances, the strong family we have mentioned is able to obtain profit not only from its own labour. We are not speaking here, of course, of those cases where individuals known as kulaks, sharks, emerge from those families; we are examining the most ordinary occurrences among the peasant population. The tables given in Volume II of the *Abstract* and in Part I of Volume VI clearly show that as the conditions of one section of the peasantry grow worse, in the majority of cases there is an increase in the prosperity of the other, smaller section, or of individual members.

"As industrial occupation spreads, intercourse with the outside world, with the town, in this case with Moscow, becomes more frequent, and some of the Moscow customs gradually penetrate into the village and are met with at first precisely in these more prosperous families. They buy samovars, table crockery and glass, they wear 'neater' clothes. Whereas at first this neatness of clothing takes the shape, among men, of boots in place of bast shoes, among the women leather shoes and boots are the crowning glory, so to speak, of neater clothing; they prefer bright, motley calicoes and kerchiefs, figured woollen shawls, and similar charms....

"...In the peasant family it has been the custom 'for ages' for the wife to clothe her husband, herself and the children.... As long as they grew their own flax, less money had to be spent on the purchase of cloth and other materials required for clothing, and this money was obtained from the sale of poultry, eggs, mushrooms, berries, a spare skein of yarn, or piece of linen. All the rest was made at home. It was such circumstances, i.e., the domestic production of all those articles which the peasant women were expected to make, and the fact that they spent on it all the time they had free from field work, that explain, in the present case, the extremely slow development of the lace industry in the villages in Voronovo Volost. Lace was made mainly by the young women of the more prosperous or of the larger families, where it was not necessary for all the women to spin flax or weave linen. But cheap calico gradually began to oust linen, and to this other circumstances were added: either the flax crop failed, or the wife wanted to make her husband a red calico shirt and herself a smarter dress, and so the custom of weaving various sorts of linen and kerchiefs at home for peasants' clothing gradually died out, or became very restricted. And the clothing itself underwent a change, partly because homespun cloth was displaced by factory-made cloth....

"...That explains why the majority of the population do all they can to make articles for sale, and even put their children to this work."

This artless narrative of a careful observer clearly shows how the process of division of social labour takes place among our peasant masses, how it leads to the enhancement of commodity production [and, consequently, of the market], and how this commodity production, of itself, i.e., by virtue of the very relations in which it places the producer to the market, leads to the purchase and sale of labour-power becoming "a most ordinary occurrence."

VIII

In conclusion, it will, perhaps, be worth while to illustrate the disputed issue which, I think, is overburdened with abstractions, diagrams and formulae—by an examination of the argument advanced by one of the latest and most prominent representatives of "current views."

I am referring to Mr. Nikolai —on.*

He regards as the greatest "obstacle" to the development of capitalism in Russia the "contraction" of the home market and the "diminution" of the purchasing power of the peasants. The capitalisation of the handicraft industries, he says, ousted the domestic production of goods; the peasants had to buy their clothing. To obtain the money for this, the peasant took to the expansion of his crop area, and as the allotments were inadequate he carried this expansion far beyond the limits of rational farming; he raised the payment for rented land to scandalous heights, and in the end he was ruined. Capitalism dug its own grave, it brought "people's economy" to the frightful crisis of 1891 and ... stopped, having no ground under its feet, unable to "continue along the same path."

---

* It goes without saying that there can be no question here of examining his entire work, a separate book would be required for that. We can only examine *one* of his favourite arguments.

Realising that "*we* have departed from the time-hallowed people's system" Russia is now waiting ... for orders from the authorities "to infuse large-scale production into the village community."

Wherein lies the absurdity of this "ever new" (for the Russian Narodniks) theory?

Is it that its author fails to understand the significance of the "production of means of production as means of production"? Of course, not. Mr. Nik. —on knows that law very well and even mentions that it operates in our country, too (pp. 186, 203-204). True, in view of his faculty for castigating himself with contradictions, he sometimes (cf. p. 123) forgets about that law, but it is obvious that the correction of such contradictions would not in the least correct the author's main (above-quoted) argument.

The absurdity of his theory lies in his inability to explain capitalism in this country and in basing his arguments about it on pure fictions.

The "peasantry," who were ruined by the ousting of home-made products by factory-made products, are regarded by Mr. Nik. —on as something homogeneous, internally cohesive, and reacting to all the events of life as one man.

Nothing of the kind exists in reality. Commodity production could not have arisen in Russia if the productive units (the peasant households) had not existed separately, and everybody knows that actually each of our peasants conducts his farming separately and independently of his fellows; he carries on the production of products, which become his private property, at his own exclusive risk; he enters into relation with the "market" on his own.

Let us see how matters stand among the "peasantry."

"Being in need of money, the peasant enlarges his crop area excessively and is ruined."

But only the prosperous peasant can enlarge his crop area, the one who has seed for sowing, and a sufficient quantity of livestock and implements. *Such* peasants (and they, as we know, are the minority) do, indeed, extend their crop areas and expand their farming to such an extent that they cannot cope with it without the aid of hired labourers. The majority of peasants, however, are quite unable to meet their need for money by expanding their farming, for they have no stocks, or sufficient means of production. *Such* a peasant, in order to obtain money, seeks "outside employments," i.e., takes his labour-power and not his product to the market. Naturally, work away from home entails a further decline in farming, and in the end the peasant leases his allotment to a rich fellow community member, who rounds off his farm and, of course, does not himself consume the product of the rented allotment, but sends it to the *market*. We get the "impoverishment of the people," the growth of capitalism and the expansion of the market. But that is not all. Our rich peasant, fully occupied by his extended farming, can no longer produce as hitherto for his own needs, let us say footwear: it is more advantageous for him to buy it. As to the impoverished peasant, he, too, has to buy footwear; he cannot produce it on his farm for the simple reason that he no longer has one. There arises a demand for footwear and a supply of grain, produced in abundance by the enterprising peasant, who touches the soul of Mr. V. V. with the progressive trend of his farming. The neighbouring handicraft footwear-makers find themselves in the same position as the agriculturists just described: to buy grain, of which the declining farm yields too little, production must be expanded. Again, of course, production is expanded only by the handicraftsman who has savings, i.e., the representative of the minority; he is able to hire workers, or give work out to poor peasants to be done at home. The members of the majority of handicraftsmen, however, cannot even think of enlarging their workshops: they are glad to "get work" from the moneyed buyer-up, i.e., to find a purchaser of their only commodity—their labour-power. Again we get the impoverishment of the people, the growth of capitalism and the expansion of the market; a new impetus is given to the further development and intensification of the social division of labour. Where will that movement end? Nobody can say, just as nobody can say where it began, and after all that is not important. The important thing is that we have before us a single, living, organic process, the process of the development of commodity economy and the growth of capitalism. "Depeasantising" in the countryside shows us the beginning of this process, its genesis, its early stages; large-scale capitalism in the towns shows us the end of the process, its tendency. Try to tear these phenomena apart, try to examine them separately and independently of each other and you will not get your argument to hang together; you will be unable to explain either one phenomenon or the other, either the impoverishment of the people or the growth of capitalism.

Mostly, however, those who advance such arguments, which have neither beginning nor end, being unable to explain the process, break off the investigation with the statement that one of the two phenomena equally unintelligible to them [and, of course, precisely the one that contradicts "the morally developed sense of the critically thinking individual"] is "absurd," "accidental," "hangs in the air."

In actual fact, what is "hanging in the air" is of course only their own arguments.

tendency? [illegible] phenomena [illegible] the [illegible] and [illegible] tendency of [illegible] you will not [illegible] argument [illegible] long [illegible] you will be unable to explain either the [illegible] of the other, [illegible] the movement of the people or the growth of population.

Many [illegible] who advance such arguments, which [illegible] be [illegible] with the [illegible] ment that one of [illegible] immutable [illegible] that contradicts the [illegible] of the [illegible]

In [illegible] the [illegible] only their own arguments.

ма. „Раскрестьяниваніе“ въ деревнѣ показываетъ намъ начало этого процесса, зарожденіе его, его раннія стадіи; крупный капитализмъ въ городахъ показываетъ намъ конецъ этого процесса, его тенденціи. Попробуйте разорвать эти явленія, попробуйте разсматривать ихъ отдѣльно и независимо другъ отъ друга, — и вы не сможете въ своемъ разсужденіи свести концевъ съ концами, не сможете объяснить ни того ни другого явленія, ни обѣдненія народа, ни роста капитализма.

При этомъ однако бываетъ большею частью такъ, что авторъ подобныхъ разсужденій безъ начала и безъ конца, не умѣя объяснить процесса, обрываетъ изслѣдованіе заявленіемъ, что одно изъ двухъ, одинаково непонятныхъ ему явленій [и притомъ конечно уже именно то, которое противорѣчитъ „нравственно развитому чувству критически мыслящей личности“] — „нелѣпо“, „случайно“, „виситъ въ воздухѣ“.

На самомъ дѣлѣ, разумѣется, „виситъ въ воздухѣ“ одно только ихъ собственное разсужденіе.

Last manuscript page of Lenin's *On the So-Called Market Question*, 1893 (*Reduced*)

WHAT THE "FRIENDS OF THE PEOPLE" ARE AND HOW THEY FIGHT THE SOCIAL-DEMOCRATS

(A REPLY TO ARTICLES IN *RUSSKOYE BOGATSTVO* OPPOSING THE MARXISTS [25])

Written in the spring and summer of 1894

First published in 1894

Published according to the hectographed edition, 1894

PART I

Russkoye Bogatstvo[26] has launched a campaign against the Social-Democrats. Last year, in issue No. 10, one of the leading lights of this magazine, Mr. N. Mikhailovsky, announced a forthcoming "polemic" against "our so-called Marxists, or Social-Democrats."[27] Then followed Mr. S. Krivenko's article "Our Cultural Free Lances" (No. 12), and Mr. N. Mikhailovsky's "Literature and Life" (*Russkoye Bogatstvo*, 1894, Nos. 1 and 2). As to the magazine's own views on our economic realities, these have been most fully expounded by Mr. S. Yuzhakov in the article "Problems of Russia's Economic Development" (in Nos. 11 and 12). While in general claiming to present the ideas and tactics of true "friends of the people" in their magazine, these gentlemen are arch-enemies of Social-Democracy. So let us take a closer look at these "friends of the people," their criticism of Marxism, their ideas and their tactics.

Mr. N. Mikhailovsky devotes his attention chiefly to the theoretical principles of Marxism and therefore makes a special investigation of the materialist conception of history. After outlining in general the contents of the voluminous Marxist literature enunciating this doctrine, Mr. Mikhailovsky opens his criticism with the following tirade:

"First of all," he says, "the question naturally arises: in which of his works did Marx expound his materialist conception of history? In *Capital* he gave us an example of the combination of logical force with erudition, with a scrupulous investigation of all the economic literature and of the pertinent facts. He brought to light theoreticians of economic science long forgotten or unknown to anybody today, and did not overlook the most minute details in factory inspectors' reports or experts' evidence before various special commissions; in a word, he examined this enormous mass of factual material, partly in order to provide arguments for his economic theories and partly to illustrate them. If he has created a 'completely new' conception of the historical process, if he has explained the whole past of mankind from a new viewpoint and has summarised all hitherto existing theories on the philosophy of history, then he has done so, of course, with equal zeal: he has, indeed, reviewed and subjected to critical analysis all the known theories of the historical process, and worked over a mass of facts of world history. The comparison with Darwin, so customary in Marxist literature, serves still more to confirm this idea. What does Darwin's whole work amount to? Certain closely interconnected generalising ideas crowning a veritable Mont Blanc of factual material. But where is the appropriate work by Marx? It does not exist. And not only does no such work by Marx exist, but there is none to be found in all Marxist literature, despite its voluminous and extensive character."

The whole tirade is highly characteristic and helps us to understand how little the public understand *Capital* and Marx. Overwhelmed by the tremendously convincing way he states his case, they bow and scrape before Marx, laud him, and at the same time entirely lose sight of the basic content of his doctrine and quite calmly continue to sing the old songs of "subjective sociology." In this connection one cannot help recalling the very apt epigraph Kautsky selected for his book on the economic teachings of Marx:

Wer wird nicht einen Klopstock loben?
Doch wird ihn jeder lesen? Nein.
Wir wollen weniger erhoben,
*Und fleissiger gelesen sein!**

---

* Who would not praise a Klopstock? But will everybody read him? No. We would like to be exalted less, but read more diligently! (Lessing).— *Ed.*

Just so! Mr. Mikhailovsky should praise Marx less and read him more diligently, or, better still, give more serious thought to what he is reading.

"In *Capital* Marx gave us an example of the combination of logical force with erudition," says Mr. Mikhailovsky. In this phrase Mr. Mikhailovsky has given us an example of a brilliant phrase combined with lack of substance—a certain Marxist observed. And the observation is a very just one. How, indeed, did this logical force of Marx's manifest itself? What were its effects? Reading the above tirade by Mr. Mikhailovsky, one might think that this force was concentrated entirely on "economic theories," in the narrowest sense of the term—and nothing more. And in order to emphasise still further the narrow limits of the field in which Marx manifested the force of his logic, Mr. Mikhailovsky lays stress on "most minute details," on "scrupulosity," on "theoreticians unknown to anybody" and so forth. It would appear that Marx contributed nothing essentially new or noteworthy to the methods of constructing these theories, that he left the bounds of economic science where the earlier economists had them, without extending them, without contributing a "completely new" conception of the science itself. Yet anybody who has read *Capital* knows that this is absolutely untrue. In this connection one cannot but recall what Mr. Mikhailovsky wrote about Marx sixteen years ago when arguing with that vulgar bourgeois, Mr. Y. Zhukovsky.[28] Perhaps the times were different, perhaps sentiments were fresher—at any rate, both the tone and the content of Mr. Mikhailovsky's article were then entirely different.

"'...It is the ultimate aim of this work, to lay bare the law of development (in the original: das oekonomische Bewegungsgesetz—the economic law of motion) of modern society,' Karl Marx says in reference to his *Capital*, and he adheres strictly to this programme." This is what Mr. Mikhailovsky said in 1877. Let us examine this programme more closely, which—as the critic admits—has been strictly adhered to. It is "to lay bare the economic law of development of modern society."

The very formulation confronts us with several questions that require explanation. Why does Marx speak of "modern" society, when all the economists who preceded him spoke of society in general? In what sense does he use the word "modern," by what features does he distinguish this modern society? And further, what is meant by the economic law of motion of society? We are accustomed to hear from economists—and this, by the way, is one of the favourite ideas of the publicists and economists of the milieu to which the *Russkoye Bogatstvo* belongs—that only the production of values is subject to solely economic laws, whereas distribution, they declare, depends on politics, on the nature of the influence exercised on society by the government, the intelligentsia and so forth. In what sense, then, does Marx speak of the economic law of motion of society, even referring to this law as a Naturgesetz—a law of nature? How are we to understand this, when so many of our native sociologists have covered reams of paper to show that social phenomena are particularly distinct from the phenomena of natural history, and that therefore the investigation of the former requires the employment of an absolutely distinct "subjective method in sociology."

All these perplexities arise naturally and necessarily, and, of course, only an absolute ignoramus would evade them when speaking of *Capital*. To elucidate these questions, we shall first quote one more passage from the same Preface to *Capital*—only a few lines lower down:

"[From] my standpoint," says Marx, "the evolution of the economic formation of society is viewed as a process of natural history."[29]

It will be sufficient to compare, say, the two passages just quoted from the Preface in order to see that it is here that we have the basic idea of *Capital*, pursued, as we have heard, with strict consistency and with rare logical force. First let us note two circumstances regarding all this: Marx speaks of one "economic formation of society" only, the capitalist formation, that is, he says that he investigated the law of development of this formation only and of no other. That is the first. And secondly, let us note the methods Marx used in working out his deductions. These methods consisted, as we have just heard from Mr. Mikhailovsky, in a "scrupulous investigation of the pertinent facts."

Now let us examine this basic idea of *Capital*, which our

subjective philosopher so adroitly tried to evade. In what, properly speaking, does the concept of the economic formation of society consist? and in what sense can and must the development of such a formation be regarded as a process of natural history?—such are the questions that now confront us. I have already pointed out that from the standpoint of the old (not old for Russia) economists and sociologists, the concept of the economic formation of society is entirely superfluous: they talk of society in general, they argue with the Spencers about the nature of society in general, about the aim and essence of society in general, and so forth. In their reasonings, these subjective sociologists rely on arguments such as—the aim of society is to benefit all its members, that justice, therefore, demands such and such an organisation, and that a system that is out of harmony with this ideal organisation ("Sociology must start with some utopia"—these words of Mr. Mikhailovsky's, one of the authors of the subjective method, splendidly typify the essence of their methods) is abnormal and should be set aside. "The essential task of sociology," Mr. Mikhailovsky, for instance, argues, "is to ascertain the social conditions under which any particular requirement of human nature is satisfied." As you see, what interests this sociologist is only a society that satisfies human nature, and not at all some strange formations of society, which, moreover, may be based on a phenomenon so out of harmony with "human nature" as the enslavement of the majority by the minority. You also see that from the standpoint of this sociologist there can be no question of regarding the development of society as a process of natural history. ("Having accepted something as desirable or undesirable, the sociologist must discover the conditions under which the desirable can be realised, or the undesirable eliminated"—"under which such and such ideals can be realised"—this same Mr. Mikhailovsky reasons.) What is more, there can be no talk even of development, but only of various deviations from the "desirable," of "defects" that have occurred in history as a result ... as a result of the fact that people were not clever enough, were unable properly to understand what human nature demands, were unable to discover the conditions for the realisation of such a rational system. It is obvious that Marx's basic idea that the development of the social-economic formations is a process of natural history cuts at the very root of this childish morality which lays claim to the title of sociology. By what means did Marx arrive at this basic idea? He did so by singling out the economic sphere from the various spheres of social life, by singling out *production relations* from all social relations as being basic, primary, determining all other relations. Marx himself has described the course of his reasoning on this question as follows:

"The first work which I undertook for a solution of the doubts which assailed me was a critical review of the Hegelian philosophy of right....[30] My investigation led to the result that legal relations as well as forms of state are to be grasped neither from themselves nor from the so-called general development of the human mind, but rather have their roots in the material conditions of life, the sum-total of which Hegel, following the example of the Englishmen and Frenchmen of the eighteenth century, combines under the name of 'civil society,' that, however, the anatomy of civil society is to be sought in political economy.... The general result at which I arrived ... can be briefly formulated as follows: in the social production of their life, men enter into definite relations ... *relations of production* which correspond to a definite stage of development of their material productive forces. The sum-total of these relations of production constitutes the economic structure of society, the real foundation, on which rises a legal and political superstructure and to which correspond definite forms of social consciousness. The mode of production of material life conditions the social, political and intellectual life process in general. It is not the consciousness of men that determines their being, but, on the contrary, their social being that determines their consciousness. At a certain stage of their development, the material productive forces of society come in conflict with the existing relations of production, or—what is but a legal expression for the same thing—with the property relations within which they have been at work hitherto. From forms of development of the productive forces these relations turn into their fetters. Then begins an epoch of social revolution. With the change of the economic foundation the entire immense superstructure is more or less rapidly transformed.

In considering such transformations, a distinction should always be made between the material transformation of the conditions of production, which should be established in terms of natural science, and the legal, political, religious, aesthetic or philosophic—in short, ideological—forms in which men become conscious of this conflict and fight it out. Just as our opinion of an individual is not based on what he thinks of himself, so can we not judge of such a period of transformation by its own consciousness; on the contrary, this consciousness must be explained rather from the contradictions of material life, from the existing conflict between the social productive forces and the relations of production.... In broad outlines Asiatic, ancient, feudal, and modern bourgeois modes of production can be designated as progressive epochs in the economic formation of society."[31]

This idea of materialism in sociology was in itself a stroke of genius. Naturally, *for the time being* it was only a hypothesis, but one which first created the possibility of a strictly scientific approach to historical and social problems. Hitherto, not knowing how to get down to the simplest primary relations such as those of production, the sociologists undertook the direct investigation and study of political and legal forms, stumbled on the fact that these forms emerge from certain of mankind's ideas in the period in question—and there they stopped; it appeared as if social relations are consciously established by men. But this conclusion, fully expressed in the idea of the *Contrat social*[32] (traces of which are very noticeable in all systems of utopian socialism), was in complete contradiction to all historical observations. It never has been the case, nor is it so now, that the members of society conceive the sum-total of the social relations in which they live as something definite, integral, pervaded by some principle; on the contrary, the mass of people adapt themselves to these relations unconsciously, and have so little conception of them as specific historical social relations that, for instance, an explanation of the exchange relations under which people have lived for centuries was found only in very recent times. Materialism removed this contradiction by carrying the analysis deeper, to the origin of man's social ideas themselves; and its conclusion that the course of ideas depends on the course of things is the only one compatible with scientific psychology. Further, and from yet another aspect, this hypothesis was the first to elevate sociology to the level of a science. Hitherto, sociologists had found it difficult to distinguish the important and the unimportant in the complex network of social phenomena (that is the root of subjectivism in sociology) and had been unable to discover any objective criterion for such a demarcation. Materialism provided an absolutely objective criterion by singling out "production relations" as the structure of society, and by making it possible to apply to these relations that general scientific criterion of recurrence whose applicability to sociology the subjectivists denied. So long as they confined themselves to ideological social relations (i.e., such as, before taking shape, pass through man's consciousness*) they could not observe recurrence and regularity in the social phenomena of the various countries, and their science was at best only a description of these phenomena, a collection of raw material. The analysis of material social relations (i.e., of those that take shape without passing through man's consciousness: when exchanging products men enter into production relations without even realising that there is a social relation of production here)—the analysis of material social relations at once made it possible to observe recurrence and regularity and to generalise the systems of the various countries in the single fundamental concept: *social formation*. It was this generalisation alone that made it possible to proceed from the description of social phenomena (and their evaluation from the standpoint of an ideal) to their strictly scientific analysis, which isolates, let us say by way of example, that which distinguishes one capitalist country from another and investigates that which is common to all of them.

Thirdly, and finally, another reason why this hypothesis for the first time made a *scientific* sociology possible was that only the reduction of social relations to production relations and of the latter to the level of the productive forces, provided a firm basis for the conception that the development of

* We are, of course, referring all the time to the consciousness of *social* relations and no others.

formations of society is a process of natural history. And it goes without saying that without such a view there can be no social science. (The subjectivists, for instance, although they admitted that historical phenomena conform to law, were incapable of regarding their evolution as a process of natural history, precisely because they came to a halt before man's social ideas and aims and were unable to reduce them to material social relations.)

Then, however, Marx, who had expressed this hypothesis in the forties, set out to study the factual (nota bene) material. He took one of the social-economic formations—the system of commodity production—and on the basis of a vast mass of data (which he studied for not less than twenty-five years) gave a most detailed analysis of the laws governing the functioning of this formation and its development. This analysis is confined exclusively to production relations between members of society: without ever resorting to features outside the sphere of these production relations for an explanation, Marx makes it possible to discern how the commodity organisation of social economy develops, how it becomes transformed into capitalist organisation, creating antagonistic classes (antagonistic within the bounds of production relations), the bourgeoisie and the proletariat, how it develops the productivity of social labour, and thereby introduces an element that becomes irreconcilably contradictory to the foundations of this capitalist organisation itself.

Such is the *skeleton* of *Capital*. The whole point, however, is that Marx did not content himself with this skeleton, that he did not confine himself to "economic theory" in the ordinary sense of the term, that, while *explaining* the structure and development of the given formation of society *exclusively* through production relations, he nevertheless everywhere and incessantly scrutinised the superstructure corresponding to these production relations and clothed the skeleton in flesh and blood. The reason *Capital* has enjoyed such tremendous success is that this book by a "German economist" showed the whole capitalist social formation to the reader as a living thing—with its everyday aspects, with the actual social manifestation of the class antagonism inherent in production relations, with the bourgeois political superstructure that protects the rule of the capitalist class, with the bourgeois ideas of liberty, equality and so forth, with the bourgeois family relationships. It will now be clear that the comparison with Darwin is perfectly accurate: *Capital* is nothing but "certain closely interconnected generalising ideas crowning a veritable Mont Blanc of factual material." And if anybody has read *Capital* and contrived not to notice these generalising ideas, it is not the fault of Marx, who, as we have seen, pointed to these ideas even in the preface. And that is not all; such a comparison is correct not only from the external aspect (which for some unknown reason particularly interests Mr. Mikhailovsky), but also from the internal aspect. Just as Darwin put an end to the view of animal and plant species being unconnected, fortuitous, "created by God" and immutable, and was the first to put biology on an absolutely scientific basis by establishing the mutability and the succession of species, so Marx put an end to the view of society being a mechanical aggregation of individuals which allows of all sorts of modification at the will of the authorities (or, if you like, at the will of society and the government) and which emerges and changes casually, and was the first to put sociology on a scientific basis by establishing the concept of the economic formation of society as the sum-total of given production relations, by establishing the fact that the development of such formations is a process of natural history.

Now—since the appearance of *Capital*—the materialist conception of history is no longer a hypothesis, but a scientifically proven proposition. And until we get some other attempt to give a scientific explanation of the functioning and development of some formation of society—formation of society, mind you, and not the way of life of some country or people, or even class, etc.—another attempt just as capable of introducing order into the "pertinent facts" as materialism is, that is just as capable of presenting a living picture of a definite formation, while giving it a strictly scientific explanation—until then the materialist conception of history will be a synonym for social science. Materialism is not "primarily a scientific conception of history," as Mr. Mikhailovsky thinks, but the only scientific conception of it.

And now, can you imagine anything funnier than the fact that there are people who have read *Capital* without discovering any materialism there! Where is it?—asks Mr. Mikhailovsky in sincere perplexity.

He has read the *Communist Manifesto* and failed to notice that the explanation it gives of modern systems—legal, political, family, religious and philosophical—is a materialist one, and that even the criticism of the socialist and communist theories seeks and finds their roots in such and such production relations.

He has read *The Poverty of Philosophy* and failed to notice that its analysis of Proudhon's sociology is made from the materialist standpoint, that the criticism of the solution propounded by Proudhon for the most diverse historical problems is based on the principles of materialism, and that the author's own indications as to where the data for the solution of these problems are to be sought all amount to references to production relations.

He has read *Capital* and failed to notice that he had before him a model of scientific, materialist analysis of one—the most complex—formation of society, a model recognised by all and surpassed by none. And here he sits and exercises his mighty brain over the profound problem: "In which of his works did Marx expound his materialist conception of history?"

Anybody acquainted with Marx would answer this question by another: in which of his works did Marx not expound his materialist conception of history? But Mr. Mikhailovsky will probably learn of Marx's materialist investigations only when they are classified and properly indexed in some sophistical work on history by some Kareyev under the heading "Economic Materialism."

But the funniest of all is that Mr. Mikhailovsky accuses Marx of not having "reviewed (sic!) all the known theories of the historical process." This is amusing indeed. Of what did nine-tenths of these theories consist? Of purely a priori, dogmatic, abstract discourses on: what is society, what is progress? and the like. (I purposely take examples which are dear to the heart and mind of Mr. Mikhailovsky.) But, then, such theories are useless because of the very fact that they exist, they are useless because of their basic methods, because of their solid unrelieved metaphysics. For, to begin by asking what is society and what is progress, is to begin at the end. Where will you get a conception of society and progress in general if you have not studied a single social formation in particular, if you have not even been able to establish this conception, if you have not even been able to approach a serious factual investigation, an objective analysis of social relations of any kind? This is a most obvious symptom of metaphysics, with which every science began: as long as people did not know how to set about studying the facts, they always invented a priori general theories, which were always sterile. The metaphysician-chemist, still unable to make a factual investigation of chemical processes, concocts a theory about chemical affinity as a force. The metaphysician-biologist talks about the nature of life and the vital force. The metaphysician-psychologist argues about the nature of the soul. Here it is the method itself that is absurd. You cannot argue about the soul without having explained psychical processes in particular: here progress must consist precisely in abandoning general theories and philosophical discourses about the nature of the soul, and in being able to put the study of the facts about particular psychical processes on a scientific footing. Therefore, Mr. Mikhailovsky's accusation is exactly similar to that of a metaphysician-psychologist, who has spent all his life writing "investigations" into the nature of the soul (without knowing exactly how to explain a single psychical phenomenon, even the simplest), and then starts accusing a scientific psychologist of not having reviewed all the known theories of the soul. He, the scientific psychologist, has discarded philosophical theories of the soul and set about making a direct study of the material substratum of psychical phenomena—the nervous processes—and has produced, let us say, an analysis and explanation of some one or more psychological processes. And our metaphysician-psychologist reads this work and praises it: the description of the processes and the study of the facts, he says, are good; but he is not satisfied. "Pardon me," he exclaims excitedly, hearing people around him speak of the absolutely new conception of psychology produced by this scientist, of his special method of scientific psychology. "Pardon me," the philosopher cries heatedly, "in what work is this method expounded? Why, this work contains 'nothing but facts.' There is no trace in it of a review of 'all the known philosophical theories of the soul.' It is not the appropriate work at all!"

In the same way, of course, neither is *Capital* the appropriate work for a metaphysician-sociologist who does not realise the sterility of a priori arguments about the nature of society and does not understand that such methods, instead of contributing to a study and elucidation of the problem, only serve to insinuate into the concept "society" either the bourgeois ideas of the British shopkeeper or the petty-bourgeois socialist ideals of the Russian democrat—and nothing more. That is why all these theories of the philosophy of history arose and burst like soap-bubbles, being at best a symptom of the social ideas and relations of their time, and not advancing one hair's breadth man's *understanding* of even a few, but real, social relations (and not such as "harmonise with human nature"). The gigantic step forward taken by Marx in this respect consisted precisely in that he discarded all these arguments about society and progress in general and produced a *scientific* analysis of *one* society and of *one* progress—capitalist. And Mr. Mikhailovsky blames him for beginning at the beginning and not at the end, for having begun with an analysis of the facts and not with final conclusions, with a study of particular, historically-determined social relations and not with general theories about what these social relations consist of in general! And he asks: "Where is the appropriate work?" O, most wise subjective sociologist!!

If our subjective philosopher had confined himself to mere perplexity as to where, in which work, materialism is substantiated, it would not have been so bad. But, despite the fact that he did not find even an exposition, let alone a substantiation, of the materialist conception of history anywhere (and maybe just because he did not), he begins to ascribe to this doctrine claims which it has never made. He quotes a passage from Blos to the effect that Marx proclaimed an entirely new *conception* of history, and without further ado goes on to declare that this theory claims to have "explained to mankind its past," to have explained "the whole (sic!!?) past of mankind," and so on. But this is utterly false! The theory only claims to explain the capitalist social organisation, and no other. If the application of materialism to the analysis and explanation of one social formation yielded such brilliant results, it is quite natural that materialism in history already ceases to be a mere hypothesis and becomes a scientifically tested theory; it is quite natural that the necessity for such a method extends to other social formations, even though they have not been subjected to special factual investigation and detailed analysis—just as the idea of transformism, which has been proved in relation to quite a large number of facts, is extended to the whole realm of biology, even though it has not yet been possible to establish with precision the fact of their transformation for certain species of animals and plants. And just as transformism does not at all claim to explain the "whole" history of the formation of species, but only to place the methods of this explanation on a scientific basis, so materialism in history has never claimed to explain everything, but merely to indicate the "only scientific," to use Marx's expression (*Capital*), method of explaining history.[33] One may therefore judge how ingenious, earnest and seemly are the methods of controversy employed by Mr. Mikhailovsky when he first misrepresents Marx by ascribing to materialism in history the absurd claims of "explaining everything," of finding "the key to all historical locks" (claims which were, of course, refuted by Marx immediately and in very biting style in his "Letter"[34] on Mikhailovsky's articles), then pulls faces at these claims of his own invention, and, finally, accurately citing Engels' ideas—accurately because in this case a quotation and not a paraphrase is given—to the effect that political economy as understood by the materialists "has still to be brought into being" and that "such economic science as we possess up to the present is limited almost exclusively to" the history of capitalist society[35]—draws the conclusion that "these words greatly narrow the field of operation of economic materialism"! What infinite naïveté, or what infinite conceit a man must have to count on such tricks passing unnoticed! First he misrepresents Marx, then pulls faces at his own pack of lies, then accurately cites precise ideas—and now has the insolence to declare that they narrow the field of operation of economic materialism!

The kind and quality of Mr. Mikhailovsky's twisting may be seen from the following example: "Marx nowhere substantiates them"—i.e., the foundations of the theory of economic materialism—says Mr. Mikhailovsky. "True, Marx and Engels thought of writing a work dealing with the history of philosophy and the philosophy of history, and even did write one (in 1845-1846), but it was never published.[36] Engels says: 'The finished portion [of this work] consists of an exposition of the materialist conception of history which proves only how incomplete our knowledge of economic history still was at that time.' Thus," concludes Mr. Mikhailovsky, "the fundamental points of 'scientific socialism' and of the theory of economic materialism were discovered, and were then expounded in the *Manifesto*, at a time when, as one of the authors himself admits, they were poorly equipped with the knowledge needed for such a work."

A charming way of criticising, is it not? Engels says that their knowledge of economic "history" was poor and that for this reason they did not publish their work of a "general" character on the history of philosophy. Mr. Mikhailovsky garbles this to make it mean that their knowledge was poor "for such a work" as the elaboration of "the fundamental points of scientific socialism," that is, of a scientific criticism of the "bourgeois" system, already given in the *Manifesto*. One of two things: either Mr. Mikhailovsky cannot grasp the difference between an attempt to embrace the whole philosophy of history, and an attempt to explain the bourgeois regime scientifically, or he imagines that Marx and Engels possessed insufficient knowledge for a criticism of political economy. In that case, it is very cruel of him not to acquaint us with his views on this insufficiency, and with his amendments and additions. The decision by Marx and Engels not to publish their work on the history of philosophy and to concentrate all their efforts on a scientific analysis of one social organisation is only indicative of a very high degree of scientific conscientiousness. Mr. Mikhailovsky's decision to twist this by the little addition that Marx and Engels expounded their views while themselves confessing that their knowledge was inadequate to elaborate them, is only indicative of methods of controversy which testify neither to intellect nor to a sense of decency.

Here is another sample: "More was done by Marx's alter ego, Engels, to substantiate economic materialism as a theory of history," says Mr. Mikhailovsky. "He wrote a special historical work, *The Origin of the Family, Private Property and the State in the Light of* (im Anschluss) *the Researches of Morgan.* This 'Anschluss' is truly noteworthy. The book of the American Morgan appeared many years after Marx and Engels had announced the principles of economic materialism and entirely independently of it." And then, says Mikhailovsky, "the economic materialists associated themselves" with this book; moreover, since there was no class struggle in prehistoric times, they introduced an "amendment" to the formula of the materialist conception of history indicating that, in addition to the production of material values, a determining factor is the production of man himself, i.e., procreation, which played a primary role in the primitive era, when the productivity of labour was still very undeveloped.

Engels says that "Morgan's great merit lies in having ... found in the groups based on ties of sex of the North American Indians the key to the most important, hitherto insoluble, riddles of the earliest Greek, Roman and German history."[37]

"And so," quoth Mr. Mikhailovsky in this connection, "at the end of the forties an absolutely new, materialist and truly scientific conception of history was discovered and proclaimed, and it did for historical science what Darwin's theory did for modern natural science." But this conception—Mr. Mikhailovsky once more repeats—was never scientifically substantiated. "Not only was it never tested in a large and varied field of factual material" (*Capital* is "not the appropriate" work: it contains only facts and painstaking investigations!), "but was not even sufficiently motivated by at least a criticism and exclusion of other systems of the philosophy of history." Engels' book—*Herrn E. Dührings Umwälzung der Wissenschaft**— represents "only witty attempts made in passing," and Mr. Mikhailovsky therefore considers it possible to ignore completely the mass of essential questions dealt with in that work, despite the fact that these "witty attempts" very wittily show the emptiness of sociologies which "start with utopias," and despite the fact that this work contains a detailed criticism

* *Herr Eugen Dühring's Revolution in Science (Anti-Dühring).—Ed.*

of the "force theory," which asserts that political and legal systems determine economic systems and is so zealously professed by the gentlemen who write in *Russkoye Bogatstvo*. Of course, it is much easier, is it not, to utter a few meaningless phrases about a work than to make a serious examination of even one of the problems materialistically solved in it. And it is also safe, for the censor will probably never pass a translation of that book, and Mr. Mikhailovsky may, without fear for his subjective philosophy, call it a witty book.

Even more characteristic and edifying (as an illustration to the saying that man was given a tongue to conceal his thoughts—or to lend vacuity the form of thought) are his comments on Marx's *Capital*: "There are brilliant pages of history in *Capital*, **but**" (that wonderful "but"! It is not so much a "but," as that famous "mais," which translated into Russian means "the ears never grow higher than the forehead") "by virtue of the very purpose of the book they are devoted to only one definite historical period, and not so much affirm the basic propositions of economic materialism as simply touch on the economic aspect of a certain group of historical phenomena." In other words, *Capital*—which is devoted solely to a study of capitalist society—gives a materialist analysis of that society and its superstructures, "**but**" Mr. Mikhailovsky prefers to pass over this analysis. It deals, don't you see, with only "one" period, whereas he, Mr. Mikhailovsky, wants to embrace all periods, and to embrace them in such a way as not to speak of any one of them in particular. Of course, there is only one way to achieve this aim—i.e., to embrace all periods without practically dealing with any one of them, and that is by uttering commonplaces and phrases, "brilliant" and empty. And nobody can compare with Mr. Mikhailovsky in the art of dismissing matters with phrases. It seems that it is not worth dealing (separately) with Marx's investigations because he, Marx, "not so much affirms the basic propositions of economic materialism as simply touches on the economic aspect of a certain group of historical phenomena." What profundity! "Does not affirm," but "simply touches on"! How simple it really is to obscure any issue by phrase-mongering! For instance, when Marx repeatedly shows how civil equality, free contract and similar principles of the law-governed state are based on relations among commodity producers—what is that? Does he thereby affirm materialism, or "simply" touch on it? With his characteristic modesty, our philosopher refrains from replying on the substance of the matter and directly draws conclusions from his "witty attempts" to talk brilliantly and say nothing.

"No wonder," the conclusion runs, "that forty years after the announcement of the theory which claimed to elucidate world history, ancient Greek, Roman and German history were still unsolved riddles for it; and the key to these riddles was provided, firstly, by a man who had absolutely no connection with the theory of economic materialism and knew nothing about it, and, secondly, with the help of a factor which was not economic. A rather amusing impression is produced by the term 'production of man himself,' i.e., procreation, which Engels seizes upon in order to preserve at least a verbal connection with the basic formula of economic materialism. He was, however, obliged to admit that for many ages the life of mankind did not proceed in accordance with this formula." Your method of controversy is indeed a "wonder," Mr. Mikhailovsky. The theory was that in order to "elucidate" history one must seek the foundations not in ideological, but in material social relations. Lack of factual material made it impossible to apply this method to an analysis of certain very important phenomena in ancient European history—for instance, that of gentile organisation[38]—which in consequence remained a riddle.* But then, the wealth of material collected by Morgan in America enabled him to analyse the nature of gentile organisation; and he came to the conclusion that its explanation must be sought not in ideological (e.g., legal or religious), but in material relations. Obviously, this fact is a brilliant confirmation of the materialist method, and nothing more. And when Mr. Mikhailovsky flings the *re-*

* Here, too, Mr. Mikhailovsky does not miss an opportunity of pulling faces: what, says he, do you mean—a scientific conception of history, yet ancient history remains a riddle! Mr. Mikhailovsky, take any textbook, and you will find that the problem of gentile organisation is one of the most difficult, and has evoked a host of theories in explanation of it.

proach at this doctrine that, firstly, the key to very difficult historical riddles was found by a man "who had absolutely no connection" with the theory of economic materialism, one can only wonder at the degree to which people can fail to distinguish what speaks in their favour from what severely trounces them. Secondly—argues our philosopher—procreation is not an economic factor. But where have you read in the works of Marx or Engels that they necessarily spoke of economic materialism? When they described their world outlook they called it simply materialism. Their basic idea (quite definitely expressed, for instance, in the passage from Marx quoted above) was that social relations are divided into material and ideological. The latter merely constitute a superstructure on the former, which take shape independent of the will and consciousness of man as (the result) the form of man's activity to maintain his existence. The explanation of political and legal forms—Marx says in the passage quoted—must be sought in "the material conditions of life." Mr. Mikhailovsky surely does not think that procreation relations are ideological? The explanation given by Mr. Mikhailovsky in this connection is so characteristic that it deserves to be dwelt on. "However much we exercise our ingenuity on the question of 'procreation,'" says he, "and endeavour to establish at least a verbal connection between it and economic materialism, however much it may be interwoven in the complex web of phenomena of social life with other, including economic, phenomena, it has its own physiological and psychical roots." (Are you telling babes and sucklings, Mr. Mikhailovsky, that procreation has physiological roots!? Who do you think you are fooling?) "And this reminds us that the theoreticians of economic materialism failed to settle accounts not only with history, but also with psychology. There can be no doubt that gentile ties have lost their significance in the history of civilised countries, but this can hardly be said with the same assurance of directly sexual and family ties. They have, of course, undergone considerable modification under the pressure of the increasing complexity of life in general, but with a certain amount of dialectical dexterity it might be shown that not only legal, but also economic relations themselves constitute a 'superstructure' on sexual and family relations.

We shall not dwell on this, but nevertheless would at least point to the institution of inheritance."

At last our philosopher has been lucky enough to leave the sphere of empty phrase-mongering* and approach facts, definite facts, which can be verified and make it less easy to "fool" people about the essence of the matter. Let us then see how our critic of Marx shows that the institution of inheritance is a superstructure on sexual and family relations. "What is transmitted by inheritance," argues Mr. Mikhailovsky, "is the products of economic production" ("the products of economic production"!! How literate! How sonorous! What elegant language!) "and the very institution of inheritance is to a certain degree determined by the fact of economic competition. But, firstly, non-material values are also transmitted by inheritance—as expressed in the concern to bring up children in the spirit of their fathers." So the upbringing of children is part of the institution of inheritance! The Russian Civil Code, for example, contains a clause saying that "parents must endeavour by home upbringing to train their" (i.e., their children's) "morals and to further the aims of government." Is this what our philosopher calls the institution of inheritance?—"and, secondly, even confining ourselves solely to the economic sphere, if the institution of inheritance is inconceivable without the products of production transmitted by inheritance, it is just as unthinkable without the products of 'procreation,' without them and without that complex and intense psychology which directly adheres to them." (Do pay attention to the language: a complex psychology "adheres to" the products of procreation! That is really exquisite!) And so, the institution of inheritance is a superstructure on family and sexual relations, because inheritance is inconceivable without procreation! Why, this is a veritable discovery of America! Until now everybody believed that procreation can explain the institution of inheritance just as little as the necessity for taking food can explain the institution of

* By what other name, indeed, can one call the device by which the materialists are accused of not having settled accounts with history, without, however, an attempt being made to examine *a single one* of the numerous materialist explanations of various historical problems given by the materialists?—or by which the statement is made that we could prove it but we shall not bother about it?

property. Until now everybody thought that if, for instance, in the era when the fief system[39] flourished in Russia, the land was not transmissible by inheritance (because it was regarded as conditional property only), the explanation was to be sought in the peculiarities of the social organisation of the time. Mr. Mikhailovsky presumably thinks that the explanation of the matter is simply that the psychology which adhered to the products of procreation of the fief-holder of that time was distinguished by insufficient complexity.

Scratch the "friend of the people"—we may say, paraphrasing the familiar saying—and you will find a bourgeois. Really, what other meaning can attach to Mr. Mikhailovsky's reflections on the connection between the institution of inheritance and the upbringing of children, the psychology of procreation, and so on, except that the institution of inheritance is just as eternal, essential and sacred as the upbringing of children? True, Mr. Mikhailovsky tried to leave himself a loophole by declaring that "the institution of inheritance is to a certain degree determined by the fact of economic competition," but that is nothing but an attempt to avoid giving a definite answer to the question, and a futile attempt at that. How can we give this statement our consideration when we are not told a single word as to exactly what "certain degree" inheritance depends on competition, and when absolutely no explanation is given on what in fact gives rise to this connection between competition and the institution of inheritance? Actually, the institution of inheritance presumes the existence of private property, and the latter arises only with the appearance of exchange. Its basis is in the already incipient specialisation of social labour and the alienation of products on the market. So long, for instance, as all the members of the primitive American Indian community produced in common all the articles they required, private property was impossible. But when division of labour invaded the community and its members proceeded, individually, to engage in the production of some one article and to sell it on the market, this material isolation of the commodity producers found expression in the institution of private property. Both private property and inheritance are categories of a social order in which separate, small (monogamous) families have already been formed and exchange has begun to develop. Mr. Mikhailovsky's example proves exactly the opposite of what he wanted to prove.

Mr. Mikhailovsky gives another factual reference—and this too is a gem in its way! "As regards gentile ties," he says, continuing to put materialism right, "they paled in the history of civilised peoples partly, it is true, under the rays of the influence of the forms of production" (another subterfuge, only more obvious still. Exactly what forms of production? An empty phrase!), "but partly they became dissolved in their own continuation and generalisation—in national ties." And so, national ties are a continuation and generalisation of gentile ties! Mr. Mikhailovsky, evidently, borrows his ideas on the history of society from the tales taught to school children. The history of society—this copybook maxim runs—is that first there was the family, that nucleus of every society,* then—we are told—the family grew into the tribe, and the tribe grew into the state. If Mr. Mikhailovsky with a solemn air repeats this childish nonsense, it merely shows—apart from everything else—that he has not the slightest notion of the course taken even by Russian history. While one might speak of gentile life in ancient Rus, there can be no doubt that by the Middle Ages, the era of the Moscovite tsars, these gentile ties no longer existed, that is to say, the state was based on associations that were not gentile at all, but local: the landlords and the monasteries acquired peasants from various localities, and the communities thus formed were purely territorial associations. But one could hardly speak of national ties in the true sense of the term at that time: the state split into separate "lands," sometimes even principalities, which preserved strong traces of the former autonomy, peculiarities of administration, at times their own troops (the local boyars went to war at the head of their own companies), their own tariff frontiers, and so forth. Only the modern period of

* This is a purely bourgeois idea: separate, small families came to predominate only under the bourgeois regime; they were entirely non-existent in prehistoric times. Nothing is more characteristic of the bourgeois than the application of the features of the modern system to all times and peoples.

Russian history (approximately from the seventeenth century) is characterised by the actual amalgamation of all such regions, lands and principalities into one whole. This amalgamation, most esteemed Mr. Mikhailovsky, was brought about not by gentile ties, nor even by their continuation and generalisation: it was brought about by the increasing exchange among regions, the gradually growing circulation of commodities, and the concentration of the small local markets into a single, all-Russian market. Since the leaders and masters of this process were the merchant capitalists, the creation of these national ties was nothing else than the creation of bourgeois ties. By both his factual references Mr. Mikhailovsky has only belaboured himself and given us nothing but examples of bourgeois banality; "banality," because he explained the institution of inheritance by procreation and its psychology, and nationality by gentile ties; "bourgeois," because he took the categories and superstructures of one historically definite social formation (that based on exchange) for categories as general and eternal as the upbringing of children and "directly" sexual ties.

What is highly characteristic here is that as soon as our subjective philosopher tried to pass from phrases to concrete facts he got himself into a mess. And apparently he feels very much at ease in this not over-clean position: there he sits, preening himself and splashing filth all around him. He wants, for instance, to refute the thesis that history is a succession of episodes of the class struggle, and so, declaring with an air of profundity that this is "extreme," he says: "The International Working Men's Association,[40] formed by Marx and organised for the purposes of the class struggle, did not prevent the French and German workers from cutting each other's throats and despoiling each other"—something, he avers, which proves that materialism has not settled accounts "with the demon of national vanity and national hatred." Such an assertion reveals the critic's utter failure to understand that the very real interests of the commercial and industrial bourgeoisie constitute the principal basis of this hatred, and that to talk of national sentiment as an independent factor is only to obscure the essence of the matter. Incidentally, we have already seen what a profound idea of nationality our philosopher has. Mr. Mikhailovsky cannot refer to the International except with the irony of a Burenin.[41] "Marx was the head of the International Working Men's Association, which, it is true, has fallen to pieces, but is due to be resurrected." Of course, if the nec plus ultra of international solidarity is to be seen in a system of "fair" exchange, on which the chronicler of home affairs expatiates with philistine banality in No. 2 of *Russkoye Bogatstvo*, and if it is not understood that exchange, fair or unfair, always presupposes and includes the rule of the bourgeoisie, and that the cessation of international clashes is impossible unless the economic organisation based on exchange is destroyed, then it is understandable that there should be nothing but sneers for the International. Then one can understand that Mr. Mikhailovsky cannot grasp the simple truth that there is no other way of combating national hatred than by organising and uniting the oppressed class for a struggle against the oppressor class in each separate country, than by uniting such national working-class organisations into a single international working-class army to fight international capital. As to the statement that the International did not prevent the workers from cutting each other's throats, it is enough to remind Mr. Mikhailovsky of the events of the Commune, which showed the true attitude of the organised proletariat to the ruling classes engaged in war.

What is particularly disgusting in all this polemic of Mr. Mikhailovsky's is the methods he employs. If he is dissatisfied with the tactics of the International, if he does not share the ideas in the name of which the European workers are organising, let him at least criticise them bluntly and openly, and expound his idea of what would be more expedient tactics and more correct views. As it is, no definite and clear objections are made, and all we get is senseless jibes scattered here and there among a welter of phrase-mongering. What can one call this but filth, especially if we bear in mind that defence of the ideas and tactics of the International is not legally allowed in Russia? Such too are the methods Mr. Mikhailovsky employs when he argues against the Russian Marxists: without taking the trouble to formulate any of their theses conscientiously and accurately, so as to subject them to direct and definite criticism, he prefers to fasten on fragments of Marxist arguments he happens to have heard and to garble them. Judge for yourselves: "Marx was too intelligent and too learned to think that it was he who discovered the idea of the historical necessity and conformity to law of social phenomena.... The lower rungs" (of the Marxist ladder)* "do not know this" (that "the idea of historical necessity is not something new, invented or discovered by Marx, but a long established truth"), "or, at least, they have only a vague idea of the centuries of intellectual effort and energy spent on the establishment of this truth."

Of course, statements of this kind may very well make an impression on people who hear of Marxism for the first time, and in their case the aim of the critic may be easily achieved, namely, to garble, scoff and "conquer" (the word used, it is said, about Mr. Mikhailovsky's articles by contributors to *Russkoye Bogatstvo*). Anybody who has any knowledge at all of Marx will immediately perceive the utter falsity and sham of such methods. One may not agree with Marx, but one cannot deny that he formulated with the utmost precision those of his views which constitute "something new" in relation to the earlier socialists. The something new consisted in the fact that the earlier socialists thought that to substantiate their views it was enough to show the oppression of the masses under the existing regime, to show the superiority of a system under which every man would receive what he himself had produced, to show that this ideal system harmonised with "human nature," with the conception of a rational and moral life, and so forth. Marx found it impossible to content himself with such a socialism. He did not confine himself to describing the existing system, to judging it and condemning it; he gave a scientific explanation of it, reducing that existing system, which differs in

* Regarding this meaningless term it should be stated that Mr. Mikhailovsky gives a special place to Marx (who is too intelligent and too learned for our critic to be able to criticise any of his propositions directly and openly), after whom he places Engels ("not such a creative mind"), next—more or less independent men like Kautsky—and then the other Marxists. Well, can such a classification have any serious value? If the critic is dissatisfied with the popularisers of Marx, what prevents him from correcting them on the basis of Marx? He does nothing of the kind. He evidently meant to be witty—but his wit fell flat.

the different European and non-European countries, to a common basis—the capitalist social formation, the laws of the functioning and development of which he subjected to an objective analysis (he showed the *necessity* of exploitation under that system). In just the same way he did not find it possible to content himself with asserting that only the socialist system harmonises with human nature, as was claimed by the great utopian socialists and by their wretched imitators, the subjective sociologists. By this same *objective* analysis of the capitalist system, he proved the *necessity* of its transformation into the socialist system. (Exactly how he proved this and how Mr. Mikhailovsky objected to it is something we shall have to refer to again.) That is the source of those references to necessity which are frequently to be met with among Marxists. The distortion which Mr. Mikhailovsky introduced into the question is obvious: he omitted the whole factual content of the theory, its whole essence, and presented the matter as though the whole theory amounts to the one word "necessity" ("one cannot refer to this alone in complex practical affairs"), as though the *proof* of the theory is that this is what historical necessity demands. In other words, saying nothing about the content of the doctrine, he seized only on its label, and again started to pull faces at that which was "simply the worn-out coin," he had worked so hard to transform into Marx's teaching. We shall not, of course, try to follow up his clowning, because we are already sufficiently acquainted with that sort of thing. Let him cut capers for the amusement and satisfaction of Mr. Burenin (who not without good reason patted Mr. Mikhailovsky on the back in *Novoye Vremya*),[42] let him, after paying his respects to Marx, yelp at him from round the corner: "his controversy with the utopians and idealists is one-sided as it is," i.e., as it is without the Marxists repeating its arguments. We cannot call such sallies anything else but yelping, because he does not adduce *one single* factual, definite and verifiable objection to this polemic, so that however willing we might be to discuss the subject, since we consider this controversy extremely important for the settlement of Russian socialist problems—we simply cannot reply to the yelping, and can only shrug our shoulders and say:

Mighty must the pug-dog be, if at the elephant barketh he![43]

Not without interest is the next thing Mr. Mikhailovsky has to say about historical necessity, because it reveals, if only partly, the real ideological stock-in-trade of "our well-known sociologist" (the title enjoyed by Mr. Mikhailovsky, equally with Mr. V. V., among the liberal members of our "cultured society"). He speaks of "the conflict between the idea of historical necessity and the significance of individual activity": socially active figures err in regarding themselves as active, when as a matter of fact they are "activated," "marionettes, manipulated from a mysterious underground by the immanent laws of historical necessity"—such, he claims, is the conclusion to be drawn from this idea, which he therefore characterises as "sterile" and "diffuse." Probably not every reader knows where Mr. Mikhailovsky got all this nonsense about marionettes and the like. The point is that this is one of the favourite hobby-horses of the subjective philosopher—the idea of the conflict between determinism and morality, between historical necessity and the significance of the individual. He has filled reams of paper on the subject and has uttered an infinite amount of sentimental, philistine nonsense in order to settle this conflict in favour of morality and the role of the individual. Actually, there is no conflict here at all; it has been invented by Mr. Mikhailovsky, who feared (not without reason) that determinism would cut the ground from under the philistine morality he loves so dearly. The idea of determinism, which postulates that human acts are necessitated and rejects the absurd tale about free will, in no way destroys man's reason or conscience, or appraisal of his actions. Quite the contrary, only the determinist view makes a strict and correct appraisal possible instead of attributing everything you please to free will. Similarly, the idea of historical necessity does not in the least undermine the role of the individual in history: all history is made up of the actions of individuals, who are undoubtedly active figures. The real question that arises in appraising the social activity of an individual is: what conditions ensure the success of his actions, what guarantee is there that these actions will not remain an isolated act lost in a welter of contrary acts? This also is a question answered differently by Social-Democrats and by the other Russian socialists: how must actions aimed at bringing about the socialist system attract the masses in order to yield serious fruits? Obviously, the answer to this question depends directly and immediately on the way in which the grouping of social forces in Russia and the class struggle which forms the substance of Russian reality are understood; and here too Mr. Mikhailovsky merely wanders all round the question, without even attempting to formulate it precisely and furnish an answer. The Social-Democratic answer to the question is based, as we know, on the view that the Russian economic system constitutes a bourgeois society, from which there can be only one way out, the one that necessarily follows from the very nature of the bourgeois system, namely, the class struggle of the proletariat against the bourgeoisie. Obviously, criticism that is serious should be directed either against the view that ours is a bourgeois system, or against the conception of the nature of this system and the laws of its development; but Mr. Mikhailovsky does not even dream of dealing with serious questions. He prefers to dispose of matters with vapid phrasemongering about necessity being too general a bracket and so on. But then, Mr. Mikhailovsky, any idea will be too general a bracket if you treat it like an egg from which you throw out the meat and then begin playing with the shell! This outer shell, which hides the really serious and burning questions of the day, is Mr. Mikhailovsky's favourite sphere, and with particular pride he stresses the point, for example, that "economic materialism ignores or throws a wrong light on the question of heroes and the crowd." Pray note—the question which are the conflicting classes that make up contemporary Russian reality and what is its basis, is probably too general for Mr. Mikhailovsky, and he evades it. On the other hand, the question of what relations exist between the hero and the crowd—whether it is a crowd of workers, peasants, factory owners, or landlords, is one that interests him extremely. Maybe these questions are "interesting," but to rebuke the materialists for devoting all their efforts to the settlement of problems that directly concern the liberation of the labouring class is to be an admirer of philistine science, nothing more. Concluding his "criticism" (?) of materialism, Mr. Mikhailovsky makes one more attempt to misrepresent the facts and performs one more manipulation. Having expressed doubt about the correctness of Engels' opinion that *Capital* was hushed up by the official economists[44] (a doubt he justifies on the curious grounds that there are numerous universities in Germany!), Mr. Mikhailovsky says: "Marx did not have this particular circle of readers" (workers) "in view, but expected something from men of science too." That is absolutely untrue. Marx understood very well how little impartiality and scientific criticism he could expect from the bourgeois scientists and in the Afterword to the second edition of *Capital* he expressed himself very definitely on this score. There he says: "The appreciation which *Das Kapital* rapidly gained in wide circles of the German working class is the best reward of my labours. Herr Mayer ... who in economic matters represents the bourgeois point of view, in a pamphlet published during the Franco-German War, aptly expounded the idea that the great capacity for theory (der grosse theoretische Sinn), which used to be considered a hereditary German possession, had almost completely disappeared amongst the so-called educated classes in Germany, but that amongst its working class, on the contrary, that capacity was celebrating its revival."[45]

The manipulation again concerns materialism and is entirely in the style of the first sample. "The theory (of materialism) has never been scientifically substantiated and verified." Such is the thesis. The proof: "Individual good pages of historical content in the works of Engels, Kautsky and some others also (as in the esteemed work of Blos) might well dispense with the label of economic materialism, since" (note the "since"!), "in fact" (sic!), "they take the sum-total of social life into account, even though the economic note predominates in the chord." And the conclusion—"Economic materialism has not justified itself in science."

A familiar trick! To prove that the theory lacks foundation, Mr. Mikhailovsky first distorts it by ascribing to it the absurd intention of not taking the sum-total of social life into account, whereas quite the opposite is the case: the materialists (Marxists) were the first socialists to raise the issue of the need to analyse all aspects of social life, and not only the economic*—then he declares that "in fact" the materialists have "effectively" explained the sum-total of social life by economics (a fact which obviously demolishes the author)—and finally he draws the conclusion that materialism "has not justified itself." Your manipulations, however, Mr. Mikhailovsky, have justified themselves magnificently!

This is all that Mr. Mikhailovsky advances in "refutation" of materialism. I repeat, there is no criticism here, it is nothing but empty and pretentious babbling. If we were to ask anybody at all what objections Mr. Mikhailovsky has raised against the view that production relations form the basis of all others; how he has refuted the correctness of the concept of the social formation and of the natural-historical development of these formations elaborated by Marx using the materialist method; how he has proved the fallacy of the materialist explanations of various historical problems given, for instance, by the writers he has mentioned—the answer would have to be that Mr. Mikhailovsky has raised no objections, has advanced no refutation, indicated no fallacies. He has merely beaten about the bush, trying to cover up the essence of the matter with phrases, and in passing has invented various paltry subterfuges.

---

* This has been quite clearly expressed in *Capital* and in the tactics of the Social-Democrats, as compared with the earlier socialists. Marx directly demanded that matters must not be confined to the economic aspect. In 1843, when drafting the programme for a projected magazine,[46] Marx wrote to Ruge: "The whole socialist principle is again only one aspect.... We, on our part, must devote equal attention to the other aspect, the theoretical existence of man, and consequently must make religion, science, and so forth an object of our criticism.... Just as *religion* represents the table of contents of the theoretical conflicts of mankind, the *political state* represents the table of contents of man's practical conflicts. Thus, the political state, within the limits of its form, expresses sub specie rei publicae (from the political standpoint) all social conflicts, needs and interests. Hence to make a most special political question—e.g., the difference between the social-estate system and the representative system—an object of criticism by no means implies descending from the hauteur des principes (the height of principles.—*Ed.*) since this question expresses in *political* language the difference between the rule of man and the rule of private property. This means that the critic not only may but must deal with these political questions (which the inveterate socialist considers unworthy of attention)."

We can hardly expect anything serious of such a critic when he continues in No. 2 of *Russkoye Bogatstvo* to refute Marxism. The only difference is that his inventiveness in the sphere of manipulations is already exhausted and he is beginning to use other people's.

He starts out by holding forth on the "complexity" of social life: why, he says, even galvanism is connected with economic materialism, because Galvani's experiments "produced an impression" on Hegel, too. Wonderful wit! One could just as easily connect Mr. Mikhailovsky with the Emperor of China! What follows from this, except that there are people who find pleasure in talking nonsense?!

"The essence of the historical process," Mr. Mikhailovsky continues, "which is elusive in general, has also eluded the doctrine of economic materialism, although this apparently rests on two pillars: the discovery of the all-determining significance of the forms of production and exchange and the incontrovertibility of the dialectical process."

And so, the materialists rest their case on the "incontrovertibility" of the dialectical process! In other words, they base their sociological theories on Hegelian triads.[47] Here we have the stock method of accusing Marxism of Hegelian dialectics, an accusation that might be thought to have been worn threadbare enough by Marx's bourgeois critics. Unable to advance any fundamental argument against the doctrine, these gentlemen fastened on Marx's manner of expression and attacked the origin of the theory, thinking thereby to undermine its essence. And Mr. Mikhailovsky makes no bones about resorting to such methods. He uses a chapter from Engels' *Anti-Dühring*[48] as a pretext. Replying to Dühring, who had attacked Marx's dialectics, Engels says that Marx never dreamed of "proving" anything by means of Hegelian triads, that Marx only studied and investigated the real process, and that the sole criterion of theory recognised by him was its conformity to reality. If, however, it sometimes happened that the development of some particular social phenomenon fitted in with the Hegelian scheme, namely, thesis—negation—negation of the negation, there is nothing surprising about that, for it is no rare thing in nature at all. And Engels proceeds to cite examples from natural history (the development of a seed) and the social sphere—as, for instance, that first there was primitive communism, then private property, and then the capitalist socialisation of labour; or that first there was primitive materialism, then idealism, and then scientific materialism, and so forth. It is clear to everybody that the main weight of Engels' argument is that materialists must correctly and accurately depict the actual historical process, and that insistence on dialectics, the selection of examples to demonstrate the correctness of the triad, is nothing but a relic of the Hegelianism out of which scientific socialism has grown, a relic of its manner of expression. And, indeed, once it has been categorically declared that to "prove" anything by triads is absurd, and that nobody even thought of doing so, what significance can attach to examples of "dialectical" processes? Is it not obvious that this merely points to the origin of the doctrine and nothing more? Mr. Mikhailovsky himself sees it when he says that the theory should not be blamed for its origin. But in order to discern in Engels' arguments something more than the origin of the theory, proof should obviously be offered that the materialists have settled at least one historical *problem* by means of triads, and not on the strength of the pertinent facts. Did Mr. Mikhailovsky attempt to prove this? Not a bit of it. On the contrary, he was himself obliged to admit that "Marx filled the empty dialectical scheme so full with factual content that it can be removed from this content like a lid from a bowl without changing anything" (as to the exception which Mr. Mikhailovsky makes here—regarding the future—we shall deal with it anon). If that is so, why is Mr. Mikhailovsky making so much fuss about this lid that changes nothing? Why does he say that the materialists "rest" their case on the incontrovertibility of the dialectical process? Why, when he is combating this lid, does he declare that he is combating one of the "pillars" of scientific socialism, which is a downright untruth?

It goes without saying that I shall not examine how Mr. Mikhailovsky analyses the examples of triads, because, I repeat, this has no connection whatever either with scientific materialism or with Russian Marxism. But there is one interesting question: what grounds had Mr. Mikhailovsky for so distorting the attitude of Marxists to dialectics?

Two grounds: firstly, Mr. Mikhailovsky, as the saying goes, heard the tolling of a bell, but whence it came he could not tell; secondly, Mr. Mikhailovsky performed (or, rather, borrowed from Dühring) one more piece of subterfuge.

Ad 1)* When reading Marxist literature, Mr. Mikhailovsky constantly came across references to the "dialectical method" in social science, "dialectical thinking," again in the sphere of social problems (which alone is in question), and so forth. In his simplicity of heart (it were well if it were only simplicity) he took it for granted that this method consists in solving all sociological problems in accordance with the laws of the Hegelian triad. Had he been just a little more attentive to the matter in hand he could not but have become convinced of the absurdity of this notion. What Marx and Engels called the dialectical method—as against the metaphysical—is nothing else than the scientific method in sociology, which consists in regarding society as a living organism in a state of constant development (and not as something mechanically concatenated and therefore permitting all sorts of arbitrary combinations of separate social elements), an organism the study of which requires an objective analysis of the production relations that constitute the given social formation and an investigation of its laws of functioning and development. We shall endeavour below to illustrate the relation between the dialectical method and the metaphysical (to which concept the subjective method in sociology undoubtedly also belongs) by Mr. Mikhailovsky's own arguments. For the present we shall only observe that anyone who reads the definition and description of the dialectical method given either by Engels (in the polemic against Dühring: *Socialism: Utopian and Scientific*) or by Marx (various comments in *Capital*, in the Afterword to the second edition, and in *The Poverty of Philosophy*)[49] will see that the Hegelian triads are not even mentioned, and that it all amounts to regarding social evolution as the natural historical process of development of social-economic formations. In confirmation of this I shall cite in extenso the description of the dialectical method given in *Vestnik Yevropy*, 1872, No. 5 (in the article "The Standpoint

* As to the first point.—*Ed.*

of Karl Marx's Critique of Political Economy"),[80] which Marx quotes in the Afterword to the second edition of *Capital*. Marx says that the method he employed in *Capital* had been poorly understood. "German reviews, of course, shriek out at 'Hegelian sophistics.'" And in order to illustrate his method more clearly, Marx quotes the description of it given in the article mentioned. The one thing of importance to Marx, it is there stated, is to find the law governing the phenomena he is investigating, and of particular importance to him is the law of change, the development of those phenomena, of their transition from one form into another, from one order of social relations to another. Consequently, Marx is concerned with one thing only: to show, by rigid scientific investigation, the necessity of the given order of social relations, and to establish, as fully as possible, the facts that serve him as fundamental points of departure. For this purpose it is quite enough if, while proving the necessity of the present order of things, he at the same time proves the necessity of another order which must inevitably grow out of the preceding one regardless of whether men believe in it or not, whether they are conscious of it or not. Marx treats the social movement as a process of natural history, governed by laws not only independent of human will, consciousness and intentions, but, rather, on the contrary, determining the will, consciousness and intentions of men. (This for the information of the subjectivist gentlemen, who separate social evolution from the evolution of natural history merely because man sets himself conscious "aims" and is guided by definite ideals.) If the conscious element plays so subordinate a part in the history of civilisation, it is self-evident that a critique whose subject is civilisation, can least of all take as its basis any form of, or any result of, consciousness. That is to say, that not the idea, but the external, objective phenomenon alone can serve as its point of departure. Criticism must consist in comparing and contrasting the given fact with another fact and not with the idea; the one thing of moment is that both facts be investigated as accurately as possible, and that they actually form, in respect of each other, different moments of development; but most important of all is that an equally accurate investigation be made of the whole series of known states, their sequence and the relation between the different stages of development. Marx rejects the very idea that the laws of economic life are one and the same for the past and the present. On the contrary, every historical period has its own laws. Economic life constitutes a phenomenon analogous to the history of evolution in other branches of biology. Earlier economists misunderstood the nature of economic laws when they likened them to the laws of physics and chemistry. A more thorough analysis shows that social organisms differ among themselves as fundamentally as plants or animals. Setting himself the task of investigating the capitalist economic organism from this point of view, Marx thereby formulates, in a strictly scientific manner, the aim that every accurate investigation into economic life must have. The scientific value of such an inquiry lies in disclosing the special (historical) laws that regulate the origin, existence, development, and death of a given social organism and its replacement by another and higher organism.

Such is the description of the dialectical method which Marx fished out of the mass of magazine and newspaper comments on *Capital*, and which he translated into German, because this description of the method, as he himself says, is absolutely correct. The question arises, is so much as even a single word said here about triads, trichotomies, the incontrovertibility of the dialectical process and suchlike nonsense, which Mr. Mikhailovsky battles against so valiantly? Following this description, Marx says plainly that his method is the "direct opposite" of Hegel's method. According to Hegel the development of the idea, in conformity with the dialectical laws of the triad, determines the development of the real world. And it is only in that case, of course, that one can speak of the importance of the triads, of the incontrovertibility of the dialectical process. "With me, on the contrary," says Marx, "the ideal is nothing but the reflection of the material." And the whole matter thus amounts to an "affirmative recognition of the existing state of things and of its inevitable development"; no other role is left for the triads than that of the lid and the shell ("I coquetted with the modes of expression peculiar to Hegel," Marx says in this same Afterword), in which only philistines could be interested. How, then, we may ask, should we judge a man who set out to criticise one of the "pillars" of scientific materialism, i.e., dialectics, and began to talk about all sorts of things, even about frogs and Napoleon, but not about what dialectics is, whether the development of society is really a process of natural history, whether the materialist concept of social-economic formations as special social organisms is correct, whether the methods of objective analysis of these formations are right, whether social ideas really do not determine social development but are themselves determined by it, and so forth? Can one assume only a lack of understanding in this case?

Ad 2)* After this "criticism" of dialectics, Mr. Mikhailovsky imputes these methods of proving things "by means of" Hegelian triads to Marx, and, of course, victoriously combats them. "Regarding the future," he says, "the immanent laws of society are based purely on dialectics." (This is the exception referred to above.) Marx's arguments on the inevitability of the expropriation of the expropriators by virtue of the laws of development of capitalism are "purely dialectical." Marx's "ideal" of the common ownership of land and capital "in the sense of its inevitability and indubitability rests entirely at the end of the Hegelian three-term chain."

This argument *is taken in its entirety* from Dühring, who expounds it in his "Kritische Geschichte der Nationaloekonomie und des Sozialismus"(3-te Aufl., 1879. S. 486-87).** But Mr. Mikhailovsky says not a word about Dühring. Perhaps, incidentally, he arrived independently at this way of garbling Marx?

Engels gave a splendid reply to Dühring, and since he also quotes Dühring's criticism we shall confine ourselves to Engels' reply.[51] The reader will see that it fully applies to Mr. Mikhailovsky.

"'This historical sketch' (of the genesis of the so-called primitive accumulation of capital in England) 'is relatively the best part of Marx's book,'" says Dühring, "'and would be even better if it had not relied on the dialectical crutch to

* As to the second point.—*Ed.*

** *A Critical History of National Economy and Socialism* (3rd edition, 1879, pp. 486-87).—*Ed.*

help out its scholarly crutch. The Hegelian negation of the negation, in default of anything better and clearer, has in fact to serve here as the midwife to deliver the future from the womb of the past. The abolition of "individual property," which since the sixteenth century has been effected in the way indicated above, is the first negation. It will be followed by a second, which bears the character of a negation of the negation, and hence of a restoration of "individual property," but in a higher form, based on common ownership of land and of the instruments of labour. Herr Marx calls this new "individual property" also "social property," and in this there appears the Hegelian higher unity, in which the contradiction is supposed to be sublated'" (aufgehoben—a specific Hegelian term), '"that is to say, in the Hegelian verbal jugglery, both overcome and preserved....

"'According to this, the expropriation of the expropriators is, as it were, the automatic result of historical reality in its materially external relations.... It would be difficult to convince a sensible man of the necessity of the common ownership of land and capital, on the basis of credence in Hegelian word-juggling such as the negation of the negation.... The nebulous hybrids of Marx's conceptions will not, however, appear strange to anyone who realises what nonsense can be concocted with Hegelian dialectics as the scientific basis, or rather what nonsense must necessarily spring from it. For the benefit of the reader who is not familiar with these artifices, it must be pointed out expressly that Hegel's first negation is the catechismal idea of the fall from grace, and his second is that of a higher unity leading to redemption. The logic of facts can hardly be based on this nonsensical analogy borrowed from the religious sphere.... Herr Marx remains cheerfully in the nebulous world of his property which is at once both individual and social and leaves it to his adepts to solve for themselves this profound dialectical enigma.' Thus far Herr Dühring.

"So," Engels concludes, "Marx has no other way of proving the necessity of the social revolution, of establishing the common ownership of land and of the means of production produced by labour, except by using the Hegelian negation of the negation; and because he bases his socialist theory on these nonsensical analogies borrowed from religion, he arrives at the result that in the society of the future there will be dominant an ownership at once both individual and social, as the Hegelian higher unity of the sublated contradiction.*

"But let the negation of the negation rest for the moment, and let us have a look at the 'ownership' which is 'at once both individual and social.' Herr Dühring characterises this as a 'nebulous world,' and curiously enough he is really right on this point. Unfortunately, however, it is not Marx but again Herr Dühring himself who is in this 'nebulous world.'... He can put Marx right à la Hegel, by imputing to him the higher unity of a property, of which there is not a word in Marx.

"Marx says: 'It is the negation of the negation. This does not re-establish private property for the producer, but gives him individual property based on the acquisitions of the capitalist era; i.e., on co-operation and the possession in common of the land and of the means of production. The transformation of scattered private property, arising from individual labour, into capitalist private property is, naturally, a process incomparably more protracted, violent, and difficult than the transformation of capitalistic private property, already practically resting on socialised production, into socialised property.' That is all. The state of things brought about through the expropriation of the expropriators is therefore characterised as the re-

* That this formulation of Dühring's views applies fully to Mr. Mikhailovsky is proved by the following passage in his article "Karl Marx Being Tried by Y. Zhukovsky." Objecting to Mr. Zhukovsky's assertion that Marx is a defender of private property, Mr. Mikhailovsky refers to this scheme of Marx's and explains it in the following manner. "In his scheme Marx employed two well-known tricks of Hegelian dialectics: firstly, the scheme is constructed according to the laws of the Hegelian triad; secondly, the synthesis is based on the identity of opposites—individual and social property. This means that the word 'individual' here has the specific, purely conditional meaning of a term of the dialectical process, and absolutely nothing can be based on it." This was said by a man possessed of the most estimable intentions, defending, in the eyes of the Russian public, the "sanguine" Marx from the bourgeois Mr. Zhukovsky. And with these estimable intentions he explains Marx as basing his conception of the process on "tricks"! Mr. Mikhailovsky may draw from this what is for him the not unprofitable moral that, whatever the matter in hand, estimable intentions alone are rather inadequate.

establishment of individual property, but *on the basis* of the social ownership of the land and of the means of production produced by labour itself. To anyone who understands German" (and Russian too, Mr. Mikhailovsky, because the translation is absolutely correct) "this means that social ownership extends to the land and the other means of production, and individual ownership to the products, that is, the articles of consumption. And in order to make the matter comprehensible even to children of six, Marx assumes on page 56" (Russ. ed., p. 30)[52] "'a community of free individuals, carrying on their work with the means of production in common, in which the labour-power of all the different individuals is consciously applied as the combined labour-power of the community,' that is, a society organised on a socialist basis; and he continues: 'The total product of our community is a social product. One portion serves as fresh means of production and *remains social.*' But another portion is consumed by the members as means of subsistence. '*A distribution of this portion among them is consequently necessary.*' And surely that is clear enough even for Herr Dühring....

"The property which is at once both individual and social, this confusing hybrid, this nonsense which necessarily springs from Hegelian dialectics, this nebulous world, this profound dialectical enigma, which Marx leaves his adepts to solve for themselves—is yet another free creation and imagination on the part of Herr Dühring....

"But what role," Engels continues, "does the negation of the negation play in Marx? On page 791 and the following pages" (Russ. ed., p. 648 et seq.)[53] "he sets out the final conclusions which he draws from the preceding 50" (Russ. ed., 35) "pages of economic and historical investigation into the so-called primitive accumulation of capital. Before the capitalist era, petty industry existed, at least in England, on the basis of the private property of the labourer in his means of production. The so-called primitive accumulation of capital consisted there in the expropriation of these immediate producers, that is, in the dissolution of private property based on the labour of its owner. This became possible because the petty industry referred to above is compatible only with narrow and primitive bounds of production and society and at a certain stage brings forth the material agencies for its own annihilation. This annihilation, the transformation of the individual and scattered means of production into socially concentrated ones, forms the prehistory of capital. As soon as the labourers are turned into proletarians, their means of labour into capital, as soon as the capitalist mode of production stands on its own feet, the further socialisation of labour and further transformation of the land and other means of production" (into capital), "and therefore the further expropriation of private proprietors, takes a new form. 'That which is now to be expropriated is no longer the labourer working for himself, but the capitalist exploiting many labourers. This expropriation is accomplished by the action of the immanent laws of capitalistic production itself, by the concentration of capital. One capitalist always kills many. Hand in hand with this concentration, or this expropriation of many capitalists by few, develop, on an ever-extending scale, the co-operative form of the labour process, the conscious technical application of science, the methodical cultivation of the soil, the transformation of the instruments of labour into instruments of labour only usable in common, the economising of all means of production by their use as the means of production of combined, socialised labour. Along with the constantly diminishing number of the magnates of capital, who usurp and monopolise all advantages of this process of transformation, grows the mass of misery, oppression, slavery, degradation, exploitation; but with this too grows the revolt of the working class, a class always increasing in numbers, and disciplined, united, organised by the very mechanism of the process of capitalist production itself. Capital becomes a fetter upon the mode of production, which has sprung up and flourished along with, and under it. Concentration of the means of production and socialisation of labour at last reach a point where they become incompatible with their capitalist integument. This integument is burst asunder. The knell of capitalist private property sounds. The expropriators are expropriated.'

"And now I ask the reader: where are the dialectical frills and mazes and conceptual arabesques; where the mixed and misconceived ideas according to which everything is all one and the same thing in the end; where the dialectical miracles for his faithful followers; where the mysterious dialectical rubbish and the maze in accordance with the Hegelian Logos doctrine, without which Marx, according to Herr Dühring, is unable to put his exposition into shape? Marx merely shows from history, and here states in a summarised form, that just as formerly petty industry by its very development, necessarily created the conditions of its own annihilation ... so now the capitalist mode of production has likewise itself created the material conditions from which it must perish. The process is a historical one, and if it is at the same time a dialectical process, this is not Marx's fault, however annoying it may be to Herr Dühring.

"It is only at this point, after Marx has completed his proof on the basis of historical and economic facts, that he proceeds: 'The capitalist mode of appropriation, the result of the capitalist mode of production, produces capitalist private property. This is the first negation of individual private property, as founded on the labour of the proprietor. But capitalist production begets, with the inexorability of a law of Nature, its own negation. It is the negation of the negation'—and so on (as quoted above).

"Thus, by characterising the process as the negation of the negation, Marx does not intend to prove that the process was historically necessary. On the contrary: only after he has proved from history that in fact the process has partially already occurred, and partially must occur in the future, he in addition characterises it as a process which develops in accordance with a definite dialectical law. That is all. It is therefore once again a pure distortion of the facts by Herr Dühring when he declares that the negation of the negation has to serve here as the midwife to deliver the future from the womb of the past, or that Marx wants anyone to be convinced of the necessity of the common ownership of land and capital ... on the basis of credence in the negation of the negation" (p. 125).

The reader will see that Engels' splendid rebuttal of Dühring applies in its entirety to Mr. Mikhailovsky, who also asserts that with Marx the future rests exclusively at the end of the Hegelian chain and that the conviction of its inevitability can be founded only on faith.*

The whole difference between Dühring and Mr. Mikhailovsky reduces itself to the following two small points: firstly, Dühring, despite the fact that he could not speak of Marx without foaming at the mouth, nevertheless considered it necessary to mention in the next section of his *History* that Marx in the Afterword[54] categorically repudiated the accusation of Hegelianism. Mr. Mikhailovsky, however, has nothing to say about the (above quoted) absolutely definite and clear statements by Marx on what he conceives the dialectical method to be.

Secondly, another peculiarity of Mr. Mikhailovsky's is that he concentrated all his attention on the use of tenses. Why, when he speaks of the future, does Marx use the present tense?—our philosopher demands with an air of triumph. You may find the answer to this in any grammar, most worthy critic: you will find that the present tense is used instead of the future when the future is regarded as inevitable and undoubted. But why so, why is it undoubted?—Mr. Mikhailovsky anxiously asks, desiring to convey such profound agitation as would justify even a distortion. But on this point, too, Marx gave an absolutely definite reply. You may consider it inadequate or wrong, but in that case you must show *how exactly* and *why exactly* it is wrong, and not talk nonsense about Hegelianism.

Time was when Mr. Mikhailovsky not only knew himself what this reply was, but lectured others on it. Mr. Zhukovsky, he wrote in 1877, had good grounds for regarding Marx's conception of the future as conjectural, but he "had no moral right" to ignore the question of the socialisation of labour, "to which Marx attributes vast

---

* It is worth while, I think, to note in this connection that the entire explanation given by Engels is contained in the same chapter in which he discusses the seed, the teaching of Rousseau, and other examples of the dialectical process. It would seem that the absurdity of accusing Marxism of Hegelian dialectics would have been made quite evident by merely comparing these examples with the clear and categorical statements by Engels (and by Marx, to whom the manuscript was read before printing), and there can be no question of trying *to prove* anything by triads or of inserting in the depiction of the real process the "conditional members" of these triads.

importance." Well, of course! Zhukovsky in 1877 had no moral right to evade the question, but Mr. Mikhailovsky in 1894 has this moral right! Perhaps, quod licet Jovi, non licet bovi?!*

I cannot help recalling here a strange notion of this socialisation once expressed in *Otechestvenniye Zapiski.*[55] In No. 7, 1883, this magazine published "A Letter to the Editor," from a certain Mr. Postoronny[56] who, like Mr. Mikhailovsky, regarded Marx's "conception" about the future as conjectural. "Essentially," this gentleman argues, "the social form of labour under capitalism amounts to this, that several hundreds or thousands of workers grind, hammer, turn, place on, place under, pull and perform numerous other operations under one roof. As to the general character of this regime it is excellently expressed by the saying: 'Every man for himself, and God for all.' Where does the social form of labour come in?"

Well, you can see at once that the man has grasped what it is all about! "The social form of labour" "amounts" to "working under one roof"!! And when such preposterous ideas are expressed in one of the, so far, best Russian magazines, they still want to assure us that the theoretical part of *Capital* is generally recognised by science. Yes, as it was unable to raise the slightest serious objection to *Capital*, "generally recognised science" began to bow and scrape to it, at the same time continuing to betray the most elementary ignorance and to repeat the old banalities of school economics. We must dwell on this question somewhat in order to show Mr. Mikhailovsky what is the essence of the matter which he, by force of habit, has passed over entirely.

The socialisation of labour by capitalist production does not at all consist in people working under one roof (that is only a small part of the process), but in the concentration of capital being accompanied by the specialisation of social labour, by a decrease in the number of capitalists in each given branch of industry and an increase in the number of separate branches of industry—in many

* What Jove may do, the bull may not.—*Ed.*

separate production processes being merged into one social production process. When, in the days of handicraft weaving, for example, the small producers themselves spun the yarn and made it into cloth, we had a few branches of industry (spinning and weaving were merged). But when production becomes socialised by capitalism, the number of separate branches of industry increases: cotton spinning is done separately and so is weaving; this very division and the concentration of production give rise to new branches—machine building, coal mining, and so forth. In each branch of industry, which has now become more specialised, the number of capitalists steadily decreases. This means that the social tie between the producers becomes increasingly stronger, the producers become welded into a single whole. The isolated small producers each performed several operations simultaneously, and were therefore relatively independent of each other: when, for instance, the handicraftsman himself sowed flax, and himself spun and wove, he was almost independent of others. It was this (and only this) regime of small, dispersed commodity producers that justified the saying: "Every man for himself, and God for all," that is, an anarchy of market fluctuations. The case is entirely different under the socialisation of labour that has been achieved due to capitalism. The manufacturer who produces fabrics depends on the cotton-yarn manufacturer; the latter depends on the capitalist planter who grows the cotton, on the owner of the engineering works, the coal mine, and so on and so forth. The result is that no capitalist can get along without others. It is clear that the saying "every man for himself" is quite inapplicable to such a regime: here each works for all and all for each (and no room is left for God—either as a supermundane fantasy or as a mundane "golden calf"). The character of the regime changes completely. When, during the regime of small, isolated enterprises, work came to a standstill in any one of them, this affected only a few members of society, it did not cause any general confusion, and therefore did not attract general attention and did not provoke public interference. But when work comes to a standstill in a large enterprise, one engaged in a highly specialised branch of industry and therefore working almost for the whole of society and, in its turn, dependent on the whole of society (for the sake of simplicity I take a case where socialisation has reached the culminating point), work is bound to come to a standstill in all the other enterprises of society, because they can only obtain the products they need from this enterprise, they can only dispose of all their own commodities if its commodities are available. All production processes thus merge into a single social production process; yet each branch is conducted by a separate capitalist, it depends on him and the social products are his private property. Is it not clear that the form of production comes into irreconcilable contradiction with the form of appropriation? Is it not evident that the latter must adapt itself to the former and must become social, that is, socialist? But the smart philistine of *Otechestvenniye Zapiski* reduces the whole thing to work under one roof. Could anything be wider of the mark! (I have described only the material process, only the change in production relations, without touching on the social aspect of the process, the fact that the workers become united, welded together and organised, since that is a derivative and secondary phenomenon.)

The reason such elementary things have to be explained to the Russian "democrats" is that they are so badly stuck in the mud of petty-bourgeois ideas that to imagine any but a petty-bourgeois order of things is quite beyond them.

Let us return, however, to Mr. Mikhailovsky. What objections did he make to the facts and arguments on which Marx based the conclusion that the socialist system is inevitable by virtue of the very laws of capitalist development? Did he show that in reality, under a commodity organisation of social economy, there is no growing specialisation of the social labour process, no concentration of capital and enterprises, no socialisation of the whole labour process? No, he did not advance a single argument in refutation of these facts. Did he shake the proposition that anarchy, which is irreconcilable with the socialisation of labour, is an inherent feature of capitalist society? He said nothing about this. Did he prove that the amalgamation of the labour processes of all the capitalists into a single social labour process is compatible with private property, or that some solution to the contradiction is possible and conceivable other than that indicated by Marx? No, he did not say a word about this.

On what, then, does his criticism rest? On manipulations, distortion, and on a spate of words which are nothing more than the noise of a rattle.

How else, indeed, are we to characterise methods employed by the critic who, after first talking a lot of nonsense about triple successive steps of history, demands of Marx with a serious air: "And what next?"—that is, how will history proceed beyond that final stage of the process he has described? Please note that from the very outset of his literary and revolutionary activities Marx most definitely demanded that sociological theory should accurately depict the real process—and nothing more (cf., for instance, the *Communist Manifesto* on the communists' criterion of theory).[57] He strictly adhered to this demand in his *Capital*: he made it his task to give a scientific analysis of the capitalist form of society—and there he stopped, after showing that the development of this organisation actually going on before our eyes has such and such a tendency, that it must inevitably perish and turn into another, a higher organisation. But Mr. Mikhailovsky, evading the whole substance of Marx's doctrine, puts his stupid question: "And what next?" And he adds profoundly: "I must frankly confess that I am not quite clear what Engels' reply would be." We, however, on our part must frankly confess, Mr. Mikhailovsky, that we are quite clear about what the spirit and methods of such "criticism" are!

Or take the following argument: "In the Middle Ages, Marx's individual property based on the proprietor's own labour was neither the only nor the predominating factor, even in the realm of economic relations. There was much more besides, but the dialectical method in Marx's interpretation" (and not in Mr. Mikhailovsky's garbled version of it?) "does not propose returning to it.... It is obvious that all these schemes do not present a picture of historical reality, or even of its proportions; they simply satisfy the tendency of the human mind to think of every object in its past, present and future states." Even your way of distorting things, Mr. Mikhailovsky, is monotonous to the point of nausea! Into Marx's scheme, which claims to formulate nothing but the actual process of development of capitalism,* he first insinuates the intention of proving everything by triads, then declares that Marx's scheme does not conform to the plan foisted on it by Mr. Mikhailovsky (the third stage restores only *one* aspect of the first stage, omitting all the others), and then in the most blatant manner draws the conclusion that "the scheme obviously does not present a picture of historical reality"!

Is any serious polemic thinkable with a man who (as Engels said of Dühring) cannot quote accurately, even by way of exception? Can there be any arguing, when the public is assured that the scheme "obviously" does not conform to reality, without even an attempt being made to show its faultiness in any respect?

Instead of criticising the real content of Marxist views, Mr. Mikhailovsky exercises his ingenuity on the subject of the categories past, present and future. Engels, for instance, arguing against the "eternal truths" of Herr Dühring, says that the "morality ... preached to us today" is a threefold morality: Christian-feudal, bourgeois and proletarian, so that the past, present and future have their own theories of morality.[58] In this connection, Mr. Mikhailovsky reasons as follows: "I think that it is the categories past, present and future that lie at the basis of all triple divisions of history into periods." What profundity! Who does not know that if any social phenomenon is examined in its process of development, relics of the past, foundations of the present and germs of the future will always be discovered in it? But did Engels, for instance, think of asserting that the history of morality (he was speaking, we know, only of the "present") was confined to the three factors indicated, that feudal morality, for example, was not preceded by slave morality, and the latter by the morality of the primitive-communist community? Instead of seriously criticising Engels' attempt to elucidate modern trends in

* The other features of the economic system of the Middle Ages are omitted because they belonged to the feudal social formation, whereas Marx investigates only the *capitalist* formation. In its pure form the process of capitalist development actually began—in England, for instance—with the system of small, isolated commodity producers and their individual labour property.

moral ideas by explaining them materialistically, Mr. Mikhailovsky treats us to the most empty phrase-mongering!

In respect of such methods of "criticism" employed by Mr. Mikhailovsky, criticism which begins with the statement that he does not know where, in what work, the materialist conception of history is expounded, it would perhaps be worth while to recall that there was a time when the author knew one of these works and was able to appraise it more correctly. In 1877, Mr. Mikhailovsky expressed the following opinion of *Capital*: "If we remove from *Capital* the heavy, clumsy and unnecessary lid of Hegelian dialectics" (How strange! How is it that "Hegelian dialectics" were "unnecessary" in 1877, while in 1894 it appears that materialism rests on "the incontrovertibility of the dialectical process"?), "then, apart from the other merits of this essay, we shall observe in it splendidly elaborated material for an answer to the general question of the relation of forms to the material conditions of their existence, and an excellent formulation of this question for a definite sphere." "The relation of forms to the material conditions of their existence"—why, that is the very problem of the interrelation between the various aspects of social life, of the superstructure of ideological social relations on the basis of material relations, a problem whose well-known solution constitutes the doctrine of materialism. Let us proceed.

"In point of fact, *the whole of 'Capital'*" (my italics) "is devoted to an inquiry into how a form of society, once it has emerged, continues to develop and accentuates its typical features, subjecting to itself and assimilating discoveries, inventions and improvements in methods of production, new markets and science itself and compels them to work for it, and of how, finally, the given form cannot stand up against further changes in material conditions."

An astonishing thing! In 1877, "the whole of *Capital*" was devoted to a materialist inquiry into a particular form of society (what else does materialism consist in, if not in explaining forms of society by material conditions?), whereas in 1894 it appears that it is not even known where, in what work, an exposition of this materialism should be sought!

In 1877, *Capital* contained an "inquiry into" how "a particular form" (the capitalist form, is it not?) "cannot" (mark that!) "stand up against further changes in material conditions,"—whereas in 1894 it turns out that there has been no inquiry at all and that the conviction that the capitalist form cannot withstand any further development of the productive forces—rests "entirely at the end of the Hegelian triad"! In 1877, Mr. Mikhailovsky wrote that "the analysis of the relations of the given form of society to the material conditions of its existence will *for ever*" (my italics) "remain a monument to the author's logical powers and vast erudition," whereas in 1894 he declares that the doctrine of materialism has never and nowhere been scientifically verified and proved.

An astonishing thing! What does it really mean? What has happened?

Two things have happened. Firstly, the *Russian*, peasant socialism of the seventies—which "snorted" at freedom because of its bourgeois character, fought the "clear-browed liberals" who zealously covered up the antagonistic nature of Russian life, and dreamed of a peasant revolution—has completely decayed and has begotten that vulgar, philistine liberalism which discerns an "encouraging impression" in the progressive trends of peasant farming, forgetting that they are accompanied (and determined) by the wholesale expropriation of the peasantry. Secondly, in 1877 Mr. Mikhailovsky was so engrossed in his task of defending the "sanguine" (i.e., revolutionary socialist) Marx from the liberal critics that he failed to observe the incompatibility of Marx's method and his own. And then this irreconcilable contradiction between dialectical materialism and subjective sociology was explained to him—explained by Engels' articles and books, and by the Russian Social-Democrats (one often meets with very apt comments on Mr. Mikhailovsky in Plekhanov's writings)—and Mr. Mikhailovsky, instead of seriously sitting down to reconsider the whole question, simply took the bit between his teeth. Instead of welcoming Marx (as he did in 1872 and 1877)[89] he now barks at him under cover of dubious praise, and rages and splutters against the Russian Marxists for refusing to rest content with the "defence of the economically weakest," with warehouses and improvements in the countryside, with museums and artels for handicraftsmen, and similar well-meaning philistine ideas of progress, and for wanting to remain "sanguine" people, advocates of social revolution, and to teach, guide and organise the really revolutionary elements of society.

After this brief excursion into the realm of the distant past, one may, we think, conclude this examination of Mr. Mikhailovsky's "criticism" of Marx's theory. Let us then try to sum up and recapitulate the critic's "arguments."

The doctrine he set out to demolish is based, firstly, on the materialist conception of history, and, secondly, on the dialectical method.

As to the first, the critic began by declaring that he did not know in which work materialism was expounded. Not having found such an exposition anywhere, he himself set about concocting an explanation of what materialism is. In order to give an idea of the excessive claims of this materialism, he concocted the story that the materialists claim to have explained the entire past, present and future of mankind—and when it was subsequently shown by reference to the authentic statements of the Marxists that they regard only one social formation as having been explained, the critic decided that the materialists narrow the scope of materialism, whereby, he asserts, they defeat themselves. In order to give an idea of the methods by which this materialism was worked out, he invented the story that the materialists themselves had confessed to the inadequacy of their knowledge for the elaboration of scientific socialism, despite the fact that Marx and Engels confessed only to the insufficiency of their knowledge (in 1845-1846) of economic history in general, and despite the fact that they never published the essay which testified to the insufficiency of their knowledge. After these preludes, we were treated to the criticism itself: *Capital* was annihilated because it dealt with only one period, whereas the critic wants to have all periods; and also because it did not affirm economic materialism, but simply touched upon it—arguments, evidently, so weighty and serious as to compel the recognition that materialism had never been scientifically substantiated. Then the fact was cited against materialism that a man totally unconnected with this doctrine, having studied prehistoric times in an entirely different country, also arrived at materialist conclusions. To show, further, that it was absolutely wrong to drag procreation into materialism, that this was nothing but a verbal artifice, the critic proceeded to prove that economic relations are a superstructure based on sexual and family relations. The statements made thereupon by our weighty critic for the edification of the materialists enriched us with the profound truth that inheritance is impossible without procreation, that a complex psychology "adheres" to the products of this procreation, and that children are brought up in the spirit of their fathers. In passing, we also learnt that national ties are a continuation and generalisation of gentile ties. Continuing his theoretical researches into materialism, the critic noted that the content of many of the Marxists' arguments consisted in the assertion that oppression and exploitation of the masses were "necessary" under the bourgeois regime and that this regime must "necessarily" turn into a socialist regime, after which he hastened to declare that necessity is too general a bracket (if we omit what, exactly, people consider necessary) and that therefore Marxists are mystics and metaphysicians. The critic also declared that Marx's polemic against the idealists was "one-sided," but he did not say a word about the relation of these idealists' views to the subjective method and the relation of Marx's dialectical materialism to these views.

As to the second pillar of Marxism—the dialectical method—one push by the bold critic was enough to cast it to the ground. And the push was very well directed: the critic toiled and moiled with prodigious effort to disprove the notion that anything can be proved by triads, ignoring the fact that the dialectical method does not consist in triads at all, but that it consists precisely in the rejection of the methods of idealism and subjectivism in sociology. Another push was specially directed at Marx: with the help of the valorous Herr Dühring, the critic ascribed to Marx the incredible absurdity of having tried to prove the necessity of the doom of capitalism by means of triads—and then victoriously combated this absurdity.

Such is the epic of the brilliant "victories" of "our well-known sociologist"! How very "edifying" (Burenin) it was to contemplate these victories!

We cannot refrain at this point from touching on another circumstance, which has no direct bearing on the criticism of Marx's doctrine, but is extremely characteristic for an understanding of the critic's ideals and of his conception of reality. It is his attitude to the working-class movement in the West.

Above we quoted Mr. Mikhailovsky's statement that materialism had not justified itself in "science" (perhaps in the science of the German "friends of the people"?); but this materialism, argues Mr. Mikhailovsky, "is really spreading very rapidly among the working class." How does Mr. Mikhailovsky explain this fact? "The success," he says, "enjoyed by economic materialism in breadth, so to speak, and its dissemination in a critically unverified form, are chiefly due to the day-to-day practice established by prospects for the future, and not to science." What other meaning can there be in this clumsy phrase about practice "established" by prospects for the future than that materialism is spreading not because it correctly explains reality, but because it turns away from reality towards prospects? And he goes on to say: "These prospects require of the German working class which is adopting them and of those who take a warm interest in its future neither knowledge nor the effort of critical thinking. They require only faith." In other words, the spread of materialism and scientific socialism in breadth is due to the fact that this doctrine promises the workers a better future! But a most elementary acquaintance with the history of socialism and of the working-class movement in the West is enough to reveal the utter absurdity and falsity of this explanation. Everybody knows that scientific socialism never painted any prospects for the future as such: it confined itself to analysing the present bourgeois regime, to studying the trends of development of the capitalist social organisation, and that is all. "We do not say to the world," Marx wrote as far back as 1843, and he fulfilled this programme to the letter, "we do not say to the world: 'Cease struggling—your whole struggle is senseless.' All we do is to provide it with a true slogan of struggle. We only show the world what it is actually struggling for, and consciousness is a thing which the world *must* acquire, whether it likes it or not."[60] Everybody knows that *Capital*, for instance—the chief and basic work in which scientific socialism is expounded—restricts itself to the most general allusions to the future and merely traces those already existing elements from which the future system grows. Everybody knows that as far as prospects for the future are concerned incomparably more was contributed by the earlier socialists, who described future society in every detail, desiring to inspire mankind with a picture of a system under which people get along without conflict and under which their social relations are based not on exploitation but on true principles of progress that conform to the conditions of human nature. Nevertheless, despite the whole phalanx of very talented people who expounded these ideas, and despite the most firmly convinced socialists, their theories stood aloof from life and their programmes were not connected with the political movements of the people until large-scale machine industry drew the mass of proletarian workers into the vortex of political life, and until the true slogan of their struggle was found. This slogan was found by Marx, "not a utopian, but a strict and, in places, even dry scientist" (as Mr. Mikhailovsky called him in the long distant past—in 1872); and it was certainly not found by means of prospects, but by a scientific analysis of the present bourgeois regime, by an elucidation of the *necessity* of exploitation under this regime, by an investigation of the laws of its development. Mr. Mikhailovsky may, of course, assure the readers of *Russkoye Bogatstvo* that neither knowledge nor an effort of thinking is required to understand this analysis, but we have already seen in his own case (and shall see it to a still greater extent in the case of his economist collaborator[61]) so gross a lack of understanding of the elementary truths established by this analysis that such a statement, of course, can only provoke a smile. It remains an indisputable fact that the working-class movement spreads and develops precisely where and to the extent that large-scale capitalist machine industry develops; the socialist doctrine is successful precisely when it stops arguing about social conditions that conform to human nature and sets about making a materialist analysis of contemporary social relations and explaining the necessity for the present regime of exploitation.

Having tried to evade the real reasons for the success of materialism among the workers by ascribing the attitude of this doctrine to "prospects" in a manner directly contrary to the truth, Mr. Mikhailovsky goes on to scoff in the most vulgar and philistine way at the ideas and tactics of the West-European working-class movement. As we have seen, he was unable to adduce a single argument against Marx's proofs of the inevitability of the capitalist system being transformed into a socialist system as a result of the socialisation of labour. And yet he jeers in the most blatant manner at the idea of an "army of proletarians" preparing to expropriate the capitalists, "whereupon all class conflict will cease and peace on earth and goodwill among men will reign." He, Mr. Mikhailovsky, knows far simpler and surer paths to the achievement of socialism than this: all that is required is that the "friends of the people" should indicate in greater detail the "clear and unalterable" paths of the "desired economic evolution"—and then these friends of the people will most likely "be called in" to solve "practical economic problems" (see the article "Problems of Russia's Economic Development" by Mr. Yuzhakov in *Russkoye Bogatstvo*, No. 11) and meanwhile—meanwhile the workers must wait, must rely on the friends of the people and not begin, with "unjustified self-assurance," an independent struggle against the exploiters. Desiring to strike a deathblow at this "unjustified self-assurance," our author waxes highly indignant at "this science that can almost fit into a pocket dictionary." How terrible, indeed! Science—and Social-Democratic penny pamphlets that can fit into the pocket!! Is it not obvious how unjustifiably self-assured are those who value science only insofar as it teaches the exploited to wage an independent struggle for their emancipation, teaches them to keep away from all "friends of the people" engaged in glossing over class antagonisms and desirous of taking the whole business upon themselves—those who, therefore, expound this science in penny publications which so shock the philistines? How different it would be if the workers placed their fate in the hands of the "friends of the people"! They would show them a real, voluminous, university and philistine science; they would acquaint them in detail with a social organisation that conforms to human nature, provided only—the workers agreed to wait and did not themselves begin the struggle with such unjustified self-assurance!

Before passing to the second part of Mr. Mikhailovsky's "criticism," which this time is not directed against Marx's theory in general but against the Russian Social-Democrats in particular, we shall have to make a little digression. When criticising Marx, Mr. Mikhailovsky not only made no attempt to give an exact exposition of Marx's theory but horribly distorted it, and in just the same way he now most unscrupulously garbles the ideas of the Russian Social-Democrats. The truth must be restored. This can be done most conveniently by comparing the ideas of the earlier Russian socialists with the ideas of the Social-Democrats. I borrow an account of the former from an article by Mr. Mikhailovsky in *Russkaya Mysl*, 1892, No. 6, in which he also spoke of Marxism (and spoke of it—be it said in reproach to him—in a decent tone, without dealing with problems which, in a censored press, can be treated only in Burenin fashion, without confusing the Marxists with all sorts of riffraff) and expounded his own views in opposition to Marxism—or, at least, if not in opposition to, then parallel to Marxism. Of course, I have not the least desire to offend either Mr. Mikhailovsky, by classing him among the socialists, or the Russian socialists, by putting Mr. Mikhailovsky on a par with them; but I think that the *line of argument* is essentially the same in both cases, the difference being only in the degree of firmness, straightforwardness and consistency of their convictions.

Describing the ideas of *Otechestvenniye Zapiski*, Mr. Mikhailovsky wrote: "We included the ownership of the land by the tiller and of the implements of labour by the producer among moral and political ideals." The point of departure, as you see, is most well-intentioned, inspired by the best wishes.... "The medieval forms of labour* still existing in our country had been seriously shaken, but we saw no reason to put a complete end to them for the sake of any doctrine whatever, liberal or non-liberal."

Strange argument! Obviously, "forms of labour" of any kind can be shaken only if they are superseded by some other forms; yet we do not find our author (nor would we find any of his like-minded friends, for that matter) even attempting to analyse and to explain these new forms, or to ascertain why they supplant the old. Stranger still is the second half of the tirade: "We saw no reason to put an end to these forms for the sake of any doctrine." What means do "we" (i.e., the socialists—see the above reservation) possess to "put an end" to forms of labour, that is, to reconstruct the existing production relations between the members of society? Is not the idea of remaking these relations in accordance with a doctrine absurd? Listen to what comes next: "Our task is not to rear, out of our own national depths, a civilisation that is positively 'original'; but neither is it to transplant Western civilisation to our own country in toto, together with all the contradictions that are tearing it apart; we must take what is good from wherever we can; and whether it be our own or foreign is not a matter of principle, but of practical convenience. Surely, this is so simple, clear and understandable that there is nothing even to discuss." Indeed, how simple it is! "Take" what is good from everywhere—and the trick is done! From the medieval forms "take" the labourer's ownership of the means of production, and from the new (i.e., capitalist) forms "take" liberty, equality, enlightenment and culture. And there is nothing to discuss! Here the whole subjective method in sociology is as clear as daylight: sociology starts with a utopia—the labourer's ownership of the land—and indicates the conditions for realising the desirable, namely, "take" what is good from here and from there. This philosopher takes a purely metaphysical view of social relations as of a simple

* "By medieval forms of labour"—the author explains in another place—"are meant not only communal landownership, handicraft industry and artel organisation. All these are undoubtedly medieval forms, but to them must be added all forms of ownership of land or implements of production by the labourer."

mechanical aggregation of various institutions, a simple mechanical concatenation of various phenomena. He plucks out one of these phenomena—the cultivator's ownership of the land in its medieval forms—and thinks that it can be transplanted to all other forms, just as a brick can be transferred from one building to another. But that is not studying social relations; it is mutilating the material to be studied. In reality, there was no such thing as the cultivator's ownership of the land existing separately and independently, as you have taken it; it was only one of the links in the then existing production relations, which consisted in the land being divided up among large landed proprietors, landlords, who allotted it to the peasants in order to exploit them, so that the land was, as it were, wages in kind: it provided the peasant with necessary products, so that he might be able to produce a surplus product for the landlord; it provided the means for the peasants to render feudal service to the landlord. Why did the author not follow up this system of production relations, instead of confining himself to plucking out one phenomenon and thus presenting it in an absolutely false light? Because the author does not know how to handle social problems: he (I repeat, I am using Mr. Mikhailovsky's arguments only as an example for criticising Russian socialism as a *whole*) does not set out at all *to explain* the then existing "forms of labour" and to present them as a definite system of production relations, as a definite social formation. To use Marx's expression, the dialectical method, which requires us to regard society as a living organism in its functioning and development, is alien to him.

Without even asking himself why the old forms of labour are supplanted by the new, he repeats exactly the same error when he discusses these new forms. For him it is enough to note that these forms "shake" the cultivator's ownership of the land—that is, speaking more generally, find expression in the separation of the producer from the means of production—and to condemn this for not conforming to the ideal. And here again his argument is utterly absurd: he plucks out one phenomenon (land dispossession), without even attempting to present it as an element of a now different system of production relations based on *commodity economy*, which necessarily begets competition among the commodity producers, inequality, the ruin of some and the enrichment of others. He noted one thing, the ruin of the masses, and put aside the other, the enrichment of the minority, and this made it impossible for him to understand either.

And such methods he calls "seeking answers to the questions of life clothed in flesh and blood" (*Russkoye Bogatstvo*, 1894, No. 1), when, as a matter of fact, quite the contrary is the case: unable and unwilling to explain reality, to look it straight in the face, he ignominiously fled from these questions of life, with its struggle of the propertied against the propertyless, to the realm of innocent utopias. This he calls "seeking answers to the questions of life in the ideal treatment of their burning and complex actual reality" (*Russkoye Bogatstvo*, No. 1), when, as a matter of fact, he did not even attempt to analyse and explain this actual reality.

Instead, he presented us with a utopia contrived by senselessly plucking individual elements from various social formations—taking one thing from the medieval form, another from the "new" form, and so on. It is obvious that a theory based on this was bound to stand aloof from actual social evolution, for the simple reason that our utopians had to live and act not under social relations formed from elements taken from here and from there, but under those which determine the relation of the peasant to the kulak (the enterprising muzhik), of the handicraftsman to the buyer-up, of the worker to the factory owner, and which they completely failed to understand. Their attempts and efforts to remould these un-understood relations in accordance with their ideal were bound to end in failure.

Such, in very general outline, was how the problem of socialism stood in Russia when "the Russian Marxists appeared on the scene."

What they began with was a criticism of the subjective methods of the earlier socialists. Not satisfied with merely stating the fact of exploitation and condemning it, they desired *to explain* it. Seeing that the whole post-Reform history of Russia consisted in the ruin of the masses and the enrichment of a minority, observing the colossal expropriation of the small producers side by side with universal technical progress, noting that these polarising tendencies arose and increased wherever, and to the extent that, commodity economy developed and became consolidated, they could not but conclude that they were confronted with a bourgeois (capitalist) organisation of social economy, *necessarily* giving rise to the expropriation and oppression of the masses. Their practical programme was directly determined by this conviction; this programme was to join in the struggle of the proletariat against the bourgeoisie, the struggle of the propertyless classes against the propertied, which constitutes the principal content of economic reality in Russia, from the most out-of-the-way village to the most up-to-date and perfected factory. How were they to join in? The answer was again suggested by reality. Capitalism had brought the principal branches of industry to the stage of large-scale machine industry; by thus socialising production, it had created the material conditions for a new system and had at the same time created a new social force—the class of factory workers, the urban proletariat. Being subjected to the same bourgeois exploitation—for such, in its economic essence, is the exploitation to which the whole working population of Russia is subjected—this class, however, has been placed in a special, favourable position as far as its emancipation is concerned: it no longer has any ties with the old society based entirely on exploitation; the very conditions of its labour and the circumstances of life organise it, compel it to think and enable it to step into the arena of political struggle. It was only natural that the Social-Democrats should direct all their attention to, and base all their hopes on, this class, that they should reduce their programme to the development of its class consciousness, and direct all their activities towards helping it rise to wage a direct political struggle against the present regime, and towards drawing the whole Russian proletariat into this struggle.

Let us now see how Mr. Mikhailovsky fights the Social-Democrats. What arguments does he level against their theoretical views, against their political, socialist activity?

The theoretical views of the Marxists are set forth by the critic in the following manner:

"The truth" (the Marxists are represented as declaring) "is that in accordance with the immanent laws of historical necessity Russia will develop her own capitalist production, with all its inherent contradictions and the swallowing up of the small capitalists by the large, and meanwhile the muzhik, divorced from the land, will turn into a proletarian, unite, become 'socialised,' and the trick is done, the hat reappears, and it only remains to put the hat on the head of now happy mankind."

And so, if you please, the Marxists do not differ in any way from the "friends of the people" in their conception of reality; they differ only in their idea of the future: they do not deal at all, it appears, with the present, but only with "prospects." There can be no doubt that this is Mr. Mikhailovsky's idea; the Marxists, he says, "are fully convinced that there is nothing utopian in their forecasts of the future, and that everything has been weighed and measured in accordance with the strict dictates of science"; finally and even more explicitly: the Marxists "believe in, and profess, the immutability of an abstract historical scheme."

In a word, we have before us that most banal and vulgar accusation against the Marxists long employed by all who have nothing substantial to bring against their views. "The Marxists profess the immutability of an abstract historical scheme!!"

But this is a downright lie and invention!

No Marxist has ever argued anywhere that there "must be" capitalism in Russia "because" there was capitalism in the West, and so on. No Marxist has ever regarded Marx's theory as some universally compulsory philosophical scheme of history, as anything more than an explanation of a particular social-economic formation. Only Mr. Mikhailovsky, the subjective philosopher, has managed to display such a lack of understanding of Marx as to attribute to him a universal philosophical theory; and in reply to this, he received from Marx the quite explicit explanation that he was knocking at the wrong door. No Marxist has ever based his Social-Democratic views on anything but the conformity of theory with reality and the history of the given, i.e., the Russian, social and economic relations; and he could not have done so, because this demand on theory was quite definitely and clearly proclaimed and made the corner-stone of the whole doctrine by the founder of "Marxism" himself—Marx.

Of course, Mr. Mikhailovsky may refute these statements as much as he pleases, by arguing that he has heard "with his own ears" the profession of an abstract historical scheme. But what does it matter to us, Social-Democrats, or to anybody else, that Mr. Mikhailovsky has had occasion to hear all sorts of absurd nonsense from people he has talked to? Does it not merely show that he is very fortunate in the choice of the people he talks to, and nothing more? It is very possible, of course, that the witty interlocutors of the witty philosopher called themselves Marxists, Social-Democrats, and so forth—but who does not know that nowadays (as was noted long ago) every scoundrel likes to array himself in "red" garments?* And if Mr. Mikhailovsky is so perspicacious that he cannot distinguish these "mummers" from Marxists, or if he has understood Marx so profoundly as not to have noticed this criterion—most emphatically advanced by Marx—of the whole doctrine (the formulation of "what is going on before our eyes"), it only proves again that Mr. Mikhailovsky is not clever, and nothing else.

At any rate, since he undertook a polemic in the press against the "Social-Democrats," he should have had in mind the group of socialists who have long borne that name and have borne it alone—so that others cannot be confused with them—and who have their literary representatives, Plekhanov and his circle.[62] And had he done so—and that obviously is what anybody with any decency should have done—and had he even consulted the first Social-Democratic work, Plekhanov's *Our Differences*, he would have found in its very first pages a categorical declaration made by the author on behalf of all the members of the circle:

"We in no case wish to cover our programme with the authority of a great name" (i.e., the authority of Marx). Do you understand Russian, Mr. Mikhailovsky? Do you understand the difference between professing abstract

* All this is said on the assumption that Mr. Mikhailovsky has indeed heard professions of abstract historical schemes and has not invented anything. But I consider it absolutely imperative in this connection to make the reservation that I give this only for what it is worth.

schemes and entirely disclaiming the authority of Marx when passing judgement on Russian affairs?

Do you realise that you acted dishonestly by representing the first opinion you happened to hear from your interlocutors as Marxist, and by ignoring the published declaration made by a prominent member of Social-Democracy on behalf of the whole group?

And then the declaration becomes even more explicit: "I repeat," Plekhanov says, "that the most consistent Marxists may disagree in the appraisal of the present Russian situation"; our doctrine is the "first attempt at applying this particular scientific theory to the analysis of very complicated and entangled social relations."

It would seem difficult to speak more clearly: the Marxists unreservedly borrow from Marx's theory only its invaluable methods, without which an elucidation of social relations is impossible, and, consequently, they see the criterion of their judgement of these relations not in abstract schemes and suchlike nonsense at all, but in its fidelity and conformity to reality.

Perhaps you think that in making these statements the author actually had something else in mind? But that is not so. The question he was dealing with was—"must Russia pass through the capitalist phase of development?" Hence, the question was not given a Marxist formulation at all, but was in conformity with the subjective methods of various native philosophers of ours, who see the criterion of this "must" in the policy of the authorities, or in the activities of "society," or in the ideal of a society that "corresponds to human nature," and similar twaddle. So it is fair to ask, how should a man who believes in abstract schemes have answered such a question? Obviously, he would have spoken of the incontrovertibility of the dialectical process, of the general philosophical importance of Marx's theory, of the inevitability of every country passing through the phase of ... and so on and so forth.

And how did Plekhanov answer it?

In the only way a Marxist could.

He left aside entirely the question of the "must," as being an idle one that could be of interest only to subjectivists, and dealt exclusively with real social and economic relations and their actual evolution. And that is why he gave no direct answer to this wrongly formulated question, but instead replied: "Russia *has entered* the capitalist path."

And Mr. Mikhailovsky talks with the air of an expert about belief in abstract historical schemes, about the immanent laws of necessity, and similar incredible nonsense! And he calls this "a polemic against the Social-Democrats"!!

If this is a polemicist, then I simply cannot understand what a windbag is!

One must also observe in connection with Mr. Mikhailovsky's argument quoted above that he presents the views of the Social-Democrats as being: "Russia *will develop* her own capitalist production." Evidently, in the opinion of this philosopher, Russia has not got "her own" capitalist production. The author apparently shares the opinion that Russian capitalism is confined to one and a half million workers. We shall later on again meet with this childish idea of our "friends of the people," who class all the other forms of exploitation of free labour under heaven knows what heading. "Russia will develop her own capitalist production with all its inherent contradictions, and meanwhile the muzhik, separated from the land, will turn into a proletarian." The farther in the wood, the more trees there are! So there are no "inherent contradictions" in Russia? Or, to put it plainly, there is no exploitation of the mass of the people by a handful of capitalists, there is no ruin of the vast majority of the population and no enrichment of a few? The muzhik has still to be separated from the land? But what is the entire post-Reform history of Russia, if not the wholesale expropriation of the peasantry, proceeding with unparalleled intensity? One must possess great courage indeed to say such things publicly. And Mr. Mikhailovsky possesses that courage: "Marx dealt with a ready-made proletariat and a ready-made capitalism, whereas we have still to create them." Russia has still to create a proletariat?! In Russia—the only country where such a hopeless poverty of the masses and such shameless exploitation of the working people can be found; which has been compared (and legitimately so) to England as regards the condition of the poor; and where the starvation of millions of people is a permanent thing existing side by side, for instance, with a steady increase in the export of grain—in Russia there is no proletariat!!

I think Mr. Mikhailovsky deserves to have a monument erected to him in his own lifetime for these classic words! *

We shall, incidentally, see later that it is a constant and most consistent tactic of the "friends of the people" to shut their eyes pharisaically to the intolerable condition of the working people in Russia, to depict this condition as having merely been "shaken," so that only the efforts of "cultured society" and the government are needed for everything to be put on the right track. These knights think that if they shut their eyes to the fact that the condition of the working masses is bad not because it has been "shaken," but because these masses are being shamelessly robbed by a handful of exploiters, that if they bury their heads in the sand like ostriches so as not to see these exploiters, the exploiters will disappear. And when the Social-Democrats tell them that it is shameful cowardice to fear to look reality in the face, when they take the fact of exploitation as their starting-point and say that its only possible explanation lies in the bourgeois organisation of Russian society, which is splitting the mass of the people into a proletariat and a bourgeoisie, and in the class character of the Russian state, which is nothing but the organ of the rule of this bourgeoisie, and that therefore *the only way out* lies in the class struggle of the proletariat against the bourgeoisie—these "friends of the people" begin to howl that the Social-Democrats want to dispossess the people of their land!! that they want to destroy our people's economic organisation!!

We now come to the most outrageous part of all this indecent, to say the least, "polemic," namely, Mr. Mikhai-

* But perhaps here, too, Mr. Mikhailovsky may try to wriggle out by declaring that he had no intention of saying that there was no proletariat at all in Russia, but only that there was no capitalist proletariat? Is that so? Then why did you not say so? The *whole question* is one of whether the Russian proletariat is a proletariat characteristic of the bourgeois or of some other organisation of social economy. Who is to blame if in the course of two whole articles you did not utter a *word* about this, the only serious and important question, but preferred instead to talk all sorts of nonsense, and reach the craziest conclusions?

lovsky's "criticism" (?) of the political activities of the Social-Democrats. Everybody realises that the activities carried on among the workers by socialists and agitators cannot be honestly discussed in our legal press, and that the only thing a decent censored periodical can do in this connection is to "maintain a tactful silence." Mr. Mikhailovsky has forgotten this very elementary rule, and has not scrupled to use his monopoly contact with the reading public in order to sling mud at the socialists.

However, means of combating this unscrupulous critic will be found even if outside of legal publications.

"As far as I understand," Mr. Mikhailovsky says with assumed naïvete, "the Russian Marxists can be divided into three categories: Marxist spectators (indifferent observers of the process), passive Marxists (they only "allay the birth pangs"; they "are not interested in the people on the land, and direct their attention and hopes to those who are already separated from the means of production"), and active Marxists (who bluntly insist on the further ruin of the countryside)."

What is this?! Mr. Critic must surely know that the Russian Marxists are socialists whose point of departure is the view that the reality of our environment is capitalist society, and that there is only one way out of it—the class struggle of the proletariat against the bourgeoisie. How, then, and on what grounds, does he mix them up with some sort of senseless vulgarity? What right (moral, of course) has he to extend the term Marxists to people who obviously do not accept the most elementary and fundamental tenets of Marxism, people who have never and nowhere acted as a distinct group and have never and nowhere announced a programme of their own?

Mr. Mikhailovsky has left himself a number of loopholes for justifying such outrageous methods.

"Perhaps," he jokes with the easy air of a society fop, "these are not real Marxists, but they consider and proclaim themselves as such." Where have they proclaimed it, and when? In the liberal and radical salons of St. Petersburg? In private letters? Be it so. Well, then, talk to them in your salons and in your correspondence! But you come out publicly and in the press against people who (under the banner of Marxism) have never come out publicly anywhere. And you have the effrontery to claim that you are polemising against "Social-Democrats," although you know that this name is borne only by *one* group of revolutionary socialists, and that nobody else should be confused with them!*

Mr. Mikhailovsky twists and turns like a schoolboy caught red-handed: I am not the least to blame here—he tries to make the reader believe—I "heard it with my own ears and saw it with my own eyes." Excellent! We are quite willing to believe that there is nobody in your field of vision but vulgarians and scoundrels. But what have we, Social-Democrats, to do with it? Who does not know that "at the present time, when" not only socialist activity, but any social activity that is at all independent and honest evokes political persecution—for every one actually working under some banner—be it Narodovolism,[63] Marxism, or even, let us say, constitutionalism—there are several score phrase-mongers who under cover of that name conceal their liberal cowardice, and, in addition, perhaps, several downright rascals who are feathering their own nests? Is it not obvious that only the meanest vulgarity could make any of these trends responsible for the fact that its banner is being soiled (privately and secretly, at that) by all sorts of riffraff? Mr. Mikhailovsky's whole argument is one chain of distortions, misrepresentations, and manipulations. We saw above that he completely distorted the "truths" which are the Social-Democrats' starting-point, presenting them

* I shall dwell on at least one *factual* reference which occurs in Mr. Mikhailovsky's article. Anybody who has read that article will have to admit that he includes even Mr. Skvortsov (author of *The Economic Causes of Starvation*) among the "Marxists." But, as a matter of fact, this gentleman does not call himself a Marxist, and the most elementary acquaintance with the works of the Social-Democrats is sufficient for anybody to see that from their standpoint he is nothing but a most vulgar bourgeois. What sort of Marxist is he if he does not understand that the social environment for which he projects his progressive schemes is a bourgeois environment, and that therefore all "agricultural improvements" actually to be observed even in peasant farming are bourgeois progress, which improves the position of a minority but proletarianises the masses! What sort of Marxist is he if he does not understand that the state to which he addresses his projects is a class state, capable only of supporting the bourgeoisie and oppressing the proletariat!

in a way in which no Marxist at any time or place has, or could have, presented them. And if he had set forth the actual Social-Democratic conception of Russian reality, he could not but have seen that one can "conform" to these views *in only one way*, namely, by helping to develop the class consciousness of the proletariat, by organising and uniting it for the political struggle against the present regime. He has, however, one other trick up his sleeve. With an air of injured innocence he pharisaically lifts up his eyes to heaven and unctuously declares: "I am very glad to hear that. But I cannot understand what you are protesting against" (that is exactly what he says in *Russkoye Bogatstvo*, No. 2). "Read my comment on passive Marxists more attentively and you will see that I say: from the ethical standpoint, no objection can be made."

This, of course, is nothing but a rehash of his former wretched subterfuges.

Tell us, please, how one would characterise the conduct of a person who declared that he was criticising social-revolutionary Narodism (at a time when no other type of Narodism had yet appeared—I take such a period), and who proceeded to say approximately the following:

"The Narodniks, as far as I understand, are divided into three categories: the consistent Narodniks, who completely accept the ideas of the muzhik and, in exact accordance with his desires, make a general principle of the birch and wife-beating and generally further the abominable policy of the government of the knout and the club, which, you know, has been called a people's policy; then, shall we say, the cowardly Narodniks, who are not interested in the opinions of the muzhik, and are only striving to transplant to Russia an alien revolutionary movement by means of associations and suchlike—against which, however, no objection can be made from the ethical standpoint, unless it be the slipperiness of the path, which may easily convert a cowardly Narodnik into a consistent or courageous one; and, lastly, the courageous Narodniks, who carry out to the full the people's ideals of the enterprising muzhik, and accordingly settle on the land in order to live as kulaks in good earnest." All decent people, of course, would characterise this as vile and vulgar scoffing. And if, furthermore, the person who said such things could not be rebutted by the Narodniks in the same press; if, moreover, the ideas of these Narodniks had hitherto been expounded only illegally, so that many people had no exact idea of what they were and might easily believe whatever they were told about the Narodniks—then whoever would agree that such a person is....

But perhaps Mr. Mikhailovsky himself has not yet quite forgotten the word that fits here.

But enough! Many similar insinuations by Mr. Mikhailovsky still remain, but I know of no job more fatiguing, more thankless and more disgusting than to have to wade through this filth, to collect insinuations scattered here and there, to compare them and to search for at least one serious objection.

Enough!

April 1894

PUBLISHER'S NOTE [64]

In the text of the article the reader will find references to a further examination of certain questions, whereas actually no such examination is made.

The reason is that the present article is only the first part of a reply to articles in *Russkoye Bogatstvo* about Marxism. Acute shortage of time prevented the timely appearance of this article, but we do not consider it possible to delay any longer; we are two months late as it is. That is why we have decided to issue an examination of Mr. Mikhailovsky's "criticism" in the meantime without waiting until the whole article is printed.

In the 2nd and 3rd parts, now in course of preparation, the reader will find, in addition to the examination here presented, a further one dealing with the social and economic views of other leading figures of *Russkoye Bogatstvo*, Messrs. Yuzhakov and S. Krivenko, in connection with an essay on the economic situation in Russia and the "ideas and tactics of the Social-Democrats" that follow therefrom.

NOTE TO THE PRESENT EDITION[63]

The present edition is an exact reproduction of the first. Having had no share whatever in compiling the text, we have not considered ourselves entitled to alter it in any way and have confined ourselves simply to the work of publication. Our motive for undertaking this work has been the confidence that the present pamphlet will serve to bring about some revival of our Social-Democratic propaganda.

Believing that one indispensable corollary of Social-Democratic convictions should be a readiness to promote such propaganda, we appeal to all who share the views of the author of the present pamphlet to assist by every means (especially, of course, by republication) in securing the widest possible circulation both of the present work and of all organs of Marxist propaganda in general. The present moment is particularly opportune. *Russkoye Bogatstvo* is assuming an increasingly provocative tone towards us. In an effort to paralyse the spread of Social-Democratic ideas in society, that magazine has gone so far as to accuse us outright of being indifferent to the interests of the proletariat and of insisting on the ruination of the masses. We make bold to think that by such methods it will only injure itself and pave the way for our victory. However, it should not be forgotten that these slanderers command all the material means for the most widespread propaganda of their slanders. They possess a magazine with a circulation of several thousand; they have reading-rooms and libraries at their disposal. Hence, if we are to prove to our enemies that even the advantages of a privileged position do not always ensure the success of insinuation, we must exert our every effort. We are fully confident that this effort will be forthcoming.

July 1894

PART III

Выпускъ III.

Что такое „друзья народа"

и

какъ они воюютъ противъ

соціал-демократовъ.

Сентябрь 1894.

Изданіе
провинціальной группы
соціал-демократовъ.

Cover of Part III, hectographed edition, of Lenin's *What the "Friends of the People" Are and How They Fight the Social-Democrats*, 1894

Reduced

Let us, in conclusion, make the acquaintance of Mr. Krivenko, another "friend of the people," who also launches open war against the Social-Democrats.

However, we shall not examine his articles ("Our Cultural Free Lances," in No. 12, 1893, and "Travel Letters," in No. 1, 1894) as we did those of Messrs. Mikhailovsky and Yuzhakov. An analysis in toto of their articles was essential to get a clear idea, in the first case, of the substance of their objections to materialism and Marxism in general, and, in the second, of their political-economic theories. Now, to get a complete idea of the "friends of the people," we shall have to acquaint ourselves with their tactics, their practical proposals and their political programme. This programme they have not anywhere set forth directly and as consistently and fully as they have set out their theoretical views. I am therefore obliged to take it from various articles in a magazine whose contributors are unanimous enough not to contradict each other. I shall give preference to the above-mentioned articles of Mr. Krivenko's merely because they furnish more material and because their author is as typical of the magazine as a practical man and a politician, as Mr. Mikhailovsky is a socialist and Mr. Yuzhakov is an economist.

However, before passing on to their programme, there is one more theoretical point we consider it absolutely essential to deal with. We have seen how Mr. Yuzhakov disposes of matters with meaningless phrases about people's land renting that supports people's economy, etc., using them to cover up the fact that he does not understand the economic life of our peasants. He did not deal with the handicraft industries, but confined himself to data on the growth of large-scale factory industry. Now Mr. Krivenko repeats exactly the same sort of phrases about handicraft industries. He flatly contrasts "our people's industry," i.e., handicraft industries, to capitalist industry (No. 12, pp. 180-81). "People's production" (sic!), says he, "in the majority of cases arises naturally," whereas capitalist industry "is very often created artificially." In another passage he contrasts "small-scale people's industry" to "large-scale, capitalist industry." If you were to ask what is the distinguishing feature of the former, you would only learn that it is "small"* and that the instruments of labour are united with the producer (I borrow this latter definition from Mr. Mikhailovsky's above-mentioned article). But this is certainly far from defining its economic organisation—and, moreover, is absolutely untrue. Mr. Krivenko says, for example, that "small-scale people's industry to this day yields a much larger total output and employs more hands than large-scale capitalist industry." The author is evidently referring to data on the number of handicraftsmen, which is as many as 4 million, or, according to another estimate, 7 million. But who does not know that the form of economy predominating in our handicraft industries is the domestic system of large-scale production? that the bulk of the handicraftsmen occupy a position in production that is not independent at all, but completely dependent, subordinate, that they do not process their own material but that of the merchant, who merely pays the handicraftsman a wage? Data on the predominance of this form have been cited even in legal literature. Let me quote, for example, the excellent work by the well-known statistician, S. Kharizomenov, published in *Yuridichesky Vestnik*[66] (1883, Nos. 11 and 12). Summarising the published data on our handicraft industries in the central gubernias, where they are most highly developed, S. Kharizomenov reached the conclusion that there is an absolute predominance of the domestic system of large-scale production, i.e., an unquestionably capitalist form of industry. "Defining the economic role of small-scale independent industry," he says, "we arrive

* The only other thing you would learn is this: "From it may develop a real (sic!) people's industry," says Mr. Krivenko. A common trick of the "friends of the people" is to utter idle and senseless phrases instead of giving a precise and direct description of reality.

at the following conclusions: in Moscow Gubernia 86.5% of the annual turnover of handicraft industry is accounted for by the domestic system of large-scale production, and only 13.5% by small-scale independent industry. In the Alexandrov and Pokrov uyezds of Vladimir Gubernia, 96% of the annual turnover of handicraft industry falls to the share of the domestic system of large-scale production and manufacture, and only 4% is accounted for by small-scale independent industry."

Nobody, as far as we know, has tried to refute these facts; nor can they be refuted. How, then, can one ignore these facts, and say nothing about them, call such industry "people's" in contradistinction to capitalist, and talk about the possibility of its developing into real industry?

There can be only one explanation of this direct ignoring of facts, namely, the general tendency of the "friends of the people," as of all Russian liberals, to gloss over class antagonism and the exploitation of the working people in Russia by representing all this as just plain "defects." But perhaps, an additional cause lies in so profound a knowledge of the subject as is revealed, for instance, by Mr. Krivenko when he calls the "Pavlovo cutlery trade"—"a trade of a semi-artisan character." The lengths of distortion to which the "friends of the people" will go are simply phenomenal! How can one speak here of artisan character, when the Pavlovo cutlers produce for the market and not to order? Or perhaps Mr. Krivenko regards as artisan industry the system under which a merchant orders articles from the handicraftsman and then sends them to Nizhni-Novgorod Fair? Funnily enough, this seems to be the case. As a matter of fact, the making of cutlery has least of all (compared with other Pavlovo industries) preserved the small-scale handicraft form, with its (seeming) independence of the producers. "The production of table and industrial cutlery,"* says N. F. Annensky, "is already largely approaching the factory, or, more correctly, the manufactory form." Of the 396 handicraftsmen engaged in the making of table cutlery in Nizhni-Novgorod Gubernia, only 62

* The largest of the Pavlovo trades, which produces 900,000 rubles' worth of goods out of a total output of 2,750,000 rubles.

(16%) work for the market, 273 (69%) work for a master,* and 61 (15%) are wage-workers. Hence, only one-sixth of them are not directly enslaved to an employer. As to the other branch of the cutlery industry—the production of folding-knives (penknives)—the same author says that it "occupies a position midway between the table-knife and the lock: the majority of the handicraftsmen in this branch are working for a master, but along with them there are still quite a number of independent handicraftsmen who have to do with the market."

In Nizhni-Novgorod Gubernia there are in all 2,552 handicraftsmen producing this sort of cutlery, of whom 48% (1,236) work for the market, 42% (1,058) work for a master, and 10% (258) are wage-workers. Consequently, here too the independent (?) handicraftsmen are in the minority. And those who work for the market are, of course, only apparently independent; actually they are no less enslaved to the *capital* of buyers-up. If we take the data for the industries of the entire Gorbatov Uyezd, Nizhni-Novgorod Gubernia, where 21,983 working people, or 84.5%, *of all who work*,** are engaged in industries, we get the following (exact data on the economics of the industry are available for only 10,808 workers, in the following industries: metal, leather goods, saddlery, felt, and hemp spinning): 35.6% of the handicraftsmen work for the market, 46.7% work for a master, and 17.7% are wage-workers. Thus, *here too we see the predominance of the domestic system of large-scale production, the predominance of relations under which labour is enslaved to capital.*

Another reason why the "friends of the people" so freely ignore facts of this kind is that their conception of capitalism has not advanced beyond the commonplace vulgar idea that a capitalist is a wealthy and educated employer who runs a large machine enterprise—and they refuse to

* I.e., for the merchant who supplies the handicraftsmen with materials and pays them ordinary wages for their labour.

** Exceptionalist Russian economists, who measure Russian capitalism by the number of factory workers (sic!), unceremoniously classify these working people, and the multitudes like them, as part of the agricultural population, who do not suffer from the yoke of capital, but from pressure artificially exerted on the "people's system" (???!!)

consider the scientific content of the term. In the preceding chapter we saw that Mr. Yuzhakov dates the beginning of capitalism directly from machine industry, omitting simple co-operation and manufacture. This is a widespread error, which, incidentally, results in the capitalist organisation of our handicraft industries being ignored.

It goes without saying that the domestic system of large-scale production is a capitalist form of industry: here we have all its features—commodity economy already at a high level of development, the concentration of the means of production in the hands of individuals, and the expropriation of the mass of the workers, who have no means of production of their own and therefore apply their labour to those of others, working not for themselves but for the capitalist. Obviously, in its organisation, handicraft industry is pure capitalism; it differs from large-scale machine industry in being technically backward (chiefly because of the preposterously low wages) and in the fact that the workers retain diminutive farms. This latter circumstance particularly confuses the "friends of the people," who, as befits true metaphysicians, are accustomed to think in naked and direct contrasts: "Yea, yea—nay, nay, and whatsoever is more than these comes from the evil one."

If the workers have no land—there is capitalism; if they have land—there is no capitalism. And they confine themselves to this soothing philosophy, losing sight of the whole social organisation of economy and forgetting the generally-known fact that ownership of land does not in the least do away with the dire poverty of these landowners, who are most shamelessly robbed by other such "peasant" landowners.

They do not know, it seems, that capitalism—while still at a comparatively low level of development—was nowhere able to completely separate the worker from the land. For Western Europe, Marx established the law that only large-scale machine industry expropriates the worker once and for all. It is therefore obvious that the stock argument of there being no capitalism in our country since "the people own land" is quite meaningless, because the capitalism of simple co-operation and manufacture has never been connected anywhere with the worker's complete separation from the land, and yet, needless to say, it has not on that account ceased to be capitalism.

As to large-scale machine industry in Russia—and this form is rapidly being assumed by the biggest and most important branches of our industry—here too, despite all the specific features of our life, it possesses the same property as everywhere in the capitalist West, namely, it absolutely will not tolerate the retention of the worker's tie with the land. This fact has been proved, incidentally, by Dementyev with precise statistical material, from which he has drawn (quite independently of Marx) the conclusion that machine production is inseparably connected with the worker's complete separation from the land. This investigation has demonstrated once again that Russia is a capitalist country, that the worker's tie with the land in Russia is so feeble and unreal, and the power of the man of property (the money owner, the buyer-up, the rich peasant, the manufactory owner, etc.) so firmly established, that one more technical advance will be enough for the "peasant" (?? who has long been living by the sale of his labour-power) to turn into a worker pure and simple.* The failure of the "friends of the people" to understand the economic organisation of our handicraft industries is far, however, from being confined to this. Their idea even of those industries where work is not done "for a master" is just as superficial as their idea of the cultivator (which we have already seen above). This, by the way, is quite natural in the case of gentlemen who presume to hold forth on questions of political economy when all they know, it seems, is that there is such a thing in the world as means of production, which "may" be united with the working people—and that is very good; but which "may" also be separated from them—and that is very bad. That will not take you far.

Speaking of industries that are becoming capitalist and of those that are not (where "small-scale production can

* The domestic system of large-scale production is not only a capitalist system, but the worst kind of capitalist system, one under which the most intense exploitation of the working people is combined with the minimum opportunity for the workers to wage a struggle for their emancipation.

freely exist"), Mr. Krivenko says, for one thing, that in certain branches "the basic expenditure on production" is very inconsiderable and that small-scale production is therefore possible. He cites as an example the brick industry, where the expenditure, he says, may be one-fifteenth of the annual turnover of the brickyards.

As this is almost the only reference the author makes to facts (it is, I repeat, the most characteristic feature of subjective sociology that it fears a direct and precise description and analysis of reality, preferring to soar into the sphere of the "ideals"... of the petty bourgeois), let us take it, in order to show what a false conception the "friends of the people" have of reality.

We find a description of the brick industry (the making of bricks from white clay) in the economic statistics of the Moscow Zemstvo (*Returns*, Vol. VII, Book 1, Part 2, etc.). The industry is chiefly concentrated in three volosts of Bogorodskoye Uyezd, where there are 233 establishments, employing 1,402 workers (567, or 41%, being family workers,* and 835, or 59%, hired), with an annual aggregate output valued at 357,000 rubles. The industry is an old one, but has developed particularly during the past fifteen years owing to the building of a railway, which has greatly facilitated marketing. Before the railway was built the family form of production predominated, but it is now giving way to the exploitation of wage-labour. This industry, too, is not exempt from the dependence of the small industrialists on the bigger ones for marketing: owing to "lack of funds" the former sell the latter their bricks (sometimes "crude"—unbaked) on the spot at terribly low prices.

However, we are also able to acquaint ourselves with the organisation of the industry apart from this dependence, thanks to the house-to-house census of handicraftsmen which is appended to the essay, where the number of workers and the annual aggregate output of each establishment are indicated.

To ascertain whether the law that commodity economy is capitalist economy—i.e., is inevitably converted into the latter at a certain stage of development—applies to

* By "family" workers, as against hired, are meant working members of the masters' families.

this industry, we must compare the size of the establishments: the problem is precisely one of the relation between the small and the large establishments according to their role in output and their exploitation of wage-labour. Taking the number of workers as a basis, we divide the establishments of the handicraftsmen into three groups: I) establishments employing 1 to 5 workers (both family and hired); II) employing 6 to 10 workers, and III) employing over 10 workers.

Examining the size of establishments, the complement of workers and the value of the output in each group, we obtain the following data:

Groups of handicraftsmen according to number of workers	Avg. number workers per establishment	Per cent		Ann. output per worker (rubles)	Percentage distribution			Absolute figures		
		Estabs. employing w.-wkrs.	Wage-workers		Establishments	Workers	Total output	Number of establishments*	Number of workers	Total output (rubles)
I. Employing 1-5 workers	2.8	25	19	251	72	34	34	167/43	476/92	119,500
II. Employing 6-10 workers	7.3	90	58	249	18	23	22	43/39	317/186	79,000
III. Employing over 10 workers	26.4	100	91	260	10	43	44	23/23	609/557	158,500
Total	6.0	45	59	254	100	100	100	233/105	1,402/835	357,000

Take a glance at these figures and you will perceive the bourgeois, or, what is the same, the capitalist organisation of the industry: the larger the establishments, the higher the productivity of labour** (the middle group is an

* The denominators indicate the number of establishments employing wage-workers and the number of wage-workers. Same in the next table.

** The annual output per worker in Group I is 251 rubles; in II—249, in III—260.

exception), the greater the exploitation of wage-labour,* the greater the concentration of production.**

The third group, which almost entirely bases its economy on wage-labour, comprises 10% of the total number of establishments but accounts for 44% of the aggregate output.

This concentration of the means of production in the hands of a minority, which is connected with the expropriation of the majority (the wage-workers), explains both the dependence of the small producers on buyers-up (the big industrialists are in fact buyers-up) and the oppression of labour in this industry. Hence we see that the *cause* of the expropriation of the working people and of their exploitation lies in the production relations themselves.

The Russian Narodnik socialists, as we know, held the opposite view and considered that the cause of the oppression of labour in the handicraft industries did not lie in production relations (which were proclaimed to be based on a principle which precludes exploitation), but in something else—in policy, namely, agrarian and fiscal policy and so on. The question arises, what was, and is, the basis of the persistence of this opinion, which has now acquired almost the tenacity of a prejudice? Maybe it is the prevalence of a *different* concept of production relations in the handicraft industries? Not at all. It persists only because no attempt whatever is made *to give an accurate and definite description of the facts, of the real forms of economic organisation*; it persists only because the production relations are not singled out and submitted to an independent analysis. In a word, it persists solely due to a failure to understand the only scientific method of social science, namely, the materialist method. We can now understand the train of thought of our old socialists. As far as the handicraft industries are concerned, they attribute the cause of exploitation to things lying *outside* production relations; as far as large-scale, factory capitalism

* The proportion of establishments employing wage-labour is 25% in Group I, 90% in II and 100% in III; the proportion of wage-workers is 19%, 58% and 91% respectively.

** Group I, comprising 72% of the total establishments, accounts for 34% of the total output; II: 18% of the establishments, 22% of the output; III: 10% of the establishments, 44% of the output.

is concerned, they could not help seeing that *there* the cause of exploitation lies precisely in the production relations. The result was an irreconcilable contradiction, an incongruity; where this large-scale capitalism could have come from, since there was nothing capitalist in the production relations of the handicraft industries (which had not been studied!)—passed comprehension. The conclusion follows naturally: failing to understand the connection between handicraft and capitalist industry they contrasted the former to the latter, as "people's" to "artificial" industry. The idea appears that capitalism contradicts our "people's system"—an idea that is very widespread and was quite recently presented to the Russian public in a revised and improved edition by Mr. Nikolai —on. This idea persists by inertia, despite its phenomenal illogicality: factory capitalism is judged on the basis of what it actually is in reality, whereas handicraft industry is judged on the basis of what it "might be"; the former on the basis of an analysis of production relations, the latter without even an attempt to examine the production relations separately, the matter being directly transferred to the sphere of politics. We have only to turn to an analysis of these production relations to find that the "people's system" consists of these very same capitalist production relations, although in an undeveloped, embryonic state; that—if we reject the naïve prejudice that all handicraftsmen are equal, and accurately set forth the differences among them—the difference between the "capitalist" of the factory and works and the "handicraftsman" will at times prove to be less than the difference between one "handicraftsman" and another; and that *capitalism does not contradict the "people's system" but is the direct, next and immediate continuation and development of it.*

Perhaps, however, it will be argued that the example quoted is unsuitable; we may be told that the percentage of wage-workers in the given case is altogether too high?* But, as a matter of fact, the important thing here is not the absolute figures but the *relations* they disclose, rela-

* This is scarcely true of the industries of Moscow Gubernia, but it may be true, perhaps, with regard to the less developed industries of the rest of Russia.

tions which are bourgeois in essence, and which do not cease to be such whether their bourgeois character is strongly or weakly marked.

If you like, I shall take another example—one deliberately chosen for its weak bourgeois character. I take (from Mr. Isayev's book on the industries of Moscow Gubernia) the pottery industry, "a purely domestic industry," as the professor calls it. This industry may, of course, be taken as representative of the small-scale peasant industries: its technique is the simplest, its equipment quite small and the articles it produces of universal and essential use. Well then, thanks to the house-to-house census of the potters giving the same particulars as in the previous case, we are in a position to study the economic organisation of this industry too, one that is undoubtedly quite typical of the numerous Russian small, "people's" industries. We divide the handicraftsmen into groups: I) those employing 1 to 3 workers (family and hired); II) those employing 4 to 5 workers, and III) those employing over 5 workers—and make the same calculation:

Groups of handicraftsmen according to number of workers	Avg. number wkrs. per establishment	Per cent		Ann. output per worker (rubles)	Percentage distribution			Absolute figures		
		Estab. employing w.-wkrs.	Wage-workers		Establishments	Workers	Total output	Number of establishments	Number of workers	Total output (rubles)
I. Employing 1-3 workers	2.4	39	19	468	60	38	36	72/28	174/33	81,500
II. Employing 4-5 workers	4.3	48	20	498	27	32	32	33/16	144/29	71,800
III. Employing over 5 workers	8.4	100	65	533	13	30	32	16/16	134/87	71,500
Total	3.7	49	33	497	100	100	100	121/60	452/149	224,800

Obviously, the *relations* in this industry too—and similar examples could be quoted indefinitely—are bourgeois: we find the same break-up arising out of commodity economy and it is a specifically capitalist break-up, leading to the exploitation of wage-labour, which already plays a primary part in the top group, where one-eighth of all the establishments and 30% of the total workers produce nearly one-third of the total output, and the productivity of labour is considerably above the average. These production relations alone are enough to explain the appearance and power of the buyers-up. We see how a minority, owning larger and more profitable establishments, and receiving a "net" income from the labour of others (in the top group of potters there is an average of 5.5 wage-workers per establishment), accumulate "savings," while the majority are ruined, and even the petty masters (not to mention the wage-workers) are unable to make ends meet. It is obvious and inevitable that the latter should be enslaved to the former—inevitable precisely because of the capitalist character of the given production relations. These relations are: the product of social labour, organised by commodity economy, passes into the hands of individuals and in their hands serves as an instrument for oppressing and enslaving the working people, as a means of personal enrichment by the exploitation of the masses. And do not think that this exploitation, this oppression, is any less marked because relations of this kind are still poorly developed, because the accumulation of *capital*, concomitant with the ruination of the producers, is negligible. Quite the contrary. This only leads to cruder, serf forms of exploitation, to a situation where capital, not yet able to subjugate the worker directly, by the mere purchase of his labour-power at its value, enmeshes him in a veritable net of usurious extortion, binds him to itself by kulak methods, and as a result robs him not only of the surplus-value, but of an enormous part of his wages, too, and, what is more, grinds him down by preventing him from changing his "master," and humiliates him by compelling him to regard as a boon the fact that capital "gives" (sic!) him work. It is obvious that not a single worker would ever consent to exchange his status for that of a Russian "independent" handicraftsman in "real," "people's" industry. It is equally obvious that all the favourite measures of the Russian radicals either will not in the least affect the exploitation of the working people and their enslavement to capital, and will remain isolated experiments (artels), or will worsen the conditions of the working people (inalienability of allotments), or, lastly, will only refine, develop and consolidate the given capitalist relations (improvement of technique, loans, etc.).

The "friends of the people," however, will never be able to grasp the fact that despite its general wretchedness, its comparatively tiny establishments and extremely low productivity of labour, its primitive technique and small number of wage-workers, peasant industry is *capitalism*. They simply cannot grasp the point that *capital* is a certain relation between people, a relation which remains the same whether the categories under comparison are at a higher or a lower level of development. Bourgeois economists have never been able to understand this; they have always objected to such a definition of capital. I recall how one of them, writing in *Russkaya Mysl* about Sieber's book (on Marx's theory), quoted this definition (capital is a relation), and indignantly put exclamation marks after it.

To regard the categories of the bourgeois regime as eternal and natural is most typical of bourgeois philosophers. That is why, for capital, too, they adopt such definitions as, for example, accumulated labour that serves for further production—that is, describe it as an eternal category of human society, thereby obscuring that specific, historically definite economic formation in which this "accumulated labour," organised by commodity economy, falls into the hands of those who do not work and serves for the exploitation of the labour of others. That is why, instead of an analysis and study of a definite system of production relations, they give us a series of banalities applicable to any system, mixed with the sentimental pap of petty-bourgeois morality.

And now look at this—why do the "friends of the people" call this industry "people's," and why do they contrast it to capitalist industry? It is only because these gentlemen are petty-bourgeois ideologists and cannot even conceive that these small producers live and operate under a system of commodity economy (that is why I call them petty bourgeois) and that their relations to the market necessarily and inevitably split them into a bourgeoisie and a proletariat. Why don't you try studying the real organisation of our "people's" industries instead of phrase-mongering about what they "might" lead to, then we will see whether you can *find in Russia any branch of handicraft industry, at all developed, which is not organised on capitalist lines.*

And if you do not agree that the monopolising of the means of production by a minority, their alienation from the majority, and the exploitation of wage-labour (speaking more generally, the essence of capitalism is the appropriation by individuals of the product of social labour organised by commodity economy) are necessary and adequate features for this concept, then be good enough to give your "own" definition and your "own" history of capitalism.

Actually, the organisation of our "people's" handicraft industries furnishes an excellent illustration to the general history of the development of capitalism. It clearly demonstrates the latter's origin, its inception, for example, in the form of simple co-operation (the top group in the pottery industry); it further shows how the "savings" that—thanks to commodity economy—accumulate in the hands of separate individuals become *capital*, which first monopolises marketing ("buyers-up" and traders), owing to the fact that only the owners of these "savings" possess the necessary funds for wholesale disposal, which enable them to wait until the goods are sold in distant markets; how, further, this merchant capital enslaves the mass of producers and organises capitalist manufacture, the capitalist domestic system of large-scale production; and how, finally, the expansion of the market and increasing competition lead to improved techniques, and how this merchant capital becomes industrial capital and organises large-scale machineproduction. And when this capital, having grown strong and enslaved millions of working people and whole districts, begins openly and brazenly to exert pressure on the government and turns it into its lackey—our ingenious "friends of the people" raise a howl about "the implanting of capitalism," about its "artificial creation"!

A timely discovery, indeed!

So that when Mr. Krivenko talks about people's, real, proper, etc., industry, he is simply trying to conceal the fact that our handicraft industries are nothing but capitalism at various stages of development. We have already become sufficiently acquainted with these methods in the case of Mr. Yuzhakov, who, instead of studying the peasant Reform, used empty phrases about the fundamental aim of the momentous Manifesto,[67] etc.; who, instead of studying land renting, dubbed it people's renting; and who, instead of studying how a home market is being formed for capitalism, philosophised about the latter's inevitable collapse from lack of markets, and so on.

To show how far Messrs. the "friends of the people" distort the facts, I shall dwell on one more example.* Our subjective philosophers so rarely condescend to give us precise references to facts that it would be unfair to ignore one of these most precise references of theirs, namely, the one Mr. Krivenko makes (No. 1, 1894) to the budgets of the Voronezh peasants. Here, on the basis of data selected by themselves, we may make quite sure which idea of reality is more correct—that of the Russian radicals and "friends of the people," or that of the Russian Social-Democrats.

Mr. Shcherbina, a Voronezh Zemstvo statistician, appends to his description of peasant farming in Ostrogozhsk Uyezd 24 budgets of typical peasant households, and analyses them in the text.**

---

* Although this example concerns the break-up of the peasantry, about which much has already been said, I consider it necessary to analyse *their own data* in order to show clearly what an insolent lie it is to assert that the Social-Democrats are interested not in reality but in "prophesying the future," and what charlatan methods the "friends of the people" use when in their controversies with us they ignore the substance of our views and dispose of them with nonsensical phrases.

** *Statistical Returns for Voronezh Gubernia*, Vol. II, Part II. *Peasant Farming in Ostrogozhsk Uyezd*, Voronezh, 1887. The budgets are given in the appendices, pp. 42-49, and the analysis in Chapter XVIII: "Composition and Budgets of Peasant Households."

Mr. Krivenko reproduces this analysis, failing, or rather refusing, to see that its methods are entirely unsuited to the purpose of getting an idea of the economy of our peasant farmers. The fact is that these 24 budgets depict entirely different households—prosperous, middle and poor—as Mr. Krivenko himself points out (p. 159); but, like Mr. Shcherbina, he simply employs *average* figures, lumping together the most different types of households, and thus completely disguises the fact of their differentiation. Yet the differentiation of our small producers is such a general, such a major fact (to which the Social-Democrats have long been drawing the attention of Russian socialists. See the works of Plekhanov.) that it is brought out quite distinctly even by the scanty data selected by Mr. Krivenko. Instead, when dealing with the *farming* of the peasants, of dividing them into categories according to the size of their farms and type of farming, he, like Mr. Shcherbina, divides them into legal categories—former state and former landlords' peasants—directing all his attention to the greater prosperity of the former as compared with the latter, and loses sight of the fact that the differences among the peasants within these categories are far greater than the differences between the categories.* To prove this, I divide these 24 budgets into three groups. I pick out a) 6 prosperous peasants, then b) 11 peasants of average prosperity (Nos. 7 to 10 and 16 to 22 in Shcherbina's table) and c) 7 poor peasants (Nos. 11 to 15, 23 and 24 in Shcherbina's table of budgets). Mr. Krivenko says, for example, that the expenditure per farm of the former state peasants is 541.3 rubles, and of the former landlords' peasants 417.7 rubles. But he overlooks the fact that the expenditures of different peasants are far from being equal: among the former state peasants, for instance, there is one with an expenditure of 84.7 rubles and another with an expenditure *ten times as large*—887.4 rubles (even if we leave out the

* Undoubtedly, the farm of a peasant who lives exclusively by agricultural pursuits and employs a labourer differs in type from the farm of a peasant who lives as a farm labourer and gets three-fifths of his earnings by farm-labouring. And among these 24 peasants there are both types. Judge for yourselves what kind of "science" will result if we lump together farm labourers and farmers who employ labourers, and make use of a general average!

German colonist with an expenditure of 1,456.2 rubles). What meaning can an average have if it is derived by lumping such magnitudes together? If we take the division into categories that I give, we find that the average expenditure per farm of a prosperous peasant is 855.86 rubles, of a middle peasant 471.61 rubles, and of a poor peasant 223.78 rubles.*

The ratio is, roughly, 4 : 2 : 1.

Let us proceed. Following in Shcherbina's footsteps, Mr. Krivenko gives the expenditure on personal requirements among the various legal categories of peasants: among the former state peasants, for example, the annual expenditure per person on vegetable food is 13.4 rubles, and among the former landlords' peasants 12.2 rubles. But if we take them according to economic categories, the figures are: a) 17.7; b) 14.5 and c) 13.1 The expenditure on meat and dairy produce per person among the former landlords' peasants is 5.2 rubles and among the former state peasants 7.7 rubles. Taken by economic categories the figures are 11.7, 5.8 and 3.6 respectively. It is obvious that calculation according to legal categories merely conceals these huge divergences and nothing more. It is, therefore, obviously worthless. The income of the former state peasants is greater than the income of the former landlords' peasants by 53.7 per cent—says Mr. Krivenko: the general average (for the 24 budgets) is 539 rubles; and for the two categories, over 600 rubles and about 400 rubles, respectively. But if graded according to economic strength, the incomes are a) 1,053.2 rubles, b) 473.8 rubles and c) 202.4 rubles, or a fluctuation of 10 : 2, and not 3 : 2.

"The capital value of a peasant farm among the former state peasants is 1,060 rubles, and among the former landlords' peasants 635 rubles," says Mr. Krivenko. But if we take the economic categories,** the figures are a) 1,737.91 rubles, b) 786.42 rubles and c) 363.38 rubles—again a fluctuation of 10 : 2, and not 3 : 2. By dividing the "peasantry" into legal categories the author prevented himself from

* The fluctuation in the size of the average family is much less: a) 7.83, b) 8.36, and c) 5.28 persons per family.

** The divergence is greater still in the value of implements owned. The average is 54.83 rubles per household. But among the forming a correct judgement of the economics of this "peasantry."

If we examine the farms of the various types of peasants according to economic strength, we find that the prosperous families have an average income of 1,053.2 rubles, and expenditure of 855.86 rubles, or a net income of 197.34 rubles. The middle family has an income of 473.8 rubles and an expenditure of 471.61 rubles, or a net income of 2.19 rubles per farm (and that without counting credit debts and arrears)—obviously, it can barely make ends meet: out of 11 farms, 5 have a deficit. The bottom, poor, group run their farms at a direct loss: with an income of 202.4 rubles their expenditure is 223.78 rubles, which means a deficit of 21.38 rubles.* It is evident that if we lump farms together and strike a general average (net income—44.11 rubles) we completely distort the real picture. We then overlook the fact (as Mr. Krivenko has done) that all the six prosperous peasants who secure a net income employ farm labourers (8 of them)—a fact which reveals the character of their farming (they are in process of becoming capitalist farmers), which yields them a net income and relieves them almost entirely of the need to resort to "industries." These farmers all together cover only 6.5% of their budgets by industries (412 rubles out of a total of 6,319.5); moreover, these industries—as Mr. Shcherbina in one place remarks—are of such a type as "carting," or even "dealing in sheep," that is, such as, far from indicating dependence, presuppose the exploitation of others (precisely in the second case: accumulated "savings" are converted into merchant *capital*). These peasants own 4 industrial establishments, which yield an income of 320 rubles (5% of the total).**

The economy of the middle peasants is of a different type: they, as we have seen, can barely make ends meet.

---

well-to-do peasants it is twice as much—111.80 rubles, and among the poor peasants one-third the amount—16.04 rubles. Among the middle peasants it is 48.44 rubles.

* It is interesting to note that the budgets of the farm labourers—two out of the seven poor peasants—show no deficit: income 99 rubles and expenditure 93.45 rubles per family. One of the farm labourers is fed, clothed and shod by his master.

** See Appendix I (p. 301 of this volume.—*Ed.*).

Farming does not cover their needs, and 19% of their income is from so-called industries. What sort of industries these are we learn from Mr. Shcherbina's article. They are given for 7 peasants: only two engage in independent industries (tailoring and charcoal-burning); the remaining 5 sell their labour-power ("went mowing in the lowlands,"* "works at a distillery," "does day-labouring at harvest-time," "herds sheep," "worked on the local estate"). These are already half peasants, half workers. Side occupations divert them from their farming and thus undermine it completely.

As to the poor peasants, they farm at a dead loss; the significance of "industries" in their budgets is still greater (providing 24% of the income), and these industries amount almost entirely (except in the case of one peasant) to the sale of labour-power. In the case of two of them, "industries" (farm-labouring) predominate, providing two-thirds of their income.

It is quite clear that what we have here is a process of the complete differentiation of the small producers, the upper groups of whom are being turned into a bourgeoisie, the lower into a proletariat. Naturally, if we take general averages we shall see nothing of this and get no idea of the economics of the countryside.

It was only his operations with these fictitious averages that enabled the author to adopt the following method. To determine the place of these typical farms in the peasant farming of the uyezd as a whole, Mr. Shcherbina groups the peasants according to the size of their allotments, and it transpires that the level of prosperity (general average) of the 24 farms selected is higher by about one-third than the average in the uyezd. This calculation cannot be regarded as satisfactory, both because there is great divergence among these 24 peasants and because the classification according to size of allotment conceals the differentiation of the peasantry: the author's thesis that the "allotments are the prime cause of the prosperity" of the peasant is absolutely wrong. Everybody knows that the "equal" distribution of land within the village community does not in any way prevent its horseless members from giv-

* Peasants from Voronezh Gubernia hired themselves out to rich Cossacks in the Don lowlands for the haymaking.—*Ed. Eng. ed.*

ing up the land, letting it, going away to work and turning into proletarians; or the members with many horses from renting large tracts of land and running big and profitable farms. If, for example, we take our 24 budgets, we shall see that one rich peasant, with 6 dessiatines of allotment land, has a total income of 758.5 rubles; a middle peasant, with 7.1 dessiatines of allotment land, 391.5 rubles; and a poor peasant, with 6.9 dessiatines of allotment land, 109.5 rubles. In general, we have seen that the ratio of the incomes of the various groups is 4 : 2 : 1; while the ratio of allotment land is 22.1 : 9.2 : 8.5, which equals 2.6 : 1.08 : 1. This is quite natural, for we find, for example, that the rich peasants, with 22.1 dessiatines of allotment land per household, rent an additional 8.8 dessiatines each, whereas the middle peasants, who have smaller allotments (9.2 dessiatines), rent less—7.7 dessiatines, and the poor peasants, with still smaller allotments (8.5 dessiatines), rent only 2.8 dessiatines.* And so, when Mr. Krivenko says: "Unfortunately, the data given by Mr. Shcherbina cannot serve as an accurate measure of the general state of affairs even in the uyezd, let alone the gubernia"—all that we can say is that they cannot serve as a measure only when you resort to the wrong method of calculating general averages (a method which Mr. Krivenko should not have resorted to), but that, generally speaking, Mr. Shcherbina's data are so comprehensive and valuable that they enable us to arrive at correct conclusions—and that if Mr. Krivenko has not done so, it is not Mr. Shcherbina who is to blame.

The latter, for example, gives on page 197 a classification of the peasants according to draught animals and not according to allotment land, that is, a classification on economic, not legal lines—and this gives us every ground for asserting that the ratios between the various categories of the selected 24 typical households are absolutely identical with the ratios between the various economic groups throughout the uyezd.

---

* Of course, I do not mean to say that the data for the 24 farms are *alone* enough to refute the thesis that the allotments are of prime importance. But above we cited data for several uyezds which totally refute it.[68]

The classification is as follows:*

Ostrogozhsk Uyezd, Voronezh Gubernia

Groups of householders according to number of draught animals owned	Number		Per household			Average family (persons)	Percentage of households					
	Householders	Percentage	Head of cattle	Land (dess.) Allotment	Land (dess.) Rented		With farm labourers	With com. or ind. estabs.	With no house	With no working member	Cultivating no land	With no implements
I. With no draught animals . . .	8,728	26.0	0.7	6.2	0.2	4.6	0.6	4.0	9.5	16.6	41.6	98.5
II. With 1 draught animal	10,510	31.3	3.0	9.4	1.3	5.7	1.4	5.4	1.4	4.9	2.9	2.5
III. With 2 or 3 draught animals. . .	11,191	33.3	6.8	13.8	3.6	7.7	8.3	12.3	0.4	1.3	0.4	—
IV. With 4 or more draught animals . . .	3,152	9.4	14.3	21.3	12.3	11.2	25.3	34.2	0.1	0.4	0.3	—
Total . . .	33,581	100.0	4.4	11.2	2.5	6.7	5.7	10.0	3.0	6.3	11.9	23.4
Of the 24 typical households**: Farm labourers			0.5	7.2	0.0	4.5						
Poor peasants			2.8	8.7	3.9	5.6						
Middle peasants . . .			8.1	9.2	7.7	8.3						
Prosperous peasants			13.5	22.1	8.8	7.8						
Total			7.2	12.2	6.6	7.3***						

* The comparison of the 24 typical households with the categories of farms for the whole uyezd has been made by the same methods as Mr. Shcherbina used in comparing the average of the 24 farms with groups based on size of allotment.

** Two farm labourers (Nos. 14 and 15 of Shcherbina's budgets) have here been eliminated from the group of poor peasants, so that only 5 poor peasants remain.

*** It must be noted in connection with this table that here too we find that the amount of rented land increases in proportion to growing prosperity, *despite* the increase in allotment land. Thus, the facts for one more uyezd confirm the fallacy of the idea that the allotments are of prime importance. On the contrary, we find that the proportion of allotment land to the total holding of a given

There can be no doubt that the general averages of the 24 typical farms are superior to the general run of peasant farm in the uyezd. But if, instead of these fictitious averages, we take economic categories, a comparison becomes possible.

We find that the farm labourers on typical farms are somewhat below the peasants who have no draught animals,

---

group diminishes as the prosperity of the group increases. Adding allotment land to rented land, and calculating the percentage of allotment land to the total, we obtain the following figures by groups: I) 96.8%; II) 85.0%; III) 79.3%; IV) 63.3%. And this is quite natural. We know that with the emancipation Reform, land in Russia became a commodity. Whoever has money can always buy land; and allotment land too must be bought. It is obvious that the prosperous peasants concentrate land in their hands, and that this concentration is more marked in the case of rented land because of the medieval restrictions on the transfer of allotments. The "friends of the people," who favour these restrictions, do not realise that this senseless reactionary measure only worsens the condition of the poor peasants: the ruined peasants, possessing no agricultural implements, are obliged, in any case, to lease their land, and any prohibition on such leasing (or sale) will lead either to land being leased secretly, and, consequently, on worse terms for those who lease it, or to the poor peasants surrendering their land for nothing to the "village community," i.e., again to the kulak.

I cannot refrain from quoting a profoundly true comment made by Hourwich on this vaunted "inalienability":

"To see our way clearly through the question at issue, we have to discover who are the buyers of the land sold by peasants. We have seen that only a minor portion of the quarterly lots have been purchased by merchants. As a rule, the small lots sold by the nobility are acquired by peasants only. The question at issue is thus one that has been settled as between peasants alone, and that affects neither the interests of the nobility nor those of the capitalistic class. In such cases it may well please the Russian government to throw a sop to the peasantists [Narodniks]. This mésalliance of oriental paternalism with some queer sort of state socialistic prohibitionism, however, would be apt to meet with opposition from the very ones who were supposed to be benefited. As the process of dissolution is obviously spreading from within, and not from without the village, inalienability of peasant land would simply mean gratuitous expropriation of the poor for the benefit of the wealthy members of the community.

"We notice that the percentage of emigrants among the quarterly possessors[69] who have enjoyed the right of alienating their land has been far greater than that among the former state peasants who live in agrarian communism: namely, in the Ranenburg district (Ryazan Gubernia) the percentage of emigrants among the former is but approach them very closely. The poor peasants approximate very closely to the owners of one draught animal (the number of cattle is less by 0.2—the poor peasants have 2.8 and the one-horse peasants 3.0—but on the other hand, their total land, both allotment and rented, is somewhat more—12.6 dessiatines as against 10.7 dessiatines). The middle peasants are only slightly above those with two or three draught animals (they have slightly more cattle and a little less land), while the prosperous peasants approximate to those who have four or more draught animals, being a little *below* them. We are therefore entitled to draw the conclusion that in the uyezd as a whole not less than one-tenth of the peasants engage in regular, profitable farming and have no need for outside work. (Their income—it is important to note—is expressed in money, and therefore presupposes agriculture of a commercial character.) To a large extent they conduct

---

17, among the latter it is 9. In the Dankov district among the former it is 12 and among the latter it is 5.

"To what is this difference due? A single concrete example will clear up the matter.

"In 1881 a small community of 5 households, former serfs of Grigorov, emigrated from the village of Bigildino, district of Dankov. Their land, 30 dessiatines, was sold to a rich peasant in consideration of 1,500 rubles. The emigrants could not make a living at home, and most of them were yearly labourers. (*Statistical Report*, Part II, pp. 115, 247.) According to Mr. Grigoryev (*Emigration of the Peasants of Ryazan Gubernia*), 300 rubles, the price of an average peasant holding of 6 dessiatines, is sufficient to enable a peasant family to start farming in Southern Siberia. A peasant who has been absolutely ruined is thus enabled, through the sale of his lot in the communal land, to rise to the position of a farmer in the new country. Devotion to the sacred customs of forefathers would hardly be able to withstand such a temptation as this, but for the helpful right hand of the most gracious Bureaucracy.

"I shall, of course, be charged with pessimism, as I have been recently on account of my views on the emigration of the peasants. (*Severny Vestnik*, 1892, No. 5, in an article by A. Bogdanovsky.) The usual method of reasoning followed takes some such course as this: Granted that the case is presented true to life as it actually stands, the evil consequences" (of emigration) "are nevertheless due to the present abnormal condition of the peasantry, and under normal circumstances, the objections are 'no good.' Unhappily, however, these very 'abnormal' conditions are developing spontaneously, while the creation of 'normal' conditions is beyond the jurisdiction of the well-wishers of the peasantry." (Op. cit., p. 137.[70])

their farming with the help of hired labourers: not less than one-fourth of all the households employ regular farm labourers, and the number employing temporary day labourers is not known. Further, more than half the peasants in the uyezd are poor (nearly six-tenths: horseless and one-horse peasants, 26% + 31.3% = 57.3%), who conduct their farming at a dead loss and are consequently sinking into ruin, steadily and inexorably being expropriated. They are obliged to sell their labour-power and about one-fourth of the peasants already gain their livelihood more by wage-labour than by agriculture. The remaining are middle peasants, who carry on somehow, farming at a regular loss made up by outside earnings, and who, consequently, have no economic stability whatever.

I have deliberately dwelt on these data in such detail in order to show how distorted is Mr. Krivenko's picture of the real situation. Without stopping to think, he takes general averages and operates with them. Naturally, the result is not even a fiction but a downright falsehood. We have seen, for example, that the net income (+197.34 rubles) of one prosperous peasant (from among the typical budgets) covers the deficits of *nine* poor households (—21.38 × 9 = —192.42), so that 10% of rich peasants in the uyezd will not only cover the deficits of 57% of poor peasants but even yield a certain surplus. And Mr. Krivenko, deriving from the average budget of the 24 farms a surplus of 44.14 rubles—or, deducting credit debts and arrears, 15.97 rubles—simply speaks of the "decline" of the middle and lower-than-middle peasants. Actually, however, one can talk of decline only in reference, perhaps, to the middle peasants,* whereas in the case of the mass of poor peasants we observe direct *expropriation*, accompanied, moreover, by the concentration of the means of production in the hands of a minority who own comparatively large and firmly-established farms.

Because he ignored this latter circumstance, the author failed to observe another very interesting feature of these budgets, namely, that they likewise prove that *the differ-*

---

* And even this would scarcely be true, because decline implies a temporary and casual loss of stability, whereas the middle peasants, as we have seen, are always in a state of instability, on the verge of ruin.

entiation of the peasantry is creating a home market. On the one hand, as we pass from the top group to the bottom, we observe the growing importance of income from industries (6.5%, 18.8% and 23.6% of the total budget of the prosperous, middle and poor peasants, respectively), that is, chiefly from the sale of labour-power. On the other hand, as we pass from the bottom to the top groups, we observe the growing commodity (nay, more: *bourgeois*, as we have seen) character of agriculture and an increase in the proportion of produce disposed of: the total income from agriculture of the categories is *a)* $\frac{3,861.7}{1,774.4}$, *в)* $\frac{3,163.8}{899.9}$, *c)* $\frac{689.9}{175.25}$. The denominator indicates the money part of the income,* which constitutes 45.9%, 28.3% and 25.4% respectively, passing from the top category to the bottom.

Here we again see clearly how the means of production taken from the expropriated peasants turn *into capital.*

It is quite obvious that Mr. Krivenko could not draw correct conclusions from the material used—or, rather, misused—in this way. After describing the money character of peasant farming in Novgorod Gubernia on the basis of what he was told by a peasant from those parts with whom he travelled by rail, he was forced to draw the correct conclusion that it is precisely this circumstance, commodity economy, that "cultivates" "special abilities" and gives rise to one preoccupation: "to get it (the hay) mown as cheaply as possible" and "sell it as dear as possible" (p. 156).** This

* A fairly complex calculation was required to arrive at the money income from agriculture (which Shcherbina does not give). It was necessary to exclude from the total income from crops the income derived from straw and chaff, which, according to the author, are used as cattle feed. The author himself excludes them in Chapter XVIII, but only for the total figures for the uyezd, and not for the given 24 households. Taking his total figures, I determined the proportion of income from grain (compared with the total income from the crops, i.e., both from grain and from straw and chaff) and on this basis excluded straw and chaff in the present case. This proportion is, for rye 78.98%, for wheat 72.67%, for oats and barley 73.32% and for millet and buckwheat 77.78%. The amount of grain sold was then determined by excluding the amount consumed on the farm itself.

** "The worker must be hired cheap and the most made out of him," Mr. Krivenko quite rightly remarks in the same passage.

serves as a "school" which "awakens" (quite true!) "and refines commercial gifts." "Talented people come to the fore to become the Kolupayevs, the Derunovs[71] and other types of blood-suckers,* while the simple-hearted and simple-minded fall behind, deteriorate, become impoverished and pass into the ranks of the farm labourers" (p. 156).

The data for a gubernia in which entirely different conditions prevail—an agricultural one (Voronezh)—lead to exactly the same conclusions. One would have thought the situation was quite clear: the system of commodity economy stands out distinctly as the main background of the economic life of the country in general and of the "community" "peasantry" in particular; the *fact* also stands out that this commodity economy, *and it alone*, is splitting the "people" and the "peasantry" into a proletariat (they become ruined, enter the ranks of the farm labourers) and a bourgeoisie (blood-suckers), i.e., it is turning into capitalist economy. But the "friends of the people" never dare look *realities* in the face and call a spade a spade (that would be too "harsh")! And Mr. Krivenko argues as follows:

"Some people consider this state of affairs quite natural" (he should have added: a quite natural consequence of the capitalist character of production relations. Then it would have been an accurate description of the views of "some people," and then it would have been impossible for him to dispose of these views with empty phrases and he would have had to make a real analysis of the matter. When the author did not deliberately set out to combat these "some people," he himself had to admit that money economy is precisely the "school" that produces "talented" blood-suckers and "simple-hearted" farm labourers) "and regard it as the irresistible mission of capitalism." (Well, of course! To believe that the struggle has to be waged against this "school" and the "blood-suckers" who dominate it, together with their administrative and intellectual lackeys, is to consider that capitalism cannot be overcome! But to leave the capitalist

* Mr. Yuzhakov, how's this! Here is your colleague saying that "talented people" become "blood-suckers," whereas you assured us that people become so only because they have "uncritical minds." That won't do, gentlemen, contradicting each other like this in one and the same magazine!

"school" with its blood-suckers in complete immunity and to want to eliminate its capitalist products by means of liberal half-measures is to be a true "friend of the people"!) "We look at the matter somewhat differently. Capitalism undoubtedly does play an important part here, as we pointed out above" (this refers to the remark about the school of blood-suckers and farm labourers), "but it cannot be said that its role is so all-embracing and decisive that no other factors are responsible for the changes taking place in the national economy, and that the future holds out no other solution" (p. 160).

There you are! Instead of giving an exact and straightforward description of the present system, instead of giving a definite answer to the question of why the "peasantry" is splitting into blood-suckers and farm labourers, Mr. Krivenko disposes of the matter with meaningless phrases. "It cannot be said that the role of capitalism is decisive." Why, that is the whole question: can it be said, or can it not?

To uphold your opinion you should have indicated what other factors are "decisive," what other "solution" there can be besides the one indicated by the Social-Democrats, namely, the class struggle of the proletariat against the blood-suckers.* But nothing is indicated. Unless, perhaps, the author regards the following as an indication? Amusing as it may be, you can expect anything from the "friends of the people."

"The first to fall into decline, as we have seen, are the weak farms poor in land"—namely, with allotments of less than five dessiatines. "But the typical farms of the state peasants, with allotments of 15.7 dessiatines, are distinguished for their stability.... True, to secure such an income (a net income of 80 rubles) they rent an additional five dessiatines but that only shows what they need."

What does this "amendment," which links up the notorious "land poverty" with capitalism, amount to? Only to

* If only urban factory workers are as yet capable of assimilating the idea of the class struggle of the proletariat against the bourgeoisie, while the rural "simple-hearted and simple-minded" farm labourers, i.e., the people who have actually lost those charming qualities so closely bound up with the "age-old basis" and the "community spirit," are not—it only proves the correctness of the Social-Democrats' theory of the progressive and revolutionary role of Russian capitalism.

this, that those who have little lose that little, while those who have much (15.7 dessiatines each) acquire still more.* But, then, this is a meaningless paraphrase of the statement that some sink into ruin while others grow rich!! It is high time to abandon this meaningless talk about land poverty, which explains nothing (because the peasants are not given allotments free but have to buy them); it only describes a process, and moreover describes it inaccurately, because one should not speak about the land alone, but about the means of production in general, and not say that the peasants have a "poor" supply of them, but that they are being *freed* from them, are *being expropriated* by growing capitalism. "We have no intention of saying," Mr. Krivenko remarks, concluding his philosophical discourse, "that agriculture should and can, under all circumstances, remain 'natural' and separated from manufacturing industry" (another phrase! Was it not you who were just obliged to admit that a school of money economy already exists, which presupposes exchange and, consequently, the separation of agriculture from manufacturing industry? Why again this sloppy talk of what can be and what should be?); "all we say is that to create a separate industry artificially is irrational" (it would be interesting to know: is the industry of the Kimry and Pavlovo handicraftsmen "separate," and who "artificially created" it, and how and when?), "and that the separation of the labourer from the land and the instruments of production is being effected not by capitalism alone, but also by other factors that precede and promote it."

Here most likely he again had in mind the profound idea that if the labourer is separated from the land, which passes into the hands of the blood-sucker, this happens because the former is "poor" and the latter is "rich" in land.

And this kind of philosophy charges the Social-Democrats with "narrowness" for regarding capitalism as the decisive factor!... I have dwelt once more in such detail on the differentiation of the peasants and handicraftsmen just because it was necessary to bring out clearly how the Social-Democrats picture the matter and how they explain

* Not to mention the absurdity of the idea that peasants with equal allotments are equal and are not also divided into "blood-suckers" and "farm labourers."

it. It was necessary to show that the facts which to the subjective sociologist mean that the peasants have "grown poor," while the "money chasers" and "blood-suckers" "derive profits for their own advantage," to the materialist mean the bourgeois differentiation of the commodity producers necessitated by commodity production itself. It was necessary to show what facts serve as the basis for the thesis (quoted above in Part 1)* that the struggle between the propertied and the propertyless is going on everywhere in Russia, not only in the mills and factories, but even in the most remote villages, and that everywhere this struggle is one between the bourgeoisie and the proletariat that emerge as a result of commodity economy. The break-up, the depeasantisation of our peasants and handicraftsmen, which can be depicted accurately thanks to the admirable material provided by Zemstvo statistics, furnishes *factual* proof of the correctness of precisely the Social-Democratic conception of Russian reality, the conception that the peasant and the handicraftsman are *petty producers* in the "categorical" meaning of the term, that is, are *petty bourgeois*. This thesis may be called the central point of the theory of **WORKING-CLASS SOCIALISM** as against the old peasant socialism, which understood neither the conditions of commodity economy in which the petty producers live, nor their capitalist differentiation due to these conditions. And, therefore, whoever wanted to criticise Social-Democracy seriously should have concentrated his argument on this, and shown that from the angle of political economy Russia is not a system of commodity economy, that it is not this which causes the break-up of the peasantry, and that the expropriation of the mass of the population and the exploitation of the working people can be explained by something other than the bourgeois, capitalist organisation of our social (including peasant) economy.

Well, just try it, gentlemen!

There is another reason why it was the data on peasant and handicraft economy that I preferred to take in illustration of the Social-Democratic theory. It would be a departure from the materialist method were I, when criticising the

* See p. 191 of this volume.—*Ed.*

views of the "friends of the people," to confine myself to contrasting their ideas with the Marxist ideas. One must in addition explain the "Narodnik" ideas, demonstrate their MATERIAL basis in our present social-economic relations. Illustrations and examples of the economy of our peasants and handicraftsmen show what this "peasant" is whose ideologists the "friends of the people" want to be. They demonstrate the bourgeois character of our rural economy and thus confirm the correctness of classifying the "friends of the people" as ideologists of the petty bourgeoisie. But this is not all; they show that there is the closest connection between the ideas and programmes of our radicals and the interests of the petty bourgeoisie. It is this connection, which will become even clearer after a detailed examination of their programme, that explains why these radical ideas are so widespread in our "society"; it also admirably explains the political servility of the "friends of the people" and their readiness for compromise.

There was, lastly, one other reason for dwelling in such detail on the economics of precisely those sides of our social life where capitalism is least developed and from which the Narodniks have usually drawn the material for their theories. A study and description of these economics was the simplest way to reply in substance to one of the most widespread objections to Social-Democracy current among people here. Proceeding from the usual idea that capitalism contradicts the "people's system," and observing that the Social-Democrats regard large-scale capitalism as progressive, that it is large-scale capitalism that they want to have as their basis in combating the present robber regime—our radicals, without more ado, accuse the Social-Democrats of ignoring the interests of the mass of the peasant population, of desiring "to put every muzhik through the factory melting pot," etc.

All these arguments are based on the amazingly illogical and strange procedure of judging capitalism by what it really is, but the countryside by what it "might be." Naturally, there could be no better reply to this than to show them the *real* countryside and its *real* economics.

Anybody who studies these economics dispassionately and scientifically will be bound to admit that rural Russia constitutes a system of small, scattered markets (or small branches of a central market), which regulate the social and economic life of separate small districts. And in each of these districts we find all the phenomena that are, in general, peculiar to the social-economic organisation whose regulator is the market: we find the division of the once equal, patriarchal direct producers into rich and poor; we find the rise of *capital*, especially of merchant capital, which spins its web around the working people and sucks the lifeblood out of them. When you compare the descriptions of peasant economy given by our radicals with precise first-hand data on rural economic life, you are astonished that there is no place in the criticised system of views for that mass of small hucksters who swarm in each of these markets, all these higglers and chafferers or whatever else the peasants call them in different localities, for all that mass of petty exploiters who dominate the markets and ruthlessly oppress the working people. They are usually simply brushed aside with the remark—"These are no longer peasants, but hucksters." Yes, you are quite right: these are "no longer peasants." But try to treat all these "traders" as a distinct group, that is, speaking in the precise language of political economy, those who engage in commercial enterprise and who appropriate, to whatever extent, the labour of others; try to express in precise figures the economic strength of this group and the part it plays in the entire economic life of the district; and then try to treat as an opposite group all those who also are "no longer peasants" because they bring their labour-power to the market, because they work for others and not for themselves—try to fulfil these elementary requisites of a dispassionate and serious inquiry and you will get such a vivid picture of bourgeois differentiation that not a trace of the "people's system" myth will remain. This mass of small rural exploiters represents a terrible force, especially terrible because they oppress the isolated, single toiler, because they fetter him to themselves and deprive him of all hope of deliverance; terrible because this exploitation, in view of the barbarism of the countryside due to the low labour productivity characteristic of the system described and to the absence of communications, constitutes not only robbery of labour, but also the Asiatic abuse of human dignity that is constantly encountered in the countryside. Now, if you compare this *real* countryside with our capitalism you will understand why the Social-Democrats regard the work of our capitalism as progressive when it draws these small, scattered markets together into one nation-wide market, when, in place of the legion of small well-meaning blood-suckers, it creates a handful of big "pillars of the fatherland," when it socialises labour and raises its productivity, when it shatters the subordination of the working people to the local blood-suckers and subordinates them to large-scale *capital*. This subordination is progressive compared with the former — despite all the horrors of the oppression of labour, of gradual extinction, brutalisation, and the crippling of the bodies of women and children, etc.—because it **AWAKENS THE MIND OF THE WORKER**, converts dumb and incoherent discontent into conscious protest, converts scattered, petty, senseless revolt into an organised class struggle for the emancipation of all working folk, a struggle which derives its strength from the very conditions of existence of this large-scale capitalism, and therefore can undoubtedly count upon **CERTAIN SUCCESS**.

In reply to the accusation of ignoring the mass of the peasantry, Social-Democrats would be quite justified in quoting the words of Karl Marx:

> "*Criticism has plucked the imaginary flowers which adorned the chain, not that man should wear his fetters denuded of fanciful embellishment, but that he should throw off the chain and reach for the living flower.*"[72]

The Russian Social-Democrats are plucking from our countryside the imaginary flowers that adorn it, are combating idealisations and fantasies, and are performing the destructive work for which they are so mortally detested by the "friends of the people," not in order that the mass of the peasantry shall remain in their present state of oppression, gradual extinction and enslavement, but in order that the proletariat may understand what sort of chains everywhere fetter the working people, that they may understand how these chains are forged, and be able to rise against them, to throw them off and reach out for the real flower.

When they bring this idea to those representatives of the working people who by virtue of their position are alone capable of acquiring class-consciousness and of launching a class struggle, they are accused of wanting to put the muzhik through the factory melting pot.

And who are the accusers?

People who themselves base their hopes for the emancipation of the working people on the "government" and on "society," that is, on the organs of that very bourgeoisie which has everywhere fettered the working people!

And these spineless creatures have the presumption to talk of the Social-Democrats having no ideals!

Let us now pass to the political programme of the "friends of the people," to whose theoretical views we have, we think, devoted far too much time. By what means do they propose to "put out the fire"? What way out do they propose in place of the one, which they claim is wrong, proposed by the Social-Democrats?

"The reorganisation of the Peasants' Bank," says Mr. Yuzhakov in an article entitled "The Ministry of Agriculture" (*Russkoye Bogatstvo*, No. 10), "the establishment of a Colonisation Department, the regulation of state land leasing in the interest of people's farming ... the study and regulation of land letting—such is the programme for the restoration of people's farming and its protection from the economic violence" (sic!) "of the nascent plutocracy." And in the article "Problems of Economic Development" this programme for "the restoration of people's farming" is supplemented by the following "first, but essential steps": "Removal of all restrictions that now encumber the village community; its release from tutelage, adoption of common cultivation (the socialisation of agriculture) and the development of the communal processing of raw materials obtained from the soil." And Messrs. Krivenko and Karyshev add: "Cheap credit, the artel form of farming, an assured market, the possibility of dispensing with employers' profit" (this will be dealt with separately below), "the invention of cheaper engines and other technical improvements," and, finally, "museums, warehouses, commission agencies,"

Examine this programme and you will find that these gentlemen wholly and completely adopt the position of modern society (i.e., that of the capitalist system, without realising it), and want to settle matters by mending and patching it up, failing to understand that all their progressive measures—cheap credit, improved machinery, banks, and so on—can only serve to strengthen and develop the bourgeoisie.

Nik. —on is quite right, of course, when he says—and this is one of his most valuable theses, against which the "friends of the people" could not help protesting—that no reforms under the present system are of any use, and that credit, migration, tax reform, the transfer of all the land to the peasants, will not appreciably change anything, but, on the contrary, are bound to strengthen and develop capitalist economy, retarded as it now is by excessive "tutelage," survivals of feudal dues, the tying of the peasantry to the land, etc. Economists, he says, who, like Prince Vasilchikov (an undoubted "friend of the people" in his ideas), desire the extensive development of credit, want the same thing as the "liberal," i.e., bourgeois, economists, and "are striving for the development and consolidation of capitalist relations." They do not understand the antagonistic character of our production relations (within the "peasantry" as within the other social estates), and instead of trying to bring this antagonism out into the open, instead of simply joining with those who are enslaved as a result of this antagonism and trying to help them rise in struggle, they dream of stopping the struggle by measures that would satisfy everybody, to achieve reconciliation and unity. The result of all these measures is naturally a foregone conclusion: one has but to recall the examples of differentiation given above to be convinced that all these credits,* improvements, banks and similar "progressive"

* This idea—of utilising credit to foster "people's farming," i.e., the farming of petty producers, where capitalist relations exist (and the "friends of the people," as we have already seen, can no longer deny that they do exist)—this meaningless idea, which reveals an inability to understand the elementary truths of theoretical political economy, quite clearly shows how vulgar is the theory advanced by these gentlemen who try to sit between two stools.

measures will be available only to the one who, possessing a properly-run and established farm, has certain "savings," i.e., the representative of an insignificant minority, the petty bourgeoisie. And however much you reorganise the Peasants' Bank and similar institutions, you will not in the least alter the fundamental and cardinal fact that the mass of the population have been and continue to be expropriated, and lack means even of subsistence, let alone of farming on proper lines.

The same must be said of "artels," and "common cultivation." Mr. Yuzhakov called the latter "the socialisation of agriculture." This is merely funny, of course, because socialisation requires the organisation of production on a wider scale than the limits of a single village, and because it necessitates the expropriation of the "blood-suckers" who have monopolised the means of production and now direct Russian social economy. And this requires struggle, struggle and struggle, and not paltry philistine moralising.

And that is why such measures of theirs turn into mild, liberal half-measures, barely subsisting on the generosity of the philanthropic bourgeois, and do much more harm by diverting the exploited from the struggle than good from the possible improvement in the position of a few individuals, an improvement that cannot but be meagre and precarious on the general basis of capitalist relations. The preposterous extent to which these gentlemen attempt to hide the antagonism in Russian life—doing so, of course, with the very best intentions in order to put an end to the present struggle, i.e., with the sort of intentions with which the road to hell is paved —is shown by the following argument of Mr. Krivenko:

"The intelligentsia direct the manufacturers' enterprises, and they could direct popular industry."

The whole of their philosophy amounts to whining that struggle and exploitation exist but that they "might" not exist if ... if there were no exploiters. Really, what did the author mean by this meaningless phrase? Can it be denied that year after year the Russian universities and other educational establishments turn out a brand of "intelligentsia" (??) whose only concern is to find someone to feed them? Can it be denied that today, in Russia, the means for maintaining this "intelligentsia" are owned only by the bourgeois minority? Can the bourgeois intelligentsia in Russia be expected to disappear because the "friends of the people" say that they "might" serve somebody other than the bourgeoisie? Yes, they "might," *if* they were not a bourgeois intelligentsia. They "might" not be a bourgeois intelligentsia, "if" there were no bourgeoisie and no capitalism in Russia! And they are content to spend their whole lives just repeating these "ifs" and "ans." What is more, these gentlemen not only decline to attach decisive importance to capitalism, but totally refuse to see anything wrong in it. If certain "defects" were removed, they would perhaps not fare so badly under it. How do you like the following statement by Mr. Krivenko:

"Capitalist production and the capitalisation of industries are by no means gates through which manufacturing industry can only depart from the people. It can depart, of course, but it can also enter the life of the people and come into closer proximity to agriculture and the raw materials industry. This can be contrived in various ways, and these gates, as well as others, can serve this purpose" (p. 161). Mr. Krivenko has a number of very good qualities—as compared with Mr. Mikhailovsky; for example, frankness and straightforwardness. Where Mr. Mikhailovsky would have filled reams with smooth and glib sentences, wriggling around the subject without ever touching it, the business-like and practical Mr. Krivenko hits straight from the shoulder, and without a twinge of conscience spreads before the reader all the absurdities of his views without reservation. "Capitalism can enter the life of the people"—if you please! That is, capitalism is possible without the working people being divorced from the means of production! This is positively delightful! At least, we now are absolutely clear as to what the "friends of the people" want. They want commodity economy without capitalism—capitalism without expropriation and without exploitation, with nothing but a petty bourgeoisie peacefully vegetating under the wing of humane landlords and liberal administrators. And, with the serious mien of a departmental official who intends to confer a boon on Russia, they set about contriving schemes under which the wolves have their fill and the sheep their skins. To get some idea of the character of these schemes we must turn to the article by the same author in No. 12 ("Our Cultural Free Lances"): "The artel and state form of industry," argues Mr. Krivenko—apparently under the impression that he has already been "called upon" to "solve practical economic problems"—"is by no means all that can be imagined in the present instance. For example, the following scheme is possible...." And he goes on to relate how an engineer visited the offices of *Russkoye Bogatstvo* with a plan for the technical exploitation of the Don Region by a joint-stock company with shares in small denominations (not exceeding 100 rubles). The author was recommended to modify his scheme roughly as follows: "The shares shall not belong to private persons, but to village communities; that part of the village population employed in the company's enterprises shall receive ordinary wages, the village communities guaranteeing that their connection with the land is maintained."

What administrative genius, is it not? With what admirable simplicity and ease capitalism is introduced into the life of the people and all its pernicious attributes eliminated! All that is required is that the rural rich should buy shares* through the communities and receive dividends from the enterprise, in which a "part of the population" will be employed and their tie with the land guaranteed—a "tie" insufficient to assure a livelihood from the land (otherwise who would go to work for "ordinary wages"?), but sufficient to bind a man to his locality, enslave him to

* I say the rich will buy the shares, despite the author's stipulation that the shares shall be owned by the communities, because, after all, he speaks of the purchase of shares with money, which only the rich have. Hence, whether the business is conducted through the agency of the communities or not, only the rich will be able to pay, just as the purchase or renting of land by the community in no way prevents the rich from monopolising this land. The dividends too must go to those who have paid—otherwise the shares will not be shares. And I understand the author's proposal to mean that a certain part of the profits will be earmarked for "guaranteeing the workers their tie with the land." If the author does not mean this (although it inevitably follows from what he says), but that the rich shall pay for the shares and not receive dividends, then all his scheme amounts to is that the rich shall share with the poor. This reminds one of the anecdote about the fly-killer which requires that you first catch the fly and put it in the dish—and it will die instantly.

the local capitalist enterprise and deprive him of the possibility of changing masters. I say master, capitalist, quite legitimately, for he who pays the labourer *wages* cannot be called anything else.

The reader is perhaps annoyed with me already for dwelling so long on such nonsense, nonsense that would seem to be undeserving of any attention. But I must say that although it is nonsense, it is a type of nonsense that is useful and necessary to study, because it reflects the social and economic relations actually existing in Russia and, as a consequence, is one of the social ideas, very widespread in our country, that Social-Democrats will have to reckon with for a long time to come. The point is that the transition from the feudal to the capitalist mode of production in Russia gave rise, and to some extent still gives rise, to a situation for the working people in which the peasant, being unable to obtain a livelihood from the land and *to pay dues from it to the landlord* (and *he pays them to this very day*), was compelled to resort to "outside employments," which at first, in the good old days, took the form either of independent occupations (for example, carting), or labour which was not independent but, owing to the poor development of these types of employment, was comparatively well paid. Under this condition the peasantry were assured of a certain well-being as compared with things today—the well-being of serfs, who peacefully vegetated under the tutelage of a hundred thousand noble police chiefs and of the nascent gatherers of Russia's land—the bourgeoisie.

And the "friends of the people" idealise this system, simply disregarding its dark sides, dream about it—"dream," because it has long ceased to exist, has long been destroyed by capitalism, which has given rise to the wholesale expropriation of the peasant farmers and turned the former "employments" into the unbridled exploitation of abundantly offered "hands."

Our petty-bourgeois knights want to preserve the peasant's "tie" with the land; but they do not want the serfdom that alone ensured this tie, and which was broken only by the commodity production and capitalism, which made this tie impossible. They want outside employments that do not take the peasant away from the land, that—while work is done for the market—do not give rise to competition, do not create *capital* and do not enslave the mass of the population to it. True to the subjective method in sociology, they want to "take" what is good from here and from there; but actually, of course, this childish desire only leads to reactionary dreaming which ignores realities, to an inability to understand and utilise the really progressive, revolutionary aspects of the new system, and to sympathy for measures which perpetuate the good old system of semi-serf, semi-free labour—a system that was fraught with all the horrors of exploitation and oppression, and held out no possibility of escape.

To prove the correctness of this explanation, which classes the "friends of the people" among the reactionaries, I shall quote two examples.

In the Moscow Zemstvo statistics we can read a description of the farm of a certain Madame K. (in Podolsk Uyezd), which (the farm, not the description) aroused the admiration both of the Moscow statisticians and of Mr. V. V., if my memory does not deceive me (he wrote about it, I think, in a magazine article).

This notorious farm of Madame K.'s was regarded by Mr. V. Orlov as "convincing practical confirmation" of his favourite thesis that "where peasant farming is in a sound condition, the private landowners' farms are also better conducted." From Mr. Orlov's account of this lady's estate, it appears that she runs her farm with the labour of the local peasants, who till her land in return for a winter loan of flour, etc. The lady is extraordinarily kind to these peasants and helps them, so that they are now the most prosperous in the volost and have enough grain "to last them almost until the new harvest (formerly, it did not even last until St. Nicholas' day)."

The question arises, does "such an arrangement" preclude "the antagonism of interests of peasant and landowner," as Messrs. N. Kablukov (Vol. V, p. 175) and V. Orlov (Vol. II, pp. 55-59 and elsewhere) think? Obviously not, because Madame K. lives on the labour of her peasants. Hence, exploitation has not been abolished at all. Madame K. may be forgiven for failing to see the exploitation behind her kindness to the exploited, but not so an economist and statistician who, in his ecstasy over the case in question, takes up exactly the same stand as those Menschenfreunde* in the West who go into ecstasies over the kindness of a capitalist to a worker, rapturously relate cases where a factory owner shows concern for his workers, provides them with general stores, dwellings, etc. To conclude from the existence (and therefore "possibility") of such "facts" that there is no antagonism of interests, is not to see the wood for the trees. That is the first point.

The second point is that we learn from Mr. Orlov's account that Madame K.'s peasants, "thanks to excellent crops (the landlady gave them good seed), have acquired livestock" and have "prosperous" farms. Let us assume that these "prosperous peasants" have become not "almost," but completely prosperous, that not the "majority," but all of them have enough grain, not "almost" until, but right until the new harvest. Let us assume that these peasants now have enough land, and that they have "cattle runs and pastures"—which they have not got at present (fine prosperity!), and which they rent from Madame K., making payment in labour. Does Mr. Orlov really believe that in that case—that is, if the peasant farming were really prosperous—these peasants would agree to "perform all the jobs on Madame K.'s estate thoroughly, punctually and swiftly," as they do now? Or perhaps gratitude to the kind lady who sweats the life-blood out of these prosperous peasants with such maternal care will be a no less potent incentive than the hopelessness of the present condition of the peasants, who, after all, cannot dispense with pastures and cattle runs?

Evidently, the ideas of the "friends of the people" are, in essence, the same: as true petty-bourgeois ideologists, they do not want to abolish exploitation, but to mitigate it, they do not want conflict, but conciliation. Their broad ideals, from the standpoint of which they so vigorously fulminate against the narrow-minded Social-Democrats, go no further than the "prosperous" peasant who performs his "duties" to the landlords and capitalists, provided the landlords and capitalists treat him fairly.

Take the other example. Mr. Yuzhakov, in his quite

---

* Philanthropists.—*Ed.*

well-known article, "Quotas for People's Landownership in Russia" (*Russkaya Mysl*, 1885, No. 9), expounded his views on what should be the dimensions of "people's" landownership, i.e., in the terminology of our liberals, the kind of landownership that excludes capitalism and exploitation. Now, after the excellent explanation given by Mr. Krivenko, we know that he too regarded things from the standpoint of "introducing capitalism into the life of the people." As the minimum for "people's" landownership he took such allotments as would cover "cereal food and payments,"* while the rest, he said, could be obtained by "employments."... In other words, he simply resigned himself to a state of affairs in which the peasant, by maintaining connection with the land, is subjected to a double exploitation—partly by the landlord, on the "allotment," and partly by the capitalist, in "employments." This state of the small producers, who are subjected to a double exploitation, and whose conditions of life, moreover, are such as inevitably breed a cowed and crushed spirit, killing all hope that the oppressed class will fight, let alone be victorious—this semi-medieval condition is the nec plus ultra of the outlook and ideals of the "friends of the people." Well then, when capitalism, which developed with tremendous rapidity throughout the whole of Russia's post-Reform history, began to uproot this pillar of old Russia—the patriarchal, semi-serf peasantry—to drag them out of these medieval and semi-feudal conditions and to place them in a modern, purely capitalist environment, compelling them to abandon their old homes and wander over the face of Russia in search of work, breaking the chains of enslavement to the local "work-giver" and disclosing the basis of exploitation in general, of class exploitation as distinct from the depredations of a particular viper—when capitalism began to draw the rest of the peasant population, cowed and forced down to the

* To show the relation between these outlays and the rest of the peasant budget, let me quote again the 24 budgets of Ostrogozhsk Uyezd. The average expenditure per family is 495.39 rubles (in kind and in cash). Of this, 109.10 rubles go for the maintenance of cattle, 135.80 rubles are spent on vegetable food and taxes, and the remaining 250.49 rubles on other expenses—non-vegetable food, clothes, implements, rent, etc. Mr. Yuzhakov allows the hay-fields and other grounds to account for the maintenance of cattle.

level of cattle, en masse into the vortex of increasingly complex social and political life, then our knights began to howl and wail about the fall and destruction of the old pillars. And they continue to this day to howl and wail about the good old times, although now, it seems, one must be blind not to see the revolutionary side of this new mode of life, not to see how capitalism is creating a new social force, which has no ties with the old regime of exploitation and is in a position to fight it.

The "friends of the people," however, show no trace of a desire for any radical change in the present system. They are entirely satisfied with liberal measures on the existing basis, and in the invention of such measures Mr. Krivenko really displays the administrative abilities of a native Jack-in-offiice.

"Generally speaking"—he argues, about the need for a "detailed study and radical transformation" of "our people's industry"—"this question calls for special investigation, and for the division of industries into those that can be applied to the life of the people" (sic!!) "and those whose application encounters serious obstacles."

Mr. Krivenko himself gives us an example of such a division when he divides the various industries into those which are not capitalised, those in which capitalisation has already taken place, and those which can "contend with large-scale industry for existence."

"In the first case," this administrator decides, "petty production can exist freely"—but can it be free of the market, whose fluctuations split the petty producers into a bourgeoisie and a proletariat? Can it be free of the expansion of the local markets and their amalgamation into a big market? Can it be free of technical progress? Or perhaps this technical progress—under commodity production—need not be capitalistic? In the last case, the author demands the "organisation of production on a large scale too": "Clearly," he says, "what is needed here is the organisation of production on a large scale too, what is needed is fixed and circulating capital, machinery, etc., or something else that will counterbalance these conditions: cheap credit, the elimination of superfluous middlemen, the artel form of farming and the possibility of dispensing with employers' profit, an assured market, the invention of cheaper engines and other technical improvements, or, finally, some reduction in wages, provided it is compensated by other benefits."

This sort of reasoning is highly characteristic of the "friends of the people," with their broad ideals in words and their stereotyped liberalism in deeds. As you see, our philosopher starts out from nothing more nor less than the possibility of dispensing with employers' profit and from the organisation of large-scale farming. Excellent: this is EXACTLY what the Social-Democrats want, too. But how do the "friends of the people" want to achieve it? To organise large-scale production without employers, it is necessary, first of all, to abolish the commodity organisation of social economy and to replace it by communal, communist organisation, under which production is not regulated by the market, as it is at present, but by the producers themselves, by the society of workers itself, and the means of production are owned not by private individuals, but by the whole of society. Such a change from the private to the communal *form of appropriation* apparently requires that the *form of production first* be changed, that the separate, small, isolated processes of production of petty producers be merged into *a single social productive process*; in a word, it requires the very material conditions which capitalism creates. But the "friends of the people" have no intention of basing themselves on capitalism. How then do they propose to act? They do not say. They do not even mention the abolition of commodity economy: evidently, their broad ideals are quite unable to transcend the bounds of this system of social production. Moreover, to abolish employers' profit it would be necessary to expropriate the employers, who obtain their "profits" precisely because they have monopolised the means of production. And to expropriate these pillars of our fatherland, a popular revolutionary movement against the bourgeois regime is required, a movement of which only the working-class proletariat, which has no ties with this regime, is capable. But the "friends of the people" have no struggle in mind at all, and do not even suspect that other types of public men, apart from the administrative organs of the employers themselves, are possible and necessary.

Clearly, they have not the slightest intention of taking any serious measures against "employers' profit." Mr. Krivenko simply allowed his tongue to run away with him. And he immediately corrected himself: why, such a thing as "the possibility of dispensing with employers' profit" can be "counterbalanced"—"by something else," namely credits, organised marketing, technical improvements. Thus everything is arranged quite satisfactorily: instead of abolishing the sacred right to "profit," a procedure so offensive to Messrs. the employers, there appear such mild, liberal measures as will only supply capitalism with better weapons for the struggle, and will only strengthen, consolidate and develop our petty, "people's" bourgeoisie. And so as to leave no doubt that the "friends of the people" champion the interests of this petty bourgeoisie alone, Mr. Krivenko adds the following remarkable explanation. It appears that the abolition of employers' profit may be "counterbalanced"... "by a reduction in wages"!!! At first glance this seems to be sheer gibberish. But, no. It is the consistent application of petty-bourgeois ideas. The author observes a fact like the struggle between big capital and small and, as a true "friend of the people," he, of course, takes the side of small ... *capital*. He has further heard that one of the most powerful weapons of the small capitalist is wage reduction—a fact that has been quite correctly observed and confirmed in a large number of industries in Russia, too, parallel to lengthening the working day. And so, desiring at all costs to save the small ... *capitalists*, he proposes "some reduction in wages, provided it is compensated by other benefits"! Messrs. the employers, about whose "profit" some queer things seemed to have been said at first, need not worry. They would, I think, be quite willing to install this brilliant administrator, who plans to fight *against* the employers by a reduction in wages, in the post of Minister of Finance.

One could quote another example of how the pure-blooded bourgeois peeps out of the humane and liberal administrators of *Russkoye Bogatstvo* as soon as they have to deal with any practical question. "The Chronicle of Home Affairs" in *Russkoye Bogatstvo*, No. 12, deals with the subject of monopoly.

"Monopoly and the syndicate," says the author, "such are

the ideals of developed industry." And he goes on to express his surprise that these institutions are appearing in Russia, too, although there is no "keen competition among the capitalists" here. "Neither the sugar industry nor the oil industry has developed to any great extent yet. The consumption of sugar and kerosene here is still practically in the embryo, to judge by the insignificant per capita consumption of these goods here as compared with that of other countries. It would seem that there is still a very large field for the development of these branches of industry and that they could still absorb a large amount of capital."

It is characteristic that as soon as it comes to a practical question, the author forgets the favourite idea of *Russkoye Bogatstvo* about the shrinking of the home market. He is compelled to admit that this market still has the prospect of tremendous development, and not of shrinkage. He arrives at this conclusion from a comparison with the West, where consumption is greater. Why? Because culture is on a higher level. But what is the material basis of this culture if not the development of capitalist technique, the growth of commodity economy and exchange, which bring people into more frequent intercourse with each other and break down the medieval isolation of the separate localities? Was not culture in France, for example, on a level no higher than ours before the Great Revolution, when the semi-medieval peasantry had still not finally split into a rural bourgeoisie and a proletariat? And if the author had examined Russian life more closely he could not have helped noticing, for example, that in localities where capitalism is developed the requirements of the peasant population are much higher than in the purely agricultural districts. This is noted unanimously by all investigators of our handicraft industries in all cases where they develop so far as to lay an industrial impress on the whole life of the population.*

The "friends of the people" pay no attention to such "trifles," because, as far as they are concerned, the expla-

* As an example let me refer, say, to the Pavlovo handicraftsmen as compared to the peasants of the surrounding villages. See the works of Grigoryev and Annensky. I again deliberately give the example of the countryside in which a specific "people's system" supposedly exists.

nation is "simply" culture or the growing complexity of life in general, and they do not even inquire into the material basis of this culture and this complexity. But if they were to examine, at least, the economics of our countryside they would have to admit that it is the break-up of the peasantry into a bourgeoisie and a proletariat that creates the home market.

They must think that the growth of the market does not by any means imply the growth of a bourgeoisie. "In view of the low level of development of production generally," continues the above-mentioned chronicler of home affairs, "and the lack of enterprise and initiative, monopoly will still further retard the development of *the country's forces.*" Speaking of the tobacco monopoly, the author calculates that it "would take 154,000,000 rubles out of *people*'s circulation." Here sight is altogether lost of the fact that the basis of our economic system is commodity economy, the leader of which, here as everywhere else, is the bourgeoisie. And instead of speaking about the bourgeoisie being hampered by monopoly, he speaks about the "country," instead of speaking about commodity, bourgeois circulation, he speaks about "people's" circulation.* A bourgeois is never able to detect the difference between these two terms, great as it is. To show how obvious this difference really is, I will quote a magazine which is an authority in the eyes of the "friends of the people," namely, *Otechestvenniye Zapiski*. In No. 2 of that magazine, 1872, in the article "The Plutocracy and Its Basis," we read the following:

"According to Marlo, the most important characteristic of the plutocracy is its love for a liberal form of government, or at all events for the principle of freedom of acquisition. If we take this characteristic and recall what the position was some eight or ten years ago, we shall find that in respect of liberalism we have made enormous strides.... No matter what newspaper or magazine you take up, they all seem more or less to represent democratic principles, they are all out for the interests of the people. But side by side with these democratic views, and even under the cloak of

* The author must be particularly blamed for this use of terms because *Russkoye Bogatstvo* loves the word "people's" as opposed to bourgeois.

them" (*mark* this), "time and again, intentionally or unintentionally, plutocratic aspirations are pursued."

The author quotes as an example the address presented by St. Petersburg and Moscow merchants to the Minister of Finance, expressing the gratitude of this most venerable body of the Russian bourgeoisie for his having "based the financial position of Russia on the widest possible expansion of private enterprise, which alone is fruitful." And the author of the article concludes: "Plutocratic elements and proclivities undoubtedly exist in our society, and in plenty."

As you see, your predecessors in the distant past, when the impressions of the great emancipatory Reform (which, as Mr. Yuzhakov has discovered, should have opened up peaceful and proper paths of development for "people's" production, but which in fact only opened up paths for the development of a plutocracy) were still vivid and fresh, were themselves forced to admit the plutocratic, i.e., bourgeois character of private enterprise in Russia.

Why have you forgotten this? Why, when you talk about "people's" circulation and the development of the "country's forces" thanks to the development of "enterprise and initiative," do you not mention the antagonistic character of this development, the exploiting character of this enterprise and this initiative? Opposition to monopolies and similar institutions can, and should, of course, be expressed, for they undoubtedly worsen the condition of the working people; but it must not be forgotten that besides all these medieval fetters the working people are shackled by still stronger ones, by modern, bourgeois fetters. Undoubtedly, the abolition of monopolies would be beneficial to the whole "people," because, bourgeois economy having become the basis of the economic life of the country, these survivals of the medieval system only add to the capitalist miseries still more bitter medieval miseries. Undoubtedly, they must definitely be abolished—and the quicker and more radically, the better—in order, by ridding bourgeois society of its inherited semi-feudal fetters, to untie the hands of the working class, to facilitate its struggle against the bourgeoisie.

That is how one should talk, calling a spade a spade—saying that the abolition of monopolies and of all sorts of other medieval restrictions (and in Russia their name is legion) is absolutely essential for the working class in order to facilitate its struggle against the bourgeois system. That is all. None but a bourgeois could see only the solidarity of the interests of the whole "people" against medieval, feudal institutions and forget the profound and irreconcilable antagonism between the bourgeoisie and the proletariat within this "people."

Incidentally, it would be absurd to think of putting the "friends of the people" to shame with this, when, for example, they say things like the following about the needs of the countryside:

"When, a few years ago," Mr. Krivenko informs us, "certain newspapers discussed what professions and what type of intellectual people the countryside needed, the list proved to be a very long and varied one and embraced nearly every walk of life: men and women doctors were followed by feldshers, then came lawyers, followed by teachers, librarians and booksellers, agronomists, forestry experts and agricultural experts generally, technicians of the most varied branches (a very extensive sphere, almost untouched as yet), organisers and managers of credit institutions, warehouses, etc."

Let us stop to consider, say, those "intellectuals" (??) whose activities directly pertain to the economic sphere, all those forestry experts, agricultural experts, technicians, etc. And how these people are needed in the countryside! But in **WHAT** countryside? It goes without saying in the countryside of the landowners, the countryside of the enterprising muzhiks, who have "savings" and can afford to pay for the services of all these "technicians" whom Mr. Krivenko is pleased to call "intellectuals." *This* countryside has, indeed, long been thirsting for technicians, for credits, for warehouses; all our economic literature testifies to this. But there is another countryside, much larger, and it would not harm the "friends of the people" to think of it a little more often; it is the countryside of the ruined, ragged and fleeced peasants, who not only have no "savings" with which to pay for the labour of "intellectuals," but have not even bread enough to save themselves from starvation. And it is *this* countryside that you want to assist with *warehouses*!! What will our one-horse and horseless peasants put in them?

Their clothes? They pawned them as far back as 1891 to the rural and urban kulaks who at that time, in fulfilment of your humane and liberal recipe, set up regular "warehouses" in their homes, taverns, and shops. All they have left is their "hands"; but even the Russian bureaucrats have so far failed to invent "warehouses" for this sort of commodity....

It would be hard to imagine more striking proof of the utter banality of these "democrats" than this sentimentality about technical progress among the "peasantry" and closing of eyes to the wholesale expropriation of this very "peasantry." For example, in *Russkoye Bogatstvo*, No. 2 ("Sketches," § XII), Mr. Karyshev, with the fervour of a liberal cretin, tells of cases of "perfections and improvements" in peasant farming—of the "spread on peasant farms of improved sorts of seed," such as American oats, Vasa rye, Clydesdale oats, etc. "In some places the peasants set special plots apart for seed and after careful tilling, they hand-plant selected samples of grain on them." "Many and very varied innovations" are noted "in the sphere of improved implements and machines,"* such as cultivators, light ploughs, threshing-machines, winnowing-machines, seed sorters. Mention is made of "a greater variety of fertilisers"—phosphates, glue waste, pigeon manure, etc. "Correspondents urge the necessity for setting up local Zemstvo stores in the villages for the sale of phosphates—and Mr. Karyshev, quoting from Mr. V. V.'s book, *Progressive Trends in Peasant Farming* (Mr. Krivenko also refers to this book), is affected by all this touching progress almost to the point of fervour:

"These reports, which we have been able to give only in brief, make a heartening and at the same time saddening impression.... Heartening, because these people, impoverished, debt-laden, very many of them horseless, work with might and main, do not give way to despair, do not change their occupation, but remain true to the land, realising that in it, in the proper treatment of it, lies their future,

---

* I remind the reader of how these improved implements are distributed in Novouzensk Uyezd: 37% of the peasants (the poor), or 10,000 out of 28,000 households, have 7 implements out of 5,724, that is, one-eighth of one per cent! Four-fifths of the implements are monopolised by the rich, who constitute only one-fourth of the total households.

their strength, their wealth." (Why, of course! It goes without saying that it is just the impoverished and horseless muzhik who buys phosphates, seed sorters, threshing-machines and Clydesdale oat seed! O, sancta simplicitas! And this is not written by a ladies' college damsel, but by a professor, a Doctor of Political Economy! No, say what you like, it can't all be due to sacred simplicity.) "They are feverishly searching for ways of effecting that proper treatment, searching for new ways, methods of cultivation, seed, implements, fertilisers, everything that will lend fertility to the soil that feeds them and that will sooner or later reward them a hundredfold....* Saddening, because" (perhaps you think that here at least this "friend of the people" mentions the wholesale expropriation of the peasantry that accompanies and engenders the concentration of land in the hands of the enterprising muzhiks, its conversion into *capital*, into the basis of *improved* farming—the expropriation that throws on the market the "free" and "cheap" "hands" which make for the success of native "enterprise" which employs all these threshing-machines, seed sorters and winnowing-machines?—Nothing of the kind!) "because ... it is we ourselves who must be roused. Where is our aid to the muzhik who is striving to improve his farming? We have at our disposal science, literature, museums, warehouses, commission agencies." (Yes, gentlemen, that's how he puts them, side by side: "science" and "commission agencies."... The time to study the "friends of the people" is not when they are fighting the Social-Democrats, because on such occasions they don a uniform sewn from tatters of their "fathers'

* You are profoundly right, venerable Mr. Professor, when you say that improved farming will reward a *hundredfold* the "people" who do not "give way to despair" and "remain true to the land." But have you not observed, O, great Doctor of Political Economy, that to acquire all these phosphates and so on, the "muzhik" must stand out from among the mass of the starving poor in having *spare* money — and money, after all, is a product of *social* labour that falls into private hands; that the appropriation of the "reward" for improved farming will be the appropriation of *other people*'s labour; and that only the most contemptible hangers-on of the bourgeoisie can see the source of this abundant reward in the personal effort of the husbandman, who "working with might and main," "fertilises the soil that feeds him"?

ideals," but in their everyday clothes, when they are discussing in detail the affairs of daily life. Then you get the full colour and flavour of these petty-bourgeois ideologists.) "Is there anything of that sort at the disposal of the muzhik? Of course, there are the rudiments of them, but somehow they are developing very slowly. The muzhik wants an example—where are our experimental fields, our model farms? The muzhik is seeking the printed word—where is our popular agronomic literature?... The muzhik is seeking fertilisers, implements, seed—where are our Zemstvo stores for all these things, wholesale buying, purchasing and distributing conveniences?... Where are you, men of affairs, private and Zemstvo? Go forth and work, the time for it has long been ripe, and

> Hearty thanks will be your meed
> From Russia's people!"[73]

N. Karyshev (*Russkoye Bogatstvo*, No. 2, p. 19.)

Here they are, these friends of the petty "people's" bourgeoisie, revelling in their petty-bourgeois progress!

One would think that, even apart from an analysis of our rural economy, it is enough to observe this striking fact in our modern economic history—namely, the generally-noted progress in peasant farming, parallel to the tremendous expropriation of the "peasantry"—to become convinced of the absurdity of picturing the "peasantry" as a single harmonious and homogeneous whole, to become convinced of the bourgeois character of all this progress! But the "friends of the people" remain deaf to all this. Having lost the good features of the old Russian social-revolutionary Narodism, they cling tightly to one of its grave errors—its failure to understand the class antagonism within the peasantry.

"The peasantist [Narodnik] of 'the seventies,'" Hourwich aptly remarks, "had no idea of class antagonism within the ranks of the peasantry themselves, regarding it as confined entirely to the 'exploiter'—kulak or *miroyed*—and his victim, the peasant imbued with the communistic spirit.* Gleb Uspensky stood alone in his scepticism, op-

* "There have arisen opposite social classes within the village community," says Hourwich elsewhere (p. 104). I quote Hourwich only to supplement the facts given above.

posing his ironical smile to the universal illusion. With his perfect knowledge of the peasantry, and his extraordinary artistic talent that penetrated to the very heart of the phenomena, he did not fail to see that individualism had become the basis of economic relations, not only as between the usurer and the debtor, but among the peasants at large. Cf. his article "Casting in One Mould" (Ravneniye pod odno), *Russkaya Mysl*, 1882, No. 1." (Op. cit., p. 106.)

It was pardonable and even natural to succumb to this illusion in the sixties and seventies, when relatively accurate information about rural economy was so scarce, and when the differentiation of the peasantry had not yet become so marked, but today one must deliberately close one's eyes not to see this differentiation. It is extremely characteristic that it is precisely of late, when the ruin of the peasantry seems to have reached its peak, that one hears so much on all sides about progressive trends in peasant farming. Mr. V. V. (also a most indubitable "friend of the people") has written a whole book on this subject. And you cannot accuse him of factual inaccuracy. On the contrary, the technical, agronomical progress of the peasantry is an undoubted fact, but so is the fact of the wholesale expropriation of the peasantry. And there you are—the "friends of the people" concentrate all their attention on the fact that the "muzhik" is feverishly searching for new methods of cultivation to help him fertilise the soil that feeds him—losing sight of the reverse side of the medal, namely, the feverish separation of that very "muzhik" from the soil. They bury their heads in the sand like ostriches so as to avoid looking facts in the face, so as not to notice that they are witnessing the process of the transformation into capital of the land from which the peasant is being separated, the process of creation of a home market.* Try to disprove the *existence* of these two opposite processes among our community peasantry, try *to explain* them in any other way than by the bourgeois character of our society! That would be too much!

* The reason the search for "new methods of cultivation" is becoming "feverish" is that the enterprising muzhik has to run a larger farm, and cannot cope with it by the old methods; that he is compelled by competition to seek new methods, inasmuch as agriculture is increasingly acquiring a commodity, bourgeois character.

Chanting hallelujahs and effusing humanitarian and benevolent phrases are the alpha and omega of their "science," of their whole political "activity."

And they even elevate this modest, liberal patching up of the present order to a regular philosophy. "Minor, genuine activity," says Mr. Krivenko, with an air of profundity, "is much better than major inactivity." How new and clever! Moreover, he goes on to say, "minor activity is by no means synonymous with minor purpose." And as examples of such "extension of activity," when minor performance becomes "proper and good," he quotes the work of a certain lady in organising schools, lawyers' activities among the peasants eliminating pettifoggers, lawyers' plans to accompany circuit courts into the provinces to act as defendant's counsel, and, lastly, what we have already heard about, the organisation of handicraftsmen's warehouses: in this case the extension of activity (to the dimensions of a great purpose) is to consist in opening warehouses "by the combined efforts of the Zemstvos in the busiest centres."

All this, of course, is very lofty, humane and liberal—"liberal," because it will free the bourgeois economic system from all its medieval handicaps and thus make it easier for the worker to fight the system itself, which, of course, will be strengthened rather than hurt by such measures; and we have long been reading about all this in all Russian liberal publications. It would not be worth opposing it if the *Russkoye Bogatstvo* gentlemen did not compel us to do so; they began advancing these "modest beginnings of liberalism" **AGAINST** the Social-Democrats and, as a lesson to them, simultaneously rebuking them for renouncing "the ideals of their fathers." That being the case, we cannot help saying that it is, at the very least, amusing to oppose the Social-Democrats with proposals and suggestions for such moderate and meticulous *liberal* (that is, bourgeois-serving) activity. As for the fathers and their ideals, it should be said that however erroneous and utopian the old theories of the Russian Narodniks were, at all events they were **ABSOLUTELY** opposed to such "modest beginnings of liberalism." I have borrowed the latter expression from Mr. N. K. Mikhailovsky's article "About the Russian Edition of K. Marx's Book" (*Otechestvenniye Zapiski*, 1872, No. 4)—an article written in a very lively and brisk style (compared with his present writings), and strongly protesting against the proposal not to offend our young liberals.

But that was long ago, so long ago that the "friends of the people" have managed to forget all about it, and have glaringly demonstrated, by their tactics, that when there is no materialist criticism of political institutions, and when the class character of the modern state is not understood, it is only one step from political radicalism to political opportunism.

Here are a few examples of this opportunism.

"The transformation of the Ministry of State Properties into the Ministry of Agriculture," declares Mr. Yuzhakov, "may profoundly influence the course of our economic development, but it may also prove to be nothing but a reshuffling of officials." (*Russkoye Bogatstvo*, No. 10.)

Everything depends, consequently, on who will be "called upon"—the friends of the people or the representatives of the interests of the landlords and capitalists. The interests themselves need not be touched.

"The protection of the economically weak from the economically strong is the first natural task of state interference," continues this same Mr. Yuzhakov in the same article; and he is supported in the same terms by the chronicler of home affairs in *Russkoye Bogatstvo*, No. 2. And so as to leave no doubt that his interpretation of this philanthropic nonsense* is the same as that of his worthy associates, the West-European liberal and radical petty-bourgeois ideologists, he at once adds:

"Gladstone's Land Bills,[74] Bismarck's workers' insurance, factory inspection, the idea of our Peasants' Bank, the organisation of migration, measures against the kulak—all these are attempts to apply this same principle of state interference for the protection of the economically weak."

This at least has the merit of being frank. The author bluntly states that, like the Gladstones and Bismarcks, he wants to adhere to the present social relations, like them he wants to patch up and darn present-day society

* It is nonsense because the strength of the "economically strong" lies, among other things, in his possession of political power. Without it he could not maintain his economic rule.

(bourgeois society—something he does not understand any more than the West-European followers of the Gladstones and Bismarcks do), and not combat it. In complete harmony with this, their fundamental theoretical tenet, is the fact that they regard as an instrument of reform an organ which has its basis in this present-day society and protects the interests of its ruling classes—the state. They positively believe the state to be omnipotent and above all classes, and expect that it will not only "assist" the working people, but create a real and proper system (as we have heard from Mr. Krivenko). But then, of course, nothing else is to be expected of them, dyed-in-the-wool petty-bourgeois ideologists that they are. For it is one of the fundamental and characteristic features of the petty bourgeoisie—one, incidentally, which makes it a reactionary class—that the petty producers, disunited and isolated by the very conditions of production and tied down to a definite place and to a definite exploiter, cannot understand the class character of the exploitation and oppression from which they suffer, and suffer sometimes no less than the proletarian; they cannot understand that in bourgeois society the state too is bound to be a class state.*

Why is it then, most worthy "friends of the people," that till now—and with particular energy since this very emancipatory Reform—our government has "supported, protected and created" only the bourgeoisie and capitalism? Why is it that such unseemly conduct on the part of this absolute, allegedly supraclass, government has coincided precisely with a historical period characterised in the country's internal life by the development of commodity economy, commerce and industry? Why do you consider these latter changes in

* That is why the "friends of the people" are arch-reactionaries when they say that it is the state's natural task to protect the economically weak (that is what it *should be* according to their banal, old wives' morality), whereas Russia's entire history and home policy testify that the task of our state is to protect only the feudal landlords and the big bourgeoisie, and to punish with the utmost brutality every attempt of the "*economically weak*" to stand up for their rights. And that, of course, is its *natural* task, because absolutism and the bureaucracy are thoroughly saturated with the feudal-bourgeois spirit, and because in the economic sphere the bourgeoisie hold undivided sway and keep the workers "as quiet as lambs."

internal life to be the effect and the government's policy the cause, despite the fact that these changes were so deep down in society that the government did not even notice them and put innumerable obstacles in their way, and despite the fact that this very same "absolute" government, under other conditions of internal life, "supported," "protected" and "created" another class?

Oh, the "friends of the people" never concern themselves with such questions! All this, you see, is materialism, dialectics, "Hegelianism," "mysticism and metaphysics." They simply think that if you plead with this government nicely enough and humbly enough, it will put everything right. And as far as humbleness is concerned, one must do *Russkoye Bogatstvo* justice: truly, it stands out even among the Russian liberal press for its inability to display the slightest independence. Judge for yourselves:

"The abolition of the salt tax, the abolition of the poll-tax and the reduction of the land redemption payments" are described by Mr. Yuzhakov as "a considerable relief to people's farming." Well, of course! But was not the abolition of the salt tax accompanied by the imposition of a host of new indirect taxes and an increase in the old ones? Was not the abolition of the poll-tax accompanied by an increase in the payments made by the former state peasants, under guise of placing them on a redemption basis? And is there not even now, after the famous reduction of redemption payments (by which the government did not even return to the peasants the profit it had made out of the redemption operations), a discrepancy between the payments and the income from the land, i.e., a direct survival of feudal quitrent? Never mind! What is important, you see, is "the first step," the "principle." As for the rest ... the rest we can plead for later on!

These, however, are only the blossoms. Now for the fruit. "The eighties eased the people's burden" (that's by the above measures!) "and thus saved them from utter ruin."

This is another phrase classic for its shameless servility, one that can only be placed, say, alongside Mr. Mikhailovsky's statement, quoted above, that we have still to create a proletariat. One cannot help recalling in this connection Shchedrin's incisive description of the evolution of the Russian liberal! This liberal starts out by pleading with the authorities to grant reforms "as far as possible," then he goes on to beg for "well, at least something," and ends by taking up an eternal and unshakable stand on "anything, however mean." And what else can one say of the "friends of the people" but that they have adopted this eternal and unshakable stand when, fresh from the impressions of a famine affecting millions of people, towards which the government's attitude was first one of a huckster's stinginess and then of a huckster's cowardice, they say in print that the government has saved the people from utter ruin!! Several years more will pass, marked by the still more rapid expropriation of the peasantry; the government, in addition to establishing a Ministry of Agriculture, will abolish one or two direct and impose several new indirect taxes; the famine will then affect 40 million people—and these gentlemen will write in the same old way: you see, 40 and not 50 million are starving, that is because the government has eased the people's burden and has saved them from utter ruin; it is because the government has hearkened to the "friends of the people" and established a Ministry of Agriculture!

Another example:

In *Russkoye Bogatstvo*, No. 2, the chronicler of home affairs arguing that Russia is "fortunately" (sic!) a backward country, "which has preserved elements that enable her to base her economic system on the principle of solidarity,"* says that she is therefore able to act "in international affairs as an exponent of economic solidarity" and that Russia's chances for this are enhanced by her undeniable "political might"!!

It is the gendarme of Europe, that constant and most reliable bulwark of all reaction, who has reduced the Russian people, themselves oppressed at home, to the shameful position of serving as an instrument for oppressing the peoples in the West—it is this gendarme who is described as an exponent of economic solidarity!

* Between whom? The landlord and the peasant, the enterprising muzhik and the tramp, the mill owner and the worker? To understand what this classical "principle of solidarity" means, we must remember that solidarity between the employer and the workman is achieved by "a reduction in wages."

This is indeed beyond all limit! Messrs. the "friends of the people" will outdo all liberals. They not only plead with the government, they not only eulogise it, they positively pray to it, pray with such obeisance, with such zeal that a stranger cannot help feeling eerie at the sound of their loyal foreheads cracking on the flagstones.

Do you remember the German definition of a philistine?

Was ist der Philister?
Ein hohler Darm,
Voll Furcht und Hoffnung,
Dass Gott erbarm.*

This definition does not quite apply to our affairs. God ... God takes a back seat with us. But the authorities ... that's a different matter. And if in this definition we substitute the word "authorities" for the word "God" we shall get an exact description of the ideological stock-in-trade, the moral level and the civic courage of the Russian humane and liberal "friends of the people."

To this absolutely preposterous view of the government, the "friends of the people" add a corresponding attitude toward the so-called "intelligentsia." Mr. Krivenko writes: "Literature ..." should "appraise phenomena according to their social meaning and encourage every active effort to do good. It has harped, and continues to harp, on the shortage of teachers, doctors, technicians, on the fact that the people are sick, poor" (there are few technicians), "illiterate, etc.; and when people come forward who are weary of sitting at card tables, participating in private theatricals and eating sturgeon patties at parties given by Marshals of Nobility, and who go out to work with rare self-sacrifice and in face of numerous obstacles" (think of it: they have sacrificed card tables, theatricals and patties!), "literature should welcome them."

Two pages later, with the business-like air of an old campaigner grown wise by experience, he reproves those who "wavered when confronted with the question whether or not to accept office as Zemsky Nachalniks,[75] town mayors, or

* What is a philistine? A hollow gut, full of fear and of hope in God's mercy (Goethe).—*Ed.*

chairmen or members of Zemstvo Boards under the new regulations. In a society with a developed consciousness of civic requirements and duties" (really, gentlemen, this is as good as the speeches of famous Russian Jacks-in-office like the Baranovs and Kosiches!), "such wavering and such an attitude to affairs would be inconceivable, because it would assimilate in its own way every reform that had any vital side to it at all, that is, would take advantage of and develop those sides of the reform that are expedient; as to the undesirable sides, it would convert them into a dead letter; and if there were nothing whatever vital in the reform it would remain an entirely alien body."

What on earth do you make of that! What miserable twopenny-ha'penny opportunism, what indulgence in self-admiration! The task of literature is to collect all the drawing-room gossip about the wicked Marxists, to bow and cringe to the government for saving the people from utter ruin, to welcome people who have grown weary of sitting at card tables, to teach the "public" not to fight shy even of such posts as that of Zemsky Nachalnik.... What is this I am reading—*Nedelya*,[76] or *Novoye Vremya*? No, it is *Russkoye Bogatstvo*, the organ of the advanced Russian democrats....

And such gentlemen talk about the "ideals of their fathers," claim that they, and they alone, guard the traditions of the days when France poured the ideas of socialism all over Europe[77]—and when, in Russia, the assimilation of these ideas produced the theories and teachings of Herzen and Chernyshevsky. This is a downright disgrace and would be positively outrageous and offensive—if *Russkoye Bogatstvo* were not so utterly amusing, if such statements in the columns of a magazine of this type did not arouse Homeric laughter, and nothing else. Yes, indeed, you are besmirching those ideals! What were actually the ideals of the first Russian socialists, the socialists of the epoch which Kautsky so aptly described in the words:

"When every socialist was a poet and every poet a socialist."

Faith in a special social order, in the communal system of Russian life; hence—*faith in the possibility of a peasant socialist revolution*—that is what inspired them and roused dozens and hundreds of people to wage a heroic struggle against the government. And you, you cannot reproach the Social-Democrats with failing to appreciate the immense historical services of these, the finest people of their day, with failing to respect their memory profoundly. But I ask you, where is that faith now? It has vanished. So utterly, that when Mr. V. V. tried to argue last year that the village community trains the people to common effort and is a centre of altruistic sentiments, etc.,[78] even Mr. Mikhailovsky's conscience was pricked and he shamefacedly began to lecture Mr. V. V. and to point out that "no *investigation* has shown a connection between our village community and altruism."[79] And, indeed, no investigation has. Yet there was a time when people had faith, implicit faith, without making any investigation.

How? Why? On what grounds?...

"Every socialist was a poet and every poet a socialist."

Moreover, adds the same Mr. Mikhailovsky, all conscientious investigators agree that the countryside is splitting up, giving rise, on the one hand, to a mass of proletarians, and, on the other, to a handful of "kulaks" who keep the rest of the population under their heel. And again he is right: the countryside is indeed splitting up. Nay more, the countryside long ago split up completely. And the old Russian peasant socialism split up with it, making way for workers' socialism, on the one hand, and degenerating into vulgar petty-bourgeois radicalism, on the other. This change cannot be described as anything but degeneration. From the doctrine that peasant life is a special social order and that our country has taken an exceptional path of development, there has emerged a sort of diluted eclecticism, which can no longer deny that commodity economy has become the basis of economic development and has grown into capitalism, but which refuses to see the bourgeois character of all the relations of production, refuses to see the necessity of the class struggle under this system. From a political programme calculated *to arouse the peasantry* for the socialist revolution *against the foundations of modern society** there has

* That, substantially, was what all our old revolutionary programmes amounted to—from those, say, of the Bakuninists and the rebels,[80] to those of the Narodniks, and finally the Narodovoltsi,

emerged a programme calculated to patch up, to "improve" the conditions of the peasantry *while preserving the foundations of modern society*.

Strictly speaking, all this should already suffice to give an idea of the kind of "criticism" to be expected from these gentlemen of *Russkoye Bogatstvo* when they undertake to "demolish" the Social-Democrats. They do not make the slightest attempt to give a straightforward and conscientious exposition of the Social-Democrats' conception of Russian realities (they could quite well do so, and get round the censorship, if they laid special stress on the economic side and kept to the general, partly allegorical terms in which they have conducted all their "polemics") and to argue against its substance, to argue against the correctness of the practical conclusions drawn from it. They prefer instead to confine themselves to the most vacuous phrases about abstract schemes and belief in them, about the conviction that every country has to pass through the phase ... and similar nonsense, with which we have already become sufficiently familiar in the case of Mr. Mikhailovsky. Often we get downright distortions. Mr. Krivenko, for example, declares that Marx "admitted that, if we desired it" (?!! So, *according to Marx*, the evolution of social and economic relations depends on human will and consciousness?? What is this—abysmal ignorance or unparalleled effrontery?!), "and acted accordingly, we could avoid the vicissitudes of capitalism and proceed by a different and more expedient path (sic!!!)."

Our knight was able to talk such nonsense by indulging in deliberate distortion. Citing the passage from the well-known "K. Marx's Letter" (*Yuridichesky Vestnik*, 1888, No. 10), where Marx speaks of his high esteem for Chernyshevsky, who thought it possible for Russia not to "undergo the tortures of the capitalist system," Mr. Krivenko closes the quotation marks, i.e., ends the reproduction of what Marx actually said (the last words of which were: "he [Chernyshevsky] pronounces in favour of this latter solution")—

---

for whom the conviction that the peasants would send an overwhelming majority of socialists to a future Zemsky Sobor[81] also occupied no small place in their thoughts.

and adds: "And I, says Marx, *share*" (Krivenko's italics) "these views" (p. 186, No. 12).

What Marx actually said was this: "And my honourable critic would have had at least as much reason for inferring from my esteem for this 'great Russian scholar and critic' that I shared his views on the question, as for concluding from my polemic against the Russian 'literary man' and Pan-Slavist[82] that I rejected them." (*Yuridichesky Vestnik*, 1888, No. 10, p. 271.)

And so Marx said that Mr. Mikhailovsky had no right to regard him as an opponent of the idea of Russia's special line of development because he also respected those who held this idea; but Mr. Krivenko misconstrues this to mean that Marx "admitted" this special line of development. This is an out-and-out distortion. Marx's statement quoted above shows quite clearly that he evaded the question as such: "Mr. Mikhailovsky could have taken as a basis either of the two contradictory remarks, i.e., he had no grounds for basing his conclusions as to my views on Russian affairs in general on either of them." And in order that these remarks should provide no occasion for misinterpretation, Marx, in this very same "letter," gave a direct reply to the question of how his theory could be applied to Russia. This reply very clearly shows that Marx avoided answering the question as such, avoided examining Russian data, which alone could decide the question: "If Russia," he replied, "is tending to become a capitalist nation on the pattern of the West-European countries—and during the last years she has been taking much trouble in this respect—she will not succeed without having first transformed a good part of her peasants into proletarians."[83]

This, I think, is perfectly clear: the question was whether Russia was tending to become a capitalist nation, whether the ruin of her peasants was the process of the creation of a capitalist system, of a capitalist proletariat; and Marx says that "if" she was so tending, she would have to transform a good part of her peasants into proletarians. In other words, Marx's theory is to investigate and explain the evolution of the economic system of certain countries, and its "application" to Russia can be only the **INVESTIGATION** of Russian production relations and their evolution, **EMPLOYING** the established practices of the **MATERIALIST** method and of **THEORETICAL** political economy.*

The elaboration of a new theory of methodology and political economy marked such gigantic progress in social science, such a tremendous advance for socialism, that almost immediately after the appearance of *Capital* "the destiny of capitalism in Russia" became the principal theoretical problem for Russian socialists; the most heated debates raged around this problem, and the most important points of programme were decided in accordance with it. And it is noteworthy that when (some ten years ago) a separate group of socialists appeared who answered in the affirmative the question of whether Russia's evolution was capitalist, and based this answer on the data of Russian economic reality, it encountered no direct and definite criticism of the point at issue, no criticism which accepted the same general methodological and theoretical principles and gave a different explanation of the data.

The "friends of the people," who have launched a veritable crusade against the Marxists, likewise do not argue their case by examining the facts. As we saw in the first article, they dispose of the matter with phrases. Mr. Mikhailovsky, moreover, never misses an opportunity to display his wit about the Marxists lacking unanimity and about their failure to agree among themselves. And "our well-known" N. K. Mikhailovsky laughs heartily over his joke about Marxists "real" and "not real." It is true that complete unanimity does not reign among the Marxists. But, firstly, Mr. Mikhailovsky misrepresents this fact; and, secondly, it demonstrates the strength and vitality of Russian Social-Democracy and not its weakness. A particularly characteristic feature of the recent period is that socialists are arriving at Social-Democratic views by various paths and for that reason, while unreservedly agreeing on the fundamental and principal thesis that Russia is a bourgeois society which has grown out of the feudal system, that its political form is a class state, and that the only way to end the exploitation

* I repeat that this conclusion could not but be clear to anybody who had read the *Communist Manifesto*, *The Poverty of Philosophy*, and *Capital*, and that a special explanation was required only for the benefit of Mr. Mikhailovsky.

of the working people is through the class struggle of the proletariat—they differ on many particular problems both in their methods of argument and in the detailed interpretation of this or that phenomenon of Russian life. I can therefore delight Mr. Mikhailovsky in advance by stating that, within the limits of the above-mentioned thesis, which is fundamental and common to all Social-Democrats, differences of opinion exist also on the problems that have been touched upon in these cursory notes, for example, the peasant Reform, the economics of peasant farming and handicraft industries, land renting, etc. The unanimity of people who content themselves with the unanimous acceptance of "lofty truths" such as: the peasant Reform *might* open for Russia peaceful paths of proper development; the state *might* call, not upon the representatives of capitalist interests, but upon the "friends of the people"; the village community *might* socialise agriculture and manufacturing industry, which *might* be developed into large-scale production by the handicraftsman; *people*'s land renting supports *people*'s farming—this touching and moving unanimity has been replaced by disagreements among persons who are seeking for an explanation of Russia's *actual*, *present* economic organisation as a system of definite production relations, for an explanation of her *actual* economic evolution, of her political and all other types of superstructure.

And if such work—while leading people from different angles to the acceptance of the common position which undoubtedly dictates joint political action and consequently confers on all who accept it the right and duty to call themselves **"SOCIAL-DEMOCRATS"**—still leaves a wide field for differences of opinion on a host of particular problems open to various solutions, it merely demonstrates, of course, the strength and vitality of Russian Social-Democracy.*

* For the simple reason that *no solution* of these problems *has so far been found*. Indeed, you cannot regard as a solution of the land-renting problem the assertion that "people's land renting supports people's farming," or the following description of the system of cultivating the landlord's land with the peasants' implements: "The peasant has proved to be stronger than the landlord," who "has sacrificed his independence for the benefit of the independent peasant";

Moreover, it would be hard to imagine anything more difficult than the conditions under which this work is being done: there is not, nor can there be, an organ to unite the various aspects of the work; in view of prevailing police conditions, private intercourse is extremely difficult. It is only natural that Social-Democrats cannot properly discuss and reach agreement on details, that they contradict each other....

This is indeed funny, is it not?

Mr. Krivenko's references, in his "polemic" against the Social-Democrats, to "neo-Marxists" may cause some perplexity. Some readers may think that something in the nature of a split has taken place among the Social-Democrats, and that "neo-Marxists" have broken away from the old Social-Democrats. Nothing of the kind. At no time or place has anybody in a public defence of Marxism criticised the theories and programme of Russian Social-Democracy, or advocated any other kind of Marxism. The fact is that Messrs. Krivenko and Mikhailovsky have been listening to drawing-room gossip about the Marxists, have been observing various liberals who use Marxism to cover up their liberal inanity, and, with their characteristic cleverness and tact, have set out with this stock-in-trade to "criticise" the Marxists. It is not surprising that this "criticism" consists of a regular chain of absurdities and filthy attacks.

"To be consistent," argues Mr. Krivenko, "we should give an affirmative answer to this" (to the question: "should we not strive for the development of capitalist industry?"), and "not shrink from buying up peasants' land or opening shops and taverns"; we should "rejoice at the success of the numerous inn-keepers in the Duma and assist the still more numerous buyers-up of the peasants' grain."

Really, that is amusing. Try to tell such a "friend of the people" that everywhere in Russia the exploitation of the working people is by its nature capitalistic, that the enterprising muzhiks and buyers-up should be classed among the representatives of capitalism because of such and such political-

"the peasant has wrested large-scale production from the grasp of the landlord"; "the people are the victors in the struggle for the form of agricultural technique." This idle liberal chatter is to be found in *The Destiny of Capitalism*, the work of "our well-known" Mr. V. V.

economic features, which prove the bourgeois character of the splitting up of the peasantry—why, he would raise a howl, call it outrageous heresy, shout about the indiscriminate borrowing of West-European formulas and abstract schemes (while at the same time most carefully evading the actual meaning of the "heretical" argument). But when pictures of the "horrors" caused by the wicked Marxists have to be painted, lofty science and pure ideals may be left aside, and it may be admitted that buyers-up of peasants' grain and peasants' land-really are representatives of capitalism, and not merely "hankerers" after other people's goods.

Try and prove to this "friend of the people" that not only are the Russian bourgeoisie already in control of the people's labour everywhere, due to the concentration of the means of production in their hands alone, but they also bring pressure to bear upon the government, initiating, compelling and determining the bourgeois character of its policy—why, he would fly into a real rage, begin to shout about the omnipotence of our government, about fatal misunderstanding and unlucky chance alone causing it always to "call upon" representatives of the interests of capitalism and not upon the "friends of the people," about its artificially implanting capitalism.... But on the sly they are themselves compelled to recognise as representatives of capitalism the innkeepers in the Duma, i.e., one of the elements of this very government that is supposed to stand above classes. But, gentlemen, are the interests of capitalism in Russia represented only in the "Duma," and only by "inn-keepers"?...

As to filthy attacks, we have had quite enough of them from Mr. Mikhailovsky, and we get them again from Mr. Krivenko, who, for example, in his eagerness to annihilate the hated Social-Democracy, relates that "some go into the factories (when, of course, they can get soft jobs as technicians or office workers), claiming that their sole purpose is to accelerate the capitalist process." There is no need, of course, to reply to such positively indecent statements. All we can do is to put a full stop here.

Keep on in the same spirit, gentlemen, keep boldly on! The imperial government, the one which, as you have just told us, has already taken measures (even though they have flaws in them) to save the people from utter ruin, will take measures, this time without any flaws whatever, to save your banality and ignorance from exposure. "Cultured society" will gladly continue as hitherto, in the intervals between sturgeon patties and the card table, to talk about the "younger brother" and to devise humane projects for "improving" his condition; its representatives will be pleased to learn from you that by taking up positions as Zemsky Nachalniks or other supervisors of the peasants' purses they display a developed consciousness of civic requirements and duties. Keep on! You may be certain not only of being left in peace but even of approval and praise ... from the lips of the Messrs. Burenins.

In conclusion it will perhaps be worth while replying to a question which has probably occurred already to more than one reader. Did it pay to argue so long with such gentlemen? Was it worth while replying seriously to this stream of liberal and censor-protected filth which they were pleased to call polemics?

I think it was, not for their sake, of course, or for the sake of the "cultured" public, but for the useful lesson which Russian socialists can and should learn from this onslaught. It provides most striking and most convincing proof that the period of Russia's social development, when democracy and socialism were merged in one inseparable and indissoluble whole (as was the case, for example, in Chernyshevsky's day), has gone never to return. Today there are absolutely no grounds for the idea, which Russian socialists here and there still cling to and which most harmfully affects their theories and practical work, that there is no profound qualitative difference in Russia between the ideas of the democrats and those of the socialists.

Quite the contrary; a wide gulf divides these ideas, and it is high time the Russian socialists understood this, understood that a **COMPLETE** and **FINAL RUPTURE** with the ideas of the democrats is **INEVITABLE** and **IMPERATIVE!**

Let us see what this Russian democrat actually was in the days which gave rise to this idea, and what he has now become. The "friends of the people" provide enough material for such a comparison.

Extremely interesting in this connection is Mr. Krivenko's attack on Mr. Struve who, in a German publication, opposed Mr. Nik. —on's utopianism (his article "On Capitalist Development in Russia," "Zur Beurtheilung der kapitalistischen Entwicklung Russlands," appeared in *Sozialpolitisches Centralblatt*,[84] III, No. 1, October 2, 1893). Mr. Krivenko launches out against Mr. Struve for, as he alleges, classing the ideas of those who "stand for the village community and the allotment" as "national socialism" (which, he says, is of a "purely utopian nature"). This terrible accusation of being concerned with socialism drives our worthy author into a rage:

"Were there," he exclaims, "no others" (apart from Herzen, Chernyshevsky and the Narodniks), "who stood for the village community and the allotment? What about those who drew up the regulation for the peasants, who made the community and the peasants' economic independence the basis of the Reform; what about the investigators of our history and of contemporary life who support these principles, and almost the whole of our serious and respectable press, which also supports these principles—are they all victims of the delusion called 'national socialism'?"

Calm yourself, most worthy "friend of the people"! You were so scared by the awful accusation of being concerned with socialism that you did not even take the trouble to read Mr. Struve's "little article" carefully. And, indeed, what a crying injustice it would be to accuse those who stand for "the village community and the allotment" of being concerned with socialism! Pray, what is there socialistic in this? Socialism, as we know, is the name given to the protest and struggle against the exploitation of the working people, a struggle for the complete abolition of this exploitation—while "to stand for the allotment" means supporting the peasant's payment of redemption money for all the land they used to have at their disposal. But even if one does not stand for land redemption but for the gratuitous retention of the land the peasants possessed before the Reform, there is nothing socialistic in it, for it is this peasant ownership of land (which evolved during the feudal period) that has everywhere in the West, as here in Russia,* been the basis of bourgeois society. "To stand for the village community," i.e., to protest against police interference in the customary methods of distributing the land—what is there socialistic in that, when everyone knows that exploitation of the working people can very well exist and is engendered within this community? That is stretching the word "socialism" to mean anything; maybe Mr. Pobedonostsev,[85] too, will have to be classed as a socialist!

Mr. Struve is not guilty of such an awful injustice at all. He speaks of the "utopianism of the national socialism" of the *Narodniks*, and we can see whom he classes as Narodniks from the fact that he refers to Plekhanov's *Our Differences* as a polemic against the Narodniks. Plekhanov, undoubtedly, polemised against socialists, against people who had nothing in common with the "serious and respectable" Russian press. Mr. Krivenko, therefore, had no right to take as applying to himself what was meant for the Narodniks. If, however, he was so anxious to know Mr. Struve's opinion about the trend to which he himself adheres, I am surprised that he paid no attention to, and *did not translate for Russkoye Bogatstvo*, the following passage in Mr. Struve's article:

"As capitalist development advances," says the author, "the philosophy" (Narodnik philosophy) "just described is bound to lose its basis. It will either degenerate (wird herabsinken) into a rather colourless reformist trend, capable of compromise and seeking for compromise,** promising rudiments of which have long been observable, or it will admit that the actual development is inevitable and will draw the theoretical and practical conclusions that necessarily follow from this—in other words, will cease to be utopian."

If Mr. Krivenko cannot guess where, in Russia, are to be found the rudiments of the trend that is only capable of compromise, I would advise him to glance at *Russkoye Bogatstvo*, at the theoretical views of that magazine, which represent a pitiful attempt to piece together fragments of the Narodnik doctrine with the recognition of Russia's cap-

---

* Proof—the break-up of the peasantry.

** Ziemlich blaße kompromißfähige und kompromißsüchtige Reformrichtung—I think this might be rendered in Russian as *kulturnichesky opportunizm* [uplift opportunism].

italist development, and at its political programme, which aims at improving and restoring the economy of the small producers on the basis of the present capitalist system.*

One of the most characteristic and significant phenomena of our social life in recent times is, generally speaking, the degeneration of Narodism into petty-bourgeois opportunism.

Really, if we take the substance of the programme of *Russkoye Bogatstvo*—the regulation of migration, land renting, cheap credit, museums, warehouses, technical improvement, artels, common land cultivation and all the rest—we shall find that it is indeed very widely circulated in the whole "serious and respectable press," i.e., in the whole liberal press, the publications that are not the organs of the feudal landlords and do not belong to the reptile press.[86] The idea that all these measures are necessary, useful, urgent, "innocuous," has taken deep root among the entire intelligentsia and is extremely widespread. You will meet with it in provincial sheets and newspapers, in all Zemstvo

* Mr. Krivenko cuts an altogether sorry figure in his attempt to wage war on Mr. Struve. He betrays a childish inability to bring forward any really valid objections, and an equally childish irritation. For example, Mr. Struve says that Mr. Nik. —on is a "utopian," and gives very explicit reasons for calling him so: 1) because he ignores the "actual development of Russia," and 2) because he does not understand the class character of our state and appeals to "society" and the "state." What arguments does Mr. Krivenko bring against this? Does he deny that our development is really capitalist? Does he say that it is of some other kind? Does he say that ours is not a class state? No. He prefers to avoid these questions altogether and to battle with comical wrath against "stereotyped patterns" of his own invention. Another example. Besides charging Mr. Nik. —on with not understanding the class struggle, Mr. Struve reproaches him with grave errors of theory in the sphere of "purely economic facts." He points out, among other things, that in speaking of the smallness of our non-agricultural population, Mr. Nik. —on "fails to observe that the capitalist development of Russia will smooth out this difference between 80%" (rural population of Russia) "and 44%" (rural population of America): "that, one might say, is its historical mission." Mr. Krivenko, firstly, garbles this passage by speaking of "our" (?) mission to deprive the peasant of his land, whereas the fact of the matter is that capitalism tends to reduce the rural population, and, secondly, without saying a single word on the substance of the question (whether a capitalism that does not lead to a reduction of the rural population is possible), he talks a lot of nonsense about "doctrinaires," etc. See Appendix II (p. 308 of this volume.—*Ed.*).

researches, abstracts, descriptions, etc., etc. If *this* is to be regarded as Narodism, then undoubtedly its success is enormous and indisputable.

Only it is not Narodism at all (in the old, customary meaning of that term), and its success and tremendously widespread character have been achieved at the cost of vulgarising Narodism, converting social-revolutionary Narodism, which was sharply opposed to our liberalism, into uplift opportunism, that merges with this liberalism and expresses only the interests of the petty bourgeoisie.

To convince ourselves of this we need but turn to the pictures of differentiation among the peasants and handicraftsmen given above—and these pictures by no means depict isolated or new facts, but are simply an attempt to portray in terms of political economy that "school" of "blood-suckers" and "farm labourers" whose existence in our countryside is not denied even by our opponents. It goes without saying that the "Narodnik" measures can only serve to strengthen the petty bourgeoisie; or else (artels and common cultivation) are bound to be miserable palliatives, remain pitiful experiments of the kind which the liberal bourgeoisie cultivated so tenderly everywhere in Europe for the simple reason that they do not in the least affect the "school" itself. For the same reason, even the Messrs. Yermolovs and Wittes[87] cannot object to progress of this kind. Quite the contrary. Do us the favour, gentlemen! They will even give you money "for experiments," if only these will divert the "intelligentsia" from revolutionary work (emphasising the antagonism, explaining it to the proletariat, attempting to bring this antagonism out on to the high road of direct political struggle) to such patching up of the antagonism, to conciliation and unification. Do us the favour!

Let us dwell a little on the process which led to this degeneration of Narodism. When it first arose, in its original form, it was a fairly well-knit theory: starting from the view of a specific way of life of the people, it believed in the communist instincts of the "communal" peasant and for that reason regarded the peasantry as a natural fighter for socialism. But it lacked theoretical elaboration and confirmation in the facts of Russian life, on the one hand, and experience in applying a political programme based on these assumed qualities of the peasant, on the other.

The development of the theory, therefore, proceeded along the two lines, the theoretical and the practical. The theoretical work was directed mainly towards studying that form of land*ownership* in which they wanted to see the rudiments of communism; and this work yielded a wealth of factual material of the most varied kind. But this material, which mainly concerned the form of land*ownership*, completely obscured the *economics* of the countryside from the investigators' eyes. This happened all the more naturally, because, firstly, the investigators lacked a sound theory of method in social science, a theory showing the need to single out and make a special study of production relations; and because, secondly, the collected factual material furnished direct evidence of the immediate needs of the peasantry, of the immediate hardships which had a depressing effect upon peasant economy. All the investigators' attention was concentrated on studying these hardships—land poverty, high payments, lack of rights, and the crushed and downtrodden condition of the peasants. All this was described, studied and explained with such a wealth of material, in such minute detail, that if ours were not a class state, if its policy were determined not by the interests of the ruling classes, but by the impartial discussion of the "people's needs," it should, of course, have been convinced a thousand times over of the need for eliminating these hardships. The naïve investigators, believing in the possibility of "convincing" society and the state, were completely submerged in the details of the facts they had collected, and lost sight of one thing, the political-economic structure of the countryside, lost sight of the main background of the economy that really was being crushed by these immediate hardships. The result, naturally, was that defence of the interests of an economy crushed by land poverty, etc., turned out to be a defence of the interests of the class that held this economy in its hands, that alone could endure and develop under the given social-economic relations *within* the community, under the given economic system in the country.

Theoretical work directed towards the study of the institution which was to serve as the basis and support for the abolition of exploitation led to a programme being drawn up which expresses the interests of the petty bourgeoisie, i.e., the very class upon which this system of exploitation rests!

At the same time, practical revolutionary work also developed in quite an unexpected direction. Belief in the communist instincts of the muzhik naturally demanded of the socialists that they set politics aside and "go among the people." A host of extremely energetic and talented persons set about fulfilling this programme, but practice convinced them of the naïveté of the idea of the muzhik's instincts being communist. It was decided, incidentally, that they did not have to do with the muzhik, but with the government—and the entire activity was then concentrated on a fight against the government, a fight then waged by the intellectuals alone; they were sometimes joined by *workers*. At first this fight was waged in the name of socialism and was based on the theory that the people were ready for socialism and that it would be possible, merely by seizing power, to effect not only a political, but also a social revolution. Latterly, this theory is apparently becoming utterly discredited, and the struggle waged by the Narodovoltsi against the government is becoming a struggle of the radicals for political liberty.

Hence, in this case, too, the work led to results diametrically opposite to its point of departure; in this case, too, there emerged a programme expressing only the interests of radical bourgeois democracy. Strictly speaking, this process is not yet complete, but is already, I think, clearly defined. This development of Narodism was altogether natural and inevitable, because the doctrine was based on the purely mythical idea of peasant economy being a special (communal) system: the myth dissolved when it came into contact with reality, and peasant socialism turned into radical-democratic representation of the petty-bourgeois peasantry.

Let me give examples of the democrat's evolution:

"We must see to it," argues Mr. Krivenko, "that instead of an integral man we do not get an all-Russian jellyfish filled only with a vague ferment of good sentiments but incapable either of real self-sacrifice or of doing anything durable in life." The homily is an excellent one, but let us see what it is applied to. "In regard to the latter," continues Mr. Krivenko, "I am acquainted with the following vexatious fact": in the South of Russia there lived some young people "who were inspired by the very best intentions and by a love for the younger brother; they showed the greatest attention and respect for the muzhik; they treated him as the guest of honour, ate out of the same bowl with him, treated him to jam and biscuits; they paid him higher prices than others did; they gave him money—as loans, or as tips, or for no reason at all, they told him about European institutions and workers' associations, etc. In the same locality there lived a young German named Schmidt, the steward of an estate, or rather just a gardener, a man without any humanitarian ideas, a real, narrow, formal German soul" (sic??!!), etc. Three or four years passed, and these people separated and went their different ways. Another twenty years passed, and the author, on revisiting the locality, learned that "Mr. Schmidt" (as a reward for his useful activities gardener Schmidt had been promoted to Mr. Schmidt) had taught the peasants grape growing, from which they now obtain "some income," 75 to 100 rubles a year, and on this account they had preserved "kind memories" of him, whereas of the "gentlemen who merely cherished kind sentiments for the muzhik but did nothing tangible (!) for him, not even the memory was left."

A calculation shows that the events described occurred about 1869-1870, that is, roughly at the time when the Russian Narodnik socialists were trying to introduce into Russia the most advanced and most important of "European institutions"—the International.[88]

Clearly, the impression created by Mr. Krivenko's account is a little too harsh, and so he hastens to make a reservation:

"I do not suggest, of course, that Schmidt was better than these gentlemen. I merely point out why, for all his defects, he left a more lasting impression in the locality and on the population." (I do not suggest that he was better, I merely point out that he left a more lasting impression—what nonsense?!) "Nor do I say that he did anything important; on the contrary, I cite what he did as an example of a most trifling, incidental deed, which cost him nothing, but which for all that was undoubtedly vital."

The reservation, you see, is very ambiguous; the point, however, is not its ambiguity, but the fact that the author, in contrasting the fruitlessness of the one activity with the success of the other, apparently does not suspect that there is a fundamental difference of tendency between these two types of activity. That is the whole point, which makes the story so characteristic in defining the contemporary democrat's physiognomy.

The young people who talked to the muzhik about "European institutions and workers' associations" evidently wanted to inspire in the muzhik a desire to alter the forms of social life (the conclusion I draw may be wrong in this instance, but everyone will agree, I think, that it is a legitimate one, for it follows inevitably from Mr. Krivenko's story), they wanted to stir him to undertake a social revolution against contemporary society, which engenders such disgraceful exploitation and oppression of the working people, accompanied by universal rejoicing over all sorts of liberal progress. "Mr. Schmidt," on the other hand, true husbandman that he was, merely wanted to help others arrange their affairs—and nothing more. Well, but how can one compare, juxtapose these two types of activity, which have diametrically opposite aims? Why, it is just as though somebody were to start comparing the failure of a person who tried to destroy a given building with the success of one who tried to reinforce it! To draw a comparison with any sense in it, he should have inquired why the efforts of the young men and women who went among the people to stimulate the peasants to revolution were so unsuccessful—whether it was because they erroneously believed that the "peasantry" really represented the working people and exploited population, whereas in fact the peasantry does not constitute a single class (—an illusion only to be explained, perhaps, by the reflected influence of the epoch of the fall of serfdom, when the peasantry did indeed come forward as a *class*, but only as a class of feudal society), for within it a bourgeois and a proletarian class are forming—in a word, he should have examined the old socialist theories and the Social-Democratic criticism of these theories. Instead, Mr. Krivenko moves heaven and earth to prove that "Mr. Schmidt's" work was "undoubtedly vital." But pardon me, most worthy Mr. "friend of the people," why hammer at an open door? Whoever doubts it? To lay out a vineyard and get an annual income of 75 to 100 rubles from it—what could be more vital?*

And the author goes on to explain that if one peasant lays out a vineyard, that is isolated activity; but if several do, that is common and widespread activity, which transforms a small job into real and proper work, *just as, for example*, A. N. Engelhardt[89] not only used phosphates on his estate but got others to use them.

Now, isn't this democrat really splendid!

Let us take another example, one from opinions on the peasant Reform. What attitude towards it had Chernyshevsky, a democrat of that epoch, when democracy and socialism were undivided? Unable to express his opinion openly, he *kept silent*, but gave the following roundabout description of the contemplated reform:

"*Suppose I was interested in taking measures to protect the provisions out of which your dinner is made. It goes without saying that if I was prompted to do so by my kind disposition towards you, then my zeal was based on the assumption that the provisions belonged to you and that the dinner prepared from them would be wholesome and beneficial to you. Imagine my feelings, then, when I learn that the provisions do not belong to you at all, and that for every dinner prepared from them you are charged a price which not only exceeds the cost of the dinner*" (this was written *before* the Reform. Yet the Messrs. Yuzhakovs assert *now* that its fundamental principle was to give security to the peasants!!) "*but which you are not able to pay at all without extreme hardship. What thoughts enter my head when I make such strange discoveries?... How stupid I was to bother about the matter when the conditions did not exist to ensure its usefulness! Who but a fool would bother about the retention of property in certain hands without first satisfying himself that those hands will receive the*

* You should have tried to thrust your offer of this "vital" work on *those* young people who talked to the muzhik about European associations! What a welcome, what a splendid retort they would have given you! You would have been as mortally afraid of their ideas as you now are of materialism and dialectics!

property, and on favourable terms? ... Far better if all these provisions are lost, for they will only cause harm to my dear friend! Far better be done with the whole business, for it will only cause your ruin!"

I have emphasised the passages which show most saliently how profoundly and splendidly Chernyshevsky understood the realities of his time, how he understood the significance of the peasants' payments, how he understood the antagonism between the social classes in Russia. It is also important to note his ability to expound such purely revolutionary ideas in the censored press. He wrote the same thing in his illegal works, but without circumlocution. In *A Prologue to the Prologue*, Volgin (into whose mouth Chernyshevsky puts his ideas) says:

"*Let the emancipation of the peasant be placed in the hands of the landlords' party. It won't make much difference.*"*
And in reply to his interlocutor's remark that, on the contrary, the difference would be tremendous, because the landlords' party was opposed to allotting land to the peasants, he replies emphatically:

"*No, not tremendous, but insignificant. It would be tremendous if the peasants obtained the land without redemption payments. There is a difference between taking a thing from a man and leaving it with him, but if you take payment from him it is all the same. The only difference between the plan of the landlords' party and that of the progressists is that the former is simpler and shorter. That is why it is even better. Less red tape and, in all probability, less of a burden on the peasants. Those peasants who have money will buy land. As to those who have none—there's no use compelling them to buy it. It will only ruin them. Redemption is nothing but purchase.*"

It required the genius of a Chernyshevsky to understand so clearly at that time, when the peasant Reform was only being introduced (when it had not yet been properly elucidated even in Western Europe), its fundamentally bourgeois character, to understand that already at that time Russian

* I quote from Plekhanov's article "N. G. Chernyshevsky," in *Sotsial-Demokrat*.[90]

"society" and the Russian "state" were ruled and governed by social classes that were irreconcilably hostile to the working people and that undoubtedly predetermined the ruin and expropriation of the peasantry. Moreover, Chernyshevsky understood that the existence of a government that screens our antagonistic social relations is a terrible evil, which renders the position of the working people ever so much worse.

"*To tell the truth,*" Volgin continues, "*it would be better if they were emancipated without land.*" (That is, since the feudal landlords in this country are so strong, it would be better if they acted openly, straightforwardly, and said all they had in mind, instead of hiding their interests as serf owners behind the compromises of a hypocritical absolute government.) "*The matter is put in such a way that I see no reason for getting excited, even over whether the peasants are emancipated or not, let alone over whether the liberals or the landlords are to emancipate them. To my mind it is all the same. It will even be better if the landlords do it.*"

Here is a passage from "Unaddressed Letters": "*They say: emancipate the peasants.... Where are the forces for it? Those forces do not yet exist. It is useless tackling a job when the forces for it are lacking. Yet you see the way things are going. They will start emancipating. But what will come of it? Well, judge for yourself what comes of tackling a job which is beyond your powers. You just botch it—and the result will be vile.*"[91]

Chernyshevsky understood that the Russian feudal, bureaucratic state was incapable of emancipating the peasants, that is, of overthrowing the feudal serf owners, that it was only capable of something "vile," of a miserable compromise between the interests of the liberals (redemption is nothing but purchase) and of the landlords, a compromise employing the illusion of security and freedom to deceive the peasants, but actually ruining them and completely betraying them to the landlords. And he protested, execrated the Reform, wanted it to fail, wanted the government to get tied up in its equilibristics between the liberals and the landlords, and wanted a crash to take place that would bring Russia out on the high road of open class struggle.

Yet *today*, when Chernyshevsky's brilliant predictions have become fact, when the history of the past thirty years has ruthlessly shown up all economic and political illusions, our contemporary "democrats" sing the praises of the Reform, regard it as a sanction for "people's" production, contrive to draw proof from it of the possibility of finding a way which would *get around* the social classes hostile to the working people. I repeat, their attitude towards the peasant Reform is most striking proof of how profoundly bourgeois our democrats have become. These gentlemen have learned nothing, but have forgotten very, very much.

For the sake of comparison, I will take *Otechestvenniye Zapiski* for 1872. I have already quoted passages from the article "The Plutocracy and Its Basis," dealing with the successes in respect of liberalism (which screened plutocratic interests) achieved by Russian society in the very first decade after the "great emancipatory" Reform.

While formerly, wrote the same author in the same article, one would often find people who whined over the reforms and wailed for the good old days, they are to be found no longer. "Everybody is pleased with the new order; everybody is happy and satisfied." And the author goes on to show how literature "itself is becoming an organ of the plutocracy," advocating the interests and aspirations of the plutocracy "under the cloak of democracy." Examine this argument a little more closely. The author is displeased with the fact that "everybody" is pleased with the new order brought about by the Reform, that "everybody" (the representatives of "society" and of the "intelligentsia," of course, not of the working people) is happy and satisfied, notwithstanding the obvious antagonistic, bourgeois features of the new order: the public fail to notice that liberalism merely screens "freedom of acquisition," acquisition, of course, at the expense and to the disadvantage of the mass of working people. And he protests. It is this protest, characteristic of the socialist, that is valuable in his argument. Observe that this protest against a plutocracy screened by democracy contradicts the general theory of the magazine: for they deny that there are any bourgeois features, elements or interests in the peasant Reform, they deny the class character of the Russian intelligentsia and of the Russian state, they deny that there is a basis for capitalism in Russia—nevertheless, they cannot but sense and perceive the capitalism and bourgeoisdom.

And to the extent that *Otechestvenniye Zapiski*, sensing the antagonism in Russian society, fought bourgeois liberalism and bourgeois democracy—to that extent it fought in a cause common to all our pioneer socialists, who, although they could not understand this antagonism, nevertheless realised its existence and desired to combat the very organisation of society which gave rise to it; to that extent *Otechestvenniye Zapiski* was progressive (from the point of view of the proletariat, of course). The "friends of the people" have forgotten this antagonism, they have lost all sensibility of the fact that in this country, too, in Holy Russia, the pure-blooded bourgeois hide "under the cloak of democracy"; and that is why they are now reactionary (in relation to the proletariat), for they gloss over the antagonism, and talk, not of struggle, but of conciliatory, "uplift" activity.

But, gentlemen, has the Russian clear-browed liberal, the democratic representative of the plutocracy of the sixties, ceased to be the ideologist of the bourgeoisie in the nineties just because his brow has become clouded with civic grief?

Does "freedom of acquisition" on a large scale, freedom to acquire big credits, big capital, big technical improvements, cease to be liberal, i.e., bourgeois, while the present social-economic relations remain unchanged, merely because its place is taken by freedom to acquire small credits, small capital, small technical improvements?

I repeat, it is not that they have altered their opinions under the influence of a radical change of views or a radical change in our order of things. No, they have simply forgotten.

Having lost the only feature that once made their predecessors progressive—notwithstanding the utter unsoundness of their theories and their naïve and utopian outlook on reality—the "friends of the people" have learnt absolutely nothing during all this time. And yet, quite apart from a political-economic analysis of Russian realities, the political history of Russia during the past thirty years alone should have taught them a great deal.

At that time, in the era of the "sixties," the power of the feudal landlords was sapped: they suffered defeat, not complete, it is true, but so decisive that they had to slink from the stage. The liberals, on the contrary, raised their heads. Streams of liberal phrase-mongering flowed about progress, science, goodness, struggle against injustice, the interests of the people, the conscience of the people, the forces of the people, etc., etc.—the very phrases which now, too, at moments of particular depression, are vomited forth by our radical snivellers in their salons, and by our liberal phrase-mongers at their anniversary dinners, and in the columns of their magazines and newspapers. The liberals proved strong enough to mould the "new order" in their own fashion—not entirely, of course, but in fair measure. Although "the clear light of the open class struggle" did not shine in Russia at that time, there was more light then than there is now, so that even those ideologists of the working people who had not the faintest notion of this class struggle, and who preferred to dream of a better future rather than *explain* the vile present, could not help seeing that liberalism was a cloak for plutocracy, and that the new order was a bourgeois order. It was the removal from the stage of the feudal landlords, who did not divert attention to still more crying evils of the day, and did not prevent the new order from being observed in its pure (relatively) form, that enabled this to be seen. But although our democrats of that time knew how to denounce plutocratic liberalism, they could not understand it and explain it scientifically; they could not understand that it was inevitable under the capitalist organisation of our social economy; they could not understand the progressive character of the new system of life as compared with the old, feudal system; they could not understand the revolutionary role of the proletariat it created; and they limited themselves to "snorting" at this system of "liberty" and "humanity," imagined that its bourgeois character was fortuitous, and expected social relations of some other kind to reveal themselves in the "people's system."

And then history showed them these other social relations. The feudal landlords, not completely crushed by the Reform, which was so outrageously mutilated in their interests, revived (for a time) and showed vividly what these other than bourgeois social relations of ours were, showed it in the form of such unbridled, incredibly senseless and brutal reaction that our democrats caught fright, subsided, instead of advancing and remoulding their naïve democracy—which was able to sense what was bourgeois but was unable to understand it—into Social-Democracy, went backwards, to the liberals, and are now proud of the fact that their snivelling—i.e., I want to say, their theories and programmes—is shared by "the whole serious and respectable press." One would have thought the lesson was a very impressive one: the illusions of the old socialists about a special mode of life of the people, about the socialist instincts of the people, and about the fortuitous character of capitalism and the bourgeoisie, had become too obvious; one would have thought that the facts could now be looked straight in the face and the admission be openly made that there had not been and were not any other social-economic relations than bourgeois and moribund feudal relations in Russia, and that, therefore, there could be no road to socialism except through the working-class movement. But these democrats had learned nothing, and the naïve illusions of petty-bourgeois socialism gave way to the practical sobriety of petty-bourgeois progress.

Today, the theories of these petty-bourgeois ideologists, when they come forward as the spokesmen of the interests of the working people, are positively reactionary. They obscure the antagonism of contemporary Russian social-economic relations and argue as if things could be improved by general measures, applicable to all, for "raising," "improving," etc., and as if it were possible to reconcile and unite. They are reactionary in depicting our state as something standing above classes and therefore fit and capable of rendering serious and honest aid to the exploited population.

They are reactionary, lastly, because they simply cannot understand the necessity for a struggle, a desperate struggle of the working people themselves for their emancipation. The "friends of the people," for example, seem to think they can manage the whole thing themselves. The workers need not worry. Why, an engineer has even visited the offices of *Russkoye Bogatstvo*, and there they have almost completely worked out a "scheme" for "introducing capitalism into the life of the people." Socialists must make a **DECISIVE** and **COMPLETE** break with all petty-bourgeois ideas and theories—**THAT IS THE PRINCIPAL USEFUL LESSON** to be drawn from this campaign.

I ask you to note that I speak of a break with petty-bourgeois ideas and not with the "friends of the people" or with their ideas—because there can be no breaking with something with which there has never been any connection. The "friends of the people" are only one of the representatives of one of the trends of this sort of petty-bourgeois socialist ideas. And if, in this case, I draw the conclusion that it is necessary to break with petty-bourgeois socialist ideas, with the ideas of the old Russian peasant socialism *generally*, it is because the campaign now launched against the Marxists by the representatives of the old ideas, scared by the growth of Marxism, has induced them to give particularly full and vivid expression to petty-bourgeois ideas. Comparing these ideas with contemporary socialism and with the facts of contemporary Russian reality, we see with astonishing clarity how outworn these ideas have become, how they have lost every vestige of an integral theoretical basis and have sunk to the level of a pitiful eclecticism, of a most ordinary opportunist uplift programme. It may be said that this is not the fault of the old socialist ideas in general, but of the gentlemen in question, whom no one thinks of classing as socialists; but such an argument seems to me quite unsound. I have throughout tried to show that such a degeneration of the old theories was inevitable. I have throughout tried to devote as little space as possible to criticism of these gentlemen in particular and as much as possible to the general and fundamental tenets of the old Russian socialism. And if the socialists should find that I have defined these tenets incorrectly or inaccurately, or have left something unsaid, then I can only reply with the following very humble request: please, gentlemen, define them yourselves, state them fully and properly!

Indeed, no one would be more pleased than the Social-Democrats of an opportunity to enter into a polemic with the socialists.

Do you think that we like answering the "polemics" of these gentlemen, or that we would have undertaken it if they had not thrown down a direct, persistent and emphatic challenge?

Do you think that we do not have to force ourselves to read, re-read and grasp the meaning of this repulsive mixture of stereotyped liberal phrase-mongering and philistine moralising?

Surely, we are not to blame for the fact that only such gentlemen now take upon themselves the job of vindicating and expounding these ideas. I ask you also to note that I speak of the need for a break with petty-bourgeois ideas about *socialism*. The petty-bourgeois theories we have examined are **ABSOLUTELY** reactionary **INASMUCH AS** they claim to be socialist theories.

But if we understand that actually there is absolutely nothing socialist in them, i.e., that all these theories completely fail to explain the exploitation of the working people and therefore cannot serve as a means for their emancipation, that as a matter of fact all these theories reflect and further the interests of the petty bourgeoisie—then our attitude towards them must be different, and we must ask: *what should be the attitude of the working class towards the petty bourgeoisie and its programmes*? And this question cannot be answered unless the dual character of this class is taken into consideration (here in Russia this duality is particularly marked owing to the antagonism between the big bourgeoisie and the petty bourgeoisie being less developed). It is progressive insofar as it puts forward general democratic demands, i.e., fights against all survivals of the medieval epoch and of serfdom; it is reactionary insofar as it fights to preserve its position as a petty bourgeoisie and tries to retard, to turn back the general development of the country along bourgeois lines. Reactionary demands of this kind, such, for example, as the notorious inalienability of allotments, as well as the many other projects for tutelage over the peasants, are usually covered up by plausible talk of protecting the working people but actually, of course, they only worsen their condition, while at the same time hampering them in their struggle for emancipation. A strict distinction should be drawn between these two sides of the petty-bourgeois programme and, while denying that these theories are in any way socialist in character, and while combating their reactionary aspects, we should not forget their democratic side. I shall give an example to show that, although the Marxists completely repudiate petty-bourgeois theories, this does not prevent them from including democracy in their programme, but, on the contrary, calls for still stronger insistence on it. We have mentioned above the three main theses that always formed the theoretical stock-in-trade of the representatives of petty-bourgeois socialism, viz., land poverty, high payments and the tyranny of the authorities.

There is absolutely nothing socialist in the demand for the abolition of these evils, for they do not in the least explain expropriation and exploitation, and their elimination will not in the least affect the oppression of labour by capital. But their elimination will free this oppression of the medieval rubbish that aggravates it, and will facilitate the worker's direct struggle against capital, and for that reason, as a democratic demand, will meet with the most energetic support of the workers. Generally speaking, the question of payments and taxes is one to which only the petty bourgeois can attach any particular significance; but in Russia the payments made by the peasants are, in many respects, simply survivals of serfdom. Such, for example, are the land redemption payments, which should be immediately and unconditionally abolished; such, too, are the taxes which only the peasants and the small townspeople pay, but from which the "gentry" are exempt. Social-Democrats will always support the demand for the elimination of these relics of medieval relations, which cause economic and political stagnation. The same can be said of land poverty. I have already given proof at length of the bourgeois character of the wailing on this score. There is no doubt, however, that the peasant Reform, for example, by permitting the cutting-off of lands[2] positively robbed the peasants for the benefit of the landlords, rendering service to this tremendous reactionary force both directly (by snatching land from the peasants) and indirectly (by the clever way the allotments were marked out). And Social-Democrats will most strenuously insist on the immediate return to the peasants of the land taken from them and on the complete abolition of landed proprietorship—that bulwark of feudal institutions and traditions. This latter point, which coincides with the nationalisation of the land, contains nothing socialist, because the capitalist-farming relations already taking shape in our country would in that case only flourish more rapidly and abundantly; but it is extremely important from the democratic standpoint as the only measure capable of completely breaking the power of the landed nobility. Lastly, only the Yuzhakovs and V. V.s, of course, can speak of the peasants' lack of rights as the cause of their expropriation and exploitation. As for the oppression of the peasantry by the authorities, it is not only an unquestionable fact, but is something more than mere oppression; it is treating the peasants as a "base rabble," for whom it is natural to be subject to the landed nobility; to whom general civil rights are granted only as a special favour (migration,* for example), and whom any Jack-in-office can order about as if they were workhouse inmates. And the Social-Democrats unreservedly associate themselves with the demand for the complete restoration of the peasants' civil rights, the complete abolition of all the privileges of the nobility, the abolition of bureaucratic tutelage over the peasants, and the peasants' right to manage their own affairs.

In general, the Russian communists, adherents of Marxism, should more than any others call themselves **SOCIAL-DEMOCRATS**, and in their activities should never forget the enormous importance of **DEMOCRACY**.**

In Russia, the relics of medieval, semi-feudal institutions are still so enormously strong (as compared with Western Europe), they are such an oppressive yoke upon the proletariat and the people generally, retarding the growth of political thought in all estates and classes, that one cannot but insist on the tremendous importance which the struggle against all feudal institutions, absolutism, the social-estate system, and the bureaucracy has for the workers. The workers must be shown in the greatest detail what a terribly reactionary force these institutions are, how they intensify

* One cannot help recalling here the purely Russian feudal arrogance with which Mr. Yermolov, now Minister of Agriculture, objects to migration in his book *Crop Failures and the Distress of the People*. Migration cannot be regarded as rational from the standpoint of the state, he says, when the landlords in European Russia still experience a shortage of labour. And, indeed, what do the peasants exist for, if not to work and feed the idle landlords and their "high-placed" servitors?

** This is a very important point. Plekhanov is quite right when he says that our revolutionaries have "two enemies: old prejudices that have not yet been entirely eradicated, on the one hand, and a narrow understanding of the new programme, on the other." See Appendix III (p. 326 of this volume.—*Ed.*).

the oppression of labour by capital, what a degrading pressure they exert on the working people, how they keep capital in its medieval forms, which, while not falling short of the modern, industrial forms in respect of the exploitation of labour, add to this exploitation by placing terrible difficulties in the way of the fight for emancipation. The workers must know that unless these pillars of reaction* are overthrown, it will be utterly impossible for them to wage a successful struggle against the bourgeoisie, because so long as they exist, the Russian rural proletariat, whose support is an essential condition for the victory of the working class, will never cease to be downtrodden and cowed, capable only of sullen desperation and not of intelligent and persistent protest and struggle. And that is why it is the direct duty of the working class to fight side by side with the radical democracy against absolutism and the reactionary social estates and institutions—a duty which the Social-Democrats must impress upon the workers, while not for a moment ceasing also to impress upon them that the struggle against all these institutions is necessary only as a means of facilitating the struggle against the bourgeoisie, that the worker needs the achievement of the general democratic demands only to clear the road to victory over the working people's chief enemy, over an institution that is purely democratic by nature, *capital*, which here in Russia is particularly in-

* A particularly imposing reactionary institution, one to which our revolutionaries have paid relatively little attention, is our *bureaucracy*, which de facto rules the Russian state. The bureaucracy being made up mainly of middle-class intellectuals are profoundly bourgeois both in origin and in the purpose and character of their activities; but absolutism and the enormous political privileges of the landed nobility have lent them particularly pernicious qualities. They are regular weathercocks, who regard it as their supreme task to combine the interests of the landlord and the bourgeois. They are Judushkas[93] who use their feudal sympathies and connections to fool the workers and peasants, and employ the pretext of "protecting the economically weak" and acting as their "guardian" against the kulak and usurer to carry through measures which reduce the working people to the status of a "base rabble," handing them over to the feudal landlords and making them all the more defenceless against the bourgeoisie. The bureaucracy are most dangerous hypocrites, who have imbibed the experience of the West-European champion reactionaries, and skilfully conceal their Arakcheyev[94] designs behind the fig-leaves of phrases about loving the people.

clined to sacrifice its democracy and to enter into alliance with the reactionaries in order to suppress the workers, to still further impede the emergence of a working-class movement.

What has been said is, I think, sufficient to define the attitude of the Social-Democrats towards absolutism and political liberty, and also towards the trend which has been growing particularly strong of late, that aims at the "amalgamation" and "alliance" of all the revolutionary groups for the winning of political liberty.[95]

This trend is rather peculiar and characteristic.

It is peculiar because proposals for "alliance" do not come from a definite group, or definite groups, with definite programmes which coincide on one point or another. If they did, the question of an alliance would be one for each separate case, a concrete question to be settled by the representatives of the uniting groups. Then there could be no special "amalgamation" trend. But such a trend exists, and simply comes from people who have cut adrift from the old, and have not moored to anything new. The theory on which the fighters against absolutism have hitherto based themselves is evidently crumbling, and is destroying the conditions for solidarity and organisation which are essential for the struggle. Well then, these "amalgamators" and "alliance advocates" would seem to think that the easiest way to create such a theory is to reduce it to a protest against absolutism and a demand for political liberty, while evading all other questions, socialist and non-socialist. It goes without saying that the bottom will inevitably be knocked out of this naïve fallacy at the very first attempts at such unity.

But what is characteristic is that this "amalgamation" trend represents one of the last stages in the process of transformation of militant, revolutionary Narodism into politically radical democracy, a process which I have tried to outline above. A durable amalgamation of all the non-Social-Democratic revolutionary groups under the banner mentioned will be possible only when a durable programme of *democratic* demands has been drawn up that will put an end to the prejudices of the old Russian exceptionalism. Of course, the Social-Democrats believe that the formation of such a democratic party would be a useful step forward and their anti-Narodnik activity should further it, should further the eradication of all prejudices and myths, the grouping of the socialists under the banner of Marxism and the formation of a democratic party by the other groups.

The Social-Democrats, who consider essential the independent organisation of the workers into a separate workers' party, could not, of course, "amalgamate" with such a party, but the workers would most strongly support any struggle waged by the democrats against reactionary institutions.

The degeneration of Narodism into the most ordinary petty-bourgeois radical theory—of which (degeneration) the "friends of the people" furnish such striking testimony—shows what a tremendous mistake is made by those who spread among the workers the idea of fighting absolutism without at the same time explaining to them the antagonistic character of our social relations by virtue of which the ideologists of the bourgeoisie also favour political liberty—without explaining to them the historical role of the Russian worker as a fighter for the emancipation of the whole working population.

The Social-Democrats are often accused of wanting to monopolise Marx's theory, whereas, it is argued, his economic theory is accepted by all socialists. But the question arises, what sense is there in explaining to the workers the form of value, the nature of the bourgeois system and the revolutionary role of the proletariat, if here in Russia the exploitation of the working people is generally and universally explained not by the bourgeois organisation of social economy, but by, say, land poverty, redemption payments, or the tyranny of the authorities?

What sense is there in explaining to the worker the theory of the class struggle, if that theory cannot even explain his relation to the employer (capitalism in Russia has been artificially implanted by the government), not to mention the mass of the "people," who do not belong to the fully established class of factory workers?

How can one accept Marx's economic theory and its corollary—the revolutionary role of the proletariat as the organiser of communism by way of capitalism—if people in our country try to find ways to communism other than through the medium of capitalism and the proletariat it creates?

Obviously, under such conditions to call upon the worker to fight for political liberty would be equivalent to calling upon him to pull the chestnuts out of the fire for the progressive bourgeoisie, for it cannot be denied (typically enough, even the Narodniks and the Narodovoltsi did not deny it) that political liberty will primarily serve the interests of the bourgeoisie and will not ease the position of the workers, but ... will ease only the conditions for their struggle ... *against this very bourgeoisie.* I say this as against those socialists who, while they do not accept the theory of the Social-Democrats, carry on their agitation among the workers, having become convinced empirically that only among the latter are revolutionary elements to be found. The theory of these socialists contradicts their practice, and they make a very serious mistake by distracting the workers from their direct task of **ORGANISING A SOCIALIST WORKERS' PARTY.***

It was a mistake that arose naturally at a time when the class antagonisms of bourgeois society were still quite undeveloped and were held down by serfdom, when the latter was evoking the unanimous protest and struggle of the entire intelligentsia, thus creating the illusion that there was something peculiarly democratic about our intelligentsia, and that there was no profound gulf between the ideas of the liberals and of the socialists. Now that economic development has advanced so far that even those who formerly denied a basis for capitalism in Russia admit our having entered the capitalist path of development—illusions on this score are no longer possible. The composition of the "intelligentsia" is assuming just as clear an outline as that of society engaged in the production of material values: while the latter is ruled and governed by the capitalist, among the former the fashion is set by the rapidly growing

* There are two ways of arriving at the conclusion that the worker must be roused to fight absolutism: *either* by regarding the worker as the sole fighter for the socialist system, and therefore seeing political liberty as one of the conditions facilitating his struggle; that is the view of the Social-Democrats; *or* by appealing to him simply as the one who suffers most from the present system, who has nothing more to lose and who can display the greatest determination in fighting absolutism. But that would mean compelling the worker to drag in the wake of the bourgeois radicals, who refuse to see the antagonism between the bourgeoisie and the proletariat behind the solidarity of the whole "people" against absolutism.

horde of careerists and bourgeois hirelings, an "intelligentsia" contented and satisfied, a stranger to all wild fantasy and very well aware of what they want. Far from denying this fact, our radicals and liberals strongly emphasise it and go out of their way to prove its immorality, to condemn it, strive to confound it, shame it ... and destroy it. These naïve efforts to make the bourgeois intelligentsia *ashamed* of being bourgeois are as ridiculous as the efforts of our petty-bourgeois economists to frighten our bourgeoisie (pleading the experience of "elder brothers") with the story that it is moving towards the ruin of the people, towards the poverty, unemployment and starvation of the masses; this trial of the bourgeoisie and its ideologists is reminiscent of the trial of the pike, which was sentenced to be thrown into the river. Beyond these bounds begin the liberal and radical "intelligentsia," who pour out innumerable phrases about progress, science, truth, the people, etc., and who love to lament the passing of the sixties, when there was no discord, depression, despondency and apathy, and when all hearts were aflame with democracy.

With their characteristic simplicity, these gentlemen refuse to understand that the cause of the unanimity that then prevailed was the then existing material conditions, gone never to return: serfdom pressed down everybody equally—the serf steward who had saved a little money and wanted to live in comfort; the enterprising muzhik, who hated the lord for exacting tribute, for interfering in and tearing him from his business; the proletarianised manor-serf and the impoverished muzhik who was sold into bondage to the merchant; it brought suffering to the merchant manufacturer and the worker, the handicraftsman and the subcontractor. The only tie that linked all these people together was their hostility to serfdom; beyond that unanimity, the sharpest economic antagonism began. How completely one must be lulled by sweet illusions not to perceive this antagonism even today when it has become so enormously developed; to weep for the return of the days of unanimity at a time when the situation demands struggle, demands that everyone who does not want to be a **WILLING** or **UNWILLING** myrmidon of the bourgeoisie shall take his stand on the side of the proletariat.

If you refuse to believe the flowery talk about the "interests of the people" and try to delve deeper, you will find that you are dealing with the out-and-out ideologists of the petty bourgeoisie, who dream of improving, supporting and restoring their ("people's" in their jargon) economy by various innocent progressive measures, and who are totally incapable of understanding that under prevailing production relations the only effect such progressive measures can have is to proletarianise the masses still further. We cannot but be grateful to the "friends of the people" for having done much to reveal the class character of our intelligentsia and for having thereby fortified the Marxist theory that our small producers are petty bourgeois. They must inevitably hasten the dissipation of the old illusions and myths that have so long confused the minds of Russian socialists. The "friends of the people" have so mauled, overworked and soiled these theories that Russian socialists who held them are confronted with the inexorable dilemma of either revising them, or abandoning them altogether and leaving them to the exclusive use of the gentlemen who announce with smug solemnity, urbi et orbi, that the rich peasants are buying improved implements, and who with serious mien assure us that we must welcome people who have grown weary of sitting at the card tables. And in this strain they talk about a "people's system" and the "intelligentsia"—talk, not only with a serious air, but in pretentious, stupendous phrases about broad ideals, about an ideal treatment of the problems of life!...

The socialist intelligentsia can expect to perform fruitful work only when they abandon their illusions and begin to seek support in the actual, and not the desired development of Russia, in actual, and not possible social-economic relations. Moreover, their **THEORETICAL** work must be directed towards *the concrete study of all forms of economic antagonism in Russia, the study of their connections and successive development*; they must *reveal this antagonism wherever it has been concealed by political history, by the peculiarities of legal systems or by established theoretical prejudice*. They must *present an integral picture of our realities as a definite system of production relations, show that the exploitation and expropriation of the working people are essential under this system, and show the way out of this system that is indicated by economic development.*

This theory, based on a detailed study of Russian history and realities, must furnish an answer to the demands of the proletariat—and if it satisfies the requirements of science, then every awakening of the protesting thought of the proletariat will inevitably guide this thought into the channels of Social-Democracy. The greater the progress made in elaborating this theory, the more rapidly will Social-Democracy grow; for even the most artful guardians of the present system cannot prevent the awakening of proletarian thought, because this system itself necessarily and inevitably entails the most intense expropriation of the producers, the continuous growth of the proletariat and of its reserve army—and this parallel to the progress of social wealth, the enormous growth of the productive forces, and the socialisation of labour by capitalism. However much has still to be done to elaborate this theory, the socialists will do it; this is guaranteed by the spread among them of materialism, the only scientific method, one requiring that every programme shall be a precise formulation of the actual process; it is guaranteed by the success of Social-Democracy, which has adopted these ideas—a success which has so stirred up our liberals and democrats that, as a certain Marxist has put it, their monthly magazines have ceased to be dull.

In thus emphasising the necessity, importance and immensity of the theoretical work of the Social-Democrats, I by no means want to say that this work should take precedence over **PRACTICAL** work,*—still less that the latter should be postponed until the former is completed. Only the admirers of the "subjective method in sociology," or the followers of utopian socialism, could arrive at such a conclusion. Of course, if it is presumed that the task of the socialists is to seek "different" (from actual) "paths of development" for the country, then, naturally, practical work becomes possible only when philosophical geniuses discover and indicate these "different paths"; and conversely, once these paths are discovered and indicated theoretical work ends, and the work of those who are to direct the "fatherland" along the "newly-discovered" "different paths"

* On the contrary, the practical work of propaganda and agitation must always take precedence, because, firstly, theoretical work only

begins. The position is altogether different when the task of the socialists is to be the ideological leaders of the proletariat in its actual struggle against actual and real enemies who stand in the *actual* path of social and economic development. Under these circumstances, theoretical and practical work merge into one aptly described by the veteran German Social-Democrat, Liebknecht, as:

Studieren, Propagandieren, Organisieren.*

You cannot be an ideological leader without the above-mentioned theoretical work, just as you cannot be one without directing this work to meet the needs of the cause, and without spreading the results of this theory among the workers and helping them to organise.

Such a presentation of the task guards Social-Democracy against the defects from which socialist groups so often suffer, namely, dogmatism and sectarianism.

There can be no dogmatism where the supreme and sole criterion of a doctrine is its conformity to the actual process of social and economic development; there can be no sectarianism when the task is that of promoting the organisation of the proletariat, and when, therefore, the role of the "intelligentsia" is to make special leaders from among the intelligentsia unnecessary.

Hence, despite the existence of differences among Marxists on various theoretical questions, the methods of their political activity have remained unchanged ever since the group arose.

The political activity of the Social-Democrats lies in promoting the development and organisation of the working-class movement in Russia, in transforming this movement from its present state of sporadic attempts at protest, "riots" and strikes devoid of a guiding idea, into an organised struggle of the **WHOLE** Russian working **CLASS** directed against the bourgeois regime and working for the

---

supplies answers to the problems raised by practical work, and, secondly, the Social-Democrats, for reasons over which they have no control, are so often compelled to confine themselves to theoretical work that they value highly every moment when practical work is possible.

* Study, propaganda, organisation.—*Ed.*

expropriation of the expropriators and the abolition of the social system based on the oppression of the working people. Underlying these activities is the common conviction of Marxists that the Russian worker is the sole and natural representative of Russia's entire working and exploited population.*

Natural because the exploitation of the working people in Russia *is everywhere capitalist in nature*, if we leave out of account the moribund remnants of serf economy; but the exploitation of the mass of producers is on a small scale, scattered and undeveloped, while the exploitation of the factory proletariat is on a large scale, socialised and concentrated. In the former case, exploitation is still enmeshed in medieval forms, various political, legal and conventional trappings, tricks and devices, which hinder the working people and their ideologists from seeing the essence of the system which oppresses the working people, from seeing where and how a way can be found out of this system. In the latter case, on the contrary, exploitation is fully developed and emerges in its pure form, without any confusing details. The worker cannot fail to see that he is oppressed by *capital*, that his struggle has to be waged against the bourgeois *class*. And this struggle, aimed at satisfying his immediate economic needs, at improving his material conditions, inevitably demands that the workers organise, and inevitably becomes a war not against individuals, but against a *class*, the class which oppresses and crushes the working people not only in the factories, but everywhere. That is why the factory worker is none other than the foremost representative of the entire exploited population. And in order that he may fulfil his function of representative in an organised, sustained struggle it is by no means necessary to enthuse him with "perspectives"; all that is needed is simply *to make him understand his position*, to make him understand the political and economic structure of the system that oppresses him, and the necessity and inevitability of class antagonisms under this system. This position of the factory worker

* Russia's man of the future is the muzhik—thought the representatives of peasant socialism, the Narodniks in the broadest sense of the term. Russia's man of the future is the worker—think the Social-Democrats. That is how the Marxist view was formulated in a certain manuscript.

in the general system of capitalist relations makes him the sole fighter for the emancipation of the working class, for only the higher stage of development of capitalism, large-scale machine industry, creates the material conditions and the social forces necessary for this struggle. Everywhere else, where the forms of capitalist development are low, these material conditions are absent; production is scattered among thousands of tiny enterprises (and they do not cease to be scattered *enterprises* even under the most equalitarian forms of communal land*ownership*), for the most part the exploited still possess tiny enterprises, and are thus tied to the very bourgeois system they should be fighting: this retards and hinders the development of the social forces capable of overthrowing capitalism. Scattered, individual, petty exploitation ties the working people to one locality, divides them, prevents them from becoming conscious of class solidarity, prevents them from uniting once they have understood that oppression is not caused by some particular individual, but by the whole economic system. Large-scale capitalism, on the contrary, inevitably severs all the workers' ties with the old society, with a particular locality and a particular exploiter; it unites them, compels them to think and places them in conditions which enable them to commence an organised struggle. Accordingly, it is on the working class that the Social-Democrats concentrate all their attention and all their activities. When its advanced representatives have mastered the ideas of scientific socialism, the idea of the historical role of the Russian worker, when these ideas become widespread, and when stable organisations are formed among the workers to transform the workers' present sporadic economic war into conscious class struggle—then the Russian **WORKER**, rising at the head of all the democratic elements, will overthrow absolutism and lead the **RUSSIAN PROLETARIAT** (side by side with the proletariat of **ALL COUNTRIES**) *along the straight road of open political struggle to* **THE VICTORIOUS COMMUNIST REVOLUTION.**

The End

1894

ными хозяйствами при самыхъ уравнительныхъ формахъ общиннаго
землевладѣнія), эксплуатируемый большею частью владѣетъ еще кро
шечнымъ хозяйствомъ и так. обр. привязывается къ той самой бу
ржуазной системѣ, противъ к-рой долженъ вести борьбу: это задержи
ваетъ и затрудняетъ развитіе тѣхъ соціальныхъ силъ, к-рыя спо
собны ниспровергнуть капитализмъ. Раздробленная, единичная, мелкая
эксплуатація привязываетъ трудящихся къ мѣсту, разобщаетъ ихъ,
не даетъ имъ возможности уразумѣть своей классовой солидарнос
ти, не даетъ возможности объединиться, понявъ, что причина угне
тенія - не та или другая личность, а вся хозяйственная систе
ма. Напротивъ, крупный капитализмъ неизбѣжно разрываетъ всякую
связь рабочаго со старымъ обществомъ, съ опредѣленнымъ мѣстомъ
и опредѣленнымъ эксплуататоромъ, объединяетъ его, заставляетъ мыс
лить и ставитъ въ условія, дающія возможность начать организо
ванную борьбу. На классъ рабочихъ и обращаютъ соціалъ-демокра
ты все свое вниманіе и всю свою дѣятельность. Когда передо
вые представители его усвоятъ идеи научнаго соціализма, идею
объ исторической роли русскаго рабочаго, когда эти идеи полу
чатъ широкое распространеніе и среди рабочихъ создадутся проч
ныя организаціи, преобразующія теперешнюю разрозненную экономичес
кую войну рабочихъ въ сознательную классовую борьбу, - тогда
русскій **РАБОЧІЙ**, поднявшись во главѣ всѣхъ демократичес
кихъ элементовъ, свалитъ абсолютизмъ и поведетъ **РУССКІЙ
ПРОЛЕТАРІАТЪ** (рядомъ съ Пролетаріатомъ **ВСѢХЪ
СТРАНЪ**) прямой дорогой открытой по
литической борьбы къ **ПОБѢДОНОСНОЙ**

КОММУНИСТИЧЕСКОЙ РЕВОЛЮЦІИ.

Конецъ
1894

Last page of Part III, hectographed edition, of Lenin's *What the "Friends of the People" Are and How They Fight the Social-Democrats*, 1894

Reduced

Appendix I

The annexed table contains the data for the 24 budgets referred to in the text.

Composition and budgets of 24 typical peasant households in Ostrogozhsk Uyezd—Summary

Explanation of the table

1) The first 21 columns have been taken bodily from the Statistical Abstract. Column 22 combines the columns in the Abstract on: rye, wheat, oats and barley, millet and buckwheat, other grain crops, potatoes, vegetables, and hay (8 columns). How the income from grain crops (Column 23), excluding chaff and straw, was computed has been explained in the text. Column 24 combines the columns in the Abstract on: horses, cattle, sheep, pigs, poultry, hides and wool, back fat and meat, dairy produce, butter (9 columns). Columns 25-29 have been taken bodily from the Abstract. Columns 30-34 combine the columns in the Abstract on: expenditure on rye, wheat, millet and buckwheat, potatoes, vegetables, salt, butter, fat and meat, fish, dairy produce, vodka and tea (12 columns). Column 35 combines the columns in the Abstract giving expenditure on: soap, kerosene, candles, clothing, and utensils (4 columns). The remaining columns require no explanation.

2) Column 8 was arrived at by adding together the area, in dessiatines, of rented land and the amount of arable in the allotment (for which there is a special column in the Abstract).

3) The bottom rows of figures in the columns "Sources of Income" and "Distribution of Expenditure" indicate the *money part of income and expenditure*. In Columns 25 to 28 and 37 to 42 the income (or expenditure) is wholly monetary. The money part was calculated (the author does not show it separately) by dedncting from gross income the amount consumed by the household itself.

CATEGORIES OF HOUSEHOLDERS AND THEIR NUMBER		Number of persons, both sexes	Number of working persons, males	Farm labourers	
				Households with farm labourers	Number (both sexes)
		1	2	3	4
6 prosperous householders	Total	47	11	6	8
	Average per householder	7.83	1.8	—	—
11 middle householders	Total	92	26	2	2
	Average per householder	8.36	2.4	—	—
7 poor householders	Total	37	10	2	2
	Average per householder	5.28	1.4	—	—
Total 24 householders	Total	176	47	10	12
	Average per householder	7.33	1.9	—	—
2 farm labourers (included among poor householders)	Total	9	2	—	—
	Average per householder	4.5	1	—	—

Allotted land (dess.)	Leased land		Total tillage	Number of buildings	Number of industrial establishments	Number of agricultural implements	Animals (head of)	
	Households	dess.					Draught animals	Total, in terms of cattle
5	6	7	8	9	10	11	12	13
132.6	6	52.8	123.4	52	4	224	35	81
22.1	—	8.8	20.6	8.6	—	37.3	5.8	13.5
101.2	10	85.5	140.2	70	—	338	40	89.1
9.2	—	7.7	12.7	6.4	—	30.7	3.6	8.1
57.8	4	19.8	49.8	31	—	108	7	15.3
8.5	—	2.8	7.1	4.4	—	15.4	1	2.2
291.6	20	158.1	313.4	153	4	670	82	185.4
12.1	—	6.6	13	6.4	—	27.9	3.4	7.7
14.4	—	—	6.8	6	—	11	—	1.1
7.2	—	—	3.4	3	—	5.5	—	0.5

CATEGORIES OF HOUSEHOLDERS AND THEIR NUMBER		Value in rubles						
		Buildings	Other immovable property	Implements	Utensils	Clothing	Livestock and bees	Total
		14	15	16	17	18	19	20
6 prosperous householders	Total	2,696	2,237	670.8	453	1,294.2	3,076.5	10,427.5
	Av. per h.holder	449.33	372.83	111.80	75.5	215.7	512.75	1,737.9
11 middle householders	Total .	2,362	318	532.9	435.9	2,094.2	2,907.7	8,650.7
	Av. per h.holder	214.73	28.91	48.44	39.63	190.38	264.33	786.4
7 poor householders	Total .	835	90	112.3	254	647.1	605.3	2,543.7
	Av. per h.holder	119.28	12.85	16.04	36.29	92.45	86.47	363.3
Total 24 householders	Total .	5,893	2,645	1,316	1,142.9	4,035.5	6,589.5	21,621.9
	Av. per. h.holder	245.55	110.21	54.83	47.62	168.14	274.56	900.9
2 farm labourers (incl. among poor householders)	Total .	155	25	6.4	76.8	129.3	9.1	401.6
	Av. per h.holder	77.5	12.5	3.2	38.4	64.65	4.55	200.8

Arrears in loans (rubles)	Sources of income							
	From agriculture		From stock raising	From bee-keeping and gardening	From industries	From establishments	From various sources	Total (rubles)
	Total	Of which grain crops						
21	22	23	24	25	26	27	28	29
80	61.2% 3,861.7 1,774.4	2,598.2 1,774.4	15.4% 972.6 396.5	4.3% 271	6.5% 412	5% 320	7.6% 482.2	100% 6,319.5 3,656.1
13.3	643.6	—	162.1	45.2	68.6	53.3	80.4	1,053.2 609.3
357	60.7% 3,163.8 899.9	2,203.8 899.9	16.1% 837.5 423.2	0.7% 36.1	18.8% 979.3	—	3.7% 195.5	100% 5,212.2 2,534
32.4	287.7	—	76.1	3.2	89	—	17.8	473.8 230
233.6	48.7% 689.9 175.25	502.08 175.24	22.9% 324.2 216.6	1.9% 27	23.8% 336.8	—	2.7% 39	100% 1,416.9 794.64
33.4	98.5	—	46.3	3.9	48.1	—	5.5	202.4 113.5
670.6	59.6% 7,715.4 2,849.54	5,304.8 2,849.54	16.5% 2,134.3 1,036.3	2.6% 334.1	13.3% 1,728.1	2.5% 320	5.5% 716.7	100% 12,948.6 6,984.74
27.9	321.5	—	88.9	13.9	72	13.3	29.9	539.5 291.03
50	59.5 3	—	5.7 4.8	—	128.8	—	4	198 140.6
25	29.75	—	2.85	—	64.4	—	2	99 70.3

CATEGORIES OF HOUSEHOLDERS AND THEIR NUMBER		Distribution					
		Food					Clothes and domestic needs
		Total	Vegetable	Other	Of which: Milk, meat, etc.	Of which: Salt, vodka, tea	
		30	31	32	33	34	35
6 prosperous householders	Total . .	29.2% 1,500.6 218.7	823.8	676.8	561.3 103.2	115.5	8.2% 423.8 58.6
	Av. per h.holder	250.1	—	—	—	—	70.63
11 middle householders	Total . .	37.6% 1,951.9 257.7	1,337.3 33.4	614.6	534.3 144	80.3	10.6% 548.1 49.5
	Av. per h.holder	177.45	—	—	—	—	49.83
7 poor householders	Total . .	42.1% 660.8 253.46	487.7 160.96	173.1	134.4 53.8	38.7	14.6% 229.6 26.8
	Av. per h.holder	94.4	—	—	—	—	32.8
Total 24 householders	Total . .	34.6% 4,113.3 729.86	2,648.8	1,464.5	1,230	234.5	10.1% 1,201.5 134.9
	Av. per h.holder	171.39	110.37	61.02	51.25	9.77	50.06
2 farm labourers (included among poor h. holders)	Total . .	81.7 50.7	72.1 42.5	9.6	6.1 4.7	3.5	14.9 4.6
	Av. per h.holder	40.85	—	—	—	—	7.45

of expenditure								
Mainte-nance of livestock	Implements and livestock	On labourers and shep-herds	Rent	Taxes and duties	Payments to priests	Miscellan-eous	Total (rubles)	Surplus (+) or deficit (—)
36	37	38	39	40	41	42	43	44
24.9% 1,276.6	9.4% 484.5	13.5% 691.7	6.5% 332	4.9% 253.5	1.1% 56	2.3% 116.5	100% 5,135.2 2,211.5	+1,184.3
212.76	80.75	115.29	55.33	42.25	9.33	19.42	855.86 368.6	+ 197.34
21.2% 1,098.2	5% 256	0.9% 47.6	6.8% 351.7	4.9% 254.9	1.3% 69.9	11.7% 609.4	100% 5,187.7 1,896.7	+ 24.5
99.84	23.27	4.33	31.97	23.17	6.35	55.4	471.6 172.5	+ 2.19
15.6% 243.7	7.1% 110.6	1.6% 24.3	6% 94.5	6.5% 101.8	1.8% 28	4.7% 73.2	100% 1,566.5 712.66	— 149.6
34.81	15.8	3.47	13.5	14.54	4	10.46	223.78 101.8	— 21.38
22.2% 2,618.5	7.1% 851.1	6.4% 763.6	6.5% 778.2	5.1% 610.2	1.3% 153.9	6.7% 799.1	100% 11,889.4 4,820.86	+1,059.2
109.1	35.46	31.82	32.43	25.43	6.41	33.29	495.39 200.87	+ 44.11
8	53.2	0.4	—	22.6	2.8	3.3	186.9 137.6	+ 11.1
4	26.6	0.2	—	11.3	1.4	1.65	93.45 68.8	+ 5.55

Appendix II

Mr. Struve quite rightly makes the corner-stone of his criticism of Nik. —on the thesis that "Marx's doctrine of the class struggle and the state is completely foreign to the Russian political economist." I do not possess the boldness of Mr. Krivenko to make this one (four-column) article by Mr. Struve the basis for a judgement of his system of views (I am not acquainted with his other articles); and I must say that I do not agree with all the statements he makes; and can, therefore, support only certain fundamental propositions he advances and not his article as a whole. But the circumstance mentioned has, at any rate, been quite correctly assessed: Mr. Nik. —on's *basic error* is, indeed, his failure to understand the class struggle inherent in capitalist society. The correction of this one error would be sufficient to ensure that Social-Democratic conclusions would be drawn from even his theoretical propositions and investigations. To overlook the class struggle is indeed to reveal a gross misunderstanding of Marxism, a misunderstanding for which Mr. Nik. —on must be all the more blamed since he is so very anxious to pass himself off as a strict adherent of Marx's principles. Can anyone with the least knowledge of Marx deny that the doctrine of the class struggle is the pivot of his whole system of views?

Mr. Nik. —on could, of course, have accepted Marx's theory with the exception of this point, on the grounds, let us say, that it does not conform to the facts of Russian history and reality. But then, in the first place, he could not have said that Marx's theory explains our system; he could not even have spoken of this theory and of capitalism, because it would have been necessary to remould the theory and to work out a conception of a different capitalism, in which antagonistic relations and the class struggle were not inherent. At any rate he should have made an explicit reservation and explained why, having accepted the *A* of Marxism he refuses to accept *B*. Mr. Nik. —on made no attempt to do anything of the kind.

And Mr. Struve quite rightly concluded that failure to understand the class struggle makes Mr. Nik. —on a *utopian*, for anybody who ignores the class struggle in capitalist society eo ipso ignores all the real content of the social and political life of this society and, in seeking to fulfil his desideratum, is inevitably doomed to hover in the sphere of pious wishes. This failure to understand the class struggle makes him a *reactionary*, for appeals to "society" and to the "state," that is, to bourgeois ideologists and politicians, can only confuse the socialists, and cause them to accept the worst enemies of the proletariat as their allies, can only hamper the workers' struggle for emancipation instead of helping to strengthen, clarify and improve the organisation of that struggle.

Since we have mentioned Mr. Struve's article, we cannot but deal with Mr. Nik. —on's reply in *Russkoye Bogatstvo*, No. 6.*

"It appears," argues Mr. Nik. —on, citing data about the slow increase in the number of factory workers, an increase lagging behind the growth of the population, "that in our country capitalism, far from fulfilling its 'historic mission,' is itself setting limits to its own development. That, incidentally, is why those who seek 'for their fatherland a path of development distinct from that which Western Europe followed and still follows' are a thousand times right." (And this is written by a man who

* Generally speaking, by his articles in *Russkoye Bogatstvo*, Mr. Nik. —on is apparently trying hard to prove that he is by no means as remote from petty-bourgeois radicalism as one might think; that he too is capable of discerning in the growth of a peasant bourgeoisie (No. 6, p. 118—the spread among the "peasants" of improved implements, phosphates, etc.) symptoms indicating that "the *peasantry* itself" (the peasantry that is being expropriated wholesale?) "realises the necessity of finding a way out of the position it is in."

admits that Russia is following this very capitalist path!) This "historic mission" is not being fulfilled, according to Mr. Nik. —on, because "the economic trend hostile to the village community (i.e., capitalism) is destroying the very foundations of its existence without providing that modicum of unifying significance so characteristic of Western Europe and which is beginning to manifest itself with particular force in North America."

In other words, what we have here is the standard argument against the Social-Democrats invented by the celebrated Mr. V. V., who regarded capitalism from the standpoint of a government official settling the state problem of the "introduction of capitalism into the life of the people"—if it is fulfilling its "mission," let it in; if not, "keep it out!" Apart from all the other virtues of this clever argument, the very "mission" of capitalism was understood by Mr. V. V., and is apparently understood by Mr. Nik. —on, in an impossibly and preposterously false and narrow fashion. And again, of course, these gentlemen unceremoniously ascribe the narrowness of their own understanding to the Social-Democrats, who can be maligned like the dead since the legal press is closed to them!

As Marx saw it, the progressive and revolutionary work of capitalism consists in the fact that, in socialising labour, it at the same time "disciplines, unites and organises the working class" by the mechanism of that very process, it trains them for the struggle, organises their "revolt," unites them to "expropriate the expropriators," seize political power and wrest the means of production from the "few usurpers" and turn them over to society (*Capital*, p. 650).[96]

That is how Marx formulates it.

Nothing, of course, is said here about the "number of factory workers": Marx speaks of the concentration of the means of production and of the socialisation of labour. It is quite clear that these criteria have nothing in common with the "number of factory workers."

But our exceptionalist interpreters of Marx misinterpret this to mean that the socialisation of labour under capitalism amounts to factory workers labouring under one roof, and that the progressiveness of the work of capitalism is therefore to be measured by ... the number of factory workers!!! If the number of factory workers is increasing, capitalism is doing its progressive work well; if the number is decreasing, it is "fulfilling its historic mission badly" (p. 103 of Mr. Nik. —on's article), and it behoves the "intelligentsia" "to seek different paths for their fatherland."

And so the Russian intelligentsia set out to seek "different paths." It has been seeking and finding them for decades, trying with might and main to prove* that capitalism is a "false" line of development, for it leads to unemployment and crises. We faced a crisis, they say, in 1880, and again in 1893; it is time to leave this path, for obviously things are going badly with us.

The Russian bourgeoisie, however, like the cat in the fable, "listens but goes on eating":[97] of course things are going "badly" when fabulous profits can no longer be made. So it echoes the song of the liberals and radicals and, thanks to available and cheaper capital, energetically sets about building new railways. Things are going badly with "us" because in the old places "we" have already picked the people clean and now have to enter the field of industrial capital, which cannot enrich us as much as merchant capital. And so "we" will go to the eastern and northern border regions of European Russia, where "primitive accumulation," which yields a profit of hundreds per cent, is still possible, where the bourgeois differentiation of the peasantry is still far from complete. The intelligentsia perceive all this and ceaselessly threaten that "we" are again heading for a crash. And a new crash is really upon us. Very many small capitalists are being crushed by the big capitalists, very many peasants are being squeezed out of agriculture, which is increasingly passing into the hands of the bourgeoisie; the sea of poverty, unemployment

---

* These proofs are wasted, not because they are wrong—the ruin, impoverishment and starvation of the people are unquestionable and inevitable concomitants of capitalism—but because they are addressed to thin air. "Society," even under the cloak of democracy, furthers the interests of the plutocracy, and, of course, the plutocracy will hardly take up the cudgels against capitalism. The "government"... I will cite the comment of an opponent, Mr. N. K. Mikhailovsky: however little we know the programmes of our government, he once wrote, we know them enough to be certain that the "socialisation of labour" has no part in them.

and starvation is increasing immensely—and the "intelligentsia," with a clear conscience, point to their prophecies and ceaselessly complain about a wrong path, citing the absence of foreign markets as proof of the instability of our capitalism.

The Russian bourgeoisie, however, "listens but goes on eating." While the "intelligentsia" seek new paths, the bourgeoisie undertake gigantic projects for the construction of railways to their colonies, where they create a market for themselves, introducing the charms of the bourgeois system to the young countries and there, too, creating an industrial and agricultural bourgeoisie with exceptional rapidity, and casting the mass of the producers into the ranks of the chronically starving unemployed.

Will the socialists really continue to confine themselves to complaining about wrong paths, and try to prove ... by the slow increase in the number of factory workers that capitalism is unstable!!?

Before discussing this childish idea,* I cannot but mention that Mr. Nik. —on very inaccurately quoted the passage from Mr. Struve's article that he criticised. This article says literally the following:

"When the author (i.e., Mr. Nik. —on) points to the difference in the occupational composition of the Russian and American populations—for Russia 80% of the total gainfully-employed population (erwerbsthätigen) are taken as engaged in agriculture, and in the United States only 44%—he does not observe that the capitalist development of Russia will work to obliterate this difference between 80% and 44%; that, one might say, is its historic mission."

It may be held that the *word* "mission" is very inappropriate here, but Mr. Struve's idea is clear: Mr. Nik. —on did not notice that the capitalist development of Russia

* How can this idea be called anything but childish, when the progressive work of capitalism is not judged by the degree of socialisation of labour, but by such a fluctuating index of the development of only *one* branch of national labour! Everybody knows that the number of workers cannot be anything but extremely inconstant under the capitalist mode of production, and that it depends upon a host of secondary factors, such as crises, the size of the reserve army, the degree of the exploitation of labour, the degree of its intensity, and so on and so forth.

(he himself admits that this development is really a capitalist one) will reduce the rural population, whereas in fact it is a general law of capitalism. Consequently, to refute this objection, Mr. Nik. —on should have shown *either* 1) that he had not overlooked this tendency of capitalism, *or* 2) that capitalism has no such tendency.

Instead, Mr. Nik. —on sets about analysing the data on the number of our factory workers (1% of the population, according to his estimate). But was Mr. Struve speaking of factory workers? Does the 20% of the population in Russia and the 56% in America represent factory workers? Are the terms "factory workers" and "population not engaged in agriculture" identical? Can it be denied that the proportion of the population engaged in agriculture is diminishing in Russia too?

Having made this correction, which I consider all the more necessary because Mr. Krivenko has already garbled this passage in this very magazine, let us pass to Mr. Nik. —on's idea itself—"our capitalism is fulfilling its mission badly."

Firstly, it is absurd to identify the number of factory workers with the number of workers engaged in capitalist production, as is done by the author of the *Sketches*.* This is repeating (*and even aggravating*) the error of the Russian petty-bourgeois economists who make large-scale machine industry the very beginning of capitalism. Are not the millions of Russian handicraftsmen who work for merchants, with the latter's material and for ordinary wages, engaged in capitalist production? Do the regular farm labourers and day labourers in agriculture not receive wages from their employers, and do they not surrender surplus-value to them? Are not the workers in the building industry (which has rapidly developed in our country since the Reform) subjected to capitalist exploitation? And so on.**

Secondly, it is absurd to compare the number of factory workers (1,400,000) with the total population and to

* N. F. Danielson, *Sketches on Our Post-Reform Social Economy*, St. Petersburg, 1893.—*Ed.*

** I confine myself here to criticising Mr. Nik. —on's *method* of judging "the unifying significance of capitalism" by the number of factory workers. I cannot undertake an analysis of the figures because I have not got Mr. Nik. —on's sources handy. One cannot.

express the ratio as a percentage. That is simply comparing incommensurables: the able-bodied population with the non-able-bodied, those engaged in the production of material values with the "liberal professions," and so on. Do not the factory workers each maintain a certain number of non-working members of the family? Do not the factory workers maintain—apart from their employers and a whole flock of traders—a host of soldiers, civil servants and similar gentry, whom you assign to the agricultural population, contrasting this hotchpotch to the factory population? And then, are there not in Russia such industries as fishing and so forth, which it is again absurd to con-

---

however, refrain from noting that he has hardly selected these sources happily. He first takes data for 1865 from the *Military Statistical Abstract* and those for 1890 from the *Directory of Factories and Works* of 1894. The number of workers he gets (exclusive of mine-workers) is 829,573 and 875,764, respectively. The increase of 5.5%is much less than the increase in population (from 61,420,000 to 91,000,000, or 48.1%). But on the *next page* different figures are taken: both for 1865 and 1890 from the *Directory* of 1893. According to these data, the number of workers is 392,718 and 716,792, respectively—an increase of 82%. But this does not include industries paying excise duties, in which the number of workers (p. 104) was 186,053 in 1865 and 144,332 in 1890. Adding these figures to the preceding ones we get the following total numbers of workers (except mine-workers): 578,771 in 1865 and 861,124 in 1890. An increase of 48.7% with a population increase of 48.1%. Thus in the space of five pages the author uses some data that show an increase of 5% and others showing an increase of 48%! And on the basis of such contradictory figures he finds that our capitalism is unstable!!

And then why did not the author take the data on the number of workers quoted in the *Sketches* (Tables XI and XII), and from which we see that it increased by 12-13% in *three years* (1886-1889), an increase that far outstrips the growth of population? The author may perhaps say that the time interval was too short. But then, in the first place, these data are homogeneous, comparable and more reliable; and in the second place, did not the author himself use these same data, despite the short time interval, to form a judgement of the growth of factory industry?

Obviously, if such a fluctuating index as the number of workers is used to indicate the state of only one branch of national labour, those data cannot be anything but shaky. And one must be a naïve dreamer indeed to base one's hopes on such data—hopes that our capitalism will collapse, crumble to dust spontaneously, without a desperate and stubborn struggle—and to use these data to question the indisputable domination and development of capitalism in all branches of national labour!

trast with factory industry and to combine with agriculture? If you wanted to get an idea of the occupational composition of the population of Russia, you should, firstly, have singled out into a special group the population engaged in the production of material values (excluding, consequently, the non-working population, on the one hand, and soldiers, civil servants, priests, etc., on the other); and, secondly, you should have tried to divide them among the various branches of national labour. If the data for this were not available, you should have refrained from undertaking such calculations,* instead of talking nonsense about

* Mr. Nik. —on attempted such a calculation in the *Sketches*, but very unsuccessfully. On p. 302, we read:

"An attempt was recently made to determine the total number of free workers in the 50 gubernias of European Russia (S. A. Korolenko, *Hired Labour*, St. Petersburg 1892). An investigation made by the Department of Agriculture estimates the able-bodied rural population in the 50 gubernias of European Russia at 35,712,000, whereas the total number of workers required in agriculture and in the manufacturing, mining, transport and other industries is estimated at only 30,124,000. Thus the number of absolutely superfluous workers reaches the huge figure of 5,588,000, which, together with their families, according to the accepted standard, would amount to no less than 15,000,000 persons." (Repeated on p. 341.)

If we turn to this "investigation," we shall find that only the hired labour employed by the landlords was "investigated"; Mr. S. Korolenko supplemented the investigation with an "agricultural and industrial survey" of European Russia. This survey makes an attempt (not on the basis of some "investigation," but on the basis of old available data) to class the working population of European Russia by occupation. The results arrived at by Mr. S. A. Korolenko are as follows: the total number of workers in the 50 gubernias of European Russia is 35,712,000, engaged in:

agriculture		27,435,400	30,124 thous.
cultivation of special crops		1,466,400	
factory and mining industry		1,222,700	
Jews		1,400,400	
lumbering	about	2,000,000	
stock-breeding	"	1,000,000	
railways	"	200,000	
fishing	"	200,000	
local and outside employment, hunting, trapping, and miscellaneous others		787,200	
Total		35,712,100	

Thus Mr. Korolenko (rightly or wrongly) classed *all* the workers by occupation, but Mr. Nik. —on arbitrarily takes the first three head-

1% (??!!) of the population being engaged in factory industry.

Thirdly—and this is the chief and most outrageous distortion of Marx's theory of the progressive and revolutionary work of capitalism—where did you get the idea that the "unifying significance" of capitalism is expressed in uniting only the factory workers? Can it be that you borrow your idea of Marxism from the articles in *Otechestvenniye Zapiski* on the socialisation of labour? Can it be that you, too, identify it with work under one roof?

But no. It would appear that Nik. —on cannot be accused of this, because he accurately describes the socialisation of labour by capitalism on the second page of his article in *Russkoye Bogatstvo*, No. 6, correctly indicating both features of this socialisation: 1) work for the whole of society, and 2) the uniting of individual labourers so as to obtain the product of common labour. But if that is so, why judge the "mission" of capitalism by the number of factory workers, when this "mission" is fulfilled by the development of capitalism and the socialisation of labour in general, by the creation of a proletariat in general, in relation to which the factory workers play the role only of front-rankers, the vanguard. There is, of course, no doubt that the revolutionary movement of the proletariat depends on the number of these workers, on their concentration, on the degree of their development, etc.; but all this does not give us the slightest right *to equate the "unifying significance" of capitalism with the number of factory workers*. To do so would be to narrow down Marx's idea impossibly.

---

ings and talks about 5,588,000 "absolutely superfluous" (??) workers!

Apart from this defect one cannot refrain from noting that Mr. Korolenko's estimates are extremely rough and inaccurate: the number of agricultural workers is computed in accordance with one general standard for the whole of Russia; the non-producing population has not been classed separately (under this heading Mr. Korolenko, in deference to official anti-Semitism, classed ... *the Jews*! There must be more than 1,400,000 non-producing workers: traders, paupers, vagabonds, criminals, etc.); the number of handicraftsmen (the last heading—outside and local employment) is preposterously low, etc. It would be better not to quote such estimates at all.

I will give you an example. In his pamphlet *Zur Wohnungsfrage*,* Frederick Engels speaks of German industry and points out that in no other country—he is referring only to Western Europe—do there exist so many wage-workers who own a garden or a plot of land. "*Rural domestic industry carried on in conjunction with kitchen-gardening or ... agriculture*," he says, "*forms the broad basis of Germany's new large-scale industry*." This domestic industry grows increasingly with the growing distress of the German small peasant (as is the case in Russia, let us add), but the **COMBINATION** of industry with agriculture is the basis not of the **WELL-BEING** of the domestic producer, the handicraftsman, but on the contrary, of his greater **OPPRESSION**. Being tied to his locality, he is compelled to accept any price, and therefore surrenders to the capitalist not only surplus-value but a large part of his wages as well (as is the case in Russia, with her vast development of the domestic system of large-scale production). "*That is one side of the matter*," Engels continues, "*but it also has its reverse side.... With the expansion of domestic industry, one peasant area after another is being dragged into the present-day industrial movement. It is this revolutionising of the rural areas by domestic industry which spreads the industrial revolution in Germany over a far wider territory than was the case in England and France.... This explains why in Germany, in contrast to England and France, the revolutionary working-class movement has spread so tremendously over the greater part of the country instead of being confined exclusively to the urban centres. And this in turn explains the tranquil, certain and irresistible progress of the movement. It is perfectly clear that in Germany a victorious rising in the capital and in the other big cities will be possible only when the majority of the smaller towns and a great part of the rural districts have become ripe for the revolutionary change*."[98]

So you see, it appears that not only the "unifying significance of capitalism," but also the success of the working-class movement depends not only on the number of factory workers, but also on the number of ... *handicraftsmen*! Yet our exceptionalists, ignoring the purely capitalist organisa-

* *The Housing Question.—Ed.*

tion of the vast majority of the Russian handicraft industries, contrast them, as a sort of "people's" industry, to capitalism and judge "the percentage of the population at the direct disposal of capitalism" by the number of factory workers! This is reminiscent of the following argument by Mr. Krivenko: the Marxists want all attention to be directed to the factory workers; but as there are only one million of them out of 100 million people, they constitute only a small corner of life, and to devote oneself to it is just like confining oneself to work in estate or charitable institutions (*Russkoye Bogatstvo*, No. 12). Mills and factories are just as small a corner of life as estate and charitable institutions!! What a genius you are, Mr. Krivenko! No doubt it is the estate institutions that produce goods for the whole of society? No doubt it is the state of affairs in the estate institutions that explains the exploitation and expropriation of the working people? No doubt it is in the estate institutions that one must look for the advanced representatives of the proletariat who are capable of raising the banner of working-class emancipation.

It is not surprising to hear such things from the lips of the minor bourgeois philosophers; but it is a pity to have to read that sort of thing in the writings of Mr. Nik. —on.

On p. 393 of *Capital*,[99] Marx quotes figures of the composition of the English population. In 1861 there was a total of 20 million people in England and Wales. Of these, 1,605,440 persons were employed in the main branches of factory industry.* Furthermore, there were 1,208,648 members of the servant class, and in a footnote to the second edition Marx refers to the very rapid growth of this class. Now just imagine that there were "Marxists" in England who divided 1,600,000 by 20,000,000 to judge the "unifying significance of capitalism"!! The result would

---

* There were 642,607 persons employed in the textile, hosiery and lace industries (in our country tens of thousands of women engaged in stocking- and lace-making are incredibly exploited by the "tradeswomen" for whom they work. Wages are sometimes as low as *three* [sic!] kopeks a day! Do you mean to say, Mr. Nik. —on, that they are not "at the direct disposal of capitalism"?), and in addition 565,835 persons were employed in coal and ore mines, and 396,998 persons in all metal works and manufactures.

be 8%—*less than one-twelfth*!!! How can one speak of the "mission" of capitalism when it has not united even one-twelfth of the population, and when, moreover, there is a more rapid increase in the "domestic slave" class—representing a dead loss of "national labour," which shows that "we," the English, are following the "wrong path"! Is it not clear that "we" must "seek different," non-capitalist "paths of development for our fatherland"?!

There is yet another point in Mr. Nik. —on's argument: when he says that capitalism here does not yield the unifying significance which is "so characteristic of Western Europe and *is beginning to manifest itself with particular force in North America*," he is apparently referring to the working-class movement. And so, we must seek different paths because capitalism here does not give rise to a working-class movement. This argument, it seems to me, was anticipated by Mr. Mikhailovsky. Marx operated with a ready-made proletariat—he admonished the Marxists. And when a Marxist told Mikhailovsky that all he saw in poverty was poverty, his reply was: this remark, as usual, was taken bodily from Marx. But if we turn to this passage in *The Poverty of Philosophy* we shall find that it is not applicable in our case and that our poverty is just poverty. As a matter of fact, however, you will still find nothing to bear you out in *The Poverty of Philosophy*. Marx there says of the communists of the old school that they saw in poverty nothing but poverty without seeing its revolutionary, destructive side, which would overthrow the old society.[100] Evidently, Mr. Mikhailovsky takes the absence of any "manifestation" of a working-class movement as grounds for asserting that it is not applicable in our case. In reference to this argument, let us remark, firstly, that only a most superficial acquaintance with the facts can give rise to the idea that Marx operated with a ready-made proletariat. Marx's communist programme was drawn up before 1848. What working-class movement* was there in Germany then? There

* The smallness of the working class at that time may be judged from the fact that *27 years later*, in 1875, Marx wrote that "the majority of the toiling people in Germany consists of peasants, and not of proletarians."[101] That is what "operating (??) with a ready-made proletariat" comes down to!

was not even political liberty at that time, and the activities of the communists were confined to secret circles (as in our country today). The Social-Democratic labour movement, which made the revolutionary and unifying role of capitalism quite clear to everybody, began two decades later, when the doctrine of scientific socialism had definitely taken shape, when large-scale industry had become more widespread, and there emerged numerous talented and energetic disseminators of this doctrine among the working class. In addition to presenting historical facts in a false light and forgetting the vast amount of work done by the socialists in lending consciousness and organisation to the working-class movement, our philosophers foist upon Marx the most senseless fatalistic views. In his opinion, they assure us, the organisation and socialisation of the workers occur spontaneously, and, consequently, if we see capitalism but do not see a working-class movement, that is because capitalism is not fulfilling its mission, and not because we are still doing too little in the matter of organisation and propaganda among the workers. This cowardly petty-bourgeois artifice of our exceptionalist philosophers is not worth refuting: it is refuted by all the activities of the Social-Democrats in all countries; it is refuted by every public speech made by any Marxist. Social-Democracy—as Kautsky very justly remarks—is a fusion of the working-class movement and socialism. And in order that the progressive work of capitalism may "manifest" itself in this country too, our socialists must set to work with the utmost energy; they must work out in greater detail the Marxist conception of the history and present position of Russia, and make a more concrete investigation of all forms of the class struggle and exploitation, which are particularly complex and masked in Russia. They must, furthermore, popularise this theory and make it known to the worker; they must help the worker to assimilate it and devise *the form of organisation* most **SUITABLE** *under our conditions for disseminating Social-Democratic ideas and welding the workers into a political force.* And the Russian Social-Democrats, far from ever having said that they have already completed, fulfilled this work of the ideologists of the working class (there is no end to this work), have always stressed the fact that they are only just beginning it, and that much effort by many, many persons will be required to create anything at all lasting.

Besides its unsatisfactory and preposterously narrow conception of the Marxist theory, this common objection that progressive work is lacking in our capitalism seems to be based on the absurd idea of a mythical "people's system."

When the "peasants" in the notorious "village community" are splitting up into paupers and rich, into representatives of the proletariat and of capital (especially merchant capital), they refuse to see that this is embryonic, medieval capitalism, and, evading the political-economic structure of the countryside, they chatter, in their search for "different paths for the fatherland," about changes in the form of peasant land*ownership*, with which they unpardonably confuse the form of economic organisation, as though a purely bourgeois differentiation of the peasantry were not in full swing within the "equalitarian village community" itself. And at a time when this capitalism is developing and outgrowing the narrow forms of medieval, village capitalism, shattering the feudal power of the land and compelling the peasant, long stripped clean and starving, to abandon the land to the community for equalitarian division among the triumphant kulaks, to leave home, to tramp the whole of Russia, unemployed for many a long day, and to hire himself now to a landlord, tomorrow to a railway contractor, then as an urban labourer or as farm labourer to a rich peasant, and so on; when this "peasant," who changes masters all over Russia, sees that wherever he goes he is most shamefully plundered; when he sees that other paupers like himself are plundered; that it is not necessarily the "lord" who robs him, but also "his brother muzhik," if the latter has the money to buy labour-power; when he sees how the government always serves his masters, restricting the rights of the workers and suppressing as riots every attempt to protect their most elementary rights; when he sees the Russian worker's labour becoming more and more arduous, and wealth and luxury growing more and more rapidly, while the worker's conditions are becoming steadily worse, expropriation more intense and unemployment a regular thing—at a time like this our critics of Marxism are seeking different paths for the fatherland; at a time like this they are occupied in pondering over the profound question of whether we can admit that the work of capitalism is progressive seeing how slow is the growth in the number of factory workers, and whether we should not reject our capitalism and consider it a false path because "it is fulfilling its historic mission badly, very, very badly."

A lofty and broadly humane occupation, is it not?

And what narrow doctrinaires these wicked Marxists are when they say that to seek different paths for the fatherland when capitalist exploitation of the working people exists all over Russia means to flee from realities to the sphere of utopia; when they find that it is not our capitalism but rather the Russian socialists who are fulfilling their mission badly, those socialists who refuse to understand that to dream about the age-old economic struggle of the antagonistic classes of Russian society dying down is tantamount to sinking to Manilovism,[102] and who refuse to realise that we must strive to impart organisation and understanding to this struggle, and to this end set about Social-Democratic work.

In conclusion, we cannot but note another attack by Mr. Nik. —on on Mr. Struve in this same issue, No. 6, of *Russkoye Bogatstvò*.

"We cannot help drawing attention," Mr. Nik. —on says, "to a certain peculiarity in Mr. Struve's methods of controversy. He was writing for the German public, in a serious German magazine; but the methods he employed seem entirely inappropriate. We may take it that not only the German but even the Russian public has grown to 'man's estate,' and will not be impressed by all the 'bugbears' in which his article abounds. 'Utopia,' 'reactionary programme' and similar expressions are to be met with in every column. But today, alas, these 'terrible words' simply do not produce the effect on which Mr. Struve apparently counts" (p. 128).

Let us try to examine whether "inappropriate methods" have been employed in this controversy between Messrs. Nik. —on and Struve, and, if they have, by whom.

Mr. Struve is accused of employing "inappropriate methods" on the grounds that in a serious article he tries to impress the public with "bugbears" and "terrible words."

To employ "bugbears" and "terrible words" means describing an opponent in terms of severe disapproval that at the same time are not clearly and precisely motivated and do not follow inevitably from the writer's standpoint (one that has been definitely stated), but simply express a desire to abuse, to dress down.

Obviously, it is only this last feature which turns epithets of severe disapproval into "bugbears." Mr. Slonimsky spoke severely of Mr. Nik. —on, but as he clearly and definitely formulated his point of view, that of an ordinary liberal who is absolutely incapable of understanding the bourgeois character of the present order, and quite explicitly formulated his phenomenal arguments; he may be accused of anything you like, but not of "inappropriate methods." Mr. Nik. —on, on his part, spoke severely of Mr. Slonimsky, quoting, incidentally, for his edification and instruction, Marx's words—which have been "justified in our country too" (as Mr. Nik. —on admits)—about the *reactionary* and *utopian* character of the defence of the small handicraft industry and small peasant landownership which Mr. Slonimsky wants, and accusing him of "narrow-mindedness," "*naïveté*," and the like. Look, Mr. Nik. —on's article "abounds" in the same epithets (underscored) as Mr. Struve's; but we cannot speak of "inappropriate methods" in this case, because it is all motivated, it all follows from the author's definite standpoint and system of views, which may be false, but which, if accepted, necessarily lead to regarding one's opponent as a naïve, narrow-minded and reactionary utopian.

Let us see how matters stand with Mr. Struve's article. Accusing Mr. Nik. —on of utopianism that leads inevitably to a reactionary programme, and of naïveté, he quite clearly indicates the grounds which led him to such an opinion. Firstly: desiring the "socialisation of production," Mr. Nik. —on "appeals to society" (sic!) "and the state." This "proves that Marx's doctrine of the class struggle and the state is completely foreign to the Russian political economist." Our state is the "representative of the ruling classes." Secondly: "If we contrast to *real* capitalism an *imaginary* economic system which *must* come about simply because we *want* it to, in other words, if we want the socialisation of production without capitalism, this is only evidence of a naïve conception, which does not conform to history." With the development of capitalism, the elimination of natural economy and the diminution of the rural population, "the modern state will emerge from the twilight in which, in our patriarchal times, it is still enveloped (we are speaking of Russia), and step out into the clear light of the open class struggle, and other forces and factors will have to be sought for the socialisation of production."

Well, is this not a sufficiently clear and precise motivation? Can one dispute the truth of Mr. Struve's specific references to the author's ideas? Did Mr. Nik. —on really take account of the class struggle inherent in capitalist society? He did not. He speaks of society and the state, and forgets this struggle, excludes it. He says, for example, that the state supported capitalism instead of socialising labour through the village community, and so on. He evidently believes that the state could have behaved this way or that, and, consequently, that it stands *above classes*. Is it not clear that to accuse Mr. Struve of resorting to "bugbears" is a *crying* injustice? Is it not clear that a man who believes that ours is a class state cannot regard one who appeals to that state to socialise labour, that is, to abolish the ruling classes as anything but a naïve and reactionary utopian? More, when one accuses an opponent of resorting to "bugbears," and *says nothing* about the views from which his opinion follows, despite the fact that he has clearly formulated these views; and when, moreover, one accuses him in a censored magazine, where these views cannot appear—should we not rather regard this as "an absolutely inappropriate method"?

Let us proceed. Mr. Struve's second argument is formulated no less clearly. That the socialisation of labour apart from capitalism, through the village community, is an imaginary system cannot be doubted, for it does not exist in reality. This reality is described by Mr. Nik. —on himself as follows: prior to 1861 the productive units were the "family" and the "village community" (*Sketches*, pp. 106-

107). This "small, scattered, self-sufficing production could not develop to any considerable extent, and its extremely routine nature and low productivity were therefore typical." The subsequent change meant that "the social division of labour became deeper and deeper." In other words, capitalism broke out of the narrow bounds of the earlier productive units and socialised labour throughout society. *Mr. Nik. —on, too, admitted this socialisation of labour by our capitalism.* Therefore, in wanting to base the socialisation of labour not on capitalism, which *has already socialised labour*, but on the village community, *the break-down of which for the first time brought about the socialisation of labour throughout society*, he is a reactionary utopian. That is Mr. Struve's idea. One may regard it as true or false, but it cannot be denied that his severe comment on Mr. Nik. —on followed with logical inevitability from this opinion, and it is, therefore, out of place to talk of "bug-bears."

Furthermore, when Mr. Nik. —on concludes his controversy with Mr. Struve by attributing to his opponent the desire to dispossess the peasantry of the land ("if by a progressive programme is meant dispossessing the peasantry of the land ... then the author of the *Sketches* is a conservative"), despite Mr. Struve's explicit statement that he desires the socialisation of labour, desires it through capitalism, and therefore desires to base himself on the forces that will be visible in "the clear light of the open class struggle"—that can only be called a version diametrically opposed to the truth. And if we bear in mind that Mr. Struve could not in the censored press speak of the forces which come forward in the clear light of the open class struggle, and that, consequently, Mr. Nik. —on's opponent was gagged—it can scarcely be denied that Mr. Nik. —on's method is altogether "inappropriate."

Appendix III

When I speak of a narrow understanding of Marxism, I have the Marxists themselves in mind. One cannot help remarking in this connection that Marxism is most atrociously narrowed and garbled when our liberals and radicals undertake to expound it in the pages of the legal press. What an exposition it is! Just think how this revolutionary doctrine has to be mutilated to fit it into the Procrustean bed of Russian censorship! Yet our publicists light-heartedly perform that operation! Marxism, as they expound it, is practically reduced to the doctrine of how individual property, based on the labour of the proprietor, undergoes its dialectical development under the capitalist system, how it turns into its negation and is then socialised. And with a serious mien, they assume that the whole content of Marxism lies in this "scheme," ignoring all the specific features of its sociological method, the doctrine of the class struggle, and the direct purpose of the inquiry, namely, to disclose all the forms of antagonism and exploitation in order to help the proletariat abolish them. It is not surprising that the result is something so pale and narrow that our radicals proceed to mourn over the poor Russian Marxists. We should think so! Russian absolutism and Russian reaction would not be absolutism and reaction if it were possible, while they exist, to give a full, accurate and complete exposition of Marxism, setting forth its conclusions without reservation! And if our liberals and radicals knew Marxism properly (if only from German literature), they would be ashamed thus to distort it in the pages of the censored press. If a theory may not be expounded—keep silent, or make the reservation that you are giving a far from complete exposition of it, that you are omitting its most essential features; but why expound only fragments of it and then howl about its being narrow?

That, indeed, is the only explanation of the absurdity, possible only in Russia, that people are regarded as Marxists who have no idea of the class struggle, of the antagonism necessarily inherent in capitalist society, and of the development of this antagonism; people who have no notion of the revolutionary role of the proletariat; even people who come out with purely bourgeois projects, provided they contain such catchwords as "money economy," its "necessity," and similar expressions, which require all the intellectual profundity of a Mr. Mikhailovsky to be regarded as specifically Marxist.

Marx, on the other hand, considered the whole value of his theory to lie in the fact that it is "in its essence critical* and revolutionary."[103] And this latter quality is indeed completely and unconditionally inherent in *Marxism*, for this theory directly sets itself the task of *disclosing* all the forms of antagonism and exploitation in modern society, tracing their evolution, demonstrating their transitory character, the inevitability of their transformation into a different form, *and thus serving the proletariat as a means of ending all exploitation as quickly and easily as possible*. The irresistible attraction of this theory, which draws to itself the socialists of all countries lies precisely in the fact that it combines the quality of being strictly and supremely scientific (being the last word in social science) with that of being revolutionary, it does not combine them accidentally and not only because the founder of the doctrine combined in his own person the qualities of a scientist and a revolutionary, but does so intrinsically and inseparably. Is it not a fact that the task of theory, the aim of science,

* Note that Marx is speaking here of materialist criticism, which alone he regards as scientific—that is, criticism which compares the political, legal, social, conventional and other facts, with economics, with the system of production relations, with the interests of the classes that inevitably take shape on the basis of all the antagonistic social relations. That Russian social relations are antagonistic can hardly be doubted. But nobody has yet tried to take them as a basis for *such* criticism.

is here defined as assistance for the oppressed class in its actual economic struggle.

"*We do not say to the world: Cease struggling—your whole struggle is senseless. All we do is to provide it with a true slogan of struggle.*"[104]

Hence, the direct task of science, according to Marx, is to provide a true slogan of struggle, that is, to be able to present this struggle objectively as the product of a definite system of production relations, to be able *to understand* the necessity of this struggle, its content, course and conditions of development. It is impossible to provide a "slogan of struggle" unless we study every separate form of the struggle minutely, unless we trace every stage of the struggle during the transition from one form to another, so that we can define the situation at any given moment, without losing sight of the general character of the struggle and its general aim, namely, the complete and final abolition of all exploitation and all oppression.

Try to compare with Marx's "critical and revolutionary" theory the colourless trash which "our well-known" N. K. Mikhailovsky, in his "criticism," expounded and which he then did battle with, and you will be astonished that there can really be people who regard themselves as "ideologists of the working people," and confine themselves ... to that "worn-out coin" into which our publicists transform the Marxist theory by obliterating everything that is vital in it.

Try to compare with the demands of this theory our Narodnik literature, which, after all, is also prompted by the desire to be the ideological spokesman of the working people, a literature devoted to the history and to the present state of our economic system in general and of the peasantry in particular, and you will be astonished that socialists could be satisfied with a theory that confines itself to studying and describing distress and to moralising over it. Serfdom is depicted not as a definite form of economic organisation which gave rise to such and such exploitation, such and such antagonistic classes, certain political, legal and other systems, but simply as abuses by the landlords and injustice to the peasants. The peasant Reform is depicted not as a clash of definite economic forms and of definite economic classes, but as a measure taken by the authorities, who "chose" a "wrong path" by mistake, despite their very best intentions. Post-Reform Russia is depicted as a deviation from the true path, accompanied by the distress of the working people and not as a definite system of antagonistic relations of production with a certain development.

Now, however, there can be no doubt that this theory is discredited, and the sooner Russian socialists realise that with the present level of knowledge there can be no revolutionary theory apart from Marxism, the sooner they devote all their efforts to applying this theory to Russia, theoretically and practically—the surer and quicker will be the success of revolutionary work.

To give a clear illustration of the corruption the "friends of the people" have caused in the "meagre Russian thought" of today by their call to the intelligentsia to exert a cultural influence on the "people" so as to "create" a real and proper industry, etc.—let us cite the opinion of people who hold views sharply distinct from ours, namely, the "Narodopravtsi," these direct and immediate offspring of the Narodovoltsi. See pamphlet, *An Urgent Issue*, 1894, published by the Narodnoye Pravo party.

After giving a splendid rebuttal to the kind of Narodniks who say that "under no circumstances, not even on condition of broad liberty, must Russia part with her economic organisation, which ensures (!) the working people an independent place in production," and that "what we need is not political reforms but systematic and planned economic reforms," the Narodopravtsi go on to say:

"We are not defenders of the bourgeoisie, still less are we admirers of their ideals; but if a malicious fate were to present the people with the choice of 'planned economic reforms' under the protection of Zemsky Nachalniks who zealously guard them from the encroachments of the bourgeoisie, or the bourgeoisie themselves on the basis of political liberty, that is, under conditions which *ensure* the people the organised defence of their interests—we think the people would obviously gain by choosing the latter. At the moment, we have no 'political reforms' which threaten to deprive the people of their pseudo-independent economic organisation; what we do have is what everybody everywhere is accustomed to regard as bourgeois policy, expressed in the grossest exploitation of the people's labour. We have neither broad nor narrow liberty; what we do have is the protection of social-estate interests, which the agrarians and capitalists of constitutional countries have ceased to dream of. We have no 'bourgeois parliamentarianism'—society is not allowed within cannon-shot of the administrative machine; what we do have is the Messrs. Naidenovs, Morozovs, Kazis and Byelovs, who demand that a Chinese Wall be set up for the safeguarding of their interests, side by side with representatives of 'our loyal nobility,' who go so far as to demand free credits for themselves to the tune of 100 rubles per dessiatine. They are invited to serve on commissions, they are listened to with respect, and they have a decisive voice in cardinal questions affecting the economic life of the country. Yet who stands up in defence of the interests of the people, and where? Is it not they, the Zemsky Nachalniks? Is it not for the people that agricultural labour squads are being projected? Has it not only just been declared, with a frankness bordering on cynicism, that the only reason the people have been granted allotments is to enable them to pay taxes and to perform services, as the Governor of Vologda put it in one of his circulars? He only formulated and expressed aloud the policy that the autocracy, or, more correctly, bureaucratic absolutism, is fatally pursuing."

However nebulous the Narodopravtsi's notions still are about the "people," whose interests they want to defend, and about "society," which they continue to regard as a trustworthy organ for the protection of the interests of labour, one cannot but admit that the formation of the Narodnoye Pravo party is a step forward, a step towards the complete abandonment of the illusions and dreams about "different paths for the fatherland," towards the fearless recognition of the real paths, and towards the search on their basis for elements for a revolutionary struggle. Here we clearly see a striving to form a democratic party. I speak only of a "striving," because, unfortunately, the Narodopravtsi do not implement their basic thesis consistently. They still talk of amalgamation and alliance with the socialists, refusing to realise that to draw the workers into mere political radicalism would only mean severing the worker intellectuals from the mass of the workers and condemning the working-class movement to impotence; for it can be strong only by defending the interests of the working class completely and in every way, by engaging in economic struggle against capital, a struggle inseparably bound up with a political struggle against the servants of capital. They refuse to realise that the "amalgamation" of all the revolutionary elements can be much better achieved by the separate organisation of the representatives of the different interests* and by the joint action of the two parties in particular cases. They still go on calling their party a "social-revolutionary" party (see the Manifesto of the Narodnoye Pravo party, dated February 19, 1894), although at the same time they confine themselves exclusively to political reforms and most carefully evade our "cursed" socialist problems. A party which so ardently calls for a fight against illusions should not foster illusions in others by the very first words of its "manifesto"; it should not speak of *socialism* where there is nothing but *constitutionalism*. But, I repeat, one cannot form a correct judgement of the Narodopravtsi unless one bears in mind that they spring from the Narodovoltsi. It must, therefore, be admitted that they are taking a step forward by basing an exclusively political struggle—unrelated to socialism—on an exclusively political programme. The Social-Democrats whole-heartedly wish the Narodopravtsi success, wish that their party may grow and develop, that they may form closer ties with those social elements which take their stand by the present economic system** and whose

* They themselves protest against faith in the miracle-working powers of the intelligentsia; they themselves talk of the need to draw the people themselves into the struggle. But this requires that the struggle be bound up with definite everyday interests and, consequently, that a distinction be made between the different interests, and that they be drawn separately into the struggle.... But if these separate interests are obscured by bare political demands that only the intelligentsia understand, will this not mean again turning back, again confining everything to the struggle of the intelligentsia alone, whose impotence has only just been admitted?

** (I.e., the capitalist system)—and not by the necessary rejection of this system and the waging of a ruthless struggle against it.

everyday interests really are most intimately bound up with *democracy*.

The conciliatory, cowardly, sentimental and dreamy Narodism of the "friends of the people" will not stand up long when attacked from both sides: by the political radicals for being capable of expressing confidence in the bureaucracy and for not realising the absolute necessity of political struggle; and by the Social-Democrats, for attempting to represent themselves almost as socialists, although they have not the slightest relation to socialism and not the slightest inkling of the causes of the oppression of the working people or of the character of the class struggle now in progress.

THE ECONOMIC CONTENT OF NARODISM AND THE CRITICISM OF IT IN MR. STRUVE'S BOOK

(THE REFLECTION OF MARXISM IN BOURGEOIS LITERATURE)

P. Struve. *Critical Remarks on the Subject of Russia's Economic Development*. St. Petersburg, 1894 [105]

Written: end of 1894-beginning of 1895
First published over the signature of K. Tulin in the miscellany entitled *Material for a Characterisation of Our Economic Development*. St. Petersburg, 1895

Published according to *Material for a Characterisation of Our Economic Development*

МАТЕРІАЛЫ

КЪ ХАРАКТЕРИСТИКѢ

НАШЕГО ХОЗЯЙСТВЕННАГО РАЗВИТІЯ.

СБОРНИКЪ СТАТЕЙ.

С.-ПЕТЕРБУРГЪ
Типографія П. П. Сойкина, Стремянная ул., № 12
1895

Title page of the miscellany in which Lenin's *The Economic Content of Narodism and the Criticism of It in Mr. Struve's Book*, 1895, was published

Mr. Struve's book is a systematic criticism of Narodism —this word to be understood in its broad sense, as a theoretical doctrine that gives a particular solution to highly important sociological and economic problems, and as "a system of dogmas of economic policy" (p. VII). The very posing of such a problem would have made the book of outstanding interest, but of still greater importance is the standpoint from which the criticism is made. Of this the author in his Preface says the following:

"While adhering, on certain basic issues, to views that have been quite definitely established in literature, he (the author) does not consider himself bound in the least by the word and letter of any doctrine whatsoever. He is not infected with orthodoxy" (IX).

The contents of the book make it clear that these "views that have been quite definitely established in literature" are those of Marxism. The question arises: which, exactly, are the "certain basic" tenets of Marxism that the author accepts, and which are those he rejects? Why and to what extent? He gives no direct answers to these questions. That is why a detailed examination will be necessary in order to make clear exactly what there is in the book that may be classed as Marxist—which of the doctrine's tenets the author accepts and how consistently he adheres to them—and which of them he rejects, and what are the results when he does so.

The contents are exceedingly varied: the author gives us, firstly, an exposition of "the subjective method in sociology" as accepted by our Narodniks, criticises it and sets against it the method "of historico-economic materialism." Then he gives an economic criticism of Narodism, firstly on the strength of "human experience" (p. IX) and, secondly, on the basis of the facts of Russia's economic history and present-day reality. A criticism of the dogmas of Narodnik economic policy is given in passing. The varied character of the contents (something quite inevitable when criticising a major trend in our public thought) determines the form in which the examination is made: we shall have to follow the author's exposition step by step, dwelling on each series of arguments.

Before, however, proceeding to examine the book, I consider it necessary to give a preliminary explanation in somewhat greater detail. The task of the present article is to criticise Mr. Struve's book from the viewpoint of one who "adheres to views that have been quite definitely established in literature" on *all* (and not merely on "certain") "basic issues."

These views have been expounded on more than one occasion for the purpose of criticism in the columns of the liberal and Narodnik press, and this exposition has abominably obscured them—has, indeed, distorted them by involving what has nothing whatever to do with them, namely, Hegelianism, "faith in the necessity of each country having to pass through the phase of capitalism" and much other purely *Novoye Vremya* nonsense.

It is above all the practical side of the doctrine, its application to Russian affairs, that has been badly distorted. Our liberals and Narodniks refused to understand that the starting-point of the Russian Marxist doctrine is a totally different concept of Russian reality, and by looking at that doctrine from the standpoint of their old views of this reality, reached conclusions that were not only absolutely absurd but that in addition levelled the most preposterous accusations at the Marxists.

It seems to me, therefore, that unless I define my attitude to Narodism exactly, it will be impossible to set about an examination of Mr. Struve's book. Furthermore, a preliminary comparison of the Narodnik and Marxist viewpoints is necessary to explain many passages in the book under review, which confines itself to the objective side of the doctrine and leaves practical conclusions almost entirely untouched.

The comparison will show us what points of departure Narodism and Marxism have in common, and in what they differ fundamentally. It will be more convenient to take the old Russian Narodism, since, firstly, it is immeasurably superior to that of today (as represented by publications such as *Russkoye Bogatstvo*) in consistency and forthrightness, and, secondly, it gives a fuller picture of the best aspects of Narodism, aspects which in some respects Marxism also adheres to.

Let us take one of the professions de foi* of the old Russian Narodism and follow the author step by step.

---

* Creeds.—*Ed.*

CHAPTER I

A LINE-BY-LINE COMMENTARY ON A NARODNIK PROFESSION DE FOI

Volume CCXLII of *Otechestvenniye Zapiski** contains an unsigned article entitled "New Shoots in the People's Fields," which graphically sets forth the progressive aspects of Narodism as against Russian liberalism.

The author begins by saying that "now" it is considered "almost treachery" to protest against "those who emerge from the midst of the people and reach a higher level of society."

"Not long ago a certain literary donkey kicked at *Otechestvenniye Zapiski* for displaying *pessimism towards the people*, as he expressed himself regarding a brief review of a book by Zlatovratsky which contained nothing pessimistic apart from pessimism towards usury and the corrupting influence of money in general; and when, later, Gleb Uspensky wrote a commentary to his latest articles (*Otechestvenniye Zapiski*, No. 11, 1878), the liberal bog heaved and surged, just as in the fairy-tale ... and all of a sudden, so many defenders of the people appeared that, verily, we were surprised to find that our people had so many friends.... I cannot but sympathise ... with the way of posing the problem of the beauteous countryside and of the attitude of the literary lads towards it, or, to put it better, not lads but old roués from among Messrs. the nobility and lackeys, and the young merchants.... To sing serenades to the countryside and "to make eyes at it" does not at all mean to love and respect it, just as pointing to its defects does not mean to be hostile towards it. Should you ask the very same Uspensky ... what is closest to his heart, where he sees the greatest guarantees for the future ... in the countryside or in the old-nobility and the new middle-class strata, can there be any doubt at all that he would say: 'The countryside.'"

This is a very typical passage. Firstly, it shows clearly the essence of Narodism: it is protest against serfdom (the

* 1879, No. 2, *Contemporary Review*, pp. 125-52.

old-nobility stratum) and bourgeoisdom (the new middle-class stratum) in Russia *from the peasant's, the small producer's, point of view.* Secondly, it shows at the same time that this protest is based on fantasy, that it turns its back on the facts.

Does the "countryside" exist somewhere *outside of* the "old-nobility" or "new middle-class" regimes? Was it not the "countryside" that representatives of both the one and the other built and are still building each after their own fashion? The countryside is in fact a "stratum" that is partly "old-nobility," and partly "new middle-class." Whichever way you look at the countryside, if you confine yourself to stating the actual situation (that is all that is at issue) and not to possibilities, you will not be able to find anything else, any third "stratum," in it. And if the Narodniks *do*, it is only because they cannot see the wood for the trees, the form of land *tenure* in the separate peasant communities prevents them from seeing the economic organisation of Russian social economy. This organisation turns the peasant into a commodity producer, transforms him into a petty bourgeois, a petty isolated farmer producing for the market. This organisation, therefore, makes it impossible to look *backwards* for "guarantees for the future" and makes it essential to look for them *ahead.* They should not be sought in the "countryside," where the combination of the "old-nobility" and "new middle-class" strata terribly worsens the position of labour and deprives it of the opportunity of fighting against the masters of the "new middle-class" order, for here the antithesis between their interests and those of labour is insufficiently developed. But they should be sought in the fully-developed stratum which is completely "new middle-class" and has entirely disposed of the blessings of the "old-nobility," has socialised labour, has brought to a head and clarified that social contradiction which, in the countryside, is still in an embryonic, suppressed condition.

Now we must indicate the theoretical differences existing between the doctrines that *lead* to Narodism and to Marxism, between the different *conceptions* of Russian reality and history.

Let us follow the author further.

He assures "spiritually indignant gentlemen" that Uspensky understands the relation between the poverty and the morality of the people

"better than many admirers of the countryside, for whom ... the countryside ... is something like the liberal passport which all intelligent and practical bourgeois usually provide themselves with in an epoch like the present."

You, Mr. Narodnik, are wondering why something so lamentable and hurtful should take place—that a man who wants to represent the interests of labour should see that which he regards as "guarantees for the future" transformed into a "liberal passport." That future has to rule out the bourgeoisie—but the way in which you wish to arrive at this future, far from being given a hostile reception by the "practical and intelligent bourgeois," is accepted willingly, is accepted as a "passport."

Do you think such a scandalous thing would be possible if you were to point to the "guarantees for the future," not where the social contradictions inherent in the system dominated by the "practical and intelligent bourgeois" are still in an undeveloped, embryonic state, but where they are developed thoroughly, to nec plus ultra, where, consequently, one cannot confine oneself to palliatives or half-measures, where the desiderata of the working people cannot be utilised for one's own benefit, and where the issue is squarely put?

Do you not yourself say further on:

"The passive friends of the people refuse to understand the simple thing that in society all active forces usually add up to two equally operating, mutually opposite ones, and that the passive forces which apparently take no part in the struggle, merely serve the force preponderant at the given moment" (p. 132).

Does not this description apply to the countryside, or is the countryside some specific kind of world devoid of these "mutually opposite forces" and struggle, a countryside that can be spoken of indiscriminately, without fear of playing into the hands of the "preponderant force"? Is it sound, since we are talking about struggle, to begin where the content of this struggle is cluttered up with a host of extraneous circumstances that prevent those mutually opposite forces from being definitely and finally separated from one another, that prevent the chief enemy from being clearly seen? Is it not obvious that the programme advanced by the author at the end of his article—education, expansion of peasant land tenure, reduction of taxes—can have no effect on the one who is preponderant, while the last point of the programme—"organisation of people's industry"—presumes, does it not, that the struggle has not only taken place, but, furthermore, has already ended in victory? Your programme fights shy of the antagonism whose existence you yourself could not help admitting. That is why it holds no terrors for the masters of the "new middle-class stratum." Your programme is a petty-bourgeois dream. That is why it is only good enough to be a "liberal passport."

"People for whom the countryside is an abstract concept, and the muzhik an abstract Narcissus, even think badly when they say that the countryside should only be praised and be told that it is standing up splendidly to all influences destructive to it. If the countryside is placed in such a position that it must fight every day for a kopek, if it is skinned by the usurers, deceived by the kulaks, oppressed by the landlords, if it is sometimes flogged in the Volost offices, can this be without influence to its moral side?... If the ruble, that capitalist moon, sails to the forefront of the rural landscape, if all eyes, all thoughts and spiritual forces are focussed on it, if it becomes the aim of life and the yardstick of individual abilities, can the fact be hidden and can we say that the muzhik is such an altruist that he needs no money at all? If in the countryside there are visible tendencies towards conflict, if kulakdom is in full bloom and is striving to enslave the weakest peasants and turn them into labourers, to wreck the village community, etc., can we, I ask, conceal all these facts?! We may wish for a more detailed and comprehensive investigation of them, we may explain them to ourselves by the oppressive conditions of poverty (hunger drives people to theft, murder, and in extreme cases even to cannibalism), but we cannot conceal them at all. To conceal them means to defend the status quo, to defend the notorious laissez faire, laissez aller until the sad phenomena assume terrible proportions. To colour the truth is never worth while."

Once again, how fine is this description of the countryside and how petty the conclusions drawn from it! How well are the facts observed and how paltry the explanation, the understanding of them! Here again we see the gigantic abyss between the desiderata of the defence of labour, and the means of fulfilling them. Capitalism in the countryside, so far as the author is concerned, is no more than a "sad phenomenon." Despite the fact that he sees the same sort of capitalism in the towns on a big scale, that he sees how capitalism has subordinated to itself not only all spheres of the people's labour but even "progressive" literature, which presents the measures of the bourgeoisie in the name and in behalf of the people, despite this, he refuses to admit that it is a matter of the specific organisation of our social economy, and consoles himself with dreams about its being merely a sad phenomenon called into existence by "oppressive conditions." And if, says he, one does not cling to the theory of non-interference, then these conditions may be eliminated. Yes, *if* ifs and ans! But Russia has never yet witnessed a policy of non-interference; there always has been interference ... for the benefit of the bourgeoisie, and only sweet dreams of "after-dinner tranquillity" can give rise to hopes of changing this without a "redistribution of the social force between the classes," as Mr. Struve puts it.

"We forget that our society needs ideals—political, civic and others—mainly so that, having acquired a stock of them, it may be able to think of nothing; that society seeks them not with youthful eagerness, but with after-dinner tranquillity, that society is not disillusioned in them with torments of the soul but with the lightness of a prince of Arcady. Such, at least, is the overwhelming majority of our society. Actually it requires no ideals because it is sated and is fully satisfied by digestive processes."

A superb description of our liberal-Narodnik society.

The question arises, who is more consistent now: the "Narodniks," who continue to fuss and bother with this "society," who regale it with a picture of the horrors of "oncoming" capitalism, of the "threatening evil,"* as the author of the article expressed it, who call on its representatives to leave the wrong road on to which "we" have deviated, etc.—or the Marxists, who are so "narrow" that they sharply fence themselves off from society and consider it necessary to address themselves exclusively to those who are not "satisfied" and *cannot be satisfied* with "digestive proc-

* Threatening what? The digestive processes? Capitalism not only does not "threaten" them, but, on the contrary, promises the most refined and dainty victuals.

esses," for whom ideals are a necessity, for whom they are a matter of daily life.

That is the attitude of a ladies' college damsel—continues the author. That

"testifies to profound corruption of thought and feelings... never has there been such decent, polished, such innocent and at the same time profound corruption. This corruption is entirely the property of our recent history, the property of middle-class culture" [i.e., of the bourgeois, capitalist order, to be more exact. K. T.*] "that has grown up on the soil of landlordism, the sentimentality, ignorance and indolence of the nobility. The middle class have introduced their own science, their own moral code and their own sophisms into life."

One would have thought that the author had so well assessed the situation that he should have understood the only possible conclusion to be drawn. If it is all a matter of our bourgeois culture, there can be no other "guarantees for the future" except in the "antipode" of this bourgeoisie, because it alone has been totally "differentiated" from this "middle-class culture," is finally and irrevocably hostile to it and is incapable of any of the compromises out of which it is so convenient to fashion "liberal passports."

But no. One may still dream. "Culture" is certainly nothing but "middle-class," nothing but corruption. But this is only because it comes from the old landlordism (he himself has just admitted that this culture is a product of contemporary history, of that history, in fact, that destroyed the old landlordism) and from indolence—something, therefore, that is fortuitous and has no firm roots, etc., etc. Then come phrases that have no meaning other than turning one's back on the facts and sentimental dreaming that ignores the *existence* of "mutually opposite forces." Listen:

"They (the middle class) have to instal them (science, the moral code) in the university chairs, in literature, in the courts and in other spheres of life." [Above we have seen that they *have already installed them* in such a profound "sphere of life" as the countryside. K. T.] "First and foremost, they do not find a sufficient number of people suitable for this, and of necessity address themselves to people of other traditions." [Is it the Russian bourgeoisie that "does not find people"?! This is

* K. T. (K. Tulin)—V. I. Lenin.—*Ed.*

not worth refuting, especially as the author refutes himself further on. K. T.] "These people have no knowledge of business" [the Russian capitalists?! K. T.], "their steps are uncertain, their movements clumsy "[their "knowledge of business" is sufficient for them to get tens and hundreds per cent profit; they are sufficiently "experienced" to practise the truck-system [106] everywhere, they are sufficiently astute to secure preferential tariffs. Only somebody who has no *immediate and direct* experience of oppression by these people, only a petty bourgeois could entertain such a fantasy. K. T.]; "they try to copy the West-European bourgeoisie, order books, study" [here the author has himself to admit the fantastic character of the dream he has now concocted about "middle-class culture" having grown up in Russia in the soil of *ignorance*. That is untrue. It is precisely the *middle-class culture* that brought culture and "education" to post-Reform Russia. "To colour the truth," to picture the enemy as impotent and devoid of foundation is "never worth while." K. T.]; "at times they become regretful about the past and at times uneasy about the future, because voices are heard from somewhere saying that the middle class are only the impertinent parvenus of the day, that their science will not bear criticism, while their moral code is no use at all."

Is it the Russian bourgeoisie that commits the sin of being "regretful about the past" and "uneasy about the future"?! You don't say! Don't some people like pulling their own legs by spreading such wholesale slander about the poor Russian bourgeoisie being embarrassed by voices proclaiming the "uselessness of the middle class." Is not the opposite the case: were not these "voices" "embarrassed" when they were given a good bawling out, is it not they who display "uneasiness about the future"?...

And gentlemen of this sort even express surprise and pretend they do not understand why they are called romantics!

"Yet we must save ourselves. The middle class do not ask, but order people, on pain of destruction, to go to work.* If you refuse, you will go without bread and will stand in the middle of the street, crying out, "Spare something for an ex-soldier!" or die of starvation altogether. And so work begins, you hear a squeaking, creaking, and clanking, there is a turmoil. The job is an urgent one that brooks no delay. Finally, the machine is set going. There seems to be less creaking and fewer strident sounds, the parts seem to work, all you hear is the din of something

---

* Note that, reader. When a Narodnik says that here, in Russia, "the middle class order people to go to work," that is the truth. But should a Marxist say that the capitalist mode of production prevails in Russia—then Mr. V. V. will set up a howl about his trying to "replace the democratic (sic!!) system by the capitalist."

clumsy. But that makes it all the more fearsome because the planks bend more and more, screws get loose and, look!—before you know where you are the whole thing may fall to pieces."

This passage is particularly typical in that it contains in graphic, laconic, and elegant form the line of argument which the Russian Narodniks like to clothe in scientific dress. Starting out from facts which are indisputable, which are beyond all doubt, and which prove the existence of contradictions under the capitalist system, the existence of oppression, starvation, unemployment, etc., they exert every effort to prove that capitalism is an exceedingly bad thing, is "clumsy" [cf. V. V., *Kablukov* (*The Workers in Agriculture*), and *partly* Mr. Nikolai —on], and "look, before you know where you are it may fall to pieces."

We are looking, we have been looking for many, many years, and see that this force, which orders the Russian people to go to work, keeps growing stronger and bigger, boasts to the whole of Europe about the might of the Russia *it* is creating, and is glad, of course, that "voices are heard" only about the need to hope that "the screws will get loose."

"Weak people are terror-stricken. 'All the better,' say reckless people. 'All the better,' say the bourgeoisie:—'the sooner we order new machinery from abroad, the sooner we prepare platforms, planks and other rough parts from our own material, the sooner we shall get skilled engineers.' In the meantime, the moral aspect of society is in a very bad way. Some people acquire a taste for the new activity and make frantic efforts, some lag behind and become disillusioned with life."

Poor Russian bourgeoisie! They make "frantic" efforts to appropriate surplus-value! and feel in a bad way in the moral sense! (Don't forget that a page earlier all this morality amounted to digestive processes and corruption.) It is clear that here there is no need for a struggle—and for a class struggle at that—against them; all that is needed is to chide them properly, and they will stop overdoing it.

"In the meantime practically nobody thinks of the people; yet, according to the rules of the bourgeoisie, everything is done for the people, on their account; yet all prominent public and literary people consider it their duty to hold forth on the people's welfare.. . This coquettish liberalism has crushed all other trends and become predominant. In our *democratic age* not only does Mr. Suvorin publicly 'confess his love for the people and say: I have always had but one love, and I shall have it till I die—that love is the people. I myself came from the people'(which in itself does not prove anything at all); even *Moskovskiye Vedomosti*[107] seems to have quite a different attitude to them... and in its own way, of course, concerns itself with their well-being. At the present time there is not one single paper like the late *Vest*, i.e., openly unfriendly to the people. But the obviously unfriendly attitude was better because the enemy was then plainly visible, as on the palm of your hand: you could see in what way he was a fool, and in what way he was a knave. Now all are friends and at the same time enemies; everything is mixed up in a general chaos. The people, as Uspensky says, are, in fact, enveloped in a sort of fog in which the inexperienced person may go astray. Formerly they saw themselves faced with just outspoken lawlessness. Now they are told that they are as free as the landlord, they are told that they manage their own affairs, they are told that they are being raised from insignificance and being put on their feet, whereas running through all these manifestations of concern there is a thin but tenacious thread of endless deceit and hypocrisy.

There's no gainsaying that!

"At that time far from everybody was engaged in organising loan-and-savings societies that encouraged the kulaks and left the genuinely poor without credits."

At first one might have thought that the author understood the bourgeois character of credit and so was bound to give a wide berth to all such bourgeois measures. But the distinctive and basic feature of the petty bourgeois is to battle against bourgeoisdom with the instruments of bourgeois society itself. That is why the author, like the Narodniks in general, *corrects* bourgeois activity by demanding more extensive credits, credits for the genuinely poor!

"... they did not talk of the need for intensive farming, which is hindered by the redistribution of fields and by the village community (?); they did not dwell on the burden of the poll-tax and did not propose an income tax, keeping silent about indirect taxation and the fact that income tax is usually turned in practice into a tax on the very same poor people; they did not speak of the need for credits with which the peasants could purchase land from the landlords at abnormally high prices, etc.... The same is the case in society: there, too, the people have such a multitude of friends that you can only marvel.... Very likely the pawnbrokers and tapsters will soon start talking about love for the people...."

This protest against bourgeoisdom is superb; but the conclusions are paltry: the bourgeoisie reign supreme both in everyday life and in society. One would have thought that the thing to do is to turn away from society and go to the antipode of the bourgeoisie.

No, the thing to do is to propagate credits for the "genuinely poor"!

"It is difficult to decide who is more to blame for such a confused state of affairs—literature or society—and it is, moreover, quite useless. They say that a fish starts rotting at the head, but I attach no significance to this purely culinary observation."

Bourgeois society is rotting—that, then, is the author's idea. It is worth emphasising that this is the starting-point of the Marxists.

"Yet while we are flirting with the countryside and making eyes at it, the wheel of history is turning, spontaneous forces are at work, or to speak more clearly and simply, all sorts of tricksters are insinuating themselves into life and remaking it after their own fashion. While literature argues about the countryside, about the kind-heartedness of the muzhik and his lack of knowledge, while the publicists exhaust bucketfuls of ink on the village community and the forms of land tenure, while the tax commission continues its discussion on tax reform, the countryside will be utterly ruined."

There you have it! "While we are talking, the wheel of history is turning, spontaneous forces are at work."

What a howl, my friends, you would raise, were it I that spoke thus! [108]

When Marxists speak of the "wheel of history and spontaneous forces," and explain specifically that the "spontaneous forces" are the forces of the rising bourgeoisie, Messrs. the Narodniks prefer to say nothing about whether or not the growth of these "spontaneous forces" is true and whether this fact has been rightly estimated; and they blather interminable asininities about those who dare to speak of "the wheel of history" and "spontaneous forces," calling them "mystics and metaphysicians."

The difference—and a very substantial one—between the above-cited admission of the Narodnik and the ordinary proposition of the Marxists is only this—for the Narodnik these "spontaneous forces" boil down to "tricksters" who "insinuate themselves into life," whereas for the Marxist the spontaneous forces are embodied in the bourgeois *class*, which is a product and expression of social "life," which in its turn constitutes the capitalist social formation, and do not "insinuate themselves into life" by accident or from somewhere outside. The Narodnik, who keeps to the surface of credits, taxes, forms of land tenure, redistribution, improvements, and so forth, cannot see that the bourgeoisie are deeply rooted in Russia's production relations and for that reason soothes himself with childish illusions about their being no more than "tricksters." And, naturally, from *this* point of view it really will be absolutely incomprehensible where the class struggle comes in, when it is all a matter of merely eliminating "tricksters." Naturally, Messrs. the Narodniks answer the Marxists' emphatic and repeated references to this struggle with the totally incomprehending silence of one who sees only the "trickster" and not the class.

A class can only be fought by *another class*, and only by one that is already totally "differentiated" from its enemy, totally opposite to it, whereas the police alone, and in an extreme case "society" and the "state," are, of course, enough to fight the "tricksters."

We shall soon see, however, what these "tricksters" are like from the description given by the Narodnik himself, how deeply rooted they are and how universal their social functions.

Then, immediately after the above-quoted words about "passive friends of the people," the author continues:

"This is something worse than armed neutrality in politics, worse because in this case active aid is always rendered to the strongest. However sincere a passive friend may be in his sentiments, however modest and unobtrusive a position he may try to assume in everyday life, he will nevertheless injure his friends...."

"For individuals of greater or lesser integrity and who sincerely love the people,* such a state of affairs finally becomes intolerably

* How vague are the features which here distinguish the "passive friends"! Among them, to be sure, there are also people of "integrity" who undoubtedly "love the people sincerely." From the previous comparison it obviously follows that we should contrast to the passive friend the one who participates in the struggle of "mutually opposite" *social forces*. Hier liegt der Hund begraben (That's the skeleton in the cupboard.—*Ed.*).

repugnant. They become ashamed and disgusted to hear this wholesale and sugary confession of love that is repeated from year to year, repeated daily in offices, fashionable salons, and in restaurants over bottles of Clicquot, and is never translated into action. That is why they finally come to the sweeping denial of all this hotchpotch."

This description of the attitude of the former Russian Narodniks to the liberals would fit the attitude of the Marxists to the present-day Narodniks almost completely. The Marxists, too, now find it "intolerable" to listen to talk of aid for the "people" in the shape of credits, land purchases, technical improvements, artels, common tillage,* etc. They also demand a "sweeping denial" of all this liberal-Narodnik hotchpotch from individuals desirous of siding ... not with the "people," no, but with him whom the bourgeoisie order to go to work. They find it "intolerable" hypocrisy to talk of choosing paths for Russia, of misfortunes from "threatening" capitalism, of the "needs of people's industry," when in all spheres of this people's industry we see the reign of capital, a smouldering battle of interests, that one must not hide but expose—one must not dream that "it would be better without struggle,"** but must *develop* the stability, continuity, consistency, and, chiefly, ideological nature of that struggle.

"That is why certain civic canons finally appear, certain categorical demands for decency, demands that are strict and on occasion even narrow, and for this reason are particularly disliked by liberals in the grand style who love wide shady spaces and forget that the demands have a logical origin."

Superb wish! There is an undoubted need for demands that are "strict" and "narrow."

The trouble, however, is that all the superb intentions of the Narodniks have remained in the realm of "pious wishes." Despite the fact that they have recognised the need for such demands, despite the fact that they have had quite enough time to give effect to them, they have not yet drawn

* G. Yuzhakov in *Russkoye Bogatstvo*, issue No. 7, 1894.

** Mr. Krivenko's expression (*Russkoye Bogatstvo*, 1894, No. 10) in reply to Mr. Struve's phrase about "the stern struggle of social classes."

them up, they have steadily merged with Russian liberal society by a whole series of gradual transitions, and continue to do so to this day.*

Therefore, they have only themselves to blame if the Marxists now put forward demands *against* them that are really very "strict" and "narrow," demands for *exclusive* service to one class *exclusively* (the class that is "differentiated from life"), to its independent development and thinking, demands that they should make a complete break with the "civic decency" of the "decent" bourgeois of Russia.

"However narrow these canons may be on particular points, at any rate one cannot say anything against the following general demand: 'one of two things: either be real friends, or turn into open enemies!'

"We are now passing through an exceedingly important historical process, namely, that of the formation of a third estate. The selection of representatives is going on before our eyes, and the organisation of the new social force that is preparing to govern life is taking place."

Only just "preparing"? But who does "govern"? What other "social force"?

Surely not the one that was expressed in newspapers of the *Vest* type? That is impossible. We are not in 1894, but in 1879, on the eve of "the dictatorship of the heart";[110] the time when, to use the expression of the author of the article, "extreme conservatives have fingers pointed at them in the street," and are "loudly laughed at."

Surely not the "people," not the working population? A negative reply is provided by the whole of the author's article.

Can they still say after that: "preparing to govern"?! No, that force "finished preparing" ages ago and has been "governing" for ages; it is only the Narodniks who "are preparing"

* Certain naïve Narodniks, who in their simplicity do not understand that their words are directed against themselves, even boast of this:

"Our intelligentsia in general, and literature in particular," writes Mr. V. V. *against* Mr. Struve, "even the representatives of the most bourgeois trends, bear, so to speak, a Narodnik character" (*Nedelya*, 1894, No. 47, p. 1506).

Just as in everyday life the small producer merges with the bourgeoisie by a series of imperceptible transitions, so in literature the pious wishes of the Narodniks become a "liberal passport" for the receptacles of digestive processes, skimmers,[109] etc.

to select the best paths to be followed by Russia, and they will, presumably, spend their time getting ready until the consistent development of class contradictions sweeps aside, jettisons all those who fight shy of them.

"This process, which began in Europe much earlier than ours did, has come to an end* in many countries; in others it is still being held up by the debris of feudalism and by the resistance of the working classes, but the wheel of history is there, too, year by year breaking up these debris to an ever greater extent and paving the way for the new order."

That is the extent to which our Narodniks misunderstand the West-European labour movement! It "holds up" capitalism, you see—and, as "debris," it is placed on a par with feudalism!

This is clear proof that in respect of not only Russia, but also of the West, our Narodniks are incapable of understanding how one can fight capitalism by speeding up its development, and not by "holding it up," not by pulling it back, but by pushing it forward, not in reactionary, but in progressive fashion.

"In its general features this process consists of the following: between the nobility and the people a new social stratum is being formed of elements that descend from above and of elements that rise from below, who, as it were, are of equal relative weight, if one may so express oneself; these elements are welding themselves closely together, are joining forces, undergoing a profound inner change and beginning to change both the upper and the lower strata, adapting them to their requirements. This process is extremely interesting in itself, but for us it is of particularly great significance. For us a whole series of questions arise: does the rule of the third estate constitute a fatal and inevitable stage in the civilisation of each people?..."

What sort of rubbish is this?! Where does "fatal inevitability" come from, and what has it to do with the matter? Did not the author himself describe, and will he not in still

* What's the meaning of "has come to an end"? Does it mean that its end is visible, that a "new force" is assembling already? In that case it is coming to an end in Russia, too. Or that there the third estate is no longer growing?—that is wrong, because there, too, small producers still exist from whom come handfuls of bourgeoisie and masses of proletarians.

greater detail describe, the domination of the third estate in *our country*, in holy Russia, in the seventies?

The author apparently accepts the theoretical arguments behind which the representatives of our bourgeoisie have hidden themselves.

Now, what else is it but dreamy superficiality to accept such inventions at their face value? Not to understand that behind these "theoretical" arguments stand *interests*, the interests of the society that has now been so rightly assessed, the interests of the bourgeoisie?

Only a romantic can think that interests are to be combated by syllogisms.

"... cannot the state pass directly from one stage to another without any of the somersaults that our over-prudent philistines see at every step, and without paying heed to the fatalists who see in history just fatal order, a consequence of which is that the domination of the third estate is as inevitable to the state as old age or youth is to man?..."

That's the kind of profound understanding the Narodniks have of our reality! If the state assists the development of capitalism it is not at all because the bourgeoisie possess material force enabling them to "send" the people "to work" and bend policy in their own will. Nothing of the sort! It is simply that the Vernadskys, the Chicherins, the Mendeleyevs and other professors hold wrong theories about a "fatal" order, and the state "takes heed" of them.

"... cannot, finally, the negative aspects of the advancing order be softened, somehow altered or the period of its domination shortened? Is the state really something so inert, involuntary and helpless that it cannot influence its own destiny and change it; is it really something like a spinning-top, released by providence, that moves only along a definite road, only for a certain time, and performs a certain number of revolutions, or like an organism of very limited will-power; is it really directed by something resembling a huge iron wheel which crushes every audacious person who dares to seek the nearest roads to human happiness?!"

This is a highly typical passage that shows with particular clarity *the reactionary*, *petty-bourgeois character* of the way in which the direct producers' interests have been and are being represented by the Russian Narodniks. Being hostile to capitalism, the small producers constitute a transitory class that is closely connected with the bourgeoisie and for that reason is incapable of understanding that the large-scale capitalism it dislikes is not fortuitous, but is a direct product of the entire contemporary economic (and social, and political, and juridical) system arising out of the struggle of mutually opposite social forces. Only inability to understand this can lead to such absolute stupidity as that of appealing to the "state" as though the political system is not rooted in the economic, does not express it, does not serve it.

Is the state really something inert? the small producer asks in despair, when he sees that as regards *his* interests it really is remarkably inert.

No, we might answer him, the state can on no account be something inert, it always acts and acts very energetically, it is always active and never passive—and the author himself a page earlier described this vigorous activity, its bourgeois character, its natural fruits. The only bad thing is that he refuses to see the connection between the character it has and the capitalist organisation of the Russian social economy, and that he is, therefore, so superficial.

Is the state really a top, is it really an iron wheel? asks the Kleinburger, when he sees that the "wheel" turns in a direction quite different from what he would like.

Oh no, we might answer him—it is not a top, nor a wheel, nor the law of fate, nor the will of providence: it is moved by "living individuals," "through a lane of obstacles"* (such, for example, as the resistance of the direct producers, or the representatives of the stratum of the old nobility), by precisely those "living individuals" who belong to the preponderant social force. And so, in order to compel the wheel of history to turn in the other direction, one must appeal to "living individuals" against "living individuals" (i.e., against social elements who do not belong to the liberal professions, but who directly reflect vital economic

* Mr. N. Mikhailovsky, in Mr. Struve's book, p. 8: "The living individual with all his thoughts and feelings becomes a history-maker at his own risk. He and not some mystic force, sets aims in history and pushes events towards them through a lane of obstacles placed before him by the spontaneous forces of nature and of historical conditions."

interests), appeal to a class against a class. For this, good and pious wishes about "nearest roads" are highly inadequate; this requires a "redistribution of the social force among the classes," this requires that one becomes the ideologist not of the direct producer who stands apart from the struggle, but of the one who stands in the midst of heated struggle, who has already become totally "differentiated from life" of bourgeois society. This is the *only* and hence the nearest "road to human happiness," a road along which one can not only soften the negative aspects of the existing state of things, not only cut its existence short by speeding up its development, but put an end to it altogether, by compelling the "wheel" (not of state, but of social forces) to turn in quite another direction.

"... We are interested only in the process of organising the third estate, in individuals, even, who emerge from the midst of the people and take their places in its ranks. These are very important individuals: they fulfil exceedingly important social functions, and the degree of the intensity of bourgeois order is directly dependent on them. No country where this order was installed could manage without them. If a country has none or insufficient of them, they have to be obtained from the ranks of the people, conditions have to be created in the life of the people to help them emerge and take shape, and then they have to be protected and assisted to grow until they get on their feet. Here we meet with direct interference in historical destiny by the most energetic individuals, who take advantage of circumstances and of the moment to serve their own interests. These circumstances consist mainly of the need for industrial progress (the replacement of handicraft production by manufacture and manufacture by factory production, the replacement of one system of farming by another, a more rational one), without which a country really cannot manage if it has a population of a certain density, if it maintains international relations and if there is political and moral dissension conditioned both by economic factors and the growth of ideas. It is these changes, urgent in political life, that shrewd people usually connect with themselves and with a certain order; this order could undoubtedly be replaced, and always can be replaced, by another, if other people are wiser and more energetic than they have been hitherto."

So then, the author cannot but admit that the bourgeoisie perform "important social functions"—functions that can be generally expressed as: the subordination to themselves of the people's labour, the direction of it and the raising of its productivity. The author cannot but see that economic "progress" is really "bound up" with these elements, i.e., that our bourgeoisie really are the vehicle of economic, or more exactly, technical progress.

Here, however, begins a radical distinction between the ideologist of the small producer and the Marxist. The Narodnik explains this *fact* (the connection between the bourgeoisie and progress) by asserting that "shrewd people" "take advantage of circumstances and of the moment to serve their own interests"—in other words, he considers this accidental and for that reason draws the following naïvely bold conclusion: "undoubtedly these people can always (!) be replaced by others" who will also provide progress, but not bourgeois progress.

The Marxist explains this fact by those social relations of people in the production of material values that take form in commodity economy, that convert labour into a commodity, subordinate it to capital and raise its productivity. He does not regard it as an accident, but a necessary product of the capitalist system of our social economy. He therefore sees a way out not in fairy-tales about what "undoubtedly can" be done by individuals who replace the bourgeois (the latter, bear in mind, have still to be "replaced"—and mere words or appeals to society and the state are not enough), but in the development of the class contradictions of the present economic order.

Everybody understands that these two explanations are diametrically opposed to each other, that from them follow two mutually exclusive systems of action. The Narodnik, who considers the bourgeoisie an accident, sees no connection between them and the state, and with the credulity of a "simple-minded muzhik" appeals for aid precisely to the one who guards bourgeois interests. His activity boils down to the modest and precise, official liberal activity that is on a par with philanthropy, for it does not seriously affect the "interests" and holds no terror for them at all. The Marxist turns his back on this hotchpotch, and says that there can be no other "guarantees for the future" than the "stern struggle of economic classes."

It is also understandable that if these differences in systems of action follow directly and inevitably from differences in *explaining* the fact of the domination of our bourgeoisie, the Marxist, when conducting a *theoretical dispute*, confines himself to proving the necessity and inevitability (under the given organisation of social economy) of this bourgeoisie (that was the case with Mr. Struve's book); and that if the Narodnik, avoiding the issue of these different methods of explanation, engages in talk about Hegelianism and about "cruelty towards the individual,"* this is merely a clear indication of his impotence.

"The history of the third estate in Western Europe is an exceedingly long one.... We, of course,shall not repeat all this history, despite the teaching of the fatalists; nor will the enlightened representatives of our third estate proceed, of course, to utilise the same means for achieving their aims as were resorted to previously, and will only take from them those that are most suitable and correspond to the conditions of place and time. To deprive the peasantry of the land and create a factory proletariat they will not, of course, resort to crude military force or the no less crude clearing of estates."

"Will not resort"...?!! Only among the theoreticians of sugary optimism can one meet such deliberate forgetfulness of past and present *facts* that have already said their "aye"—and rose-spectacled trustfulness that the future will, of course, yield "no." Of course that is false.

"... but they will resort to the abolition of communal landownership, to the creation of capitalist farmers, a numerically small class of wealthy peasants,** and will, in general, resort to means that allow the economically weak to perish of himself. They will not now start setting up guilds but will organise credit, raw-material, consumers' and producers' associations which, with their promise of general happiness, will only help the strong to become still stronger, and the weak to become still weaker. They will not bother about the patrimonial court, but will bother about legislation to encourage assiduity, sobriety and education, which will be pursued only by the young bourgeoisie, since the masses will continue as hitherto to get drunk, will be ignorant and will work for others."

How well described are all these credit, raw-material, and miscellaneous other associations, all these measures for encouraging assiduity, sobriety and education, towards

---

* Mr. Mikhailovsky in *Russkoye Bogatstvo*, No. 10, 1894.

** That is being superbly put into effect even without the abolition of the village community which does not in the least eliminate the split among the peasantry—as has been established by Zemstvo statistics.

which such a touching attitude is displayed by our contemporary liberal-Narodnik press, including the *Russkoye Bogatstvo*. All that remains for the Marxist is to emphasise what has been said, to agree fully that *all this is mere representation of the third estate*, and, consequently, those who show tender concern for it are nothing more than *little bourgeois* people.

This quotation is a sufficient answer to the present-day Narodniks, who draw the conclusion from the contemptuous attitude of the Marxists to such measures that they want to be mere "spectators" and do nothing. True enough, they will never set their hands to bourgeois activity; as far as that is concerned they will always be "spectators."

"The role of this class (these offspring of the people—the petty bourgeoisie), which forms the outposts, the sharpshooters and vanguard of the bourgeois army, has been, unfortunately, of very little interest to historians and economists, whereas its role, we repeat, is an exceedingly important one. When the destruction of the village community and the alienation of the peasants' land took place, it was not done by the lords and knights alone, but by their own folks, i.e., again by offspring of the people, offspring endowed with practical shrewdness and a flexible spine, who had been awarded by the lord's grace, who had fished some capital out of troubled waters or had acquired it by plunder, individuals to whom the upper estates and the legislature stretched out their hands. They were called the most industrious, capable and sober elements of the people...."

This observation is a very true one as far as the facts go. Really, the alienation of the peasants' land was done mainly by "their own folks," by the petty bourgeois. But the Narodnik understands this fact unsatisfactorily. He does not distinguish two antagonistic classes, the feudal lords and the bourgeoisie, the representatives of the "old-nobility" and of the "new middle-class" systems, does not distinguish between different systems of economic organisation, does not see the progressive significance of the second class as compared with the first. That is the first point. Secondly, he attributes the rise of the bourgeoisie to plunder, to shrewdness, servility, etc., whereas small-scale farming based on commodity production makes a petty bourgeois of the most sober, hard-working peasant: he accumulates "savings" and by virtue of environmental relations they turn into *capital*. Read about this in the descriptions of handicraft industries and peasant farming, in the works of our Narodnik men of letters.

"... They are not the sharpshooters and vanguard even, they are the main bourgeois army, the lower ranks, formed into units under the command of staff and senior officers, commanders of separate units and the General Staff, made up of publicists, speakers and scientists.* Without this army the bourgeoisie could have done nothing. Could the English landlords, who number less than 30,000, have been able to govern the hungry mass of tens of millions without the capitalist farmers?! The farmer is a real fighting man in the political sense and a little expropriating nucleus in the economic sense.... In the factories the role of the farmers is fulfilled by the foremen and assistant foremen, who get a very good wage not only for more skilled work, but for keeping a watch on the workers, for being the last to leave the bench, for preventing the workers from putting forward demands for wage increases or for reduction of working hours, and for enabling the employers to say as they point at them: 'See how much we pay those who work and are of benefit to us'; by the shopkeepers, who maintain the closest relations with the employers and factory managements; by the office staff, all sorts of supervisors and suchlike small fry, in whose veins workers' blood still flows, but over whose minds capital has already taken complete control." [Quite true! K. T.] "Of course, the things we see in Britain are also to be seen in France, Germany and other countries."[Quite true! And in Russia, too. K. T.] "The only difference in some cases is in details, and even those in greater part remain unchanged. The French bourgeoisie, who at the end of last century triumphed over the nobility, or to put it better, who took advantage of the people's victory, produced from among the people a petty bourgeoisie that helped to fleece the people, and themselves fleeced the people and delivered them into the hands of adventurers.... At a time when in literature hymns were being sung to the French people, when their greatness, magnanimity and love of liberty were being lauded to the skies, when all this adulation was enveloping France in a cloud, the bourgeois cat was eating the chicken, disposing of it almost entirely and leaving only the bones for the people. The much vaunted people's land tenure turned out to be microscopic, measured in metres and often incapable even of covering taxation expenditure...."

Let us pause here.

Firstly, we would like to ask the Narodnik: who in our country "took advantage of the victory over serfdom," over

* And administrators and the bureaucracy, it should be added. Otherwise the reference to the composition of the "General Staff" will suffer from an impossible incompleteness—impossible in the conditions peculiar to Russia.

the "old-nobility stratum"? Not the bourgeoisie, of course? What was going on in our country among the "people" when "hymns," now quoted by the author, "were being sung in literature" about the people, love for the people, magnanimity, community peculiarities and qualities, the "social mutual adaptation and joint activity" within the village community, about Russia being a single artel, and the community being "all that is in the minds and actions of village folk," etc., etc., etc., hymns that continue to be sung to this day (though in a minor key) in the columns of the liberal-Narodnik press? The land, of course, was not taken from the peasantry; the bourgeois cat, of course, did not make a hearty meal of the chicken, did not dispose of it almost entirely; "the much vaunted people's land tenure" did not "turn out to be microscopic," it contained no excess of expenditure over income?* No, only "mystics and metaphysicians" are capable of asserting that, of considering it to be a fact, of making that fact the starting-point of their opinions about our affairs, of their activity, which is aimed not at seeking for "different paths for the fatherland," but at working along the present, now quite established, capitalist path.

Secondly. It is interesting to compare the author's *method* and the *method* of the Marxists. One can far better understand wherein they differ on the basis of specific judgements than by way of abstract thinking. Why does the author say of the French "bourgeoisie" that it triumphed at the end of last century over the nobility? Why is activity that consisted chiefly and almost exclusively of the activity of the intelligentsia, called bourgeois? And then, was it not the government that acted, depriving the peasantry of the land, and imposing heavy payments, etc.? Finally, these personalities surely spoke of their love for the people, of equality and universal happiness, as the Russian liberals and Narodniks did and are doing now? Under these circumstances can one see just the "bourgeoisie" in all this? Is not this view a "narrow" one, reducing political and ideological movements to Plusmacherei?** Just note, these are the same questions

* And not only "often," as in France, but as a general rule, the excess running not only into tens, but into hundreds per cent.

** Profit-hunting.—*Ed.*

as those with which the Russian Marxists are flooded when they say identical things about our peasant Reform (seeing it as differing merely in "details"), about post-Reform Russia in general. I speak here, I repeat, not of the factual correctness of our view, but of the *method* used in the given case by the Narodnik. He takes as his *criterion* the results ("it turned out" that the people's land tenure was microscopic, the cat "was eating" and "ate up" the chicken), and what is more—exclusively economic *results.*

The question arises: why does he apply this *method* only to France, and refuse to employ it for Russia, too? Surely, the method should be universal. If in France you seek for *interests* behind the activity of the *government* and the *intelligentsia,* why do you *not seek* them in holy Russia? If *there* your criterion raises the question of what the character of people's land tenure "*turned out*" to be, why is what it "may" turn out to be made the criterion *here*? If there, phrases about the people and its magnanimity, while the "chicken was being eaten," fill you with legitimate disgust, why do you not *here* turn your backs, as you would on bourgeois philosophers, on those who, while the "eating" undoubtedly exists and is recognised by you, can talk of "social mutual adaptation," the "community spirit of the people," the "*needs of people's industry*" and suchlike things?

There is only one answer. It is because you are an ideologist of the petty bourgeoisie, because your ideas, i.e., Narodnik ideas in general, and not the ideas of Tom, Dick, and Harry—are the result of their reflecting the interests and the viewpoint of the small producer, and not at all the result of "pure"* thought.

"But particularly instructive for us in this respect is Germany, which was late, as we were, with her bourgeois reform and for that reason made use of the experience of other nations, in the negative and not the positive sense, of course." The composition of the peasantry in Germany—says the author, paraphrasing Vasilchikov—was heterogeneous: the peasants were divided up according to their rights and the land they held, i.e., the size of their allotments. The entire process led to the formation of a "peasant aristocracy," an "estate of small landowners not of noble origin," to the transformation of the

* Mr. V. V.'s expression. See *Our Trends,* and also *Nedelya,* Nos. 47-49, 1894.

mass from "householders to unskilled labourers." "Finally the finishing touch was given, and all legal roads to an improvement of the workers' conditions were cut off by the semi-aristocratic, semi-middle-class constitution of 1849, which gave the vote only to the nobility and the wealthy middle class."

An original way of arguing. The constitution "*cut off*" legal roads?! This again is a reflection of the good old theory of the Russian Narodniks, according to which the "intelligentsia" were invited to sacrifice "freedom," since, we are told, it would be of service to them alone, while the people would be surrendered to the "wealthy middle class." We are not going to argue against this stupid and reactionary theory, because it has been rejected by the contemporary Narodniks in general and our immediate opponents, Messrs. the publicists of *Russkoye Bogatstvo*, in particular. We must, however, note that by rejecting this idea, by taking a step towards openly recognising Russia's *existing* paths instead of palavering about the possibility of different paths, these Narodniks reveal their petty-bourgeois nature once and for all; their insistence on paltry, middle-class reforms, arising out of their absolute inability to understand the class struggle, places them on the side of the liberals against those who take the side of the "antipode," seeing in it the only creator, so to speak, of the good things in question.

"In Germany, too, there were many people at that time who only waxed enthusiastic over the emancipation, and did so for ten, twenty, thirty years and more; people who considered all scepticism, all dissatisfaction with the Reform playing into the hands of reaction and cursed the sceptics and the grumblers. The simple-minded among them imagined the people as a horse that had been set at liberty and could be put back into the stable again and could go once more into the mail-coach (something by no means always possible). But there were also knaves who flattered the people and who, pursuing another line on the quiet, tacked themselves on to these simpletons who were full of sincere love of the people, and could be tricked and exploited. Oh, those sincere simpletons! When civic struggle begins, by no means everybody is ready for it and by no means everybody has an aptitude for it."

Splendid words that give a good summary of the best traditions of the old Russian Narodism and that we can utilise to characterise the attitude of the Russian Marxists to *contemporary* Russian Narodism. To make such use of them not much has to be changed—so *identical* is the process of capitalist development in both countries; so *identical* are the social and political ideas reflecting this process.

In our country, too, "progressive" literature is governed and guided by individuals who talk of "fundamental differences between our peasant Reform and that of the West," about the "sanction of people's (sic!) production," about the great "allotment of land" (land redemption is called that!!), etc., and who therefore await the dispensation by their superiors of a miracle called the "socialisation of labour," wait for "ten, twenty, thirty years and more," while the cat—of which we have spoken earlier—eats the chicken, looking with the tenderness of a sated and satisfied animal at the "sincere simpletons" who talk of the need to choose another path for the fatherland, of the harm of "threatening" capitalism, and of measures for assisting the people with credits, artels, common cultivation of the land and suchlike innocent patching. "Oh, those sincere simpletons!"

"And now we, too, and mainly our peasantry, are experiencing this process of the formation of a third estate. Russia is in this respect behind the whole of Europe, even behind its college companion, or to be more exact 'teacher-in-training,' Germany. The towns were the main breeding ground and ferment of the third estate everywhere in Europe. In our country the opposite is the case"—we have far fewer urban inhabitants.... "The chief cause of this difference is our people's system of land tenure, which keeps the population in the countryside. The increase in the urban population in Europe is closely bound up with the separation of the people from the land and with factory industry which, under capitalist conditions of production, requires cheap labour and a surplus of it. The European peasantry, driven out of the villages, went to earn a living in the towns, whereas our peasantry keep to the land as long as they possibly can. Land tenure by the people is the principal strategic point, the principal key to the peasant position, a key whose significance is perfectly well understood by the leaders of the middle class, and that is why they direct all their art and all their energy against it. This is the origin of all these attacks on the village community, this is the source of the great number of projects of different kinds about the alienation of the peasants' land, for the sake of rational farming, for the sake of industrial prosperity, for the sake of national progress and glory!"

This shows clearly the superficiality of the Narodnik theory which, as a result of dreams about "different paths," quite wrongly assesses the real situation: it sees the "principal point" in such juridical institutions, which play no fundamental role, as the forms of peasant land *tenure* (community or household); it sees something peculiar in our small peasant economy, as though it is not the ordinary economy of small producers, of the same kind—as to the type of their political and economic organisation—as the economy of the West-European handicraftsmen and peasants, but some "people's" (?!) system of land tenure. According to the terminology established in our liberal and Narodnik press, the meaning of the word "people's" is one that rules out the exploitation of the one who works—so that by the definition he gives the author actually conceals the undoubted fact that in our peasant economy there is the very same appropriation of surplus-value, the very same work for others as prevail outside of the "community," and so opens the doors wide to sentimental and unctuous Pharisaism.

"Our present village community, land-poor and weighed down by taxation, is not much of a guarantee. The peasant had little land as it was, but now, as a result of the growing population and declining fertility, has still less, and the burden of taxation is not lessening, but increasing; there are few industries; there are still fewer local employments; life in the countryside is becoming so difficult that the peasants of entire villages go far away in search of employment, leaving only their wives and children at home. In this way entire uyezds become deserted.... Influenced by these hard conditions of life, on the one hand, a special class of people emerges from among the peasantry—the young bourgeoisie, who try to buy land on the side, each on his own, try to engage in other occupations—trade, usury, the organisation of workers' artels headed by themselves, to get all sorts of contracts and in similar petty business."

It is worth dwelling in great detail on this passage.

We see here, firstly, the statement of certain facts that can be expressed in a couple of words: the peasants are fleeing; secondly, an assessment of the facts (a negative one), and thirdly, an explanation of them from which there directly follows an entire programme, here not expounded, but well enough known (add land, reduce taxes; "raise" and "develop" peasant industries).

It must be emphasised that from the viewpoint of the Marxist both the *first* and the *second* are wholly and undoubtedly correct (except, as we shall see, that they are expressed in an extremely unsatisfactory way). But the *third** is absolutely useless.

Let me explain this. The first is correct. The fact is correct that our village community is no guarantee, that the peasantry are abandoning the village, leaving the land; he should have said: are being expropriated, because they possessed (on a private property basis) certain means of production and are losing them (among them land by special right, which, however, allowed land *redeemed* by the community to be also privately exploited). It is correct that handicraft industries "are declining", i.e., the peasants here too are being expropriated, are losing their means and instruments of production, are giving up domestic weaving and are leaving to work on railway construction jobs or hiring themselves out as bricklayers, unskilled labourers, etc. The means of production from which the peasants are freed pass into the hands of an insignificant minority, and serve as a source of exploitation of labour-power—*as capital.* That is why the author is right when he says that the owners of these means of production become a "bourgeoisie," i.e., a class which under the capitalist organisation of social economy holds in its hands the "people's" labour. All these facts are correctly stated and truly assessed for their exploiting significance.

But from the description given the reader has, of course, seen that the Marxist *explains* these facts in a totally different way. The Narodnik sees the causes of these things in that "there is little land," taxes are burdensome, and "earnings" are falling—i.e., in peculiarities *of policy*—land, taxation, industrial—and not in the peculiarities *of the social organisation of production*, an organisation from which the *given* policy inevitably follows.

There is little land—argues the Narodnik—and it is becoming less. (I do not even necessarily take the statement made by the author of the article, but the general proposition of the Narodnik doctrine.) Quite correct, but why do you merely say that there is *little* land, and not add that there is *little on sale.* Surely you are aware that

* That is why the theoreticians of Marxism, in combating Narodism, lay the stress on explanation and understanding, on the objective side.

our peasants are *redeeming* their allotments from the landlords. Why, then, do you concentrate your attention mainly on what there is *little* of, and not on what is *on sale*?

The very fact of sale, of redemption by purchase points to the domination of principles (the acquisition of the means of production for money) which, in any case, leave the peasants without the means of production whether few or many of them are sold. By ignoring this fact you ignore the capitalist mode of production on which basis alone the sale became possible. By ignoring this you take the side of that bourgeois society and turn into a plain political jobber who argues about whether much or little land should be on sale. You do not see that the very fact of the redemption by purchase proves that "*capital* has already taken complete control" over the "minds" of those in whose interests the "great" Reform was carried through, who themselves accomplished it; you do not see that it is the "capitalist moon" that casts the only light existing for all this liberal-Narodnik "society" which bases itself on the system created by the Reform speechifying on how to make various improvements in that system. That is why the Narodnik so savagely attacks those who adhere consistently to a basis that is different in principle. He raises a cry about their not being concerned about the people, about their wanting to take the land away from the peasants!!

He, the Narodnik, is concerned about the people, he does not want the peasant to lose his land, he wants him to have more of it (*sold* to him). He is an honest shopkeeper. True, he keeps silent about the fact that land is sold and not supplied gratis, but then, does anybody in the corner shops say that goods have to be paid for? As it is, everybody knows it.

It is understandable that he hates the Marxists, who say that we must address ourselves exclusively to those who are already "differentiated" from this shopkeepers' society, "excommunicated" from it, if one may use these highly characteristic petty-bourgeois expressions of the Messrs. Mikhailovskys and Yuzhakovs.*

* Apart from ignoring and failing to understand the capitalist character of land redemption, Messrs. the Narodniks also modestly

Let us proceed. "There are few industries"—such is the Narodnik's viewpoint on handicraft industries. And again he is silent on the way the industries are organised. He complacently shuts his eyes to the fact that both the industries that are "declining" and those that "are developing" are similarly organised on capitalist lines, labour being totally enslaved to the capital of buyers-up, merchants, etc., and confines himself to petty-bourgeois demands for progressive measures, improvements, artels, etc., as though such measures can in any way influence the *fact* of the domination of capital. In the sphere of both agriculture and of manufacturing industry he accepts their existing organisation, and does not fight against the organisation itself, but against its various imperfections. As to taxes, here the Narodnik has refuted himself by bringing into sharp relief the basic characteristic feature of Narodism—the capacity for compromise. Earlier on he himself asserted that every tax (even income tax) would hit at the workers where a system of appropriating surplus-value exists—nevertheless, he does not in the least object to discussing with the members of liberal society whether taxes are large or small and to offering, with "civic decency," the appropriate advice to the Department of Taxes and Levies.

In short, the cause—in the Marxist's view—lies neither in policy, nor in the state, nor in "society," but in the present system of Russia's economic organisation; the point is not that "shrewd people" or "tricksters" fish in troubled waters, but that the "people" constitute two opposite, mutually exclusive, classes: "in society all active forces add up to two equally operating, mutually opposite ones."

"People who are interested in installing the bourgeois order, when they see the collapse of their projects,* do not stop at that:

---

avoid the fact that side by side with the peasants' "land poverty" there are some very nice pieces of land in the possession of the representatives of the "old-nobility" stratum.

* So then, the collapse of the project to abolish the village community means victory over those who want to "install the bourgeois order"!!

Having concocted a petty-bourgeois utopia about the "community," the Narodnik goes so far in his dreams as to ignore reality that he sees in the project against the community nothing less than the in-they hourly repeat to the peasantry that the blame for everything lies with the community, collective responsibility, the redistribution of the fields, the whole system of the village community, which favour idlers and drunkards; they organise loan-and-savings societies for the prosperous peasants and busy themselves about small land credits for plot holders; in the towns they arrange technical, handicraft and various other schools, entrance to which is again available only to the children of well-to-do folk, whereas the mass are without schools; they help the rich peasants to improve their cattle by means of exhibitions, prize awards, supplying pure-bred sires on hire from depots, etc. All these petty efforts go to make up a considerable force that has a degenerating effect on the countryside and increasingly splits the peasantry into two."

The description of the "petty efforts" is a good one. The author's idea that all these petty efforts (which *Russkoye Bogatstvo* and our entire liberal and Narodnik press now uphold so zealously) signify, express and further the "new middle-class" stratum, the capitalist system, is quite a correct one.

This is precisely the reason for the Marxists' negative attitude to such efforts. And the fact that these "efforts" are undoubtedly the immediate desiderata of the small producers—proves, in their view, that their main thesis is correct that the representative of the idea of labour is not to be seen in the peasant, since he, being a petty bourgeois under the capitalist organisation of economy, takes, accordingly, the side of this system, adheres in certain aspects of his life (and of his ideas) to the bourgeoisie.

It will be worth while to utilise this passage to stress the following. The negative attitude of Marxists to "petty

---

stalling of the bourgeois order, whereas it is simply political jobbery based on the already fully "installed" bourgeois system.

To him the most forceful argument against the Marxist is the question that he asks with an air of final triumph: just tell me, now, do you want to destroy the community or not, yes or no? For him the whole question is that of "installation." He absolutely refuses to understand that from the Marxist's viewpoint the "installation" is a long-established and irrevocable fact that will not be affected either by the destruction or the consolidation of the community—just as the domination of capital is the same in the community village and in a village consisting of individual peasant households.

The Narodnik tries to advance a profounder protest against "installation" by an apology for the installation. A drowning man clutches at a straw.

efforts" particularly evokes complaints from the Narodnik gentlemen. By reminding them of their forefathers we show that there was a time when the Narodniks took a different view of this, when they were not so eager and zealous in their compromises [although they did compromise even then, as the same article proves], when they—I will not say understood—but at least sensed the bourgeois character of all such efforts, and when the denial of them was condemned as "pessimism towards the people" by only the most naïve of liberals.

The pleasant intercourse of the Narodnik gentlemen with the latter, as representatives of "society," apparently yielded good fruit.

The fact that one cannot content oneself with the "petty efforts" of bourgeois progress by no means signifies absolute rejection of partial reforms. Marxists by no means deny that these measures are of some (albeit miserable) benefit they can result in some (albeit miserable) improvement in the working people's conditions; they speed up the process of extinction of particularly backward forms of capital, usury, bondage, etc., they speed up their transformation into the more modern and humane forms of European capitalism. That is why Marxists, if they were asked whether such measures should be adopted, would, of course, answer: they should—but would thereupon explain their attitude in general to the capitalist system that is improved by these measures, would motivate their agreement by their desire to speed up the development of this system, and, consequently its downfall.*

"If we bear in mind that in this country, as in Germany, the peasantry are divided up according to rights and tenure, into various categories (state, appanage and former landlords' peasants, among them being those who received full allotments, medium and quarter lots, as well as manor serfs); that our community way of life is not the universal way of life; that in the south-west, among private landowners, we again meet with peasants owning draught animals, and footers,** market gardeners, farm labourers and *chinsh* peasants,[111]

* This refers not only to "technical and other schools," to technical improvements for peasants and handicraftsmen but also to "the extension of peasant land tenure" and to "credit," etc.

** See p. 45 of this volume.—*Ed.*

some of whom possess 100 dessiatines and more, while others have not an inch of soil; that in the Baltic gubernias the agrarian system is a perfect copy of the German agrarian system, etc., then we shall see that we too have a basis for a bourgeoisie."

One cannot but note here that fanciful exaggeration of the significance of the community from which the Narodniks have always suffered. The author expresses himself as though "community life" ruled out a bourgeoisie, ruled out the splitting up of the peasants! Now that is totally untrue!

Everybody knows that the community peasants are also split up according to rights and allotments; that in every village where the community is strong the peasants are again split up both "according to rights" (landless, allotment-holding, ex-manor serfs, paid-up allotment-holder, registered, etc., etc.) and "according to tenure": peasants who have rented out their allotments, who have been deprived of them for arrears in taxes or for not cultivating and letting them fall into neglect or who lease the allotments of others; peasants who own land in "perpetuity" or who "purchase a few dessiatines for several years"; lastly, homeless peasants, peasants owning no cattle, peasants owning no horses and those owning many horses. Everybody knows that in every village where the community is strong this economic fragmentation and commodity economy provide a basis for the full blossoming of usury capital, for bondage in all its forms. And the Narodniks continue telling sugary tales about something they call "community life"!

"Our young bourgeoisie is indeed growing by leaps and bounds, and is growing not only in the Jewish border areas, but in the heart of Russia. As yet it is difficult to express their number in figures, but when we look at the growing number of landowners, at the increasing number of commercial certificates, at the increasing number of complaints from the villages about the kulaks and the blood-suckers and other evidence,* there are grounds for thinking that their number is already considerable."

* To which should be added purchases with the aid of the Peasant Bank, "progressive trends in peasant farming" such as technical and agronomical improvements, introduction of improved implements, grass-growing, etc., the development of small-scale credits and organisation of a market for handicraftsmen, etc.

Quite true! It is this fact, that was true in 1879 and is still more true in 1895, that serves as one of the mainstays of the Marxist understanding of Russian reality.

Our attitude to this fact is equally negative; we are both agreed that it expresses phenomena opposed to the interests of the direct producers—but we *understand* these facts in quite different ways. I have already described the theoretical aspect of the difference above, and I shall now turn to the practical aspect.

The bourgeoisie, especially those of the countryside, are **still** weak in this country; they are only just coming into existence, says the Narodnik. Hence one can **still** wage a struggle against them. The bourgeois trend is still not very strong—therefore we can **still** turn back. It is not too late.

Only the metaphysical sociologist (who in practice becomes a cowardly reactionary romanticist) can argue that way. I shall not bother to say that the "weakness" of the bourgeoisie in the countryside is to be explained by the departure of their strong elements, their top-rankers, to the towns—that only the "rank and file" are in the villages, whereas in the towns we have the "general staff"—I shall not bother to speak of all these thoroughly obvious distortions of fact by the Narodniks. There is another mistake in this argument, one that makes it metaphysical.

We are faced with a certain social relation, a relation between the village petty bourgeois (the rich peasant, shopkeeper, kulak, blood-sucker, etc.), and the "labouring" peasant, labouring "for others," of course.

This relation exists—the Narodnik will not be able to deny its generally widespread character. But it is weak, says he, and for that reason may *still* be corrected.

History is made by "living individuals," we tell this Narodnik, offering him his own wares. It is, of course, possible to correct, to change social relations, but only when such action originates *from the people themselves whose social relations are being corrected or changed.* This is as clear as the clearest daylight. The question arises: can the "labouring" peasant change this relation? What does it consist of? Of the fact that two small producers operate under the system of commodity production, that this commodity economy splits them into "two," to one it gives *capital*, and the other it compels to work "for others."

How can our labouring peasant change this relation if he himself is half-rooted in what has to be changed? how can he understand that isolation and commodity economy are no good to him if he himself is isolated and works at his own risk and responsibility for the market? if these conditions of life evoke in him "thoughts and feelings" that are peculiar to one who works on his own for the market? if he is isolated by the very material conditions, by the size and character of his farm, and if by virtue of this his contradiction to capital is still so little developed that he cannot understand that he is faced by *capital* and not merely by "tricksters" and shrewd people?

Is it not obvious that one should turn to where *this same* (N. B.) social relation is *fully* developed, where those involved in this social relation, the immediate producers, are themselves fully "differentiated" and "excommunicated" from the bourgeois order, where the contradiction is already so far developed as to be self-evident, and where it is impossible to raise the problem like a dreamer, in half-hearted fashion? And when the immediate producers in these advanced conditions are "differentiated from life" of bourgeois society not only *in fact* but also *in their minds*—then the labouring peasantry, who are in backward and worse conditions, will see "how it is done," and will join with their fellow workers "for others."

"When people speak here of cases of peasants buying land, and explain that the peasantry buy land privately or as a whole community, they almost never add that purchases by the community are only rare and insignificant exceptions to the general rule of private purchases."

The author further quoted figures to show that the number of private landowners was 103,158 in 1861 and reached a total of 313,529 according to data for the sixties; he said that the explanation of this is that small proprietors of peasant origin were not included under serfdom but were included on the second occasion and continued:

"These are our young rural bourgeoisie, who immediately border on and are linked up with the small landed nobility."

True—is what we say to that—quite true, especially that about them "bordering on" and being "linked up"! And that is why we class as petty-bourgeois ideologists those who attach serious importance (in the sense of the interests of the immediate producers) to "the extension of peasant land tenure," i.e., including the author, who on page 152 says just this.

That is why we consider as no more than political jobbers people who discuss the problem of purchases made privately and by the community as though "installing" the bourgeois order depended on it in the slightest degree. We place both the one and the other case in the bourgeois category, for purchase is purchase, money is money in both cases, i.e., the sort of commodity that only falls into the hands of the petty bourgeois,* irrespective of whether he is united with others by the community "for social mutual adaptation and joint activity" or is isolated by having a plot of land of his own.

"Incidentally, they (the young rural bourgeoisie) are not shown here to the full. The word 'blood-sucker' (*miroyed*) is not new in Russia, but it has never had the meaning it now has, it has never exerted such pressure on fellow villagers as it does now. Compared with the blood-sucker of today, the old miroyed was a patriarchal sort of individual who was always subordinated to the community and was sometimes merely an idler who did not particularly hunt after profit. The word miroyed has now acquired a different meaning and, in the majority of gubernias, is merely a generic term that is relatively little used and has been replaced by such words as: kulak, welsher, merchant, publican, cat-skinner, contractor, pawnbroker, etc. This splitting up of one term into several, into words, some of which are not new either, and some quite new or have not hitherto been current among peasants, shows first and foremost that a division of labour has taken place in the exploitation of the people, and that there has been an extensive development of rapacity and that it has become specialised. In almost every village and every hamlet there are one or several such exploiters."

Without a doubt the fact of the development of rapacity has been correctly noted. It is, however, to no purpose that the author, like all Narodniks, refuses despite all these facts to understand that this systematic, universal, regular (even with division of labour) kulak activity is a manifestation of capitalism in agriculture, is the domination of capital

* This does not refer, of course, to such money as merely serves for the acquisition of necessary articles of consumption, but to *free* money that can be saved for the purchase of means of production.

in its primary forms, capital which, on the one hand, engenders the urban, banking, and in general European, capitalism that the Narodniks consider to be something adventitious, and, on the other hand, is supported and fed by this capitalism —in a word that it is one of the aspects of the capitalist organisation of the Russian national economy.

In addition, the description of the "evolution" of the blood-sucker enables us to catch the Narodnik once again.

In the Reform of 1861 the Narodnik sees the sanction of people's production, discerns in it features that are fundamentally different from those of Western reform.

The measures that he now thirsts for amount equally to similar "sanction"—of the community, etc., and to similar "provisions of allotments" and means of production in general.

Why, then, Mr. Narodnik, did the Reform, which "sanctioned people's (and not capitalist) production," merely result in the "patriarchal idler" turning into a relatively energetic, lively, civilisation-adorned vulture? merely result in a change in the *form* of rapacity, as did the corresponding great reforms in the West?

Why do you imagine that the next steps in "sanctioning" (which are quite possible in the shape of an extension of peasant land tenure, migration to other areas, regulation of land rentings and other undoubtedly progressive measures—although they are bourgeois progressive measures)—why do you imagine that they will lead to something other than a further change in the *form*, a further Europeanisation of *capital*, its transformation from merchant's into productive, from medieval into modern?

It cannot be otherwise—for the simple reason that such measures do not in the least affect *capital*, i.e., that relation between people under which money, the product of *social* labour organised by commodity economy, is accumulated in the hands of some, while others have nothing but free "hands,"* free precisely of the product that is concentrated in the possession of the previous category.

* "*The masses* will, *as hitherto* ... work *for others*" (see article under discussion, p. 135): if they were not "free" (free de facto, though de jure they may even be "provided with an allotment"), this, of course, could not take place.

..."Of them (of these kulaks, etc.) the smaller fry possessing no capital usually attach themselves to the big merchants, who supply them with credit or instruct them to make purchases on their account; the more prosperous ones carry on independently, are themselves in touch with big commercial cities and ports, send waggonloads there in their own name and go themselves for goods required locally. If you travel on any railway line you will invariably meet in the 3rd (rarely in the 2nd) class dozens of people of this type on their way somewhere on business. You will recognise them by the specific clothes they wear, by their extremely bad manners, and by their boisterous laughter at some lady who asks them not to smoke, or at a *muzhichok*"* [that's what it says: muzhichok. K. T.], "who is on his way somewhere to get work and who is 'ignorant' because he understands nothing of commerce, and wears bast shoes. You will also recognise these people by their conversation. They usually talk about calf-hides, vegetable oils, leather, smelt, millet, etc., and you will hear cynical stories about the swindling they do and the way they fake their goods, about how 'strong smelling' salt beef was 'palmed off on a factory,' about how 'anybody can give tea a colour if you show him once,' about 'how you can add three pounds' weight of water to a sugar loaf in such a way that the customer won't notice anything,' etc. All this is spoken of with such frankness and impudence that you can easily see that the only reason why these people do not steal spoons from public dining-rooms and do not turn out station gas lamps is because they are afraid of landing in jail. Morally these people are below the most elementary standards; their morals are all based on the ruble and are limited to aphorisms, such as: trading means twisting; keep your eyes skinned; don't miss your chance; look for what you can easily lay your hands on; use the moment when nobody's looking; don't pity the weak; bow and scrape when necessary." An item is then quoted from a newspaper about how a publican and usurer named Volkov set fire to his house which he had insured for a big sum. This person "... is considered to be their most respected acquaintance by the local teacher and priest," one "teacher, in return for wine, writes his legal letters for him." "The Volost Clerk promises to bamboozle the Mordovians for him." "A Zemstvo agent, at the same time a member of the Zemstvo Board, insures him his old house for 1,000 rubles," and so on. "Volkov is no isolated example, but a type. There is no locality without its Volkovs, where they tell you not only about similar fleecing and enslaving of the peasants, but also of cases of the same sort of fires...."

"... But what is the attitude of the peasantry to such people? If they are stupid, grossly heartless and petty like Volkov, the peasantry have no love for them, and fear them, because those people can play all sorts of dirty tricks on them, while they can do nothing in return; the homes of those people are insured, they have fast horses, strong locks, fierce dogs and connections with the local authorities.

* *Muzhichok*—a diminutive of muzhik, a peasant.—*Ed. Eng. ed.*

But if those people are cleverer and more cunning than Volkov, if they give their fleecing and enslaving of the peasantry a decent form, if, while robbing them of a ruble, they make an ostensible reduction of a farthing, and if they do not begrudge an extra supply of vodka or a couple of buckets of millet for a burnt-out village, they are held in honour and respect and enjoy authority among the peasants as benefactors, as fathers of the peasant poor, who, no doubt, would be lost without them. The peasantry regard them as clever people, and even let their children be trained by them, considering it an honour for their boy to have a job in a shop, and fully confident that it will make a man of him."

I deliberately copied out the author's argument in great detail so as to cite a description of our young bourgeoisie made by an *opponent* of the proposition that the organisation of Russia's social economy is bourgeois. An examination of this description can clear up many points in the theory of Russian Marxism, in the character of the current attacks made on it by *contemporary* Narodism.

It would seem from the beginning of this description that the author understands how deeply-rooted this bourgeoisie is, understands its connections with the big bourgeoisie, to which the petty bourgeoisie "attaches itself," and its connections with the peasantry, who let their "children be trained" by them. The examples given by the author show, however, that he is far from adequately appraising the strength and stability of this phenomenon.

The examples he gives deal with crime, swindling, arson, etc. One gets the impression that the "fleecing and enslaving" of the peasantry is a matter of accident, the result (as the author expressed himself above) of severe conditions of living, of the "grossness of moral ideas," of obstacles to "making literature accessible to the people" (p. 152), etc.—in a word, that all this does not inevitably result from the present-day organisation of our social economy.

The Marxist adheres to this latter view; he asserts that all this is no accident at all, but a necessity, a necessity conditioned by the capitalist mode of production prevailing in Russia. Once the peasant becomes a commodity producer (and all peasants have already become such), his "morality" will inevitably be "based on the ruble," and we have no grounds for blaming him for this, as the very conditions of life compel him to catch this ruble by all sorts of trading devices.* Under these conditions, without resort to any crime, servility, or falsification, the "peasantry" split into rich and poor. The old equality cannot hold out against the fluctuations of the market. This is not mere talk—it is a fact. And it is a fact that under these conditions the "wealth" of the few becomes *capital*, while the "poverty" of the masses compels them to sell their hands, to work for other people. Thus, from the Marxist's viewpoint capitalism has already taken firm root, taken definite shape not only in factory industry but also in the countryside and all over Russia in general.

You can imagine now how witty the Narodniks are when, in reply to the Marxist's argument that the cause of all these "unfortunate things" in the villages is not politics, land poverty, payments, or bad "personalities," but capitalism, that all this is *necessary* and inevitable where the capitalist mode of production exists, where the bourgeois class prevails—when in reply to this the Narodnik begins to howl that the Marxists want to deprive the peasantry of the land, that they "prefer" the proletarian to the "independent" peasant, that they display—as provincial ladies say and as Mr. Mikhailovsky does in reply to Mr. Struve—"contempt and cruelty" towards the "individual."

In this picture of the countryside, which is interesting because it has been drawn by an opponent, we see clearly the absurdity of the current objections made against the Marxists, how artificial they are—they avoid the facts, and forget their earlier statements—all in order to save, coûte que coûte,** the theories made up of dreams and compromises which fortunately no power is now able to save.

When they talk of capitalism in Russia the Marxists borrow ready-made schemes, dogmatically repeat propositions that are copied from quite different conditions. They make capitalist production in Russia, which is infinitesimal in development and significance (all told, 1,400,000 people are employed in our factories and works), cover the mass of the peasantry, who still own land. Such is one of the favourite objections raised in the liberal and Narodnik camp.

* Cf. Uspensky. [112]
** At all costs.—*Ed.*

Now from that same picture of the countryside we see that when the Narodnik describes the way of life of the "community" and "independent" peasants, he cannot manage without this very category of the bourgeoisie derived from abstract schemes and alien dogmas, he cannot avoid stating that it is a village type and not an isolated case, that it is bound by the strongest ties to the big urban bourgeoisie, that it is also bound to the peasantry, who "let their children be trained by them," and from whom, in other words, this young bourgeoisie emerge. We see, consequently, that the young bourgeoisie grow within our "community," and not outside of it, that they are brought into existence by the very social relations that exist among the now commodity-producing peasantry; we see that not only "1,400,000 people," but the entire mass of Russian village folk work for *capital*, are "superintended" by it. Who is it that draws more correct conclusions from these facts, which are not stated by some "mystic and metaphysician," not stated by a Marxist, who believes in "triads," but by a Narodnik exceptionalist who is well able to appreciate the peculiarities of Russian life? Is it the Narodnik, when he talks of the choice of a better path, as though capital has not already made its choice—when he talks of the turn to another system expected from "society" and the "state," i.e., from such elements as have arisen only on the basis of this choice and *in support of it*?—or the Marxist, who says that to dream of different paths means to be a naïve romanticist, since reality shows most obviously that the "path" has already been chosen, that the domination of capital is a fact not to be evaded by reproaches and censures, a fact that only direct producers can reckon with?

Another current reproach. The Marxists consider large-scale Russian capitalism to be progressive. They thus prefer the proletarian to the "independent" peasant, favour the alienation of the land from the people and, from the viewpoint of a theory that makes its ideal the ownership of the means of production by the workers, favour the separation of the worker from the means of production, i.e., fall into an irreconcilable contradiction.

Yes, the Marxists do consider large-scale capitalism progressive—not, of course, because it replaces "independence" by dependence, but because it creates conditions for abolishing dependence. As to the "independence" of the Russian peasant, it is a sugary Narodnik fairy-tale, and nothing else; actually it is non-existent. And the picture that has been cited (as well as all works about and investigations of the economic condition of the peasantry) also contains an admission of this fact (that actually independence is non-existent): the peasantry, like the workers, work "for others." This was admitted by the old Russian Narodniks. But they failed to understand the causes and character of this *lack* of independence, failed to understand that it is also *capitalist* lack of independence, differing from that of the towns in being less developed, and containing greater relics of medieval, semi-feudal forms of capital, and nothing more. Let us compare, say, the village depicted by the Narodnik with the factory. The only difference (as regards independence) is that in the former we see "small fry" and in the latter large, in the former exploitation singly, by semi-feudal methods—in the latter, exploitation of the masses, and what is more, purely capitalist exploitation. Of course, the latter is progressive: the very capitalism that is undeveloped in the village and, therefore, abounds in usury, etc., is developed in the factory; the very antagonism existing in the countryside is fully expressed in the factory; here the split is complete and the question cannot be posed in the half-hearted way that satisfies the small producer (and his ideologist), who is capable of upbraiding, reproaching and cursing capitalism, but not of abandoning the basis* of this capitalism, of abandoning his faith in its servants, of abandoning his roseate dreams about its being "better without struggle," as the splendid Mr. Krivenko said. *Here* dreams are not possible—and that alone is a tremendous step forward; here it is clearly evident which side possesses the strength, and there can be no talk of choosing the path, for it is clear that at first this strength has to be "redistributed."

* To avoid misunderstanding, let me explain that by "basis" of capitalism I infer the social relation that in various forms prevails in capitalist society and which Marx expressed in the formula: money—commodity—money with a surplus.

The measures proposed by the Narodniks *do not touch* on this relation, and do not affect either commodity production, which places

"Sugary optimism"—is the way Mr. Struve described Narodism, and it is profoundly true. What else is it but optimism when the complete domination of capital in the countryside is ignored, passed over in silence, pictured as something accidental, when all sorts of credits, artels, and common land cultivation are proposed, just as if all these kulaks, vampires, merchants, publicans, contractors, pawnbrokers, etc., as though all this "young bourgeoisie" did not already hold "every village" "in their hands." What else is it but sugary talk when people continue to talk of "ten, twenty, thirty years and more," of "better without struggle," at the very time when the struggle is already on, a smouldering struggle, it is true, unconscious, and not illumined by an idea.

"Cross over now to the towns, reader. There you will encounter the young bourgeoisie in still larger numbers and still greater variety. All who become literate and consider themselves suitable for more honourable activity, all who consider themselves worthy of a better fate than the miserable lot of the rank-and-file peasant, all, finally who under these conditions find no place in the countryside, now make their way to the towns...."

Nevertheless, the Narodnik gentlemen engage in sugary talk about the "artificial character" of urban capitalism, about its being a "hothouse plant," that will die of itself if not looked after, etc. One has only to take a plainer view of the *facts* to see clearly that this "artificial" bourgeoisie is simply the village blood-suckers who have settled in the towns, and who are growing quite spontaneously on soil illumined by the "moon of capitalism" which compels every rank-and-file peasant to buy cheaper and sell dearer.

... "Here you meet salesmen, clerks, petty tradesmen, pedlars, all sorts of contractors (plasterers, carpenters, bricklayers, etc.), conductors, senior porters, policemen, artel captains, owners of ferry-boats, eating-and lodging-houses, proprietors of various workshops, factory foremen, etc., etc. All these are the real young bourgeoisie, with

---

money—the product of social labour—into the hands of private individuals, or the split of the people into paupers and owners of this money.

The Marxist turns to the most developed form of this relation, to the form that is the quintessence of all the other forms, and shows the producer that the aim and object to follow is the abolition of this relation and its replacement by another.

all their characteristic features. Their code of morals is not a very broad one, either: their entire activity is based on the exploitation of labour,* and their object in life is to acquire capital, big or small, with which stupidly to pass away their time...." "I know that many people rejoice when they look at them, see cleverness, energy and enterprise in them, consider them to be the most progressive elements among the people, see in them a straight and natural step forward in their country's civilisation, the unevenness of which will be smoothed out by time. Oh, I have long known that a top-rank bourgeoisie has been formed in this country out of educated people, merchants and nobles who either failed to sustain the crisis of 1861 and went under, or were caught by the spirit of the period; that this bourgeoisie has already formed cadres of a third estate and that all it lacks is precisely those elements from the people which it likes because it can do nothing without them...."

A loophole has been left here, too, for "sugary optimism": the big bourgeoisie "lacks only" bourgeois elements from the people!! But where did the big bourgeoisie come from, if not from the people? Surely the author will not deny the ties between our "merchants" and the peasantry!

We see here a tendency to depict this rise of a young bourgeoisie as a matter of chance, the result of policy, etc. This superficiality in understanding things, incapable of seeing the roots of the phenomenon in the very economic structure of society, capable of giving a most detailed enumeration of the different representatives of the petty bourgeoisie, but incapable of understanding that the peasant's and the handicraftsman's small independent undertaking itself is not, under the present economic order, a "people's" undertaking at all, but a *petty-bourgeois* one—is highly typical of the Narodnik.

---

* Not exact. What distinguishes the petty from the big bourgeois is that he works himself, as the categories enumerated by the author do. There is, of course, exploitation of labour, but more than mere exploitation.

One more remark. The object in life of those who are not satisfied with the peasant's lot is to acquire capital. This is what the Narodnik says (in his sober moments). The tendency of the Russian peasantry is not towards the community, but towards the petty-bourgeois system. That is what the Marxist says.

What is the difference between these two propositions? Is it not merely that the former constitutes an empirical observation of life while the latter generalises the facts observed (which express the real "thoughts and feelings" of real "living individuals") and makes of them a law of political economy?

..."I know that many descendants of ancient families are now engaged in distilling and in running taverns, railway concessions, and in prospecting, have ensconced themselves on the boards of joint-stock banks, have even established themselves in the literary sphere and are now singing other songs. I know that many of the literary songs are extremely tender and sentimental, that they deal with the needs and desires of the people; but I also know that it is the duty of decent literature to lay bare the intention of offering the people a stone instead of bread."

What an Arcadian idyll! Only the "*intention*" as yet of offering?!

And how it harmonises: he "knows" that a bourgeoisie has "long" been formed—and still thinks that his task is to "lay bare the intention" of establishing a bourgeoisie!

And this is what is called "serenity of the spirit" when in sight of the already mobilised army, in sight of the arrayed "rank and file" united by a "long" established "general staff," people still talk of "laying bare intentions," and not of an already fully disclosed battle of interests.

..."The French bourgeoisie also identified themselves with the people and always presented their demands in the name of the people, but always deceived them. We consider the bourgeois trend taken by our society in recent years to be harmful and dangerous to the people's morals and well-being."

The petty-bourgeois character of the author is, I imagine, most clearly expressed in these sentences. He declares the bourgeois trend to be "harmful and dangerous" to the morals and well-being of the people! Which "people," respected Mr. Moralist? Those who worked for the landlords under the serfdom that fostered the "family hearth," "settled living" and the "sacred duty of labour,"* or those who subsequently went away to earn money to pay off land redemption fees? You are well aware that the payment of this money was the main and chief condition of the "emancipation," and that the peasant could only get this money from Mr. Coupon.[113] You yourself have described how this gentleman carried on his business, how "the middle class have introduced their own science, their own moral code and their own sophisms into life," how a literature has already been formed praising the "cleverness, enterprise and energy" of the bourgeoisie. Clearly,

* Terms used by Mr. Yuzhakov.

it all boils down to one form of social organisation being succeeded by another: the system of appropriating the surplus labour of tied-to-the-land serf peasants created feudal morality; the system of "free labour for others," for the owners of money, created bourgeois morality to replace it.

The petty bourgeois, however, is afraid to look things straight in the face, and to call a spade a spade. He turns his back on these undoubted facts, and begins to dream. He considers only small independent undertakings (*for the market*—he keeps a modest silence about that) to be "moral," while wage-labour is "immoral." He does not understand the tie—an indissoluble tie—between the one and the other, and considers bourgeois morality to be a chance disease, and not a direct product of the bourgeois order that grows out of commodity economy (which, in fact, he has nothing against).

So he begins his old-womanish sermon about its being "harmful and dangerous."

He does not compare the modern form of exploitation with the previous one, that of serfdom; he does not look at the changes that it has introduced into the relations between the producer and the owner of the means of production—he compares it with a senseless, philistine utopia, with the sort of "small independent undertakings" that, while being commodity economy, should not lead to what it actually does lead to (see above: "kulakdom is in full bloom, is striving to enslave the weakest, and turn them into farm labourers," etc.). That is why his protest against capitalism (as such, as a protest, it is quite legitimate and fair) becomes a reactionary lamentation.

He does not understand that, by replacing the form of exploitation which tied the working man to his locality with one that flings him from place to place all over the country, the "bourgeois trend" has done a good job; that, by replacing the form of exploitation under which the appropriation of the surplus product was tangled up in the personal relations between the exploiter and the producer, in mutual civic political obligations, in the "provision of an allotment," etc.,—by replacing this with a form of exploitation that substitutes "callous cash payment" for all that and equates labour-power with any other commodity or thing, the "bourgeois trend" strips exploitation of all its obscurities and illusions, and that to do so is a great service.

Then, take note of the statement that the bourgeois trend has been taken by our society "in recent years." Only "in recent years"? Was it not quite clearly expressed in the sixties, too? Was it not predominant throughout the seventies?

The petty bourgeois tries to smooth things out here as well, to present the bourgeois features that have characterised our "society" during the entire post-Reform period as some temporary infatuation, fashion. Not to see the wood for the trees is the main feature of the petty-bourgeois doctrine. Behind the protest against serfdom and bitter attacks on it, he (the ideologist of the petty bourgeoisie) does not see bourgeois reality, the reason being that he fears to look straight at the economic basis of the system that has been built up while he has been shouting vociferously. Behind the talk in all advanced ("liberal-coquettish," p. 129) literature about credits, and loan-and-savings societies, about the burden of taxation, about the extension of landownership and other such measures of helping the "people" he only sees the bourgeois features of "recent years." Finally, behind the complaints about "reaction," behind the wailing about the "sixties" he totally fails to see the bourgeois features underlying all this, and that is why he merges increasingly with this "society."

Actually, during all these three periods of post-Reform history our ideologist of the peasantry has always stood and marched alongside "society," not understanding that the bourgeois features of this "society" rob his protest against them of all strength and inevitably doom him either to dream or indulge in miserable petty-bourgeois compromises.

Many people find this closeness of our Narodniks (who "in principle" are hostile to liberalism) to liberal society very touching, and Mr. V. V. (cf. his article in *Nedelya*, 1894, Nos. 47-49) continues to find it so even to this day. From this the conclusion is drawn that the bourgeois intelligentsia in this country are weak or maybe even non-existent, a point that these people connect with the absence of a basis for Russian capitalism. Actually, however, the very opposite is the case. This closeness is a powerful argument against Narodism, a direct confirmation of its petty-bourgeois character. Just as in everyday life the small producer merges with the bourgeoisie by the fact of his isolated production of commodities for the market, by his chances of getting on in the world, and of becoming a big proprietor, so the ideologist of the small producer becomes a liberal when discussing problems of credits, artels, etc.; just as the small producer is incapable of fighting the bourgeoisie and hopes for such measures of assistance as tax reduction, land extension, etc., so the Narodnik places his trust in liberal "society" and its chatter, clothed in "endless deceit and hypocrisy," about the "people." If he occasionally abuses "society," he immediately adds that only "in recent years" has it become spoilt, but that generally speaking it is not bad in itself.

"*Sovremenniye Izvestia* [*Contemporary News*] recently made a study of the new economic class that has taken shape in this country since the Reform and gave the following good description of it: 'Modest and bearded, wearing well-greased top boots, the old-time millionaire, who humbled himself before a junior official, has rapidly turned into the European type of jaunty and even offhanded and haughty entrepreneur, occasionally wearing a very noticeable decoration and holding a high office. When you take a good look at these unexpectedly thriving people you notice with surprise that most of these luminaries are yesterday's publicans, contractors, stewards, etc. The new arrivals have enlivened, but not improved, urban life. They have introduced bustle into it, and extreme confusion of concepts. Increased turnover and capital requirements have intensified the feverish activity of the enterprises, which has turned into the excitement of a gamble. The numerous fortunes have been made overnight, have increased the appetite for profit beyond all bounds, etc....

"Undoubtedly, such people exert a most ruinous influence on public morals" [that's the trouble—the spoiling of morals, and not capitalist production relations at all! K. T.] "and while we do not doubt the fact that town workers are more corrupted than village workers, there is still less doubt, of course, that this is due to their being much more surrounded by such people, breathing the same air, and living the life that they established."

Clear confirmation of Mr. Struve's opinion about the reactionary character of Narodism. The "corruption" of the town workers scares the petty bourgeois, who prefers the "family hearth" (with its immorality and club rule), "settled life" (accompanied by crushing oppression and savagery) and does not understand that the awakening of the man in "the beast of burden,"[114] an awakening of such enormous and epoch-making significance that all sacrifices made to achieve it are legitimate, cannot but assume tempestuous forms under capitalist conditions in general, and Russian in particular.

"The Russian landlord was distinguished for his barbarism, and required but a little scratching for the Tatar in him to be seen, whereas the Russian bourgeois does not even need to be scratched. The old Russian merchant class created a realm of darkness, whereas now, with the aid of the new bourgeoisie, it will create darkness in which all thought, all human feeling will perish."

The author is sadly mistaken. The past tense should be used here, not the future, and should have been used when those words were written, in the seventies.

"The hordes of new conquerors disperse in all directions and meet with no opposition anywhere or from anybody. The landlords patronise them and give them a welcome reception; the Zemstvo people give them huge insurance bonuses; school-teachers write their legal papers, the priests visit them, while District Clerks help them to bamboozle the Mordovians."

Quite a correct description! "far from meeting with opposition from anybody," they meet with support from the representatives of "society" and the "state," of whom the author gives a rough list. Hence—exceptionalist logic!—in order to change matters, we should advise the choosing of another path, advise "society" and the "state" to do so.

"What, however, is to be done against such people?"

..."To await the mental development of the exploiters and an improvement in public opinion is impossible from the viewpoint either of justice, or of the morals and politics which the state must adopt."

Please note: the state must adopt a "moral and political viewpoint"! This is nothing but phrase-mongering. Do not the representatives and agents of the "state" just described (from the District Clerks upwards) possess a "political" viewpoint [cf. above ... "many people rejoice ... consider them to be the most progressive elements among the people, see in them a straight and natural step forward in their country's civilisation"] and a "moral" one [cf. ibid.:

"cleverness, energy, enterprise"]? Why do you obscure the split in moral and political ideas which are just as hostile to those "whom the bourgeoisie order to go to work" as "new shoots" are undoubtedly hostile in life? Why do you cover up the battle of these ideas, which is only a superstructure to the battle of social classes?

All this is the natural and inevitable result of the petty-bourgeois viewpoint. The petty producer suffers severely from the present system, but he stands apart from the forthright, fully disclosed contradictions, fears them, and consoles himself with naïvely reactionary dreams that "the state must adopt a moral point of view," namely, the viewpoint of the morality that is dear to the small producer.

No, you are not right. The state to which you address yourselves, the contemporary, the present state *must* adopt the viewpoint of the morality that is dear to the top bourgeoisie, *must* because such is the distribution of strength among the existing classes of society.

You are indignant. You start to howl about the Marxist defending the bourgeoisie, when he admits this "must," this necessity.

You are wrong. You feel that the facts are against you, and so resort to trickery: to those who refute your petty-bourgeois dreams about choosing a path without the bourgeoisie by referring to the domination of the latter as a *fact*; to those who refute the suitability of your petty, paltry measures against the bourgeoisie by referring to their deep roots in the economic structure of society, to the economic struggle of classes that is the basis of "society" and the "state," to those who demand of the ideologists of the toiling class that they make a complete break with these elements and exclusively serve those who are "differentiated from life" in bourgeois society—to all these you attribute a desire to defend the bourgeoisie.

> "We do not, of course, consider the influence of literature to be quite powerless, but if it is not to be powerless it must, firstly, better understand its mission and not confine itself to merely (sic!!!) educating the kulaks, but must rouse public opinion."

There you have the petit bourgeois in the pure form! If literature educates the kulaks, it is because it badly understands its mission!! And these gentlemen are surprised when they are called naïve, and when people say of them that they are romantics!

On the contrary, respected Mr. Narodnik: the "kulaks"* educate literature—they give it ideas (about cleverness, energy, enterprise, about the natural step forward in their country's civilised development), they give it resources. Your reference to literature is just as ridiculous as if somebody, in full sight of two opposing armies, were to address to the enemy field marshal's aide the humble request to "act in greater harmony." That is just what it is like.

The same is true of the desire—"to rouse public opinion." The opinion of the society that "seeks ideals with after-dinner tranquillity"? That is the customary occupation of Messrs. the Narodniks, one to which they have devoted themselves with such splendid success for "ten, twenty, thirty years and more."

Try a little more, gentlemen! The society that delights in after-dinner slumber sometimes bellows—that very likely means that it is ready to act in harmony against the kulaks. Talk a little more with that society. Allez toujours.**

..."and secondly, it must enjoy greater freedom of speech and greater access to the people."

A good wish. "Society" sympathises with this "ideal." But since it "seeks" this ideal, too, with after-dinner tranquillity, and since it fears more than anything else to have this tranquillity disturbed ... it hastens very slowly, progresses so wisely that with every passing year it gets farther and farther behind. Messrs. the Narodniks imagine that this is an accident, and that their after-dinner slumber will soon end and real progress begin. So keep waiting!

"Nor do we consider the influence of education and training to be quite powerless, but we presume, first of all: 1) that education should be given to each and every person, and not merely to exceptional persons, taking them out of their environment and turning them into kulaks...."

---

* This is too narrow a term. The more precise and definite term "bourgeoisie" should have been used.

** Keep going!—*Ed.*

"Each and every person" ... that is what the Marxists want. But they think this is unattainable under the present social and economic relations, because even if tuition is free and compulsory, money will be needed for "education," and only the "offspring of the people" have that. They think that here, too, there is no way out except "the stern struggle of social classes."

..."2) That public schools should be accessible not only to retired parsons, officials, and all sorts of good-for-nothings, but also to individuals who are really decent and sincerely love the people."

Touching! But surely those who see "cleverness, enterprise and energy" in the "offspring of the people," also assert (and not always insincerely) that they "love the people," and many of them are undoubtedly "really decent" people. Who will be the judge? Critically thinking and morally developed personalities? But did not the author himself tell us that you cannot influence these offspring with scorn?*

We again, in conclusion, meet with the same basic feature of Narodism which we noted at the very outset, namely, that it turns its back on the facts.

When a Narodnik gives us a description of the facts, he is always compelled to admit that reality belongs to capital, that our actual evolution is capitalist, that strength is in the hands of the bourgeoisie. This has now been admitted, for example, by the author of the article under review, who established the point that "middle-class culture" has been set up in this country, that the people are ordered to go to work by the bourgeoisie, that bourgeois society is occupied only with digestive processes and after-dinner slumber, that the "middle class" have even created bourgeois science, bourgeois morals, bourgeois political sophisms, and bourgeois literature.

Nevertheless, *all* Narodnik arguments are *always* based on the opposite assumption, viz.: that strength is not on the side of the bourgeoisie, but on the side of the "people." The Narodnik talks about the choice of the path (while at the same time admitting the capitalist character of the actual path), about the socialisation of labour (which is

* P. 151: "... do they not scorn in advance (take good note of the "in advance") those who might scorn them?"

under the "management" of the bourgeoisie), about the state having to adopt a moral and political point of view, and about its being the Narodniks who have to teach the people, etc.—as though strength were already on the side of the working people and their ideologists, and all that remained was to indicate the "immediate," "expedient," etc., methods of using this strength.

This is a sickening lie from beginning to end. One can well imagine that such illusions had a raison d'être half a century ago, in the days when the Prussian Regierungsrat[115] was exploring the "village community" in Russia; but now, after a history of over thirty years of "free" labour, it is either a mockery, or Pharisaism and sugary hypocrisy.

It is the basic theoretical task of Marxism to destroy this lie, however good the intentions and however clear the conscience of its author. The prime task of those who wish to seek "roads to human happiness" is not to hoodwink themselves, but to have the courage openly to admit the existence of what exists.

And when the ideologists of the toiling class have understood and felt this, then they will admit that "ideals" do not mean constructing better and immediate paths, but the formulation of the aims and objects of the "stern struggle of social classes" that is going on before our eyes in our capitalist society; that the measure of the success of one's aspirations is not the elaboration of advice to "society" and the "state," but the degree to which these ideals are spread in a definite class of society; that the loftiest ideals are not worth a brass farthing so long as you fail to merge them indissolubly with the interests of those who participate in the economic struggle, to merge them with those "narrow" and petty everyday problems of the given class, like that of a "fair reward for labour," which the grandiloquent Narodnik regards with such sublime disdain.

..."But that is not enough; intellectual development, as we unfortunately see at every step, does not guarantee man against rapacious proclivities and instincts. Hence, immediate measures must be taken to safeguard the countryside against rapacity; measures must be taken, above all, to safeguard our village community, as a form of public life that helps correct the moral imperfection of human nature. The village community must be safeguarded once and for all. But that, too, is not enough. The village community, under its present economic conditions and tax burdens, cannot exist, and so measures should be taken to extend peasant ownership of land, to reduce the taxes, and to organise people's industry.

Such are the measures against the kulaks with which all decent literature must be at one about and stand for. These measures are, of course, not new; the point, however, is that they are the only ones of their kind, but far from everybody is as yet convinced of this." (End.)

There you have the programme of the grandiloquent Narodnik! From the description of the facts we have seen that a complete contradiction of economic interests is everywhere revealed—"everywhere" meaning not only in both town and country, both within and without the village community, both in factory and in "people's" industry, but also outside the bounds of economic phenomena—in both literature and "society," in the sphere of moral, political, juridical and other ideas. Our petty-bourgeois knight, however, sheds bitter tears and appeals for "immediate measures to be taken to safeguard the countryside." The petty-bourgeois superficiality of understanding, and the readiness to resort to compromise is perfectly evident. The countryside itself, as we have seen, constitutes a split and a struggle, constitutes a system of opposite interests—but the Narodnik does not see the root of the evil in the system itself, but in its particular shortcomings, and does not build up his programme to provide an ideological basis for the struggle that is now going on, but makes "safeguarding" the countryside against chance, illegitimate, extraneous "plunderers" his basis! And who, worthy Mr. Romantic, should take measures to safeguard? Should it be the "society" that is content with digestive processes at the expense of just those who should be safeguarded? Or the Zemstvo, Volost and all other sorts of agents who live off fractions of surplus-value and therefore, as we have just seen, offer assistance but not resistance?

The Narodnik finds that this is a lamentable accident, and nothing more—the result of a poor "understanding of the mission"; that it is sufficient to issue a call to "be at one and work as a team," for all such elements to "leave the wrong path." He refuses to see that in economic relations the Plusmacherei system has taken shape, a system under which only the "offspring of the people" can have the means and the leisure for education, while the "masses" have "to remain ignorant and work for others"; the direct and immediate consequence is that only members of the former make their way into "society," and that it is only from this same "society" and from the "offspring" of the people that there can be recruited the District Clerks, Zemstvo agents and so on whom the Narodnik is naïve enough to consider as people standing *above* economic relations and classes, *over* them.

That is why his appeal to "safeguard" is directed to quite the wrong quarter.

He satisfies himself either with petty-bourgeois palliatives (struggle against the kulaks—see above about loan-and-savings societies, credits, legislation to encourage temperance, industry and education; extension of peasant land-ownership—see above about land credits and land purchase; tax reduction—see above about income tax), or with rosy, ladies' college dreams of "organising people's industry."

But is it not already organised? Have not all the young bourgeoisie described above already organised this "people's industry" after their own, bourgeois fashion? Otherwise how could they "hold every village in their hands"? How could they "order people to go to work" and appropriate surplus-value?

The Narodnik reaches the height of righteous indignation. It is immoral—he howls—to consider capitalism to be an "organisation" when it is based on the anarchy of production, on crises, on permanent, regular and ever-increasing mass unemployment, on the utmost deterioration of the conditions of the working people.

On the contrary. It is immoral to colour the truth, to picture the order that characterises the whole of post-Reform Russia as something accidental and incidental. That every capitalist nation is a vehicle of technical progress and of the socialisation of labour, but at the cost of crippling and mutilating the producer, is something that was established long ago. But to turn this *fact* into material for discussing morals with "society," and, closing one's eyes to the struggle going on, to murmur with after-dinner composure: "safeguard," "ensure," "organise"—means to be a romantic, and a naïve and reactionary romantic at that.

It will very likely seem to the reader that this commentary has no connection whatever with an analysis of Mr. Struve's book. In my opinion, only an external connection is missing.

Mr. Struve's book does not discover Russian Marxism at all. It merely introduces into our press for the first time theories that have taken shape and been stated previously.* This introduction was preceded, as has already been noted, by a furious criticism of Marxism in the liberal and Narodnik press, a criticism that confused and distorted matters.

Unless this criticism was answered, it was impossible, firstly, to approach the contemporary position of the problem; secondly, it was impossible to understand Mr. Struve's book, its character and designation.

The old Narodnik article was taken as the subject for reply because a principled article was required, and, moreover, one retaining at least some of the old Russian Narodnik precepts that are valuable to Marxism.

By means of this commentary we have tried to show the artificiality and absurdity of the current methods of liberal and Narodnik polemics. Arguments about Marxism being connected with Hegelianism,** with belief in triads, in abstract dogmas and schemes that do not have to be proved by facts, in the inevitability of every country passing through the phase of capitalism, etc., turn out to be empty blather.

Marxism sees its criterion in the *formulation* and theoretical *explanation* of the struggle between social classes and economic interests that is going on before our eyes.

Marxism does not base itself on anything else than the facts of Russian history and reality; it is also the ideology of the labouring class, only it gives a totally different explanation of the generally known facts of the growth and achievements of Russian capitalism, has quite a different understanding of the tasks that reality in this country places before the ideologists of the direct producers. That is why, when the Marxist speaks of the necessity, inevita-

* Cf. V. V. *Essays on Theoretical Economics.* St. Petersburg, 1895, pp. 257-58.[116]

** I am speaking, of course, not of the historical origin of Marxism, but of its content today.

bility, and progressiveness of Russian capitalism, he proceeds from generally established facts which are not always cited precisely because of their being generally established, because of their not being new; his explanation is different from the one that has been told and retold in Narodnik literature — and if the Narodnik replies by shouting that the Marxist refuses to face the facts, he can be exposed even by simply referring to any principled Narodnik article of the seventies.

Let us now pass to an examination of Mr. Struve's book.

CHAPTER II

A CRITICISM OF NARODNIK SOCIOLOGY

The "essence" of Narodism, its "main idea," according to the author, lies in the "theory of Russia's exceptional economic development." This theory, as he puts it, has "two main sources: 1) a definite doctrine of the role of the individual in the historical process, and 2) a direct conviction that the Russian people possess a specific national character and spirit and a special historical destiny" (2). In a footnote to this passage the author declares that "Narodism is characterised by quite definite social ideals,"* and adds that he gives the economic world outlook of the Narodniks later on in the book.

This description of the essence of Narodism, it seems to me, requires some correction. It is too abstract and idealistic; it indicates the prevailing theoretical ideas of Narodism, but does not indicate either its "essence" or its "source." It remains absolutely unclear why the ideals indicated were combined with a belief in an exceptional Russian development and with a specific doctrine of the role of the individual, and why these theories became "the most influential" trend in our social thought. If, when speaking of "the socio-

* Of course, this expression "quite definite ideals" must not be taken literally, that is, as meaning that the Narodniks "quite definitely" knew what they wanted. That would be absolutely untrue. "Quite definite ideals" should be understood as meaning nothing more than the ideology of direct producers, even though this ideology is a very vague one.

logical ideas of Narodism" (the title of the first chapter), the author was unable to confine himself to purely sociological questions (method in sociology), but also dealt with the Narodniks' views on Russian economic reality, he should have explained to us the essence of these views. Yet in the footnote referred to this is only half accomplished. The essence of Narodism is that it represents the producers' interests from the standpoint of the small producer, the petty bourgeois. In his German article on Mr. N.—on's book (*Sozialpolitisches Centralblatt*, 1893, No. 1), Mr. Struve called Narodism "national socialism" (*Russkoye Bogatstvo*, 1893, No. 12, p. 185). Instead of "national" he should have said "peasant" in reference to the old Russian Narodism, and "petty bourgeois" in reference to contemporary Russian Narodism. The "source" of Narodism lies in the predominance of the class of small producers in post-Reform capitalist Russia.

This description requires explanation. I use the expression "petty bourgeois" not in the ordinary, but in the political-economic sense. A small producer, operating under a system of commodity economy—these are the two features of the concept "petty bourgeois," Kleinbürger, or what is the same thing, the Russian *meshchanin*. It thus includes both the peasant and the handicraftsman, whom the Narodniks always placed on the same footing—and quite rightly, for they are both producers, they both work for the market, and differ only in the degree of development of commodity economy. Further, I make a distinction between the old* and contemporary Narodism, on the grounds that the former was to some extent a well-knit doctrine evolved in a period when capitalism was still very feebly developed in Russia, when nothing of the petty-bourgeois character of peasant economy had yet been revealed, when the practical side of the doctrine was purely utopian, and when the Narodniks gave liberal "society" a wide berth and "went among the people." It is different now: Russia's capitalist path of development is no longer denied by anybody, the break-up of the

* By the old Narodniks I do not mean those who backed the *Otechestvenniye Zapiski*, for instance, but those who "went among the people."

countryside is an undoubted fact. Of the Narodniks' well-knit doctrine, with its childish faith in the "village community," nothing but rags and tatters remain. From the practical aspect, utopia has been replaced by a quite un-utopian programme of petty-bourgeois "progressive" measures, and only pompous phrases remind us of the historical connection between these paltry compromises and the dreams of better and exceptional paths for the fatherland. In place of aloofness from liberal society we observe a touching intimacy with it. Now it is this change that compels us to distinguish between the ideology of the peasantry and the ideology of the petty bourgeoisie.

It seemed all the more necessary to make this correction concerning the real content of Narodism since Mr. Struve's aforementioned abstractness of exposition is his fundamental defect. That is the first point. And secondly, "certain basic" tenets of the doctrine by which Mr. Struve is not bound demand that social ideas be reduced to social-economic relations.

And we shall now endeavour to show that unless this is done it is impossible to understand even the purely theoretical ideas of Narodism, such as the question of method in sociology.

Having pointed out that the Narodnik doctrine of a special method in sociology is best expounded by Mr. Mirtov[117] and Mr. Mikhailovsky, Mr. Struve goes on to describe this doctrine as "subjective idealism," and in corroboration quotes from the works of the authors mentioned a number of passages on which it is worth while dwelling.

Both take as a corner-stone the thesis that history was made by "solitary fighting individuals." "Individuals make history" (Mirtov). Mr. Mikhailovsky is even more explicit: "The living individual, with all his thoughts and feelings, becomes a history-maker on his own responsibility. He, and not some mysterious force, sets aims in history and moves events towards them through a lane of obstacles placed before him by the elemental forces of nature and of historical conditions" (8). This thesis that history is made by individuals is absolutely meaningless from the theoretical standpoint. All history consists of the actions of individuals, and it is the task of social science to explain these actions, so that the reference to "the right of interfering in the course of events" (Mr. Mikhailovsky's words, quoted by Mr. Struve on p. 8), is but empty tautology. This is very clearly revealed in Mr. Mikhailovsky's last effusion. The living individual, he argues, moves events through a lane of obstacles placed by the elemental forces of historical conditions. And what do these "historical conditions" consist of? According to the author's logic, they consist in their turn of the actions of other "living individuals." A profound philosophy of history, is it not? The living individual moves events through a line of obstacles placed by other living individuals! And why are the actions of some living individuals called elemental, while of the actions of others it is said that they "move events" towards previously set aims? It is obvious that to search for any theoretical meaning here would be an almost hopeless undertaking. The fact of the matter is that the historical conditions which provided our subjectivists with material for the "theory" consisted (as they still consist) of antagonistic relations and gave rise to the expropriation of the producer. Unable to understand these antagonistic relations, unable to find *in these latter* the social elements with which the "solitary individuals" could join forces, the subjectivists confined themselves to concocting theories which consoled the "solitary" individuals with the statement that history is made by "living individuals." The famous "subjective method in sociology" expresses nothing, absolutely nothing, but good intentions and bad understanding. Mr. Mikhailovsky's further reasoning, as quoted by the author, is striking confirmation of this.

European life, Mr. Mikhailovsky says, "took shape just as senselessly and immorally as a river flows or a tree grows in nature. A river flows along the line of least resistance, washes away whatever it can, even if it be a diamond mine, and flows around whatever it cannot wash away, even if it be a dunghill. Sluices, dams, outlet and inlet canals are built on the initiative of human reason and sentiment. Such reason and sentiment, it may be said, were absent (?—P. S.) when the present economic system in Europe arose. They were in an embryonic state, and their influence on the natural elemental course of things was insignificant" (9).

Mr. Struve inserts a mark of interrogation, but what

perplexes us is why he inserts it only after one word and not after all of them, so meaningless is this whole effusion! What nonsense it is to say that reason and sentiment were absent when capitalism arose! Of what does capitalism consist if not of definite relations between people—and people without reason and sentiments are so far unknown. And what an untruth it is to say that only "insignificant" influence of the reason and sentiment of "individuals living" at that time was brought to bear on the "course of things"! Quite the contrary. People in sound mind and judgement then erected extremely well-made sluices and dams, which forced the refractory peasant into the mainstream of capitalist exploitation; they created extremely artful by-pass channels of political and financial measures through which swept capitalist accumulation and capitalist expropriation that were not content with the action of economic laws alone. In a word, all Mr. Mikhailovsky's statements here quoted are so preposterously false that they cannot be attributed to theoretical mistakes alone. They are entirely due to the author's petty-bourgeois standpoint. Capitalism has already revealed its tendencies quite clearly; it has developed its inherent antagonism to the full; the contradiction of interests has already begun to assume definite forms, and is even reflected in Russian legislation, but the small producer stands apart from this struggle. He is still tied to the old bourgeois society by his tiny farm, and for that reason, though he is oppressed by the capitalist system, he is unable to understand the real causes of his oppression and consoles himself with illusions about the whole trouble lying in the fact that the reason and sentiment of people are still in an "embryonic state."

"Of course," continues the ideologist of this petty bourgeois, "people have always endeavoured to influence the course of things in one way or another."

But "the course of things" consists of nothing else but actions and "influences" of people, and so this again is an empty phrase.

"But they were guided in this by the promptings of the most meagre experience and by the grossest interests; and it is obvious that it was very rarely and only by chance that these guides could indicate the path suggested by modern science and modern moral ideas" (9).

This is a petty-bourgeois morality, which condemns "grossness of interests" because it is unable to connect its "ideals" with any immediate interests—it is a petty-bourgeois way of shutting one's eyes to the split which has already taken place and which is clearly reflected both in modern science and in modern moral ideas.

Naturally, the peculiarities of Mr. Mikhailovsky's reasoning remain unchanged even when he passes to Russia. He "welcomes with all his heart" the equally strange stories of a Mr. Yakovlev that Russia is a tabula rasa, that she can begin from the beginning, avoid the mistakes of other countries, and so on and so forth. And all this is said in the full knowledge that this tabula rasa still affords a very firm foothold for representatives of the "old-nobility" system, with its large-scale landed proprietorship and tremendous political privileges, and that it provides the basis for the rapid development of capitalism, with all its diverse "progress." The petty bourgeois faint-heartedly closes his eyes to these *facts* and flies to the realm of innocent day-dreams, such as that "we are beginning to live, now that science has already mastered certain truths and gained some prestige."

And so, the class origin of the sociological ideas of Narodism is already clear from those arguments of Mr. Mikhailovsky's which Mr. Struve quotes.

We must object to a remark which Mr. Struve directs against Mr. Mikhailovsky. "According to his view," the author says, "there are no insurmountable historical tendencies which, as such, should serve on the one hand as a starting-point, and on the other as unavoidable bounds to the purposeful activity of individuals and social groups" (11).

That is the language of an objectivist, and not of a Marxist (materialist). Between these conceptions (systems of views) there is a difference, which should be dwelt on, since an incomplete grasp of this difference is one of the fundamental defects of Mr. Struve's book and manifests itself in the majority of his arguments.

The objectivist speaks of the necessity of a given historical process; the materialist gives an exact picture of the given social-economic formation and of the antagonistic relations to which it gives rise. When demonstrating the necessity for a given series of facts, the objectivist always runs the risk of becoming an apologist for these facts: the materialist discloses the class contradictions and in so doing defines his standpoint. The objectivist speaks of "insurmountable historical tendencies"; the materialist speaks of the class which "directs" the given economic system, giving rise to such and such forms of counteraction by other classes. Thus, on the one hand, the materialist is more consistent than the objectivist, and gives profounder and fuller effect to his objectivism. He does not limit himself to speaking of the necessity of a process, but ascertains exactly what social-economic formation gives the process its content, *exactly what class* determines this necessity. In the present case, for example, the materialist would not content himself with stating the "insurmountable historical tendencies," but would point to the existence of certain classes, which determine the content of the given system and preclude the possibility of any solution except by the action of the producers themselves. On the other hand, materialism includes partisanship, so to speak, and enjoins the direct and open adoption of the standpoint of a definite social group in any assessment of events.*

From Mr. Mikhailovsky the author passes to Mr. Yuzhakov, who represents nothing independent or interesting. Mr. Struve quite justly describes his sociological arguments as "florid language" "devoid of all meaning." It is worth dwelling on an extremely characteristic (for Narodism in general) difference between Mr. Yuzhakov and Mr. Mikhailovsky. Mr. Struve notes this difference by calling Mr. Yuzhakov a "nationalist," whereas, he says, "all nationalism has always been absolutely alien" to Mr. Mikhailovsky, for whom, as he himself says, "the question of the people's truth embraces not only the Russian people but the labouring folk of the whole civilised world." It seems to me that behind this difference there is also visible the reflection of the dual position of the small producer, who is a progressive element inasmuch as he begins, to use Mr. Yuzhakov's unconsciously

* Concrete examples of Mr. Struve's incomplete application of materialism and the lack of consistency in his theory of the class struggle will be given below in each particular instance.

apt expression, "to differentiate from society," and a reactionary element inasmuch as he fights to preserve his position as a small proprietor and strives to retard economic development. That is why Russian Narodism, too, is able to combine progressive, democratic features in its doctrine with the reactionary features which evoke the sympathy of *Moskovskiye Vedomosti*. As to the latter features, it would be difficult, it seems to me, to express them more graphically than was done by Mr. Yuzhakov in the following passage, quoted by Mr. Struve.

"Only the peasantry has always and everywhere been the vehicle of the pure idea of labour. Apparently, this same idea has been brought into the arena of modern history by the so-called fourth estate, the urban proletariat. But the substance of the idea has undergone such considerable changes that the peasant would hardly recognise it as the customary basis of his way of life. The *right* to work, instead of the sacred *duty* of working, the duty of earning one's bread by the sweat of one's brow" [so that is what was concealed behind the "pure idea of labour"! The purely feudal idea of the "duty" of the peasant to earn bread ... so as to perform his services? This "sacred" duty is preached to the poor beast of burden that is browbeaten and crushed by it!!*]; "then, the separation and rewarding of labour, all this agitation about a fair reward for labour, as though labour does not create its own reward in its fruits"; ["What is this?" Mr. Struve asks, "sancta simplicitas, or something else?" Worse. It is the apotheosis of the docility of the labourer tied to the soil and accustomed to work for others for almost nothing]; "the differentiation of labour from life into some abstract (?!—P.S.) category depicted by so many hours of work in the factory and having no other (?!—P.S.) relation, no tie with the daily interests of the worker" [the purely petty-bourgeois cowardice of the small producer, who at times suffers very severely from the modern capitalist organisation, but who fears nothing on earth more

* The author—as befits a little bourgeois—is presumably unaware that the West-European toiling folk have long outgrown the stage of development in which they demanded the "right to work," and that they are now demanding the "right to be lazy," the right to rest from the excessive toil which cripples and oppresses them.

than a serious movement against this organisation on the part of elements who have become completely "differentiated" from every tie with it]; "finally, the absence of a settled life, a domestic hearth created by labour, the changing field of labour—all this is entirely alien to the idea of peasant labour. The labour hearth, inherited from their fathers and forefathers; labour, whose interests permeate the whole of life and build its morals—love of the soil, watered by the sweat of many generations—all this, which constitutes an inalienable and distinguishing feature of peasant life, is absolutely unknown to the proletarian working class; and, therefore, although the life of the latter is a worker's life, it is built up on bourgeois morality (an individualist morality based on the principle of acquired right) or, at best, on abstract philosophical morality, but peasant morality has its basis in labour—in the logic of labour and its demands" (18). Here the reactionary features of the small producer appear in their pure form: his wretchedness, which induces him to believe that he is fated for ever to the "sacred duty" of being a beast of burden; his servility, "inherited from his fathers and forefathers"; his attachment to a tiny individual farm, the fear of losing which compels him to renounce even the very thought of a "fair reward" and to be an enemy of all "agitation," and which, because of the low productivity of labour and the fact of the labouring peasant being tied to one spot, turns him into a savage and, by virtue of economic conditions alone, necessarily engenders his wretchedness and servility. The breakdown of these reactionary features must unquestionably be placed to the credit of our bourgeoisie; the progressive work of the latter consists precisely in its having severed all the ties that bound the working people to the feudal system and to feudal traditions. It replaced, and is still replacing, the medieval forms of exploitation—which were concealed by the *personal* relations of the lord to his vassal, of the local kulak and buyer-up to the local peasants and handicraftsmen, of the patriarchal "modest and bearded millionaire" to his "lads," and which as a result gave rise to ultra-reactionary ideas—replacing them by the exploitation of the "European type of jaunty entrepreneur," exploitation which is impersonal, naked and unconcealed, and which therefore shatters absurd illusions and dreams. It has destroyed the old isolation ("settled life") of the peasant, who refused to know, *and could not* know, anything but his plot of land, and has begun—by socialising labour and vastly increasing its productivity—to force the producer into the arena of social life.

With respect to Mr. Yuzhakov's argument here given, Mr. Struve says: "Thus Mr. Yuzhakov quite clearly documents the Slavophil roots of Narodism" (18); and later, summarising his exposition of the sociological ideas of Narodism, he adds that the belief in "Russia's exceptional development" constitutes a "historical tie between Slavophilism and Narodism," and that therefore the dispute between the Marxists and the Narodniks is "a natural continuation of the differences between Slavophilism and Westernism" (29). This latter statement, it seems to me, requires limitation. It is indisputable that the Narodniks are very much to blame for a jingoism of the lowest type (Mr. Yuzhakov, for instance). It is also indisputable that to ignore Marx's sociological method and his presentation of questions concerning the direct producers is, to those Russian people who desire to represent the interests of these direct producers, equivalent to complete alienation from Western "civilisation." But the essence of Narodism lies deeper, it does not lie in the doctrine of exceptional development nor in Slavophilism, but in representing the interests and ideas of the Russian small producer. This is why among the Narodniks there were writers (and they were the best of the Narodniks) who, as Mr. Struve himself admitted, had nothing in common with Slavophilism, and who even admitted that Russia had entered the same road as Western Europe. You will never understand Russian Narodism through the medium of such categories as Slavophilism and Westernism. Narodism reflected a fact in Russian life which was almost non-existent in the period of the rise of Slavophilism and Westernism, namely, the contradiction between the interests of labour and of *capital*. It reflected this *fact* through the prism of the living conditions and interests of the small producer, and therefore did so in a distorted and cowardly way, creating a theory which did not give prominence to the antagonism of social interests, but to sterile hopes in a different path of development. And it is our duty to correct this mistake of

Narodism, to show which social group can become the real representative of the interests of the direct producers.

Let us now pass to the second chapter of Mr. Struve's book.

The author's plan of exposition is as follows: first he outlines the general considerations which lead us to regard materialism as the only correct method of social science; then he expounds the views of Marx and Engels; and, finally, he applies the conclusions reached to certain phenomena of Russian life. In view of the particular importance of the subject of this chapter, we shall endeavour to analyse its contents in greater detail and to note those points which provoke disagreement

The author begins with the entirely correct contention that a theory which reduces the social process to the actions of "living individuals," who "set themselves aims" and "move events," is the result of a misunderstanding. Nobody, of course, ever thought of ascribing to "a social group an existence independent of the individuals forming it" (31), but the point is that "the concrete individual is a product of all past and contemporary individuals, i.e., of a social group" (31). Let us explain the author's idea. History, Mr. Mikhailovsky argues, is made by "the living individual with all his thoughts and feelings." Quite true. But what determines these "thoughts and feelings"? Can one seriously support the view that they arise accidentally and do not follow necessarily from the given social environment, which serves as the material, the object of the individual's spiritual life, and is reflected in his "thoughts and feelings" positively or negatively, in the representation of the interests of one social class or another? And further, by what criteria are we to judge the *real* "thoughts and feelings" of *real* individuals? Naturally, there can be only one such criterion—the *actions* of these individuals. And since we are dealing only with social "thoughts and feelings," one should add: the *social actions* of individuals, i.e., *social facts.* "When we separate the social group from the individual," says Mr. Struve, "we understand by the former all the varied interactions between individuals which arise out of social life and acquire objective form in custom and law, in morals and morality, in religious ideas" (32). In other words: the materialist sociologist, taking the definite social relations of people as the object of his inquiry, by that very fact also studies the real *individuals* from whose actions these relations are formed. The subjectivist sociologist, when he begins his argument supposedly with "living individuals," actually begins by endowing these individuals with such "thoughts and feelings" as he considers rational (for by isolating his "individuals" from the concrete social environment he deprived himself of the possibility of studying their *real* thoughts and feelings), i.e., he "starts with a utopia," as Mr. Mikhailovsky was obliged to admit.* And since, further, this sociologist's own ideas of what is rational reflect (without his realising it) the given social environment, the final conclusions he draws from his argument, which seem to him a "pure" product of "modern science and modern moral ideas" in fact only reflect the standpoint and interests ... of the petty bourgeoisie.

This last point—i.e., that a special sociological theory about the role of the individual, or about the subjective method, replaces a critical, materialist inquiry by a utopia—is particularly important and, since it has been omitted by Mr. Struve, it deserves to be dwelt on a little.

Let us take as an illustration the common Narodnik argument about the handicraftsman. The Narodnik describes the pitiable condition of this handicraftsman, the miserable level of his production, the monstrous way in which he is exploited by the buyer-up, who pockets the lion's share of the product and leaves the producer a few coppers for a 16 to 18 hour working day, and concludes that the wretched level of production and the exploitation of the handicraftsman's labour are an ugly side of the present system. But the handicraftsman is not a wage-worker; that is a good side. The good side must be preserved and the bad side destroyed, and for this purpose handicraft artels must be organised. Here you have the complete Narodnik argument.

The Marxist argues differently. Acquaintance with the condition of an industrial pursuit evokes in him, in addition

---

* *Works*, Vol. III, p. 155, "Sociology Must Start with Some Utopia."

to the question of whether it is good or bad, the question of how the industry is organised, i.e., what are the relations between the handicraftsmen in the production of the given product *and why just these and no others*. And he sees that this organisation is commodity production, i.e., production by *separate* producers, connected with one another by the *market*. The product of the individual producer, destined for consumption by others, can reach the consumer and give the producer the right to receive another social product only after assuming the form of *money*, i.e., after undergoing preliminary social evaluation, both qualitatively and quantitatively. And this evaluation takes place behind the back of the producer, through market fluctuations. These market fluctuations, which are unknown to the producer and independent of him, are bound to cause inequality among the producers, are bound to accentuate this inequality, impoverishing some and putting others in possession of money=the product of social labour. The cause of the power of the money owner, the buyer-up, is therefore clear: it is that he alone, among the handicraftsmen who live from day to day, at most from week to week, possesses money, i.e., the product of earlier *social* labour, which in his hands becomes *capital*, an instrument for appropriating the surplus product of other handicraftsmen. Hence, the Marxist concludes, under such a system of social economy the expropriation and the exploitation of the producer are absolutely inevitable, and so are the subordination of the propertyless to the propertied and the contradiction between their interests which provides the content of the *scientific* conception of the *class struggle*. And, consequently, the interests of the producer do not, in any way, lie in reconciling these contradictory elements, but, on the contrary, in developing the contradiction and in developing the consciousness of this contradiction. We see that the growth of commodity production leads to such a development of the contradiction here in Russia, too: as the market widens and production grows, merchant capital becomes industrial capital. Machine industry, by finally destroying small, isolated production (it has already been radically undermined by the buyer-up), socialises labour. The system of Plusmacherei, which in handicraft production is obscured by the apparent independence of the handicraftsman and the apparent fortuitousness of the power of the buyer-up, now becomes clear and is fully revealed. "Labour," which even in handicraft industry participated in "life" only by presenting the surplus product to the buyers-up, is now finally "differentiated from life" of bourgeois society. This society discards it with utter frankness, giving full fruition to its basic principle that the producer can secure the means of subsistence only when he finds an owner of money who will condescend to appropriate the surplus product of his labour. And what the handicraftsman [and his ideologist—the Narodnik] could not understand—the profound class character of the aforementioned contradiction—becomes self-evident to the producer. That is why the interests of the handicraftsman can be represented only by this advanced producer.

Let us now compare these arguments from the angle of their sociological method.

The Narodnik assures us that he is a realist. "History is made by living individuals," and I, he declares, begin with the "feelings" of the handicraftsman, whose attitude is hostile to the present system, and with his thoughts about the creation of a better system, whereas the Marxist argues about some sort of necessity and inevitability; he is a mystic and a metaphysician.

It is true, this mystic rejoins, that history is made by "living individuals"—and I, when examining why social relations in handicraft industry have assumed such a form and no other (you have not even raised this question!), in fact examined *how* "living individuals" *have made their history* and are still making it. And I had a reliable criterion to show that I was dealing with real, "living" individuals, with real thoughts and feelings: this criterion was that their "thoughts and feelings" had already found expression in actions and had created definite social relations. True, I never say that "history is made by living individuals" (because it seems to me that this is an empty phrase), but when I investigate *actual* social relations and their *actual* development, I am in fact examining the product of the activities of living individuals. But though you talk of "living individuals," you actually make your starting-point not the "living individual," with the "thoughts and feelings" actually created by his conditions of life, by the given system of relations of production, but a marionette, and stuff its head with your own "thoughts and feelings." Naturally, such a pursuit only leads to pious dreams; life passes you by, and you pass life by.* But that is not all. Just see *what* you are stuffing into the head of this marionette, and what measures you are advocating. In recommending the artel as "the path suggested by modern science and modern moral ideas," you did not pay attention to one little circumstance, namely, the whole organisation of our social economy. Since you did not understand that this is a capitalist economy, you did not notice that *on this basis* all possible artels are nothing but petty palliatives, which do not in the least remove either the concentration of the means of production, including money, in the hands of a minority (this concentration is an indisputable fact), or the complete impoverishment of the vast mass of the population—palliatives which at best will only elevate a handful of individual handicraftsmen to the ranks of the petty bourgeoisie. From an ideologist of the working people you turn into an ideologist of the petty bourgeoisie.

Let us, however, return to Mr. Struve. Having shown the emptiness of the Narodniks' arguments regarding the "individual," he continues: "That sociology does indeed always strive to reduce the elements of individuality to social sources is corroborated by every attempt to explain any big phase in historical evolution. When the 'historical individual' or the 'great man' is referred to, there is always a tendency to represent him as the 'vehicle' of the spirit of a certain era, as the representative of his time—and his actions, his successes and failures, as a necessary result of the whole preceding course of affairs" (32). This general tendency of every attempt to *explain* social phenomena, i.e., to create a social science, "is clearly expressed in the doctrine that the class struggle is the basic process in social evolution. Since

* "Practice mercilessly curtails it" ("the possibility of a new historical path"); "it shrinks, one might say, from day to day" (Mr. Mikhailovsky, as quoted by P. Struve, p. 16). What shrinks, of course, is not the "possibility," which never existed, but illusions. And a good thing, too.

the individual had been discarded, some other element had to be found. The social group proved to be such an element" (33). Mr. Struve is absolutely right when he says that the theory of the class struggle crowns, so to speak, the general endeavour of sociology to reduce "the elements of individuality to social sources." Furthermore, the theory of the class struggle for the first time pursues this endeavour so completely and consistently as to raise sociology to the level of a science. This was achieved by the materialist definition of the concept "group." In itself, this concept is still too indefinite and arbitrary: religious, ethnographical, political, juridical and other phenomena may also be considered as criteria distinguishing "groups." There is no firm token by which particular "groups" in each of these spheres can be distinguished. The theory of the class struggle, however, represents a tremendous acquisition for social science for the very reason that it lays down the methods by which the individual can be reduced to the social with the utmost precision and definiteness. Firstly, this theory worked out the concept of the *social-economic formation*. Taking as its starting-point a fact that is fundamental to all human society, namely, the mode of procuring the means of subsistence, it connected up with this the relations between people formed under the influence of the given modes of procuring the means of subsistence, and showed that this system of relations ("relations of production," to use Marx's terminology) is the *basis* of society, which clothes itself in political and legal forms and in definite trends of social thought. According to Marx's theory, each such system of production relations is a specific social organism, whose inception, functioning, and transition to a higher form, conversion into another social organism, are governed by specific laws. This theory applied to social science that objective, general scientific criterion of repetition which the subjectivists declared could not be applied to sociology. They argued, in fact, that owing to the tremendous complexity and variety of social phenomena they could not be studied without separating the important from the unimportant, and that such a separation could be made only from the viewpoint of "critically thinking" and "morally developed" individuals. And they thus happily succeeded in transforming social science into a series of sermons on petty-bourgeois morality, samples of which we have seen in the case of Mr. Mikhailovsky, who philosophised about the inexpediency of history and about a path directed by "the light of science." It was these arguments that Marx's theory severed at the very root. The distinction between the important and the unimportant was replaced by the distinction between the economic structure of society, as the *content*, and the political and ideological *form*. The very concept of the economic structure was exactly explained by refuting the views of the earlier economists, who saw laws of nature where there is room only for the laws of a specific, historically defined system of relations of production. The subjectivists' arguments about "society" in general, meaningless arguments that did not go beyond petty-bourgeois utopias (because even the possibility of generalising the most varied social systems into special types of social organisms was not ascertained), were replaced by an *investigation* of definite forms of the structure of society. Secondly, the actions of "living individuals" within the bounds of each such social-economic formation, actions infinitely varied and apparently not lending themselves to any systematisation, were generalised and reduced to the actions of groups of individuals differing from each other in the part they played in the system of production relations, in the conditions of production, and, consequently, in their conditions of life, and in the interests determined by these conditions—in a word, to the actions of *classes*, the struggle between which determined the development of society. This refuted the childishly naïve and purely mechanical view of history held by the subjectivists, who contented themselves with the meaningless thesis that history is made by living individuals, and who refused to examine what social conditions determine their actions, and exactly in what way. Subjectivism was replaced by the view that the social process is a process of natural history—a view without which, of course, there could be no social science. Mr. Struve very justly remarks that "ignoring the individual in sociology, or rather, removing him from sociology, is essentially a particular instance of the striving for scientific knowledge" (33), and that "individualities" exist not only in the spiritual but also in the physical world. The whole point is that the reduction of "individualities" to certain general laws was accomplished for the physical realm long ago, while for the social realm it was firmly established only by Marx's theory.

Another objection made by Mr. Struve to the sociological theory of the Russian subjectivists is that, in addition to all the above-mentioned arguments, "sociology cannot *under any circumstances* recognise what we call individuality as a primary fact, since the very concept of individuality (which is not subject to further explanation) and the fact that corresponds to it are the result of a long social process" (36). This is a very true thought, and is all the more worthy of being dwelt on because the author's argument contains certain inaccuracies. He cites the views of *Simmel*, who, he declares, proved in his *Social Differentiation* the direct interdependence between the development of the individual and the differentiation of the group to which the individual belongs. Mr. Struve contrasts this thesis with Mr. Mikhailovsky's theory of the inverse dependence between the development of the individual and the differentiation ("heterogeneity") of society. "In an undifferentiated environment," Mr. Struve objects, "the individual will be 'harmoniously integral'... in his 'homogeneity and impersonality.' A real individual cannot be 'an aggregate of all the features inherent in the human organism in general,' simply because such a fulness of content exceeds the powers of the real individual" (38-39). "In order that the individual may be differentiated, he must live in a differentiated environment" (39).

It is not clear from this exposition how exactly Simmel formulates the question and how he argues. But as transmitted by Mr. Struve the formulation of the question suffers from the same defect that we find in Mr. Mikhailovsky's case. Abstract reasoning about how far the development (and well-being) of the individual depends on the differentiation of society is quite unscientific, because no correlation can be established that will suit every form of social structure. The very concepts "differentiation," "heterogeneity," and so on, acquire absolutely different meanings, depending on the particular social environment to which they are applied. Mr. Mikhailovsky's fundamental error consists precisely in the abstract dogmatism of his reasoning, which endeavours to embrace "progress" in general, instead of studying the concrete "progress" of some concrete social formation. When Mr. Struve sets his own general theses (described above) against Mr. Mikhailovsky, he repeats the latter's mistake by abandoning the depiction and explanation of a concrete progress in the realm of nebulous and unfounded dogmas. Let us take an example: "The harmonious integrity of the individual is determined as to its content by the degree of development, i.e., differentiation of the group," says Mr. Struve, and puts this phrase in italics. But what are we to understand here by the "differentiation" of the group? Has the abolition of serfdom accentuated or weakened this "differentiation"? Mr. Mikhailovsky answers the question in the latter sense ("What Is Progress?"); Mr. Struve would most likely answer it in the former sense, on the grounds of the increased social division of labour. The former had in mind the abolition of social-estate distinctions; the latter, the creation of economic distinctions. The term, as you see, is so indefinite that it can be stretched to cover opposite things. Another example. The transition from capitalist manufacture to large-scale machine industry may be regarded as diminution of "differentiation," for the detailed division of labour among specialised workers ceases. Yet there can be no doubt that the conditions for the development of the individuality are far more favourable (for the worker) precisely in the latter case. The conclusion is that the very formulation of the question is incorrect. The author himself admits that there is also an antagonism between the individual and the group (to which Mr. Mikhailovsky also refers). "But life," he adds, "is never made up of *absolute* contradictions: in life everything is *mobile* and *relative*, and at the same time all the separate sides are in a state of constant interaction" (39). If that is so, why was it necessary to speak of absolute interrelations between the group and the individual, interrelations having no connection with the strictly defined phase in the development of a definite social formation? Why could not the whole argument have been transferred to the concrete process of evolution of Russia? The author has made an attempt to formulate the question in this way, and had he adhered to it consistently his argument would have gained a great deal. "It was only the division of labour—

mankind's fall from grace, according to Mr. Mikhailovsky's doctrine—that created the conditions for the development of the 'individual' in whose name Mr. Mikhailovsky justly protests against the modern forms of division of labour" (38). That is excellently put; only in place of "division of labour" he should have said "capitalism," and, even more narrowly, *Russian capitalism*. Capitalism is progressive in its significance precisely because it has destroyed the old cramped conditions of human life that created mental stultification and prevented the producers from taking their destinies into their own hands. The tremendous development of trade relations and world exchange and the constant migrations of vast masses of the population have shattered the age-old fetters of the tribe, family and territorial community, and created that variety of development, that "variety of talents and wealth of social relationships,"* which plays so great a part in the modern history of the West. In Russia this process has been fully manifested in the post-Reform era, when the ancient forms of labour very rapidly collapsed and prime place was assumed by the purchase and sale of labour-power, which tore the peasant from the patriarchal, semi-feudal family, from the stupefying conditions of village life and replaced the semi-feudal forms of appropriation of surplus-value by purely capitalist forms. This economic process has been reflected in the social sphere by a "general heightening of the sense of individuality," by the middle-class intellectuals squeezing the landlord class out of "society," by a heated literary war against senseless medieval restrictions on the individual, and so on. The Narodniks will probably not deny that it was post-Reform Russia which produced this heightened sense of individuality, of personal dignity. But they do not ask themselves what material conditions led to this. Nothing of the kind, of course, could have happened under serfdom. And so the Narodnik welcomes the "emancipatory" Reform, never noticing that he is guilty of the same short-sighted optimism as the bourgeois historians of whom Marx wrote that they regarded the peasant Reform through the clair-obscure of "emancipation," without observing that this "emancipation" only consisted

* K. Marx, *Der achtzehnte Brumaire*, S. 98, u.s.w.[118]

in the replacement of one form by another, the replacement of the feudal surplus product by bourgeois surplus-value. Exactly the same thing has happened in our country. The "old-nobility" economy, by tying men to their localities and dividing the population into handfuls of subjects of individual lords, brought about the suppression of the individual. And then capitalism freed him of all feudal fetters, made him independent in respect of the market, made him a commodity owner (and as such the equal of all other commodity owners), and thus heightened his sense of individuality. If the Narodnik gentlemen are filled with pharisaic horror when they hear talk of the progressive character of Russian capitalism, it is only because they do not reflect on the material conditions which make for those "benefits of progress" that mark post-Reform Russia. When Mr. Mikhailovsky begins his "sociology" with the "individual" who protests against Russian capitalism as an accidental and temporary deviation of Russia from the right path, he defeats his own purpose because he does not realise that it was capitalism alone that created the conditions which made possible this protest of the individual. From this example we see once again the changes needed in Mr. Struve's arguments. The question should have been made entirely one of Russian realities, of ascertaining what actually exists and why it is so and not otherwise. It was not for nothing that the Narodniks based their whole sociology not on an analysis of reality but on arguments about what "might be"; they could not help seeing that reality was mercilessly destroying their illusions.

The author concludes his examination of the theory of "individuals" with the following formulation: "To sociology, the individual is a function of the environment," "the individual is here a formal concept, whose content is supplied by an investigation of the social group" (40). This last comparison brings out very well the contrast between subjectivism and materialism. When they argued about the "individual," the subjectivists defined the *content* of this concept (i.e., the "thoughts and feelings" of the individual, his social acts) a priori, that is, they insinuated their utopias instead of "investigating the social group."

Another "important aspect" of materialism, Mr. Struve continues, "consists in economic materialism subordinating the idea to the fact, and consciousness and what should be to being" (40). Here, of course, "subordinating the idea" means assigning to it a subordinate position in the explanation of social phenomena. The Narodnik subjectivists do exactly the opposite: they base their arguments on "ideals," without bothering about the fact that these ideals can only be a certain reflection of reality, and, consequently, must be verified by facts, must be based on facts. But then this latter thesis will be incomprehensible to the Narodnik without explanation. How is that?—he asks himself; ideals should condemn facts, show how to change them, they should verify facts, and not be verified by them. To the Narodnik, who is accustomed to hover in the clouds, this appears to be a compromise with facts. Let us explain.

The existence of "working for others," the existence of exploitation, will always engender ideals opposite to this system both among the exploited themselves and among certain members of the "intelligentsia."

These ideals are extremely valuable to the Marxist; he argues with Narodism only on the basis of these ideals; he argues exclusively about the construction of these ideals and their realisation.

The Narodnik thinks it enough to note the fact that gives rise to such ideals, then to refer to the legitimacy of the ideal from the standpoint of "modern science and modern moral ideas" [and he does not realise that these "modern ideas" are only concessions made by West-European "public opinion" to the new rising force], and then to call upon "society" and the "state" to ensure it, safeguard it, organise it!

The Marxist proceeds from the same ideal; he does not compare it with "modern science and modern moral ideas, however,"* but *with the existing class contradictions*, and therefore does not formulate it as a demand put forward by

* Engels, in *Herrn E. Dührings Umwälzung der Wissenschaft* (*Herr Eugen Dühring's Revolution in Science* [*Anti-Dühring*]—*Ed.*), very aptly points out that this is the old psychological method of comparing one's own concept with another concept, with a cast of another fact, and not with the fact it reflects.[119]

"science," but by such and such a class, a demand engendered by such and such social relations (which are to be objectively investigated), and achievable only in such and such a way in consequence of such and such properties of these relations. If ideals are not based on facts *in this way*, they will only remain pious wishes, with no chance of being accepted by the masses and, hence, of being realised.

Having thus stated the general theoretical propositions which compel the recognition of materialism as the only correct method of social science, Mr. Struve proceeds to expound the views of Marx and Engels, quoting principally the works of the latter. This is an extremely interesting and instructive part of the book.

The author's statement that "nowhere does one meet with such misunderstanding of Marx as among Russian publicists" (44) is an extremely just one. In illustration, he first of all cites Mr. Mikhailovsky, who regards Marx's "historico-philosophical theory" as nothing more than an explanation of the "genesis of the capitalist system." Mr. Struve quite rightly protests against this. Indeed, it is a highly characteristic fact. Mr. Mikhailovsky has written about Marx many times, but he has never even hinted at the relation of *Marx's method* to the "subjective method in sociology." Mr. Mikhailovsky has written about *Capital* and has declared his "solidarity" (?) with Marx's economic doctrine, but he has passed over in complete silence the question—for example—of whether the Russian subjectivists are not following the method of Proudhon, who wanted to refashion commodity economy in accordance with his ideal of justice.* In what way does this criterion (of justice—justice éternelle) differ from Mr. Mikhailovsky's criterion: "modern science and modern moral ideas"? Mr. Mikhailovsky has always protested vigorously against identifying the method of social sciences with that of the natural sciences, so why did he not object to Marx's statement that Proudhon's method is as absurd as would be that of a chemist who wanted to transform metabolism in accordance with the laws of "affinity" instead of studying the "real laws of metabolism"? Why did he not object to Marx's view that the social process is a "process of

* *Das Kapital*, I. B. 2te Aufl. S. 62, Anm. 38.[120]

natural history"? It cannot be explained by non-acquaintance with the literature; the explanation evidently lies in an utter failure or refusal to understand. Mr. Struve, it seems to me, is the first in our literature to have pointed this out—and that is greatly to his credit.

Let us now pass to those of the author's statements on Marxism which evoke criticism. "We cannot but admit," says Mr. Struve, "that a *purely philosophical proof* of this doctrine has not yet been provided, and that it has not yet coped with the vast concrete material presented by world history. What is needed, evidently, is a reconsideration of the facts from the standpoint of the new theory; what is needed is a criticism of the theory from the angle of the facts. Perhaps much of the one-sidedness and the over-hasty generalisations will be abandoned" (46). It is not quite clear what the author means by "a purely philosophical proof." From the standpoint of Marx and Engels, philosophy has no right to a separate, independent existence, and its material is divided among the various branches of positive science. Thus one might understand philosophical proof to mean *either* a comparison of its premises with the firmly established laws of other sciences [and Mr. Struve himself admitted that even psychology provides propositions impelling the abandonment of subjectivism and the adoption of materialism], *or* experience in the application of this theory. And in this connection we have the statement of Mr. Struve himself that "materialism will always be entitled to credit for having provided a profoundly scientific and truly *philosophical* (author's italics) interpretation of a number (N.B.) of vastly important historical facts" (50). This latter statement contains the author's recognition that materialism is the only scientific method in sociology, and hence, of course, a "reconsideration of the facts" is required from this standpoint, especially a reconsideration of the facts of Russian history and present-day reality, which have been so zealously distorted by the Russian subjectivists. As regards the last remark about possible "one-sidedness" and "over-hasty generalisations," we shall not dwell on this general, and therefore vague, statement, but shall turn directly to one of the amendments made by the author, "who is not infected with orthodoxy," to the "over-hasty generalisations" of Marx.

The subject is the state. Denying the state, "Marx and his followers ... went ... too far in their criticism of the *modern state*" and were guilty of "one-sidedness." "The state," Mr. Struve says, correcting this extravagance, "is first of all the *organisation of order*; it is, however, the organisation of rule (class rule) in a society in which the subordination of certain groups to others is determined by its economic structure" (53). Tribal life, in the author's opinion, knew the state; and it will remain even after classes are abolished, for the criterion of the state is coercive power.

It is simply amazing that the author, criticising Marx from his professorial standpoint, does so with such a surprising lack of arguments. First of all, he quite wrongly regards coercive power as the distinguishing feature of the state: there is a coercive power in every human community; and there was one in the tribal system and in the family, but there was no state. "An essential feature of the state," says Engels in the work from which Mr. Struve took the quotation about the state, "is a public power distinct from the mass of the people" (*Ursprung der Familie* u.s.w., 2te Aufl., S. 84. Russ. trans., p. 109);[121] and somewhat earlier he speaks of the institution of the naucrary[122] and says that it "undermined the tribal system in two ways: firstly, by creating a public power (*öffentliche Gewalt*), which simply no longer coincided with the sum-total of the armed people" (ib., S. 79; Russ. trans., p. 105).[123] Thus the distinguishing feature of the state is the existence of a separate class of people in whose hands *power* is concentrated. Obviously, nobody could use the term "state" in reference to a community in which the "organisation of order" is administered in turn by *all* its members. Furthermore, Mr. Struve's arguments are still more unsubstantial in relation to the modern state. To say of it that it is "first of all (sic!?!) the organisation of order" is to fail to understand one of the most important points in Marx's theory. In modern society the bureaucracy is the particular stratum which has power in its hands. The direct and intimate connection between this organ and the bourgeois class, which dominates in modern society, is apparent both from history (the bureaucracy was the first political instrument of the bourgeoisie against the feudal lords, and against the representatives of the "old-nobility" system in general, and marked the first appearance in the arena of political rule of people who were not high-born landowners, but commoners, "middle class") and from the very conditions of the formation and recruitment of this class, which is open only to bourgeois "offspring of the people," and is connected with that bourgeoisie by thousands of strong ties.* The author's mistake is all the more unfortunate because it is precisely the Russian Narodniks, against whom he conceived the excellent idea of doing battle, who have no notion that every bureaucracy, by its historical origin, its contemporary source, and its purpose, is purely and exclusively a bourgeois institution, an institution to which only ideologists of the petty bourgeoisie are capable of turning in the interests of the producer.

It is also worth while to dwell a little on the attitude of Marxism to ethics. On pp. 64-65 the author quotes the excellent explanation given by Engels of the relation between freedom and necessity: "Freedom is the appreciation of necessity."[125] Far from assuming fatalism, determinism in fact provides a basis for reasonable action. One cannot refrain from adding that the Russian subjectivists could not understand even such an elementary question as freedom of will. Mr. Mikhailovsky helplessly confused determinism with fatalism and found a solution ... in trying to sit between two stools; not desiring to deny the functioning of laws, he asserted that freedom of will is a fact of our consciousness (properly speaking, this is Mirtov's idea borrowed by Mr. Mikhailovsky) and can therefore serve as a basis of ethics. It is clear that, applied to sociology, these ideas could provide nothing but a utopia or a vapid morality which ignores the class struggle going on in society. One therefore cannot deny the justice

---

* Cf. K. Marx, *Bürgerkrieg in Frankreich*, S. 23, Leipzig, 1876, and *Der achtzehnte Brumaire*, S. 45-46. Hamburg, 1885).[124] "But it is precisely with the maintenance of that extensive state machine in its numerous ramifications "[referring to the bureaucracy]" that the *material interests* of the French bourgeoisie are interwoven in the closest fashion. Here it finds posts for its surplus population and makes up in the form of state salaries for what it cannot pocket in the form of profits, interest, rents and honorariums."

of Sombart's remark that "in Marxism itself there is not a grain of ethics from beginning to end"; theoretically, it subordinates the "ethical standpoint" to the "principle of causality"; in practice it reduces it to the class struggle.

Mr. Struve supplements his exposition of materialism by an evaluation from the materialist standpoint of "two factors which play a very important part in all Narodnik arguments"—the "intelligentsia" and the "state" (70). This evaluation again reflects the author's "unorthodoxy" noted above in regard to his objectivism. "If ... all social groups in general represent a real force only to the extent that ... they constitute social classes or adhere to them, then, evidently, 'the non-estate intelligentsia' is not a real social force" (70). Of course, in the abstract and theoretical sense the author is right. He takes the Narodniks at their word, so to speak. You say it is the intelligentsia that must direct Russia along "different paths"—but you do not understand that since it does not adhere to any class, it is a cipher. You boast that the Russian non-estate intelligentsia has always been distinguished for the "purity" of its ideas—but that is exactly why it has always been impotent. The author's criticism is confined to comparing the absurd Narodnik *idea* of the omnipotence of the intelligentsia with his own perfectly correct *idea* of the "impotence of the intelligentsia in the economic process" (71). But this comparison is not enough. In order to judge of the Russian "non-estate intelligentsia" as a special group in Russian society which is so characteristic of the whole post-Reform era—an era in which the noble was finally squeezed out by the commoner—and which undoubtedly played and is still playing a certain historical role, we must compare the ideas, and still more the programmes, of our "non-estate intelligentsia" *with the position and the interests of the given classes of Russian society.* To remove the possibility of our being suspected of partiality, we shall not make this comparison ourselves, but shall confine ourselves to referring to the Narodnik whose article was commented on in Chapter I. The conclusion that follows from all his comments is quite definite, namely, that Russia's advanced, liberal, "democratic" intelligentsia was a bourgeois intelligentsia. The fact of the intelligentsia being "non-estate" in no way precludes the class origin of its ideas. The bourgeoisie has always and everywhere risen against feudalism in the name of the abolition of the social estates—and in our country, too, the old-nobility, social-estate system was opposed by the non-estate intelligentsia. The bourgeoisie always and everywhere opposed the obsolete framework of the social estates and other medieval institutions in the name of the whole "people," within which class contradictions were still undeveloped. And it was right, both in the West and in Russia, because the institutions criticised were actually hampering *everybody*. As soon as the social-estate system in Russia was dealt a decisive blow (1861), antagonism within the "people" immediately became apparent, and at the same time, and by virtue of this, antagonism became apparent within the non-estate intelligentsia—between the liberals and the Narodniks, the ideologists of the peasants (among whom the first Russian ideologists of the direct producers did not see, and, indeed, it was too early for them to see, the formation of opposed classes). Subsequent economic development led to a more complete disclosure of the social contradictions within Russian society, and compelled the recognition of the fact that the peasantry was splitting into a rural bourgeoisie and a proletariat. Narodism has rejected Marxism and has become almost completely the ideology of the petty bourgeoisie. The Russian "non-estate intelligentsia," therefore, represents "a real social force" *inasmuch as it defends general bourgeois interests.** If, nevertheless, this force was not *able* to create institutions suitable to the interests it defended, if it was unable to change "the atmosphere of contemporary Russian culture" (Mr. V. V.), if "active democracy in the era of the political struggle" gave way to "social indifferentism" (Mr. V. V. in *Nedelya*, 1894, No. 47), the cause of this lies not only in the dreaminess of

* The petty-bourgeois nature of the vast majority of the Narodniks' wishes has been pointed out in Chapter I. Wishes that do not come under this description (such as "socialisation of labour") hold a minute place in modern Narodism. Both *Russkoye Bogatstvo* (1893, Nos. 11-12, *Yuzhakov*'s article on "Problems of Russia's Economic Development") and Mr. V. V. (*Essays on Theoretical Economics*, St. Petersburg, 1895) protest against Mr. N.—on, who commented "severely" (Mr. Yuzhakov's word) on the outworn panacea of credits, extension of land tenure, migration, etc.

our native "non-estate intelligentsia," but, and chiefly, in the position of those classes from which it emerged and from which it drew its strength, in their duality. It is undeniable that the Russian "atmosphere" brought them many disadvantages, but it also gave them certain advantages.

In Russia, the class which, in the opinion of the Narodniks, is not the vehicle of the "pure idea of labour" has an especially great historical role; its "activity" cannot be lulled by tempting promises. Therefore, the references of the Marxists to this class, far from "breaking the democratic thread"—as is asserted by Mr. V. V., who specialises in inventing the most incredible absurdities about the Marxists—catch up this "thread," which an indifferent "society" allows to fall from its hands, and demand that it be developed, strengthened and brought closer to life.

Connected with Mr. Struve's incomplete appraisal of the intelligentsia is his not altogether happy formulation of the following proposition: "It must be proved," he says, "that the disintegration of the old economic system is inevitable" (71). Firstly, what does the author mean by "the old economic system"? Serfdom? But its disintegration does not have to be proved. "People's production"? But he himself says later, and quite justly, that this word-combination—"does not correspond to any real historical system" (177), that in other words, it is a myth, because after "serfdom" was abolished in Russia, commodity economy began to develop very rapidly. The author was probably referring to that stage in the development of capitalism when it had not yet entirely disentangled itself from medieval institutions, when merchant capital was still strong and when the majority of the producers were still engaged in small-scale production. Secondly, what does the author regard as the criterion of this inevitability? The rule of certain classes? The properties of the given system of production relations? In either case it amounts to *recording the existence* of one or another (capitalist) system; it amounts to *recording a fact*, and under no circumstances should it have been transplanted to the realm of reflections about the future. Such reflections should have left the monopoly of the Narodnik gentlemen, who are seeking "different paths for the fatherland." The author himself says on the very next page that every state is "an expression of the rule of definite social classes" and that "there must be a redistribution of the social force between various classes for the state to radically change its course" (72). All this is profoundly true and very aptly aimed at the Narodniks, and the question should accordingly have been put in a different way: the *existence* (and not the "inevitability of disintegration," etc.) of capitalist production relations in Russia must be proved; it must be proved that the Russian data also justify the law that "commodity economy is capitalist economy," i.e., that in our country, too, commodity economy is growing everywhere into capitalist economy; it must be proved that everywhere a system prevails which is bourgeois in essence, and that it is the rule of this class, and not the famous Narodnik "chance happenings" or "policy," etc., that lead to the liberation of the producer from the means of production and to his working everywhere for others.

With this let us conclude our examination of the first part of Mr. Struve's book, which is of a general character.

CHAPTER III

THE PRESENTATION OF ECONOMIC PROBLEMS BY THE NARODNIKS AND BY MR. STRUVE

After finishing with sociology, the author proceeds to deal with more "concrete economic problems" (73). He considers it "natural and legitimate" to start from "general propositions and historical references," from "indisputable premises established by human experience," as he says in the preface.

One cannot but note that this method suffers from the same abstractness noted at the beginning as being the main defect of the book under review. In the chapters we are now coming to (the third, fourth, and fifth), this defect has resulted in undesirable consequences of a twofold nature. On the one hand, it has weakened the definite theoretical propositions advanced by the author against the Narodniks. Mr. Struve argues *in general*, describes the transition from natural to commodity economy, points out that, as a rule, such and such happened on earth, and with a few cursory remarks proceeds to deal with Russia, applying to it, too, the general process of the "historical development of economic life." There can be no doubt that it is quite legitimate to apply the process in this way, and that the author's "historical references" are absolutely necessary for a criticism of Narodism, which falsely presents history, and not only Russian history. These propositions should, however, have been expressed more concretely, and been more definitely set against the arguments of the Narodniks, who say that it is wrong to apply the general process to Russia; the Narodniks' particular way of understanding Russian reality should have been compared with the Marxists' *other* way of understanding *that same* reality. On the other hand, the abstract character of the author's arguments leads to his propositions being stated incompletely, to a situation where, though he correctly indicates the existence of a process, he does not examine what classes arose while it was going on, what classes were the vehicles of the process, overshadowing other strata of the population subordinate to them; in a word, the author's objectivism does not rise to the level of materialism—in the above-mentioned significance of these terms.*

Proof of this appraisal of the above-mentioned chapters of Mr. Struve's work will be adduced as we examine some of its most important propositions.

Very true is the author's remark that "almost from the outset of Russian history we find that the direct producers' dependence (juridical and economic) on the lords has been the historical accompaniment of the idyll of 'people's production'" (81). In the period of natural economy the peasant was enslaved to the landowner, he worked for the boyar, the monastery, the landlord, but not for himself,

---

* This relation between objectivism and materialism was indicated, incidentally, by Marx in his preface to his *Der achtzehnte Brumaire des Louis Bonaparte*. Marx, after mentioning that Proudhon wrote of the same historical event (in his *Coup d'état*), says the following of how the latter's viewpoint is opposed to his own:

"Proudhon, for his part, seeks to represent the coup d'état [of Dec. 2] as the result of an antecedent historical development. Unnoticeably, however, his historical construction of the coup d'état becomes a historical *apologia* for its hero. Thus he falls into the error of our so-called *objective* historians. I, on the contrary, demonstrate how the *class struggle* in France created circumstances and relationships that made it possible for a grotesque mediocrity to play a hero's part" (Vorwort).[126]

and Mr. Struve has every right to set this *historical fact* against the tales of our exceptionalist sociologists about how "the means of production belonged to the producer" (81). These tales constitute one of the distortions of Russian history, meant to suit the philistine utopia in which the Narodniks have always lavishly indulged. Fearing to look reality in the face, and fearing to give this oppression its proper name, they turned to history, but pictured things as though the producer's ownership of means of production was an "ancient" principle, was the "age-old basis" of peasant labour, and that the modern expropriation of the peasantry is therefore to be explained not by the replacement of the feudal surplus product by bourgeois surplus-value, not by the capitalist organisation of our social economy, but by the accident of unfortunate policy, by a temporary "diversion from the path prescribed by the entire historical life of the nation" (Mr. Yuzhakov, quoted by P. Struve, p. 15). And they were not ashamed to tell these absurd stories about a country which had but recently seen the end* of the feudal exploitation of the peasantry in the grossest, Asiatic forms, when not only did the means of production not belong to the producer but the producers themselves differed very little from "means of production." Mr. Struve very pointedly sets against this "sugary optimism" Saltykov's sharp rejoinder about the connection between "people's production" and serfdom, and about how the "plenty" of the period of the "age-old basis" "fell only" [note that!] "to the lot of the descendants of the leibkampantsi[127] and other retainers" (83).

Further, let us note Mr. Struve's following remark, which definitely concerns definite facts of Russian reality and contains an exceptionally true thought. "When the producers start working for a distant and indefinite and not for a local, exactly delimited market, and competition, the struggle for a market develops, these conditions lead to technical progress.... Once division of labour is possible,

* Even today it cannot be said to have ended altogether. On the one hand, we have the land-redemption payments (and it is well known that they include not only the price of the land, but also the redemption from serfdom); on the other hand, labour service by the peasants in return for the use of "cut-off lands," for example, are a direct survival of the feudal mode of production.

it has to be carried out as widely as possible, but before production is technically reorganised, the influence of the new conditions of exchange (marketing) will be felt in the fact of the producer becoming economically dependent on the merchant (the buyer-up), and socially this point is of decisive significance. This is lost sight of by our 'true Marxists' like Mr. V. V., who are blinded by the significance of purely technical progress" (98). The reference to the decisive significance of the appearance of the buyer-up is profoundly true. It is decisive in that it proves beyond doubt that we have here the capitalist organisation of production, it proves the applicability to Russia, too, of the proposition that "commodity economy is money economy, is capitalist economy," and creates that subordination of the producer to capital from which there can be no other way out than through the independent activity of the producer. "From the moment that the capitalist entrepreneur comes between the consumer and the producer—and this is inevitable when production is carried on for an extensive and indefinite market—we have before us one of the forms of capitalist production." And the author rightly adds that "if *handicraft* production is understood as the kind under which the producer, who works for an indefinite and distant market, enjoys *complete economic independence*, it will, I think, be found that in Russian *reality* there is none of this true handicraft production." It is only a pity that use is made here of the expression "I think," along with the future tense: the predominance of the domestic system of large-scale production and of the utter enslavement of the handicraftsmen by buyers-up is the all-prevailing *fact* of the actual organisation of our handicraft industries. This organisation is not only capitalist, but as the author rightly says, is also one that is "highly profitable to the capitalists," ensuring them enormous profits, abominably low wages and hindering in the highest degree the organisation and development of the workers (pp. 99-101). One cannot help noting that the fact of the predominance of capitalist exploitation in our handicraft industries has long been known, but the Narodniks ignore it in the most shameless fashion. In almost every issue of their magazines and newspapers dealing with this subject, you come across complaints about the government "artificially" supporting large-scale capitalism [whose entire "artificiality" consists in being large-scale and not small, factory and not handicraft, mechanical and not hand-operated] and doing nothing for the "needs of *people*'s industry." Here stands out in full relief the narrow-mindedness of the petty bourgeois, who fights for small against big *capital* and stubbornly closes his eyes to the categorically established fact that a similar opposition of interests is to be found in this "people's" industry, and that consequently the way out does not lie in miserable credits, etc. Since the small proprietor, who is tied to his enterprise and lives in constant fear of losing it, regards all of this as something awful, as some sort of "agitation" in favour of "a fair reward for labour, as though labour itself does not create that reward in its fruits," it is clear that only the producer employed in the "artificial," "hothouse" conditions of factory industry can be the representative of the working handicraftsmen.*

Let us deal further with Mr. Struve's argument about agriculture. Steam transport compels a transition to exchange economy, it makes agricultural production commodity production. And the commodity character of production unfailingly requires "its economic and technical rationality" (110). The author considers this thesis a particularly important argument against the Narodniks, who triumphantly claim that the advantages of large-scale production in agriculture havenot been proved. "It ill becomes those," says the author in reply, "who base themselves on Marx's teachings, to deny the significance of the economic and technical peculiarities of agricultural production thanks to which small undertakings in some cases possess economic advantages over big ones—even though Marx himself denied the importance of these peculiarities" (111). This passage is very unclear. What peculiarities is the author speaking of? Why does he not indicate them exactly? Why does he not indicate where and how Marx expressed his

* "The entire process is expressed in the fact of petty production (handicraft) approximating to 'capitalism' in some respects, and in others to wage-labour separated from the means of production" (p.104).

views on the matter and on what grounds it is considered necessary to correct those views?

"Small-scale agricultural production," continues the author, "must increasingly assume a commodity character, and the small agricultural undertakings, if they are to be viable *enterprises*, must satisfy the general requirements of economic and technical rationality" (111). "It is not at all a matter of whether the small agricultural enterprises are absorbed by the big ones—one can hardly anticipate such an outcome to economic evolution—but of the metamorphosis to which the entire national economy is subjected under the influence of exchange. The Narodniks overlook the fact that the ousting of natural economy by exchange economy in connection with the above-noted 'dispersal of industry' completely alters the entire structure of society. The former ratio between the agricultural (rural) and non-agricultural (urban) population is changed in favour of the latter. The very economic type and mental make-up of the agricultural producers is radically changed under the influence of the new conditions of economic life" (114).

The passage cited shows us what the author wished to say by his passage about Marx, and at the same time clearly illustrates the statement made above that the dogmatic method of exposition, not supported by a description of the concrete process, obscures the author's thoughts and leaves them incompletely expressed. His thesis about the Narodniks' views being wrong is quite correct, but incomplete, because it is not accompanied by a reference to the new forms of class antagonism that develop when irrational production is replaced by rational. The author, for example, confines himself to a cursory reference to "economic rationality" meaning the "highest rent" (110), but forgets to add that *rent* presupposes the *bourgeois organisation of agriculture*, i.e., firstly, its complete subordination to the market, and, secondly, the formation in agriculture of the same classes, bourgeoisie and proletariat, as are peculiar to capitalist industry.

When the Narodniks argue about the non-capitalist, as they believe, organisation of our agriculture, they pose the problem in an abominably narrow and wrong way, reducing everything to the ousting of the small farms by the big, and nothing more. Mr. Struve is quite right in telling them that when they argue that way they overlook the general character of agricultural production, which can be (and really is in our country) bourgeois even where production is small-scale, just as West-European peasant farming is bourgeois. The conditions under which small-scale independent enterprise ("people's"—to use the expression of the Russian intelligentsia) becomes bourgeois are well known. They are, firstly, the prevalence of commodity economy, which, with the producers isolated* from one another, gives rise to competition among them, and, while ruining the mass, enriches the few; secondly, the transformation of labour-power into a commodity, and the means of production into capital, i.e., the separation of the producer from the means of production, and the capitalist organisation of the most important branches of industry. Under these conditions the small independent producer acquires an exceptional position in relation to the mass of producers—just as now *really independent* proprietors constitute in our country an exception among the masses, who work for others and, far from owning "independent" enterprises, do not even possess means of subsistence sufficient to last a week. The condition and interests of the independent proprietor isolate him from the mass of the producers, who live *mainly* on wages. While the latter raise the issue of a "fair reward," which is necessarily the gateway to the fundamental issue of a different system of social economy, the former have a far more lively interest in quite different things, namely, credits, and particularly small "people's" credits, improved and cheaper implements, "organisation of marketing," "extension of land tenure," etc.

The very law of the superiority of large enterprises over small is a law of commodity production alone and consequently is not applicable to enterprises not yet entirely drawn into commodity production, not subordinated to

* This, of course, refers to their being isolated *economically*. Community *landownership* does not eliminate this in the least. Even where the land re-allotments are "equalitarian" in the highest degree the peasant farms single-handed on his own strip of land; hence he is an isolated producer working on his own.

the market. That is why the line of argument (in which, by the way, Mr. V. V. also exercised himself) that the decline of the nobles' farms after the Reform and the renting of privately-owned land by the peasants refute the view of the capitalist evolution of our agriculture, merely proves that those who resort to it have absolutely no understanding of things. Of course, the destruction of feudal relations, under which *cultivation* had been in the hands of the peasants, caused a crisis among the landlords. But, apart from the fact that this crisis merely led to the increasing employment of farm labourers and day labourers, which replaced the obsolescent forms of semi-feudal labour (labour service); apart from this, the peasant farm itself began to change fundamentally in character: it was compelled to work for the market, a situation that was not long in leading to the peasantry splitting into a rural petty bourgeoisie and a proletariat. This split settles once and for all the issue of capitalism in Russia. Mr. Struve explains the process in Chapter V, where he remarks: "There is differentiation among the small farmers: there develops, on the one hand, an 'economically strong'" [he should have said: bourgeois] "peasantry, and, on the other—a proletarian type of peasantry. Features of people's production are combined with capitalist features to form a single picture, above which is clearly visible the inscription: here comes Grimy" (p. 177).

Now it is to this aspect of the matter, to the *bourgeois organisation* of the new, "rational" agriculture that attention should have been directed. The Narodniks should have been shown that by ignoring the process mentioned they change from ideologists of the peasantry into ideologists of the petty bourgeoisie. "The improvement of people's production," for which they thirst, can only mean, under such an organisation of peasant economy, the "improvement" of the petty bourgeoisie. On the other hand, those who point to the producer who lives under the most highly developed capitalist relations, correctly express the interests not only of this producer, but also of the vast mass of the "proletarian" peasantry.

Mr. Struve's exposition is unsatisfactory in character, is incomplete and sketchy; on account of this, when dealing with rational agriculture, he does not describe its social and economic organisation, and, when he shows that steam transport replaces irrational by rational production, natural by commodity production, he does not describe the new form of class antagonism that then takes shape.

This same defect in the presentation of problems is to be observed in most of the arguments in the chapters under examination. Here are some more examples to illustrate this. Commodity economy—says the author—and extensive social division of labour "develop on the basis of the institution of private property, the principles of economic freedom, and the sense of individualism" (91). The progress of national production is bound up with the "extent to which the institution of private property dominates society." "Maybe it is regrettable, but that is how things happen in actual life, it is empirically, historically established coexistence. At the present time, when the ideas and principles of the eighteenth century are treated so light-heartedly —the mistake it made being in fact repeated—this cultural-historical tie between economic progress and the institution of private property, the principles of economic freedom, and the sense of individualism is too often forgotten. Only by ignoring this tie can one expect economic progress to be possible in an economically and culturally undeveloped society, without the principles mentioned being put into effect. We feel no particular sympathy for these principles and perfectly well understand their historically *transient* character, but at the same time we cannot help seeing in them a tremendous cultural force, of not only a negative, but also a positive character. Only idealism which, in its hypotheses, imagines it has no ties with any historical succession, can fail to see it" (91).

The author is quite right in his "objective" statement of "historical coexistences"; all the more pity that his argument is incompletely stated. One would like to say to him: complete the argument! reduce all these general propositions and historical notes to a definite period of our Russian history, formulate them in such a way as to show why and in precisely what way your conception differs from that of the Narodniks, contrast them with the reality that has to serve as the criterion for the Russian Marxist, show the class contradictions that are concealed by all these examples of progress and of culture.*

The "progress" and the "culture" that post-Reform Russia brought in its train are undoubtedly bound up with the "institution of private property"—it was not only introduced for the first time in all its fulness by the creation of a new "contentious" civil process which ensured the same sort of "equality" in the courts as was embodied in life by "free labour" and its sale to capital; it covered the holdings both of the landlords, rid of all obligations and duties to the state, and of the peasants, turned into peasant *proprietors*; it was even made the basis of the political rights of "citizens" to participate in local government (the qualification), etc. Still more undoubted is the "tie" between our "progress" and the "principles of economic freedom": we have already heard in Chapter I from our Narodnik how this "freedom" consisted in liberating the "modest and bearded" gatherers of Russia's land from the need to "humble themselves to a junior police official." We have already spoken of how the "sense of individualism" was created by the development of commodity economy. By combining all these features of Russia's progress, one cannot but reach the conclusion (drawn, too, by the Narodnik of the seventies) that this progress and culture were thoroughly bourgeois. Contemporary Russia is far better than pre-Reform Russia, but since all this improvement is wholly and exclusively due to the bourgeoisie, to its agents and ideologists, the producers have not profited by it. As far as they are concerned the improvements have only meant a change in the form of the surplus product, have only meant improved and perfected methods of separating the producer from the means of production. That is why the Narodnik gentlemen display the most incredible "flippancy" and forgetfulness when they address their protest against Russian capitalism and bour-

* Contra principia negantem disputari non potest (you cannot argue against one who denies principles.—*Ed.*)—says the author about an argument with the Narodniks. That depends on how these principia are formulated—as general propositions and notes, or as a *different understanding* of the *facts* of Russian history and present-day reality.

geoisdom to those who in fact were their vehicles and exponents. All you can say of them is: "they came unto their own, and their own received them not."

To agree with that description of post-Reform Russia and "society" will be beyond the capacity of the contemporary Narodnik. And to challenge it, he would have to deny the bourgeois character of post-Reform Russia, to deny the very thing for which his distant forefather, the Narodnik of the seventies, rose up and "went among the people" to seek "guarantees for the future" among the direct producers themselves. Of course, the *contemporary* Narodnik will possibly not only deny it, but will perhaps seek to prove that a change for the better has taken place in the relation under review; by doing so, however, he would merely show all who have not yet seen it, that he is absolutely nothing more than the most ordinary *little bourgeois* individual.

As the reader sees, I have only to round off Mr. Struve's propositions, to formulate them in another way, "to say the same thing, only differently." The question arises: is there any need for it? Is it worth while dealing in such detail with these additions and conclusions? Do they not follow automatically?

It seems to me that it is worth while, for two reasons. Firstly, the author's narrow objectivism is extremely dangerous, since it extends to the point of forgetting the line of demarcation between the old professorial arguments about the paths and destiny of the fatherland, so rooted in our literature, and a precise characterisation of the actual process impelled by such and such classes. This narrow objectivism, this inconsistency in relation to Marxism, is the main defect of Mr. Struve's book, and it will be necessary to dwell on it in particularly great detail, so as to show that it originates not from Marxism but from its inadequate application; not from the author seeing criteria of his theory other than reality, from his drawing other practical conclusions from the doctrine (they are impossible, I repeat, unthinkable unless you mutilate all its main tenets), but from the fact that the author has limited himself to one, the most general aspect of the theory, and has not applied it quite consistently. Secondly, one cannot but agree with the idea which the author expressed in his preface that before criticising Narodism on secondary issues, it was necessary "to disclose the very fundamentals of the disagreement" (VII) by way of a "principled polemic." But in order to ensure that the author's aim should not remain unachieved a more concrete meaning must be given to almost all his propositions, all his rather general remarks must be applied to the concrete problems of Russian history and present-day reality. On all these problems the Russian Marxists still have much to do to "reconsider the facts" from the materialist standpoint—to disclose the class contradictions in the activities of "society" and the "state" that lay behind the theories of the "intelligentsia," and, finally, to establish the tie between all the separate, endlessly varied forms of appropriating the surplus product in Russia's "people's" enterprises, and the advanced, most developed, capitalist form of this appropriation, which contains the "guarantees for the future" and now puts in the forefront the idea and the historical task of the "producer." Consequently, however bold the attempt to indicate the solution of these problems may seem, however numerous the changes and corrections that result from further, detailed study, it is none the less worth indicating specific problems, so as to evoke as general and broad a discussion of them as possible.

The culminating point of Mr. Struve's narrow objectivism, which gives rise to his vrong presentation of problems, is the way he argues about List, about his "splendid doctrine" concerning a "confederation of national productive forces," about the importance for agriculture of developing factory industry, and about the superiority of the manufacturing and agricultural state over the purely agricultural, etc. The author finds that this "doctrine" very "convincingly speaks of the historical inevitability and legitimacy of capitalism in the broad sense of the term" (123), and about the "cultural-historical might of triumphant commodity production" (124).

The professorial character of the arguments of the author, who rises, as it were, above all definite countries, definite historical periods, and definite classes, stands out here in particular relief. However you look at this argument—whether from the purely theoretical or from the practical aspect, such an assessment will be equally correct. Let us begin from the former. Is it not strange to think of being able to "convince" anybody at all of the "historical inevitability and legitimacy of capitalism" in a particular country by advancing abstract, dogmatic propositions about the significance of factory industry? Is it not a mistake to raise the problem in this way, so beloved of the liberal professors of *Russkoye Bogatstvo*? Is it not obligatory for a Marxist to reduce everything to ascertaining what is, and why it is so, and not otherwise?

The Narodniks consider capitalism in this country to be an artificial, hothouse plant, because they cannot understand the connection between it and the entire commodity organisation of our social economy, and fail to see its roots in our "people's production." Show them these connections and roots, show them that capitalism also dominates in its least developed and therefore worst form in people's production, and you will prove the "inevitability" of Russian capitalism. Show them that this capitalism, by raising labour productivity and socialising labour, develops and renders clear the class, social contradiction that has come into being everywhere in "people's production"—and you will prove the "legitimacy" of Russian large-scale capitalism. As to the practical aspect of this argument, which touches on the problem of commercial policy, the following may be noted. Although they stress primarily and most emphatically that the problem of free trade and protection is a capitalist problem, one of bourgeois policy, the Russian Marxists must stand for free trade, since the reactionary character of protection, which retards the country's economic development, and serves the interests not of the entire bourgeois class, but merely of a handful of all-powerful magnates, is very strongly evident in Russia, and since free trade means accelerating the process that yields the means of deliverance from capitalism.

The last section (XI) of the third chapter is devoted to an examination of the concept "capitalism." The author very rightly remarks that this word is used "very loosely" and cites examples of a "very narrow" and "very broad" way of understanding it, but lays down no precise attributes of it; the concept "capitalism," despite the author's analysis, has not been analysed. Yet, one would have thought it should present no particular difficulty, since the concept was introduced into science by Marx, who substantiated it by facts. But here, too, Mr. Struve would not let himself be infected with "orthodoxy." "Marx himself," says he, "viewed the process of the transformation of *commodity* production into *commodity-capitalist* production as perhaps more precipitate and straightforward than it is in actual fact" (p. 127, footnote). Perhaps. But since it is the only view substantiated scientifically and supported by the history of capital, and since we are unacquainted with other views, which "perhaps" are less "precipitate" and "straightforward," we turn to Marx. The essential features of capitalism, according to his theory, are (1) commodity production, as the *general* form of production. The product assumes the form of a commodity in the most diverse social production organisms, but only in capitalist production is that form of the product of labour *general*, and not exceptional, isolated, accidental. The second feature of capitalism (2)—not only the product of labour, but also labour itself, i.e., human labour-power, assumes the form of a commodity. The degree to which the commodity form of labour-power is developed is an indication of the degree to which capitalism is developed.* With the aid of this definition we shall easily see our way among the examples of incorrect understanding of this term cited by Mr. Struve. Undoubtedly, the contrasting of the Russian system to capitalism, a contrast based on the technical backwardness of our national economy, on the predominance of hand production, etc., and so often resorted to by the Narodniks, is quite absurd, since capitalism exists both where technical development is low and where it is high; in *Capital* Marx repeatedly stresses the point that capital first subordinates production as it finds it, and only subsequently

* *Das Kapital*, II Band (1885), S. 93. The reservation must be made that in the passage referred to Marx gives no *definition* of capitalism. In general, he did not offer definitions. Here he only refers to the relation between commodity and capitalist production, the point dealt with in the text.[128]

transforms it technically. Undoubtedly, the German Hausindustrie and the Russian "domestic system of large-scale production" are capitalist-organised industry, for not only does commodity production dominate, but the owner of money also dominates the producers and appropriates surplus-value. Undoubtedly, when the Russian "land-holding" peasantry is contrasted to West-European capitalism—something the Narodniks are so fond of doing—that, too, merely shows a lack of understanding of what capitalism is. As the author quite rightly remarks, "peasant semi-natural economy" (124) is also to be found in some places in the West, but neither in the West nor in Russia does this do away with either the predominance of commodity production, or the subordination of the overwhelming majority of the producers to capital: before this subordination reaches the highest, peak level of development, it passes through many stages that are usually ignored by the Narodniks despite the very precise explanation given by Marx. The subordination begins with *merchant's* and *usury capital*, then grows into industrial capitalism, which in its turn is at first technically quite primitive, and does not differ in any way from the old systems of production, then organises manufacture—which is still based on hand labour, and on the dominant handicraft industries, without breaking the tie between the wage-worker and the land—and completes its development with large-scale machine industry. It is this last, highest stage that constitutes the culminating point of the development of capitalism, *it alone* creates the fully expropriated worker* who is as free as a bird, *it alone* gives rise (both materially and socially) to the "unifying significance" of capitalism that the Narodniks are accustomed to connect with capitalism in general, *it alone* opposes capitalism to its "own child."

The fourth chapter of the book, "Economic Progress and Social Progress," is a direct continuation of the third chapter, and covers that part of the book which advances data of "human experience" against the Narodniks. We shall

* The Narodniks always describe things as though the worker separated from the land is a necessary condition of capitalism *in general*, and not of machine industry alone.

have to deal here in detail, firstly, with the author's wrong view [or clumsy expression?] concerning Marx's followers and, secondly, with the way the tasks of the economic criticism of Narodism are formulated.

Mr. Struve says that Marx conceived the transition from capitalism to the new social system as the sudden downfall, the collapse of capitalism. (He thinks that "certain passages" in Marx give grounds for this view; as a matter of fact, it runs through *all the works* of Marx.) The followers of Marx fight *for reforms.* An "important correction has been made" to the viewpoint that Marx held in the forties: instead of the "chasm" separating capitalism from the new system, a "number of transitional stages" have been admitted.

We cannot under any circumstances admit this to be right. No "correction" whatever, either important or unimportant, has been made to Marx's viewpoint by the "followers of Marx." The fight for reforms does not in the least imply a "correction," does not in the least correct the doctrine of the chasm and sudden downfall, because this struggle is waged with a frankly and definitely admitted aim, that of reaching the "fall"; and the fact that this requires a "number of transitional stages"—from one phase of the struggle to another, from one stage to the next—was admitted by Marx himself in the forties when he said in the *Manifesto* that the movement towards the new system cannot be *separated* from the working-class movement (and, hence, from the struggle for reforms), and when he himself, in conclusion, proposed a number of practical measures.[129]

If Mr. Struve wanted to indicate the *development* of Marx's viewpoint, he was, of course, right. But then, this is not a "*correction*" to his views, but the very opposite—their *application*, their *realisation.*

Nor can we agree with the author's attitude towards Narodism.

"Our Narodnik literature," he says, "seized upon the contrast between national wealth and the well-being of the people, social progress and progress in distribution" (131).

Narodism did not "seize upon" this contrast, but merely *stated* the fact that in post-Reform Russia the same contradiction was to be observed between progress, culture, wealth and—the separation of the producer from the means of production, the diminution of the producer's share in the product of the people's labour, and the growth of poverty and unemployment—as that which had led to this contrast being made in the West, too.

"...Owing to its humanity and its love for the people, this literature immediately settled the problem in favour of the well-being of the people, and as certain forms of people's economy (village community, artel) apparently embodied the ideal of economic equality and thus guaranteed the well-being of the people, and as the progress of production under the influence of increased exchange held out no promise for these forms, whose economic and psychological foundations it abolished, the Narodniks, pointing to the sad experience of the West in regard to industrial progress based on private property and economic liberty, countered commodity production—capitalism, with a so-called 'people's industry' that guarantees the well-being of the people, as a social and economic ideal for the preservation and further development of which the Russian intelligentsia and the Russian people should fight."

This argument clearly reveals the flaws in Mr. Struve's thesis. Narodism is depicted as a "humane" theory which "seized upon" the contrast between national wealth and the poverty of the people and "settled the problem" in favour of distribution, because the "experience of the West" "held out no promise" for the well-being of the people. And the author begins to argue against this "settlement" of the problem, forgetting that he is only arguing against the idealist and, moreover, naïve daydreams that are the cloak of Narodism, and not against its content, forgetting that he is committing a serious error by presenting the question in the professorial manner usually adopted by the Narodniks. As we have already stated, the *content* of Narodism reflects the viewpoint and the interests of the Russian small producer. The "humanity and love for the people" expressed in the theory derive from the downtrodden condition of our small producer, who has suffered severely both from the "old-nobility" system and traditions, and from the oppression of big capital. The attitude of Narodism towards the "West" and towards its influence upon Russia was determined, of course, not by the fact that it "seized upon" this or that idea coming from the West, but by the small producer's conditions of life: he saw that he was up against large-scale capitalism which was borrowing West-European technique,* and, oppressed by it, built up naïve theories which explained capitalism by politics instead of capitalist politics by capitalist economy, and which declared large-scale capitalism to be something alien to Russia, introduced from outside. The fact that he was tied to his separate, small enterprise prevented him from understanding the true character of the state, and he appealed to it to help develop small ("people's") production. Owing to the undeveloped condition of class antagonisms characteristic of Russian capitalist society, the theory of these petty bourgeois ideologists was put forward as representing the interests of labour in general.

Instead of showing the absurdity of Narodniks' presentation of the problem and explaining their "settlement" of it by the material conditions of the small producer's life, the author himself, in his own presentation of the problem, betrays a dogmatism which reminds one of the Narodniks' "*choice*" between economic and social progress.

"The task of criticising the economic principles of Narodism ... is ... to prove the following:

"1) Economic progress is a necessary condition for social progress: the latter emerges historically from the former, and, at a certain stage of development, organic interaction between, interdependence of, these two processes should, and in fact does, manifest itself" (133).

Speaking generally, this is, of course, a perfectly true statement. But it indicates the tasks of criticising the sociological rather than the economic principles of Narodism: in essence, it is a different way of formulating the doctrine that the development of society is determined by the development of the productive forces which we discussed in chapters I and II. It is, however, inadequate for the criticism of the "*economic principles* of Narodism." The problem must be formulated more concretely, it must be reduced from progress in general to the "progress" of

* Cf. above-mentioned article in *Otechestvenniye Zapiski*.

capitalist society in Russia, to those errors in understanding *this* progress which gave rise to the ridiculous Narodnik fables about the tabula rasa, about "people's production," about Russian capitalism having no basis, etc. Instead of talk about interaction manifesting itself between economic and social progress, the definite symptoms of social progress in Russia of which the Narodniks fail to see *such and such* economic roots, must be shown (or at least indicated).*

"2) For that reason, the question of the organisation of production and of the level of labour productivity is one that takes precedence over the question of distribution; under certain historical conditions, when the productivity of the people's labour is extremely low, both absolutely and relatively, the predominant importance of the factor of production makes itself felt very acutely."

The author here bases himself on Marx's doctrine of the subordinate importance of distribution. As an epigraph to Chapter IV a passage is taken from Marx's criticism of the Gotha Programme[130] where he contrasts vulgar socialism to scientific socialism, which attaches no great importance to distribution, explains the social system by the way the *relations of production* are organised and considers that such organisation already includes a definite system of distribution. This idea, as the author quite justly remarks, runs through the whole of Marx's theory, and is extremely important for an understanding of the petty-bourgeois content of Narodism. But the second part of Mr. Struve's sentence greatly obscures this idea, particularly because of the vague term he uses, "the factor of production." Some confusion may arise as to the sense in which this term is to be understood. The Narodnik adopts the viewpoint of the small producer, whose explanations of the misfortunes he suffers are very superficial; for example, he is "poor," while his neighbour, the buyer-up, is "rich";

* It may be argued that I am running too far ahead, for did not the author say that he intended to proceed gradually from general problems to concrete ones, which he examines in Chapter VI? The point is, however, that the abstractness of Mr. Struve's criticism to which I refer, is a distinguishing feature of the *whole* of his book—of Chapter VI and even of the concluding part. What most of all requires correcting is his way of *presenting problems*.

the "authorities" only help big capital, etc.; in a word, his misfortunes are due to the specific features of distribution, to mistakes in policy, etc. What viewpoint does the author oppose to that of the Narodnik? The viewpoint of big capital, who looks down with contempt upon the miserable little enterprise of the peasant-handicraftsman and who is proud of the high degree of development of his own industry, proud of the "service" he has rendered by raising the absolute and relative low productivity of the people's labour? Or the viewpoint of its antipode, who is now living in relationships which are so far developed that he is no longer satisfied with references to policy and distribution, and who is beginning to understand that the causes lie much deeper, in the very organisation (social) of production, in the very system of social economy based on individual property and controlled and guided by the market? This question might quite naturally arise in the reader's mind, especially since the author sometimes uses the term "factor of production" side by side with the word "economy" (see p. 171: the Narodniks "ignore the factor of production to a degree that is tantamount to denying the existence of any system of economy"), and especially since, by comparing "irrational" with "rational" production, the author sometimes obscures the relationship between the small producer and the producer who has lost the means of production altogether. It is perfectly true that from the *objective point of view* the author's exposition is no less correct on account of this and that it is easy for anyone who understands the antagonism inherent in the capitalist system to picture the situation from the angle of the latter relationship. But, as it is well known that the Russian Narodnik gentlemen do not understand this, it is desirable in controversy with them to be more definite and thorough and to resort to the fewest possible general and abstract postulates.

As we tried to show by a concrete example in Chapter I, the difference between Narodism and Marxism lies *wholly in the character of their criticism of Russian capitalism.* The Narodnik thinks that to criticise capitalism it is sufficient to indicate the existence of exploitation, the interaction between exploitation and politics, etc. The Marxist thinks it necessary to explain and also to link together the phenomena of exploitation as a system of certain relations in production, as a special social-economic formation, the laws of the functioning and development of which have to be studied objectively. The Narodnik thinks it sufficient, in criticising capitalism, to condemn it from the angle of his ideals, from the angle of "modern science and modern moral ideas." The Marxist thinks it necessary to trace in detail the classes that are formed in capitalist society, he considers valid only criticism made from the viewpoint of a definite class, criticism that is based on the precise formulation of the social process actually taking place and not on the ethical judgement of the "individual."

If, with this as our starting-point, we tried to formulate the tasks of criticising the economic principles of Narodism, they would be defined approximately as follows:

It must be shown that the relation between large-scale capitalism in Russia and "people's production" is the relation between a completely developed and an undeveloped phenomenon, between a higher stage of development of the capitalist social formation and a lower stage;* that the separation of the producer from the means of production and the appropriation of the product of his labour by the owner of money are to be explained, both in the factory and even in the village community, not by politics, not by distribution, but by the production relations that necessarily take shape under commodity economy, by the formation of classes with antagonistic interests which is characteristic of capitalist society;** that the reality (small production) which

* An analysis of the economic side should, of course, be supplemented by an analysis of the social, juridical, political, and ideological superstructures. The failure to understand the connection between capitalism and "people's production" gave rise among the Narodniks to the idea that the peasant Reform, state power, the intelligentsia, etc., were *non-class* in character. A materialist analysis, which reduces all these phenomena to the class struggle, must show concretely that our Russian post-Reform "social progress" has only been the result of capitalist "economic progress."

** A "reconsideration of the facts" of Russian economic realities, especially those from which the Narodniks obtain the material for their schoolgirl dreams, i.e., peasant and handicraft economy, should show that the cause of the producer's oppressed condition does not lie in distribution ("the muzhik is poor, the buyer-up is rich"), but the Narodniks want to raise to a higher level, bypassing capitalism, already contains capitalism with its antagonism of classes and clashes between them—only the antagonism is in its worst form, a form which hampers the independent activity of the producer; and that by ignoring the social antagonisms which have already arisen and by dreaming about "different paths for the fatherland," the Narodniks become utopian reactionaries, because large-scale capitalism only develops, purges and clarifies the content of these antagonisms, which exist all over Russia.

Directly connected with the over-abstract formulation of the tasks of the economic criticism of Narodism is the author's further exposition, in which he seeks to prove the "inevitability" and "progressive character," not of Russian capitalism, but of West European. Without directly touching on the economic content of the Narodnik doctrine, this exposition contains much that is interesting and instructive. In Narodnik literature voices have been heard time and again expressing distrust towards the West-European labour movement. This was most strikingly expressed during the recent polemics of Messrs. Mikhailovsky and Co. (*Russkoye Bogatstvo*, 1893-1894) against the Marxists. We have seen no good from capitalism yet, Mr. Mikhailovsky wrote at that time.* The absurdity of these petty-bourgeois views is excellently proved by Mr. Struve's data, especially since they are drawn from the latest bour-

---

in the very production relations, in the very social organisation of present-day peasant and handicraft economy. This will show that in "people's" production, too, "the problem of the organisation of production takes precedence ver the problem of distribution."

* We must mention that in Mr. Struve's reply Mr. Mikhailovsky finds that Engels betrays "self-admiration" when he says that the dominating, overwhelming fact of modern times, which makes these times better than any other epoch and justifies the history of their origin, is the working-class movement in the West.

This positively atrocious reproach hurled at Engels is extremely typical of contemporary Russian Narodism.

These people can talk a lot about "people's truth," they know how to talk to our "society" and to reprove it for making a wrong selection of the path for the fatherland, they can sing sweetly about "now or never," and sing it for "ten, twenty, thirty years and more," but they are absolutely incapable of understanding the all-embracing significance of independent action by those in whose name these sweet songs have been sung.

geois literature, which can on no account be accused of exaggeration. The passages quoted by the author show that in the West everybody, even the bourgeois, realises that the transition of capitalism to a new social-economic formation is inevitable.

The socialisation of labour by capital has advanced so far that even bourgeois literature loudly proclaims the necessity of the "planned organisation of the national economy." The author is quite right when he says that this is a "sign of the times," a sign of the complete break-up of the capitalist system. He quotes extremely interesting statements by bourgeois professors and even by conservatives who are compelled to admit that which Russian radicals to this very day like to deny—the fact that the working-class movement was created by the material conditions brought into existence by capitalism and not "simply" by culture or other political conditions.

After all that has been said, it is hardly necessary for us to deal with the author's argument that distribution can make progress only if based on rational production. Clearly, the meaning of this postulate is that only large-scale capitalism based on rational production creates conditions that enable the producer to raise his head, to give thought and show concern both for himself and for those who, owing to the backward state of production, do not live in such conditions.

Just a word or two about the following sentence which occurs in Mr. Struve's book: "The extreme inequality of distribution, which retards economic progress, was not created by capitalism: capitalism inherited it" from the epoch which romantics picture as flowing with milk and honey (p. 159). That is true if all the author wanted to say was that unequal distribution existed even before capitalism, something Narodnik gentlemen are inclined to forget. But it is not true if it includes a denial that capitalism has increased this inequality. Under serfdom there was not, nor could there be, that sharp inequality between the absolutely impoverished peasant or tramp, and the bank, railway, or industrial magnate, which has been created by post-Reform capitalist Russia.

Let us pass to Chapter V. Here the author gives a general description of "Narodism as an economic philosophy." "The Narodniks," in Mr. Struve's opinion, are the "ideologists of natural economy and primitive equality" (167).

We cannot agree with this description. We shall not repeat here the arguments advanced in Chapter I, proving that the Narodniks are the ideologists of the small producer. In that chapter we showed exactly how the small producer's material conditions of life, his transitory, intermediate position between the "masters" and the "workers" lead to the Narodniks' failure to understand class antagonisms, and the queer mixture of progressive and reactionary points in their programme.

Here let us merely add that its former, i.e., progressive, side brings Narodism close to West-European democracy, and for that reason the brilliant description of democracy given over forty years ago in connection with events in French history can be applied to it in its entirety:

"The democrat, because he represents the petty bourgeoisie, that is, a *transition class*, in which the interests of two classes are simultaneously mutually blunted, imagines himself elevated above class antagonism generally. The democrats concede that a privileged class confronts them, but they, along with all the rest of the nation, form the *people*. What they represent is the *people's rights*; what interests them is the *people's interests*. Accordingly... they do not need to examine the interests and positions of the different classes. They do not need to weigh their own resources too critically.... * If in the performance their interests prove to be uninteresting and their potency *impotent*, then either the fault lies with pernicious sophists, who split the *indivisible people* into different hostile

* The Russian Narodniks are exactly the same. They do not deny that there are classes in Russia which are antagonistic to the producer, but they lull themselves with the argument that these "pirates" are insignificant compared with the "people" and refuse to make a careful study of the position and interests of the respective classes, to examine whether the interests of a certain category of producers are interwoven with the interests of the "pirates," thus weakening the former's power of resistance against the latter.

camps* ... or the whole thing has been wrecked by a detail in its execution, or else an unforeseen accident has this time spoilt the game. In any case, the democrat comes out of the most disgraceful defeat just as immaculate as he was innocent when he went into it, with the newly-won conviction that he is bound to win, not that he himself and his party have to give up the old standpoint, but, on the contrary, that conditions have to ripen to suit him" (ihm entgegenzureifen haben. *Der achtzehnte Brumaire, u.s.w.*, S. 39).[131]

The very examples which the author himself quotes prove that the description of the Narodniks as ideologists of natural economy and primitive equality is wrong. "As a *curiosity* it is worth mentioning," says Mr. Struve, "that to this day Mr. —on calls Vasilchikov a liberal economist" (169). If we examine the *real essence* of this designation we shall find that it is by no means curious. In his programme Vasilchikov has the demand for cheap and widespread credit. Mr. Nikolai —on cannot fail to see that in the capitalist society which Russian society is, credit will only strengthen the bourgeoisie, will lead to "the development and consolidation of capitalist relationships" (*Sketches*, p. 77). By the practical measures he proposes, Vasilchikov, like all the Narodniks, represents nothing but the interests of the petty bourgeoisie. The only thing that is curious about this is that Mr. —on, sitting as he does side by side with the *Russkoye Bogatstvo* publicists, has "to this day" not noticed that they are exactly the same type of little "liberal economists" as Prince Vasilchikov. Utopian theories easily reconcile themselves in practice with petty-bourgeois progress. This description of Narodism is still further confirmed by Golovachov, who admits that to distribute allotments to everybody is absurd and suggests that "cheap credits be provided for working folk." In criticising this "astonishing" theory, Mr. Struve calls attention to the absurdity

* In the opinion of the Russian Narodniks the pernicious Marxists are to blame for artificially implanting capitalism and its class antagonisms in the soil in which the flowers of "social mutual adaptation" and "harmonious activity" bloom so beautifully (Mr. V. V., quoted by Struve, p. 161).

of the theory, but he appears not to have observed its petty-bourgeois content.

When speaking of Chapter V, we too cannot help dealing with Mr. Shcherbina's "law of average requirements." This is important in estimating Mr. Struve's Malthusianism, which stands out clearly in Chapter VI. The "law" is as follows: when you classify the peasants *according to allotment* you get very little fluctuation (from group to group) in the average magnitude of peasant family requirements (i.e., of expenditure on various needs); Mr. Shcherbina calculates this expenditure per head of the population.

Mr. Struve emphasises with satisfaction that this "law" is "tremendously important," since, he avers, it confirms the "well-known" law of Malthus that "the living standard and the reproduction of the population are determined by the means of subsistence they have at their disposal."

We cannot understand why Mr. Struve is so pleased with this law. We cannot understand how one can see a "law," and what is more, a "tremendously important" one, in Mr. Shcherbina's calculations. It is quite natural that where the manner of life of different peasant families does not differ very considerably we get averages that vary little if we divide the peasants into groups; particularly if, when making the division into groups, we take as the basis the size of the allotment, which is no direct index of a family's living standard (since the allotment may be leased out, or additional land may be rented) and is equally available to both the rich and the poor peasant possessing an equal number of taxable members in the family. Mr. Shcherbina's calculations merely prove that he chose a wrong method of classification. If Mr. Shcherbina thinks he has discovered some law here, it is very strange. It is equally strange to find confirmation of the law of Malthus here, as though one can judge of the "means of subsistence at the peasant's disposal" from the size of the allotment when one disregards the leasing out of land, "outside employments," the peasant's economic dependence on the landlord and the buyer-up. About this "law" of Mr. Shcherbina's (the way Mr. Shcherbina expounds this "law" indicates that the author attaches incredibly great importance to his average figures, which prove absolutely nothing) Mr. Struve says:

"'People's production' in the present case simply means production without the employment of wage-labour. It is undoubted that where production is organised in that way the 'surplus-value' remains in the hands of the producer" (176). And the author points out that where labour productivity is low, this does not prevent the representative of such "people's production" living worse than the worker. The author is carried away by the Malthusian theory, and this has led him to formulate inexactly the proposition cited. Merchant's and usury *capital* subordinates labour to itself in every Russian village and—without turning the producer into a wage-worker—deprives him of as much surplus-value as industrial capital takes from the working man. Mr. Struve rightly indicated earlier on that capitalist production sets in from the moment the *capitalist* steps between the producer and the consumer, even though he buys the ready-made ware from the independent (apparently independent) producer (p. 99 and note 2), and it would be no easy job to find among the Russian "independent" producers those that do not work for a capitalist (merchant, buyer-up, kulak, etc.). One of the biggest mistakes of the Narodniks is that they do not see the very close and indissoluble tie between the capitalist organisation of Russian social economy and the absolute dominion of merchant's capital in the countryside. The author therefore is perfectly correct when he says that the "very combination of the words 'people's production' in the sense they are used by the Narodnik gentlemen does not fit in with any actual historical order. Here in Russia 'people's production' before 1861 was closely connected with serfdom, and then after 1861 there was a rapid development of commodity economy, which could not but distort the purity of people's production" (177). When the Narodnik says that the ownership of the means of production by the producer is the age-old basis of the Russian way of life, he is simply distorting history to suit his utopia, and does so by playing tricks with words: under serfdom means of production were supplied to the producer by the landlord *in order that* the producer could engage in corvée service for him; the allotment was a sort of wages in kind—the "age-old" means of appropriating the surplus product.

The abolition of serfdom did not mean the "emancipation" of the producer at all; it only meant a *change in the form* of the surplus product. While in, say, England the fall of serfdom gave rise to really independent and free peasants, our Reform immediately effected the transition from the "shameful" feudal surplus product to "free" bourgeois surplus-value.

CHAPTER IV

HOW MR. STRUVE EXPLAINS SOME FEATURES OF RUSSIA'S POST-REFORM ECONOMY

The last (sixth) chapter of Mr. Struve's book is devoted to the most important problem, that of Russia's economic development. Its theoretical contents are divided up into the following sections: 1) over-population in agricultural Russia, its character and causes; 2) the differentiation of the peasantry, its significance and causes; 3) the part played by industrial capitalism in ruining the peasantry; 4) private-landowner farming; the character of its development, and 5) the problem of markets for Russian capitalism. Before proceeding to examine Mr. Struve's line of argument on each of these problems, let us examine what he says about the peasant Reform.

The author voices his protest against the "idealistic" understanding of the Reform and points to the requirements of the state, which needed greater labour productivity, to *land redemption*, and to the pressure "from below." It is a pity the author did not make his legitimate protest a thorough one. The Narodniks explain the Reform by the development in "society" of "humane" and "emancipatory" ideas. This is an undoubted fact, but thus *to explain* the Reform means to slip into empty tautology and to reduce "emancipation" to "emancipatory" ideas. The materialist requires a special examination of the *content* of the measures effected to put those ideas into practice. History has never known a single important "reform," even though it has been of a class character, which has not had lofty words and lofty ideas advanced in its support. This is equally true of the peasant Reform. If we pay attention to the actual content of the changes it has effected, we shall see that their character is as follows: some of the peasants were deprived of the land, and—this is the chief thing—the rest of the peasants, who retained part of their land, had to *redeem* it from the landlords, as though it was something to which they had absolutely no right, and what is more, to redeem it at an artificially high price. Not only here in Russia, but also in the West, such reforms were invested with theories about "freedom" and "equality," and it has already been shown in *Capital* that it was commodity production that provided the basis for the ideas of freedom and equality. At any rate, however complicated the bureaucratic machine that put the Reform into effect in Russia, however *apparently* * distant it was from the bourgeoisie themselves, it remains an undoubted fact that only the *bourgeois system* could develop on the basis of *such* a reform. Mr. Struve is quite right in pointing out that the stock way of contrasting the peasant Reform in Russia to those in Western Europe is wrong: "it is quite wrong (*in so general a form*) to assert that in Western Europe the peasants were emancipated without the land, or, in other words, were deprived of the land by legislation" (196). I underscore the words "in so general a form," because separation of the peasants from the land by legislation was an undoubted historical fact wherever a peasant Reform was carried through, but it is not a universal fact, for in the West *part* of the peasants, when emancipated from feudal dependence, *redeemed* the land from the landlords, and are doing so in Russia. Only the bourgeoisie are capable of hiding the fact of *redemption* and of asserting that the "emancipation of the peasants with land ** made a tabula rasa of Russia" (the words of a Mr. Yakovlev, "heartily welcomed" by Mr. Mikhailovsky—see p. 10 of P. Struve's work).

* Actually, as has already been indicated, this machine could only serve the bourgeoisie by virtue both of its composition and of its historical origin.

** To speak the truth one should say: make it possible for *part* of the peasants to *redeem part of their* allotment land from the landlords *at double the proper price*. And even the words "make it possible" are no good, because the peasant who refused such "provision of an allotment" was faced with the threat of a flogging at the Volost Administration offices.

I

Let us proceed to Mr. Struve's theory about the "character of over-population in agrarian Russia." This is one of the most important points in which Mr. Struve departs from the "doctrine" of Marxism for that of Malthusianism. The essence of his views, developed by him in his controversy with Mr. N. —on, is that over-population in agricultural Russia is "not capitalist, but, so to speak, simple over-population, that goes with natural economy."*

Since Mr. Struve says that his objection to Mr. N. —on "fully conforms with F. A. Lange's general objection to Marx's theory of relative over-population" (p. 183, footnote), we shall first turn to this "general objection" of Lange's and examine it.

Lange discusses Marx's law of population in his *Labour Problem*, Chapter V (Russian trans., pp. 142-78). He begins with Marx's main proposition that "every special historic mode of production has its own special laws of population, historically valid within its limits alone. An abstract law of population exists for plants and animals only."[132] Lange's comment is:

"May we be permitted to note firstly that, strictly speaking, there is no abstract law of population for plants and animals either, since abstraction is, on the whole, merely the extraction of the general from a whole number of similar phenomena" (143), and Lange explains in detail to Marx what abstraction is. Evidently, he simply did not understand the meaning of Marx's statement. In this respect Marx contrasts man to plants and animals on the grounds that the former lives in *diverse* historically successive *social organisms* which are determined by the system of social production, and, hence, distribution. The conditions for human reproduction are directly dependent on the structure of the different social organisms; that is why the law of population must be studied in relation to each organism separately, and not "abstractly," without

* That is how it is formulated by Mr. Struve in his article in *Sozialpolitisches Centralblatt* (1893, No. 1 of October 2). He adds that he does not consider this view to be "Malthusian."

regard to the historically different forms of social structure. Lange's explanation that abstraction means to extract the general from *similar* phenomena turns right against himself: only the conditions of existence of animals and plants can be considered similar, but this is not so with regard to man, because we know that he has lived in organisationally different types of social association.

Having expounded Marx's theory of relative over-population in a capitalist country, Lange goes on to say: "At first sight it may seem that this theory breaks the lengthy thread that runs through the whole of organic nature up to man, that it explains the basis of the labour problem as though general investigations into the existence, reproduction and perfection of the human race were quite superfluous to our purpose, i.e., to an understanding of the labour problem" (154).*

The thread that runs through the whole of organic nature up to man is not at all broken by Marx's theory, which merely requires that the "labour problem"—since it only exists as such in capitalist society—be solved not on the basis of "general investigations" into human reproduction, but on the basis of specific investigations of the laws of capitalist relations. Lange, however, is of a different opinion: "Actually, however," says he, "this is not so. Above all it is clear that factory labour from the very outset presumes *poverty*" (154). And Lange devotes a page and a half to proving this proposition, which is self-evident and does not advance us a single hair's breadth: firstly, we know that poverty is created by capitalism itself at a stage of its development prior to the factory form of production, prior to the stage at which the machines create surplus population; secondly, the form of social structure preceding capitalism—the feudal, serf system—itself created a poverty of its own, one that it handed down to capitalism.

---

* And what can these "general investigations" consist of? If they ignore the specific economic formations of human society, they will be mere banalities. And if they are to embrace several formations, it is obvious that they must be preceded by specific investigations of each separate formation.

"But even with such a powerful assistant [i.e., want], only in rare cases does the first employer succeed in winning over large numbers of workers to the new kind of activity. Usually what happens is the following. From the locality where factory industry has already won itself citizenship rights the employer brings with him a contingent of workers; to them he adds a few landless peasants,* who at the moment are workless, and the further supplementation of the existing factory contingent is done from among the *rising generation*" (156). Lange places the last two words in italics. Evidently, the "general investigations into the existence, reproduction and perfection of the human race" were expressed in precisely the postulate that the factory owner recruits new workers among the "rising generation," and not among decrepit old folk. The good Lange spends a whole page more (157) on these "general investigations" and tells the reader that parents try to give their children an assured existence, that the idle moralists are wrong in condemning those who try to work their way out of the condition into which they were born, that it is quite natural to try to arrange for children to earn their own living. Only after we have got over all these reflections, which may be in place in copybooks, do we get down to business:

"In an agrarian country where the soil belongs to small and big owners—provided that the tendency of voluntary birth-control has not firmly gripped the people's morals—there inevitably arises a constant surplus of hands and consumers who wish to exist on the products of the given territory" (157-58). This purely Malthusian proposition is put forward by Lange without offering any proof. He repeats it again and again and says: "In any case, even if such a country is thinly populated in the absolute sense, there are usually signs of relative over-population" and "on the market the supply of labour is *constantly in excess* and the demand insignificant" (158)—but all these

* By the way, where have these "landless peasants" come from? Very likely, Lange imagines, they are not the left-overs of the serf system, or the product of the rule of capital, but the result of the fact that "the tendency towards voluntary birth-control has not firmly gripped the people's morals" (p.157)?

assertions are totally unsupported. Whence does it follow that a "surplus of workers" was really "inevitable"? Whence does the connection arise between this surplus and the absence in the people's morals of a tendency to voluntary birth-control? Ought he not, before arguing about the "people's morals," to take a glance at the production relations in which the people live? Let us imagine, for example, that the small and big proprietors to whom Lange refers were connected in the production of material values as follows: the small proprietors received allotments from the big landowners on which they could exist, and in return engaged in corvée service for the big landowners, cultivating their fields. Let us imagine, further, that these relations have been shattered, that humane ideas have turned the heads of the big proprietors to such an extent that they have "emancipated their peasants with land," i.e., have cut off approximately 20% of the allotment land of the peasants, and compelled them to pay for the remaining 80% a purchase price that has been raised 100%. Naturally, with such a guarantee against the "ulcer of the proletariat" the peasants still have to continue working for the big proprietors in order to exist, although they do not now work on the instructions of the feudal steward, as formerly, but on the basis of free contract—hence they snatch the work out of one another's hands, since they are no longer bound together, and each one farms on his own account. This way of snatching up work inevitably forces some peasants out: because their allotments have grown smaller and their payments bigger, they have become weaker in relation to the landlord, and so competition among them increases the rate of surplus product, and the landlord can manage with a smaller number of peasants. However much the tendency to voluntary birth-control becomes entrenched in the people's morals, the formation of a "surplus" is inevitable. Lange's line of argument, which ignores social-economic relations, merely serves as striking proof that his methods are useless. And apart from such arguments he gives us nothing new. He says that the factory owners willingly transfer industry into the depths of the countryside, because there "*the requisite amount of child labour is always ready to hand for any undertaking*" (161), without investigating what history, what mode of social production has created this "readiness" on the part of parents to place their children in bondage. The methods he uses are most clearly seen from the following of his arguments: he quotes Marx, who says that machine industry, by enabling capital to buy female and child labour, makes the worker a "slave-dealer."

"So that's what he's getting at!" cries Lange triumphantly. "But is it to be expected that the worker, whom want forces to sell his own labour-power, would so lightly sell his wife and children, if he were not impelled to take this step by want, on the one hand, and by temptation, on the other?" (163).

The good Lange has carried his zeal to the point of defending the worker against Marx, to whom he proves that the worker is "prompted by want."

..."And what, indeed, is this ever-growing want but the metamorphosis of the struggle for existence?" (163).

Such are the discoveries resulting from "general investigations into the existence, reproduction and perfection of the human race"! Do we learn anything at all about the causes of "want," about its political-economic content and course of development if we are told that it is the metamorphosis of the struggle for existence? Why, that can be said about anything you like—about the relation of the worker to the capitalist, the landowner to the factory owner and to the peasant serf, etc., etc. We get nothing but such vapid banalities or naïveties from Lange's attempt to correct Marx. Let us now see what Lange's follower, Mr. Struve, gives us in support of this correction, in discussing the specific problem of over-population in agrarian Russia.

Commodity production, begins Mr. Struve, increases the capacity of the home market. "Exchange exerts such an effect not only by the complete technical and economic reorganisation of production, but also in those cases where the technique of production remains at the former level, and natural economy retains its former dominant role in the general economy of the population. In that case, however, 'over-population' inevitably sets in after a brief revival; but if commodity production is to blame, it is only: 1) as the *exciter*, 2) as the complicating factor" (182). Over-population would set in without commodity economy: it is non-capitalist in character.

Such are the propositions advanced by the author. From the very outset one is struck with the fact that these propositions are just as unsubstantiated as those of Lange. The assertion is made that over-population is inevitable under natural economy, but no explanation is given of exactly what process gives rise to it. Let us turn to the facts in which the author finds confirmation of his views.

The data for 1762-1846 show that the population in general did not multiply so rapidly, the annual increase being from 1.07 to 1.5%. What is more, the increase was more rapid, according to Arsenyev, in the "grain-growing" gubernias. This "fact," concludes Mr. Struve, "is highly characteristic of the primitive forms of people's economy, where reproduction is directly dependent on natural fertility, a dependence which one can feel with one's hands, so to speak." This is the action of "the law of the correlation of the growth of the population with the means of subsistence" (185). "The wider the expanse of territory, and the higher the natural fertility of the soil, the greater is the natural growth of the population" (186). The quite unsubstantiated conclusion drawn is the following: the one fact that in the central gubernias of European Russia the growth of the population between 1790 and 1846 was smallest in Vladimir and Kaluga gubernias is made the basis for a whole law correlating the growth of the population with the means of subsistence. But can one judge of the population's means of subsistence from the "expanse of territory"? (Even if we were to admit that such few data enable us to draw general conclusions.) The "population," after all, did not divert to their own use the products of the "natural fertility" they had secured: they shared them with the landlords, with the state. Is it not clear that the different types of landlord farming—quitrent or corvée, the size of tributes and the methods of exacting them, etc.—exerted a far greater influence on the amount of "means of subsistence" available to the population than the expanse of territory, which was not in the exclusive and free possession of the producers? More than that. Irrespective of the social relations that were expressed in serfdom, the population was bound together, even then, by exchange: "The separation of manufacturing industry from agriculture," rightly says the author, "i.e., the social, national division of labour, existed in the pre-Reform period, too" (189). The question, then, arises why should we presume that the marsh-dwelling Vladimir handicraftsman or cattle-dealer had a less abundant supply of "means of subsistence" than the rude tiller of Tambov with all his "natural fertility of the soil"?

Then Mr. Struve cites data about the decline in the serf population before the emancipation. The economists whose opinion he quotes attribute this to a "decline in living standards" (189). The author concludes:

"We have stopped to deal with the fact of the decline in the serf population before the emancipation, because, in our view, it throws clear light on the economic situation in Russia at that time. A considerable part of the country had ... the maximum population for the given technical-economic and social-juridical conditions: the latter were very unfavourable for any rapid increase as far as almost 40% of the population was concerned" (189). What has the Malthusian "law" of the correlation of population increase and means of subsistence to do with the matter, when the feudal social order directed these means of subsistence into the possession of a handful of big landowners, and passed over the mass of the population, the growth of which is under investigation? Can any value be attached, for example, to the author's argument that the growth in population was smallest either in the less-fertile gubernias where industry was poorly developed, or in the thickly populated and purely agricultural gubernias? Mr. Struve wishes to see in this a manifestation of "non-capitalist over-population," which was bound to have set in even without commodity economy, and which "corresponds to natural economy." But one might say with equal, if not greater, justice that this over-population corresponded to feudal economy, that the slow increase in the population was due most of all to the increased exploitation of peasant labour that resulted from the growth of commodity production on the landlords' farms, when they began using corvée labour to produce grain *for sale*, and not merely for their own needs. The author's examples tell against him: they tell of the impossibility of constructing an abstract law of population, according to the formula about correlation of growth and the means of subsistence, while ignoring historically specific systems of social relations and the stages of their development.

Passing to the post-Reform period, Mr. Struve says: "In the history of the population following the collapse of serfdom we see the same basic feature as before the emancipation. The dynamics of population increase are directly dependent on the expanse of territory and the land allotment" (198). This is proved by a small table, which groups the peasants according to size of allotment, and shows that the greater the size of the allotment, the greater the increase in population. "*And it cannot be otherwise under natural*, 'self-consumer'... economy that serves primarily to satisfy the direct needs of the producer himself" (199).

Truly, *if this were so*, if the allotments served primarily to satisfy the direct needs of the producer, if they were the only source of satisfying these needs, one could then, and only then, evolve a general law of population increase from these data. But we know that this is not the case. The allotments serve "primarily" to satisfy the needs of the landlords and the state: they are taken away from their owners, if these "needs" are not satisfied on time; payments are levied on the allotment in excess of the peasants' paying capacity. Further, they are not the peasants' only resources. A farming deficit—says the author—is bound to be reflected preventively and repressively on the population. Furthermore, outside employments, by diverting the adult male population, retard reproduction (199). But if the deficit from allotment farming is covered by renting land or by outside earnings, the peasant's means of subsistence may prove to be adequate enough for "energetic reproduction." Undoubtedly, such a favourable turn of events may be the lot of only a minority of the peasants, but, where no special examination is made of production relations existing within the peasantry, there is nothing to show that this growth proceeds evenly, that it is not called forth mainly by the prosperity of the minority. Finally, the author himself makes natural economy a condition of the demonstrability of his thesis, whereas after the Reform, on his own admission, commodity production penetrated in a broad stream into the hitherto existing life. The author's data are obviously quite inadequate *for establishing a general law of reproduction.* More, the abstract "simplicity" of this law which presumes that the means of production in the society under review "serve primarily to satisfy the direct needs of the producer himself" gives absolutely wrong, and totally unsupported, treatment of highly complicated facts. For example, after the emancipation—says Mr. Struve—it was to the landlords' advantage to lease their land to the peasants. "Thus, the food area available to the peasantry, i. e., their means of subsistence, has increased" (200). To assign the whole of the rented land in this forthright way to the category of "food area" is quite unfounded and wrong. The author himself points out that the landlords appropriated the lion's share of the produce raised on their land (200), so that it is still a question whether such renting of land (on a labour-service basis, for example) has not worsened the conditions of the tenants, whether it has not placed obligations on them that have led, in the final analysis, to the food area declining. Further, the author himself points out that the renting of land is only within the capacity of the prosperous (216) peasants, in whose hands it serves as a means of expanding commodity farming rather than consolidating "self-consumer" farming. Even if it were proven that generally speaking the renting of land improved the position of the "peasantry," of what importance could that be when, to use the words of the author himself, the peasant poor have been ruined by renting land (216)—i. e., improvement for some meant worsening for others? Evidently in the peasant renting of land the old, feudal and the new, capitalist relationships intertwine; the author's abstract reasoning, which takes no account of either the one or the other, confuses matters instead of helping to achieve clarity about these relationships.

There remains one more reference by the author to data supposedly confirming his views. It is where he says that "the old word *land-poverty* is merely the term commonly used to express what science calls over-population" (186). The author thus bases himself, as it were, on the whole of our Narodnik literature, which established the fact beyond doubt that the peasant allotments were "inadequate," and which "fortified" thousands of times over their desire for the "expansion of peasant land tenure" with the "simple" argument: the population has increased; the allotments have been split up—naturally, the peasants are being ruined. However, this hackneyed Narodnik argument about "land-poverty can hardly be of any scientific* value, it can hardly be of use for anything but "loyal speeches" in a commission dealing with the painless advance of the fatherland along the right road. In this argument the wood cannot be seen for the trees, the basic social-economic background of the picture cannot be seen for the outer contours of the object. The fact of a huge mass of land belonging to members of the "old-nobility" system, on the one hand, and the acquisition of land by purchase, on the other—such is the basic background under which every "expansion of land tenure" will be a miserable palliative. Both the Narodnik arguments about land-poverty, and the Malthusian "laws" about population increase being correlated to the means of subsistence are at fault in their abstract "simplicity," which ignores the given, specific social-economic relations.

This review of Mr. Struve's arguments leads us to the conclusion that his thesis—over-population in agrarian Russia is to be explained by reproduction not being correlated to the means of subsistence—is absolutely unproved. He concludes his arguments as follows: "And so, we are faced with a picture of natural-economic over-population complicated by commodity-economic factors and other important features inherited from the social structure of the feudal epoch" (200). Of course, one can say that any economic phenomenon in a country undergoing a transition from "natural" to "commodity" economy is a "natural-economic" phenomenon complicated by "commodity-economic factors." The opposite can also be said: "a commodity-economic" phenomenon "complicated by natural-economic factors,"—but all this, far from giving a "picture," cannot give even

* That is to say, this argument is of no use whatever as an *explanation* of the ruin of the peasantry and of over-population, though the very fact of "insufficiency" is beyond argument, just as is its accentuation as a result of the growth of the population. What is needed is not a statement of the fact, but an explanation of its origin.

the slightest idea of *exactly how* over-population is created on the basis of the *given social-economic relations*. The author's final conclusion against Mr. N. —on and his theory of capitalist over-population in Russia reads: "Our peasants produce insufficient food" (237).

The peasants' agricultural work continues to this day to yield produce that goes to the landlords, who, through the medium of the state, receive redemption payments; peasant production serves as a constant object of merchant's and usury *capital* operations, depriving vast masses of the peasantry of a considerable part of their produce; finally, among the "peasantry" itself this production is distributed in so complicated a fashion that the general and average gain (renting) turns out to be a loss for the masses, and Mr. Struve cuts all this network of social relations, like a Gordian knot, with the abstract and totally unsupported solution: "production is insufficient." But no, this theory will not hold water at all: it merely encumbers that which is to be investigated, namely, production relations in peasant agricultural economy. The Malthusian theory pictures matters as though we are confronted by a tabula rasa, and not by feudal and bourgeois relations interwoven in the contemporary organisation of Russian peasant economy.

It goes without saying that we cannot be satisfied with merely criticising Mr. Struve's views. We must in addition ask ourselves the questions: what is the basis of his mistakes? And who of the contending parties (Mr. N.—on and Mr. Struve) is right in his explanation of over-population?

Mr. N. —on bases his explanation of over-population on the fact of masses of workers being "freed" because of the capitalisation of the peasant industries. And he merely cites data relating to the growth of large-scale factory industry, and disregards the parallel fact of the growth of handicraft industries, which expresses the deepening of the social division of labour.* He transfers his expla-

* It is a known fact that our handicraft industries have grown and that a mass of new ones have appeared since the Reform. The theoretical explanation of this fact and of the capitalisation of other peasant industries is also known; it was given by Marx to explain the "creation of the home market for industrial capital" [*Das Kapital*, 2. Aufl., S. 776 u. ff.].[133]

nation to agriculture, without even attempting to give an exact description of its social-economic organisation and the *degree of its development*.

Mr. Struve indicates in reply that "capitalist over-population in Marx's sense is closely connected with technical progress" (183), and since he, together with Mr. —on, finds that the "technique" of peasant "farming has made practically no progress" (200), he refuses to recognise the over-population in agricultural Russia to be capitalist, and seeks for other explanations.

Mr. Struve's remarks in reply to Mr. N. —on are correct. Capitalist over-population is due to *capital* taking possession of production; by reducing the number of necessary workers (necessary for the production of a given quantity of products) it creates a surplus population. Marx, speaking of capitalist over-population in agriculture, says the following:

"As soon as capitalist production takes possession of agriculture, and in proportion to the extent to which it does so, the demand for an agricultural labouring population falls absolutely, while the accumulation of the capital employed in agriculture advances, without this repulsion being, as in non-agricultural industries, compensated by a greater attraction. Part of the agricultural population is therefore constantly on the point of passing over into an urban, or manufacturing proletariat....* (Manufacture is used here in the sense of all non-agricultural industries.) This source of relative surplus population is thus constantly flowing. But the constant flow towards the towns presupposes, in the country itself, a constant latent surplus population, the extent of which becomes evident only when its channels of outlet open to exceptional width. The agricultural labourer is therefore reduced to the minimum of wages, and always stands with one foot already in the swamp of pauperism" (*Das Kapital*, 2 Aufl., S. 668).[134]

* Incidentally. Observation of this fact very likely gave Lange an excuse to concoct an amendment to Marx's theory, which he did not fully understand. When analysing this fact he should have made his starting-point the given (capitalist) mode of social production and followed its manifestation in agriculture; instead he took it into his head to invent all sorts of peculiarities in the "people's morals."

Mr. N. —on *did not prove* the capitalist character of over-population in agrarian Russia, because he did not connect it with capitalism in agriculture: confining himself to a cursory and incomplete reference to the capitalist evolution of private-landowner farming, he completely overlooked the bourgeois features of the organisation of peasant farming. Mr. Struve should have corrected this unsatisfactory feature of Mr. N. —on's exposition, which is of very great importance, for ignoring capitalism in agriculture, its domination, and at the same time its still weak development, naturally led to the theory of the absence or the contraction of the home market. Instead of reducing Mr. N. —on's theory to the concrete data of our agricultural capitalism, Mr. Struve fell into another error—he denied the capitalist character of over-population completely.

The invasion of agriculture by *capital* is characteristic of the entire history of the post-Reform period. The landlords went over (whether slowly or quickly is another matter) to hired labour, which became very widespread and even determined the character of the major part of peasant earnings; they introduced technical improvements and brought machines into use. Even the dying feudal system of economy—the provision of land to the peasants in return for labour service—underwent a bourgeois transformation due to competition among the peasants; this led to a worsening of the position of tenants, to severer conditions,* and, consequently, to a decline in the number of workers. In peasant economy the splitting up of the peasantry into a village bourgeoisie and proletariat was quite clearly revealed. The "rich" extended their tillage, improved their farms [cf. V. V., *Progressive Trends in Peasant Farming*] and were compelled to resort to wage-labour. All these are long established, generally recognised facts which (as we shall see in a moment) are referred to by Mr. Struve himself. Let us take as a further example the following

* See, for example, Karyshev (*Results of Zemstvo Statistical Investigations*, Vol. II, p. 266)—reference in the Rostov-on-Don Uyezd Abstract to the gradual reduction in the peasant's share in *skopshchina*.[185] Ibid. Chapter V, § 9—additional payments made in the form of labour by peasants engaged in share-cropping.

case, a usual one in the Russian village: a "kulak" has wrested the best slice of allotment land from the "village community," or more exactly, community members of the proletarian type, and is farming it with the labour and the implements of the very same "allotment-provided" peasants who have become enmeshed in debts and obligations and are tied to their benefactor—for social mutual adaptation and common action—by the strength of the community principles beloved of the Narodniks. His farm is better run, of course, than those of the ruined peasants, and far fewer workers are required than when this slice of land was held by several small peasant farmers. No Narodnik can deny that these are not isolated but common facts. Their theories are exceptionalist only in their refusal to call facts by their real name, in their refusal to see that these facts signify the *domination of capital in agriculture.* They forget that the initial form of *capital* has always and everywhere been merchant's, money capital, that capital always takes the technical process of production as it finds it, and only subsequently subjects it to technical transformation. They therefore do not see that by "upholding" (in words, of course—no more than that) the contemporary agricultural order against "oncoming" (?!) capitalism, they are merely upholding *medieval* forms of capital against the onslaught of its latest, purely bourgeois forms.

Thus, one cannot deny the capitalist character of overpopulation in Russia, just as one cannot deny the domination of capital in agriculture. But it is quite ridiculous, of course, to ignore the *degree of the development of capital,* as Mr. N. —on does; in his enthusiasm he presents it as almost completed and for that reason concocts a theory about the contraction or the absence of the home market, whereas actually, though capital is dominant, it is in a relatively very undeveloped form; there are still many intermediate phases before it reaches full development, before the producer is completely divorced from the means of production, and every step forward by agricultural capitalism means a *growth* of the home market, which, according to Marx's theory, is created precisely by agricultural capitalism—and which in Russia is not contracting, but, on the contrary, is taking shape and developing.

Further, we see from this albeit very general description of our agricultural capitalism* that it does not embrace *all* social-economic relations in the countryside. Alongside of it we still see feudal relations—in both the economic sphere (e.g., the leasing of cut-off lands in return for labour service and payments in kind—here you have all the features of feudal economy: the natural "exchange of services" between the producer and the owner of the means of production, and the exploitation of the producer by *tying* him to the land, and not separating him from the means of production), and still more in the social and the juridical-political sphere (compulsory "provision of allotment," tying to the land, i.e., absence of freedom of movement, payment of redemption money, i.e., the same quitrent paid to the landlord, subordination to the privileged landowners in the courts and administration, etc.); these relations also undoubtedly lead to the ruin of the peasants and to unemployment, an "over-population" of farm labourers tied to the land. The capitalist basis of contemporary relations should not hide these still powerful relics of the "old-nobility" stratum which have *not yet been destroyed* by capitalism precisely because it is undeveloped. The undeveloped condition of capitalism, "Russia's backwardness," considered by the Narodniks to be "good fortune,"** is only "good fortune" for the titled exploiters. Contemporary "over-population," consequently, contains feudal in addition to its basic capitalist features.

If we compare this latter thesis with Mr. Struve's thesis that "over-population" contains natural-economic features and commodity-economic features, we shall see that the former do not rule out the latter, but, on the contrary, are included in them: serfdom relates to "natural-economic," and capitalism to "commodity-economic" phenomena. Mr. Struve's thesis, on the one hand, does not exactly indicate precisely which *relations* are natural-economic and which commodity-economic, and, on the other hand, leads us back to the unfounded and meaningless "laws" of Malthus.

* It will be dealt with in greater detail further on, taking the peasants and the landlords separately.

** Mr. Yuzhakov in *Russkoye Bogatstvo*.

These defects naturally gave rise to the unsatisfactory character of the following passage. "In what way," asks the author, "on what basis *can* our national economy be reorganised?" (202) A strange question, formulated again in a very professorial style, precisely as Messrs. the Narodniks are accustomed to put questions when they proclaim the unsatisfactory character of the present situation and select the best paths for the fatherland. "Our national economy" is a capitalist economy, the organisation and "reorganisation" of which is determined by the bourgeoisie, who "manage" this economy. Instead of the question of possible reorganisation, what should have been put is the question of the successive stages of the development of this bourgeois economy; and it should have been put from the viewpoint of precisely that theory in whose name the author so splendidly replies to Mr. V. V., who describes Mr. N. —on as an "undoubted Marxist," that this "undoubted Marxist" has no idea of the class struggle and of the class origin of the state. Had the author altered the manner of posing the question in the sense indicated it would have saved him from the confused arguments about the "peasantry" that we read on pages 202-04.

The author begins with the statement that the peasantry have insufficient allotment land, that even if they cover this insufficiency by renting land, "a considerable part of them" nevertheless *always* have a deficit; one cannot talk of the peasantry as a whole, for that means to talk of a fiction* (p. 203). And the conclusion directly drawn from this is:

"In any case, insufficient production is the *basic and dominating* fact of our national economy" (p. 204). This is quite unfounded and totally unconnected with what was said earlier: why is not the fact that the peasantry as one whole is a fiction, because antagonistic classes are taking shape within it, made the "basic and dominating fact"? The author draws his conclusion without any data, without any analysis of the facts relating to "insufficient production" [which, however, does not prevent a minority from becoming affluent at the expense of the majority], or to the splitting up

* "The main defect of Mr. Golubev's arguments in his fine articles is that he cannot rid himself of this fiction" (203).

of the peasantry—simply due to some prejudice in favour of Malthusianism. "Therefore," he continues, "an increase in the productivity of agricultural labour is a plain benefit and blessing to the Russian peasantry" (204). We are at a loss: the author has only just advanced against the Narodniks the serious (and to the highest degree legitimate) accusation of arguing about a "fiction"—the "peasantry" in general—and now he himself introduces this fiction into his analysis! If the relations within the ranks of this "peasantry" are such that a minority become "economically strong," while the majority become proletarians, if a minority expand their landownership and wax rich, while the majority always have a deficit and become ruined, how can one speak of the process in general being a "benefit and blessing"? Very likely the author wanted to say that the process is of benefit to both the one and the other section of the peasantry. But then, firstly, he should have examined the position of each group and have investigated it separately, and, secondly, in view of the antagonism existing between the groups he should have definitely established from *which* group's viewpoint reference is made to the "benefit and blessing." This example goes to confirm over and over again the unsatisfactory and incomplete character of Mr. Struve's objectivism.

Since Mr. N. —on holds an opposite view on this subject and asserts that an "increase in the productivity of agricultural labour* cannot serve to raise the national well-being if the goods are produced as commodities" (*Sketches*, p. 266), Mr. Struve now proceeds to refute this opinion.

Firstly, he says, the peasant who has been hit by the full weight of the contemporary crisis, produces grain for his own consumption; he does not sell grain, but buys extra supplies of it. For such peasants—and they constitute as much as 50% (one-horse and horseless) and certainly not less than 25% (horseless)—increased labour productivity is at any rate beneficial, despite the drop in the price of grain.

Yes, of course, an increase in productivity would be beneficial to such a peasant, if he could retain his farm and

* "However desirable and necessary" it "may be," adds Mr. N. —on.

raise it to a higher level. But the trouble is that the one-horse and horseless peasants do not enjoy these conditions. They are not able to retain their present farms, with their primitive implements, careless cultivation of the soil, etc., let alone improve their farming technique. Technical improvement is the result of the growth of commodity economy. And if, at the present stage of the development of commodity economy, even those peasants who have to buy extra supplies for themselves find it necessary to sell grain, then, at the following stage, such sales will be still more essential (the author himself recognises the need for a transition from natural to commodity economy), and the competition of peasants who have improved their farming methods will inevitably and immediately expropriate proletarians who are tied to the land and turn them into proletarians who are as free as birds. I have no wish to say that such a change will be of no benefit *to them*. On the contrary, once the producer has fallen into the clutches of capital—and this is an undoubtedly accomplished fact as regards the group of the peasantry under examination—complete freedom, which enables him to change masters, and gives him a free hand, is very much of "a benefit and a blessing" to him. But the controversy between Messrs. Struve and N.—on is not at all conducted around *such* considerations.

Secondly, continues Mr. Struve, Mr. N.—on "forgets that an increase in the productivity of agricultural labour is only possible by effecting changes in the *technique* and in the *system* of farming or crop growing" (206). Certainly, Mr. N.—on forgets that, but this consideration merely strengthens the thesis of the inevitability of the total expropriation of the economically weak peasants, the "proletarian type" of peasants. To effect technical improvements money resources must be available, but these peasants do not even possess enough food resources.

Thirdly, concludes the author, Mr. N.—on is wrong in asserting that a rise in the productivity of agricultural labour will compel competitors to lower prices. For such a price reduction—Mr. Struve rightly remarks—it is necessary that the productivity of our agricultural labour should not only catch up with that of Western Europe [in that case we shall sell produce at the level of socially necessary labour], but even outstrip it. That objection is quite a sound one, but it tells us nothing whatever about which particular section of the "peasantry" will benefit from this technical improvement and why.

"In general, Mr. N. —on has no reason to fear an increase in the productivity of agricultural labour" (207). He does so, in Mr. Struve's view, because he cannot imagine agricultural progress except as the progress of extensive agriculture, accompanied by the ever-increasing elimination of workers by machines.

The author very aptly describes Mr. N. —on's attitude to the growth of agricultural technique with the word "fear"; he is quite right in saying that this fear is absurd. But his line of argument does not, we think, touch the basic error of Mr. N. —on.

While Mr. N. —on apparently adheres to the strict letter of the doctrine of Marxism, he none the less draws a sharp distinction between the capitalist evolution of agriculture and the evolution of manufacturing industry in capitalist society, the distinction being that he recognises the progressive work of capitalism with regard to the latter—the socialisation of labour—and does not do so with regard to the former. That is why he "does not fear" an increase in the productivity of labour with regard to manufacturing industry, but "does fear" it as regards agriculture, *although the social-economic aspect of the matter and the reflection of this process on the different classes of society are exactly the same in both cases*.... Marx expressed this point very strikingly in the following remark: "Philanthropic English economists, like Mill, Rogers, Goldwin Smith, Fawcett, etc., and liberal manufacturers like John Bright and Co., ask the English landed proprietors, as God asked Cain after Abel, where are our thousands of freeholders gone? But where do *you* come from, then? From the destruction of those freeholders. Why don't you ask further, where are the independent weavers, spinners, and artisans gone?" (*Das Kapital*, I, S. 780, Anm. 237.)[136] The last sentence clearly identifies the fate of the small producers in agriculture with the fate of those in manufacturing industry, and emphasises the formation of the classes of bourgeois society in both cases.* Mr. N.—on's chief error lies precisely in the fact that he ignores these classes, their formation among our peasantry, and does not set himself the aim of following, with the utmost precision, every successive stage in the development of the antithesis between these classes.

But Mr. Struve deals with the problem quite differently. Far from correcting the error of Mr. N.—on that we have mentioned, he *himself repeats it*, arguing from the viewpoint of a professor standing *above* classes about the "benefit" of progress to the "peasantry." This attempt to rise above classes leads the author to extreme haziness in stating his points, a haziness so great that the following bourgeois conclusions may be drawn from them: in opposition to the undoubtedly correct thesis that capitalism in agriculture (as capitalism in industry) worsens the conditions of the producer, he advances the thesis of the "benefit" of these changes *in general*. This is the same as if someone were to argue about machines in bourgeois society and refute the romantic economist's theory that they worsen the conditions of the working people by proofs of the "benefit and blessing" of progress in general.

In reply to Mr. Struve's view the Narodnik will very likely say: what Mr. N.—on fears is not increased productivity of labour, but bourgeoisdom.

There is no doubt that technical progress in agriculture under our capitalist system is connected with bourgeoisdom, but the "fear" displayed by the Narodniks is, of course, quite absurd. Bourgeoisdom is a fact of actual life, labour is subordinated to capital in agriculture too, and what is to be "feared" is not bourgeoisdom, but the producer's lack of consciousness of this bourgeoisdom, his inability to defend his interests against it. That is why it is not the retardation of the development of capitalism that is to be desired, but on the contrary, its full development, its thorough development.

To show with as great detail and precision as possible the basis of the error committed by Mr. Struve in treating agriculture in capitalist society, let us try to depict (in

---

* See particularly § 4 of Chapter XXIV: "Genesis of the Capitalist Farmer." Pp. 773-76.[137]

the most general outline) the process of the formation of classes together with the technical changes that gave grounds for the argument. In this connection Mr. Struve distinguishes strictly extensive agriculture and intensive, seeing the root of Mr. N. —on's misapprehensions in his refusal to recognise anything but extensive agriculture. We shall endeavour to prove that Mr. N. —on's *chief* error lies not in this, and that as agriculture becomes intensive the formation of the classes of bourgeois society is essentially identical with that taking place as extensive agriculture develops.

There is no need to say much about extensive agriculture, because Mr. Struve also admits that here the "peasantry" are ousted by the bourgeoisie. Let us merely note two points. Firstly, technical progress is evoked by commodity economy; to bring it about the proprietor must have free, surplus *monetary* resources [surplus in relation to his consumption and the reproduction of his means of production]. Where can these resources be got? Obviously from no other source than the conversion of the cycle: commodity—money—commodity into the cycle: money—commodity—money with a surplus. In other words, these resources can be got exclusively from capital, *from merchant's and usury capital*, from the same "welshers, kulaks, merchants," etc., whom the naïve Russian Narodniks assign *not* to capitalism *but* to "rapacity" (as though capitalism is not rapacity! as though Russian reality does not show us the interconnection of all possible varieties of this "rapacity"—from the most primitive and primeval kulakdom to the very latest, rational enterprise!)* Secondly, let us note Mr. N. —on's strange

* Messrs. the Narodniks have another, very profound, method of covering up the roots of our industrial capitalism in "people's production," i.e., in "people's" usury and kulakdom. The kulak takes his "savings" to the state bank; his deposits enable the bank, by basing itself on the growth of the people's wealth, people's savings, people's enterprise, people's solvency, to borrow money from the Englishman. The "state" directs the borrowed money to the aid of ...—what a short-sighted policy! what deplorable ignoring of "modern science" and "modern moral ideas"!—*...the capitalists.* The question now arises: is it not clear that if the state directed this money (of the capitalists) not to capitalism but to "people's production," -- we here in Russia would have not capitalism but "people's production"!

attitude to this question. In the second note to page 233 he refutes V. Y. Postnikov, author of *Peasant Farming in South Russia*, who points out that machines have exactly doubled the working area of the peasant household, from 10 to 20 dessiatines per worker, and that for that reason the cause of "Russia's poverty" is "the small size of the peasant farm." In other words, technical progress in bourgeois society leads to the expropriation of the small and backward farms. Mr. N. —on objects: tomorrow technique may raise the working area three times over. Then the 60-dessiatine farms will have to be turned into 200- and 300-dessiatine farms. Such an argument against the thesis of our agriculture being bourgeois is as ridiculous as somebody setting out to prove the weakness and impotence of factory capitalism on the grounds that the steam-engine of today will have to be replaced "tomorrow" by the electric motor. "Nor is it known where the millions of released labourers get to"—adds Mr. N. —on, who sets himself up as judge of the bourgeoisie and forgets that the producer himself is the only one to judge them. The formation of a reserve army of unemployed is just as necessary a result of the use of machinery in bourgeois agriculture as in bourgeois industry.

And so, with regard to the development of extensive agriculture there is no doubt that technical progress under commodity economy leads to the transformation of the "peasant" into a capitalist farmer, on the one hand (understanding by farmer the entrepreneur, the capitalist in agriculture), and a farm labourer or day labourer, on the other. Let us now examine the case where extensive agriculture becomes intensive. It is from this process that Mr. Struve expects "benefit" for the "peasant." To prevent any argument about the suitability of the material we are using to describe this transition, let us make use of Mr. A. I. Skvortsov's* *The Influence of Steam Transport on*

* It is customary in our literature to regard him as a Marxist. There is just as little grounds for that as there is for placing Mr. N. —on among the Marxists. Mr. A. Skvortsov is also unacquainted with the theory of the class struggle and the class character of the state. His practical proposals in his *Economic Studies* are no different from ordinary bourgeois proposals. He takes a far more sober view of Rus-

Agriculture, who has earned such boundless praise from Mr. Struve.

In Chapter 3 of the fourth section of his book, Mr. A. Skvortsov examines the "change in agricultural technique under the influence of steam transport" in countries employing extensive and intensive farming. Let us take his description of this change in the *thickly-populated extensive countries*. One might think that central European Russia would fit into that category. Mr. Skvortsov foresees for such a country the changes that, in Mr. Struve's opinion, will inevitably take place in Russia too, namely, transformation into a country of intensive agriculture with developed factory production.

Let us follow Mr. A. Skvortsov (§§ 4-7, pp. 440-51).

A country of extensive* agriculture. A very considerable part of the population is engaged in agriculture. Uniformity of occupation leads to the absence of a market. The population is poor, firstly, because of the small size of the farms and, secondly, because of the absence of exchange: "requirements other than food, which is raised by the agriculturist himself, are satisfied exclusively, it can be said, by the products of primitive artisan establishments, known as handicraft industry in Russia."

The building of a railway raises the price of agricultural produce and, consequently, increases the purchasing power of the population. "Together with the railway the country is flooded with the cheap products of the manufactories and mills," which ruin the local handicraftsmen. This is the first cause of the "collapse of many farms."

The second cause of the collapse is crop failures. "Agriculture has also been conducted hitherto in a primitive

---

sian reality than Messrs. the Narodniks do, but then on those grounds *alone* B. Chicherin and many others should also be regarded as Marxists.

* Mr. A. Skvortsov points out that by a country employing extensive agriculture a thinly-populated one is usually understood (footnote to page 439). He considers this a wrong definition and gives the following as the features of extensive farming: 1) considerable harvest fluctuations; 2) homogeneity of crops and 3) absence of home markets, i.e., of big towns where manufacturing industry is concentrated.

fashion, i.e., always in an irrational way and, consequently, harvest failures are no rare occurrence, but with the building of the railway line the rise in the price of the product, that formerly resulted from crop failure, either does not take place at all or in any case is considerably smaller. That is why the natural consequence of the very first crop failure is usually the collapse of many farms. The smaller the surpluses left from normal harvests and the more the population have had to count on earnings from handicraft industries, the more rapidly the collapse occurs."

In order to manage without handicraft industries and to guarantee oneself against crop failures by going over to intensive (rational) agriculture, the following are necessary: firstly, big monetary surpluses (from the sale of agricultural produce at higher prices), and, secondly, the intellectual force of the population, without which no increased rationality and intensity is possible. The mass of the population do not, of course, enjoy these conditions: they apply to a minority only.*

"The surplus population thus formed" [i.e., as a result of the "liquidation" of many farms ruined by the failure of handicraft industries and by the greater demands on agriculture] "will partly be swallowed up by the farms that emerge from this situation more happily and that are able to increase the intensity of production" (i.e., of course they will be "swallowed up" as wage-workers, farm labourers and day labourers. Mr. A. Skvortsov does not say that, maybe because he considers it too obvious). A great expenditure of human energy will be required, since the proximity of the market brought about by improved communications makes it possible to raise perishable produce, and "the latter, in most cases, entails a considerable expenditure of manpower." "Usually, however," continues Mr. Skvortsov, "the process of destruction proceeds much more rapidly than the process of improving the surviving farms, and part of the ruined peasants have to move, at least to the towns, if not right out of the country. It is this part that has con-

* "For such a country (with a population dense for the given level of economic efficiency) we must assume that, on the one hand, small surpluses, and, on the other, the population's low educational level, force many farms into liquidation under the changed conditions" (442).

stituted the main contingent added to the population of European cities since the railways were built."

Further. "Surplus population means cheap hands." "The soil being fertile (and the climate favourable ...) all the conditions are created for the cultivation of plants and in general of raising agricultural produce that requires a large expenditure of labour-power per land unit" (443), especially since the small size of the farms ("although they will perhaps increase as compared with their former size") makes the introduction of machines difficult. "In addition to this, fixed capital will not remain unchanged, and first and foremost it is farm implements that will change their character." And apart from machines "the need for better cultivation of the soil will lead to the replacement of the former primitive implements by more up-to-date ones, and of wood by iron and steel. This transformation will lead of necessity to the establishment here of factories engaged in the production of such implements, for they cannot be produced even tolerably well by handicraft methods." The development of this branch of industry is favoured by the following conditions: 1) the need to get a machine or part of it rapidly; 2) "hands are here in abundance, and they are cheap"; 3) fuel, buildings and land are cheap; 4) "the small size of the economic units leads to an increased demand for implements, for it is well known that small farms require relatively more equipment." Other kinds of industries also develop. "In general there is a development of urban life." There is a development, out of necessity, of *mining industries*, "since, on the one hand, a mass of free hands is available and, on the other, thanks to the railways and the development of the mechanised manufacturing and other industries there is an increased demand for the products of the mining industry.

"Thus, such a district, which before the railway was built was thickly populated and whose agriculture was extensive, turns more or less quickly into a district of very intensive agriculture with more or less developed factory production." Increased intensity is manifested by the change in the system of crop raising. The three-field system is impossible because of harvest fluctuations. A transition has to be made to a "crop rotation system," which does away with harvest fluctuations. Of course, the *complete crop rotation system*,* which requires a very high level of intensity, cannot be introduced immediately. At first, therefore, *grain crop rotation* [proper succession of crops] is introduced; cattle-raising, and the *planting of fodder crops* are developed.

"Finally, therefore, our thickly-populated extensive farming district turns more or less rapidly, as railways develop, into one of highly intensive farming, and its intensity, as has been said, will grow primarily on account of an increase in variable capital."

This detailed description of the process of development of intensive farming shows clearly that in this case, too, technical progress under commodity production leads to bourgeois economy, splits the direct producers into the *farmer*, who enjoys all the advantages of intensive farming, improvement of implements, etc., and the *worker*, who with his "freedom" and his "cheapness" provides the most "favourable conditions" for the "progressive development of the entire national economy."

Mr. N. —on's chief error is not that he ignores intensive agriculture and confines himself to extensive agriculture, but his vapid lamentations about "us" going the wrong way to which he treats the reader, instead of analysing the class contradictions in the sphere of Russian agricultural production. Mr. Struve repeats this error by obscuring the class contradictions with "objective" arguments, and only corrects Mr. N. —on's secondary errors. It is all the more strange since he himself quite rightly chides this "undoubted Marxist" with failing to understand the theory of the class struggle. It is all the more regrettable since Mr. Struve, by that error, weakens the force of his quite correct idea that "fear" of technical progress in agriculture is absurd.

To finish with this problem of capitalism in agriculture, let us sum up what has been said. How does Mr. Struve pose the problem? He starts out from the a priori, unfounded explanation of over-population being the result of population increases not conforming to the means of subsistence;

* Its distinctive features are: 1) all the land is put under the plough; 2) fallow is eliminated as far as possible; 3) there is a regular succession of crops in the rotation; 4) cultivation is as thorough as possible; 5) cattle are kept in stalls.

then he points out that the production of food by our peasant is "inadequate," and settles the problem by arguing that technical progress is beneficial to the "peasantry," and that "agricultural productivity must be raised" (211). How should he have presented the problem had he been "bound by the doctrine" of Marxism? He should have *begun* with an analysis of the given production relations in Russian agriculture, and, after showing that the oppression of the producer is to be explained not by chance or by politics but by the domination of *capital*, which necessarily comes into being on the basis of commodity economy—he should then have shown how this capital destroys small production and what forms class contradictions assume in the process. He should then have shown how further development leads to capital growing from merchant's into industrial (assuming such and such forms under extensive farming, and such and such under intensive), developing and accentuating the class contradiction whose basis was firmly laid under its old form, and once and for all opposing "free" labour to "rational" production. It would then have been sufficient simply to contrast these two successive forms of bourgeois production and bourgeois exploitation, in order that the "progressive" character of the change, its "advantage" to the producer should be quite evident: in the first case the subordination of labour to capital is covered up by thousands of the remnants of medieval relations, which prevent the producer from seeing the essence of the matter and arouse in his ideologist's mind absurd and reactionary ideas about the possibility of expecting aid from "society," *etc.*; in the second case this subordination is quite free of medieval fetters, and the producer is enabled to engage in and understands the necessity for independent, conscious activity against his "antipode." Instead of arguments about a "difficult and painful transition" to capitalism we would have had a theory that not only spoke of class contradictions but also really disclosed them in each form of "irrational" and "rational" production, and of "extensive" and "intensive" farming.

The results we reach from our examination of the first part of Chapter VI of Mr. Struve's book, which is devoted to the "character of over-population in agrarian Russia," can be formulated as follows: 1) Mr. Struve's Malthusianism is not supported by any factual data and is based on methodologically incorrect and dogmatic postulates. 2) Over-population in agrarian Russia is explained by the domination of capital and not by a lack of conformity between the increase in the population and the means of subsistence. 3) Mr. Struve's thesis about the natural-economic character of over-population is only true in the sense that the survival of feudal relations holds back agricultural capital in forms that are undeveloped and are therefore particularly hard for the producer. 4) Mr. N. —on did not prove the capitalist character of over-population in Russia because he did not investigate the domination of capital in agriculture. 5) Mr. N. —on's main error, repeated by Mr. Struve, is that he did not analyse the classes that come into being where bourgeois agriculture develops. 6) This ignoring of class contradictions by Mr. Struve naturally led to the fact that the quite correct thesis of the progressiveness and desirability of technical improvements was expressed in an extremely vague and unsatisfactory form.

II

Let us now pass to the second part of Chapter VI, which is devoted to the problem of the break-up of the peasantry. This part is directly and immediately connected with the previous part, and serves as additional material on the problem of capitalism in agriculture.

Indicating the rise in the prices of agricultural produce during the first 20 years following the Reform, and to the extension of commodity production in agriculture, Mr. Struve quite rightly says that "in the main it was the landowners and prosperous peasants who benefited" from it (214). "Differentiation among the peasant population had to increase, and its first successes relate to this epoch." The author cites the remarks of local investigators to the effect that the building of railway lines merely raised the living standard of the prosperous part of the peasantry, that the renting of land gives rise to a "regular battle" among the peasants, which always leads to the victory of the economically strong elements (216-17). He cites V. Postnikov's research, according to which the farms of the prosperous peasants are already so far subordinated to the market that 40% of the sown area yields produce for sale, and, adding that at the opposite pole the peasants "lose their economic independence and, by selling their labour-power, are on the verge of becoming farm labourers," rightly concludes: "Only the penetration of exchange economy explains the fact that the economically strong peasant farms can derive benefit from the ruin of the weak households" (223). "The development of money economy and the growth of the population," says the author, "lead to the peasantry splitting into two parts: one that is economically strong and consists of representatives of a new force, of capital in all its forms and stages, and the other, consisting of semi-independent peasants and real farm labourers" (239).

Brief as they are, the author's remarks on this "differentiation" nevertheless enable us to note the following important features of the process under examination: 1) It is not confined just to the creation of property inequality: a "new force" is created—*capital*. 2) The creation of this new force is accompanied by the creation of new types of peasant farms: firstly, of a prosperous, economically strong type that engages in developed commodity economy, crowds out the peasant poor in the renting of land, and resorts to the exploitation of the labour of others;* secondly, of a "proletarian" peasantry, who sell their labour-power to capital. 3) All these phenomena have grown directly and immediately on the basis of commodity production. Mr. Struve himself has pointed out that without commodity production they were impossible, but with its penetration into the countryside they became necessary. 4) These phenomena (the "new force," the new types of peasantry) relate to the sphere of *production*, and are not confined to the sphere of exchange, commodity circulation: capital is manifested in agricultural *production*; the same is true of the sale of labour-power.

* Mr. Struve makes no mention of this feature. It is also expressed in the use of wage-labour, which plays no small part on the farms of the prosperous peasants, and in the operations of the usury and merchant's capital in their hands, which likewise deprives the producer of surplus-value. In the absence of this feature we cannot speak of "capital."

It would seem that these features of the process are a direct indication that we have to do with a purely capitalist phenomenon, that the *classes* typical of capitalist society, bourgeoisie and proletariat, are taking shape within the peasantry. Moreover, these facts bear witness not only to the domination of capital in agriculture, but also to capital having already taken a second step, if one may put it that way. From merchant's it turns into industrial capital, from a dominant force on the market into a dominant force in production; the class antithesis between the rich buyer-up and the poor peasant turns into the antithesis between the rational bourgeois employer and the free seller of free hands.

Even here Mr. Struve cannot get along without his Malthusianism; in his view only *one side* of the matter finds expression in the process mentioned ("only the progressive side"), but in addition to it he sees another, the "technical irrationality of all peasant economy": "in it expression is given, so to speak, to the retrogressive side of the whole process," it "levels" the peasantry, smooths out inequality, operating "in connection with the growth of the population" (223-24).

The only thing that is clear in this rather hazy argument is that the author prefers extremely abstract propositions to concrete statements, that he tacks on to everything the "law" that increases in population conform to the means of subsistence. I say "tacks on" because, even if we confine ourselves strictly to the facts cited by the author himself, we can find no indication of any concrete features of the process that do not fit in with the "doctrine" of Marxism and that require the recognition of Malthusianism. Let us go over this process once again: we start with natural producers, peasants more or less of one type.* The penetration of commodity production into the countryside makes the wealth of the individual peasant household dependent on the market, thus

---

* *Working for the landlord*. This aspect is set aside, in order that the transition from natural to commodity economy may stand out in greater relief. It has already been said that the remnants of the "old-nobility" relations worsen the conditions of the producers and make their ruin particularly onerous.

creating inequality by means of market fluctuations and accentuating it by concentrating free money in the hands of some, and ruining others. This money naturally serves for the exploitation of the propertyless, turns into capital. Capital can exploit peasants in the grip of ruin as long as they retain their farms, and, letting them carry on as before, on the old, technically irrational basis, can exploit them by purchasing the product of their labour. But the peasant's ruin finally develops to such a degree that he is compelled to give up his farm altogether: he can no longer sell the product of his labour; all he can do is to sell his labour. Capital then takes charge of the farm, and is now compelled, by virtue of competition, to organise it on rational lines; it is enabled to do so thanks to the free monetary resources previously "saved"; capital no longer exploits the peasant farmer but a farm labourer or a day labourer. One can well ask: what are the two sides the author finds in this process? How does he find it possible to draw the monstrous Malthusian conclusion that "the technical irrationality of the farm, and not capitalism" [note the "and not"] "is the enemy that deprives our peasantry of their daily bread" (224). As though this daily bread ever went in its entirety to the producer, and was not divided into the necessary product and the surplus, the latter being acquired by the landlord, the kulak, the "strong" peasant, the capitalist!

One must, however, add that on the question of "levelling" the author gives some further explanation. He says that the "result of the levelling referred to above" is the "*decline* or *even the disappearance of the middle section of the peasant population* noted in many places" (225). Citing a passage from a Zemstvo publication which notes "a still greater increase in the distance separating the rural rich from the landless and horseless proletariat," he concludes: "The *levelling* in the present case is, of course, at the same time *differentiation*, but on the basis of *such* differentiation only *bondage* develops, which can be nothing more than a brake on economic progress" (226). And so it now turns out that the differentiation created by commodity economy should not be contrasted to "levelling," but to differentiation as well, only differentiation *of another kind*, namely, bondage. But since bondage is a "brake" on "economic progress," the author calls this "side" "regressive."

The argument is based on extremely strange methods that are not Marxist at all. A comparison is made between "bondage" and "differentiation" as between two independent, special "systems"; one is praised for assisting "progress"; the other is condemned for being a brake on progress. What has become of Mr. Struve's demand for an analysis of class contradictions, for lack of which he so rightly attacked Mr. N. —on; of the theory of the "spontaneous process" of which he spoke so well? Why, this bondage which he has now demolished as retrogressive is nothing but the initial manifestation of capitalism in agriculture, of that very same capitalism which leads later to sweeping technical progress. And what, indeed, is bondage? It is the dependence of the peasant who owns his means of production, and is compelled to work for the market, on the owner of money—a dependence that, however differently it may express itself (whether in the form of usury capital or of the capital of the buyer-up, who monopolises marketing)—always leads to an enormous part of the product of labour falling into the hands of the owner of money and not of the producer. Hence, it is purely capitalist in essence,* and the entire peculiarity consists in the fact that this initial, embryonic form of capitalist relations is totally enmeshed in the feudal relations of former times: here there is no free contract, but a forced deal (sometimes by order of "those at the top," sometimes by the desire to keep their undertakings, sometimes by old debts, etc.); the producer is here tied to a definite place and to a definite exploiter: as against the impersonal charac-

* All the features are here present: commodity production as the basis; monopoly of the product of social labour in the form of money as the result; the turning of this money into capital. I do not in the least forget that in some cases these initial forms of *capital* were encountered even before the capitalist system came into being. The point, however, is that in contemporary Russian peasant economy they are not isolated cases but the rule, the dominant system of relations. They have now linked up (through commercial deals and the banks) with large-scale factory machine capitalism and have thereby shown their tendency; they have shown that the representatives of this "bondage" are merely rank-and-file soldiers of the army of the bourgeoisie, one and indivisible.

ter of the commodity deal that is peculiar to purely capitalist relations, here the deal always has the personal character of "aid," "benefaction,"—and this character of the deal inevitably places the producer in a position of personal, semi-feudal dependence. Such of the author's expressions as "levelling," "brake on progress," "regression," mean nothing but that capital first takes hold of production on the old basis, and subordinates the technically backward producer. The author's remark that the presence of capitalism does not entitle us "to blame it for all misfortunes" is true in the sense that our peasant who works for others suffers not only from capitalism, but also from the insufficient development of capitalism. In other words, among the huge mass of the peasantry there are now practically none who produce independently for themselves; in addition to work for "rational" bourgeois farmers we only see work for the owners of money capital, i.e., also capitalist exploitation, but exploitation which is undeveloped and primitive, and because of this it, firstly, worsens the conditions of the labouring peasant tenfold, involving him in a network of specific and additional encumbrances, and, secondly, prevents him (and his ideologist, the Narodnik) from understanding the class character of the "annoyances" inflicted on him and from regulating his activities in accordance with this character of the annoyances. Consequently, the "progressive side" of "differentiation" (to use the language of Mr. Struve), is that it brings into the light of day the contradiction hidden behind the bondage and deprives the former of its "old-nobility" features. Narodism, which stands for levelling out the peasants (before ... the kulak), is "regressive" because it desires to keep capital within those medieval forms that combine exploitation with scattered, technically backward production and with personal pressure on the producer. In both cases (in the case of "bondage" and of "differentiation") the cause of oppression is *capitalism* and the author's statements to the contrary, that it is "not capitalism" but "technical irrationality," that "it is not capitalism that is to blame for the poverty of the peasants," etc., merely show that Mr. Struve has been carried too far in his support of the correct idea that developed capitalism is to be preferred to undeveloped, and as a result of the abstractness of his propositions he has contrasted the former to the latter not as two successive stages of the development of the given phenomenon, but as two separate cases.*

III

The author also lets himself get carried away in the following argument, when he says that it is not large-scale capitalism which causes the ruin of the peasantry. He enters here into a controversy with Mr. N.—on.

The cheap production of manufactured goods, says Mr. N.—on, speaking of factory-made clothing, has caused a reduction in their domestic production (p. 227 of Mr. Struve's book).

"Here the cart is put before the horse," exclaims Mr. Struve, "as can be proved without difficulty. The reduction in the peasant output of spinning materials led to an increase in the production and consumption of the goods of the capitalist cotton industry, and not the other way round" (227).

The author hardly puts the issue properly, hiding the essence of the matter under details of secondary importance. If we start from the fact of the development of factory industry (and Mr. N.—on makes precisely the observation of that fact his starting-point), we cannot deny that the cheapness of factory goods also speeds up the growth of commodity economy, speeds up the ousting of home-made goods. By objecting to this statement of Mr. N.—on's, Mr. Struve merely weakens his argument against that author, whose main error is that he tries to present the "factory" as something isolated from the "peasantry," as something that has come down upon them accidentally, from outside, whereas, in fact, the "factory" (both according to the theory that Mr. N.—on desires loyally to support, and according to

* On what grounds, the reader will possibly ask, does this relate only to Mr. Struve's being *carried away*? On the ground that the author quite definitely recognises capitalism to be the main background against which all the phenomena described take place. He quite clearly pointed to the rapid growth of commodity economy, to the splitting-up of the peasantry, and to the "spread of improved implements" (245), etc., on the one hand—and to the "separation of the peasants from the land, the creation of a rural proletariat" (238), on the other. He himself, finally, characterised it as the creation of a new force—*capital*, and noted the decisive importance of the appearance of the capitalist between the producer and the consumer.

the data of Russian history) is merely the final stage of the development of the commodity organisation of the entire social and, consequently, peasant economy. Large-scale bourgeois production in the "factory" is the direct and immediate continuation of petty-bourgeois production in the village, in the notorious "village community" or in handicraft industry. "In order that the 'factory form' should become 'cheaper,'" Mr. Struve quite rightly says, "the peasant has to adopt the viewpoint of economic rationality, on condition that money economy exists." "If the peasantry had adhered to ... natural economy ... no textile fabrics ... would have tempted them."

In other words, the "factory form" is nothing more than *developed* commodity production, and it developed from the *undeveloped* commodity production of peasant and handicraft economy. The author wishes to prove to Mr. N. —on that the "factory" and the "peasantry" are interconnected, that the economic "principles" of their organisation are not contradictory,* but identical. To do that he should have reduced the problem to that of peasant economic organisation, and opposed Mr. N. —on by the thesis that our small producer (the peasant-agriculturist and the handicraftsman) is a petty bourgeois. By posing the problem that way he would have transferred it from the sphere of arguments on what "should" be, what "may" be, etc., into the sphere of explaining *what is*, and *why it is that way, and not otherwise*. To refute this thesis the Narodniks would have either to deny generally-known and undoubted facts about the growth of commodity economy and the splitting-up of the peasantry [*and these facts prove* the petty-bourgeois character of the peasantry], or else to deny the elementary truths of political economy. To accept this thesis would mean to admit the absurdity of contrasting "capitalism" to the "people's system," to admit the reactionary character of schemes to "seek different paths for the fatherland" and address requests for "socialisation" to bourgeois "society" or to a "state" that is still half "old-nobility" in character.

* The Narodniks said this openly and directly, but the "undoubted Marxist," Mr. N. —on, presents this same nonsense in vague phrases about a "people's system" and "people's production" garnished with quotations from Marx.

Instead, however, of beginning at the beginning,* Mr. Struve begins at the end: "We reject," says he, "one of the most fundamental postulates of the Narodnik theory of Russia's economic development, the postulate that the development of large-scale manufacturing industry ruins the peasant agriculturist" (246). Now that means, as the Germans say, to throw out the baby with the bath water! "The development of large-scale manufacturing industry" means and expresses the development of capitalism. And that it is capitalism which ruins the peasant is by no means a corner-stone of Narodism, but of *Marxism*. The Narodniks saw and continue to see the causes of the separation of the producer from the means of production in the policy of the government, which, according to them, was a failure ("we" went the wrong way, etc.), in the stagnancy of society which rallied insufficiently against the vultures and tricksters, etc., and not in that specific organisation of the Russian social economy which bears the name of capitalism. That is why their "measures" amounted to action to be taken by "society" and the "state." On the contrary, when it is shown that the existence of the capitalist organisation of social economy is the cause of expropriation this leads inevitably to the theory of the *class struggle* (cf. Struve's book, pp. 101, 288 and many other pages). The author expresses himself inexactly in speaking of the "*agriculturist*" in general, and not of the opposing classes in bourgeois agriculture. The Narodniks say that capitalism ruins *agriculture* and for that reason is incapable of embracing the country's entire production and leads this production the wrong way; the Marxists say that capitalism, both in manufacturing industry and in agriculture, oppresses the *producer*, but by raising production to a higher level creates the conditions and the forces for "socialisation."**

* That is to say, beginning with the petty-bourgeois character of the "peasant agriculturist" as proof of the "inevitability and legitimacy" of large-scale capitalism.

** The rationalising of agriculture, on the one hand, which makes it for the first time capable of operating on a social scale, and the reduction *ad absurdum* of property in land, on the other, are the great achievements of the capitalist mode of production. Like all of its other historical advances, it also attained these by first completely impoverishing the direct producers" (*Das Kapital*, III. B., 2. Th. p. 157). [138]

Mr. Struve's conclusion on this point is as follows: "One of Mr. N. —on's cardinal errors is that he has completely transferred notions and categories from the *established* capitalist system to the contemporary economy of the peasant, which to this day is more natural than money economy" (237).

We have seen above that only Mr. N. —on's complete ignoring of the concrete data of Russian agricultural capitalism led to the ridiculous mistake of talking about a "contraction" of the home market. He did not, however, make that mistake because he applied all the categories of capitalism to the peasantry, but because he did not apply any *categories of capitalism* to the data on agriculture. The classes of the bourgeoisie and the proletariat are, of course, a most important "category" of capitalism. Mr. N. —on not only did not "transfer" them to the "peasantry" (i.e., did not give an analysis of exactly to what groups or sections of the peasantry these categories apply and how far they are developed), but, on the contrary, he argued in purely Narodnik fashion, ignoring the opposite elements within the "village community," and arguing about the "peasantry" in general. It was this that led to his thesis on the capitalist character of over-population, on capitalism as the cause of the expropriation of the agriculturist, remaining unproven and merely serving to build a reactionary utopia.

IV

In § VIII of the sixth chapter, Mr. Struve sets forth his ideas about private-landowner farming. He quite rightly shows how closely and directly the forms assumed by this sort of farming depend on the ruin of the peasants. The ruined peasant no longer "tempts" the landlord with "fabulous rental prices," and the landlord goes over to the employment of farm labourers. Extracts in proof of this are cited from an article by Raspopin, who analysed Zemstvo statistical data on landlord economy, and from a Zemstvo publication on current statistics which notes the "enforced" character of the increase in the cultivation of landlord estates on capitalist lines. In reply to Messrs. the Narodniks, who so willingly hide the fact of capitalism's present domination in agriculture beneath arguments about its "future" and its "possibility," the author makes a precise reference to the *actual situation.*

We must stop here just to deal with the author's estimation of this phenomenon, who calls it the "progressive trends in private-landowner farming" (244) and says that these trends are created by the "inexorable logic of economic evolution" (240). We fear that these quite correct propositions, by reason of their abstractness, will be unintelligible to the reader who is not acquainted with Marxism; that the reader will not understand—unless definite reference is made to the succession of such and such systems of economy, such and such forms of class antagonism—why the given trend is "progressive" (from the only viewpoint, of course, from which the Marxist can pose the problem, from the viewpoint of a definite class), why, exactly, is the evolution that is taking place "inexorable." Let us therefore try to depict this succession (at least in the most general outline) parallel to the Narodnik representation of the matter.

The Narodnik presents the process of the development of the economy of farm labourers as a transition from "independent" peasant farming to dependent farming, and, naturally, considers this to be regression, decline, etc. Such a picture of the process *is quite untrue in fact*, does not correspond to reality at all, and hence the conclusions drawn from it are also absurd. By presenting things in this optimistic way (optimistic in relation to the past and the present), the Narodnik simply *turns his back on the facts* established by Narodnik literature itself, and turns his face towards utopias and possibilities.

Let us start from pre-Reform feudal economy.

The main content of the production relations at that time was as follows: the landlord supplied the peasant with land, timber for building, the means of production in general (sometimes even the means of livelihood) for each separate household and, while letting the peasant gain his own livelihood, compelled him to work *all the surplus time* doing corvée service for him, the landlord. I underscore the words "all the surplus time" in order to note that there can be no question, under this system, of the peasant's "independence."* The "allotment" with which the landlord "supplied" the peasant was nothing more than *wages in kind*, served wholly and exclusively for the exploitation of the peasant by the landlord, to "supply" the landlord with hands and actually never to provide for the peasant himself.**

Then, however, came the invasion of commodity economy. The landlord began to produce grain for sale and not for himself. This gave rise to intensified exploitation of peasant labour and then to difficulties with the allotment system, since it had become unprofitable for the landlord to supply members of the rising generation of peasants with allotments, and it was possible to settle accounts in money. It became more convenient to separate the peasants' land once and for all from that of the landlord (particularly if in the process part of the allotments were cut off and if they were redeemed at a "fair" price) and to use the labour of *the very same* peasants, placed in materially worse conditions and forced to compete with former manor serfs, "gift-landers,"[139] the more prosperous former state, appanage peasants, etc.

Serfdom collapses.

The system of economy—now serving the market (and this is very important)—changed, but did not do so at once. New features and "principles" were added to the old. These new features consisted of the following: the supplying of the peasant with means of production was no longer made the basis of Plusmacherei, but, on the contrary, it was his "separation" from the means of production, his need of money; the basis was no longer natural economy, natural exchange of "services" (the landlord gives the peasant land, while the peasant provides the products of his surplus labour, grain, linen, etc.), but commodity, "free" money contract. It was this form of economy, which combined old and new features, that has been predominant in Russia since the Reform. The old-time methods of lending out land in return for work (farming in return for cut-off lands, for

* I confine myself *exclusively* to the economic aspect of the matter.

** That is why reference to the feudal "allotment of land" as proof of the means of production belonging to the producer "from time immemorial" is false through and through.

example) were supplemented by "winter hire"—the lending of money in return for work when the peasant is in particular need of money and sells his labour for a song, the lending of grain in return for labour service, etc. The social-economic relations in the former "patriarchal estate" were reduced, as you see, to the most ordinary *usurer's* deal: they consisted of operations quite analogous to the operations of the buyer-up in relation to the handicraftsmen.

There can be no doubt that this form of economy has become typical since the Reform, and our Narodnik literature has supplied superb *descriptions* of this particularly unattractive form of Plusmacherei combined with feudal traditions and relations, and with the utter helplessness of the peasant tied to his "allotment."

But the Narodniks refused, and still refuse, to see the precise economic basis of these relations.

The basis of domination is now not only the possession of the land, as in the old days, but also the possession of money, which the peasant is in need of (and money is a product of the social labour organised by commodity economy), and the "separation" of the peasant from the means of livelihood. Obviously, this is a capitalist, bourgeois relationship. The "new" features are nothing but the initial form of the domination of *capital* in agriculture, a form not yet freed of the "old-nobility" fetters, a form that has created the class contradiction peculiar to capitalist society, but has not yet finally established it.

With the development of commodity economy, however, the ground slips from under this initial form of the domination of capital: the impoverishment of the peasantry has now developed to the point of utter ruin, the point when the peasants have lost their implements, by which the feudal and the bonded forms of labour were maintained—and the landlord is thus compelled to go over to the use of his own implements, and the peasant to become a farm labourer.

That this transition has begun in post-Reform Russia is again an undoubted fact. This fact shows the line of development of the bonded form, which the Narodniks view in a purely metaphysical way—disregarding connections with the past, disregarding the urge to develop; this same fact shows the *further* development of capitalism, the further development of the class contradiction that is peculiar to our capitalist society and that in the preceding epoch was expressed in the relation between the "kulak" and the peasant, and is now beginning to find expression in the relation between the rational farmer and the farm labourer and day labourer.

Now it is this latter change that evokes the despair and horror of the Narodnik, who begins to howl about "deprivation of the land," "loss of independence," "installation of capitalism" and the ills "threatening" as a result, etc., etc.

Look at these arguments impartially and you will see, firstly, that they contain a *falsehood*, even though a well-intentioned one, since the economy of farm labourers is not preceded by peasant "independence" but by other ways of handing the surplus product over to some one who takes no part in its production. Secondly, you will see the superficiality and the pettiness of the Narodnik protest, which make it vulgar socialism, as Mr. Struve aptly puts it. Why is this "installation" merely seen in its second form, and not in both forms? Why is the protest not directed against the basic historical fact that concentrated the means of production in the hands of "private landowners," instead of merely against one of the methods of utilising this monopoly? Why is the root of the evil not seen in production relations that subordinate labour far and wide to the owner of money, instead of merely in the inequality of distribution that stands out in such relief in the *latest* form of these relations? It is this basic circumstance—a protest against capitalism based on those same capitalist relations—that makes the Narodniks the ideologists of the petty bourgeoisie, who do not fear bourgeois reality, but merely its accentuation, which alone leads to a fundamental change.

V

Let us pass to the last point in Mr. Struve's theoretical arguments, namely, to the "problem of markets for Russian capitalism" (245).

The author begins his examination of the Narodnik-devised theory about there being no markets in this country, with the question: "What does Mr. V. V. understand by capitalism?" That question is a very relevant one, since Mr. V. V. (and all Narodniks in general) have always compared the Russian order of things with some "English form" (247) of capitalism and not with its basic features, which have a different appearance in each country. It is only a pity that Mr. Struve does not give a complete definition of capitalism, but points in general to the "domination of exchange economy" [that is one feature; the second is the appropriation of surplus-value by the owner of money, his domination over labour], to "the system we see in Western Europe" (247), "with all its consequences," with the "concentration of industrial production, capitalism in the narrow sense of the word" (247).

"Mr. V. V.," says the author, "did not go into an analysis of the concept 'capitalism,' but took it from Marx, who mainly had in view capitalism in the narrow sense, as the already fully established product of relations developing on the basis of the subordination of production to exchange" (247). One cannot agree with that. Firstly, had Mr. V. V. really taken his idea of capitalism from Marx, he would have had a correct idea of it, and could not have confused the "English form" with capitalism. Secondly, it is quite unfair to assert that Marx mainly had in view the "centralisation or concentration of industrial production" [that is what Mr. Struve understands by capitalism in the narrow sense]. On the contrary, he followed up the development of commodity economy from its initial steps, he analysed capitalism in its primitive forms of simple co-operation and manufacture—forms centuries apart from the concentration of production by machines—and he showed the connection between capitalism in industry and in agriculture. Mr. Struve himself narrows down the concept of capitalism when he says: "The object of Mr. V. V.'s study was the *first* steps of the national economy on the path from natural to commodity organisation." He should have said: the *last* steps. Mr. V. V., as far as we know, only studied Russia's post-Reform economy. *The beginning of commodity* production relates to the pre-Reform era, as Mr. Struve himself indicates (189-90), and even the *capitalist* organisation of the cotton industry took shape before the emancipation of the peasants. The Reform gave an impulse to the *final* development in this sense; it pushed the commodity form of labour-power and not the commodity form of the product of labour to the forefront; it sanctioned the domination of capitalist and not of commodity production. The hazy distinction between capitalism in the broad and in the narrow sense* leads Mr. Struve apparently to regard Russian capitalism as something of the future and not of the present, not as something already and definitely established. He says, for example:

"Before posing the question: is it inevitable for Russia to have capitalism in the English form, Mr. V. V. should have posed and settled a different one, a more general and hence more important question: is it inevitable for Russia to pass from natural to money economy, and what is the relation between capitalist production sensu stricto and commodity production in general?" (247). That is hardly a convenient way of posing the question. If the present, existing system of production relations in Russia is clearly explained, then the problem of whether this or that line of development is "inevitable" will be settled eo ipso. If, however, it is not explained, then it will be insoluble. Instead of arguments about the future (arguments beloved of Messrs. the Narodniks) an *explanation* of the present should be given. An outstanding fact in post-Reform Russia has been the outward, if one may so call it, manifestation of capitalism, i.e., manifestation of its "heights" (factory production, railways, banks, etc.), and theoretical thought was immediately faced with the problem of capitalism in Russia. The Narodniks have tried to prove that these heights are something accidental, unconnected with the entire economic system, without basis and therefore impotent; and they have used the term "capitalism" in too narrow a sense, forgetting that the enslavement of labour to capital covers very long and diverse stages from merchant's capital to the "English form." It is the job of Marxists to prove that these heights are nothing more than the last step in the development of the commodity economy that took shape

* There is nothing to show what criterion the author uses to distinguish these concepts. If by capitalism in the narrow sense is meant only machine industry, then it is not clear why manufacture should not be singled out, too. If by capitalism in the broad sense is meant only commodity economy, then there is no capitalism in it.

long ago in Russia and *everywhere*, in all branches of production, gives rise to the subordination of labour to capital.

Mr. Struve's view of Russian capitalism as something of the future and not of the present was expressed with particular clarity in the following argument: "So long as the contemporary village community exists, registered and consolidated by law, relations will develop on the basis of it that have nothing in common with the 'people's well-being.'" [Surely not just "will develop"; did they not develop so long ago that the whole of Narodnik literature, from its very outset, over a quarter of a century ago, described them and protested against them?] "In the West we have several examples of the existence of individual farmsteads alongside of large-scale capitalist farming. Our Poland and our south-west territory belong to the same order of things. It may be said that in Russia, both the community villages and those consisting of individual farms approach this type, inasmuch as the impoverished peasantry remain on the land and levelling influences among them are proving stronger than differentiating influences" (280). Is it merely a matter of approaching, and not of already being that *type* at this very moment? To determine "type," one has, of course, to take the basic economic features of the system, and not legal forms. If we look at these basic features of the economy of the Russian countryside, we shall see the isolated economy of the peasant households on small plots of land, we shall see growing commodity economy that already plays a dominant role. It is these features that give content to the concept "small individual farming." We shall see further the same peasant indebtedness to usurers, the same expropriation to which the data of the West testify. The whole difference lies in the specific character of our juridical system (the peasants' civic inequality; forms of land tenure), which retains stronger traces of the "old regime" as a result of the weaker development of our capitalism. But these specific features do not in the least disturb the uniformity of *type* of our peasant system and that of the West.

Proceeding to deal with the theory of markets itself, Mr. Struve notes that Messrs. V. V. and N. —on are caught in a vicious circle: while the development of capitalism requires the growth of the market, capitalism ruins the population. The author very unsuccessfully corrects this vicious circle with his Malthusianism, placing the blame for the ruin of the peasantry on the "growth of the population" and not on capitalism!! The mistake of the authors mentioned is quite a different one: capitalism not only ruins, but *splits* the peasantry into a bourgeoisie and a proletariat. This process does not cut down the home market, but *creates* it: commodity economy grows at both poles of the differentiating peasantry, both among the "proletarian" peasantry, who are compelled to sell "free labour," and among the bourgeois peasantry, who raise the technical level of their farms (machinery, equipment, fertilisers, etc. Cf. Mr. V. V.'s *Progressive Trends in Peasant Farming*) and develop their requirements. Despite the fact that this conception of the process is directly based on Marx's theory of the relation between capitalism in industry and in agriculture, Mr. Struve ignores it—possibly because he has been led astray by Mr. V. V.'s "theory of markets." This latter person, supposedly basing himself on Marx, has presented the Russian public with a "theory" claiming that in developed capitalist society a "surplus of goods" is inevitable; the home market cannot be sufficient, a foreign one is necessary. "This theory is a true one" (? !), declares Mr. Struve, "inasmuch as it states the fact that surplus-value cannot be realised from consumption either by the capitalists or by the workers, but presumes consumption by third persons" (251). We cannot agree with this statement at all. Mr. V. V.'s "theory" (if one may speak of a theory here) is simply that of ignoring the distinction between personal and productive consumption, the distinction between the means of production and articles of consumption, a distinction without which it is impossible to understand the reproduction of the aggregate social capital in capitalist society. Marx showed this in the greatest detail in Volume II of *Capital* (Part III: "The Reproduction and Circulation of the Aggregate Social Capital") and dealt with it vividly in Volume I as well, when criticising the thesis of classical political economy according to which the accumulation of capital consists only of the transformation of surplus-value into wages, and not into constant capital (means of production) plus wages. To confirm this description of Mr. V. V.'s theory let us confine ourselves to two quotations from the articles mentioned by Mr. Struve.

"Each worker," says Mr. V. V. in his article "The Excess in the Market Supply of Commodities," "produces more than he consumes himself, and all these surpluses accumulate in few hands; the owners of these surpluses consume them themselves, for which purpose they exchange them within the country and abroad for the most varied objects of necessity and comforts; but however much they eat, drink or dance (sic!!)—they cannot dispose of the whole of the surplus-value" (*Otechestvenniye Zapiski*, 1883, No. 5, p. 14), and "to be more convincing" the author "examines the chief expenditures" of the capitalist, such as dinners, travelling, etc. We get it still more vividly in the article "Militarism and Capitalism": "The Achilles' heel of the capitalist organisation of industry is the impossibility of the employers consuming the whole of their income" (*Russkaya Mysl*, 1889, No. 9, p. 80). "Rothschild could not consume the entire increment to his income ... for the simple reason that this ... increment constitutes such a considerable mass of articles of consumption that Rothschild, whose every whim is satisfied as it is, would find himself in very great difficulties," etc.

All these arguments, as you see, are based on the naïve view that the capitalist's purpose is only personal consumption and not the accumulation of surplus-value, on the mistaken idea that the social product splits up into $v+s$ (variable capital+surplus-value) as was taught by Adam Smith and all the political economists before Marx, and not into $c+v+s$ (constant capital, means of production, and then into wages and surplus-value), as was shown by Marx. Once these errors are corrected and attention is paid to the circumstance that in capitalist society an enormous and ever-growing part is played by the means of production (the part of the social products that is used for productive and not personal consumption, not for consumption by people but by capital) the whole of the notorious "theory" collapses completely. Marx proved in Volume II that capitalist production is quite conceivable without foreign markets, with the growing accumulation of wealth and without any "third persons," whose introduction by Mr. Struve is extremely unfortunate. Mr. Struve's reasoning on this subject evokes amazement, especially as he himself points to the overwhelming significance of the home market for Russia and catches Mr. V. V. tripping on the "programme of development of Russian capitalism" based on a "strong peasantry." The process of the formation of this "strong" (that is, bourgeois) peasantry that is now taking place in our countryside clearly shows us the rise of capital, the proletarianisation of the producer and the *growth of the home market*: the "spread of improved implements," for example, signifies precisely the accumulation of capital as means of production. On this problem it was particularly necessary, instead of dealing with "possibilities," to outline and explain the actual process expressed in the creation of a home market for Russian capitalism.*

With this we conclude our examination of the theoretical part of Mr. Struve's book, and can now try to give a general, comprehensive, so to speak, description of the main methods used in his arguments, and thus approach the solution of the problems raised at the outset: "Exactly what in this book may be assigned to Marxism?" "Which of the doctrine's (Marxism's) tenets does the author reject, supplement or correct, and with what results?"

The main feature of the author's arguments, as we noted from the start, is his narrow objectivism, which is confined to proving the inevitability and necessity of the process and makes no effort to reveal at each specific stage of this process the form of class contradiction inherent in it—an objectivism that describes the process in general, and not each of the antagonistic classes whose conflict makes up the process.

We understand perfectly well that the author had his grounds for confining his "notes" to just the "objective" and, what is more, the most general side; his grounds were, firstly, that in his desire to confront the Narodniks with the principles of hostile views, he set forth principia and

* As this is a very important and complicated problem, we intend to devote a special article to it.[140]

nothing more, leaving their development and more concrete examination to the further development of the controversy, and, secondly, we tried in Chapter I to show that *all* that distinguishes Narodism from Marxism is the *character of the criticism* of Russian capitalism, the different *explanation* of it—from which it naturally follows that the Marxists sometimes confine themselves just to general "objective" propositions, and lay emphasis exclusively on what distinguishes our understanding (*of generally-known facts*) from that of the Narodniks.

Mr. Struve, however, it seems to us, went too far in this respect. Abstractness of exposition frequently yielded propositions that could not but cause misunderstanding; the way the problem was posed did not differ from the methods current and dominant in our literature, the method of arguing in professorial style, from on high, about the paths and destiny of the fatherland and not about specific classes pursuing such and such a path; the more concrete the author's arguments, the more impossible did it become to explain the principia of Marxism and remain on the heights of general abstract propositions, the more necessary it was to make definite reference to such and such a condition of such and such classes of Russian society, to such and such a relation between the various forms of Plusmacherei and the interests of the producers.

That is why we thought that an attempt to supplement and explain the author's thesis, to follow his exposition step by step, so as to show the need for a *different* way of posing the problem, the need for a *more consistent* way of applying the theory of class contradictions, would not be out of place.

As to Mr. Struve's direct deviations from Marxism—on problems of the state, over-population, and the home market—sufficient has already been said about them.

VI

In addition to a criticism of the theoretical content of Narodism, Mr. Struve's book contains, among other things, several remarks relating to Narodnik economic policy. Although these remarks are given cursorily and are not developed by the author, we nevertheless must touch on them in order to leave no room for any misunderstanding.

These remarks contain references to the "rationality," progressiveness, "intelligence," etc., of the liberal, i.e., bourgeois policy as compared to the policy of the Narodniks.*

The author evidently wanted to contrast two policies that keep to the existing relations—and *in this sense* he quite rightly pointed out that a policy is "intelligent" if it develops and does not retard capitalism, and it is "intelligent" not because it serves the bourgeoisie by increasingly subordinating the producer to them [the way in which various "simpletons" and "acrobats" try to explain it], but because, by accentuating and refining capitalist relations, it brings clarity to the *mind* of the one on whom alone change depends, and gives him a free hand.

It must, however, be said that this quite true proposition is badly expressed by Mr. Struve, that owing to the abstractness peculiar to him he voices it in such a way that one sometimes wishes to say to him: let the dead bury the dead. In Russia there has never yet been a shortage of people who have devoted themselves, heart and soul, to creating theories and programmes that express the interests of our bourgeoisie, that express all these "urgent needs" of strong and big capital to crush small capital and to destroy its primitive and patriarchal methods of exploitation.

If the author had here also adhered strictly to the requirements of the Marxist "doctrine," demanding that exposition be reduced to the formulation of the actual process, and that the class contradictions behind each "intelligent," "rational"

---

* Let us indicate some examples of these remarks: "If the state ... desires to strengthen small but not large landownership, then under the present economic conditions it cannot achieve this aim by chasing after unrealisable economic equality among the peasantry, but only by supporting its viable elements, by creating an economically strong peasantry out of them" (240). "I cannot fail to see that the policy which is aimed at creating *such* a peasantry (namely, "economically strong, adapted to commodity production") will be the only intelligent and progressive policy" (281). "Russia must be transformed from a poor capitalist country into a rich capitalist country" (250), etc., up to the concluding phrase: "Let us go and learn from capitalism."

and progressive policy be disclosed, he would have expressed the same thought differently, would have posed the question in another way. He would have drawn a parallel between those theories and programmes of liberalism, i.e., of the bourgeoisie, which have sprung up like mushrooms since the great Reform, and factual data on the development of capitalism in Russia. In this way he would have used the Russian example to show the connection between social ideas and economic development, something he tried to prove in the first chapters and that can only be fully established by a materialist analysis of Russian data. In this way he would have shown, secondly, how naïve the Narodniks are when they combat bourgeois theories in their publications, and do so as though these theories are merely mistaken reasoning, and do not represent the interests of a powerful class which it is foolish to admonish, and which can only be "convinced" by the imposing force of another class. In this way he would have shown, thirdly, which class actually determines "urgent needs" and "progress" in this country, and how ridiculous the Narodniks are when they argue about which "path" "to choose."

Messrs. the Narodniks have seized on these expressions of Mr. Struve's with particular delight, gloating over the fact that the unhappy way they have been formulated has enabled various bourgeois economists (like Mr. Yanzhul) and champions of serfdom (like Mr. Golovin) to seize upon some phrases torn out of the general context. We have seen in what way Mr. Struve's position, that has placed such a weapon into the hands of his opponents, is unsatisfactory.

The author's attempts to criticise Narodism merely as a theory that wrongly indicates the path for the fatherland,* led to the hazy formulation of his attitude to the "economic policy" of Narodism. This may be regarded as a wholesale denial of the policy, and not only of a half of it. It is, therefore, necessary to dwell on this point.

Philosophising about the possibility of "different paths for the fatherland" is merely the outer vestment of Naro-

* The author of *Critical Remarks* indicates the economic basis of Narodism (pp. 166-67), but in our view does so inadequately.

dism. But its content is representation of the interests and viewpoint of the Russian small producer, the petty bourgeois. That is why the Narodnik, in matters of theory, is just as much a Janus, looking with one face to the past and the other to the future, as in real life the small producer is, who looks with one face to the past, wishing to strengthen his small farm without knowing or wishing to know anything about the general economic system and about the need to reckon with the class that controls it—and with the other face to the future, adopting a hostile attitude to the capitalism that is ruining him.

It is clear from this that it would be absolutely wrong to reject the whole of the Narodnik programme indiscriminately and in its entirety. One must clearly distinguish its reactionary and progressive sides. Narodism is reactionary insofar as it proposes measures that tie the peasant to the soil and to the old modes of production, such as the inalienability of allotments, etc.,* insofar as it wants to retard the development of money economy, and insofar as it expects not partial improvements, but a change of the path to be brought about by "society" and by the influence of representatives of the bureaucracy (example: Mr. Yuzhakov, who argued in *Russkoye Bogatstvo*, 1894, No. 7, about common tillage as projected by a Zemsky Nachalnik and engaged in introducing amendments to these projects). Unconditional warfare must, of course, be waged against such points in the Narodnik programme. But there are also other points, relating to self-government, to the "people's" free and broad access to knowledge, to the "raising" of the "people's" (that is to say, small) economy by means of cheap credits, technical improvements, better regulation of marketing, etc., etc. That such general democratic measures are progressive is fully admitted, of course, by Mr. Struve, too. They will not retard, but accelerate Russia's economic development along the capitalist path, accelerate the establishment of a home market, accelerate the growth of technique and machine industry by improving the conditions of the

* Mr. Struve very rightly says that these measures might merely "bring to fruition the ardent dreams of certain West-European and Russian landowners about farm labourers who are strongly bound to the land" (279).

working man and raising the level of his requirements, accelerate and facilitate his independent thinking and action.

The only question that might here arise is: who indicates such undoubtedly desirable measures with greater accuracy and ability—the Narodniks or publicists like Skvortsov who has so much to say in favour of technical progress and to whom Mr. Struve is so extremely well disposed? It seems to me that from the Marxist viewpoint there can be no doubt that Narodism is absolutely to be preferred *in this respect*. The measures proposed by the Messrs. Skvortsov relate to the interests of the entire class of small producers, the petty bourgeoisie, in the same measure as the programme of *Moskovskiye Vedomosti* relates to those of the big bourgeoisie. They are designed not for all,* but only for certain of the elect, who are vouchsafed the attention of the authorities. They are, lastly, abominably crude because they presume police interference in the economy of the peasants. Taken all in all, these measures provide no serious guarantees and chances of the "productive progress of peasant economy."

The Narodniks *in this respect* understand and represent the interests of the small producers far more correctly, and the Marxists, while rejecting all the reactionary features of their programme, must not only accept the general democratic points, but carry them through more exactly, deeply and further. The more resolute such reforms are in Russia, the higher they raise the living standard of the working masses—the more sharply and clearly will the most important and fundamental (already today) social antagonism in Russian life stand out. The Marxists, far from "breaking the democratic thread" or trend, as Mr. V. V. slanderously asserts they do, want to develop and strengthen this trend, they want to bring it closer to life, they want to take up the "thread" that "society" and the "intelligentsia" are letting slip out of their hands.**

---

* That is to say, of course, for all *to whom* technical progress *is accessible*.

** In *Nedelya*, No. 47, 1894, Mr. V. V. writes: "In the post-Reform period of our history, social relations in some respects have approx-

This demand—not to discard the "thread," but, on the contrary, to strengthen it—is not the accidental result of the personal mood of some "Marxists" or other, but is necessarily determined by the position and interests of the class they wish to serve, is necessarily and unconditionally dictated by the fundamental requirements of their "doctrine." I cannot, for reasons that are easily understandable, pause here to examine the first part of this proposition, to characterise the "position" and "interests"; here, I think, matters speak for themselves. I shall only touch on the second part, namely, the relation of the Marxist doctrine to problems that express the "breaking thread."

The Marxists must *raise* these problems *differently* than Messrs. the Narodniks do. The latter pose the problem from the viewpoint of "modern science, modern moral ideas"; the matter is presented as though there are no profound causes of the failure to implement such reforms, causes contained within *production relations* themselves, as though the obstacle lies only in grossness of feelings, in the feeble "ray of reason," etc.; as though Russia is a tabula rasa on which nothing has to be done except properly outline the right paths. *That way of presenting the problem*, of course, guaranteed it the "purity" of which Mr. V. V. boasts, and which is merely the "purity" of ladies' college daydreams, of the kind that makes Narodnik reasoning so fit for armchair conversations.

The way these same problems are posed by the Marxists must necessarily be quite different.* Obliged to seek for the roots of social phenomena in production relations obliged to reduce them to the *interests* of definite classes, they must formulate these desiderata as being the "desires" of

---

imated to those of Western Europe, with active democracy in the epoch of political struggle and with social indifferentism in the subsequent period." We tried to show in Chapter I that this "indifferentism" is no accident, but an inevitable result of the position and the interests of the class from which the representatives of "society" emerge and which in addition to disadvantages derives by no means unimportant advantages from contemporary relations.

* If they pursue their theory consistently. We have already said much about Mr. Struve's exposition being unsatisfactory precisely because of his failure to adhere to this theory with greatest strictness.

such and such social elements and meeting the opposition of such and such elements and classes. Such a way of posing the problem will absolutely eliminate the possibility of their "theories" being utilised for professorial arguments that rise *above* classes, for projects and reports that promise "splendid success."* That, of course, is just an indirect merit of the change of viewpoint referred to, but it is also a very great one, if we bear in mind how steep is the slope down which *contemporary* Narodism is slipping into the bog of opportunism. But the matter is not limited to mere indirect merit. If the same problems are posed in their application to the theory of class antagonism [and this, of course, requires a "reconsideration of the facts" of Russian history and reality], then the replies to them will provide a formulation of the vital interests of certain classes; these replies will be intended for practical utilisation** by those interested classes and by them alone—these replies will, to use the splendid expression of a certain Marxist, break out of the "cramped chamber of the intelligentsia" towards those who themselves participate in production relations in their most highly developed and pure form, towards those who are most strongly affected by the "breaking of the thread," and who "need" "ideals" because they are badly off without them. Such a way of raising issues will instil a new stream of life into all these old problems—taxes, passports, migration, Volost boards of administration, etc.—problems that our "society" has discussed and interpreted, chewed over again and again, solved and re-solved, and for which it has now begun to lose all taste.

So then, no matter how we approach the problem, whether we examine the content of the system of economic relations prevalent in Russia and the various forms of this system in

* Mr. Yuzhakov's expression.

** Of course, for *this* "utilisation" to take place a tremendous amount of preparatory work is required, and what is more, work that by its very nature goes unseen *Before* this utilisation takes place a more or less considerable period may pass during which we shall say outright that there is no force capable of providing better paths for the fatherland—as against the "sugary optimism" of Messrs. the Narodniks who assert that such forces exist and that all that remains to be done is to advise them to "leave the wrong path."

their historical connection and in their relation to the interests of the working people, or whether we examine the problem of the "breaking of the thread" and the reasons for its "breaking," we arrive, in either case, at one conclusion, that of the great significance of the historical task of "labour differentiated from life," a task advanced by the epoch in which we live, that of the universal significance of the idea of this class.

NOTES

[1] The article *New Economic Developments in Peasant Life.* (On V. Y. Postnikov's *Peasant Farming in South Russia*) is the earliest of V. I. Lenin's works that has been preserved. It was written in Samara in the spring of 1893, and the manuscript was read in circles attended by young Marxists of that town. Lenin intended to have it printed in the liberal magazine *Russkaya Mysl* (*Russian Thought*), published in Moscow, but it was rejected by the editorial board "as unsuited to the policy of the magazine." In a letter dated May 30, 1894, Lenin said the following: "I was even naïve enough to send it to *Russkaya Mysl*, but of course they turned it down. The thing became quite clear to me when I read in No. 2 of that magazine an article about Postnikov by 'our well-known' liberal vulgarian, Mr. V. V. One must surely be an artist to be able to completely distort magnificent material and to obscure all the facts with phrase-mongering!"

The Institute of Marxism-Leninism of the C.C. C.P.S.U. possesses two manuscript copies of the article *New Economic Developments in Peasant Life*. The first (rough) copy was found among Lenin's personal papers; the second, which contains some additions made by Lenin when it was finally copied, was handed by him to S. I. Mickiewicz, from whom it was confiscated during a search on December 3, 1894. The manuscript was discovered in 1923 in the records of the Moscow Law Court, and was then published for the first time in the miscellany *The Twenty-Fifth Anniversary of the First Party Congress (1898-1923)*. In the present edition, the article *New Economic Developments in Peasant Life* is printed according to the text of the second manuscript, as corrected by V. I. Lenin.

The Institute of Marxism-Leninism also possesses a copy of V. Y. Postnikov's book *Peasant Farming in South Russia* bearing Lenin's comments.

Lenin used the most important material of this article in the second chapter of his *The Development of Capitalism in Russia*, written in 1896-1899 and published in March 1899. p. 11

Zemstvos—local self-government bodies, in which the nobility dominated. The Zemstvos were established in 1864 in the central gubernias of tsarist Russia, their competence being confined to purely local economic affairs (hospital and road building, statistics, insurance, etc.). They functioned under the control of the Gubernia

Governors and the Minister of Home Affairs, who could invalidate decisions undesirable to the government.

The statistical sections, bureaux, and commissions of Gubernia and Uyezd Zemstvo Boards, engaged in statistical research (house-to-house censuses of peasant farms and handicraft establishments, determination of profitability of lands, revaluations of land and property liable to Zemstvo taxation, study of peasant budgets, etc.) and issued numerous reviews and statistical abstracts covering uyezds or gubernias, and containing a wealth of factual material.

Lenin had a high opinion of the Zemstvo statistical data, and pointed out that "a close study of Russian Zemstvo statistics by Europeans would no doubt give a strong impetus to the progress of social statistics in general." (*The Agrarian Question and the "Critics of Marx."* See present edition, Vol. 5.) At the same time Lenin criticised the methods of analysing and grouping statistical data used by the Zemstvo statisticians. "This is the greatest weakness of our Zemstvo statistics, that are magnificent in the thoroughness and detail with which they are compiled," wrote Lenin. (*The Tasks of Zemstvo Statistics*. See present edition, Vol. 20.) The Zemstvo statisticians, many of whom were Narodniks in outlook, were frequently biassed in their approach to the statistical data. In their treatment of these data, essential differences and features of the various peasant groups formed in the course of capitalist development were hidden behind columns of figures.

Lenin studied, checked and analysed Zemstvo statistical data, made his own calculations, drew up tables and summaries, and gave a Marxist analysis and scientific classification of data on peasant farms and handicraft establishments. He used the wealth of material contained in the Zemstvo statistics to expose the far-fetched schemes of the Narodniks, and drew a real picture of Russia's economic development. He made extensive use of the data in his writings, and especially in his book *The Development of Capitalism in Russia*. (On Zemstvo statistics see V. I. Lenin's paper *The Tasks of Zemstvo Statistics*, written in 1914.) p. 13

[3] Reference is made to the collection entitled *Results of the Economic Investigation of Russia According to Zemstvo Statistical Data*, of which Vol. I is: V. V.—*The Peasant Community*; Vol. II: N. Karyshev—*Peasant Rentings of Non-Allotment Land*, Dorpat, 1892. Both the books expressed liberal-Narodnik views. V. V. was the pseudonym of V. P. Vorontsov, an ideologist of liberal Narodism of the 1880s and 1890s. p. 14

[4] The *village community* (*obshchina* or *mir*) in Russia was the communal form of peasant use of the land, characterised by compulsory crop rotation, and undivided woods and pastures. Its principal features were collective responsibility (compulsory collective responsibility of the peasants for making their payments in full and on time, and the performance of various services to the state and the landlords), the regular redistribution of the land with no right to refuse the allotment given, the prohibition of its purchase and sale.

The Russian village community was known in ancient times, and in the course of historical development gradually became one of the pillars of feudalism in Russia. The landlords and the tsarist government used the village community to intensify feudal oppression and to squeeze redemption payments and taxes out of the people. Lenin pointed out that the village community "does not save the peasant from turning into a proletarian; actually it serves as a medieval barrier dividing the peasants, who are as if chained to small associations and to 'categories' which have lost all 'reason for existence.'" (*The Agrarian Question in Russia Towards the Close of the Nineteenth Century*. See present edition, Vol. 15.)

The problem of the village community aroused heated arguments and was the subject of an extensive economic literature. The Narodniks displayed particularly great interest in the village community, seeing in it the guarantee of Russian development to socialism by a special path. By tendentiously gathering and falsifying facts, and employing so-called "average figures," the Narodniks sought to prove that the community peasantry in Russia possessed a special sort of "steadfastness," and that the peasant community protected the peasants against the penetration of capitalist relations into the village, and "saved" the peasants from ruin and class differentiation. As early as the 1880s, G. V. Plekhanov showed how unfounded were the Narodniks' illusions about "community socialism," while in the 1890s V. I. Lenin completely destroyed the Narodniks' theories. Lenin cited a tremendous amount of factual and statistical material to show how capitalist relations were developing in the Russian village, and how capital, by penetrating into the patriarchal village community, was splitting the peasantry into the antagonistic classes of kulaks and poor peasants.

In 1906 the tsarist minister Stolypin issued a law benefiting the kulaks; it allowed peasants to leave the community and to sell their allotments. This law laid the basis for the official abolition of the rural community system and intensified the differentiation among the peasantry. In nine years following the adoption of the law, over two million peasant householders withdrew from the communities. p. 19

[5] This refers to *registered* males subject to the poll-tax in feudal Russia (the peasantry and lower urban categories were chiefly affected), and to this end recorded in special censuses (so-called "registrations"). Such "registrations" began in 1718, the tenth and last being made in 1857-1859. In a number of districts redistribution of the land within the village communities took place according to the number of registered males in the family. p. 20

[6] *Dessiatiners*—peasants in South Russia who rented land for part of the harvest and not for a money payment. p. 28

[7] *Mennonites*—members of a religious sect who came to Russia from West Europe at the end of the eighteenth century. Their name was derived from that of their founder, the Dutchman Menno Simons. They settled mainly in the Yekaterinoslav and Taurida gubernias.

The farms of the Mennonite colonists were mostly prosperous, kulak farms. p. 34

[8] *The Peasant Reform of 1861*, which abolished serfdom in Russia, was effected by the tsarist government in the interests of the serf-owning landlords. The Reform was made necessary by the entire course of Russia's economic development and by the growth of a mass movement among the peasantry against feudal exploitation. The "peasant Reform" was feudal in character, but by force of the economic development that had drawn Russia on to the capitalist path the feudal form was given a capitalist content, and "this was the more evident the *less* the land was filched from the peasants, the *more fully* the land of the peasants was separated from that of the landlords, the *less* the tribute (i.e., "redemption") paid to the serf owners." (See present edition, Vol. 17, *The "Peasant Reform" and Proletarian-Peasant Revolution.*) The "peasant Reform" marked a step towards Russia's transformation into a bourgeois monarchy. On February 19, 1861, Alexander II signed a Manifesto and "Regulations" for the peasants, who were being released from serf dependence. In all, 22,500,000 serfs, formerly belonging to landlords, were "emancipated." Landed proprietorship, however, remained, the peasants' lands were declared the property of the landlords and the peasant could only get a land allotment of the size established by law (and even then by agreement with the landlord) for which he had to pay (redeem). The peasants made their redemption payments to the tsarist government, which had paid the established sums to the landlords. Approximate estimates show that after the Reform, the nobility possessed 71,500,000 dessiatines of land and the peasants 33,700,000 dessiatines. Thanks to the Reform the landlords cut off and appropriated from one to two-fifths of the lands formerly cultivated by the peasants.

The Reform merely undermined but did not abolish the old corvée system of farming. The landlords secured possession of the best parts of the peasants' allotments (the "cut-off lands," woods, meadows, watering-places, grazing grounds, and so on), without which the peasants could not engage in independent farming. Until the redemption arrangements were completed the peasants were considered to be "temporarily bound," and rendered services to the landlord in the shape of quitrent and corvée service. To compel the peasants to redeem their own allotments was sheer plunder on the part of the landlords and the tsarist government. The peasants were given a period of 49 years in which to pay off the debt, with an interest of 6%. Arrears grew from year to year. The former landlords' peasants alone paid the tsarist government a total of 1,900 million rubles in redemption money, whereas the market price of the land that passed into their possession did not exceed 544 million rubles. The peasants had to pay hundreds of millions of rubles for what was actually their own land; this ruined their farms and resulted in the impoverishment of the peasant masses.

The Russian revolutionary democrats, headed by N. G. Chernyshevsky, criticised the "peasant Reform" for its feudal character.

V. I. Lenin called the "peasant Reform" of 1861 the first mass act of violence against the peasantry in the interests of nascent capitalism in agriculture—the landlords were "clearing the estates" for capitalism. p. 35

[9] The manuscript contained some slight inaccuracies in the figures used to illustrate Lenin's argument. The total area under crops should be 1,651 dessiatines; the volume of the money demand on the market, reckoning only farms with over 5 dessiatines per household under crops—22,498 rubles. The total area under crops, reckoning farms with over 5 dessiatines per household under crops, should be 1,603 dessiatines. The general conclusions, however, are not affected by these inaccuracies. p. 42

[10] *Yoking*—an old elementary form of joint work by the village poor. Several peasant households combined their working animals and other means of production for farm work. V. I. Lenin, in the second chapter of *The Development of Capitalism in Russia*, calls yoking "the co-operation of tottering farms which are being ousted by the peasant bourgeoisie." (See present edition, Vol. III.) p. 45

[11] *Village court* (in Russian: *rasprava*)— a special court for state-owned peasants founded in tsarist Russia according to the Regulation of 1838, and consisting of the village elder (chairman) and two elected peasants. The village court, being a court of first instance, examined unimportant civil cases and misdemeanours, imposed fines, passed sentences of hard labour or flogging. The village court of second instance was the volost (district) court. In 1858 these courts were abolished, but the term rasprava continued to be used as referring to the primary village courts. p. 49

[12] *Russkaya Mysl* (*Russian Thought*)—a monthly magazine, liberal-Narodnik in trend; appeared in Moscow from 1880 onwards. In the 1890s, during the polemics between the Marxists and the liberal Narodniks, the Narodnik editors of the magazine occasionally allowed articles by Marxists to be published in its columns. Items by the progressive writers A. M. Gorky, V. G. Korolenko, D. N. Mamin-Sibiryak, G. I. Uspensky, A. P. Chekhov, and others, were published in the magazine's literature section.

After the 1905 Revolution, *Russkaya Mysl* became the organ of the Right wing of the Cadet party, and was edited by P. B. Struve. It was closed down in the middle of 1918. p. 54

[13] *Long-tract system*—peasant allotments that stretched in a narrow tract for many miles on either side of the village, some of them being 15-20 miles away in one direction or another. The long-tract system was common in the southern and the eastern steppe regions of Russia, where big villages prevailed, each embracing several hundred peasant households. p. 58

[14] *Vestnik Yevropy* (*European Messenger*)—a monthly magazine devoted to politics, history and literature, bourgeois liberal in trend, that appeared in St. Petersburg from 1866 to 1918. It published articles directed against the revolutionary Marxists. p. 62

[15] *Uyezd Boards of Peasants' Affairs* were established in tsarist Russia in 1874 to supervise the village and volost "peasant public administration" bodies. The Boards were directed by Uyezd Marshals of the Nobility and consisted of police chiefs, justices of the peace, and chairmen of Uyezd Zemstvo Boards. The Uyezd Boards of Peasants' Affairs were subordinate to the Gubernia Boards, which were headed by the governors. p. 67

[16] Reference is made to the famine of 1891 which was very severe in the eastern and south-eastern gubernias of Russia. This famine was more extensive than any similar natural calamity the country had ever experienced. The working people suffered incredible hardships as a result of the famine, which ruined masses of peasants and at the same time hastened the creation of a home market for the development of capitalism in Russia. p. 69

[17] Lenin's work *On the So-Called Market Question* was written in St. Petersburg in the autumn of 1893.

The main points contained in this work were first outlined by Lenin at a circle meeting of St. Petersburg Marxists (known as the circle of "the ancients") when a discussion took place on G. B. Krasin's lecture on "The Market Question." According to participants in the circle meeting, Lenin's paper created a tremendous impression on all present. N. K. Krupskaya wrote in her reminiscences of Lenin:

"The question of markets was treated with ultra-concreteness by our new Marxist friend. He linked it up with the interests of the masses, and in his whole approach one sensed just that live Marxism which takes phenomena in their concrete surroundings and in their development." (N. K. Krupskaya, *Reminiscences of Lenin*, Moscow, 1959, p. 12.)

In his speech at the circle meeting, and also in the paper entitled *On the So-Called Market Question*, Lenin pointed to the errors of Krasin, who considered the existence of foreign markets to be a necessary condition of capitalist production and denied any connection between the two subdivisions of social production. At the same time, Lenin severely criticised the views of the liberal Narodniks on the destiny of capitalism in Russia, and also the outlook of the representatives of nascent "Legal Marxism."

Lenin's work *On the So-Called Market Question* went the rounds of the Social-Democratic circles in St. Petersburg and other cities, and was a powerful weapon in the fight against Narodism and "Legal Marxism." The principal conclusions drawn in this work were developed later by Lenin in his book *The Development of Capitalism in Russia.*

The manuscript of *On the So-Called Market Question*, which for a time was considered lost, came into the possession of the Institute of Marxism-Leninism of the C.C. C.P.S.U. only in 1937.

It was first published in the journal *Bolshevik*, issue No. 21, 1937, and in 1938 was issued in book form by the Institute. p. 75

[18] The scheme of expanded reproduction taking account of technical progress is given exactly as it is in V. I. Lenin's manuscript; occa-

sional inaccuracies in figures do not affect the line of argument and the general conclusions. p. 87

[19] The column "Means of production as means of consumption" contains the total sum I (v+m), which includes the part intended for accumulation. It should be borne in mind that part of the newly-created value in Department I is embodied in instruments and materials which are not means of production for Department II, but additional means of production (exceeding replacement) for Department I. The part of the produced means of production intended for Department II, and that remaining in Department I can be seen from the magnitude of the constant capital that actually functions in both Departments in the following year.

Two errors slipped into V. I. Lenin's manuscript, viz.: 3,172 instead of $3{,}172\frac{1}{2}$, and $10{,}828\frac{1}{2}$ instead of 10,830, as can be seen from the scheme given in the text. p. 87

[20] See K. Marx, *Capital*, Vol. II, Moscow, 1957, p. 438. p. 89

[21] See K. Marx, *Capital*, Vol. I, Moscow, 1959, p. 106. p. 100

[22] *Nik. —on* or *N. —on* was the pseudonym of N. F. Danielson, one of the ideologists of liberal Narodism of the 1880s and 1890s. The book by Nikolai —on quoted here is called *Sketches on Our Post-Reform Social Economy*, St. Petersburg, 1893. p. 101

[23] *Plyushkin*, a character in N. V. Gogol's *Dead Souls*. The name Plyushkin, a tight-fisted landlord, has come to typify extreme avarice. p. 105

[24] See K. Marx, *Capital*, Vol. II, Moscow, 1957, p. 316 (footnote 32). p. 106

[25] V. I. Lenin's book *What the "Friends of the People" Are and How They Fight the Social-Democrats* (Reply to Articles in *Russkoye Bogatstvo* Opposing the Marxists) was written in 1894 (the first part was finished in April, and the second and the third in the summer). Lenin started working on this book in Samara in 1892-93. In the Samara Marxist circle he delivered lectures in which he severely criticised the anti-Marxist liberal Narodniks V. V. (Vorontsov), Mikhailovsky, Yuzhakov, and Krivenko. These lectures served as preparatory material for the book.

In the autumn of 1894 Lenin read his work, *What the "Friends of the People" Are and How They Fight the Social-Democrats*, to members of the St. Petersburg Marxist circle. "I remember," wrote N. K. Krupskaya in her reminiscences, "how it thrilled us all. The aims of the struggle were set forth in the pamphlet with admirable clarity. Hectographed copies of it circulated afterwards from hand to hand under the name of "The Yellow Copy-Books." They were unsigned. Fairly widely read, they undoubtedly had a strong influence on the Marxist youth at the time." (N. K. Krupskaya, *Reminiscences of Lenin*, Moscow, 1959, p. 15.)

Lenin's book was published in separate parts. The first part was hectographed in June 1894 in St. Petersburg, and was illegally circulated there and in other cities. A second edition of this first part, printed the same way, appeared in July 1894. About 100 copies of the first and second parts were printed by A. A. Ganshin in August in Gorki (Vladimir Gubernia) and in September in Moscow. In September of the same year A. A. Vaneyev, in St. Petersburg, hectographed 50 more copies of the first part (that was the fourth edition), and approximately the same number of copies of the third part. This edition of the book had the following note on the cover: "Published by a provincial group of Social-Democrats." This was made necessary by the illegal conditions under which the book was produced. Local organisations made copies of Lenin's work by various means, some parts being handwritten, others typewritten, etc. A group of Social-Democrats in Borzna Uyezd of Chernigov Gubernia hectographed copies of the book in 1894; copies of this edition were circulated in Chernigov, Kiev, and St. Petersburg. At the end of 1894 the book was being read in Vilno; in 1895 in Penza; and at about the same time in Vladimir. In 1895-1896 it circulated among Marxist students in Tomsk. At the same time it was being read in Rostov-on-Don; in 1896, in Poltava and other towns.

Lenin's book was well known to the Emancipation of Labour group, and also to other Russian Social-Democratic organisations abroad.

Copies of the hectographed edition of the first and the third parts of the book were discovered in the early part of 1923 in the archives of the Berlin Social-Democratic organisation, and almost simultaneously in the State Saltykov-Shchedrin Public Library in Leningrad.

In the first, second and third editions of V. I. Lenin's *Collected Works*, it was printed according to the hectographed editions of 1894 discovered in 1923.

In 1936, the Institute of Marxism-Leninism acquired a further copy of the hectographed edition of 1894. This copy contains numerous editorial corrections, apparently made by Lenin when preparing to have the book published abroad.

The text of *What the "Friends of the People" Are* published in the present edition conforms to the text of the hectographed copy acquired by the Institute in 1936, account being taken of the corrections made. According to the authorised copy, inverted commas have been replaced in some passages by italics, while a number of interpolations that were in brackets in the text have been given as footnotes. Lenin's explanation to the table (Appendix I), omitted from previous editions, is also given.

The second part of the book has still not been found. p. 129

[26] *Russkoye Bogatstvo* (*Russian Wealth*)—a monthly magazine published in St. Petersburg from 1876 to the middle of 1918. In the beginning of the 1890s it became the organ of the liberal Narodniks, and was edited by S. N. Krivenko and N. K. Mikhailovsky. The magazine advocated reconciliation with the tsarist government and waged a bitter struggle against Marxism and the Russian Marxists.

In 1906 it became the organ of the semi-Cadet Popular Socialist party. p. 133

[27] The article referred to is N. K. Mikhailovsky's "Literature and Life," published in *Russkoye Bogatstvo*, No. 10, 1893. Marxists commented on the article in letters addressed to Mikhailovsky. Some of the letters were published in the magazine *Byloye* (*The Past*), No. 23, 1924. p. 133

[28] The article referred to is N. K. Mikhailovsky's "Karl Marx Being Tried by Y. Zhukovsky," published in the magazine *Otechestvenniye Zapiski* (*Fatherland Notes*), No. 10, October 1877. p. 135

[29] See Karl Marx, *Capital*, Vol. I, Moscow, 1959, Preface to the first German edition, p. 10. p. 136

[30] The article referred to is K. Marx's *A Criticism of Hegel's Philosophy of Law*, written in Kreuznach in the summer of 1843. The Institute of Marxism-Leninism at the C.C. C.P.S.U. possesses the unfinished manuscript of this essay containing an exhaustive critical analysis of §§ 261-313 of Hegel's *Principles of the Philosophy of Law*. Marx intended to prepare for publication an extensive essay, *A Criticism of Hegel's Philosophy of Law*, following the appearance of the Introduction to this work in the *Deutsch-Französische Jahrbücher* (*German-French Yearbooks*) in 1844. He was, however, unable to carry out his intention. Marx's manuscript was published for the first time in the language of the original in 1927, by the Institute of Marxism-Leninism. p. 138

[31] Lenin's quotation is from the preface to *A Contribution to the Critique of Political Economy*. (See K. Marx and F. Engels, *Selected Works*, Vol. I, Moscow, 1958, pp. 362-63.) p. 139

[32] *Contrat social*—one of the chief works of Jean-Jacques Rousseau. Its full title is *Du contrat social; ou, Principes du droit politique*. (*The Social Contract; or the Principles of Political Law.*) It was published in Amsterdam in 1762 and translated into Russian in 1906. The main idea in the book was the assertion that every social system should be the result of a free agreement, of a contract between people. Fundamentally idealistic though it was, the "social contract" theory, advanced in the eighteenth century on the eve of the French bourgeois revolution, nevertheless played a revolutionary role. It expressed the demand for bourgeois equality, the abolition of the privileges of the feudal estates, and the establishment of a bourgeois republic. p. 139

[33] See K. Marx, *Capital*, Vol. I, Moscow, 1959, p. 373. p. 146

[34] *Letter from Karl Marx to the Editorial Board of "Otechestvenniye Zapiski"* was written at the end of 1877 in connection with N. K. Mikhailovsky's article "Karl Marx Being Tried by Y. Zhukovsky." The letter was copied and sent to Russia by Engels after Marx's death. Engels stated that this letter "for a long time circulated in Russia in manuscript copies taken from the French original, and later a Russian translation of it was published in *Vestnik Narodnoi Voli* (*People's Will Messenger*), (No. 5.—*Ed.*), in 1886, in Geneva, and subsequently in Russia. This letter, like everything that

came from Marx's pen, aroused considerable attention in Russian circles." (*Internationales aus dem Volksstaat* (1871-1875), Berlin, 1894, S. 68.) It was first published in Russian in the magazine *Yuridichesky Vestnik* (*The Legal Messenger*), No. 10, 1888. (See K. Marx and F. Engels, *Selected Correspondence*, Moscow, pp. 376-79.) p. 146

[35] See F. Engels, *Anti-Dühring, Herr Eugen Dühring's Revolution in Science* (Part II. Political Economy, Chapter One. Subject Matter and Method), Moscow, 1954, pp. 207-8. p. 146

[36] *German Ideology* was written jointly by Marx and Engels in the years 1845-1846.

The manuscript, amounting to nearly 800 printed pages, was in two volumes, the first of which was mainly devoted to an elaboration of the basic theses of historical materialism and to a criticism of the philosophical views of Ludwig Feuerbach, B. Bauer and M. Stirner, and the second, to a criticism of the views of various representatives of "true socialism."

In 1846-1847 Marx and Engels made repeated attempts to find a publisher in Germany who would issue their work. They were, however, unsuccessful, due to the obstacles raised by the police and because the publishers, themselves interested parties, were champions of the very trends combated by Marx and Engels and refused to handle it. Only one chapter appeared during the lifetime of Marx and Engels. That was Chapter IV, Volume II of *German Ideology*, which was published in the magazine *Das Westphalische Dampfboot* (*Westphalean Steamer*), August and September 1847. The manuscript was pigeonholed for dozens of years in the archives of the German Social-Democratic Party. The German text was first published in full in 1932 by the Institute of Marxism-Leninism of the C.C. C.P.S.U. A Russian translation appeared in 1933.

The characterisation of *German Ideology* given by Engels is taken from the Preface to his *Ludwig Feuerbach and the End of Classical German Philosophy*. (See K. Marx and F. Engels, *Selected Works*, Vol. II, Moscow, 1958, p. 359.) p. 147

[37] See F. Engels, Preface to the first German edition of "The Origin of the Family, Private Property and the State." (K. Marx and F. Engels, *Selected Works*, Vol. II, Moscow, 1958, p. 171.) p. 148

[38] *The gentile, clan organisation of society*. This was the system of primitive communism, or the first social-economic formation in human history. The clan system began to take shape when the modern type of man was fully formed. The clan community was a collective unit of blood relations, united by economic and social ties. In its development, the clan system passed through two periods, matriarchy and patriarchy. Patriarchy came to an end when primitive society became class society and the state emerged. The basis of production relations in the primitive-communal system was the social ownership of the means of production and the equal distribution of products. In the main this corresponded to the low level of development of the productive forces, and to their character at that period. Stone implements, and later the bow and arrow, ruled

out the possibility of men combating natural forces and wild animals individually.

On the system of primitive communism, see K. Marx's *Synopsis of L. H. Morgan's "Ancient Society"* and F. Engels' *The Origin of the Family, Private Property and the State.* p. 150

[39] The *fief* (*pomestye*) system—the specific system of feudal landownership that arose and became firmly established in Russia in the fifteenth, and particularly the sixteenth century. The fief system was closely bound up with the formation of a centralised state and the establishment of a centralised army. The fief lands, considered the property of the feudal ruler, were distributed by the government among those who served in the armed forces or at court. The amount of land received depended on the duties of the landholder. The fief, as distinct from the *votchina*, the absolute and hereditary landed property of the boyar, was the conditional and temporary property of a nobleman who had rendered these services.

From the middle of the sixteenth century the fief was gradually transformed into an hereditary estate, and increasingly approximated to the votchina. In the seventeenth century the difference between these two forms of feudal landownership disappeared, and the feudal rights of votchina and fief owners became identical. Following Peter I's ukase on inheritance issued in 1714 the fief once and for all became the private property of the landed nobility. The term fief (pomestye) continued to be used in Russia throughout the entire feudal epoch. p. 153

[40] *The First International—The International Working Men's Association*—the first international organisation of the proletariat, founded by Karl Marx in 1864 at an international workers' conference in London convened by British and French workers. The First International was the result of years of hard work by Marx and Engels to establish a revolutionary working-class party. As V. I. Lenin noted, the First International "laid the foundation of an international organisation of the workers for the preparation of their revolutionary onslaught on capital," "laid the foundation of the proletarian, international struggle for socialism." (*The Third International and Its Place in History*. See present edition, Vol 29.)

The central directing body of the First International was the General Council of the International Working Men's Association, of which Marx was a life member. Marx worked to overcome the petty-bourgeois influences and sectarian tendencies then prevailing in the working-class movement (craft unionism in Britain, and Proudhonism and Anarchism in the Romance countries), gathering round himself the most class-conscious members of the General Council (including F. Lessner, E. Dupont, and H. Jung). The First International directed the economic and political struggle of the workers of different countries and strengthened the bonds of solidarity between them. It played a tremendous part in disseminating Marxism, in introducing socialism into the working-class movement.

After the defeat of the Paris Commune the working class was faced with the task of organising national mass parties based on the principles advanced by the First International. "... As I view European conditions it is quite useful to let the formal organisation of the International recede into the background for the time being." (K. Marx and F. Engels, *Selected Correspondence*, Moscow, p. 348.) In 1876, at a conference held in Philadelphia, the First International was officially liquidated. p. 155

[41] Lenin used the name of V. Burenin, a contributor to the reactionary paper *Novoye Vremya* (*New Times*), as a synonym for dishonest methods of controversy. p. 156

[42] *Novoye Vremya* (*New Times*)—a daily paper that appeared in St. Petersburg from 1868 to 1917; it belonged to different publishers at different times and repeatedly changed its political line. At first it was moderately liberal, but from 1876 it became the organ of reactionary circles among the aristocracy and the bureaucracy. From 1905 it became the organ of the Black Hundreds. After the bourgeois-democratic revolution of February 1917, it gave full support to the counter-revolutionary policy of the bourgeois Provisional Government and conducted a furious campaign against the Bolsheviks. On November 8 (October 26, old style), 1917, it was closed down by the Revolutionary Military Committee of the Petrograd Soviet. Lenin called *Novoye Vremya* a typical example of the venal press.

In an item, "Critical Notes," published in *Novoye Vremya* of February 4, 1894, V. Burenin praised Mikhailovsky for fighting the Marxists. p. 158

[43] The words are from I. A. Krylov's fable "The Elephant and the Pug-Dog." p. 159

[44] See F. Engels Preface to the first edition of "The Origin of the Family, Private Property and the State." (K. Marx and F. Engels, *Selected Works*, Vol. II, Moscow, 1958, p. 170.) p. 161

[45] See K. Marx, *Capital*, Vol. I, Moscow, 1959, p. 13. p. 161

[46] Reference is to the journal *Deutsch-Französische Jahrbücher* (*German-French Yearbooks*) published in Paris under the editorship of K. Marx and A. Ruge in the German language. Only one issue, a double number, appeared in February 1844. The main reason why publication was discontinued, was Marx's differences in principle with the bourgeois radical Ruge. p. 162

[47] *Triad* (Greek, *trias*)—in philosophy it is the formula of three-stage development. The idea of three-stage development was first formulated by the Greek Neo-Platonic philosophers, particularly by Proclus, and was expressed in the works of the German idealist philosophers Fichte and Schelling. The triad was, however, developed most fully in the idealist philosophy of Hegel, who considered that every process of development traverses three stages—thesis, antithesis, and synthesis. The second stage is the negation of the first, which transformed into its opposite by transition to the second stage. The third stage is the negation of the second, i.e., the nega-

tion of the negation, which means a return to the form existing at the outset that is now enriched by a new content and is on a higher level. Hegel's triad is a scheme into which reality was fitted artificially; the arbitrary construction of the triad scheme distorted the real development of nature and society. K. Marx, F. Engels and V. I. Lenin had a high opinion of the rational elements in Hegel's dialectics, but they critically refashioned his dialectical method and created materialist dialectics, which reflect the most general laws of the development of the objective world and human thought. p. 163

[48] See F. Engels, *Anti-Dühring* (First Part. Philosophy. Chapter Thirteen. Dialectics. Negation of the Negation). p. 163

[49] A systematic exposition and further development of the Marxist dialectical method is given in V. I. Lenin's *Materialism and Empirio-Criticism*, *Philosophical Notebooks*, *Karl Marx*, etc. p. 165

[50] The author of the article (I. K—n) was Professor I. I. Kaufman of St. Petersburg University. In Marx's view, the article was one of the best expositions of the dialectical method. (See K. Marx, *Capital*, Vol. I, Moscow, 1959. Afterword to the second edition pp. 17-19.) p. 166

[51] Further on in the text (on pages 168-73 of the present volume) V. I. Lenin cites an extract from F. Engels' *Anti-Dühring* (Part One. Philosophy. Chapter Thirteen. Dialectics. Negation of the Negation). p. 168

[52] See K. Marx, *Capital*, Vol. I, Moscow, 1959, p. 78. p. 171

[53] See K. Marx, *Capital*, Vol. I, Moscow, 1959, pp. 761-63. p. 171

[54] Reference is made to the Afterword to the second edition of Volume I of K. Marx's *Capital*. p. 174

[55] *Otechestvenniye Zapiski* (*Fatherland Notes*)—a literary-political magazine that began publication in St. Petersburg in 1820. From 1839 it became the best progressive publication of its day. Among its contributors were V. G. Belinsky, A. I. Herzen, T. N. Granovsky, and N. P. Ogaryov. Following Belinsky's departure from the editorial board in 1846, *Otechestvenniye Zapiski* began to lose its significance. In 1868 the magazine came under the direction of N. A. Nekrasov and M. Y. Saltykov-Shchedrin. This marked the onset of a period in which the magazine flourished anew, gathering around itself the revolutionary-democratic intellectuals of Russia. When Nekrasov died (in 1877), the Narodniks gained dominant influence in the magazine.

The *Otechestvenniye Zapiski* was continually harassed by the censors, and in April 1884 was closed down by the tsarist government. p. 175

[56] *Postoronny* (*Outsider*)—pen-name of N. K. Mikhailovsky. p. 175

[57] Reference is made to the following theses formulated by Marx and Engels in the *Manifesto of the Communist Party*:

"The theoretical conclusions of the Communists are in no way based on ideas or principles that have been invented, or discovered by this or that would-be universal reformer.

"They merely express, in general terms, actual relations springing from an existing class struggle, from a historical movement going on under our very eyes." (See K. Marx and F. Engels, "Manifesto of the Communist Party," *Selected Works*, Vol. I, Moscow, 1958, p. 46.) p. 178

[58] See F. Engels. *Anti-Dühring* (Part One. Philosophy. Chapter Nine. Morality and Law. Eternal Truths), Moscow, 1959, p. 130. p. 179

[59] Reference is made to N. K. Mikhailovsky's articles "About the Russian Edition of Karl Marx's Book" (*Otechestvenniye Zapiski*, No. 4, April 1872), and "Karl Marx Being Tried by Y. Zhukovsky" (*Otechestvenniye Zapiski*, No. 10, October 1877). p. 181

[60] Lenin quotes from K. Marx's letter to A. Ruge (dated September 1843). p. 185

[61] Lenin refers to S. N. Yuzhakov, whose political and economic views he criticised more particularly in the second part of *What the "Friends of the People" Are*. Neither the manuscript, nor a copy of the hectographed edition of the second part of this book has been found. p. 185

[62] Reference is made to the Emancipation of Labour group, the first Russian Marxist group, founded by G. V. Plekhanov in Geneva in 1883. Apart from Plekhanov, P. B. Axelrod, L. G. Deutsch, V. I. Zasulich, and V. N. Ignatov belonged to the group.

The Emancipation of Labour group played a great part in disseminating Marxism in Russia. The group translated into Russian, published abroad and distributed in Russia the works of the founders of Marxism: *Manifesto of the Communist Party* by Marx and Engels; *Wage-Labour and Capital* by Marx; *Socialism: Utopian and Scientific* by Engels, etc. Plekhanov and his group dealt a severe blow to Narodism. In 1883 and 1885 Plekhanov wrote two drafts of a programme for Russian Social-Democrats, which were published by the Emancipation of Labour group. This was an important step forward in preparing the ground for, and in the establishment of, a Social-Democratic Party in Russia. An important part in spreading Marxist views in Russia was played by Plekhanov's essays: *Socialism and the Political Struggle* (1883), *Our Differences* (1885) and *The Development of the Monist View of History* (1895). The Emancipation of Labour group, however, committed serious errors; they clung to remnants of the views of the Narodniks, underestimated the revolutionary capacity of the peasantry, and overestimated the role of the liberal bourgeoisie. These errors were the embryo of the future Menshevik views held by Plekhanov and other members of the group. The Emancipation of Labour group had no practical ties with the working-class movement. V. I. Lenin pointed out that the Emancipation of Labour group "only theoretically founded the Social-Democracy and took the first step in the direction of the working-class movement." (*The Ideological Struggle in the Working-Class Movement*. See present edition, Vol. 20.)

At the Second Congress of the R.S.D.L.P. held in August 1903, the Emancipation of Labour group announced that it had ceased its activity as a group. p. 193

[63] *Narodovolism*, the tenets of the *Narodovoltsi*—members of the secret Narodnik terrorist political organisation Narodnaya Volya (People's Will), which arose in August 1879, following the split in the secret society Zemlya i Volya (Land and Liberty). The Narodnaya Volya was headed by an Executive Committee which included A. I. Zhelyabov, A. D. Mikhailov, M. F. Frolenko, N. A. Morozov, V. N. Figner, S. L. Perovskaya, A. A. Kvyatkovsky. The immediate object of the Narodnaya Volya was the overthrow of the tsarist autocracy, while their programme provided for the organisation of a "permanent popular representative body" elected on the basis of universal suffrage; the proclamation of democratic liberties; the land to be given to the people; and the elaboration of measures for factories to pass into the hands of the workers. The Narodovoltsi were unable, however, to find the road to the masses of the people, and took to political conspiracy and individual terror. The terroristic struggle of the Narodovoltsi was not supported by a mass revolutionary movement, and enabled the government to crush the organisation by resorting to fierce persecution, death sentences and provocation.

After 1881 the Narodnaya Volya fell to pieces. Repeated attempts to revive it during the 1880s ended in failure—for example, the terrorist group organised in 1886, headed by A. I. Ulyanov (V. I. Lenin's brother) and P. Y. Shevyryov, which shared these traditions. After an unsuccessful attempt to assassinate Alexander III, the group was exposed, and its active members executed.

While he criticised the erroneous, utopian programme of the Narodovoltsi, Lenin expressed great respect for the selfless struggle waged by its members against tsarism. In 1899, in the "Protest by Russian Social-Democrats," he pointed out that "the representatives of the old Narodnaya Volya managed to play an enormous role in the history of Russia despite the fact that only narrow social strata supported the few heroes, and despite the fact that it was by no means a revolutionary theory that served as the banner of the movement." ("A Protest by Russian Social-Democrats." See present edition, Vol. 4.) p. 198

[64] *Publisher's Note*—the Afterword to the first edition of the first part of V. I. Lenin's *What the "Friends of the People" Are and How They Fight the Social-Democrats*. p. 201

[65] *Note to the present edition*—Afterword to the second edition of the first part of *What the "Friends of the People" Are* written in July 1894. p. 202

[66] *Yuridichesky Vestnik* (*The Legal Messenger*)—a monthly magazine, bourgeois-liberal in trend, published in Moscow from 1867 to 1892. p. 206

[67] The Manifesto abolishing serfdom in Russia signed by Tsar Alexander II on February 19, 1861. p. 219

[68] The *data for several uyezds*, dealing with the differentiation of the peasantry, mentioned by V. I. Lenin, were included in the second part (not yet found) of *What the "Friends of the People" Are*.

In his *Development of Capitalism in Russia*, Lenin deals with this problem in detail particularly in the second chapter: "The Differentiation of the Peasantry." p. 224

[69] State peasants with quarter holdings—the name given in tsarist Russia to the category of former state peasants, descendants of lower-rank servicemen who in the sixteenth to seventeenth centuries were settled in the border lands of the state of Muscovy. For their services in guarding the state frontiers the settlers (Cossacks, musketeers, soldiers) were given the usufruct of small plots of land either temporarily or in perpetuity. The area of such a plot amounted to a so-called *quarter* [1.35 acres]. From the year 1719 such settlers were called *odnodvortsi* [i.e., those possessing only their own farmsteads]. Formerly they enjoyed various kinds of privileges and had the right to own peasants, but during the course of the nineteenth century were gradually deprived of these rights and reduced to the status of ordinary peasants. By a regulation of the year 1876 the quarter lots were recognised as the private property of the former *odnodvortsi* (quarter-lot peasants) and their descendants. p. 226

[70] Here and in other parts of the present volume, V. I. Lenin quotes from I. A. Hourwich's *The Economics of the Russian Village*, published in New York in 1892. A Russian translation of this book appeared in 1896. Lenin had a high opinion of Hourwich's book, which contains valuable factual material. p. 227

[71] *Kolupayev and Derunov*—types of capitalist sharks portrayed in the works of the Russian satirist M. Y. Saltykov-Shchedrin. p. 230

[72] V. I. Lenin quotes from Karl Marx's *A Criticism of Hegel's Philosophy of Law*. (See Marx-Engels, *Gesamtausgabe*, Bd. I, Abt. 1, Erster Halbband, S. 608 2 bas.) p. 236

[73] From "To the Sowers" by the Russian poet N. A. Nekrasov. p. 255

[74] The *Gladstone Land Bills*—the land laws adopted in Britain by Gladstone's Liberal Ministry in the 1870s and 1880s. With a view to mitigating the struggle between the tenant farmers and the landlords and to securing the votes of the former, the Gladstone government introduced some minor measures limiting the tyranny of the landlords, who had driven masses of tenants off the land. The government also promised to regulate the question of tenants' arrears, to set up special land courts that would establish "fair" rents, etc. The Gladstone Land Bills were typical of the social demagogy of the liberal bourgeoisie. p. 258

[75] In 1889, the tsarist government, desirous of strengthening the landlords' power over the peasants, introduced the administrative post of Zemsky Nachalnik. The Zemsky Nachalniks, who were appointed from among the local landlord nobility, were given tremendous powers both administrative and juridical to deal with the peasants.

These powers included the right to arrest peasants and administer corporal punishment. p. 262

[76] *Nedelya* (*Week*)—a liberal-Narodnik political and literary newspaper. Appeared in St. Petersburg from 1866 to 1901. Was opposed to fighting the autocracy, and advocated the so-called theory of "minor matters," i.e., appealed to the intelligentsia to abstain from revolutionary struggle and to engage in "cultural activity." p. 263

[77] This refers to French utopian socialism, which was widespread at the beginning of the nineteenth century and was one of the main ideological trends of the time.

The social-economic basis to which French utopian socialism owed its origin was the increased exploitation of the toiling masses, the appearance of irreconcilable contradictions between the proletariat and the bourgeoisie. The most prominent representatives of French utopian socialism were Saint-Simon and Charles Fourier, whose views were widely held not only in France, but also in other countries. The French utopian socialists were, however, unable to expose the essence of capitalist relations and capitalist exploitation with consistency or to discover the basic contradiction of the capitalist mode of production. In conformity with the utopian character of their social and political ideals, they based the need for the socialist reorganisation of society on the need for reason to conquer ignorance, for truth to conquer falsehood. The immaturity of their views is to be explained by the social conditions of the epoch, by the insufficient development of large-scale capitalist industry, and of the industrial proletariat. For a more detailed account of French socialism, see F. Engels' *Socialism: Utopian and Scientific* and *Anti-Dühring*. Lenin described the teachings of the French utopian socialists, in connection with French revolutionary teachings in general, as one of the mainsprings of Marxism.

The Russian revolutionary democrats A. I. Herzen, V. G. Belinsky, N. G. Chernyshevsky, and N. A. Dobrolyubov accepted the ideas of the French Enlighteners, but differed from the representatives of many West-European trends of utopian socialism in advocating the idea of mass struggle to overthrow the autocracy, the idea of a peasant revolution. However, they mistakenly imagined that the path to socialism lay through the semi-feudal peasant community. Since Russia's economic development was still weak the Russian revolutionary democrats, headed by Chernyshevsky, were unable to show the decisive role of the working class in the building of socialist society. p. 263

[78] This refers to V. V.'s (V. P. Vorontsov's) *Our Trends*, which appeared in 1893. p. 264

[79] N. K. Mikhailovsky replied to V. V. in the article "Literature and Life" published in *Russkoye Bogatstvo*, issue No. 10, 1893. p. 264

[80] *The Bakuninists and the rebels*—supporters and followers of M. A. Bakunin (1814-1876), the ideologist of anarchism and a bitter enemy of Marxism and scientific socialism. The Bakuninists carried

on a stubborn struggle against the Marxist theory and tactics of the working-class movement. The main plank of the Bakuninist platform was the complete rejection of any form of state, including the dictatorship of the proletariat. They did not understand the epoch-making role of the proletariat. Bakunin put forward the idea of the "levelling" of classes, the organisation of "free associations" from below. In the Bakuninists' view, a secret revolutionary society, made up of "outstanding" individuals, was to direct popular revolts, which were to take place immediately. Thus the Bakuninists believed that the peasantry in Russia were ready to rise up in rebellion without delay. Their tactics of conspiracy-making, of hasty revolts and of terrorism were adventurist and hostile to Marxist teachings on insurrection. Bakuninism was close to Proudhonism, the petty-bourgeois trend that reflected the ideology of the ruined petty proprietor. One of the Bakuninists in Russia, S. G. Nechayev, was in close contact with Bakunin, who lived abroad. The Bakuninists expounded the programme of the conspiratorial society in the "Revolutionary Catechism." In 1869 Nechayev tried to found a narrow conspiratorial "People's Reprisal" organisation in Russia. He succeeded, however, in organising only a few circles in Moscow. "The People's Reprisal" was soon exposed, and in December 1869 was broken up by the tsarist government. The theory and tactics of the Bakuninists were severely condemned by Marx and Engels. Lenin described Bakuninism as the world outlook "of the petty bourgeois who despairs of his salvation." (*In Memory of Herzen.* See present edition, Vol. 18.) Bakuninism was one of the ideological sources of Narodism. p. 264

[81] A central representative assembly is referred to. In 1873 Marx and Engels wrote the following on this subject: "At that time the demand was raised for the convention of a Zemsky Sobor. Some demanded it with a view to settling financial difficulties, others—so as to end the monarchy. Bakunin wanted it to demonstrate Russia's unity and to consolidate the tsar's power and might." (L'alliance de la Démocratie Socialiste et l'association Internationale des travailleurs. Rapport et documents publiés par ordre du congrès international de la Haye. 1873. p. 113.)

Many Russian revolutionaries equated the convocation of a Zemsky Sobor with the overthrow of the tsarist dynasty.

The convocation of a Zemsky Sobor representing all citizens to draw up a constitution was one of the programmatic demands of the Russian Social-Democratic Party. p. 265

[82] Reference is made to N. G. Chernyshevsky and A. I. Herzen. See Marx's letter to the editorial board of *Otechestvenniye Zapiski* (K. Marx and F. Engels, *Selected Correspondence*, Moscow, p. 377). p. 266

[83] See K. Marx and F. Engels, *Selected Correspondence*, Moscow, pp. 378-79. p. 266

[84] *Sozialpolitisches Centralblatt* (*Central Social Political Sheet*)—organ of the Right wing of German Social-Democracy. First appeared in 1892. p. 272

[85] *Pobedonostsev, K. P.*—Procurator General of the Synod, an extreme reactionary who inspired the feudal policy of Alexander III. p. 273

[86] Lenin refers to the venal press—newspapers and magazines that were in the pay of the tsarist government and fawned on it. p. 274

[87] *Yermolov, A. S.*—Minister of Agriculture and State Properties in 1893-1905; he voiced the interests of the feudal landlords and his policy was one of retaining the relics of serfdom.

Witte, S. Y.—an influential Minister in tsarist Russia; was for many years (1892-1903) Minister of Finance. The measures he adopted in the sphere of finance, customs policy, railway construction, etc., were in the interests of the big bourgeoisie and promoted the development of capitalism in Russia. p. 275

[88] Lenin refers to the *Group of Narodnik Socialists*, Russian revolutionary émigrés headed by N. I. Utin, A. D. Trusov, and V. I. Bartenev. This group published the magazine *Narodnoye Dyelo* (*People's Cause*) in Geneva. At the beginning of 1870 it set up the Russian section of the International Working Men's Association (First International). On March 22, 1870, the General Council of the International accepted the affiliation of the Russian section. At the section's request, Marx undertook to serve as its representative on the General Council. "I gladly accept the honourable duty that you offer me, that of your representative on the General Council," wrote Marx on March 24, 1870, to the members of the Committee of the Russian section (Marx-Engels, *Ausgewahlte Briefe*, M.-L., 1934, S. 234). The members of the Russian section of the First International supported Marx in his struggle against the Bakuninist anarchists, propagated the revolutionary ideas of the International, did what they could to strengthen the ties between the Russian revolutionary movement and the West-European, and took part in the working-class movements of Switzerland and France. However, the members of the Russian section were not consistent Marxists, their views still contained much of Narodnik utopianism; specifically they idealised the village community, calling it "a great achievement of the Russian people." The section failed to establish close ties with the revolutionary movement in Russia, which, in the final analysis, was the main reason for its collapse in 1872. p. 278

[89] *Engelhardt, A. N.*—a Narodnik publicist, who became widely known for his social and agronomic activities and his experiment in organising rational farming on his own estate in Batishchevo, Smolensk Gubernia. A description of the farming methods is given by Lenin in his *Development of Capitalism in Russia* (See present edition, Vol. 3, Chapter 3). p. 280

[90] *Sotsial-Demokrat* (*Social-Democrat*)—a literary political review published abroad (London-Geneva) by the Emancipation of Labour group in 1890-1892. It played a great part in spreading Marxist ideas in Russia. In all, four issues appeared. The leading contributors to the magazine were G. V. Plekhanov, P. B. Axelrod, and V. I. Zasulich.

Lenin here quotes Plekhanov's article "N. G. Chernyshevsky" (See *Sotsial-Demokrat*, No. 1, 1890, pp. 138-39). p. 281

[91] From N. G. Chernyshevsky's novel *Prologue*. p. 282

[92] See Note 8. p. 289

[93] Lenin refers to *Judas Golovlyov*—a sanctimonious, hypocritical landlord serf owner described in M. Saltykov-Shchedrin's *The Golovlyov Family*. p. 291

[94] Lenin uses as an epithet the name Arakcheyev—the brutal favourite of tsars Paul I and Alexander I; a period of reactionary police despotism and gross domination of the military is connected with his activities. A characteristic feature of the Arakcheyev regime was the brutal measures employed against the revolutionary movement of the oppressed masses and against any manifestation of liberty. p. 291

[95] Lenin refers to the Narodnoye Pravo (People's Right) party, an illegal organisation of the Russian democratic intelligentsia founded in the summer of 1893. Among the founders were such former Narodovoltsi as O. V. Aptekman, A. I. Bogdanovich, A. V. Gedeonovsky, M. A. Natanson and N. S. Tyutchev. The members of the Narodnoye Pravo set themselves the aim of uniting all opposition forces, with a view to conducting a struggle for political reform. The Narodnoye Pravo party issued two programme documents, a "Manifesto" and "An Urgent Issue." In the spring of 1894 the party was broken up by the tsarist government. For Lenin's assessment of the Narodnoye Pravo as a political party see pages 329-32 of the present volume, and also the pamphlet *The Tasks of the Russian Social-Democrats* (Vol. 2). The majority of the Narodnoye Pravo members subsequently joined the Socialist-Revolutionary Party. p. 292

[96] See K. Marx, *Capital*, Vol. I, Moscow, 1959, p. 763. p. 310

[97] Lenin quotes from I. A. Krylov's fable "The Cat and the Cook." p. 311

[98] Here and further on Lenin quotes from the Preface to the second edition o F. Engels' *The Housing Question*. (See K. Marx and F. Engels, *Selected Works*, Vol. I, Moscow, 1958, pp. 550, 554-55.) p. 317

[99] See K. Marx, *Capital*, Vol. I, Moscow, 1959, p. 446. p. 318

[100] Lenin refers to the principles expressed by Marx in the second chapter of *The Poverty of Philosophy*, an essay directed against Proudhon. (See K. Marx, *The Poverty of Philosophy*, Moscow, pp. 140-41.) p. 319

[101] Lenin quotes from Marx's *Critique of the Gotha Programme*. (See K. Marx and F. Engels, *Selected Works*, Vol. II, Moscow, 1958, p. 31.) p. 319

[102] *Manilovism*—derived from the name of Manilov, one of the characters in N. V. Gogol's *Dead Souls*. Manilov is a sentimental, "high-souled" landlord in whom Gogol has embodied the typical

features of the weak-willed dreamer, empty visionary, and inert tattler. Lenin uses the name Manilov as an epithet to describe the liberal Narodniks. p. 322

[103] See Afterword to the second edition of Volume One of Marx's *Capital* (K. Marx, *Capital*, Vol. I, Moscow, 1959, p. 20). p. 327

[104] Lenin quotes from Marx's letter to Ruge (dated September 1843). Fuller quotations from this letter will be found on pages 184-85 of this volume. p. 328

[105] The essay, *The Economic Content of Narodism and the Criticism of It in Mr. Struve's Book* (*The Reflection of Marxism in Bourgeois Literature*). *P. Struve: Critical Remarks on the Subject of Russia's Economic Development, St. Petersburg, 1894*, was written by V. I. Lenin in St. Petersburg at the end of 1894 and the beginning of 1895. It was the first of Lenin's works to be printed legally. In this essay Lenin continued the criticism of Narodnik views that he had begun in his previous writings, and gave a comprehensive criticism of the mistaken views of the legal Marxists. Lenin was the first to recognise the liberal-bourgeois nature of legal Marxism. As early as 1893, in his work *On the So-Called Market Question* Lenin not only exposed the views of the liberal Narodniks, but also criticised the legal Marxist outlook that was then emerging.

In the autumn of 1894 Lenin read a paper in the St. Petersburg Marxists' circle directed against Struve and other legal Marxists. This paper served as the basis for the essay *The Economic Content of Narodism and the Criticism of It in Mr. Struve's Book*. Lenin wrote the following in 1907 about his reading of the paper in the St. Petersburg Marxists' circle: "In this circle I read a paper entitled *The Reflection of Marxism in Bourgeois Literature*." As the heading shows, the controversy with Struve was here far sharper and more definite (as to Social-Democratic conclusions) than in the article printed in the spring of 1895. It was toned down partly because of censorship considerations and partly due to the "alliance" with legal Marxism for joint struggle against Narodism. That the "push to the left" then given to Mr. Struve by the St. Petersburg Social-Democrats was not entirely without result is clearly shown by Mr. Struve's article in the Miscellany which was burned (1895), and some of his articles in *Novoye Slovo* (*New Word*) (1897). *Preface to the Miscellany "Twelve Years."* (See present edition, Vol. 13.)

The Economic Content of Narodism and the Criticism of It in Mr. Struve's Book was printed (under the pen-name of *K. Tulin*) in the Miscellany entitled *Material for a Characterisation of Our Economic Development*. An edition of 2,000 copies of the Miscellany was printed in April 1895, but its circulation was banned by the tsarist government, which, after retaining the ban for a full year, confiscated the edition and had it burned. It only proved possible to save about 100 copies, which were secretly circulated among Social-Democrats in St. Petersburg and other cities.

Lenin's article was the most militant and politically acute in the Miscellany. The censor, in his report on *Material for a Characterisation of Our Economic Development*, dwells in particular detail on

Lenin's work. Pointing out that the contributors to the Miscellany put forward Marx's theory about the inexorable advance of the capitalist process, the censor stated that K. Tulin's article contained the most outspoken and complete programme of the Marxists.

At the end of 1907, Lenin included *The Economic Content of Narodism and the Criticism of It in Mr. Struve's Book* in Volume One of the Miscellany *Twelve Years*, and gave it the sub-heading "The Reflection of Marxism in Bourgeois Literature." The first volume of this Miscellany was published by the Zerno Book Publishers in the middle of November 1907 (the title-page is dated 1908). Of the three volumes intended for publication, the publishers succeeded in issuing only Volume One, and part one of Volume Two. Apart from the paper mentioned, Volume One contained the following works by Lenin: *The Tasks of the Russian Social-Democrats*, *The Persecutors of the Zemstvo and the Hannibals of Liberalism*, *What Is To Be Done?*, *One Step Forward, Two Steps Back*, *The Zemstvo Campaign and "Iskra's" Plan*, and *Two Tactics of Social-Democracy in the Democratic Revolution*. Volume One was confiscated soon after its appearance, but a considerable part of the edition was salvaged, and the book continued to circulate illegally. p. 333

[106] The *truck-system*—the system of paying the workers wages in the shape of goods and foodstuffs from the employer's shop. This system was an additional means of exploiting the workers, and was particularly widespread in Russia, in the areas where there was handicraft industry. p. 346

[107] *Moskovskiye Vedomosti* (*Moscow Recorder*)—a Russian newspaper of long standing, first issued in 1756 as a small sheet by Moscow University. From the 1860s it pursued a monarchist-nationalist line, its views being those of the most reactionary landlords and clergy. From 1905 onwards it was one of the principal organs of the Black Hundreds. Continued publication until the October Revolution of 1917.

Vest (*News*)—a reactionary feudalist newspaper that appeared in Russia in the 1860s and 1870s. p. 348

[108] Lenin quotes from I. A. Krylov's fable "The Wolf and the Shepherds." p. 349

[109] *Skimmers*—ironical expression repeatedly used by M. Y. Saltykov-Shchedrin in his works to describe the bourgeois liberal press and its representatives. In Chapter V of *The Diary of a Provincial in St. Petersburg*, Saltykov-Shchedrin bitterly derides the liberals, and writes: "For want of real work to do, and by way of an innocent pastime they have established a learned literary society, "The Free League of Skimmers." Saltykov-Shchedrin describes the "duties" of this "League" as follows: "Not to miss a single contemporary problem, but to discuss everything in such a manner as to ensure that no result shall ever be achieved." p. 352

[110] *Dictatorship of the heart*—ironical term used to indicate the short-lived policy of flirting with the liberals pursued by the tsarist official Loris-Melikov. In 1880 he was first appointed chief of the Supreme Control Commission for combating "sedition," and then

Minister of Home Affairs. Loris-Melikov tried to base his policy on promises of "concessions" to the liberals and on ruthless persecution of revolutionaries. The revolutionary situation of 1879-80 gave rise to this balancing policy, the purpose of which was to weaken the revolutionary movement and to win over to tsarism the oppositional liberal bourgeoisie. After suppressing the revolutionary wave of 1879-1880, the tsar's government abandoned the policy of the "dictatorship of the heart" and hastened to issue a manifesto on the "inviolability" of the autocracy. In April 1881, Loris-Melikov had to resign. p. 352

[111] *Chinsh* peasants—those entitled to the hereditary possession of the land in perpetuity, and who had to pay a quitrent that rarely changed, known as chinsh. In tsarist Russia, the chinsh system operated mainly in Poland, Lithuania, Byelorussia, and the Black Sea littoral of the Ukraine. p. 370

[112] See, for example, Gleb Uspensky's stories and essays "From a Village Diary," "Cheque-Book," "Mid-Journey Letters," "Unbroken Ties," "Living Figures." p. 378

[113] *Mr. Coupon*—a term adopted in the literature of the 1880s and 1890s to indicate capital and capitalists. The expression "Mr. Coupon" was put in circulation by the writer Gleb Uspensky in his essays "Grave Sins." p. 383

[114] "*Beast of burden*"—the downtrodden poor peasant, exhausted by excessive toil, typified by M. Y. Saltykov-Shchedrin in his satirical tale *Konyaga* (literally—overworked nag). In this tale the author speaks allegorically of the "unmoving enormity of the fields" which shall keep man in bondage until he releases the "magic force" from captivity. At the same time Saltykov-Shchedrin derides the Narodniks' vulgar arguments that the "real labour" which the "konyaga" found for himself is the guarantee of the peasant's invulnerability, spiritual equilibrium, clarity and integrity. p. 387

[115] *The Prussian Regierungsrat* (*State Counsellor*)—refers to the German economist, Baron A. Haxthausen, who visited Russia in the 1840s. In his book *Studies of Internal Relations in Popular Life and Particularly of Rural Institutions of Russia*, Haxthausen gave a detailed description of the Russian village community, in which he saw a means of consolidating feudalism. He sang the praises of Russia under Tsar Nicholas I, considering it to be superior to Western Europe in that it did not suffer from the "ulcer of proletarianism." Marx and Engels showed the reactionary character of Haxthausen's conclusions, and his views were also severely criticised by A. I. Herzen and N. G. Chernyshevsky. p. 391

[116] Owing to the censorship, Lenin could make no direct reference to the Marxist works published by the Emancipation of Labour group. He refers the reader to V.V.'s (Vorontsov's) work *Essays on Theoretical Economics* (St. Petersburg, 1895), which, on pages 257-58, contains a lengthy extract from Plekhanov's article "Domestic Review," that appeared in the *Sotsial-Demokrat* (*Social-Democrat*), Book Two, August 1890. p. 394

[117] *Mirtov*—pseudonym of P. L. Lavrov (1820-1900); a Narodnik ideologist in the 1870s. Was a member of the Narodnik secret society Zemlya i Volya (Land and Liberty), and then of the Narodnaya Volya (People's Will) party. In the 1870s he advocated the need to "go among the people." Was the founder of the idealist "subjective school" in sociology. p. 397

[118] See K. Marx and F. Engels, "The Eighteenth Brumaire of Louis Bonaparte," *Selected Works*, Vol. I, Moscow, 1958, p. 334. p. 414

[119] See F. Engels, *Anti-Dühring*, Moscow, 1959, p. 133. p. 416

[120] See K Marx, *Capital*, Vol. I, Moscow, 1959, pp. 84-85, Footnote 2. p. 417

[121] See K. Marx and F. Engels, "Origin of the Family, Private Property and the State," *Selected Works*, Vol. II, Moscow, 1958, p. 272. p. 419

[122] *Naucrary*—small territorial districts in the ancient Athenian Republic. Naucraries were united in phyles. The collegium of naucrars (naucrary chiefs) conducted the finances of the Athenian State. It was the duty of each naucrary to build, equip, and man a warship and to provide two horsemen to meet the military needs of the state. p. 419

[123] See K. Marx and F. Engels, op. cit., in *Selected Works*, Vol. II, Moscow, 1958, p. 269. p. 419

[124] See K. Marx and F. Engels, "Civil War in France" and "The Eighteenth Brumaire of Louis Bonaparte," *Selected Works*, Vol. I, Moscow. 1958, pp. 284, 516-17. p. 420

[125] See F. Engels, *Anti-Dühring*, Moscow, 1959, p. 157. p. 420

[126] See K. Marx and F. Engels, "The Eighteenth Brumaire of Louis Bonaparte," *Selected Works*, Vol. I, Moscow, 1958, p. 244.
The book by Proudhon mentioned in the text is called *The Social Revolution Demonstrated by the Coup d'État*. p. 425

[127] *Leibkampantsi*, from Leibkompanie (personal bodyguard), the title of honour bestowed on the Grenadier Company of the Preobrazhensky Regiment in 1741 by Tsarina Yelizaveta Petrovna for having placed her on the Russian throne. They were given estates and all sorts of special privileges, while those of them who were not of noble origin were made hereditary nobles. The nickname "Leibkampantsi" was put in circulation by M. Y. Saltykov-Shchedrin in his *Poshekhon Tales*. p. 426

[128] See K. Marx, *Capital*, Vol. II, Moscow, 1957, pp. 116-17. p. 437

[129] See K. Marx and F. Engels, "Manifesto of the Communist Party," *Selected Works*, Vol. I, Moscow, 1958, pp. 53-54. p. 439

[130] *Gotha Programme*—the programme of the German Social-Democratic Party adopted in 1875 at the Gotha congress, where unity was established between the two German socialist parties that had previously existed separately; they were the Eisenachers (who were led by Bebel and Liebknecht, and were under the ideological influence of Marx and Engels), and the Lassalleans. The programme suffered from eclecticism, and was opportunist, since the Eisenachers made

concessions to the Lassalleans and accepted their formulations on vitally important points. Marx and Engels subjected the Gotha draft programme to withering criticism, for they regarded it as a considerable step backwards even as compared with the Eisenach programme of 1869. (See K. Marx and F. Engels, "Critique of the Gotha Programme," *Selected Works*, Vol. II, Moscow, 1958, pp. 13-48.) p. 442

[131] See K. Marx and F. Engels, "The Eighteenth Brumaire of Louis Bonaparte," *Selected Works*, Vol. I, Moscow, 1958, pp. 278-79. p. 448

[132] See K. Marx, *Capital*, Vol. I, Moscow, 1959, p. 632. p. 453

[133] Lenin refers to Chapter XXX, Vol. I, *Capital* (Reaction of the Agricultural Revolution on Industry. Creation of the Home Market for Industrial Capital). (See K. Marx, *Capital*, Vol. I, Moscow, 1959, p. 745.) p. 463

[134] K. Marx, *Capital*, Vol. I, Moscow, 1959, p. 642. p. 464

[135] *Skopshchina*—the name given in the southern parts of Russia to a type of rent in kind, on terms of bondage, the tenant paying the landowner *s kopny* (from the corn-shock) a portion of the harvest (a half, and sometimes more), and usually fulfilling miscellaneous labour services in addition. p. 465

[136] See K. Marx, *Capital*, Vol. I, Moscow, 1959, p. 749, Footnote 2. p. 471

[137] See K. Marx, *Capital*, Vol. I, Moscow, 1959, pp. 742-44. p. 472

[138] See K. Marx, *Capital*, Vol. III, Moscow, 1959, p. 604. p. 488

[139] *Gift-landers or gift-land peasants*, peasants who were formerly landlords' serfs and who, at the time of the Reform of 1861, by "agreement" with their landlords received allotments gratis (without having to pay redemption money for them). The gift-lander received a miserable strip, amounting in all to a quarter of the so-called "top" or "statutory" allotment established by law for the given locality. All the rest of the lands that had constituted the peasants' allotments before the Reform were seized by the landlord, who held his "gift-landers," forcibly dispossessed of their land, in a state of economic bondage even after serfdom was abolished. The "gift-land" allotment came to be known among the people as a "quarter," "orphan's," "cat's," or "gagarin" allotment (the last epithet being derived from the name of the initiator of the law on "gift-land" allotments, Prince P. P. Gagarin). p. 491

[140] Lenin deals with this problem in detail in his book *The Development of Capitalism in Russia* (1899). See present edition, Vol. 3. p. 499

THE LIFE AND WORK OF

V. I. LENIN

Outstanding Dates

(1870-1894)

1870

April 10 (22 new style)	Vladimir Ilyich Ulyanov (Lenin), born in Simbirsk (now Ulyanovsk).

1879

August 16(28)	Lenin is accepted into Simbirsk classical Gymnasium.

1886

January 12(24)	Ilya Nikolayevich Ulyanov, Lenin's father, dies.

1887

March 1(13)	Lenin's elder brother, Alexander Ilyich Ulyanov, is arrested for participating in an attempt on the life of Alexander III.
May 8(20)	Alexander Ulyanov and other participants in the attempt are executed.
June 10(22)	Lenin graduates Simbirsk Gymnasium, winning a Gold Medal.
End of June	The Ulyanov family moves to Kazan.
August 13(25)	Lenin enters Kazan University.
September-November	Lenin participates in a revolutionary students' circle in Kazan.
December 4(16)	Lenin participates in a students' rally in Kazan University.
December 5(17)	Lenin is arrested for participation in the students' revolutionary movement.

December 7(19)	Lenin is expelled from the university and exiled from Kazan to the village of Kokushkino, under the secret surveillance of the police.

1888

September 23 (October 5)	Lenin's application for permission to go abroad "to continue my education" is rejected by Police Department.
Beginning of October	Lenin receives permission to return from Kokushkino village to Kazan, where the Ulyanov family settle.
Autumn	Lenin studies K. Marx's *Capital*, and joins a Marxist circle organised by N. Y. Fedoseyev.

1889

May 3-4(15-16)	Lenin moves from Kazan to a hamlet near the village of Alakayevka, Samara Gubernia.
June 14(26)	Lenin is informed of the rejection of his application to go abroad "for treatment."
July 13(25)	N. Y. Fedoseyev and members of the Marxist circles he organised in Kazan are arrested. Among the arrested are members of the circle to which Lenin had belonged.
October 11(23)	Lenin moves from the hamlet near Alakayevka village to Samara.

1890

End of 1889-1890	In Samara Lenin continues his study of Marx and Engels, translates *The Manifesto of the Communist Party*, which is subsequently read in illegal circles in Samara (no copy of the translation remains). Lenin becomes acquainted with A. P. Sklyarenko and engages in Marxist propaganda among the youth of Samara.
May 17(29)	Lenin receives permission to sit for the final examinations at the Law Faculty of St. Petersburg University as an external student.
End of August (beginning of September)	Lenin's first visit to St. Petersburg in connection with the examinations at St. Petersburg University.

August 26-September 1(Sept. 7-13)	On his way to St. Petersburg Lenin stops in Kazan.
October 24 (November 5)	Lenin leaves St. Petersburg to return to Samara.

1891

April 4-24 (April 16-May 6)	Lenin sits for the final examinations at the Law Faculty of St. Petersburg University (spring session).
May 17(29)	Lenin leaves St. Petersburg for Samara.
Summer-beginning of September	Lenin lives in Samara and at the hamlet near the village of Alakayevka.
September 16(28)-November 9(21)	Lenin sits for the last of the examinations at St. Petersburg University (autumn session).
November 12(24)	Lenin returns from St. Petersburg to Samara.

1892

January 14(26)	Lenin receives a University Graduation Diploma, First Class, from the Head Office of the St. Petersburg Educational District.
January 30 (February 11)	By decision of the Samara Circuit Court Lenin is entered on the rolls of Junior Barristers.
July 23 (August 4)	Lenin granted the right to practise law.
Summer of 1892-winter of 1892-1893	Lenin writes papers criticising the views of the Narodniks, and reads them at meetings of illegal circles. These papers constitute the preparatory material for work *What the "Friends of the People" Are*.

1893

Spring-summer	First circle of Samara Marxists (including A. P Sklyarenko and I. K. Lalayants) is formed. Lenin is central figure in the circle. He prepares and reads the paper (article) entitled *New Economic Developments in Peasant Life* (on V. Y. Postnikov's Book).
End of August (beginning of September)	On his way from Samara to St. Petersburg Lenin stops at Nizhni-Novgorod and makes the acquaintance of local Marxists.

August 31 (September 12)	Lenin arrives in St. Petersburg.
September 3(15)	Lenin is registered as Junior Barrister to M. F. Wolkenstein.
September 25 (October 7)	Lenin travels to Vladimir for a meeting with N. Y. Fedoseyev which does not take place because Fedoseyev was still not released from prison.
Autumn	In St. Petersburg Lenin joins a Marxist circle of Technological Institute students (S. I. Radchenko, V. V. Starkov, P. K. Zaporozhets, G. M. Krzhizhanovsky and others), and at a circle meeting criticises G. B. Krasin's paper "The Market Question." Lenin writes the paper "On the So-Called Market Question," which he reads to the Marxist circle.
Autumn and winter 1893-1894	Lenin establishes contact with progressive workers of St. Petersburg factories (V. A. Shelgunov, I. V. Babushkin and others). Lenin's speeches strongly impress participants in Marxist circles of St. Petersburg. His exceptionally profound knowledge of Marxist theory, his ability to apply Marxism constructively to Russia's economic and political situation, his fervent and unshakable belief in the victory of the workers' cause, his outstanding organisational talent—all this makes Lenin the recognised leader of the St. Petersburg Marxists.

1894

Beginning of January	Lenin comes to Moscow for the winter holidays.
January 9(21)	At an illegal meeting in Moscow Lenin opposes the Narodnik V. V. (V. P. Vorontsov), subjecting his views to annihilating criticism.
January	Lenin visits Nizhni-Novgorod and reads a paper at the local Marxist circle on V. V.'s book *The Destiny of Capitalism in Russia.* Lenin returns to St. Petersburg, where he leads the St. Petersburg group of Social-Democrats and the central workers' circle, and conducts workers' classes outside the Nevskaya Toll gates and in other parts of the city.
March-June	Lenin writes *What the "Friends of the People" Are and How They Fight the Social-Democrats,* the first part of which appeared that spring.

First half of the year	In a Marxist circle in St. Petersburg, Lenin reads a paper in which he critically analyses the book by the Narodnik N. Karyshev *Peasant Rentings of Non-Allotment Land*
June 14(26)	Lenin leaves for Moscow to spend the summer with relatives. He also visits Sàmara.
July	The second edition of part one of *What the "Friends f the People" Are* appears in St. Petersburg.
August 27 (September 8)	Lenin returns from Moscow to St. Petersburg.
End of August (first half of September)	The first edition of part two and the third edition of part one of Lenin's *What the "Friends of the People" Are* appear (in Gorki, Vladimir Gubernia).
September	The first edition of part three and the fourth edition of part one of Lenin's *What the "Friends of the People" Are* appear in St. Petersburg.
October	Lenin reads *What the "Friends of the People" Are* to the members of a St. Petersburg Marxist circle.
Autumn	At a meeting of a St. Petersburg Marxists' circle, Lenin reads his paper "The Reflection of Marxism in Bourgeois Literature," in which he severely criticises the bourgeois distortions of Marxism in Struve's book *Critical Remarks on the Subject of Russia's Economic Development.*
After December 24 (after January 5)	Assisted by the worker I. V. Babushkin, Lenin drafts a leaflet to the workers of the Semyannikov factory dealing with the unrest there. This is the first leaflet issued by Russian Marxists.
End of 1894-beginning of 1895	Lenin writes *The Economic Content of Narodism and the Criticism of It in Mr. Struve's Book.*

В. И. ЛЕНИН

СОЧИНЕНИЯ

Том 1

На английском языке

35